Handbook of Research on Technology Project Management, Planning, and Operations

Terry T. Kidd
Texas A&M University, USA

INFORMATION SCIENCE REFERENCE

Hershey · New York

Director of Editorial Content:	Kristin Klinger
Senior Managing Editor:	Jamie Snavely
Managing Editor:	Jeff Ash
Assistant Managing Editor:	Carole Coulson
Typesetter:	Carole Coulson
Cover Design:	Lisa Tosheff
Printed at:	Yurchak Printing Inc.

Published in the United States of America by
    Information Science Reference (an imprint of IGI Global)
    701 E. Chocolate Avenue
    Hershey PA 17033
    Tel: 717-533-8845
    Fax: 717-533-8661
    E-mail: cust@igi-global.com
    Web site: http://www.igi-global.com/reference

and in the United Kingdom by
    Information Science Reference (an imprint of IGI Global)
    3 Henrietta Street
    Covent Garden
    London WC2E 8LU
    Tel: 44 20 7240 0856
    Fax: 44 20 7379 0609
    Web site: http://www.eurospanbookstore.com

Library of Congress Cataloging-in-Publication Data

Handbook of research on technology project management, planning, and operation / Terry T. Kidd, Editor.
    p. cm.
  Includes bibliographical references and index.
  Summary: "This book provides a compendium of terms, definitions and explanations of concepts, processes and acronyms that reflect the growing trends, issues, and applications of technology project management"--Provided by publisher.
   ISBN 978-1-60566-400-2 (hardcover : alk. paper) -- ISBN 978-1-60566-401-9 (ebook : alk. paper) 1. Project management. 2. Information technology-- Management. I. Kidd, Terry T. HD69.P75H355 2009
   658.4'04--dc22
                        2008047728

British Cataloguing in Publication Data
A Cataloguing in Publication record for this book is available from the British Library.

All work contributed to this book is new, previously-unpublished material. The views expressed in this book are those of the authors, but not necessarily of the publisher.

List of Contributors

Table of Contents

Section I
Overview of Technology Project Management

Chapter I

> *James W. Price Jr., Kennesaw State University, USA*
> *Pamila Dembla, Kennesaw State University, USA*

Chapter II

> *A. J. Gilbert Silvius, Utrecht University of Applied Sciences, The Netherlands*

Chapter III

> *Gregory J. Skulmoski, Zayed University, UAE*
> *Francis T. Hartman, University of Calgary, Canada*

Section II
Leadership, Management & Decision Making in Technology Project Management,
Planning, and Operations

Chapter IV

> *Ralf Müller, Umeå School of Business, Sweden & BI Norwegian School of Management, Norway*

Section V
Case Study Examples in Technology Project Management, Planning, and Operations

Section VI
Issues & Trends in Technology Project Management, Planning, and Operations

Detailed Table of Contents

Section I
Overview of Technology Project Management

Section I provides both an introduction and an overview of technology project management, planning and operations beginning with a foundational knowledge to understanding technical projects through an analytical framework. Chapters in this section present ideas for project management competencies, IT project complexities, and then a brief look into the evolution of project management from 2007.

Chapter I
    James W. Price Jr., Kennesaw State University, USA
    Pamila Dembla, Kennesaw State University, USA

The aim of this chapter is to assess if Sun-Tzu's application of Taoist principles are applicable to the problem domain of Enterprise Resource Planning Management (ERPM). The chapter argues that an ERP's complexity not only shares conceptually The Art of War's historical context, but can be understood to be a disequilibrium force best understood using Taoist principles. Sun-Tsu's The Art of War (AW) has been adapted successfully to the military domain (MD); and, MD has been adapted to strategic management (SM). If an ERP's business drivers can be mapped to a firm's strategic goals, one may conclude Sun-Tzu's Art of War can be adapted to an ERP implementation (AW→MD→SM→ERP). Therefore, the authors hope to explore the applicability of Sun-Tzu's Five Factors of Initial Estimation (Five Factors), an Eastern philosophy (a non-linear thought process) to ERP-related Western-oriented project management techniques (a linear though process).

Chapter II

A. J. Gilbert Silvius, Utrecht University of Applied Sciences, The Netherlands

This chapter examines the expected development of the competences of the project manager in the year 2027. In the study the 46 competences of the International Competence Baseline 3 (ICB 3) were tested against the expectations of the respondents for the development of project management. Based on four scenarios for the future of Europe, the members indicated which of the competences are expected to become more important, equally important or less important than today.

Chapter III

Gregory J. Skulmoski, Zayed University, UAE
Francis T. Hartman, University of Calgary, Canada

The purpose of this chapter was to investigate the soft competencies by project phase that IT project managers, hybrid and technical team members require for project success. The authors identified the key competencies for the three types of job roles. The research participants offered their opinions of what are the most important competencies from the following competence categories: Personal Attributes (e.g. eye for details), Communication (e.g. effective questioning), Leadership (e.g. create an effective project environment), Negotiations (e.g. consensus building), Professionalism (e.g. life long learning), Social Skills (e.g. charisma), and Project Management Competencies (e.g. manage expectations).

Section II
Leadership, Management & Decision Making in Technology Project Management, Planning, and Operations

Section II lays a thorough foundation of project leadership, decision making, and management for the overall success of a technology based project. Leadership is essential to the success or failure of a project. This section will highlight processes to ensure project success and frameworks to build effective leadership and decision making capacities of project managers.

Chapter IV

Ralf Müller, Umeå School of Business, Sweden & BI Norwegian School of Management, Norway

This chapter addresses various leadership styles of project managers from the perspective of those involved in technology intensive projects. The chapter starts by defining and outlining the need for technology based leadership, and then describes the historical recent schools of leadership theory.

A project manager's role on any project goes far beyond task-related deliverables. Although the project manager must be able to effectively manage goals related to time, scope and cost, his or her work does not stop here since the project manager must also be able to manage numerous issues and goals, and be able to lead the people performing them. The desired leadership qualities for a project manager are discussed.

This chapter introduces the concept of technology management by objectives. Technology is one of the fastest moving elements in the 21st Century, which could be well explained using the growth theory. The growth theory is defined on the basis of the economic growth from the increasing returns that is associated with the new knowledge. The knowledge has various dimensions in today's world, one of which is the technology. The major portion of any improvement or any development in any sector is due to technology or due to a change in technology. Technology in any organization can improve, sustain, and diminish the business based on the approaches used in the model. The ability to connect technology and gain organization advantage depends upon how efficiently and effectively the technology is managed within the organization.

Chapter VII

This study adopts a stakeholder analysis framework to examine stakeholders' roles in influencing organizational decisions to abandon information technology projects. By providing a better understanding of the project stakeholders' perception, expectations and their interrelationship, this study provides practitioners with useful insights to managing project stakeholders during information technology development projects. For researchers, our contribution lies in the development of a project cancellation review model that adds a stakeholder perspective.

Chapter VIII

This chapter provides practical recommendations for developers and managers who wish to increase the utilization of their products by bringing the user into the development process. The practical recommendations include Ely's (1999) conditions that facilitate the implementation of innovations.

This chapter discussed various system development life cycles (SDLC) found in the information technology project management arena. A comprehensive overview of the SDLCs history as well as the trigger that instigated its development is be laid out in this chapter.

Chapter X

This chapter uses the Diffusion of Innovations (DOI) theory to examine a business case, highlighting certain gaps in the theory. The hope is to foster an understanding of "real world" business cases to give academics insights into the relationship between innovation and its diffusion as well as teach practitioners the caveats of a business case.

Chapter XI

This chapter introduces the firm-level value creation model as a means of planning information systems projects based on their potential for generating business value. Further, the chapter presents a review of economic literature on firm-level value creation based on the premise that ex-ante economic inefficiencies embedded in the firm processes are the key enabler of effectiveness in IT project implementations. After presenting a detailed case study on the banking industry, the chapter presents a description of how to implement a practical assessment of the potential effectiveness of any IT project. By presenting the underlying theoretical foundations of the business value generation mechanism, the author intends to contribute to the academy by bringing the economic theories to the center of the analysis of IT value generation.

Chapter XII

In this chapter the author investigates the management of service innovation projects while asking the questions if ICT-based service innovation be facilitated by traditional project management thinking. Or should the initiators strive for more interaction with users and other stakeholders, thus organizing the initiatives much looser than what the traditional project work method allows?

This chapter provides a framework for technology project implementation in systems where the human is an integral element of the completed project. Unlike logically devised software codes and performance tested hardware components, human responses can be unpredictable when faced with the combined stressors of technological and organizational change, which occur when management dictates a technological upgrade. An analysis of peer-reviewed literature combined with the author's industrial experience provides a ten-step process for converting an existing manual system to an automated or computerized version with emphasis on integrating the human element.

Section III
Project Quality and Risk Management

Section III provides an overview of quality and risk management for technology projects. This section first reviews the basic principles, techniques, and their application to the development of quality. The reader is then provided with a review of basic risk management concepts, including the Integrated Project Risk Model. The balance of the section discusses how quality techniques are both a contributor to, as well as a mitigator of risk.

Project management is carefully planned, organized effort to manage the resources in order to successfully accomplish specific project goals and objectives. This chapter covers the entire life cycle of a project right from the feasibility study of the project, project planning, implementation, evaluation, support, and maintenance of the project. Each phases of the project is a vast topic within project management. The topic of interest here is the quality assurance in project management.

This chapter provides a fundamental yet comprehensive coverage of quality management. Bringing managers and engineers the most up-to-date quality management tools, research, and theory, this chapter shows readers how to plan for quality and achieve quality control. Broad in scope and inclusive in methodology, the material covered in this chapter will be useful for anyone concerned with quality management and control in business and industry. Topics covered include planning and organizing for quality, total quality management, quality improvement, statistical quality control, and ISO 9000.

Chapter XVI

Dawn M. Owens, University of Nebraska at Omaha, USA
Deepak Khazanchi, University of Nebraska at Omaha, USA

Successful implementation of IT (information technology) projects is a critical strategic and competitive necessity for firms in all industrial sectors today. However, due to cost overruns, schedule delays, unfilled requirements and poor quality, it is reported that less than 30% of IT projects are perceived to be successful. Much has been written about causes of project failure and many have provided best practices and critical success factors for effective management projects, yet projects still continue to fail. As a first step to overcome systemic causes of project failure the authors propose a unified definition of software quality assurance (SQA). They use this definition to develop and present an approach to SQA that focuses on controlling risks and provide a framework for assuring the development and project management life cycles.

Chapter XVII

Fayez Ahmed Albadri, ADMA-OPCO, Abu Dhabi, UAE

An overwhelming number of information technology (IT) projects experience persistent problems and failures. This chapter reflects on some of the important aspects of IT project management as applied to the implementation and post-implementation of enterprise information systems and ERP applications. By investigating 25 major IT projects and analysing the variables that influence project performance, the research has successfully developed, tested and refined a hypothesised risk-based management model. With its components, processes, metrics and tools clearly defined and characterised, the integrated project-risk management (IPRM) model and system are presented as viable alternatives to conventional project management approaches and tools.

Chapter XVIII

Pete Hylton, Indiana University Purdue University Indianapolis, USA

In today's highly competitive industrial environment, many high-tech businesses are using technical risk management (TRM) in their engineering design programs as a means of improving the chances of success. TRM allows program mangers to pinpoint potential failure modes of a project early in the process, so that corrective actions can be taken in the most effective manner. TRM also allows managers to appropriately prioritize program tasks so as to achieve optimum use of available technical resources. TRM requires that a methodology of practices and processes be implemented on an ongoing basis.

These processes identify, evaluate, mitigate, and manage technical risks effecting program success. This chapter will discuss implementation of the TRM process and provide a simple example to show how the process works.

Section IV
Project Planning and Assessment

Project planning is a critical and complex component of IT project process. This section provides the reader with a critical framework on how to plan a project, how to assess the project and then how to determine when to outsource a project.

Chapter XIX

IT projects across all sectors are relying on more iterative methodologies that can employ early and frequent assessment and evaluation processes in order to ensure that project deliverables are satisfactory. This chapter provides a practical overview of assessment and evaluation processes and how they can be built into any of the various project management and development models. Methods discussed include: audience and needs assessment; approaches for maintaining engagement with stakeholder audiences; requirements and feedback-gathering methods including focus groups, surveys, and other communications; and evaluation and review methods such as usability testing and user acceptance testing. Iterative cycles of assessment, prototyping, evaluation, and implementation will be demonstrated through examples and process model flow diagrams.

Chapter XX

Considering the high failure rate of information technology (IT) projects over the last 40 years, project managers should use all the tools at their disposal in order to make their project a success; however, more than half of all project managers fail to use a powerful tool that is readily available – a development methodology. A development methodology provides structure to a project, which facilitates communication, establishes expectations, enhances quality and promotes consistency. While empirical research in this area is lacking, a review of the extant literature reveals several factors that are important when choosing a development methodology. In this chapter, many of these factors are identified, a model for categorizing them is proposed, and a model for selecting a methodology is presented.

Chapter XXI

In this chapter, the author describes how one can implement and incorporate creative techniques to design, develop, document and disseminate a systematic process for conducting assessment, whether it be in a multinational corporation or it be in a small business environment. The author accomplishes this by providing models, samples and established guidelines for effectively using assessment results for continuous quality improvement. The author focuses on the importance of adopting modern techniques and stresses that technology should not be viewed just as a growing trend. The author shows how technology can be intelligently implemented as an invaluable assessment tool that can quickly identify areas for improvement so that a given corporation can continue to climb the ladder of success in a competitive global market of the 21st Century.

Chapter XXII

It is well-known that well managed and controlled projects are more likely to be delivered on time and within budget. The construction of a (resource-feasible) baseline schedule and the follow-up during execution are primary contributors to the success or failure of a project. Earned value management systems have been set up to deal with the complex task of controlling and adjusting the baseline project schedule during execution. Although earned value systems have been proven to provide reliable estimates for the follow-up of cost performance, they often fail to predict the total duration of the project. In this chapter, results of a large simulation study to evaluate the forecast accuracy of earned value based predictive metrics are presented. No detailed mathematical calculations are presented in the chapter, but instead an overview from a project life cycle point-of-view is presented.

Section V
Case Study Examples in Technology Project Management, Planning, and Operations

Section V presents the unique opportunity for readers to learn strategies of technology project management, planning and operations through a variety of case studies that span business, industry, and education. Gaining knowledge from the successes and failures of others is an effective way to learn and this section presents innovation case studies to facilitate such learning.

Chapter XXIII

This chapter presents a technology exploration process designed to support service innovation for information and communication technologies in a university environment. The mission of the technology exploration is to highlight possible applications of new technologies on the basis of prototypes which, following an evaluation phase, are used to develop new services.

Chapter XXIV

Planning for Technology Integration 385

Henryk R. Marcinkiewicz, Aramco Services Company, USA

This chapter presents three models that discuss the planning for technology integration into instruction. Institutional needs are assessed for three dimensions suggested in Gilbert's, "Model of Human Competence." The areas needing addressing are typically within instruction; therefore, the process steps of a generic instructional design model are used. Within designing for instruction, Bransford's, "variables affecting learning," are the focal points organizational planners need to consider in planning instruction. Instruction is framed as "faculty-as-learner centered instruction." The variables are also a significant aspect of the content of instruction for faculty because faculty will use them in planning their own instruction integrated with technology.

Chapter XXV

University Task Force Deepens Academic Involvement in ERP 397

Michael Crow, Kansas State University, USA

This case study explores the evolution of a task force from its beginnings, springing out of an update session with an academic policy and procedure committee to the point that the task force eventually supplanted the Project Steering Committee as the primary conduit of information exchange between the project team and the academic community.

Chapter XXVI

Production, Publication, and Use of Educational Multimedia Content in Brazil: Challenges and Opportunities in Real World Technology Projects 406

Joni A. Amorim, Universidade Estadual de Campinas (UNICAMP), Brazil

Carlos Machado, PST Electronics, Brazil

Rosana G. S. Miskulin, Universidade Estadual Paulista "Júlio de Mesquita Filho" (UNESP), Brazil

Mauro S. Miskulin, Universidade Estadual de Campinas (UNICAMP), Brazil

The production of quality educational multimedia content involves both publication and use. In Brazil, there are many challenges and opportunities in real world technology projects. This is particularly true for the field of education. Challenges may involve not only strategy and project engineering issues, but also the management of change in the creation of virtual groups focused on multimedia production. This chapter intends to highlight the complexities involved in a pioneer project that was to provide secondary students with free content by connecting to the Internet.

Chapter XXVII

Instructional Technology Plans for Higher Education 419

Hasan Tinmaz, Educational Technologist, Turkey

Technology planning is an indispensable activity for all higher education institutions. A major purpose of technology planning is to utilize technologies effectively and implement them for communicative, managerial and instructional purposes. This chapter offers a dynamic and adaptable framework for technology planning project in higher education institutions.

Chapter XXVIII

The rapid proliferation of e-learning tools that offer low or no cost investment and are not housed on institutional servers have made it very attractive for faculty to move learning experiences online. Yet institutions are often unaware of the technology project practices of instructors, thereby investing time, effort, and funding into tools and infrastructure than may not be the best support for learning outcomes. This chapter describes shifts in the use of learning technologies to illustrate a high level overview for assessing current use and practice, and provides a framework for selecting delivery solutions and tools that can best support instructional goals.

Chapter XXIX

Original equipment manufacturers (OEMs) in the automotive industry are faced with the conflicting goals of creating vehicles with higher reliability, increased feature content and quality while lowering model runs, reducing costs, and shorter developmental times. However, to achieve these goals, it is very difficult in a global product development environment that involves globally distributed OEMs while suppliers work on the same components and subsystems. This chapter attempts to narrow down this gap by presenting a lean and global product development (GPD) framework and the necessary enablers to achieve this end. The framework is demonstrated through an automotive industry case study.

Section VI
Issues & Trends in Technology Project Management, Planning, and Operations

Technology project management, planning activities, and operational strategies ensure a higher chance for organizations to reach their project related goals. Technology project management streamlines processes, coordinate projects and enable more efficiency in day-to-day operations while planning of technology projects. As more companies see the relevance of technology project management, these trends will become increasingly important to overall technology project management, planning, and operation strategies.

The business world is running at a faster pace than ever before. Globalization has partnered the world and new ways of doing business to meet increasing demands are inevitable. Teams now have members dispersed around the globe, distanced by location and brought together by technology. Where these geographically dispersed teams work is known as a "virtual" world. The "virtual" team is different from the traditional team many are familiar with requiring that new skills be learned to be a successful member. This chapter will introduce the virtual team and discuss how it is different from traditional teams. The skills required of the leadership and members of a virtual team will be identified and detailed. The various types of virtual teams will be examined to determine how they are utilized in today's business world.

Chapter XXXI

Social networking technologies—such as Wikis, blogs and instant messaging—are increasingly being employed in business settings to support communication, collaboration and knowledge management. In this chapter, the authors discuss how a Wiki was used to facilitate project management in a large system implementation for a decentralized organization. Further, the authors show how it continues to add value to the organization after the project's completion, supporting operational management activities while at the same time providing a platform for fostering and promoting innovation. They introduce important implementation considerations for deploying a Wiki in your organization, in addition to sharing observations from their own implementation that saw both successes and failures.

Chapter XXXII

Higher education IT project managers have always relied on user activity data as logged in one form or another. Summarized counts of users and performance trends serve as essential sources of information for those who need to analyze problems, monitor security, improve software, perform capacity planning, and so forth. This chapter examines how data mining solutions – particularly Web usage mining methods– are being taken up in three open systems project management contexts: digital libraries, online museums, and course management systems. In describing the issues and challenges that motivate data mining applications in these three contexts, the chapter provides an overview of how data mining integrates within project management processes. The chapter also touches on ways in which data mining can be augmented by the complementary practice of data visualization.

Foreword

Successful technology project management, planning, and operations are increasingly vital to all organizations, driven by the demands of global competition, rapid technological growth, and faster time to
market. For those in technology fields, project management skills are a major core competency needed
for serious competition. Those who have mastered these skills will continue to be in high demand
worldwide, commanding higher salaries than those around them. However, how does one extend those
skills or acquire them in the first place? *The Handbook of Research on Technology Project Management,
Planning, and Operations* is a great place to start.

I am pleased and honored to write a foreword to this book on behalf of the Chief Editor Professor
Terry T. Kidd, as its scope and content provide organizations with the essential ingredients for implementing and managing technology based projects. Kidd has done it again, synthesizing internationally
renowned scholars and practitioners in the field to publish such a volume. Whether the projects are associated with office, a government computing systems, or a management information system, technology
project management, planning, and operations provide crucial support for developing and implementing
strategies for overall project success. The integrative approach is particularly welcome.

It is important to understand that technology project management, planning and operations are a critical
resource for organizations. Virtually every government agency and many businesses spend substantial
time and resources collecting, distributing, analyzing, transforming, and using information. In the past,
manual procedures provided the only means for manipulating information. Today, technology represents
powerful tools for maximizing the value of information. As a major resource and asset, technology requires effective planning, management, and operations. In this respect, technology project management
has much in common with other types of assets, such as human resources, capital facilities, and financial
resources. All require some degree of formal structure to promote effective use and management.

In my role as Executive Director of Project White Hat, an information security and research firm, I
am able to have firsthand experience with technology project management, planning, and operations.
Further, I have a unique experience with personnel from a wide venue of clientele who seek professional
guidance on the technology project management. I believe that these people will benefit from reading
this book for its extensive source of information.

This book merges the academic and the hands-on knowledge of the authors, to assist organizations
in gaining benefits from both perspectives. It offers the practical knowledge derived from technology
project management, based on the wide-ranging consulting and project management fieldwork of the
Project Management Institute. Further this book combines extensive academic research and real world
case studies that have been performed by scholars in the discipline of information systems, engineering,
education, and business administration.

This book cuts through much of the hype associated with technology project management and provides the real with the bare bones needed to get the job done. The book provides a thorough examination

of business contexts that influence the ways that technology projects are managed. Further, the book beyond mere research, but provides a framework for requirements assessment, evaluation, quality, risk management, leadership, and project management tools, along with examples to assist with analysis and specification of technology project management solutions. A highlight of the book is the fact that the text provides extensive checklists and case studies to assist organizations with their technology project requirements.

With the rapid progress in technology, systems planning and management have become increasingly important in this digital economy. New technologies that can have significant implications for corporate strategies are developed constantly. The incredible growth of technologies and the demand for a new generation of technology stakeholders have facilitated the introduction of Technology Project Management programs in many higher education institutions in the United States and around the world. *The Handbook of Research on Technology Project Management, Planning and Operations* will provide a broad scope of information technology project and resources for researchers, educators, students, and industry practitioners to share and exchange their research ideas, practical experiences, challenges, and opportunities concerning technology project management. This book will help those organizations to progress and implementation of the next generation of technology project management solutions.

I am pleased to be able to recommend this book to readers across the globe. Whether they those looking for substantive material on knowledge strategy, those looking to understand an important aspect of technology project management, planning and operations, or those about to embark on the journey of a technology based project. Regardless of the focus, this book is for you. I wish you the very best successes with this book for Kidd have synthesized yet another piece where all can benefit.

Robert K. Hiltbrand, MS.
Executive Director, Project Whitehat

Robert K. Hiltbrand *is the executive director of Project White Hat, an information securities and technology project management consulting firm. He has over 15 years of experience in information systems administration, information security, and IT project management. He has Bachelors of Arts in sociology from Southwest Texas State University and a Masters of Science in Technology Project Management - Information Systems Security from the University of Houston, where his expertise lies within in the concept of the LiveCD as a desktop platform for general-purpose computing needs within a public access environment.*

Preface

Technology project management, planning, and operational strategies are critical resources for organizations. In the past, manual procedures provided the only means for manipulating information. Today, technology represents powerful tools for maximizing the value of information. As a major resource and asset, technology requires effective planning, management, and operations. In this respect, technology project management has much in common with other types of assets, such as human resources, capital facilities, and financial resources. All require some degree of formal structure to promote effective use and management.

Looking back at recent innovations within technology, we can trace these innovations back to a project: the behind the scenes work that, when managed correctly, results in a new system, a new technology, or a new product in the marketplace. Technology project management refers to the field of study and practice utilizing management and administrative principles as a means to controlling the bounds of a technology-based project to solve business and organizational challenges and human performance issues. Within the field of technology project management, there are many specific areas of focus. While technology project management can apply to the military and corporate settings, it is also applied to the school setting including charter schools, public schools, online, higher education or anywhere a technology project or initiative can be initiated.

With the rapid progress in technologies, systems planning and management have become increasingly important in this digital economy. New technologies that can have significant implications for corporate strategies are developed constantly. The incredible growth of technology and the demand for a new generation of technology stakeholders have facilitated the introduction of technology project management programs in many higher education institutions in the United States and around the world. *The Handbook of Research on Technology Project Management, Planning and Operations* provides a broad scope of technology project strategies for researchers, educators, students, and industry practitioners to share and exchange their research ideas, practical experiences, challenges, and opportunities concerning technology project management.

Successful technology project management, planning, and operations are increasingly vital to all organizations, driven by the demands of global competition, rapid technological growth, and faster time to market. For those in technology fields, project management skills are a major core competency needed for serious competition. Those who have mastered these skills will continue to be in high demand worldwide, commanding higher salaries than those around them. However, how does one extend those skills or acquire them in the first place? *The Handbook of Research on Technology Project Management, Planning, and Operation* is a great place to start.

Technology Project Management is the discipline of planning, organizing, and managing resources to bring about the successful completion of specific project goals and objectives within a technology driven organization. A technology project is a finite endeavor (having specific start and completion dates) undertaken to create a unique product or service which brings about beneficial change or added value. This finite characteristic of projects stands in sharp contrast to processes, or operations, which are permanent or semi-permanent functional work to repetitively produce the same product or service. In practice, the management of these two systems is often found to be quite different, and as such requires the development of distinct technical skills and the adoption of separate management philosophy.

The primary challenge of project management is to achieve all project goals and objectives while adhering to classic project constraints, including scope, quality, time and budget. The secondary and more ambitious challenge is to optimize the allocation and integration of inputs necessary to meet pre-defined objectives.

Technology project management is quite often the province and responsibility of an individual project manager combined with technological expertise. This individual seldom participates directly in the activities that produce the end result, but rather strives to maintain the progress and productive mutual interaction of various parties in such a way that overall risk of failure is reduced.

Further, a technology project manager can be a client representative. This representative has to determine and implement the exact needs of the client, based on knowledge of the firm they are representing.

An organizations vision for technology project management should speaks "to achieve the objectives of the project on time and within budget." This vision, goals, and priorities of an organization provides context for the technology project management planning and operations process. In addition, good technology project management planning and operations should help to achieve certain principles for technology-based projects. These include:

- Technology must serve and respond to the mission, goals, and priorities of the sponsoring entity.
- Assessing and possibly redesigning the business process must precede decisions about applying a specific information technology solution.
- The planning, operations and management process should treat projects as a strategic resource that has value and should explore ways to maximize this value.
- Technology projects belong to the enterprise, and sponsoring entities should incorporate data sharing and the needs of other users in their plans, subject to privacy and confidentiality requirements.
- Technology projects should be scalable, reliable, and efficient.

Like any human undertaking a technology-based projects, projects needs to be performed and delivered under certain constraints. Traditionally, these constraints have been listed as "scope," "time," and "cost". A further refinement of the constraints separates product "quality" or "performance" from scope, and turns quality into a fourth constraint.

The time constraint refers to the amount of time available to complete a project. The cost constraint refers to the budgeted amount available for the project. The scope constraint refers to what must be done to produce the project's end result. These three constraints are often competing constraints: increased scope typically means increased time and increased cost, a tight time constraint could mean increased costs and reduced scope, and a tight budget could mean increased time and reduced scope.

The discipline of technology project management is about providing the tools and techniques that enable the project team (not just the project manager) to organize their work to meet these constraints.

Of the hundreds of project management books on the market, few address the unique needs of the technology project manager or projects undertaken in a technology driven organization. Unlike most other project management books, *The Handbook of Research of Technology Project Management, Planning, and Operations* tackles the specific issues that technology professionals must face, such as understanding technology resources, managing project scope and feature creep, quality, risk management, assessment, project evaluation, meeting client expectations, leadership, outsourcing, among many others.

Whether you're a college student, a software engineer, an IT professional, or a scholar in the field, *The Handbook of Technology Project Management, Planning, and Operations* will help you gain a comprehensive understanding of the technology project management life cycle and learn how to manage it – from first steps on through to intermediate topics (as well as some advanced ones).

With *The Handbook of Research on Technology Project Management, Planning, and Operations* you will:

- Discover the reasons projects fail
- Understand keys features to project success
- Explore the components of the technology project lifecycle
- Review the documents necessary for technology project management and learn how to complete a post project evaluation
- Understand the warning signs of a project in trouble and learn how to get it back on track
- Learn quality and risk management practices in easy-to-understand terms
- Acquire practical ways to develop effective leadership and team-building skills

The *Handbook of Research on Technology, Project Management, Planning and Operations* provides a compendium of terms, definitions and explanations of concepts, processes and acronyms. Additionally, this volume feature chapters authored by leading experts offering an in-depth description of key terms and concepts related to different areas, issues and trends in technology project management, technology management, technology planning, and technology operations in modern organizations worldwide.

Technology project management, planning, and operational strategies ensure a higher chance for organizations to reach their technology based goals. Technology project management streamlines processes, coordinate projects and enable more efficiency in day-to-day operations and planning of technology project management. As more companies see the relevance of technology project management, these trends will become increasingly important to overall technology project management, planning, and operations design.

In order to provide the best balanced coverage of concepts and issues related to the topics of this handbook, current researchers from around the world were asked to submit their chapter describing their unique coverage of technology project management planning and operations. Each chapter submission began with the proposal phase. Following the submission phase, each proposal was submitted for blind reviewed by a team of reviewers who indicated the accepted or rejection of the chapter proposal. Following the proposal review phase, each author was then given permission to complete their own chapters for the handbook. After completing their respective chapter, the chapter was then submitted once again for blind peer review once more. After a two round rigorous referred processed of two reviewers, the chapters that were strong and favorable from the reviewers were chosen as entries for this handbook. The idea here was to assemble the best minds in the field from all over the world to contribute entries to the handbook. As a result of the double blind submission process, this handbook includes more than 30 entries highlighting current concepts, issues and emerging trends relating to technology project management planning, and operations. All entries are written by knowledgeable, distinguished scholars from many prominent research institutions around the world.

This book can provide valuable information to wide-range audience. This audience includes members from higher education, K-12 education, business and industry, as well as federal, state, and local governments and the military. Whether one is planning, managing, implementing or evaluating a technology-based project, researchers and practitioners alike will need to be informed concerning technology project management, planning activities, and operational strategies.

In particular, this handbook will be valuable to corporate executives, information technology professionals, project managers, and scholars in the field who are seeking sound theoretically and practically informed strategies of how to effectively manage technology-based projects. Managers may take advantage of examples from this book to help justify project management tools, offices, initiatives and strategic plans. This book also appeals to higher education IT professionals and administrators struggling with issues on where to place value and resources as it relates to technology projects. Clarification of the range of technology project management models can help administrators and staff members. Whether one is planning, managing, implementing or evaluating a technology-based project researchers and practitioners alike will need information concerning technology project management, planning, and operations. Those in the field conducting research will benefit from reading chapters on the current research and applications both from the corporate perspective. Finally, policy makers reading or accessing this book will discover the value and power in technology project management to promote excellence in technology project management. Hence governmental funding for these types of initiatives and projects needs to reflect this fact.

The chapters authored in this collection were selected because of their expertise and leadership roles within the field as well as the unique perspective they had to tell. With the mix of corporate and military training, non profit organizations, K-12 school, higher education institution, and industry, a wide range of perspectives are covered in this book. This book highlights technology project management as a growing field of study which uses technological interventions as a means to solve project related challenges challenges. The chapters are not organized by industry. Instead, they are divided into six major themes. Section I provides both an introduction and an overview of technology project management, planning and operations beginning with a foundational knowledge to understanding technical projects through an analytical framework. Chapters in this section present to the author project management, competencies, IT project complexities, and then a brief look at project management from 2027. Section II lays a thorough foundation of project leadership, decision making, and management for the overall success of a technology based project. Leadership is essential to the success or failure of a project. Section III provides an overview of quality and risk management for technology projects. This section first reviews the basic principles, techniques, and their application to the development of quality. The reader is then provided with a review of basic risk management concepts, including the Integrated Project Risk Model. The balance of the section discusses how quality techniques are both a contributor to, as well as a mitigator of risk. Project planning is a most critical and complex part of entire IT project process. Section IV provides the reader with critical information on how to plan planning a project, how to assess the project and then how to determine when to outsource a project. Section V presents the unique opportunity for the reader to learn of technology project management, planning and operations through a variety of case studies that span business, industry, and education. Gaining knowledge from the successes and failures of others is an effective way to learn and this section presents innovation case studies to facilitate such learning. Section VI, presents future trends within the field of Technology Project Management, Planning, and Operations As more companies see the relevance of technology project management, these trends will become increasingly important to overall technology project management, planning, and operations design.

For all practical purposes this handbook discusses various methods and tools for assessment, testing and evaluation of technology project management strategies, case studies, opportunities and challenges. For future development of technology project management, this book gives information about the trends and issues facing the field. At the end of this book, there is a wide range of ideas, examples, guidelines, stories, models, and solution all with the basic premise of technology project management.

With the diverse and comprehensive coverage of multiple perspectives in the field, this authoritative handbook will contribute to a better understanding all topics, research, and discoveries in this evolving, significant field of study. Furthermore, the contributions included in this handbook will be instrumental in expanding of the body of knowledge in this vast field. The coverage of this handbook provides strength to this reference resource for technology project management, planning, and operations research and also decision makers in obtaining a greater understanding of the concepts, issues, problems, trends, challenges and opportunities. It is my sincere hope that this publication and the amount of information and research presented will assist colleagues, faculty, students, teachers, and organizational decision makers in enhancing their understanding of this discipline and to effectively integrate technology planning and operations and technology project management to meet the needs of our diverse organizations. Perhaps this publication will inspire its readers to contribute to the current body of research in this immense field, tapping into possibilities to assist organizations in making technology project management opportunities open to success.

Terry T. Kidd
Texas A&M University, USA
October 2008

Acknowledgment

Completing a project of this magnitude is an opportunity many choose never to undertake. It is with the help of many who have inspired me to complete the journey that was ahead.

I would first like to take this opportunity to acknowledge the considerable time and effort the authors have invested in their respective publications in this book. The authors presented within this book are intelligence and well seasoned in their practice and respective areas. Without the hard work, dedication, and in some cases sacrifice, this book would not be made into reality without the assistance of the authors. Thank you for being so gracious and patient under fire and accepting to my comments and ideas on your chapters. I would like to send a special acknowledge and thanks to Mrs. Peggy Powell and Mrs. Julee Rendon from the University of Texas Health Science Center School of Public Health for assisting me during this project.

Gratitude and acknowledgements go out to the reviewers who spent countless hours reading, proofing, and articulating their comments from the proposal stage to the final chapter revisions.

Special thanks also must go to the IGI Global publishing team, and in particular Ms. Rebecca Beistline and Ms. Julia Mosemann, for their continued administrative support and hard work in helping me bring this vision to a reality. Without them, this would not have been made possible.

I would also like to acknowledge and thank Dr. Carolyn Ashe and Dr. Chynette Nealy, from the University of Houston-Downtown, Dr. Curtis J. Bonk of Indiana University, Dr. Gene Schroder of the University of Texas School of Public Health, and Dr. Jean Madsen of the Texas A&M University for their encouragement, advice, and mentorship in my career. I would also like to thank my good friend, Ms. Taresa Mikle, for her continued support and humor while working on this project.

Lastly, I would like to thank and acknowledge Ms. Virginia Ilene Johnson, Mrs. Susan McKrell, and Ms. Kathy Moseley who believed in me when others did not. I would also like to thank my good friends for their continued support.

In closing, I wish to pay a special tribute to Ada Lovelace who started a revolution in the world of computing. This book is dedicated to her memory of her work in the field.

Terry T. Kidd
Texas A&M University, USA
October 2008

Section I
Overview of Technology Project Management

Chapter I
The Tao to Understanding Enterprise Resource Planning Complexity:
Sun–Tzu's Five Factors Revisited

James W. Price Jr.
Kennesaw State University, USA

Pamila Dembla
Kennesaw State University, USA

ABSTRACT

As exploratory research, the chapter's aim is to assess if Sun-Tzu's application of Taoist principles are applicable to the problem domain of Enterprise Resource Planning Management (ERPM). It argues that an ERP's complexity not only shares conceptually The Art of War's historical context, but also can be understood to be a disequilibrium force best understood using Taoist principles. Sun-Tsu's The Art of War (AW) has been adapted successfully to the military domain (MD); and, MD has been adapted to strategic management (SM). If an ERP's business drivers can be mapped to a firm's strategic goals, one may conclude Sun-Tzu's Art of War can be adapted to an ERP implementation (AW→MD→SM→ERP). Therefore, the authors hope to explore the applicability of Sun-Tzu's Five Factors of Initial Estimation (Five Factors), an Eastern philosophy (a non-linear thought process) to ERP-related Western-oriented project management techniques (a linear thought process).

INTRODUCTION

In spite of advances in project management, statistics and lessons learned from past failures, "…big IT projects, whether major technology installations or new growth strategies fail at an astonishing rate. These efforts consume tre- mendous resources over months or even years and the toll they take is not just financial…" (Marchewka, 2006, pp.109-114). The myriad of strategic goals for an Enterprise Resource Planning (ERP) implementation include, afforded business process reengineering, enabled ability to derive additional value from supply chain, enhanced ability to future e-Commerce integration as well as integration with other internal business information systems, improved management of inventory costs, enabled replacement in part or whole legacy systems, empowered management of multinational enterprise competitiveness on a per unit basis, enhancing enterprise images, and further evolution of the e-business strategy. With such varied strategic drivers, ERP implementation rests on a host of forces whose impact can vary considerably from company to company (Fang & Lin, 2006). Though ERP systems are considered as technically complex projects, failure to plan well has been identified as the main obstacle to effectively deploying large-scale systems (Chen, 2001; McAfee, 2003; Muscatello & Parente, 2006).

If research has concluded that ERP implementations are challenged not by the technology, instead by lack of planning; one might conclude top management's failure to plan may be related to its lack of understanding an ERP's true nature. Instead of reinventing the wheel with another paradigm, top management may find it efficient and effective to explore eastern philosophies accumulation of over five thousand years of knowledge

on achieving balance in dynamic environments (e.g. *Chou I (Book of Changes)*, Confucius, Lao-Tzu, Sun-Tzu and others). Thus, this paper's aim is to explore the applicability of Sun-Tzu's Five Factors of Initial Estimation (Five Factors), an Eastern philosophy (non-linear thought process) to ERP-related Western-oriented project management techniques (linear thought process).

The chapter's format is as follows: First, the underlying conceptual foundation is developed by exploring Sun-Tzu's historical context. Second, a logical reasoning is offered as to why Sun-Tzu's teachings may be applicable to ERPM. Then, an attempt to map terminology between the *Art of War* and project management entities is offered as bridge to developing a model. This is followed by a discussion of three case studies and case analysis. In closing, the ERPM Five Factors of Analysis (working model) will be explained. The model serves as merely a novel first step to understanding ERP's complexity using a non-linear process. The paper's concludes with a discussion of its Implications and Conclusion.

As shown in Figure 1, Sun-Tzu's Five Factors consist of *Tao, Heaven, Earth, General, and*

Figure 1. Sun-Tzu's Five Factors of initial estimations

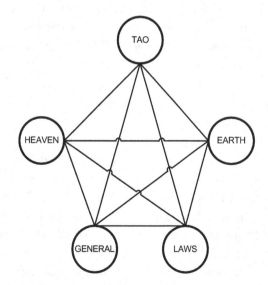

Figure 2. Traditional single factor classification

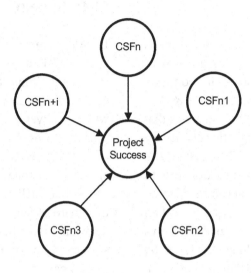

Laws (Sawyer, 1996). The research goal of this paper is to compare and create a working model for Enterprise IT Project Management (a linear thought process) with the help of Sun-Tzu's Five Factors of Initial Estimation Approach (a non-linear process). Figure 2 will be re-introduced later in the paper with additional detail to further capture Sun-Tzu and Taoist's teachings.

LITERATURE REVIEW

Sun-Tzu

It has been generally accepted that *The Art of War* was written towards the end of China's Spring and Autumn Period, 722-481 B.C.E, and the beginning of the Warring States Period, 403-221 B.C.E. (Sawyer, 1996; Tusi, 1999). During this period seven kingdoms namely Zhoa, Wu, Han, Qin, Qi, Yuëh, Chin, Chou, and Ch'u existed comprising of hundreds of smaller states, and competing against each other. This period was "characterized by great personalities, inescap-

able intrigue, murder, ever-expanding warfare, and the unfolding of astounding drama in which entire states rose and perished, often at the whims of dominant individuals" (Sawyer, 1996, pp.1). Though seven kingdoms existed, not all were of the same size or relative strength. Ch'u was considered to be the strongest and Wu (where the *Art of War* is believed to be penned and applied) was not considered a powerful state. Similar to enterprise IT projects, Sun-Tzu's environment consisted of a myriad of stakeholders with varied interests, and fierce competition within and outside the seven kingdoms. In such a dynamic environment, Sun-Tzu clearly understood warfare's true nature, a disequilibrium force, and the kingdom of Wu's need to properly assess its every move in such a volatile environment. If one equates warfare and ERP implementations as disequilibrium forces, an ERP implementation strategy should be to achieve maximum results with minimum exposure, limiting the destruction to be inflicted and suffered. Also, the dynamic environment and warfare nature necessitates a constant assessment of the environment.

Rationale for Equating Sun-Tzu and ERPM: Strategy

A common Chinese phrase, 'the marketplace is a battlefield' reflects an understanding that warfare and marketplace strategies share common characteristics (Lee, 2001; Wu, Chou, & Wu 2004). Also, Michael Porter (1995) suggests that strategic management is the adaptation of military strategy to the business world. Thus, just as *The Art of War* (AW) can be adapted successfully to the military domain (MD); MD can be adapted to strategic management (SM). In addition, if an ERP's business drivers can be mapped to a firm's strategic goals, one may conclude Sun-Tzu's *Art of War* can be adapted to an ERP implementation (AW→MD→SM→ERP).

Wong, Thomas & George (1998) suggested a plethora of research relating Sun-Tzu's *Art of War* to the business domain. Further, they extended Sun-Tzu's Five Factors to the analysis of Western firms operating in China's dynamic and complex marketplace. In doing so, they went beyond traditional analysis of Sun-Tzu work which typically centered on firms competing head-to-head. They expanded the breadth of analysis to include dynamic elements, such as stakeholders and business counterparts. Table 1 below reflects a comparison of Sun-Tzu's historical context and content-analysis of Wong et al., (1998) application of Sun-Tzu to the business domain.

Mapping Sun-Tzu Terminology to the ERP Domain

In order to map Sun-Tzu's *Art of War's* terminology to ERP, a correlation of terms is in order. In ancient China, the emperor with input from a war council decided whether or not to pursue war. Once war was decided, a general would be selected to draw-up battle plans and would be provided officers and troops. In today's business climate, someone from top management would sponsor an ERP project. If it is a large firm, then the Board of Directors would make the ultimate decision as to whether or not to pursue an ERP system. If approval is granted by the Board or top management, in general, a Senior Project Manager (PM) would be selected and someone from top management would serve as the Project's Champion or Sponsor. The PM, as Sun-Tzu's general, is primarily tasked with drawing up plans to coordinate and control the work effort needed to achieve an ERP's Critical Success Factors (CSF). Given the similarities between Sun-Tzu and modern-day business practices, Table 2 is suggested to correlate terminology.

With a simplified appreciation of Sun-Tzu's *Art of War,* the discussion shall now turn to the methodology used to analyze Sun-Tzu's Five Factors.

Table 1. Mapping of Sun-Tzu to the business domain

China Historical Context Salient Points (Sawyer, 1996)	Dynamics of Western Firms in China (Wong, et al., 1998)
Large Number of Stakeholder w/ Varied Interests	-Business Counterparts
Environment of Great Uncertainty/Unpredictability	-Stakeholders Actions cannot always be predicted -New experimentation with capital markets -No Industry Standards
Wu – Warfare is a Tactical Strategic Response	-Strategic Initiative -No Rules of the Game
Constant Assessment of the Environment	-Marketplace is Constantly Changing

Table 2. Mapping Sun-Tzu terminology to the ERP domain

Sun-Tzu's Terminology (Sawyer, 1996)	ERPM Terminology
1. Emperor	1. Board and/or Top management
2. Troops	2. Project Team
3. Warfare	3. ERP Project
4. Generals	4. Project Champion, Senior Project Manager
5. Battle Plans	5. Implementation Strategy, Work-Break-Structure

Table 3. Framework of mapping of Sun Tsu's five factors to ERPM

Sun-Tzu's Five Factors (Sawyer, 1996)	Business Domain Mapping of Five Factors (Wong et al, 1998)	ERPM Principles
Tao	Permeating Force	
Heaven	Uncontrollable External Factors	
Earth	Semi-Controllable Environmental Factors	
Generals	Business Manager	
Laws	Capabilities	

METHODOLOGY

The research methodology consists of qualitative multi-case analysis compliment with additional research finding related to each factor. Three case studies are analyzed; two successful ERP cases and one failed ERP implementation of similar size and scope. Wong et al.'s (1998) mapping of Sun-Tzu's Five Factors to the business domain was used as a template to mapping Sun-Tzu to ERP domain, by inference to the ERPM domain. Table 3 above is suggested as a guide. Ultimately, the table will be populated and re-analyzed at the conclusion of the analysis of Sun-Tzu's Five Factors of Initial Estimation section.

Before we begin the Sun-Tzu's Five Factors of Initial Estimation section, below is a brief introduction to each business.

Case Studies Introduction

The qualitative multi-case study analysis rests primarily on three ERP implementations: Cisco Systems, Tektronix, and FoxMeyer. Though all three ERP implementations occurred in the early 1990's; they represent issues encountered by firms almost fifteen years later as well. To further complicate ERP implementations, top management must plan to (1) extend beyond the enterprise and connect its ERP to external vendor's ERP systems and the web; and (2) evaluate the impact or incorporation of new technologies such as, Open ERP, SOA and XML into existing ERP systems or planned systems.

Case Study 1

Founded in 1984, Cisco Systems had grown to a five hundred (500) million dollar company by 1994. In order to grow into a five billion dollar plus company, Cisco's Top management needed an IT infrastructure capable of supporting such growth (Cotteller, Austin, & Nolan, 1999; Nolan, 2005). In support of Cisco's growth goals, CIO Peter Solvik foresaw a need (a) to change Cisco's internal-IT perception and (b) to overall the current IT infrastructure. In addition, about six months prior to the project's launch, Cisco core legacy systems failed which resulted in a 2-day company shutdown. Therefore, the need for a new system became a priority. Ultimately, KPMG was chosen as the primary consulting firm and Oracle as the ERP platform (Cotteller, et al., 1999).

Case Study 2

In 1993 FoxMeyer was a five billion dollar, pharmaceutical firm. SAP's R/3 package (dubbed Delta III Project) was to replace its Unisys-mainframe system and Pinnacle data warehousing-automation software (Scott, 1999). To integrate the two projects, Andersen Consulting was chosen. With a stated goal of improved IT capabilities and business operations, the Delta project was envisaged as a client/server SAP R/3 solution to be integrated with the automated warehouse project. However FoxMeyer's implementation failed and resulted in litigation, so exact details are limited. In spite of this, there is enough information to understand how a multitude of forces doomed this implementation.

Case Study 3

Tektronix was a billion dollar global firm specializing in electronic tools and devices. Its organizational structure reflected three autonomous business units. Prior to the ERP project, Tektronix was plagued with an IT infrastructure characterized by over 460 legacy systems in just the United States alone. The infrastructure offered no global standards, no integration of systems, and no inventory visibility. It was identified that the legacy system impeded ability to set global standardized business processes, limited financial data to divest any portions of the business, impacted ability to devise a flexible strategy, required at times for orders to be manually entered into multiple systems which allowed for order errors in different systems, impacted customer service, conferred limited ability to gauge performance of business units and to integrate acquisitions, and prohibited ability to manage customer accounts and to offer credit on a global basis (Westerman, Cotteler, & Austin, 1999). Though a clear business case for a global ERP was obvious, top management was concerned given its past problem implementing large-scale IT systems. Therefore, a clear vision was required to overcome any resistance to implement a global system (Westerman et al., 1999).

Sun-Tzu's Five Factors of Initial Estimation

In order to assess war, Sawyer's (1996) translation of the *Art of War* named these five factors, *Tao, Heaven, Earth, General, Laws of Military Organization and Discipline (Laws)*. Sun-Tzu suggested analyzing each factor using estimations in order to properly understand each factor's true nature. Sun-Tzu advised that one should only pursue war if a majority of the factors have been determined to be in accord with the kingdom's long-term strategic goals. Wong et al. (1998) suggested these five factors to serve as the cornerstones of a firm's strategic assessment of itself and its external environment as well as to build robust organizations. The discussion shall now turn to an analysis of each factor, starting with *Tao* and ending with the *Laws*.

Tao

Tao is an ancient, universal construct whose traditional meaning could be understood as a path or way to achieving a balanced existence (Wong et al., 1998). Sun-Tzu described *Tao* as a catalyst to a desired outcome. In mapping *Tao* to the business domain, Wong et al (1998) suggested, *"Tao seems to start[s] at the top and flow down to the lowest levels of the organization, just as national goals are first established by a country's leaders and are then translated into economic, social and military objectives"*. Further, Mei-Yeh & Lin (2006) suggested that top management view an ERP system as a tool to facilitate its strategic goals. Additionally, top management's initial selection of ERP business drivers can impact a firm's post-ERP implementation performance.

Case Study 1

In 1994, Cisco embarked on a 15 million dollar ERP implementation to replace all of its core legacy systems (Cotteller et al,, 1999; Nolan, 2005). Prior to the ERP project, the CIO had made changes which conferred the ability of each business unit to build its own system. McAfee (2003) noticed that for unknown reasons none of the three business unit managers offered a joint solution or attempted to provide a solution for their own division. Such indecision can be described as inertia, one of the five pitfalls of process-enabling IT projects. The backing of the Senior VP Manufacturing for a shared solution provided the needed push so that all impacted Senior VPs would ultimately agree to a single shared system. Therefore, the project's Tao would rest on the combined strength of alignment among the three divisions.

An Executive Steering Committee comprising of the VP of Manufacturing, the VP of Customer Advocacy, Corporate Controller, CIO, Oracle's Senior VP of Applications, and KPMG's Partner-in-Charge of West Coast Consulting was appointed to align the major stakeholders'

interest and ensure good communication. The Executive Steering Committee along with the CEO demonstrated the project's importance to everyone. In short, everybody in the company knew this was happening and it was a priority for the business.

Case Study 2

As previously defined, Tao entails that all of ERP's stakeholders must work in tandem to ensure success. In the case of FoxMeyer, two primary stakeholders; the top management and warehouse employees (end-users) clashed from the very beginning. Though top management's support was high, research suggested warehouse employees were disillusioned because the warehouse automation project would result in the closing of warehouses and threatened warehouse employees' jobs. Even before the project had started, its Tao seemed to be in question. Woltz Consulting had previously warned the initial project duration of eighteen months as unrealistic, but the top management did not heed to the advice and decided not to deviate from its plan (Scott 1999).

Case Study 3

The CFO/Project Manager was given absolute authority by the CEO to lead effort using three broad guidelines: (1) Businesses Unit Autonomy - each division would have its own database instance with all business units having standardized business processes; (2) Leveraging Shared Services – top management assumed that they would be significant saving by consolidating shared functions among the three business units, and (3) "As "plain vanilla" as Possible" – only if the system could not implement a process which afforded competitive advantage would the ERP software be changed (Westerman et al., 1999). In addition, the Executive Steering Committee was tasked by the Project Manager to with developing a global business framework which provided further guidance to the systems' expected business value.

In summary, the term, *Tao of Aligned Interests*

can be used to capture the top management's need to ensure that all relevant stakeholders' interests match with the ERP's strategic goals. Though the analysis above centered on top management, end-users and vendors; other key stakeholders may exist. As noted in the ERP literature review, communication barriers between IT and non-IT entities can be a barrier to success. The critical task for top management is to identify all relevant stakeholders and then assess the degree of alignment among all parties' interests.

Going forward, each termed offered by the authors to map Sun-Tzu to ERP will be appended with *Tao of Aligned Interests* in appreciation that every process or effort has its own *Tao* (Wong et al., 1998).

Heaven

As with *Tao, Heaven* is an ancient, universal construct of unknown date of origination or author. Sun-Tzu applied *Heaven* in its traditional meaning, an external force beyond anyone's control.

Though top management may strive to manage costs, an ERP project may be impacted by external forces which can drive costs beyond initial estimates. In the event of spiraling costs, Muscatello & Parente (2006) concluded top management must make decision in relation to the strength of the ERP's business case, not entirely on a change in the initial, in-complete estimates. Muscatello & Parente (2006) also noted that ERP project costs are often incomplete, in part, due to the inability of initial planners to capture all future costs, such as implementation and training. To leverage the benefit of *Heaven,* the use of a phased implementation approach was suggested to top management to (a) assess each project phase as a success or failure, (b) to build off lessons learned from a real-world implementation, and (c) to allow top management's business decisions' impact on cost to be contained to the individual implementation.

Therefore, the criteria to analyzing *Heaven's* impact on the case studies is not only to assess top management's efforts to identify unpredictable critical process/activities, but also their ability to devise a strategy to both mitigate risk and leverage opportunities.

Case Study 1

Given a tight timeline of only nine months to replace all of its core systems, the team utilized the "rapid iterative prototyping" methodology. The implementation was broken into a series of phases called "Conference Room Pilots" (CRP) (Cotteller et al., 1999; Nolan, 2005). Using such an approach, the team was able to leverage knowledge gained in prior iterations. Overall, the methodology required four phases before going live. The first phase, CPR0, resulted in the realization that an unmodified implementation was not tenable and significant modifications were to be expected. During phase two, CPR1, the degree and magnitude of modification became quite apparent.

As a result of proactively managing the implementation's unpredictability, thirty or so developers were quickly recruited. This iteration also determined that an after-sale application was needed. In spite of the added complexity, top management decided to Go-Live with both applications on the same day. The third phase, CPR2, identified the need for even further modification and a requirement for a data warehouse. A data warehouse afforded Cisco the ability to connect all of its systems to a single source of data. The goal of the final phase, CPR3, was to test the entire system. With roughly 60 days to spare, the project was able to eventually resolve all outstanding issues and the project was deemed a success. Though not explicitly stated, one could surmise the co-project leaders expected major problems after going-live. Therefore, they knew the earlier they went live, the more time available to solve unanticipated problems.

Case Study 2

Given the project's complexity and infancy of the technology, top management should have better managed its position and reduced implementation risk by first changing business processes to match the application to reduce the uncertainty of being an early adopter of technology in a new business domain (Scott, 1999). FoxMeyer clearly understood that it was "betting the company" by being the first major installation of using SAP R/3 in a distribution environment, as opposed to its normal manufacturing environment. As one of first distribution companies to implement SAP's R/3, FoxMeyer could have spread the impact of failure by tying the project's success and Accenture's fees together. Instead of mitigating the uncertainty of such a risky endeavor, the top management further complicated matters by adding a warehouse automation project.

Case Study 3
The top management chose a "wave implementation approach" to both mitigate and leverage *Heaven's* impact. The project was divided into five sub-implementations with each sub-implementation headed by the impacted division's President and the division's Director as the Project Manager. The 'wave approach' afforded to the project team excellent feedback as to a real-world implementation and afforded scheduling flexibility to program managers (Westerman et al., 1999).

The US site used a beta-version which delayed the rollout due to debugging, but was ultimately a success. The 'wave approach' allowed domestic program managers to perform future system upgrades before any new functionality was to be added. The phased approach also assured top management that the project's length and costs were justified and each successful wave positively affected overall team morale. Additionally, the US rollout leveraged *Heaven's* uncertainty, because rollout afforded the project team with needed lessons learned from an actual implementation, enhanced understanding of the needed work effort, and established need for standardized practices.

After the US rollout was a success, Holland for used as a test site for Europe. Soon, a series of pilot rollouts in Europe and non-EU nations were performed to truly understand the endeavor's opportunities, difficulties and costs. With the knowledge gained from the previous implementations, top management was empowered to go with the Big Bang approach for the rest of Europe. In spite of success in Europe and US, top management was unable to rollout simultaneously to Mexico, Brazil, and Canada due to geographic distances and non-synergies among businesses. Instead of working against its *Tao* and mindful of unanticipated problems, top management implemented Oracle in each country separately without any major impact to operations. As with Europe, the approach taken in Asia was to implement first in an English-speaking countries (India and Singapore) and with knowledge gained from the experience turned to Korea, Taiwan and Hong Kong. Using a phased approach, the project team was able to implement Oracle in 23 countries in under five hundred (500) days without any serious interruption to operations (Westerman et al., 1999).

Based on the analysis above, the authors suggest the term, *Tao of Global Impacts*, to capture the need for top management to assess and understand how to leverage the impact of external, unpredictable forces and to devise strategies in relation to the degree and magnitude of uncertainties.

Earth

As with *Tao* and *Heaven*, the construct of *Earth* is an ancient, universal construct whose author and date of origination is unknown. In regard to military planning, Sun-Tzu extended the idea of *Earth* to stress that one must consider how the landscape may impact the army's ability. Further, Sun-Tzu advised that a General should be able to leverage the landscape to the army's advantage (Sawyer, 1996).

Consistent with Sun-Tzu's teachings, Muscatello & Parente (2006) concluded that an ERP's scope should be established prior to the start of work. Without a solid understanding of the overall effort involved or realization that a void in understanding exists, initial estimates as to factors related to scope are useless. Further, McAfee (2003) suggested that if inertia, resistance and misspecification are likely pitfalls; implementation leaders should consider throttling back the project scope prior to start. In addition, top management must have the courage to reduce the endeavor's scale once top management realizes the scope is unattainable or has become unmanageable. In the case studies to follow, the assessment criteria are to assess top management's ability to understand the scope and its ability to put in-place measures to manage a project's scope.

Case Study 1

To manage the scope of the project, Cisco's Top management along with KPMG created a twenty member 'Tiger Team' to truly understand the project's scope (Cotteller et al., 1999; Nolan, 2005). Within seventy five days of its creation, KPMG and the 'Tiger Team' selected Oracle as the ERP vendor and then set out to estimate the project's duration and budget. Interestingly, the project's duration of nine months was a reflection of Cisco's business cycle, not technology.

Given its aggressive implementation schedule and rough estimation of the project's scope and budget, the project team utilized an iterative developmental methodology to truly understand the project's scope and the breath and depth of missed requirements. Further, top management used various methods to manage scope creep. For scope related problem which could be resolved by the project team, top management utilized Project Management Office and, if still unresolved, the Executive Steering Committee made the final decision. As iterations uncovered additional requirements, top management added resources and relied on the internal-IT department to maintain schedule. It is important to note, top management did not merely restrict all scope changes. Instead,

top management weighed scope changes against schedule and proprietary advantages.

Case Study 2

FoxMeyer competed on price and volume in the marketplace (Scott, 1999). Initial testing of Andersen's design and platform indicated a system capable of handling needed volume, but by 1994 the R/3 could process only 10,000 customer orders per night, compared with 420,000 under FoxMeyer's original mainframe system (Jesitus, 1997). In addition, the top management took an "unprecedented" large, volume contract which resulted in the focus of the project dramatically changing, contributing to rising project costs (eventually over $100 million), and lowering FoxMeyer's already narrow margins and erasing its profitability.

Ultimately, improper testing failed to catch the system's lack of processing capability, and FoxMeyer's failure to change business practices added additional uncertainty to top management's ability to manage or understand the project's overall scope. The addition, the warehouse project only served to add another unknown variable to a sea of unknown variables.

Case Study 3

Though a non-modified ERP application was desired as a means to help manage scope, ultimately modifications were needed. The scope was further managed by (1) the CFO's use of high-level guiding principles; (2) firm's commitment to change non-competitive business practices to match ERP's functionality; and (3) the utilization of a phased implementation approach afforded the additional benefits of allowing top management to manage project's scope.

As an example, during the European rollout, the project team's scope had to be expanded to satisfy the environment's multiple languages. Though top management had wanted an English-only solution, the lack of multi-language support threatened competitive advantage. So as not to sacrifice schedule, ultimately a multi-language module was designed but not included in the heart of the package. Such a strategy preserved the application's integrity and allowed for planner to get a head-start on identifying future multi-language modules needed for future implementations. Lastly, top management's willingness to sacrifice short-run costs to maintain schedule allowed for the procurement of needed resources and afforded ability to further manage the project's scope.

Based on the analysis above, we suggest the term; *Tao of Estimates* to stress that failure to estimate a project's work effort or at least understand the project's environmental variables can impede top management's ability to manage a project's scope.

General

In the business domain, Wong et al. (1998) used the term "Effective Leadership" and went on to describe how a business manager must posses each characteristics. In mapping Sun-Tzu's *General* to an ERP implementation, the breadth of the project requires a broader understanding of a *General* to account for a firm's multiple-layers of leadership (e.g., from Board, Top management, Executive Steering Committee, Project Management Office, Middle Management, Front-Line Managers, and so forth). Further, each layer's *General* is capable of impacting the success or failure of an ERP project.

To maintain control of large-scaled implementations, Nolan (2005) noted that Mellon Financial, Novell, Home Depot, Procter & Gamble, Wal-Mart and Fed Ex have used IT Governance Committees as an additional technique to offer guidance to top management. McAfee (2003) recommended that for process-enabling IT projects, such as an ERP, a high-ranking member of top management should be the project manager. A high ranking project manager can manage "above the interfaces" of ERP's stakeholders whose interests may conflict. Additionally, such a project manager afforded the

ability to make decisions to overcome the lethal forces of inertia and resistance. Lastly, Davenport, Harris, & Cantrell (2004) offered top management must assess the impact of the proposed solution across all levels of an organization.

Case Study 1
The impact of top management's various Generals has been previously discussed. During the second phase of software development, the need for a shared data warehouse solution called on Cisco's internal IT department to take on a General's role. The data warehouse solution needed Cisco's internal-IT's intimate knowledge of the infrastructure in order to build the system and maintain schedule. After going live, Cisco's internal-IT stepped up once again and resolved technical problems associated with the new system.

As Cisco's internal IT department stepped up, so did Cisco's hardware vendor evolve into a *General*. The contract with the vendor suggested that any problems attributed to the hardware resulted in the vendor to bear the full cost to resolve. Since, the ERP's instability was attributed, largely to the hardware platform, the hardware vendor's President led the post-implementation Executive Steering Committee and avoided legal action. In the end, the implementation's various *Generals* stabilized the system within the nine month deadline and project was deemed a success (Cotteller et al., 1999; Nolan, 2005).

Case Study 2
Since there is litigation pending in this case, there is very little information available to explain the top management's reasoning. FoxMeyer overspent and bit off more than they could chew, since they lacked available users on staff with the sophistication to handle a fast-track installation (Scott 1999).

Case Study 3
In addition to the CFO, CIO, Executive Steering Committee, the ERP's hierarchy of *Generals*

consisted of Sponsors, Champions, Program Management, User Project Leaders, Global Leaders, Power Users, Functional Experts, and Change Control Agents.

As the project's leader, the CFO used his authority to force decisions, influence compliance with the project goals and principles, break log jams, challenge current processes, help maintain schedules and momentum, and authorize funding. As previously discussed, each of the five sub-projects was led by the division's President and Director.

As to ensuring that needed resources were in-place for each rollout, a sole person was tasked and assigned the title of Program Management Officer. For each geographical region's rollout, a tenured employee served as User Project Leader and was tasked with being a promoter for the region's business entities. Further, the User Project Leader served as an enterprise business analyst, junior project manager, and conflict manager. Both the Program Management Officer and the User Project Leader, served under a Global Leader whose familiarity with all phases of the rollout facilitated requirements prioritization, global business analysis and business process change management. Additionally, a global Test Team was created on a cross-business, cross-geographical basis to test the impact of proposed functionality, create test scripts and post-implementation improvements.

On each wave, power users, functional experts, and change control agents were established (Westerman, et al. 1999). Power users leverage their knowledge of the basic system to address training issues, define requirements, gap functionality analysis, and system testing. Functional Experts afforded the team intimate knowledge from the systems and business perspectives. So as to mitigate the implementation's potential impact on operations, change control agents focused on analyzing any system changes prior to implementation. Lastly, a world-wide post-implementation was created to assess any the impact of new system changes.

To capture the importance of an ERP's hierarchy of *Generals*, the phrase *Tao of Commanding Heights* is suggested.

Laws of Military Organization and Discipline

To understand how Laws relates conceptually to an ERP project, one must first understand the tie between command, logistics and warfare. In the military domain, command and logistics combine to offer an army its capability to wage war.

In the extension of *Laws* to the assessment of an ERP project, top management must assess the firm's internal capabilities to support the project. Top management must understand not only the project's scope, but also understand how the firm's internal dynamics can enhance or impede project success. Palmer (2004) suggested that understanding the impact of change as a result of human factors is more critical than technical considerations. Furthermore, firms should first access their capacity for change; then apply techniques to overcome any resistance to change.

Deemed to be critical to ERP implementation's success, Muscatello & Parente (2006) suggested that top management must devise an effective training schedule. A formal training program including re-fresh training should be considered. As we extend Sun-Tzu to an ERP project, the focus is on the firm's internal capabilities. Therefore, the criterion to access the case studies is to focus on top management's ability to assess and/or leverage its firm's internal capabilities.

Case Study 1
Cisco's top management understood its internal limitations, such as its legacy systems, internal-IT department's lack of ERP-specific technical knowledge, and that its overall workforce limitations necessitated a strong implementation partner for success. KPMG was sought after by Cisco's top management for its seasoned professionals.

Cisco leveraged its partner knowledge to build-up its employees' knowledge-base. In addition, it realized that if no knowledge transferred between KPMG and its project team, then the project's total cost of ownership would steadily rise over time. To avoid this situation, project managers' ensured that Cisco employees were paired with KPMG's seasoned consultants with functional expertise to facilitate proper knowledge transfer.

Case Study 2

Since FoxMeyer suffered from a lack of a competent staff to implement the two systems; it had no choice but to rely heavily on Andersen Consulting and SAP's staff (Scott 1999). However, misalignment of interests among the three stakeholders exasperated the project's demise. Though the project had begun to show early warning of trouble and out right failure, potential bad publicity and loss of consulting fees prevented Andersen Consulting and SAP from scaling back the project. Further, FoxMeyer's lawyers alleged that Andersen's consultants, almost fifty at the project's peak, were inexperienced and turnover was high and that Andersen consultants used the Delta project as a "training ground" for "consultants who were very inexperienced" (Computergram International 1998). In addition, FoxMeyer claimed that SAP treated it like "its own research and development guinea pig" (Scott, 1999).

Case Study 3

Tektronix relied heavily on external vendors to help drive their ERP implementation. In regard to the Oracle Financial modules, Aris Consulting began from a small fixed priced role, and became a major contributor to the project's success. As a small firm whose founders were former Oracle employees, Aris Consulting clearly had a stake in the ERP implementation success

During the implementation of the Order Management/Account Receivable module, the initial large consulting firm was replaced with Aris Consulting, Oracle, and other consultants. Once

creditable consulting resources were identified, project managers ensured their employees were paired with consultants with functional expertise to facilitate knowledge transfer.

In closing, we have chosen the phrase, the Tao *of Capabilities,* to demonstrate that top management must assess the firm's internal capabilities in relation to its ability to impact a project.

ERP Project Management Five Factors of Initial Estimations Framework

Based on the analysis above, Table 4 is suggested as the adaptation of Sun-Tzu's five factors to the realm of ERP implementations. The key to understanding the table is to reflect on how each of the five factors, in isolation or combination, can permeate throughout an ERP's life cycle.

The figures below are an attempt to graphically represent the mapping of Sun-Tzu to the domain of ERP implementations. The five point star diagram (Figure 3) represents a visual display of all five factors and the doubled-arrow lines reflect the potential for each factor to act in combination and isolation. The signs in the circles reflect each factor's ability to positively or negatively impact a project. The Ying-Yang diagram (Figure 4) has the five factors transposed upon the traditional Ying-Yang diagram. The Ying-Yang diagram visually captures that each circle (factor) has a dual nature and the lines indicate that each factor can act in combination and/or isolation with other factors.

IMPLICATIONS AND CONCLUSION

As noted previously, each case study was purposely chosen to reflect the challenges faced by the early 1990's adopters of ERP. In spite of the litany of research as to an ERP's best practices and critical success factors, ERP implementations are still a challenge and the need to assess additional

Table 4. Mapping of Sun Tsu's five factors to ERPM

Sun-Tzu's Five Factors (Sawyer, 1996)	Business Domain Mapping of Five Factors (Wong et al, 1998)	ERPM Principles
Tao	Permeating Force	Tao of Aligned Interests
Heaven	Uncontrollable External Factors	Tao of Global Impacts
Earth	Semi-Controllable Environmental Factors	Tao of Estimation
Generals	Business Manager	Tao of Commanding Heights
Laws	Capabilities	Tao of Capabilities

Figure 3. Five-Point Star, five factors of analysis

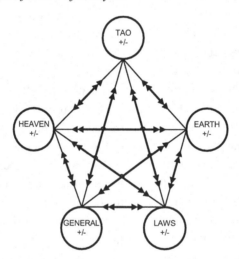

Figure 4. Sun-Tzu five factors of ERPM analysis

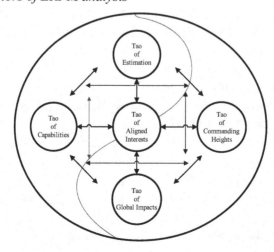

technologies/systems such as Open-source ERP, e-biz, CRM and Web Services/XML, have added even more complexities to an already complex endeavor. Further research and refinement of the framework may ultimately conclude that the ERP Five Factors of Initial Estimations Framework can be adapted to any IT project which spans an organization. Researchers may also find it beneficial to revisit Chinese philosophies to discern if additional treasures can be mined from these ancient texts and then applied to creating multi-dimensional risk-based IT project management frameworks. Another line of research could be to explore if the *Art of War* can serve as a methodology to teach Strategic Management and/or Project Management principles to the uninitiated. Lastly, researchers may explore if the *Book of Changes* universal concepts of *Tao, Heaven, and Earth* (Kidder, 1999) can serve as a conceptual taxonomy to a universal lexicon of project management principles in order to overcome culture and languages differences.

If accepted, the model can serve as a medium between Chinese and Western executives' decision making styles and may be beneficial to both countries and ultimately lead to universal, non-cultural business practices and shared understanding.

REFERENCES

Austin R., Nolan R., & Cotteler, M. (1999). *Cisco Systems, Inc.: Implementing ERP*. Harvard Business School case no. 9-699-022, Boston: Harvard Business School Publishing.

Bryce, D. (2005). *Tao-Te-Ching / Lao-Tzu*. New York: Gramercy Books.

Chen, M. (1994). Sun Tzu's strategic thinking and contemporary business. *Business Horizons, 37*(2), 42.

Computergram International, July 20, 1998. Article's URL <a href="http://findarticles.com/p/articles/mi_m0CGN/is_n143/ai_20920858">

Cotteller, M., Austin, R. D., & Nolan, R. L. (1998). *Cisco System, Inc.: Implementing ERP*. Boston: Harvard Business School Publishing.

Davenport, T., Harris J. G., & Cantrell, S. (2004). Enterprise systems and ongoing process change. *Business Process Management Journal, 10*(1), 16-26.

Jesitus, J. (1997). Broken promises?; FoxMeyer 's Project was a disaster. Was the company too aggressive or was it misled? *Industry Week*, November 3, 31-37.

Kidder, S. (1999). I Ching: The classic of change / The classic of changes: A new translation of the I Ching as interpreted by Wang Bi / The Columbia I Ching on CD-ROM. *Philosophy East and West, 49(3), 377.*

Lee, J. (2001). The Tao of Business. *Asian Business, 37(8), 48.*

Marchewka, J. T. (2006). *Information Technology Project Management: Providing Measurable Organizational Value*. Hoboken, NJ: Wiley.

McAfee, A. (2003). When too much IT knowledge is a dangerous thing. *MIT Sloan Management Review, 44*(2), 83.

Mei-Yeh, F., & Lin, F. (2006). Measuring the performance of ERP system – From the balanced scorecard perspectives. *The Journal of American Academy of Business, 10*(1), 256-263.

Muscatello, J. R. & Parente, D.H. (2006). Enterprise resource planning: A postimplementation cross-case analysis. *Information Resources Management Journal, 19*(3), 61-80.

Nolan, R. (2005). *Cisco Systems Architecture: ERP and Web-enabled IT*, case no. 9-301-099. Boston: Harvard Business School Publishing.

Palmer (2004). Overcoming resistance to change. *Quality Progress, 7*(4), 35-39

Porter, M. E. (1985). What is strategy? *Harvard Business Review, 74*(6), 61.

Sawyer, R. D. (1996). *The complete art of war / Sun Tzu, Sun Pin; translated, with historical introduction and commentary, by Ralph D. Sawyer; with the collaboration of Mei-chu̇n Lee Sawyer.* Boulder, CO: Westview Press.

Scott, J. E. (1999). *The FoxMeyer Drugs bankruptcy: Was it a failure of ERP?* Paper presented at The 5th Americas Conference on Information Systems (AMCIS), Milwaukee, WI .

Ted, L. (2002). Managing the chaos of change. *The Journal of Business Strategy, 23*(5), 11.

Tsui, Y.-K. A. (1999). *A holistic model for driving improvement.* Dominguez Hills: California State University.

Wee, C. H. (1994). Sun Tzu's art of war: Selected applications to strategic thinking and business practices. *International Review of Strategic Management, 5*, 83.

Westerman, Cotteleer, Austin & Nolan. (1999). *Tektronix, Inc.: Global ERP Implementation,* Harvard Business School, case no. 9-699-043. Boston: Harvard Business School Publishing.

Wong, Y. Y., Thomas, M., & George, L. (1998). The strategy of an ancient warrior: An inspiration for international managers. *Multinational Business Review, 6(1), 83.*

Wu, W. Y., Chou, C. H., & Wu, Y.A. Wu (2004). A study of strategy implementation as expressed through Sun Tzu's principles of war. *Industrial Management + Data Systems 104*(5/6), 396.

KEY TERMS AND DEFINITIONS

The Art of War is said to have been written by Sun Tzu. It presents a complete philosophy of war for managing conflicts and winning clear victories. It is widely accepted as a masterpiece on strategy and has been referenced by generals and theorists throughout history.

China is one of the world's oldest uninterrupted civilizations, consisting of states and cultures dating back more than six millennia.

EnterpriseResource Planning (ERP) systems in businesses maintain a single database for the data needed for a variety of business functions such as Manufacturing, Supply Chain Management, Financials, Projects, Human Resources and Customer Relationship Management. ERP systems are also referred to as Enterprise Information Technology Projects.

A **Framework** is a basic conceptual composition used to solve or address complicated issues.

Sun Tzu, is the author of the *Art of War* and a legendary figure in China. He had a great impression on Chinese and Asian history and culture.

Taoism (also spelled **Daoism**) refers to a variety of related thoughts and spiritual traditions and concepts. These traditions have inspired East Asia for over two thousand years and some have spread internationally.

Chapter II
Project Management 2027:
The Future of Project Management

A. J. Gilbert Silvius
Utrecht University of Applied Sciences, The Netherlands

ABSTRACT

This chapter describes a study into the expected development of the competences of the project manager in the year 2027. The study was performed amongst the members of IPMA-The Netherlands during the summer of 2007. In the study the 46 competences of the International Competence Baseline 3 (ICB 3) were tested against the expectations of the respondents for the development of project management. Based on four scenarios for the future of Europe, the members indicated which of the competences are expected to become more important, equally important or less important than today. The aim of the study was to provide insight in the expected future development of the project management competences. This goal is relevant for both practitioners and educators. The conclusions are that the study shows indications that project management is developing from an 'occupation' into a true "profession". Part of this development is a broader orientation of the project manager in which especially the competences related to the relationship of the project with its environment grow strongly in importance.

INTRODUCTION

'Panta rhei' was the immortal wisdom, spoken 2500 years ago by the Greek philosopher Herakleitos. 'Everything flows', everything changes, and nothing remains the same. Organizations are continuously adapting to changes in their environment. Many of these changes are managed like projects, unique efforts that require the mobilization of resources of different disciplines, capabilities and organizational units. Organizing and managing change in an effective and efficient way is becoming a critical success factor for business agility and in fact sustainable success. Given the rise of project management standards and certificates, the task of managing projects is developing into a 'real' profession.

For Utrecht University of Applied Sciences this development implies the desire to include project management competences in the different curricula that are taught at the university. But for a professional educator it is not sufficient to teach just what is required for the professional of today; we educate professionals for the next 20 to 40 years. That is why the Research Centre for Innovation and Business conducted a study into the development of project management in the year 2027.

The question how project management will evolve in the next 20 years is relevant for educators, but also for professionals. For that reason Project Management 2027 is a cooperation between the Dutch chapters of the International Project Management Association (IPMA), and the IT Service Management Forum (itSMF) and Utrecht University of Applied Sciences.

This report first presents some visions of the year 2027. These visions evolve into four scenarios for the future of Europe and the Netherlands. The next paragraph than looks into the competences of the professional project manager. After this groundwork has been done, the research project is explained and the results shown. The report is concluded by discussing the interpretation and implications of the study.

THE FUTURE OF PROJECT MANAGEMENT

The future of project management is frequently addressed in visionary papers and presentations. Table 1 provides an overview of studies in the last ten years.

Table 1. Studies into the future of project management

Authors	Main findings
Jaafari (1998)	This paper makes a case for a fundamental shift in the preparation of the next generation project managers and in re-definition and registration of project managers. The traditional models of project management are increasingly inadequate in the highly turbulent and technology dependent world. There is an increasing trend to require project managers to accept part responsibility for the eventual facility and its commercial success. In order to do so project managers must be proficient in the core technology of their client's operation, be capable of integration and addition of value to information, be IT literate and be capable of operating within a concurrent engineering/construction environment. Preparation of such professionals will require skills in systems engineering and knowledge management.
Barnes (2000)	This paper describes a new model for project management drawing upon experience of the last thirty years in a number of sectors. The new model is presented for debate. If accepted, it will make a significant difference to how project management is defined, taught and applied in the future. Its adoption will make application of project management in both traditional and new areas easier and more effective than it has been up to now. The paper begins with analysis of the key areas and proposals for components of the new model. It ends with a summary of the features of the new model.
Gorrino-Arriaga & Eraso (2000)	This paper discusses the new processes and competencies that will be needed to cope with the future trends of project management. The study has been performed on the basis of substantial literature review.
Woollett (2000)	The author argues that the project management now practiced is out of date and still stuck in the 1980s. Projects now exist in an environment of globalisation, free markets, borderless worlds, mobile capital, international benchmarks and momentous advances in technology and communication. How should the project management profession and individual practitioners reclaim the management of projects from accountants, lawyers, and charlatans that now seek to practice it.

continued on following page

Table 1. continued

Hartman (2001)	The author argues that the next step for project management lies in the needs of organizations tomorrow. These needs are being defined by today's trends and challenges. As part of an on-going project, this paper presents this year's crop of trends, failures, successes and breakthroughs that point to where project management is going. The paper starts with some examples of what was predicted in the past and how accurate those predictions were. Some guesses were right, others were wrong. These are reviewed and the lessons learned are discussed. Based on this, the new predictions are made. Some of the trends and changes are then discussed and their contribution to the forecast of what is important in the future are presented. The paper uses the visible trends to present some of the impacts that these trends will have on project management. Project management is being used as the preferred way of implementing technological and other change in a growing number of businesses. The newest connection for project management is to management of enterprises as a whole so that they can remain competitive. Competitiveness today requires constant change. The ability of organizations - the way they are structured today - to absorb such rapid change is severely limited. The limitation lies in the static nature of the organizational model itself. The paper concludes with some of the implications of the next generation of organization - the dynamic one. These organizations will be founded on a variant of project management. The paper closes with some future picture of what this evolution of project management will look like and how we can prepare to take advantage of these changes.
Heerkens (2001)	In this paper it is argued that, until now, most have viewed the project manager's role as largely that of a producer of technical solutions who is immutably bound by the triple constraints. That view will undoubtedly change dramatically within the next few years. Organizations wishing to thrive (and perhaps just survive) in the turbulent, competitive, and rapidly changing environment of the future will need to give their project managers the opportunity and the latitude to act in a more entrepreneurial fashion. And for the most part, the measure of the project manager's entrepreneurial expertise will be evaluated by their ability to demonstrate and apply sound business judgement. In short, mastering business skills is one of the biggest things on the horizon for today's project manager. The project managers of the future will still have to produce deliverables that function as expected and satisfy requirements - it's unlikely that part of the job will change or go away. The difference will be that the project managers of the future will not only be expected to produce technical and/or functional success, they'll be expected to do it in a way that ensures a positive contribution to the bottom line. Metrics such as profitability, cash flow, life cycle cost, and strategic alignment will gradually begin to eclipse scope, cost, and schedule as the essential measures of project success. This notion is somewhat foreign to many of today's project managers, and is therefore practiced little. The business success of the project has not ordinarily been defined as one of their key areas of responsibility.
Foti (2001)	The author looks at the future of project management as he looks at the future of business. He argues that the two are synonymous and asks whether project management will go the same path as Total Quality Management or whether it will become a standard operating procedure for smart companies. Either way he believes the future will be interesting.
Baumann, et al. (2002)	This study compares the approach to project management within different countries and industry sectors and presents conclusions on best practices as well as pitfalls to be avoided. It explores the organisational structures, tools and processes used by successful companies. Further more, the study envisions potential future scenarios, and presents new, though provoking perspectives for project managers.
Bigelow, et al. (2002)	The millennium, with all its technological advancements, has unveiled a new management approach – virtual management. After five years of building and managing a virtual organization with virtual project teams, the author outlines challenges encountered and benefits to be had under this new and ever-increasing wave of the future.
Brochta (2002)	The author argues that the future of project management involves being more successful more of the time. But what are the criteria for determining project success, and whose opinion about success counts? This paper examines the widely differing viewpoints about project success and presents a best practice approach to improve the odds that projects will be viewed as successful.
Hutson (2002)	This paper describes the future of global organizations. Besides the traditional goals of financial success, high quality goods and services delivered on time and within budget, and satisfied employees, customers and stakeholders, future organizations will aim at the conversion of matter into spirit as the purpose of our human existence in our business environment.
Lambert (2002)	Winning the war against project failure requires the business world to equip and train its project management soldiers and then empower them to fight the good fight. In this article, a battle-hardened project management professional explains how.

continued on following page

Table 1. continued

Zwerman, et al. (2002)	This research was performed to begin the development of a framework within which to consider the professionalization possibilities of project management. The paths other occupations have taken to establish their lines of work are examined for knowledge that can be used to further the cause of professionalization for project management.
Bames (2002)	This paper reviews the past of project management and suggests how its future might evolve. Can its current energy be maintained? Will its impact increase or decrease as the new century unfolds? Is it a secure profession or is project management just a rather long-lived management fad?
Kloppenburg, et al. (2002)	This paper describes the methodology and results of a research effort that identified the project management research published in English since 1960. An annotated bibliography was created of 3,554 articles, papers, dissertations, and government research reports. Trends were identified in each of the nine PMBOK Guide knowledge areas. A workshop was conducted with experienced practitioners to help interpret the identified trends and to predict future directions for project management research.
Soderlund (2004)	Project management has long been considered as an academic field for planning-oriented techniques, and, in many respects, an application of engineering science and optimization theory. Much research has also been devoted to the search for the generic factors of project success. Project management has, however, in the last decade received wider interest from other academic disciplines. As the field rapidly expands, the need for an internal discussion and debate about project management research increases. Project management and project organisation is a complex subject and, we argue, is usefully examined from several perspectives. In this paper, the author discusses the emerging perspectives within the project field. The paper also presents a number of questions that project research to a greater extent should acknowledge. The questions concern issues such as why project organisations exist, how they behave and why they differ. The principal argument is that too much effort has been dedicated to clarifying the reasons of project success and failure, while downplaying a number of important research questions that need to be discussed in order to further the knowledge about project management.
Ingason & Jonasson (2006)	This paper reports the vision of an Icelandic Think-tank on the development of project management from 2006 to 2020. In general they expect project management to become human and soft-value oriented, with focus on achieving strategic goals.

Overlooking these studies, a few issues stand out.

First of all, most authors seem to share the believe that competitiveness of organizations in the future requires constant change of these companies. This change will mostly be organized in projects and project management therefore becomes a core competence of any organization.

This development requires project management in the future to be more oriented on the business context of a project and less on the (triple) constraints of a projects itself. This necessary shift in orientation seems to result from an increasingly dynamic and turbulent environment which does not allow for fixed goals over any realistic period of time.

Thirdly, and aligned with the development described above, 'soft values' and leadership tend to become more important compared to technical project management skills.

Fourthly and finally the authors seem to agree on the observation that the sometimes accidental job of project manager is developing into a profession. At this moment still an emerging profession, but the rising academic interest for project management also adds to this development.

The development summarized here is acknowledged by the International Project Management Association (IPMA) in version 3 of the International Competence Baseline (ICB), presented in October 2006. This ICB provides the official definition of the competences expected from project management personnel by the IPMA for certification using the universal IPMA certification system. It is the common framework document that all IPMA Member Associations and Certification Bodies abide by to ensure that consistent and harmonized standards are applied.

In ICB3 IPMA added two new groups of competences to the baseline: behavioral and contextual. ICB3 now breaks professional project management down into 46 competences that cover the following categories:

- Technical competences for project management
- Behavioral competences of project personnel
- Contextual competences of projects, programs and portfolios

The explicit recognition of these last two categories fit the development of project management that the studies show. The studies listed in table 1 were in general expert opinions by sometimes one author based on analysis of the literature or by a panel of specialists. In Project Management 2027 we add to these expert opinions the vision of the practitioners.

RESEARCH DESIGN

Project Management 2027 studied the expected development of project management competences given a number of specified scenarios for the future of Europe in 2027.

The research questions of the study were:

- How will the competences of the project manager develop in the future, according to practitioners?
- Which project management competences will grow in importance and which will decline?
- Do future expectations differ by the four scenarios for the future of Europe?
- Are the future expectations of project managers influenced by personal or work related variables?

The study was conducted in the Netherlands amongst the members of IPMA and itSMF, using a structured Web-survey, the respondents were asked to indicate whether they thought a specific project management competence would in 2027 be less important, equally important or more important than today. This question was asked for all 46 project management competences of the ICB3 and related to four scenarios of the future. A 7 point Likert-type scale was used with 'equally important' as the middle score.

PROJECT MANAGEMENT

Project Management can be defined as the application of knowledge, skills, tools, and techniques to project activities to meet the project requirements (Project Management Institute, 2004). The comments on this definition are that it is technically correct, but does not help a lot in understanding more of the tasks of the project manager. For the purpose of the Project Management 2027 study however, a recognized definition of project management competences is more important than to settle the discussions about the definition of project management in general. A well recognized baseline for the competences of the project manager is provided by the ICB3 that was mentioned above.

As stated ICB3 breaks professional project management down into 46 competences in three categories:

- Technical competences for project management (20 competences)
- Behavioral competences of project personnel (15 competences)
- Contextual competences of projects, programs and portfolios (11 competences)

These competences are specified in Table 2 and briefly described in annex A.

The ICB3 represents the integration of all the elements of project management as seen through the eyes of the project manager when evaluating a specific situation.

THE WORLD IN 2027

Research into the future is not about fortune-telling. Some developments, like demographic developments, can be calculated with high precision. A more difficult factor to foresee is technical development. It is now expected that Moore's law, an important and remarkably reliable indicator for information technology development in the past 35 years, will continue to predict the growth of computer processing power for another 20 years to go (Dubash, 2005).

More uncertain than long-run developments in, for instance demography and technology, are the responses to them by societies. Both at an international and at a national level, institutions are under pressure. International organizations must find ways to improve their decision making. Whether they succeed depends on both the ability and the willingness of member countries to cooperate, which renders the outcome uncertain. National governments can maintain strong public responsibilities or move towards more private initiatives. It is uncertain which choices countries will make and whether they are able to avoid potential pitfalls along each of these routes.

In order to present the respondents of the study a specified and validated view of the future, we built upon the study 'Four Futures of Europe' by the Dutch Bureau for Economic Policy Analysis (Mooij, 2006). This study into the future of Europe and the Netherlands reports four scenarios

Table 2. Project management competences in the ICB3

Technical competences	*Behavioral competences*	*Contextual competences*
1.01 Project management success	2.01 Leadership	3.01 Project orientation
1.02 Interested parties	2.02 Engagement & motivation	3.02 Program orientation
1.03 Project requirements & objectives	2.03 Self-control	3.03 Portfolio orientation
1.04 Risk & opportunity	2.04 Assertiveness	3.04 Project, program & portfolio orientation
1.05 Quality	2.05 Relaxation	3.05 Permanent organization
1.06 Project organization	2.06 Openness	3.06 Business
1.07 Teamwork	2.07 Creativity	3.07 Systems, products & technology
1.08 Problem resolution	2.08 Results orientation	3.08 Personnel management
1.09 Project structures	2.09 Efficiency	3.09 Health, security, safety & environment
1.10 Scope & deliverables	2.10 Consultation	3.10 Finance
1.11 Time & project phases	2.11 Negotiation	3.11 Legal
1.12 Resources	2.12 Conflict & crisis	
1.13 Cost & finance	2.13 Reliability	
1.14 Procurement & contract	2.14 Values appreciation	
1.15 Changes	2.15 Ethics	
1.16 Control & reports		
1.17 Information & documentation		
1.18 Communication		
1.19 Start-up		
1.20 Close-out		

for the future of Europe. The scenarios provide a structure for discussing the uncertain future of Europe in a comprehensive framework. In this way, the scenarios may yield early warnings to policy makers about particular challenges in the future. The scenarios may also serve as a tool for policy analyses with a long-term character.

The four scenarios for the future of Europe resulted from two 'key-uncertainties'. The first key-uncertainty concerns international cooperation: to what extent are member states willing and able to cooperate within international organizations like the World Trade Organization and the European Union? The second key-uncertainty concerns national institutions: to what extent will the mix of public and private responsibilities change?

Combining the two key uncertainties, the degree of international cooperation and the mix of public and private responsibilities creates the following four scenarios for the future of Europe (Mooij, 2006).

Regional Communities

In the first scenario, the European Union cannot adequately cope with the Eastern enlargement and fails to reform her institutions. As an alternative, a core of rich European countries emerges. More generally, the world is fragmented into a number of trade blocks, and multilateral cooperation is modest.

European countries rely on collective arrangements to maintain an equitable distribution of welfare and to control local environmental problems. At the same time, governments in this scenario are unsuccessful in modernizing welfare-state arrangements. A strong lobby of vested interests blocks reforms in various areas. Together with an expanding public sector, this development puts a severe strain on European economies.

Transatlantic Market

In Transatlantic Market, countries are reluctant to give up their sovereignty. Reforms of EU decision making fail. Instead, the European Union redirects her attention to the United States; they agree upon transatlantic economic integration. This yields welfare gains on both sides of the Atlantic. This, however, sharpens the distinction between the club of rich countries and the group of developing countries.

Following social preferences for individual freedom and diversity, European countries limit the role of the state and rely more on market exchange. This boosts technology-driven growth. At the same time, it increases inequality. The heritage of a large public sector in European countries is not easily dissolved. New markets, e.g. for education and social insurance, lack transparency and competition. The elderly dominate political markets. In this scenario, they effectively oppose comprehensive reforms of the pay-as-you-go systems in continental Europe.

Strong Europe

In this scenario, reforming the process of EU decision-making lays the foundation for a successful, strong European Union. The enlargement is a success and integration proceeds further, both geographically, economically and politically. Europe is the driving force behind broad international cooperation, not only in the area of trade, but also in other areas such as climate change and poverty reduction.

European countries maintain social cohesion through public institutions, accepting that this course limits the possibilities of improving economic efficiency. Nevertheless, they cannot prevent that some groups in society lose (in relative terms). The reason is that governments respond to the growing pressure on the public sector by undertaking selective reforms in the labor market, social security and public production. Combined with early measures to accommodate the effects of ageing, this policy helps to maintain a stable and growing economy.

Global Economy

Economic integration in the second scenario is broad and global. As countries find it in their mutual interest, the new WTO round succeeds and economic integration in an enlarging European Union intensifies. Closer cooperation in non-trade areas is not feasible; international organizations in these areas cannot overcome the problem of conflicting interests and free riding. The problem of climate change intensifies.

National institutions become increasingly based on private initiatives and market-based solutions. European governments concentrate on their core tasks, such as the provision of pure public goods and the protection of property rights. They engage less in income redistribution (not only between rich and poor but also between young and old) and public insurance. Incomes become more unequal, but grow relatively fast on average. Besides, social-economic mobility is high.

DESCRIPTIVE STATISTICS

For the survey the members of the Dutch chapters of IPMA and itSMF were approached. In total 107 complete responses were received. 87% Of the respondents were male, 13% female.

Age Distribution

Figure 1 shows the age distribution of the respondents compared to the normal age distribution of higher educated professionals.

The age distribution of the respondents shows that seniority counts in project management. Compared to the normal age distribution of higher educated professionals, the classes over 44 years are overrepresented.

Experience

The work experience in or with projects is shown in Figure 2. The pattern arising from the survey shows a quite regular distribution. The average work experience in or with projects is 11.5 years.

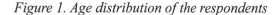

Figure 1. Age distribution of the respondents

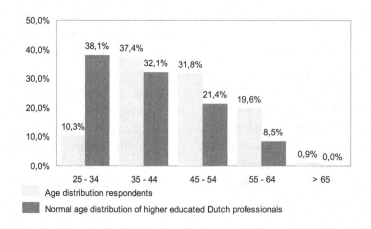

Figure 2. Work experience of the respondents

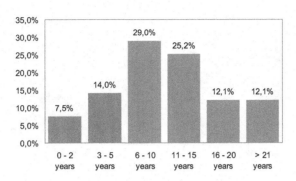

Table 3. Positions of the respondents

Position	% respondents
Portfolio Manager	4,6
Program Manager	12,2
Project Manager	38,3
Project Support Officer	4,1
Project Worker	2,0
Financial Manager	0,5
ICT Manager	4,1
General Manager	8,2
Quality Manager	4,6
Consultant	11,7
Educator / Trainer	9,7

Education

Ninety two percent of respondents have a college education (undergraduate of graduate). 4% has just vocational training and another 4% has a PhD or doctorate.

Position

Project and Program Managers make up for 50% of the response. Table 3 shows the full list of positions of the respondents.

Industry Sectors

Regarding industry sectors, the response is quite diverse (Figure 3). Relatively high scores the public sector (21.6%), financial services (15.2%), IT services (12.0%) and industry (10.8%).

Company Size

Regarding size, the market for project managers shows in the answers. In the organizations where the respondents are employed, small organizations are overrepresented. In the organizations where

Figure 3. Industry sectors of the respondents

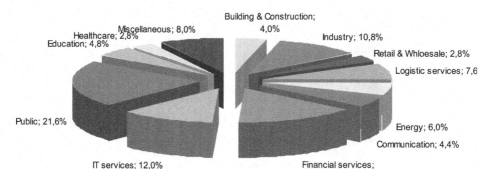

Figure 4. Company size

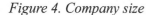

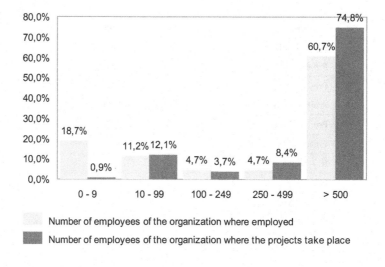

Number of employees of the organization where employed

Number of employees of the organization where the projects take place

the projects take place, larger organizations are overrepresented.

Types of Projects

Most projects worked on by the respondents are ICT projects (55%). Organizational changes account for 21% of the response whereas building and construction projects for a mere 11%. Research and development projects reach no higher than 8%.

Project Duration

The duration of the projects is one (38%) to more than one (44%) year. Almost 46% of the respondents works in international projects.

SURVEY RESULTS

Development of Competences

The respondents were asked to indicate whether they thought a specific competence would in

Figure 5. Types of projects

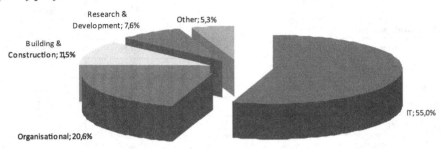

Research & Development; 7,6%

Other; 5,3%

Building & Construction; 11,5%

IT; 55,0%

Organisational; 20,6%

2027 be less important, equally important or more important than today. A 7 point Likert-type scale was used with a value of '1' attached to the 'far less important' answer and '7' to the 'far more important' answer. The 'equally important' middle score was than of course rewarded a value of '4'.

Table 4 shows the mean values and standard deviations for all competences, over all scenarios.

The results of the survey indicate that the respondents expect that all competences will be more important in the future. This may be resulting from an overestimating effect as is found in other fields (e.g. Posavac, 2008). This effect causes the respondents to overestimate the importance of the information, in this case the competence, they are asked to judge.

The growing importance of all competences can also be interpreted as in indicator for the growing complexity of project management in the future. This growing complexity may result from the increasingly dynamic environment in which projects take place. The result of the expectations for the four scenarios, shown in the next paragraph, provides some support for this interpretation.

The expected growth in importance however is not equally spread over the competences. A typical administrative competence as 'Information & documentation' is expected to more or less remain at its current importance whereas competences

like 'project orientation', 'legal', 'interested parties', 'health, security, safety & environment' and 'start up' are expected to increase substantially in importance. These last competences have in common that they all concern the relationship of the project and its environment. Not surprisingly, given the attention for the 'soft' side of project management amongst professionals, the competence 'communication' is expected to gain most importance.

Although the expectations are not equally spread over the competences, this does not strongly reflect in the expected growth in importance of the three groups of competences. Table 5 shows the summarized results for the three groups of competences.

The groups differ not significantly in expected development and standard deviation. The expectation that was derived from earlier studies, behavioral and contextual competences will grow more in importance compared to technical competences, is not confirmed by the practitioners in this study. We have to note however that most of the competences that are expected to develop most strongly are related to the relationship of the project with its environment.

Development by Scenario

Analysis of the results for each future scenario shows remarkably the same pattern of develop-

Table 4. Development of competences, average of all four scenarios

	Mean	StDev.
Technical competences		
1.01 Project management success	4,68	0,90
1.02 Interested parties	4,82	0,96
1.03 Project requirements & objectives	4,49	0,88
1.04 Risk & opportunity	4,75	0,97
1.05 Quality	4,70	0,97
1.06 Project organisation	4,53	0,99
1.07 Teamwork	4,67	0,96
1.08 Problem resolution	4,55	0,98
1.09 Project structures	4,66	0,96
1.10 Scope & deliverables	4,39	0,92
1.11 Time & project phases	4,43	0,94
1.12 Resources	4,52	0,83
1.13 Cost & finance	4,52	0,91
1.14 Procurement & contract	4,70	1,04
1.15 Changes	4,49	0,94
1.16 Control & reports	4,40	0,86
1.17 Information & documentation	4,10	0,90
1.18 Communication	5,25	1,11
1.19 Start-up	4,85	1,10
1.20 Close-out	4,61	0,96
Average Technical competences	4,61	0,95

	Mean	StDev.
Behavioral competences		
2.01 Leadership	4,62	0,95
2.02 Engagement & motivation	4,41	0,87
2.03 Self-control	4,41	0,91
2.04 Assertiveness	4,71	0,97
2.05 Relaxation	4,76	1,00
2.06 Openness	4,48	0,90
2.07 Creativity	4,71	1,00
2.08 Results orientation	4,51	0,89
2.09 Efficiency	4,34	0,83
2.10 Consultation	4,60	0,92
2.11 Negotiation	4,61	0,91
2.12 Conflict & crisis	4,66	0,94
2.13 Reliability	4,36	0,85
2.14 Values appreciation	4,68	1,02

continued on following page

Table 4. continued

2.15 Ethics	4,43	0,87
Average Behavioral competences	4,55	0,92

	Mean	StDev.
Contextual competences		
3.01 Project orientation	4,90	1,00
3.02 Programme orientation	4,67	1,00
3.03 Portfolio orientation	4,67	1,06
3.04 Project, programme & portfolio orientation	4,58	1,04
3.05 Permanent organisation	4,50	0,95
3.06 Business	4,45	0,97
3.07 Systems, products & technology	4,42	0,89
3.08 Personnel management	4,48	0,96
3.09 Health, security, safety & environment	4,74	1,12
3.10 Finance	4,26	0,83
3.11 Legal	4,90	1,06
Average Contextual competences	4,60	0,99

Average all competences	4,59	0,95

Table 5. Development of competences, summarized per group of competences

	Mean	StDev.
Average Technical competences	4,61	0,95
Average Behavioral competences	4,55	0,92
Average Contextual competences	4,60	0,99

ment of the competences over all four scenarios (Figure 6). However, the intensity of development differs per scenario. The scenario Global Economy shows the largest increase in importance of the competences. Second in line is Strong Europe, followed by Transatlantic Markets. The scenario Regional Communities shows the least development of the competences.

The growth in intensity over the four scenarios is similar to the expected economic growth in these scenarios. This is projected to be strongest in Global Economy and weakest in Regional Communities. An explanation for this similarity could be that with an increasing economic growth also the rate of change of the environment grows. This would especially effect the contextual competences. The typical technical project management competences could be expected to be equally important in all scenarios.

Figure 6. Development of competences by scenario

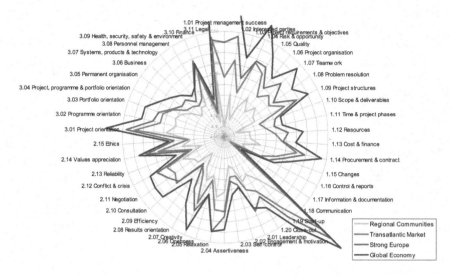

(center = equally important as now; outside ring = more important than now)

Differing Opinions?

Another interesting analysis is whether certain characteristics of the respondents or their working environment are relevant for their expectations of the future development of the project management competences.

The analysis shows that the expectations were not sensitive to most of the personal characteristics of the respondents. Gender, experience as project manager, level of education and job did all not provide significantly different results. This is in itself surprising because some difference in opinion between professionals working within projects and professionals working in the environment of projects was expected. The fact that no difference showed may be an indication that projects are more and more a 'normal' business activity.

The only personal characteristic that delivered differing results was the age of the respondent.

Both relatively young respondents (<35 years of age) and relatively old respondents (>55 years of age) are 'stronger' in their expectations than their colleagues with an age between 35 and 55. This is shown in Figure 7.

Regarding the working environment none of the variables (company size, industry sectors, type of projects and duration of projects) deliver differing results.

CONCLUSION

This chapter describes a study into the expected development of the competences of the project manager in the year 2027. The study was performed amongst the members of IPMA-Netherlands during the summer of 2007. In the study the 46 competences of the International Competence Baseline 3 (ICB 3) were tested against the expectations of the respondents for the development of

Figure 7. Development of competences by age group

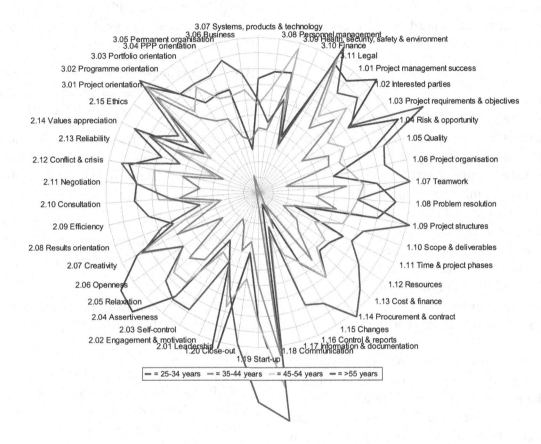

project management. Based on four scenarios for the future of Europe, the members indicated which of the competences are expected to become more important, equally important or less important than today.

The aim of the study was to provide insight in the expected future development of the project management competences. The scope of the study was restricted by the two starting points of the study: the ICB 3 for the identification and definition of project management competences and the 'Four Futures of Europe' for the scenarios of the future.

The research questions of the study were:

• How will the competences of the project manager develop in the future, according to practitioners?

• Which project management competences will grow in importance and which will decline?

• Do future expectations differ by the four scenarios for the future of Europe?

• Are the future expectations of project managers influenced by personal of work related variables?

Regarding the first two questions it can be concluded that the study shows indications of the development of project management from an 'occupation' into a true 'profession'. Part of this development is a broader orientation of the project manager in which the contextual competences grow strongly in importance. In the even more dynamic environment of the future, the project manager cannot take the assignment as a fixed and given goal. He or she has to develop also as a consultant and advise the organization on the appropriateness of the project goal. The study shows that the respondents believe that all competence will grow in importance in the future, indicating a growing importance of project management as a profession. The study also shows that the development of the importance of project management competences is related to the expected economic growth.

Regarding influences of personal or work related variables, the study shows that respondents in the young (25-34 years) and old (>55 years) age groups have different expectations than the group in between (35-54 years of age). Other variables did not provide a significant influence on the expectations.

As an overall conclusion the study shows indications that project management is developing from an 'occupation' into a true 'profession'. Part of this development is a broader orientation of the project manager in which especially the competences related to the relationship of the project with its environment grow strongly in importance.

REFERENCES

Baccarini, D. (2001). The future of project management. *Australian Project Manager, 20*(2), 28-9.

Barnes, M. (2000, May 22-25). A better model for project management in the 21st century. *Congress 2000. 15th IPMA World Congress on Project Management*. AIPM. Zurich, Switzerland: International Project Management Association.

Barnes, M. (2002). A long term view of project management - Its past and its likely future. *16th World Congress on Project Management*, Berlin.

Baumann, T., Cruse, A., Poli, F., & Asum, H. (2002). The evolution of PM: Status and trends. *16th IPMA World Congress on Project Management*, Berlin. Notes: PowerPoint Presentation.

Bigelow, D. (2002). The reality of virtual project management. *PMI Seminars and Symposium Proceedings AIPM (CDRom)*. USA: PMI.

Brochta, M. (2002). Project success - What are the criteria and whose opinion counts. *PMI Seminars and Symposium Proceedings, AIPM* (CDRom). USA: PMI.

Dubash, M. (2005). *Moore's Law is dead, says Gordon Moore*. Retrieved April 20, 2008, from http://www.techworld.com/opsys/news/index.cfm?NewsID=3477

Foti, R. (2001). Forecasting the future of project management. *PM Network, 15*(10), 28-31.

Gorrino-Arriaga, J. P., & Eraso, J. C. (2000). Future trends of project management. Congress 2000. *15th IPMA World Congress on Project Management*. Additional Papers. Zurich, Switzerland, International Project Management Association.

Hartman, F. T. (2001). The key to enterprise evolution - Future PM. *PMI Seminars and Symposium Proceedings AIPM (CDRom)*. USA: PMI.

Heerkensm G. R. (2001). How to become the successful project manager of the future - Be business savvy! *PMI Seminars and Symposium Proceedings AIPM (CDRom)*. USA: PMI.

Hutson, N. J. (2002). Top four components of successful future organisations. *PMI Seminars and Symposium Proceedings*.

IPMA (2006). *International Competence Baseline version 3.0.* ISBN 0-9553213-0-1, IPMA, Nijkerk, The Netherlands.

Jaafari, A. (1998). Project managers of the next millenium: Do they resemble project managers of today? *14th World Congress on Project Manage-*

ment, Proceedings, Volume 2, AIPM. Slovenia: International Project Management Association.

Kloppenborg, T. J., Bycio, P., Cagle, J., Clark, T., Cunningham, M., Finch, M. et al. (2000). Forty years of project management research: trends, interpretations and predictions. Project management research at the turn of the millenium. In *Proceedings of PMI Research Conference, AIPM.* Pennsylvania: Project Management Institute.

Kloppenborg, T. J., & Opfer, W. A. (2002). The current state of project management research: Trends, interpretations, and predictions. *Project Management Journal, 33*(2).

Lambert, L. R. (2002). The future of project management. *Business managers and project managers working as a team.* ESI Horizons.

Levene, R. (2002). Service delivery - preparing for a new future in projects. Frontiers of project management research and application.In *Proceedings of PMI Research Conference, AIPM.* USA: PMI.

Mooij, R. de (2006). *Four futures of Europe.* ISBN 90-5833-135-0. CPB, The Hague, the Netherlands.

Posavac, S. S. (2008). Overestimating the importance of the given information in multi attribute consumer judgment. *Journal of Consumer Psycholog.* Forthcoming.

Project Management Institute (2004). *A guide to project management body of knowledge,* Third edition. ISBN 193069945X. Newtown Square, PA: Project Management Institute.

Soderlund, J. (2004). Building theories of project management: Past research, questions for the future. *International Journal of Project Management, 22*(3), 183-191.

Telaro, D. (1999). The "next generation." *Project Manager. PM Network, 13*(1), 43-5.

White, T. S. (1998). Next generation project management: Back to the future. *Tides of Change '98 PMI. Proceedings of the 29th Annual Project Management Institute 1998 Seminars and Symposiums.* AIPM. PMI.

Woollett, J. (2000). Innovate or die - The future for project management. Prosperity through partnership. *World Project Management Week. Incorporating Project Management Global Conference, AIPM (CD-Rom).*

Zwerman, B. L., Thomas, J. L., & Haydt, S. M. (2002). Exploring the past to map the future: Investigating the development of established professions to understand the professionalisation of project management. *Frontiers of Project Management Research and Application: Proceedings of PMI Research Conference, AIPM .*

KEY TERMS AND DEFINITIONS

Competence: Competence is the demonstrated ability to apply knowledge and/or skills, and, where relevant, demonstrated personal attributes

ICB3: International Competence Baseline version 3.0 as published by the International Project Management Association in June 2006. The ICB3 provides an overview of project management competences.

Project: A project is a time and cost constrained operation to realise a set of defined deliverables (the scope tofulfil the project's objectives) up to quality standards and requirements.

Project Manager: The person responsible for the management of a project.

Scenario: A plausible and consistent potential future situation.

ANNEX A.

Description of the project management competences of the ICB3.

Technical competences	
Competence	*Brief description*
1.01 Project management success	The project manager recognizes and appreciates the criteria and conditions of project success in the eyes of the interested parties.
1.02 Interested parties	The project manager recognizes and identifies the different interested parties in the project. (Note: 'interested parties' is used as synonym with stakeholders.)
1.03 Project requirements & objectives	The project manager recognizes and understands the goals, requirements and conditions of the project.
1.04 Risk & opportunity	The project manager recognizes and understands the risks of the project and manages these adequately.
1.05 Quality	The project manager understands the quality aspects of both project result as project execution and manages the realization of these aspects.
1.06 Project organization	The project manager designs, establishes and maintains an efficient and effective division of tasks in appropriate roles, responsibilities and capabilities for the project.
1.07 Teamwork	The project manager recognizes the distinct qualities of the different team members and moulds them into an effective team.
1.08 Problem resolution	The project manager identifies (potential) problems in an early stage and is capable of solving the issues at hand.
1.09 Project structures	The project manager organizes the project team and its relations with stakeholders in effective organizational and communication structures.
1.10 Scope & deliverables	The project manager specifies the project objective and assignment in specific project results, activities and work packages and understands how these are interrelated.
1.11 Time & project phases	Understanding the interrelations, the project manager plans and schedules the project activities and groups them into a clear project phasing.
1.12 Resources	The project manager identifies, recognizes and organizes the (personal as well as material) resources required for the project.
1.13 Cost & finance	The project manager plans and manages the cash flows related to the project and acquires sufficient funding.
1.14 Procurement & contract	The project manager qualifies, selects and contracts suppliers to the project, plans the purchases and coordinates the deliveries.
1.15 Changes	The project manager handles requests for change efficiently and effectively taking into account the scope of the project and the impact of the changing requirements.
1.16 Control & reports	The project manager directs the realization of the project plan, monitors the progress of activities, reports project progress and anticipates contingencies.
1.17 Information & documentation	The project manager plans, collects, archives and analyzes the project documentation and information.
1.18 Communication	The project manager is skilled in communication and deploys his skills efficiently and effectively. He is also perceptive of verbal and non-verbal communication of others.
1.19 Start-up	The project manager realizes an adequate project start-up that creates commitment of team members and interested parties for the project goal and plan.
1.20 Close-out	The project manager realizes an adequate project closure that transfers the results of the project to the project owner and dismisses the project organization from their duties.

Behavioral competences

continued on following page

ANNEX A. CONTINUED

Competence	Brief description
2.01 Leadership	The project manager stimulates and motivates team members and interested parties to act in the interest of the project and show efficient and effective behavior.
2.02 Engagement & motivation	The project manager is personally committed to and motivated for the project.
2.03 Self-control	The project manager organizes his job effectively and efficiently and dismisses unnecessary tension or pressure.
2.04 Assertiveness	The project manager is adequately assertive and convincing to ensure successful project realization
2.05 Relaxation	The project manager de-escalates conflicts and tension and facilitates effective teamwork.
2.06 Openness	The project manager creates an open atmosphere within his project team that allows new team members to immediately feel at ease. He is also open to feedback and comments.
2.07 Creativity	The project manager explores problems and issues from different and unexplored angles and is able to develop new and innovative solutions.
2.08 Results orientation	The project manager does not loose his focus on the project goals and the interests of the interested parties and achieves project results.
2.09 Efficiency	The project manager utilizes project resources and team members efficiently and effectively.
2.10 Consultation	The project manager analyses issues and situations, seeks advice and new insights, weights pros and cons of different alternatives and makes informed decisions.
2.11 Negotiation	The project manager creates consensus and cooperation for his decisions.
2.12 Conflict & crisis	The project manager anticipates on or recognizes potential conflicts of interest or crises in an early stage and develops solutions that prevent or solve the issue.
2.13 Reliability	The project manager is reliable in his beviour and does not harm the confidence put in him.
2.14 Values appreciation	The project manager recognizes the beliefs and values of team members and interested parties and respects these.
2.15 Ethics	The project manager understands ethic and moral values and acts accordingly.

Contextual competences	
Competence	Brief description
3.01 Project orientation	The project manager understands the rationale for the project and is aware of the organizational context of the project.
3.02 Program orientation	The project manager is capable of aligning program goals to business strategy and develops new proposals for new projects supporting this strategy.
3.03 Portfolio orientation	The project manager advises the organization about effective project and program priorities and about the portfolio management process.
3.04 Project, program & portfolio orientation	The project manager creates awarenes in the organization of the role of portfolios, programs and projects in the realization of the organization's strategy.
3.05 Permanent organization	The project manager is aware of the complex relations between the project its surrounding organizations and is capable these relations in an effective manner.
3.06 Business	The project manager has knowledge and understanding of the specific business and business processes of the project owner's organization.

continued on following page

ANNEX. A CONTINUED

3.07 Systems, products & technology	The project manager understands the causes of developments and the effects of actions in the project and is able manage these relations effectively.
3.08 Personnel management	The project manager recruits, selects, develops, appraises and rewards his team members in a way that stimulates effective behaviour and succesful teamwork.
3.09 Health, security, safety & environment	The project manager is aware of health, security, safety and environmental aspects of the project and manages these adequately.
3.10 Finance	The project manager has adequate knowledge of and insight in the financial and administrative processes of the project and integrates these aspects in his actions.
3.11 Legal	The project manager is aware of legal, compliancy and liability aspects of the project and manages these adequately.

Chapter III
The Progression Towards Project Management Competence

Gregory J. Skulmoski
Zayed University, UAE

Francis T. Hartman
University of Calgary, Canada

ABSTRACT

The purpose of this research was to investigate the soft competencies by project phase that IT project managers, hybrid and technical team members require for project success. The authors conducted qualitative interviews to collect data from a sample of 22 IT project managers and business leaders located in Calgary, Canada. They identified the key competencies for the three types of job roles. The research participants offered their opinions of what are the most important competencies from the following competence categories: Personal Attributes (e.g. eye for details), Communication (e.g. effective questioning), Leadership (e.g. create an effective project environment), Negotiations (e.g. consensus building), Professionalism (e.g. life long learning), Social Skills (e.g. charisma) and Project Management Competencies (e.g. manage expectations). The authors discuss the progression of competence through these job roles. They identified and discuss the interplay between a change in job role and the required competencies necessary for IT project success from a neuro-science perspective.

INTRODUCTION

More and more organizations have organized their work into project based work in order to achieve their mission and objectives; we have become a project oriented society (Gareis & Huemann, 1999; Huemann, Turner, & Keegan, 2004). We need project management to be successful. But which competencies do we need? Do project managers need the same project management competencies as other team members? What project management competencies, if any, do technical team members require? What hard and soft project management competencies do team members (including the project manager) require? In this chapter, we detail the competencies that are critical for IT project success that team members require as they progress in their careers from junior technical positions, to senior technical or hybrid positions (where they are responsible for a mix between technical and managerial outcomes), and to that of project manager.

BACKGROUND

Project management is a relatively new discipline where its practitioners and researchers are increasingly interested in project manager competency (Leybourne, 2007; Loo, 2002; Morris, Jones, & Wearne, 1998). However, we also need to be concerned with the competence of other members of the project team because they are important contributors to project success (Artto, 2000). Understanding competency is important: "Today's focus on competence is driven largely by economics: the fact is it pays to be competent" (Frame, 1999 p. 23). There is a positive relationship between project management competence and project management effectiveness (Crawford, 2005), as well as between project management competence and project success (J. Jiang, Klein, & Balloun, 1996; Lechler, 1998; Pinto & Kharbanda, 1995). Crawford (2001) links project management competence, project performance and organizational performance. Thus, we have a strong case for understanding and improving project management competencies of those who are involved in project work. This is especially important in the information technology and information systems fields where repeatable project success can be elusive (Anonymous, 2004).

Before delving too deeply into this research, we need to define competence. Competence is a widely used but problematic term; it means many different things to different people (Crawford, 1998a). Competence has also been used as an umbrella term covering almost everything that might affect performance (Bassellier, Reich, & Benbasat, 2001). There are no generally agreed upon definitions or theories of competence (Seppanen, 2002). Competency definitions are often poor and contradictory (Robertson, Gibbons, Baron, MacIver, & Nyfield, 1999), and too restrictive (Rolstadas, 2000). Indeed, definitions of competence change from one place or time to another (Sandford, 1988). It is problematic to define competency and competencies because these terms reflect both an individual's perception and that of the organization's culture (Holman & Hall, 1996). Frame (1999) suggests that socially rooted competencies – soft or personal competencies – are very subjective, more difficult to deal with than hard skills, and are more likely to lead to project failure if they are deficient. Some have even cautioned against defining competence because it may unacceptably narrow down the complex realities of managerial behavior (Robotham & Jubb, 1996). Some have argued that definitions should allow some ambiguity and reflect personal definitions (Holman & Hall, 1996). Indeed, some believe that the focus of human resource practice will increasing rely on less precise definitions of competency (Athey & Orth, 1999).

In this research, we have taken a broad view of competence as have others (Athey & Orth, 1999; Boyatzis, 1982; Crawford, 2001; Spencer & Spencer, 1993): it is performance-based and includes knowledge, skills, attitudes, personal characteristics that can be improved with experience and/or training. However, it is not our competence definition that is critical; rather it is the research participants' definition and understanding of competence that is important. We did not provide a competence definition for the research participants because we did not want to influence or curtail any answers.

While much of the practitioner literature surrounding project management competence is simplistic, anecdotal or theoretical, there is a large body of empirical research that has been focused on the technical skills of the project manager (Brown, 2000; Gale, 1999; Lei, Hitt, & Bettis, 1996; Pinto & Kharbanda, 1995; Thamhain, 1991). However, competency research is shifting – as has the general body of project management research (Leybourne, 2007) – reflecting a movement away from a technical bias to more emphasis on behavioral approaches (Cheng, Dainty, & Moore, 2005). A behavioral approach to competency includes knowledge, qualifications, skills, personal characteristics (e.g. motives, traits and self-concept) (Crawford, 2001). The behavioral approach may also be used to predict project management performance based on measurable competencies and traits (Cheng, Dainty, & Moore, 2005). Posner (1987) examined project management skills, traits and characteristics and ranked as important: interpersonal skills, management skills, team building skills, leadership skills, coping skills such as flexibility and creativity and technological skills. Posner concludes that the challenge for project managers is to develop interpersonal skills, which are more important than technical skills. Myers Briggs leadership styles were correlated with project leadership styles where INTJ, ENTJ and ESTJ being the personality types containing the most traits that enable project leadership (Gehring, 2007). The project manager's leadership style has also been related to project type (Muller & Turner, 2007). The most important leadership and managerial behaviors of female project managers have also been identified (Neuhauser, 2007). Thus, to understand the relationship between competence and project success, we employ a broad definition of what entails competence so that we better understand what influences project success. By taking a broader and behavioral view of competence (e.g. soft skills), we are making important discoveries.

Lechler (1998) argues that soft competencies contribute more to project success than hard competencies required for technical activities like planning and control. Soft competencies, like personality traits and attitudes, have received little attention. Traditional project management skills are entry-level skills, but in themselves, do not lead to superior performance as do soft skills (B. Jiang, 2002; Turner & Muller, 2003). Personal competence may be a better predictor of a person's potential to perform than one's functional competence (Cheetham & Chivers, 1998). Skulmoski, Hartman and DeMaere (2000b) investigated the threshold and superior competencies of both project participants and project managers. Threshold competencies are those, which a person requires to be regarded as minimally competent; the person is just competent enough to be able to keep his job. Those who excel in their roles often have additional competencies called superior competencies. Another empirical investigation into project manager competencies was conducted by El-Sabaa (2001). The results indicate that human skills (e.g. personal characteristics, traits and skills) of the best project manager have the greatest influence on project management practices. Technical skills, on the other hand had the least influence. El Sabaa's supports Lechler's (1998) conclusion that soft or personal skills contribute greatly to project performance and success; more so than technical skills like scheduling. While we have lists of soft competencies that contribute to project success, we do not fully understand which competencies are important for the different team members. For example, does the junior technical person need the same soft competencies as a project manager? We do not know. The IT literature is also silent in this regard.

Much of the research in IT in the last several decades has focused on identifying the technical skills required for improving the performance of IT professionals (Bassellier, Reich, & Benbasat, 2001). The required software development skills are detailed in The Guide to the Software Engineering Body of Knowledge (Abran, Moore, Baourque, Dupuis, & Tripp, 2004). The technical knowledge and skill requirements have been reviewed from 1970 to 1990 for programmers, systems analysts and IT managers (Todd, Mc-Keen, & Gallupe, 1995). The technical skill and knowledge requirements of systems analysts have also been studied (Lee, Trauth, & Farwell, 1995; Nord & Nord, 1995), cross-cultural comparisons established (Hunter & Beck, 1996), and their relationship with the maturity of the organization studied (Benbasat, Dexter, & Mantha, 1980).

Non-technical skills of IT staff, such as business process reengineering (Im, El Sawy, & Hars, 1999), and trustworthiness and credibility (Bashein & Markus, 1997) are increasingly other areas of research interest. The perceptions of systems analysts skills and project failure have also been investigated (Klein, Jiang, Shelor, & Balloun, 1999). Research has also been completed on the perceptions, preferences, age and gender of systems analysts (Lerouge, Newton, & Blanton, 2005). The most important behavioral skills of IT project managers were shown to be interviewing, directing and managing (J. Jiang & Klein, 1998). Systems analysts orientation to work (user-oriented, technically-oriented, and politically-oriented) and their perceived skills have also been studied (J. Jiang, Klein, & Means, 1999). The skills necessary for successful outsourced software development projects is another competency research area (Seppanen, 2002). Understanding and measuring end user competence in information systems has been an enduring stream of research efforts (Igbaria & Iivaria, 1995; Igbaria, Kassicieh, & Silver, 1999; Marcolin, Compeau, Munro, & Huff, 2000; Marcolin, Munro, & Campbell, 1997; Munro, Huff, Marcolin, & Compeau, 1997). Thus, most of the IT competency literature has been focused on the operations phase after the project has been completed, or on the technical skills of staff (e.g. programmer). The progression of competence from junior to senior technical roles, to that of

project manager has not been determined in IT body of knowledge. With this in mind, our research question was: "what soft competencies are required by team members in the junior technical role, the hybrid role (both technical and managerial responsibilities) and project manager role that lead to successful IT projects?"

RESEARCH METHOD

We used qualitative interviewing to answer our research question. We discussed questions (Appendix A) with our sample during two rounds of interviews, facilitated by a ranking style of questionnaire (Appendix B), followed by verification and generalization interviews with a different sample. We followed a qualitative interview method primarily based on the methodology and methods described by Mason (1996), and Rubin and Rubin (1995). We used a semi-structured interview format, and deviated from the standardized questions (Appendix A) only when they needed to be modified for either clarity, or to probe new and emerging ideas.

The first round of interviews had three purposes: (i) introduce the research and myself so as to build trust, (ii) collect demographic information and general data about competency and success, and, (iii) explain the survey instrument. In the second round, we sought to confirm and narrow the results of the first round of interviews, discuss their survey results, understand the rationale of their competency ranking, explore emerging trends and ideas, and understand the limitations and generalizability of the research.

During the pilot testing of the interview questions, the research participants had some difficulty discussing competence broadly and deeply. They recommended that we use a survey to facilitate the interview. Upon this advice, we developed a survey based on the competencies identified in the first round of interviews. We provided the interviewees with a list of competencies to rank.

They had twenty-five points to use to rank and weight the competencies within the list. They could distribute their twenty-five points within each category in any way they felt appropriate. An advantage of this type of ranking method is that it provides research participants great flexibility regarding choice.

Much of the sample (Tables 1 and 2) was generated through referrals also known as the "snowball technique" (Mason, 1996). We interviewed twenty-one people over two rounds of interviews for thirty-three total interviews. Fourteen people participated in the first round. From this group, two could not participate in the second round.

Theoretical saturation began to occur in round one after eleven interviews. To ensure saturation occurred, we invited three new participants to interviews in the second round. During these two rounds, one of the participants was from outside the IT discipline for the purposes of immediate scrutiny and generalization of emerging results. We interviewed a further four non-IT discipline participants at the end of the data collection phase to test validity and for generalization purposes.

Our sample included very senior people in organizations from Calgary, Canada with approximately twenty-one years of experience (Table 2). They represented primarily senior management,

Table 1. Sample participation

Participation	Round 1	Round 2	Generalization Validation
Total Interviews = 33 = 14 + 15 + 4	14	15	4
Total Participants = 21 = 14 + 3 + 4	14	12 + 3	4

Table 2. Demographics

Interview Sample Demographics	Total
Snowball Sample	13
Researcher Selected	8
Male	18
Female	3
Role = Managerial	12
Role = Supervisory and Technical	5
Role = Technical	4
Bachelor Degree	18
Graduate Degree	7
Project Management Professional (PMP)	4
Other Professional Qualifications	12
Experience	**Years Experience**
Professional Work Experience (average)	21
Maximum	38
Minimum	4
International Experience (total)	17
IT/IT Experience (average)	14

but technical and supervisory project team members also participated. They were well qualified and most had some international experience.

RESEARCH RESULTS

By analyzing the interview transcripts, we were better able to understand the competencies required of the technical, hybrid and project manager roles for successful IT projects. When one reviews the results, one sees a progression of competencies required for project and career success.

The Junior Technical Role

Obviously, technical skills and knowledge are fundamental to the technical role; and it is primarily for this reason that technical people are on projects. In fact, it is desirable they be leaders in their technical discipline and be objective about what can and cannot be delivered in the project. Technical people require the ability to focus on the details of their task delegated to them by the project manager. If they find that they are lacking in some area, they should ask for help or quickly learn the required skills. Along with technical skills, they need rudimentary project management skills so that they can work within project management processes (e.g. can help develop a work breakdown structure or schedule for their assigned tasks). Here we see the inter-relationships between competencies: for example, they have to apply their technical skills within the context of the budget and schedule.

Technical people also require soft skills because they will end up spending time with the client. Sometimes they need development in this area, so as part of their personal growth, they need to be presented with opportunities to work with the client. Usually technical people become involved in projects to provide technical solutions to problems. Therefore, they require problem solving skills. They need to be able to both define the

problem and recommend possible and sometimes creative solutions. They need to be able to reach a consensus with those involved, which may require cross-functional and multi-disciplinary involvement. Since they will be working with others (e.g. during the planning and testing phases), technical people need to be able to collaborate. They need to be realistic about what they propose because some technical people have the tendency to propose cutting-edge solutions when simple solutions are appropriate. Such tendencies may subside the more they work with clients, and when they better understand the business environment. The technical team members have to take ownership for not only their tasks but also for the entire project during all project phases. Such behavior reduces stovepipe mentality and the associated problems. They should be results driven and motivate themselves to complete project work to meet schedule requirements.

Finally, technical team members need an assortment of communication skills. These skills do not have to be as accomplished as a project manager (e.g. they may not need sophisticated presentation skills) but they do require the ability to present technical concepts to technical and non-technical people during project meetings. For many junior technical people, communicating technical information to less technically oriented people is a difficult task. They may be required to explain technical aspects of the project to both the project manager, the client and to others throughout the project life cycle. The research participants considered listening skills almost as important as technical skills. In order to understand what is required, they need very good listening skills because the client may not be able to articulate a problem or requirement; the technical person therefore needs to "read between the lines." They also should be able to ask good questions to get at the root of the problem; this may go beyond what the client says is the problem. To round out their communication skills, they require very good writing and documentation skills. Too often technical people lack the ability to write clearly and any deficiency in this area is evident in poor documentation. Thus, the fundamental competencies for the technical role include technical, listening and communication abilities.

The Project Manager Role

The project manager's role differs from the technical person in that he is likely to have less involvement in technical matters, but focus on project management activities. Thus, the heart of the project management role is managerial, rather than technical. The project manager has to create an effective environment for the project, lead the team to plan and successfully complete the project, and help the team solve problems (See Table 3). The project manager creates an effective project environment primarily through leadership, communication, and project management tools and processes. An effective project environment facilitates project work. An effective environment does not just happen; it needs to be planned, facilitated and nurtured. In such an environment team members share common goals, respect the needs of others on the team, are willing to do what is necessary to make sure that their views are understood, take risks, and will compromise

when necessary. An effective environment is one where all project participants are required to voice an opinion; it is not optional to be silent. You cannot remain quiet because you want to avoid conflict. The project manager should create a culture where the team takes responsibility for their tasks. Without this fundamental characteristic of the environment, projects fall apart. An effective project environment also includes goal setting, incentive schemes, defining clear relationships within the team and implementing a clear issue management process. The project manager needs to remove the barriers to communication that may exist in the project environment so that open communication can occur. There is a relationship between the environment and competencies: an effective project environment necessitates certain competencies. For example, if individual goal setting and responsibility for tasks is required, then the team needs these competencies to work successfully in that environment. Therefore, not only does the project manager need to create such an environment, he needs to make sure that the team has the competencies required to flourish in that environment.

In addition to creating an effective environment, the project manager requires project management skills to manage the project. He needs

Table 3. Effective environment characteristics the project manager must develop and maintain

Effective Environment Characteristics	
Fun*	Trust*
Creativity	Risk Taking
Goal Setting	Tribal Mentality*
Common Goals	Problem Solving
Active Contribution	Respect Others
Ownership of Tasks	Clear Role Relationships
Barrier Free Open Communications	Transparent Management Process
* Identified in previous research (Hartman & Skulmoski, 1999)	

to have a history of project success before he can lead and manage others. The manager needs to be self-motivated and organized. He likely has these skills; otherwise, he would not be a project manager. If he lacks these skills, then project failure is almost certain. To manage the project he first has to manage the IT project planning process. A difficulty with many IT projects is that the project requirements are vague which requires the project manager to deal with ambiguity, and to check that the project contributes to achieving the firm's business goals. Measuring this contribution is often problematic with IT projects because there are often other factors that contribute to business goal attainment other than an effective IT. The project manager needs the difficult combination of both having an eye for detail (micro focus), but also seeing the big picture (macro focus). The project manager needs to be able to articulate the business problem, and sell the solution to the stakeholders. He has to make sure the team clearly understands how each of their assigned technical pieces help to solve the business problem. The project manager needs the stakeholders to be open or else he will not fully understand the business problem. Experience in the business, creativity and communication skills help to draw out these requirements.

The project manager should be competent with project management tools and processes which may be immature in their organization. He needs to use judgment to select the appropriate tools and techniques since there is often multiple tools or processes to potentially fit the task. A lack of either competence or appreciation by the client and/or the project team of the importance of some of the tools may complicate this. For example, they may not be familiar with Monte Carlo simulations or range estimates, which may make the project manager's task more difficult. He has to be able to get buy in from the organization and team to use the appropriate tools and processes. He should to be able to develop, implement, monitor and control an integrated project plan. Some technical

skills and knowledge are necessary for the project manager; for example, he may need to challenge technical comments during planning sessions. Project managers need to be able to multitask because they very often are working on multiple projects at a time and in different phases of the same project at any given time; thus, they need temporal skills.

The project manager has the prime responsibility to lead the project. Perhaps leadership is a critical skill for a project manager to have and the other required competencies help to facilitate leadership. We hire project managers to lead the team and all of the other competencies help the project manager to lead. Project managers need to take the initiative and be decisive. We can enhance leadership when we align the project with the goals and mission of the organization. The project manager is responsible for aligning the project. He needs to explain how alignment works, and how different pieces of the project contribute to alignment. You cannot assume that technical people see how their piece fits in with the whole IT project. He needs to align team members for project success with the attitude that "if we loose, we all loose." Teams need to take winning personally.

It is the role of the project manager or the person in contact with the client, to manage expectations. This is especially important when there is a politically charged environment. Often clients have high expectations of what they want delivered which are not always feasible. He has to bring reality back into contact with desires. Often you need to scale back functionality or scope due to budget or schedule shortcomings, and then you need to manage expectations. If you cannot manage expectations, more projects will be terminated, especially in the first phase of the project. The project manager has to manage expectations that there are degrees of success: for example, the project can be successful if the team delivers 80% of the core project. Managing expectations requires a high degree of political tact because projects are often very political. The project manager needs to manage the expectations of his team who may be optimists regarding the initial charter; managing their expectations is achieved through open and effective communication.

The project manager should be able to communicate effectively using a broad range of communication styles. This means that the effective project manager will develop different modes of communication to accommodate all types of communication styles. He also has to remove barriers to communication; this is related to creating an effective environment. For example, some people believe it is good to hoard information and not share power. He should be able to break down the project into pieces so that others can understand. The project manager needs the ability to listen to what is said, rather than hearing the loudest person in the room. He needs to know that some people need to "sleep on issues", and should provide for opportunities to participate later. This ability to generate feedback is therefore temporal.

The project manager has to lead and manage the team. He needs to be able to delegate tasks to others, but allow them the freedom to determine the means by which to complete their tasks. While the project manager requires an eye for details, he delegates the majority of this responsibility regarding technical matters to the technical and hybrid roles; his focus is to deliver the "big picture". Project managers have to be able to harness the energies of people who are doers; some people want to start working, rather than be involved with comprehensive planning.

The manager needs to be responsible for motivating his team. However, if he has picked a good team, there is less need to motivate them because they will be self-motivating. The ease of which one motivates a team is related to how successful the project is which is related to the competence of the project manager and team. Part of motivation is protecting your team; you want them to know that you are always backing them, which gives them both confidence and the ability

to focus on their tasks. The project manager has to be able to tell a team member who does not get along with others that they are no longer part of the project. When a team member lacks a certain skill, the project manager may manage it rather than try to develop it.

The project manager needs to help the team with problem solving. This begins with making sure that the team takes ownership for their tasks and their problems. It is not acceptable to bring only problems to the project manager to solve; team members need to bring potential solutions. The project manager needs to be proactive so that he can minimize future problems, which can derail a project. He should help his team be proactive as well. The project manager is responsible for facilitating both conflict and dispute resolution, and consensus building. If he cannot do this, then the project will fail. He will see more conflicts and disputes during the implementation phase than any other phase due to the tendency of problems to arise during this phase. The project manager has to encourage and manage open and honest discussion, which can lead to disputes, but increases understanding. The project manager needs to facilitate negotiations so that the team can make compromises. The goal is to achieve a win-win solution, which does not usually result with mediation. When successful mediation occurs, you usually have two losers.

The project manager has to be able to end project activities; projects cannot just continue. An amiable type of personality may let project activities drag on, while a driving type of project manager will focus on project termination according to the schedule. However, driving project managers are likely to alienate the team in the long term resulting in a dysfunctional environment. If the project is contractual, there are additional activities for the project manager to perform (e.g. disband the team and closeout the contracts) which require supplementary skills. Thus, the project manager requires a broad range of competencies to manage and lead the project and stakeholders throughout the project lifecycle.

Finally, a project manager will require a greater number of competencies than a technical person because their scope of responsibilities is often much broader. Indeed, he requires most of the skills listed in the survey instrument (Appendix B). Thus, the most important skills the project manager requires are project management skills and knowledge, vision oriented/articulate the business problem, open communication, and the ability to create an effective environment for the project.

The Hybrid Role

The hybrid role is the go-between the project manager and the technical person. The project manager delegates some managerial and supervisory responsibilities to the person carrying out a hybrid role. For example, the senior technical person performing the hybrid role could closely monitor and control the technical activities carried out by a team of junior technical team members. This would free up time for the project manager to carry out other project management activities. Therefore, people in a hybrid role require most of the same competencies as both the technical and project management roles except that these hybrid competencies are not as highly honed as those either of the other roles (Figure 1). That is,

they need a broader range of competencies than either the junior technical person or the project manager, but these competencies do not have to be as developed. The research participants emphasized two competencies for the hybrid role: effective questioning and the ability to generate feedback. These are critical competencies for the hybrid role because they spend a great deal of time communicating with the project manager and the technical team.

Threshold Competencies

There were certain competencies that all project participants required regardless of what role they play in projects. Without these threshold competencies, the project participant will not be successful in their jobs. These threshold competencies include:

1. Understand basic principles of IT with rudimentary project management skills;
2. Display leadership abilities, especially in their technical area;
3. Conduct themselves professionally and deliver high quality products;
4. Commitment to the project and work independently according to the project's schedule;

Figure 1. Responsibility array

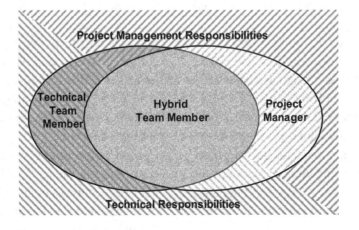

Figure 2. Competence configuration

Hybrid	
Effective Questioning	Ability to Generate Feedback

Technical Team Member	Project Manager
Technical Abilities Open Communication Listening Skills	Project Management Abilities Vision Oriented Articulate the Business Problem Open Communication Create an Effective Environment

Threshold	
Proactive	Flexibility
Confidence	Verbal Skills
Commitment	Participate Fully
Professionalism	Problem Solving
Work Independently	Risk Awareness
Deliver Quality Outputs	Share Information
Subject Matter Leadership	Integration Perspective
Basic Project Management	Ability to Get Along

5. Display confidence in their abilities;
6. Understand how their work integrates with the overall project;
7. Ability to get along with others, share information and participate fully;
8. Verbal skills since this is the backbone of project communications;
9. Problem solving, risk awareness and proactive behaviors to reduce or minimize problems in projects; and
10. Flexibility to work in an ambiguous environment.

With these threshold competencies, the team member is at least minimally competent and can develop through project experience, formal and informal training and education.

CONCLUSION

From this research, it is clear that as duties change, the required competencies to successfully complete those duties also change. To contribute to IT projects, all team members, including the project manager, require at least threshold competencies to be considered minimally competent (Figure 2). Without these threshold competencies, the project team member will struggle to contribute to the IT project. In addition to the threshold skills, technical people require both technical and soft skills to be successful. The technical position is not only about technical work; it is working with others to plan, organize and implement technical plans. To work effectively with others, technical team members need soft skills such as the ability to listen and communicate openly.

The project manager's focus is more on planning, managing and controlling, rather than on technical details of the IT project. While they do not need to be technically superior, the project manager needs both to understand the basic elements of information technologies and needs to delegate technical responsibilities to other members of the team (e.g. technical team and hybrid members). Therefore, their required competencies begin with solid project management competencies. They also require leadership competencies such as articulating the business problem, then developing and advancing the project's vision. These require open communications. They also have to create an effective environment for the team. The project manager needs the threshold competencies in addition to these competencies. Team members wishing to progress into a project management role; will need to develop these competencies as they progress from a junior role.

The hybrid team members require both technical and managerial competencies, in addition to the threshold competencies. They are the supervisory go between the technical team and the project manager. They are delegated the responsibility to ensure the technical deliverables are completed. To fulfill these responsibilities, they need most of the competencies of both the project manager and the technical team but not to the depth of expertise of either. However, hybrid team members usually come from the ranks of the technical team and slowly given supervisory and project management responsibilities. They often develop project management and supervisory skills on an ad hoc basis with very little formal training.

To be successful in IT projects, the team and the project manager requires competencies beyond mere technical skills. All participants require project management skills as well as solid communication skills. The technical team members under the supervision of both the hybrid team members and project manager complete project work. When their competence is increased, there is a greater likelihood of IT project success. Can the team learn these competencies so that the progression of competence is planned and facilitated?

The team members can develop many of these threshold competencies through training (e.g. problem solving, verbal communication and basic project management skills such as estimating task durations). However, some of these threshold competencies are traits (e.g. confidence) and motives (e.g. professionalism) that are more difficult to develop. Nonetheless, they need to be present and applied by people in projects. If we

are to better understand the development of these competencies and we wish to examine the nature versus nurture dilemma, then we need do look further in to the development of these skills and competencies. The neuro-science of learning and decision-making may offer some insights to this and help us understand the processes and experiences that good project managers need to work through to develop the required skills to be truly successful. This is of growing importance as we work through the significant change in the demographics of the workplace that has already started and will likely continue for the next decade.

Hartman looked to exceptional project managers to try to understand the traits that their peers recognize as the "best". He identified these project managers and met with over a period of about 15 years. Through discussion, a pattern emerged that supported a common set of attributes of these managers:

1. All were able to identify problems and their impact either instantly or could predict issues and challenges, and be ready to deal with them effectively. Resulting decisions were generally considered sound
2. All demonstrated exceptional skills in building and maintaining relationships. This was underpinned by good communication skills
3. There was a high level of trust between the project manager and other stakeholders

We know that different parts of the brain perform different and specific functions. From this, we have been able to challenge many assumptions that current knowledge has been based upon. For example, experiments with fMRI devices have shown that in common decision-making situations people do not necessarily act rationally.

We might quite safely assume that the brain is the single most important instrument used by project managers. We need to develop the programs and provide the right data for project managers to work with the full range of decisions, relationships and other challenges they face. In the world of project management, we often refer to "hard" tools and to "soft" issues. Typically, most people who are attracted to project management as a profession find the "hard" stuff easy and the "soft" stuff hard!

Let us consider one of the threshold competencies we identified: *"Display confidence in their abilities"*. There is a correspondence between intuition and implicit and explicit self-esteem (Lieberman, Jarcho, & Satpute, 2004). They identified that multiple self-knowledge systems may exist. High experience based judgment activity occurred in the in X-System Neural structure, while low experience-based judgment occurred in the in C-System neural structure, for effortful social cognition and prepositional thought. The C-System is so named based on (C in reflective) work by Lieberman' research team (Lieberman, Gaunt, Gilbert, & Trope, 2002). In this work, they identified brain activity associated with articulating words such as RED when it is printed in blue letters and the subject was asked what color the ink was. The C-system regions include the lateral prefrontal cortex, Posterior parietal cortex and Hippocampus. The X-system regions (from the X in reflexive) include prefrontal cortex, basal langlia and amygdala. A key observation in this study was that there is slow change in self-knowledge and resistance to external feedback. Thus, through neuro-science we can start to understand the brain mechanisms behind the traits we are looking for. From this we may be able to develop (and explicitly test) different learning experiences for future project managers.

We know that we learn, in part, by developing synaptic connections. Synaptic connections in the average human brain peak at about the age of 6 years. At this stage in our development, we purge many weak synaptic connections. Learning before this "purge" of weak and little used connections appears to be relatively judgment-free, allowing young people under the age of six to learn languages, develop ambidextrous skills and more, relatively easily. Possibly, at this point, after the purge of synaptic connections, judgment, bias or preferences start to influence the learning process and it is harder to change ideas and learn new concepts. The logical extension of this is to find new and more effective ways to develop synaptic connections in our brains to help us think more effectively, leading to better pattern recognition, improved use of our experience and development of new knowledge that will lead to improved "Project Management Wisdom". That is a topic for a future book.

REFERENCES

Abran, A., Moore, J., Baourque, P., Dupuis, R., & Tripp, L. (2004). *Guide to the software engineering body of knowledge*. Los Alamitos, CA: IEEE Computer Software.

Anonymous. (2004). CHAOS Chronicles. Retrieved February 5, 2008, from http://www.softwaremag.com/L.cfm?Doc=newsletter/2004-01-15/Standish

Artto, K. (2000). What do you manage: Processes or personnel's competencies for managing the processes? *Project Management, 6*(1), 4-9.

Athey, T., & Orth, M. (1999). Emerging competency methods for the future. *Human Resource Management, 38*(3), 215-225.

Bashein, B., & Markus, M. L. (1997). A credibility equation for IT specialists. *Sloan Management Review*, 35-44.

Bassellier, G., Reich, B., & Benbasat, I. (2001). Information technology competence of business managers: A definition and research model. *Journal of Management Information Systems, 17*(4), 159-182.

Benbasat, I., Dexter, A., & Mantha, R. (1980). Impact of organizational maturity on information system skill needs. *MIT Quarterly, 4*(1), 21-34.

Boyatzis, R. (1982). *The Competent manager.* New York: John Wiley & Sons Inc.

Brown, K. (2000). Developing project management skills: A service learning approach. *Project Management Journal, 31*(4), 53-58.

Cheetham, G., & Chivers, G. (1998). The reflective (and competent) practitioner: A model of professional competence which seeks to harmonize the reflective practitioner and competence-based approaches. *Journal of European Industrial Training, 22*(7), 267-276.

Cheng, M.-I., Dainty, A. R. J., & Moore, D. R. (2005). What makes a good project manager. *Human Resources Management Journal, 15*(1), 25-37.

Crawford, L. (1998a, June 10 - 13). *Project management competence for strategy realization.* Paper presented at the Strategy and Startup: Proceedings of the 14th World Congress on Project Management, Ljubljana.

Crawford, L. (2001). *Project management competence: The value of standards.* Uxbridge, UK: Brunel University.

Crawford, L. (2005). Senior management perceptions of project management competence. *International Journal of Project Management, 23,* 7-16.

Dietz, T. (1987). Methods for analyzing data from Delphi panels: Some evidence from a forecasting study. *Technological Forecasting and Social Change, 31*(1), 79-85.

El-Sabaa, S. (2001). The skills and career path of an effective project manager. *International Journal of Project Management, 19*(1), 1-7.

Frame, D. (1999). *Building project management competence: Building key skills for individuals, teams, and organizations.* San Francisco: Jossey-Bass.

Gale, A. (1999, November 17 - 20). *How to know what: Setting the project management competency agenda.* Paper presented at the PM Days '99: Projects and Competencies, Vienna, Austria.

Gareis, R., & Huemann, M. (1999, November 17 - 20). *Specific competences in the project-oriented society.* Paper presented at the PM Days '99: Projects and Competencies, Vienna, Austria.

Gehring, D. R. (2007). Applying traits theory of leadership to project management. *Project Management Journal, 38*(1), 44-54.

Hartman, F., & Skulmoski, G. (1999). Quest for team competence. *Project Management, 5*(1), 10-15.

Holman, D., & Hall, L. (1996). Competence in management development: Rites and wrongs. *British Journal of Management, 7*(2), 191-202.

Huemann, M., Turner, J. R., & Keegan, A. (2004, July 11 - 14). *The role of human resource management in project oriented organizations.* Paper presented at the PMI Research Conference, London.

Hunter, M. G., & Beck, J. (1996). A cross-cultural comparison of 'excellent' systems analysts. *Information Systems Journal, 6*(4), 245-260.

Igbaria, M., & Iivaria, J. (1995). The effects of self-efficacy on computer usage. *Omega: International Journal of Management Science, 25*(6), 587-605.

Igbaria, M., Kassicieh, S., & Silver, M. (1999). Career orientations and career success among research, and development and engineering professionals. *Journal of Engineering and Technology Management, 16*(1), 29-54.

Im, I., El Sawy, O., & Hars, A. (1999). Competence and impact of tools for BPR. *Information & Management, 36*(6), 301-311.

Jiang, B. (2002). Key elements of a successful project manager. *Project Management, 8*(1), 14-19.

Jiang, J., & Klein, G. (1998). Important behavioral skills for IT project managers: The judgments of experienced IT professionals. *Project Management Journal, 29*(1), 39-44.

Jiang, J., Klein, G., & Balloun, J. (1996). Ranking of system implementation success factors. *Project Management Journal, 27*(4), 23-30.

Jiang, J., Klein, G., & Means, T. (1999). The missing link between systems analysts' actions and skills. *Information Systems Journal, 9*(1), 21-33.

Klein, G., Jiang, J., Shelor, R., & Balloun, J. (1999). Skill coverage in project teams. *Journal of Computer Information Systems, 40*(1), 76-81.

Lechler, T. (1998, July 6 - 8). *When it comes to project management, it's the people that matter.* Paper presented at the IRNOP III: The Nature and Role of Projects in the Next 20 Years: Research Issues and Problems, Calgary, Canada.

Lee, D., Trauth, E., & Farwell, D. (1995). Critical skills and knowledge requirements of IT professionals: A joint academic/industry investigation. *MIT Quarterly, 19*(3), 313-340.

Lei, D., Hitt, M., & Bettis, R. (1996). Dynamic core competences through meta-learning and strategic context. *Journal of Management, 22*(4), 549-569.

Lerouge, C., Newton, S., & Blanton, J. E. (2005). Exploring the systems analyst skill set: Perceptions, preferences, age, and gender. *The Journal of Computer Information Systems, 45*(3), 12-24.

Leybourne, S. A. (2007). The changing bias of project management research: A consideration of the literatures and an application of extant theory. *Project Management Journal, 38*(1), 61-73.

Lieberman, M. D., Gaunt, R., Gilbert, D. T., & Trope, Y. (2002). Reflection and reflexion: A social cognitive neuroscience approach to attributional inference. *Advances in Experimental Social Psychology, 34*, 199-249.

Lieberman, M. D., Jarcho, J. M., & Satpute, A. B. (2004). Evidence-based and intuition-based self-knowledge: An fMRI study. *Journal of Personality and Social Psychology, 87*, 421-435.

Loo, R. (2002). Working towards best practices in project management: A Canadian study. *International Journal of Project Management, 20*(2), 93-98.

Marcolin, B., Compeau, D., Munro, M., & Huff, S. (2000). Assessing user competence: Conceptualization and measurement. *Information Systems Research, 11*(1), 37-60.

Marcolin, B., Munro, M., & Campbell, K. (1997). End user ability: Impact of job and individual differences. *Journal of End User Computing, 9*(3), 3-12.

Mason, J. (1996). *Qualitative researching.* Thousand Oaks, CA: Sage Publications.

Morris, P., Jones, I., & Wearne, S. (1998, July 6 - 8). *Current research directions in the management of projects at UMITT.* Paper presented at the IRNOP III: The Nature and Role of Projects in the Next 20 Years: Research Issues and Problems, Calgary, Canada.

Muller, R., & Turner, J. R. (2007). Matching the project manager's leadership style to project type. *International Journal of Management, 25*(1), 21-32.

Munro, M., Huff, S., Marcolin, B., & Compeau, D. (1997). Understanding and measuring user competence. *Information & Management, 33*(1), 45-57.

Neuhauser, C. (2007). Project manager leadership behaviors and frequency of use by female project managers. *Project Management Journal, 38*(1), 21-31.

Nord, G. D., & Nord, J. (1995). Knowledge and skill requirements important for success as a systems analyst. *Journal of Information Technology Management, 6*(3), 47-52.

Pinto, J., & Kharbanda, O. (1995). *Successful Project Managers: Leading Your Team to Success.* New York: Van Nostrand Reinhold.

Robertson, I., Gibbons, P., Baron, H., MacIver, R., & Nyfield, G. (1999). Understanding management performance. *British Academy of Management, 10*(1), 5-12.

Robotham, D., & Jubb, R. (1996). Competencies: Measuring the unmeasurable. *Management Development Review, 9*(6), 25-29.

Rolstadas, A. (2000, January 9 - 12). *Project 2000: A university/industry alliance to develop competence for the projectised business.* Paper presented at the IRNOP IV: Paradoxes of Project Collaboration in the Global Economy: Interdependence, Complexity and Ambiguity, Sydney, Australia.

Sandford, B. (1988). *Strategies for maintaining professional competence.* Toronto, ON: Canadian Scholar's Press, Inc.

Seppanen, V. (2002). Evolution of competence in software contracting projects. *International Journal of Project Management, 20*, 155-164.

Skulmoski, G., Hartman, F., & DeMaere, R. (2000b). Superior and threshold project competencies. *Project Management, 6*(1), 10-15.

Spencer, L., & Spencer, S. (1993). *Competence At work: Models for superior performance.* New York: John Wiley & Sons, Inc.

Thamhain, H. (1991). Developing project management skills. *Project Management Journal, 12*(3), 39-44.

Todd, P., McKeen, J., & Gallupe, R. B. (1995). The evolution of IT Job Skills: A content analysis of IT job advertisements from 1970 to 1990. *MIT Quarterly, 19*(1), 1-27.

Turner, J. R., & Muller, R. (2003). On the nature of the project as a temporary organization. *International Journal of Project Management, 21*, 1-8.

KEY TERMS AND DEFINITIONS

Competence: Is performance-based and includes knowledge, skills, traits, motives, self-image and social role that can be improved with experience and/or training. Knowledge is the understanding of some concept (e.g. to comprehend that IT projects face risks requiring risk management techniques). A skill is the ability to complete a task (e.g. determine the critical path through a logic network). A trait is a characteristic way in which a person responds to a set of stimuli [8]. People who believe they have control over their future have the efficacy trait. In projects, when these people encounter a problem, they take the initiative to discover solutions. They do not wait for someone else to fix the problem or expect luck to take care of it. Motives drive people's behavior [8]. For example, people who are motivated to improve or compete against a standard have the achievement motive. When people with a high achievement motive are given measurable objectives in the project setting, they are more likely to work to achieve the objectives. Self-image refers to a person's perception of himself or herself. A positive self-image of one's capability will likely help a person work on a novel project even though the person has not previously performed the assigned tasks. Finally, social role is a person's perception of the social norms and behaviors that are acceptable to the group or organizations to which he or she belongs. Professionalism, punctuality for meetings, and preparedness are all behaviors that may be important norms of a particular project team. Competence is performance-based because one needs to use a combination of knowledge, skills, traits, motives, self-image and social role to achieve the desired result. One is not considered competent if they have the necessary knowledge, skills, traits, motives, self-image and social role but do not use them.

Hard Skills: Is the ability to successfully complete a technical task (e.g. calculate the load capacity of a network, construct a work breakdown structure or configure a firewall). Initially, the IT discipline was focused on identifying and understanding hard skills. However, the IT community discovered through research and practical experience that soft skills were just as important to achieve IT project success.

Hybrid Role: Is performed by someone who is responsible for both technical and managerial tasks. This person may have started from a technical role (e.g. hardware technician) but with time, the person was given some management responsibilities (e.g. supervise junior hardware technicians during a hardware upgrade project.) Others have only a managerial focus with minimal or no technical responsibilities (e.g. project accountant).

Neuro-Science: Is the study of the nervous system. It has become a multidisciplinary field of research that has attracted researchers from biology, computer science, statistics, pharmacology, physics and now, project management. A principle focus in behavioral neuro-science is to understand the relationship between brain activity and thought, emotion and behavior.

Open Communication: Is different from effective communication. Effective communication occurs when the receiver understands the message as intended by the sender. Open communication occurs when the sender and receiver share all the necessary information for both of them to complete their assigned tasks. There are no hidden agenda or misrepresentation of information. Open communication is facilitated by effective communication. However, open communication does not mean everything is communicated; sensitive or private information need not be shared. Researchers are increasingly recognizing the importance of open communication to IT project success.

Soft Skills: These comprise personal qualities such as traits, motives, self-image and social role that lie behind performance. Creativity and sensitivity are examples of soft skill competencies. Soft skills are recognized as being critical to professional and project success.

Threshold Competencies: Threshold competencies include basic knowledge, skills, traits, motives, self-image and social role and are essential for performing a job. Without these, some areas of performance will be substandard. To move beyond minimal performance, additional competencies are required.

APPENDIX A. INTERVIEW QUESTIONS

1. Please define competence. How is it measured/described?

2. Please define Project Success. How is it measured?

3. What competencies lead to project success?

4. What elements affect the Competencies => Project Success relationship?

5. Which competencies are important for performance for the different project participant roles (Technical, Mixed and Managerial) on the Managerial/Technical Continuum (Figure 3)?

6. Do the required competencies differ whether or not the project participant contributes to project work directly or indirectly?

7. Are there other dimensions of competency other than the ones already mentioned?

8. Which competencies can be acquired?

9. Which competencies are inherent in people?

Figure 3. Managerial/Technical Continuum

Technical Focus	Mixed Focus			Managerial Focus
	Business Analyst		Project Manager	Project Director
Programmer		Senior Programmer		
	Technical Writer		Project Scheduler	

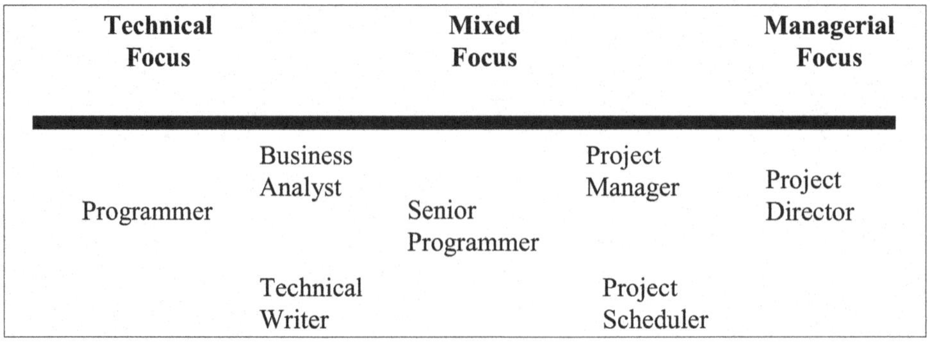

APPENDIX B. SURVEY INSTRUMENT: COMPETENCIES BY PROJECT PARTICIPANT ROLE

From the list, vote which competencies that are most critical for each type of project participant role. The first column is the list of competencies. You have a total of twenty-five votes with which to vote for the most critical competencies for project success for each of the three role (twenty-five votes per role). The competencies have been categorized for your convenience; do not vote within the category, rather, use your twenty-five votes for the competencies from the entire list. [Notice that for Questions 1 and 3 you were asked to vote within the categories and that "Total Votes for this Category (25)" was displayed for each category. For this question, you are not asked to vote within the category; instead you have only twenty-five votes for the entire list.

COMPETENCIES IMPORTANT FOR IT PROJECT SUCCESS	IT PROJECT ROLES		
	Technical	Hybrid	Managerial
Communication			
Collaborate			
Effective Questioning/Generate Feedback			
Listening Skills			
Open Communication			
Presentation Skills			
Writing Skills			
Verbal Skills			
Other:			
Leadership			
Create an Effective Environment			
Decisiveness			
Motivate Self and Others			
Objectivity			
Ownership of Tasks			
Political Awareness/Agility/Tact			
Protect the Team			
Share – Information and Credit			
Vision Oriented/Articulate the Business Problem			
Other:			
General/Project Management Skills			
Alignment			
Business Know-how/Change Management			
Human Resource Management			
Issue Formulation			
Manage Expectations			

continued on following page

APPENDIX B. CONTINUED

Project Management Skills and Knowledge			
Scout			
Team Building/Delegation			
Training/Mentoring			
Other:			

COMPETENCIES IMPORTANT FOR IT PROJECT SUCCESS	IT PROJECT ROLES		
	Technical	Hybrid	Managerial
Negotiation Skills			
Compromise			
Conflict/Dispute Resolution			
Consensus Building			
Mediation/"Umpire" Skills			
Negotiation/Facilitation Skills			
Persuasiveness/Marketing/Selling			
Other:			
Personal Attributes			
80/20 Perspective/Pareto Principle			
Ability to Learn/Self-evaluation			
Analytical/Eye for Details			
Concern for Impact			
Confident/Realistic			
Creativity/Innovative/Resourceful			
Flexibility/Deal With Ambiguity			
High Level Perspective			
Judgment			
Mental Capability			
Energetic/Committed/Focused			
Initiative/Proactive			
Problem Solving/Solution Oriented			
Risk Aware/Risk Taking			
Sense of Humour/Happy			
Self-organization/Self-directed			
Other:			

continued on following page

APPENDIX B. CONTINUED

Professional Conduct			
Lifelong Learning			
Ownership of Tasks/Results Oriented			
Pride in Workmanship/Quality			
Ethical Conduct			
Participate and Contribute Fully			
Technical Skills/Theoretical Knowledge			
Other:			
Social Skills			
Ability to Get Along/Team Player			
Charisma			
Empathy			
Respectful/Punctual/ Polite			
Sensitivity			
Trust/Trusting			
Truthful/Honest			
Other:			
Total Votes (25)	**25**	**25**	**25**

Section II
Leadership, Management & Decision Making in Technology Project Management, Planning, and Operations

Chapter IV
Leadership in Technology Project Management

Ralf Müller
Umeå School of Business, Sweden & BI Norwegian School of Management, Norway

ABSTRACT

This chapter addresses project managers' leadership styles, mainly from the perspective of technology projects. It starts by defining and outlining the need for leadership, and then describes the historical schools and the recent schools of leadership theory. Subsequently the focus turns to current leadership research in project management, and its related theories. Subsequently, the personality profiles of successful project managers in different types of projects are presented. The chapter ends with some managerial and theoretical implications, as well as scholarly challenges for further research and future developments in this area.

INTRODUCTION

Leadership and management are terms often used interchangeably in day-to-day business. There are, however, significant differences between the two.

Management refers to the *professional administration of business concerns or public undertakings* (Oxford Concise Dictionary, 1995). It is often related to guidance and coordination of people towards a defined goal, through a person granted management authority by higher levels in an organization's hierarchy.

Contrarily, leadership is defined as *a relationship through which one person influences the behavior of other people* (Mullins, 1996). Discussions on leadership often refer to the sum of traits, behaviors and characteristics of people being followed by others, independent of their formal authority in an organization. Bennis and

Nanus (1985) define management and leadership and the difference thereof as:

To manage means to bring about, to accomplish, to have responsibility for, to conduct. Leading is influencing, guiding in direction, course, action, and opinion. This distinction is crucial. Managers are people who do things right and leaders are people who do the right things.

Parry (2004) showed that with increasingly higher levels in a corporate hierarchy the need for management decreases, whereas the need for leadership increases.

The project management literature, for example the International Project Management Association's (IPMA) Competence Baseline (IPMA, 2007, p. 86), refers to leadership as:

Leadership involves providing direction and motivating others in their role or task to fulfill the project's objectives. It is a vital competence for project managers.

This definition identifies leadership as a key competence for project managers.

The mission of the chapter is to provide insight into the current state of leadership research and contemporary leadership theories and their relevance for project management. The chapter shows the fit of different leadership styles with different types of projects, and its relation to project success.

The Role of Leadership in the Project Management Literature

While the management tasks of project managers are well described, leadership is rarely addressed in the project management literature. Sometimes team roles are applied to leadership styles, such as the well known Myers-Briggs, FIRO-B, Belbin, or 16PF (Bryggs-Myers, 1995; Schultz, 1955; Belbin, 1986; Cattell *et al*, 1970 respectively). However,

there is little correlation between competencies of leaders and commonly identified team roles and behaviors (Dulewicz & Higgs, 2005), even though many of these are used as part of the recruitment process of managers and executives. Team roles are different from leadership styles, and only very few team roles and personality factors are correlated with leadership performance, according to Dulewicz and Higgs (2005):

1. **Belbin:** Only the roles of resource investigator and team worker are correlated to performance as a leader. The coordinator and implementer roles are weakly correlated to performance as a leader.
2. **16PF:** Extroverts and more emotionally stable individuals are likely to be better leaders. There is also some correlation with some of the other factors.

To understand the leadership role of project managers, we now turn to the literature on leadership, and then describe contemporary research results in leadership research in project management, and finish with theoretical and practical implications thereof.

LEADERSHIP LITERATURE

A comprehensive review of the literature on leadership theory and its relation to project management can be found in (Turner & Müller, 2006). The following is a summary thereof.

By doing a chronological review of leadership literature two classical theories of leadership can be found, dating back to 500 and 300 BC. More recently an early work on the function of the leader, and six different schools of leadership were developed. Research on leadership in project management was only addressed in recent years. All are described in the in the following.

As early as 500 BC Confucius identified the virtues (*de*) of effective leaders, which were *jen* (love), *li* (proper conduct), *xiao* (piety), *zhang rong* (the doctrine of the mean). Already this text showed the importance of interpersonal factors for effective leadership. Two hundred years later Aristotle (300 BC) developed these into the three steps of good leadership, which were:

1. **Pathos:** First build relationships with those being led
2. **Ethos:** Then sell the moral vision
3. **Logos:** Then and only then persuade by logic to manage actions

He showed that effective leaders follow the three steps above, whereas managers go straight in with the logos.

Interestingly, 2,300 years later most of the marketing and sales training in the industry still follows these steps.

Leadership Theories in the 20th Century

Among the first writers on the function in leaders was Barnard (1938). He identified both managerial and emotional functions for executive managers, which he called cognitive and cathectic functions respectively, where:

*   Cognitive functions relate to guiding, directing, as well as constraining choices and actions of those being delegated a task
*   Cathectic functions relate to emotional and motivational aspects of goal setting, and developing faith and commitment to a larger moral purpose

This is similar to Aristotle's view of pathos, ethos, and logos. Today, the cognitive roles are often associated with a transactional, and the cathectic roles with a transformational leadership style.

Over the last seventy years six main schools of leadership theory developed, (Handy, 1982; Partington, 2003; Dulewicz and Higgs, 2005):

1. The trait school
2. The behavioral or style school
3. The contingency school
4. The visionary or charismatic school
5. The emotional intelligence school
6. The competency school

The Trait School

This school was popular up to the 1940s. It assumes that effective leaders posses common traits, and that leaders are born not made or developed. The traits of effective leaders were clustered into three main areas:

*   **Abilities:** Hard management skills
*   **Personality:** Such as self-confidence and emotional variables
*   **Physical appearance:** Including size and appearance

More recently

*   Kirkpatrick and Locke (1992) identified six traits of effective leaders:
    o   Drive and ambition
    o   The desire to lead and influence others
    o   Honesty and integrity
    o   Self-confidence
    o   Intelligence
    o   Technical knowledge
*   Turner (1999) identified seven traits of effective project managers:
    o   Problem solving ability
    o   Results orientation
    o   Energy and initiative
    o   Self-confidence
    o   Perspective

    o   Communication
    o   Negotiating ability

So the traits school has been subject of interest for project management even in recent times.

The Behavioral or Style School

This school was popular from the 1940s to the 1960s. According to this school, effective leaders adopt certain styles of behaviors, which can be learned. So that effective leaders can be developed. Theories in this school often characterize managers or leaders against a few parameters, and place them on a continuum or in a two-dimensional matrix. Examples are, for instance, Blake and Mouton (1978), Tannenbaum and Schmidt (1958), Adair (1983), Hershey and Blanchard (1988), Slevin (1989). The parameters include:

1. Concern for people or relationships
2. Concern for production
3. Use of authority
4. Involvement of the team in decision-making (formulating decisions)
5. Involvement of the team in decision-taking (choosing options)
6. Flexibility versus the application of rules

The Contingency School

In the 1960s and 1970s, this school became popular (see Krech *et al*, 1962; Fiedler, 1967; House, 1971; Robbins, 1997). Aim was to identify effective leadership behavior in different situations. So the understanding of leadership moved away from universal theories to situational contingency theories. These theories typically:

1. Assessed the characteristics of the leader
2. Evaluated the situation in terms of key contingency variables
3. Aimed for identification of a match between the leader and a particular situation.

Especially popular became the path-goal theory by House (1971). It suggests that a leader must help the team find its path to their goals and then help them in the process to achieve their goals. Leadership behaviors identified here were directive, supportive, participative, and achievement-oriented. To identify the best match with a situation these four behaviors were matched against environmental and subordinate factors, which include environmental factors such as: task structure, formal authority system; as well as workgroup factors such as; subordinate factors, locus of control, experience, and perceived ability.

Another popular contingency theory was developed by Fiedler (1967). He recommends different leadership styles, depending on the favorability of the leadership situation. Here favorability is determined by the relationship between leader and those being led (level of trust), the structure of the task (clearness of task and instructions), and position power. He distinguishes between task oriented and participative leadership. A least-preferred-coworker (LPC) score is used for assigning team members to leaders depending on a particular leadership situation. In very favorable and very unfavorable situations **task oriented leaders** (having a low LPC score) are assigned to achieve effectiveness through a directive and controlling style. In moderately favorable situations **participative leaders** (high LPC score) are assigned for high effectiveness through interpersonal relationship orientation.

Frame (1987) suggested four contingent leadership styles for project managers as appropriate at different stages of the project life-cycle and with different team structures, Table 1.

The Visionary or Charismatic School

Popular during the 1980s and 1990s, this school derived from research on effective leadership in organizational change projects. Representative for this school is the transactional and transformational leadership style theory (Bass, 1990), in:

Table 1. Leadership styles, project team types and the project life-cycle

Leadership style	Stage	Team type	Team nature
Laissez-faire	Feasibility	Egoless	Experts with shared responsibility
Democratic	Design	Matrix	Mixed discipline working on several tasks
Autocratic	Execution	Task	Single discipline working on separate tasks
Bureaucratic	Close-out	Surgical	Mixed working on a single task

1. Transactional leadership:
   - Team members are rewarded for achievement of specific performance targets.
   - Managers mainly get involved when things are not going according to plan.
2. Transformational leadership:
   - Managers use charisma and vision, plus pride, respect and trust in team and task.
   - Managers set high expectations, inspire and motivate by providing intellectual stimulation, and challenging team members with new ideas and approaches.
   - Team members are allowed to be creative in problem solving.
   - Managers consider the individual, showing respect and personality.

Different combinations of the two styles are appropriate in different situations. As mentioned above, the transactional style refers to Barnard's cognitive roles and Aristotle's *logos*. The transformational style resembles Barnard's cathectic roles, as well as Aristotle's *pathos* and *ethos*.

Keegan and den Hartog (2004) took this school into the world of project management. They hypothesized that project managers mainly use transformational leadership styles, but could not find empirical support for their hypothesis. However, Dominick, Artonson and Lechler (2007) found a correlation between transformational style and project success. So transformational style

contributes to success, but is not necessarily more often used than transactional style. Turner and Müller (2006) identified transactional style for simple engineering projects and transformational style in more complex projects.

The Emotional Intelligence School

Since the late 1990s, the Emotional Intelligence School became increasingly popular. This school assumes a reasonable level of intelligence among all managers, so that it is not the intellectual intelligence that differentiates success of leaders, but their emotional response to situations. So a leader's emotional intelligence has a greater impact on success as a leader and the performance of the team than the intellectual intelligence (Goleman, Boyatzis & McKee, 2002). They identified four dimensions of emotional intelligence, based on nineteen underlying competencies: these are listed and described in the Appendix.

Six management styles for different leadership situations derived from that. Each style is associated with a different leadership competencies profile. Of those six styles, four (visionary, coaching, affiliative, and democratic) are applicable for situations requiring a medium to long-term perspective. These styles foster resonance among the team members and improve team performance when used in appropriate circumstances. The other two (pacesetting and commanding) are applicable for turnaround or recovery situations with a short tem perspective. These styles can foster dissonance and need to be used with care. Thus, Goleman *et al* (2002), and later on others, showed a contingency between situational particularities and appropriate leadership styles.

The Competency School

Since the late 1990s, the emphasis has been to identify the competencies of effective leaders. Following Boyatzis (1982) and Crawford (2003) competences are:

- Knowledge
- Skills
- Personal characteristics

that allow to deliver superior results.

So competence covers personal characteristics, (traits as understood by the traits school and emotional intelligence), knowledge and skills, (including intelligence and problem solving ability as well as management skills).

While, at first glance, this looks like a return to the trait approach, it differs from earlier schools by:

- The underlying assumption that competencies can be learned. Therefore leaders can be made or developed, not just born.
- The assumption that different combinations of competencies will lead to different leadership styles. These styles then are appropriate for different situations. Examples are transactional leaders in circumstances of low complexity and transformational leaders in circumstances of high complexity.
- Not being a singular new school, but encompassing all the earlier schools

The competence school shows that different competence profiles are appropriate in different circumstances, covering the trait, contingency, visionary & charismatic, as well as the emotional intelligence school.

Types of Competence

Dulewicz and Higgs (2005) found that the majority of researchers in the competency school identified up to four different types of competencies that impact leadership performance. These are:

1. Cognitive competencies
2. Emotional competencies
3. Behavioral competencies
4. Motivational competencies

Cognitive competencies are associated with Confucius's *li* and Barnard's cognitive functions. Emotional, behavioral and motivational competencies are associated with Confucius's *ren* and *yi,* and Barnard's cathectic functions.

Based on their research, analyses, and literature review Dulewicz and Higgs (2005) identified fifteen leadership competencies. These are categorized in seven emotional (EQ) competencies, three intellectual (IQ) ones and five managerial (MQ) ones, Table 2.

By tabulating their identified competences against those suggested by others, Dulewicz and Higgs found quite strong support in the literature. They go on to show that intellectual competence (IQ) accounts for 27% of leadership performance, managerial competence (MQ) accounts for 16%, and emotional competence (EQ) accounts for 36%. Emotional competence is therefore the most significant, but the other two are important as Barnard and Confucius suggested (Dulewicz & Higgs, 2000).

Contemporary Research in Project Management Related Leadership

Relationship Between Personality, Project Type and Project Success

A study by Dvir, Sadeh and Malach-Pines (2006) showed tentative support for the hypotheses that projects are more successful if personality

Table 2. Fifteen leadership competencies as suggested by Dulewicz and Higgs (2005)

Group	Competency
Intellectual (IQ)	1. critical analysis and judgement 2. vision and imagination 3. strategic perspective
Managerial (MQ)	4. engaging communication 5. managing resources 6. empowering 7. developing 8. achieving
Emotional (EQ)	9. self-awareness 10. emotional resilience 11. motivation 12. sensitivity 13. influence 14. intuitiveness 15. conscientiousness

characteristics match project profiles, and that project managers are more attracted to and more successful with projects that fit their personality. The researchers used a four dimensional model of project complexity, pace, novelty and technology to classify projects and identify associated leadership styles during project initiation and recruiting of team members, as well as for different structures, processes, and tools.

Leadership Competences of Successful Project Managers in Different Types of Projects

The importance of leadership competencies for project success in different types of projects was investigated by Turner and Müller (2006). They used the Leadership Development Questionnaire (LDQ) developed by Dulewicz and Higgs (2005) as part of the competency school of leadership.

Here intellectual leadership competencies (IQ) are understood as the rational capabilities of the project manager. Managerial leadership competencies (MQ) as the competencies to lead teams towards pre-defined goals. It allows the leader to

adjust the amount of management and control to the expectations of those being led. This includes open communication and the ability to manage people, empower and develop them, as well as giving them a sense of achievement. Emotional leadership competencies (EQ) set the right tone and social relationship. These were measured as the degree of a project manager's awareness and ability to manage their own feelings and their appearance to other people.

EQ competencies correlated positively with success across all types of projects. Strategic perspective (IQ), however, was negatively related to project success. There were also two exceptions: on successful mandatory projects and projects under a fixed price contract MQ is stronger related to project success than EQ. These are project types where managers cannot negotiate project scope. So they have to rely on their managerial competences to lead the project team and deliver the project as required.

At the more detailed level they identified different combinations of the underlying 15 competencies in successful projects of different type. These are described next.

Engineering and Construction Projects

Three of the 15 leadership competencies shown in Table 4 correlate positively with success. They explain 43% of the variance in success measures for these projects.

These competencies are:

- **Conscientiousness**, an emotional competency, where the project manager displays clear commitment to a course of action in the face of challenges and matches 'words and deeds' in encouraging others to support the chosen direction.
- **Interpersonal sensitivity**, another emotional competency, where the project manager is aware of, and takes account of, the needs and perceptions of others in arriving at decisions and proposing solutions to problems and challenges
- **Engaging communication**, a managerial competency, where the project manager is approachable and accessible, engages others and wins their support through communication tailored for each audience.

So a sense of duty and good interpersonal communication are the project managers' leadership attributes contributing to project success in engineering and construction projects.

Information Technology and Telecommunication Projects

The important competencies correlating positively with success are once again engaging communication, plus:

- **Self-awareness**, an emotional competency, where the project manager is aware of his or her own feelings and able to recognize them
- **Developing resources**, a managerial competency, where project managers encourage

others to take on ever more demanding tasks, roles, and accountabilities. He or she develops others' competencies and invests time and effort in coaching them.

This combination explains 21% of success in these projects. The 'soft' factors make IT projects successful. Finding the right 'tone' with others, together with good control over their own feelings, and helping project team members to take on challenging tasks, are the attributes of successful leadership in these projects.

Organizational Change Projects

Another set of competencies influences success in organizational change projects and explains 17% of success in these projects. Here again, engaging communication is important, but also:

- **Motivation**, an emotional competency, where the project manager shows drive and energy to achieve clear results and make an impact

Therefore, actively creating the required dynamics for change, together with accommodation of those involved helps organizational change projects to be successful.

However, one competency correlates negatively with success in all types of projects:

- **Vision and imagination**, an intellectual competency, where the project manager is imaginative and innovative, with a clear vision of the future. He or she foresees the impact of changes on implementation issues and business realities.

Visionary and imaginative leaders are without doubt needed for projects to succeed. So this role should be assumed by the project sponsor, who by default sets the vision and projected end-state of a project and its outcome.

Having identified the leadership dimensions correlated with project success in different types of projects (Müller & Turner, 2007) the researchers also identified the extent the different leadership dimensions are expressed (from low to high) within successful project managers (Müller & Turner, 2006). For that they looked at managers of projects with above average performance and identified the leadership profile of these managers for three different types of projects, Figure 1.

The competency most strongly expressed in successful project managers is conscientiousness. All other profile dimensions differ by project type.

Differences Between Functional Managers and Project Managers

This study by Dulewicz, Turner and Müller (2006) identified the differences between leadership profiles of line (or functional) managers and project managers.

Project managers scored higher than line managers on:

- Critical analysis (IQ)
- Conscientiousness (EQ)
- Sensitivity (EQ)

Line managers scored higher than project managers on:

- Communication (MQ)
- Developing (MQ)

The study showed also differences in explained leadership performance, depending on line or project manager role.

- For project managers leadership success is explained to 21% by EQ dimensions, 22% by IQ dimensions, and 30% by MQ dimensions
- For line (functional) managers leadership performance is explained to 36% by EQ, 27% by IQ, and 16% by MQ dimensions.

Requirement for EQ and IQ leadership competencies are higher and for MQ competencies lower in line management functions.

Figure 1. Leadership competency profiles of successful project managers

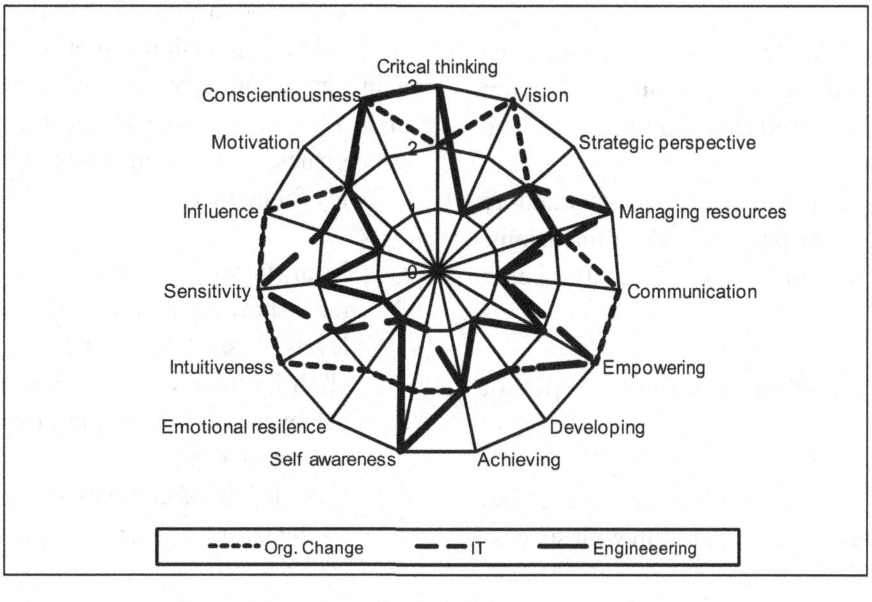

Agile Project Managers' Leadership Competencies

Porthouse and Dulewicz (2007) investigated the differences in leadership competencies between project managers using Agile/Scrum approaches and line managers. These projects are managed using more interactive and team-based approaches than traditional project management methodologies, because of a shift in management style from controlling to facilitating and the use of self organizing teams. They found:

- Intuitiveness and sensitivity significantly higher in Agile project managers
- Motivation and emotional resilience significantly lower in Agile project managers

Then they compared Agile/Scrum project managers with international project managers from the Turner and Müller (2006) study. They found:

- Intuitiveness, communication, development significantly higher in Agile project managers
- Motivation and conscientiousness significantly lower in Agile project managers

Thirteen of the 15 leadership dimensions (Table 4) correlated with success in Agile/Scrum projects: These were all except intuitiveness and vision & imagination.

Leadership performance was explained to 40% by EQ dimensions, 19% MQ dimensions, and only 4% by IQ dimensions (the latter being insignificant).

Leadership profiles in different types of complexity

By taking further their original study on leadership competences and their relationship with success in different project types, Müller, Geraldi and Turner (2007) looked into the different leadership profiles for success in projects of different types of complexity. The complexity model was adopted from Geraldi and Adlbrecht (2007) and consisted of three main dimensions for complexity:

- **Complexity of fact:** Structural complexity, including measures for the amount of information to analyse, or the number of organizations and people involved in a project

- **Complexity of faith:** Uncertainty, including measures for severity and frequency of scope changes, level of immaturity of the project team, and level of multi-disciplinarity

- **Complexity of interaction:** Inter-personal relationships, with measures for level of transparency in the team and level of inter-nationality

The results were drawn mainly from IT projects. They show different leadership profiles for projects with different types of complexity, Figure 2.

Projects dominated by either complexity of faith or interaction require relatively small expressions of the leadership dimensions. Successful managers of projects dominated by complexity of fact are stronger in achievement, emotional competencies and management of resources.

They found that:

- In any type of complexity project managers must show their commitment through high levels of conscientiousness
- High levels of complexity of fact requires achievement competency (MQ) from the project manager
- High levels of complexity of fact require strong emotional and interpersonal skills

They also conclude that projects with tangible outcomes, such as in construction or engineering, demand achievement competencies. Projects with intangible outcomes, such as IT or organizational change, demand competencies in interpersonal sensitivity.

FUTURE TRENDS

The importance of leadership on the side of the project manager is a young subject in the project management area. It was not until 2006 that major studies identified the fit between different leadership styles and project success in different types of projects, thus until the project manager was identified as a key success factor. With the momentum gained in current years, leadership in project management will be addressed both from a research as well as from a practitioner perspective.

Near Term Implications for Practitioners

Leadership will increasingly become part of project manager education and training. Assessments of leadership styles and their fit or development towards an organization's project types will increase, allowing for better project results.

The approach described above allows existing project managers to develop their own leadership competencies to make them fit for their particular project type. After taking the LDQ assessment, they can use the information on the relevant dimensions for project success and the 'target' profile of successful project managers to identify the gap between their own profile and that of successful managers. By taking into account which leadership dimensions correlate with success in their particular project type, they then identify and prioritize training needs for their own development.

Human resource departments will most likely make use of LDQ or similar assessment tools to

Figure 2. Leadership profiles of successful managers of IT projects of different type of complexity

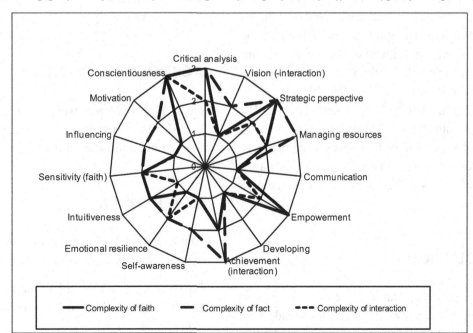

Table 3. Reoccurring dimensions of leadership

	People	*Vision*	*Process*
Confucius 500BC	Jen	Xiao	Li
Aristotle 300BC	Pathos	Ethos	Logos
Dulewicz & Higgs 2005	EQ	IQ	MQ

identify best suitable candidates for their projects, or use the above profiles as targets for development of their workforce.

Near Term Implications for Academia

The research on leadership's importance and impact on projects will continue. While writing this chapter, the Project Management Institute (PMI) decided to sponsor a further study on the development of project managers' emotional competencies for better project results. This trend will continue. Possible areas to investigate in the coming years include the different requirements for leadership training for line and project managers, as well as managers of different types of projects and in different cultures. A better understanding of these implications will allow for development of improved interaction and collaboration in international, virtual, and cross-industry teams. This will impact the ability to manage long-term projects successfully and sustainably.

Along with that, leadership competence will be accepted into the project management bodies of knowledge as a complement to existing management competences, thus contribute to a balance of 'hard' and 'soft' factors for the management of projects.

CONCLUSION

This chapter gave an overview of leadership theories and current research results on leadership in projects. The degree of influence of different leadership competences on success in different types of projects was shown, together with the presence of leadership competencies in managers of successful projects of different type.

By going back 2,500 years to the classic writings on leadership and reviewing the six schools of leadership theories of the last 70 years we see three main dimensions of leadership pervading all work, from ancient to recent times. These are people, vision, and process, Table 3.

While this bears the question of how far we have come within the last 2,500 years, it also shows the need to continue to research, to understand and apply new learning in the area. Its importance should not be underestimated, as this *new science of human relationship* (Goleman, 2006) comes close to a *DNA of leadership*, which can migrate continually.

ACKNOWLEDGMENT

Parts of this chapter were written jointly with Prof. Rodney Turner of the Graduate School of Management in Lille, France.

REFERENCES

Adair, J. (1983). *Effective deadership: A self-development manual*. Adershott, UK: Gower.

Barnard, C. I. (1938). *The functions of the executive*. Cambridge, MA: Harvard University Press.

Bass, B.M. (1990). From transactional to transformational leadership: Learning to share the vision. *Organisational Dynamics, 18*(3), 19-31.

Belbin, R. M. (1986). *Management teams*. London: Heinemann.

Bennis, W., & Nanus, B. (1985). *Leaders: The strategies for taking charge*. New York: Harper and Row.

Blake, R. R., & Mouton, S. J. (1978). *The new managerial grid*. Houston, TX: Gulf.

Boyatzis, R. E. (1982). *The Competent Manager: a model for effective performance*. New York, NY: Wiley.

Briggs-Myers, I. (1992). *Gifts differing*. Palo Alto, CA: Consulting Psychologists Press.

Cattell, R. B., Eber, H. W., & Tatsuoka, M. M. (1970). *Handbook for the 16PF*. Illinois: IPAT.

Crawford, L. H. (2003). Assessing and developing the project management competence of individuals. In J. R. Turner, (Ed.), *People in project management*. Aldershot, UK: Gower.

Dominick, P., Aronson, Z., & Lechler, T. (2007). Transformational leadership and project success. In R. R. Reilly (Ed.), *The human side of project leadership,* (pp. 1-30). Newton Square, PA: Project Management Institute.

Dulewicz, V., & Higgs, M. J. (2000). Emotional intelligence: a review and evaluation study. *Journal of Managerial Psychology, 15*(4), 341–368.

Dulewicz, & Higgs, M. (2005). Assessing leadership styles and organisational context. *Journal of Managerial Psychology, 20*(1), 105-123.

Dulevicz, V., Turner, J. R., & Müller, R. (2006). *Assessment of project managers using the leadership dimensions questionnaire: An international study* (Henley Working Paper Series). Henley Management College, Henley-on-Thames, UK.

Dvir, D., Sadeh, A., & Malach-Pines, A. (2006). Project and project managers: The relationship between project manager's personality, project types and project success. *Project Management Journal*, 37(5), 36-48.

Fiedler, F. E. (1967). *A theory of leadership effectiveness*. New York: McGraw-Hill.

Frame, J. D. (1987). *Managing projects in organizations*. San Francisco: Jossey Bass.

Geraldi, J., & Adlbrecht, G. (2007). On faith, fact, and interaction in projects. *Project Management Journal, 38*(1), 32-43.

Goleman, D. (2006). *Social intelligence: The new science of human telationships*. London: Hutchinson.

Goleman, D., Boyatzis, R., & McKee, A. (2002). *The new leaders*. Boston: Harvard Business School Press.

Handy, C. B. (1982). *Understanding organizations*. London: Penguin

Hershey, P., & Blanchard, K. H. (1988). *Management of organizational behaviour,* 5th ed. Englewood Cliffs, NJ: Prentice Hall.

House, R. J. (1971). A path-goal theory of leader effectiveness. *Administrative Science Quarterly*, September, 321-338.

IPMA (2007). *ICB: IPMA competence baseline Version 3.0*. In C. Caupin, H. Knöpfl, G. Koch., H. Pannenbäcker, F- Pérez-Polo, & C. Seabury (Eds.), Njkerk, The Netherlands: International Project Management Association.

Keegan, A. E., & Den Hartog, D. N. (2004). Transformational leadership in a project-based environment: a comparative study of the leadership styles of project managers and line managers. *International Journal of Project Management, 22*(8), 609-618.

Kirkpatrick, S. A., & Locke, E. A. (1991). Leadership traits do matter. *Academy of Management Executive,* March, 44-60.

Krech, D., Crutchfield, R. S., & Ballachey, E. L. (1962). *Individual in society.* New York: McGraw-Hill.

Müller, R., Geraldi, J., & Turner, J. R. (2007, September). *Linking complexity and leadership competences of project managers.* Paper presented at IRNOP VIII Conference (International Research Network for Organizing by Projects), Brighton, UK.

Müller, R., & Turner, J. R. (2006). Leadership competences and their successful application in different types of project. In L. Ou & R. Turner (Ed.), *Proceedings of IRNOP VII (International Research Network for Organizing by Projects),* Northwestern Polytechnic University, Xi'an, China.

Müller, R., & Turner, J. R. (2007a). Matching the project manager's leadership style to project type. *International Journal of Project Management, 25*(1), 21-32.

Müller, R., & Turner, J. R. (2007b).The influence of project managers on project success criteria and project success by type of project. *European Management Journal, 25*(4), 289-309.

Mullins, L. J. (1996). *Management and organizational behavior.* London: Pitman.

Oxford Concise Dictionary (1995). 9th edn. UK: Oxford University Press.

Parry, K. (2004). *The seven sins and the seven virtues of leadership: Which path do we follow?* (The Leading Matters Symposium Series). Centre for Leadership & Management in Education, Graduate School of Management, Griffith University, Australia, Griffith University EcoCentre.

Partington, D. A. (2003). Managing and leading. In J. R. Turner (Eds.), *People in project management.* Aldershott, UK: Gower.

Porterhouse, M., & Dulewicz, V. (2007). *Agile project managers' leadership competencies* (Henley Working Paper Series). Henley Management College, Henley-on-Thames, UK.

Robbins, S. P. (1997). *Essentials of organizational behaviour.* Englewood Cliffs, NJ: Prentice Hall.

Schultz, W. C. (1955). *FIRO: A three dimensional theory of interpersonal behaviour.* New York: Holt, Rinehart, Winston.

Slevin, D. P. (1989). *The Whole Manager.* New York, NY: Amacom.

Tannenbaum, R. & Schmidt, K. H. (1958). How to choose a leadership style. *Harvard Business Review,* March-April.

Turner, J. R. (1999). *The handbook of project-based management: Improving the processes for achieving strategic objectives.* London: McGraw-Hill.

Turner, J. R., & Müller, R. (2006). *Choosing appropriate project managers.* Newton Square, PA: Project Management Institute.

KEY TERMS AND DEFINITIONS

Behavioral or Style School: A school of leadership theories which assumes that effective leaders adopt certain styles of behaviors, which can be learned. So that effective leaders can be developed.

Competency School: A school of leadership theories which encompasses all earlier schools. It is multidimensional and includes the personal characteristics, knowledge and skills of the leader. The competency school assumes that different competence profiles are appropriate in different circumstances.

Contingency School: A school of leadership theories which assumed that effective leadership occurs through a particular leadership style which fits the idiosyncrasies of a situation.

Emotional Intelligence School: A school of leadership theories that emphasizes the social interaction between people. It assumes that the leader's emotional response to a situation has more impact on the success than the intellectual capabilities of the leader.

Emotional Leadership Competencies (EQ): A group of behavioral and motivational competencies of leaders for handling themselves and their relationships.

Intellectual Leadership Competencies (IQ): A group of cognitive competencies encompassing intelligence in form of critical analysis, strategic perspective, vision and imagination.

Leadership: A relationship through which one person influences the behavior of other people (Mullins, 1996).

Leadership Profile: The specific combination of the expression of the 15 leadership competencies in the personality of an individual.

Managerial Leadership Competencies (MQ): A group of cognitive leadership competencies encompassing the knowledge and skills of management functions.

Management: Professional administration of business concerns or public undertakings (Oxford Concise Dictionary, 1995)

Project Types: A categorization of projects, typically by project purpose or project attributes. Often done in order to prioritize projects, or to assign resources and develop or assign appropriate capabilities to manage the projects of a particular category.

Trait School: A school of leadership theories which assumes that effective leaders posses common traits, and that leaders are born not made or developed.

Visionary or Charismatic School: A school of leadership theories which emphasizes the balance between concern for relationships and concern for process and its different combinations in different situations

APPENDIX

Emotional Intelligence (EI)	EI dimension	Underlying competency	Description
Personal competencies	Self-awareness	Emotional self-awareness	• read and understand your emotions • recognize their impact on job performance and relationships.
		Accurate self-assessment	• realistically evaluate your strengths and limitations
		Self-confidence	• keep a realistically positive sense of self-worth
	Self-management	Self-control	• keep disruptive emotions and impulses under control
		Transparency	• be honest, authentic, and have integrity
		Initiative	• have a sense of efficacy and seize opportunities as they arise
		Adaptability	• adjust to changing situations and overcome obstacles
		Optimism	• view setbacks as opportunities instead of threats
		Achievement	• set realistic goals and seek for performance improvements
Social competencies	Social awareness	Empathy	• sensing a wide range of emotional signals • understanding others' perspectives • taking an active interest in their concerns
		Organizational awareness	• read the currents of organizational life • build social networks • navigate politics
		Service	• recognize and meet customers' needs
	Relationship management	Influence	• sending clear, convincing, and well-tuned messages
		Inspiration	• inspire and move people with a compelling vision
		Catalyst for change	• challenge the status quo and champion the new order

Chapter V
The Importance of Leadership in Project Management

Melanie S. Karas
TWU School of Management, USA

Mahesh S. Raisinghani
TWU School of Management, USA

Kerry S. Webb
TWU School of Management, USA

ABSTRACT

A project manager's role on any project goes far beyond task-related deliverables. Although the project manager must be able to effectively manage goals related to time, scope and cost, his or her work does not stop here since the project manager must also be able to manage numerous issues and goals, and be able to lead the people performing them. The desired leadership qualities for a project manager are discussed. As the project manager develops his or her leadership skills and uses them to encourage, motivate, and relate to the members on his or her team, he or she can expect to see the emergence of a more positive environment. Not only will such an environment improve job satisfaction and make the overall functioning of the team easier to handle, studies have also shown evidence of improved job performance and productivity, as well as a decline in the undesirable qualities that are known to occur on a project.

INTRODUCTION

Have you ever been a part of a team that had great potential but could not achieve excellence because of the components of the team? Have you ever been a part of a team whose components seemed to be lacking until everyone pulled together to accomplish something great? Why do these things happen? What is the difference between those two scenarios? The difference is the leadership. A poor leader fails to bring out the best of an already great team, but a great leader can create winners out of a team of individuals who may seem to lack ability. Leadership is a critical and essential component for any project management team.

To better understand the impact of leadership, it may be helpful to consider the following definitions of leadership:

- Leadership is the capacity to translate vision into reality (Bennis, 2003).
- Leadership is the art of influencing others to their maximum performance to accomplish any task, objective or project (Cohen and March, 1974).
- Leadership is the process of influencing the activities of an individual or a group in efforts toward goal achievement in a given situation (Hersey and Blanchard, 1984).
- Leadership is the ability of an individual to influence, motivate, and enable others to contribute toward the effectiveness and success of the organization (House, 1996).
- Leadership is the art of mobilizing others to want to struggle for shared aspirations (Kouzes and Posner, 2007).
- Leadership is a process whereby an individual influences a group of individuals to achieve a common goal (Northouse, 2007).
- Leadership is the process of influencing others to understand and agree about what needs to be done and how it can be done effectively, and the process of facilitating individual and collective efforts to accomplish shared objectives (Yukl, 2002).

Leadership involves the ability to influence people to take actions toward completing a goal or project. Projects contain a number of components – the main three being scope, cost, and time. For the project team to effectively meet scope, cost,

and time goals, one must appreciate the impact of positive leadership. It is up to the project manager to manage issues related to scope, cost, and time, as well as to lead the team to successful completion of these goals and the project as a whole.

CREATION OF A TEAM AND INTRODUCTION OF THE PROJECT

Step one of a project is to identify the project; step two is the essential step of forming the project team. This team should not include just anyone; rather, it is critical to have the "right people" on the team. Although members may be added, removed, or replaced throughout the course of the project, the core members should be selected; then, it is time to move forward with developing a team contract. The team contract will improve team relations, enhance communication, provide a clear direction, and increase the commitment of the team members (Schwalbe, 2006).

With the initial pieces in place, the project manager needs to introduce the project to the team of people who will be working together. In doing so, the manager should deliver the information clearly and with genuine enthusiasm. If the project manager has not displayed excitement toward this project previously, now is the time to start. Upon going forward with the project, the project manager must realize his or her role as a leader. As a matter of fact, this person should not think of himself or herself as the project *manager*, but rather as the project *leader*.

From this point forward, the terms "project manager" and "leader" will be used interchangeably. The leader must motivate his or her team and provide continued direction, information, goals, adjustments, and helpful feedback throughout the project. The presence of motivation does not promise great success, but the absence of motivation has great potential to damage the team in the long run (Levin and Rad, 2006). The leader is responsible to maintain the team's momentum throughout the process from the project's inception to its closure. With the abundance of information, work, details, changes, and other issues that will arise, the project manager must understand the role and skills of a leader and how to avoid or quickly address situations that could be detrimental to the completion of the project.

Since the project team has been established, it is possible that the team includes some of the right people as well as some of the wrong people for the job. The leader must be able to identify the strengths and weaknesses of each team member, assess what they bring to or take away from the team, and address those issues accordingly. It is up to the leader to manage the people on the team and make necessary modifications as situations require (Levin and Rad, 2006). The project manager must also be able to identify and understand any possible hidden agendas that individuals on the team may possess, determine whether they are positive or negative, and be ready to take the appropriate action if needed.

NEGATIVE LEADERSHIP/ MEMBERSHIP ON THE TEAM

Dr. Harold Kerzner identifies different types of team members that a project manager may encounter and separates these people into two categories—destructive and supportive members. Destructive characters include the roles of aggressor, dominator, devil's advocate, topic jumper, recognition seeker, withdrawer, and blocker (Salidas, 2007b). The characteristics of each are as follows:

- **Aggressor:** Criticizes team members and challenges ideas
- **Dominator:** Manipulates and tries to take control
- **Devil's advocate:** Challenges ideas and finds fault in suggestions

- **Topic jumper:** Moves from one subject to the next and creates a lack of focus
- **Recognition seeker:** Argues their position and wants credit for success
- **Withdrawer:** Withholds information and does not participate
- **Blocker:** Provides reasons why ideas will not work (Establishing the Roles, 2007)

When performed appropriately and in moderation, some of these behaviors may prove helpful in project development, but when done in excess or at inappropriate moments they become undesirable. Challenging ideas, for example, can be a positive trait when trying to develop a process as it can facilitate deeper thinking, enhanced development, and an advanced outcome. However, a team member who challenges ideas and continues to do so after a decision has been made can lower the team morale and may quickly turn the environment into a negative one.

Levin and Rad (2006) identify additional traits that may be present in a team, including argumentative members who constantly reference "how we used to do it," back-stabbers who criticize other members and spread gossip, and those who transfer their own responsibilities to other members of the team. Needless to say, these types of individuals fail to add value to the environment and can change the team environment from positive to negative. It is important for the leader to know, understand and identify these characteristics and be prepared to address the behaviors before the attitudes and actions lead to the deterioration of the team's performance.

POSITIVE LEADERSHIP/ MEMBERSHIP ON THE TEAM

Saladis (2007b) discusses Kerzner's list of positive team member roles and responsibilities. These roles include the initiator, information seeker, information giver, encourager, clarifier, harmonizer, and gate keeper. The traits of these team members are as follows:

- **Initiator:** Looks for new ideas and supports trying different things
- **Information seeker:** Desires information to become better informed, looks for resources and supporting information
- **Information giver:** Shares gained knowledge with the team and increases the team's knowledge
- **Encourager:** Supports team members' ideas
- **Clarifier:** Makes sure everyone on the team understands information and decisions
- **Harmonizer:** Creates feelings of unity among team members
- **Gate Keeper:** Keeps team focused and makes sure information stays relevant

These positive traits enhance the overall functioning of the team and encourage a greater sense of synergy. The characteristics listed promote positive energy and a supportive environment among the team members and are traits that a leader should work to encourage and enhance. The more emphasis put toward these qualities, the stronger they will develop, and the more contagious the positive environment will become. When a manager is supportive and gives attention to modeling positive behaviors and affirming helpful interactions among team members, the behavior patterns are more likely to be repeated and a more contagious positive environment will result.

Research has shown that the more senior the leader, the more important emotional competencies become (Goleman, 2002). Managers who are best at identifying others' emotions and responding appropriately have been shown to be more successful in their work as well as in their social lives (Rosenthal, 1977).

IMPORTANCE OF LEADER TO ADDRESS NEGATIVE AND ENHANCE POSITIVE

Leadership plays a critical role in the success of a project. While *managing* utilizes tactical skills to focus on the tasks at hand and working to ensure that details are met, *leading* tends to utilize "soft skills" to relate to the people who are responsible for completing the tasks, to understand others' needs and drives, and to provide a positive influence to achieve the timely, successful completion of the project. Both management and leadership functions are important, but without leadership the management process may increase negative attitudes and behaviors and decrease workers' motivation and efforts to complete the project effectively if the environment becomes too controlling (Bass, 1985).

Once a leader has identified the roles of the people on the team, he or she must understand how to influence the team members. As Jim Collins discusses in his book *Good to Great* (2001), an important step to ensure great results is getting the right people on the bus and the wrong people off the bus. Collins also emphasizes the importance of getting the right people into the right seats or positions to positively impact the organizational results.

Often, managers do everything in their power to get the right people on the team, but fail to address the negative behaviors and attitudes of people who are already on the team. When the leader is passive about addressing the "wrong actions" and fails to communicate clearly by defining roles and unacceptable behavior, the result is the reinforcement of negative attitudes which work counter to the successful completion of the project at hand. Sometimes managers do not realize that despite efforts to enhance and empower the right people, the presence of negative people with detrimental behaviors can hold back the "right people" with their destructive attitudes and interactions.

When a project manager stops controlling and starts leading, he or she affirms the human element in the work situation and understands the importance of correcting or removing the negative or "wrong" people. The project leader must take responsibility for removing negative influences before they damage the organization or hinder team players (Sanders, 2008). This concept is critical when dealing with a project since there are definitive time, scope, and cost goals that must be met. Any force pulling the project team away from such goals must be handled immediately. There is no time during a project to be passive about dealing with individuals who are slowing the team's progress and productivity. Leaders play a vital role in keeping the project team running like a well-oiled machine.

Once negative issues and/or destructive individuals have been adequately dealt with, the leader must take one additional step. The leader must recognize the importance and benefit of affirming and encouraging the positive people and beneficial attitudes on his team. It is important for the leader to acknowledge the strengths and helpful attributes that each member of his team brings to the table and to encourage and nurture positive behaviors. This can be done through recognition (e.g., publicly thanking them in front of their peers), additional incentives (e.g., giving someone a bonus when they went above and beyond during the project), and/or a promotion within the project team or within the company. Recognition meets one of a person's most primal needs – to feel valued and significant. Incentives and rewards will encourage the positive behavior of individuals and give team members something to strive for. Rewarding positive behavior is an effective way to encourage and promote success at the project management level as well as in other areas of an organization.

Turk (2005) reiterates the importance of developing a positive environment and emphasizes common-sense points that are often overlooked, such as the need for open communication. The notion that getting the right people involved in the project is critical, guidance is necessary, reviews and feedback are vital practices, creativity and flexibility must be encouraged, and any problems that arise should be resolved immediately and at the lowest possible level without escalating problems unnecessarily (Turk, 2005). The characteristics and qualities of good leadership in project management are rather consistent across the board. Although leadership practices are fairly straightforward, effective project managers must understand how to implement leadership skills and seek training or coaching in any areas they want to strengthen as part of their personal and professional development.

ADDITIONAL LEADERSHIP ROLES

Aside from identifying the negative and positive team members and addressing situations accordingly, there are a number of other ways that a leader can encourage his team throughout the project.

♦ Once the project manager has been able to exterminate negative actions and attitudes, he or she must be aware of signs of frustration and stress among team members. Despite the initial energy and willingness to participate, once the project is underway stress, frustration, or feelings of being overwhelmed may set in (Levin and Rad, 2006). When members of the team receive their assignments and become fully engaged in the project, they will come face-to-face with the reality of a multitude of decisions, obstacles, and challenges that stand between them and successful completion of the project. It is at these impasses where the leader must provide emotional support to encourage the members in addition to providing the team with the technical support, tools, and knowledge needed to move forward.

If the leader ignores stressors as they arise, workers may develop negative feelings, lack the desire or willingness to move forward, perform only the minimum work necessary rather than going above and beyond, or perhaps worst – spread their attitudes to other team members (Levin and Rad, 2006). As mentioned above, a positive team environment can become contagious if it is promoted, but this does not take away from the old adage that misery loves company. It can be easier for a team to fall into negative patterns of behavior than to remain focused and positive without supportive leadership. If the leader allows the work situation to decline to this level, he can potentially set the team up for failure. A leader's job is not just to motivate workers at the beginning of the project, but he or she also must continue to utilize motivational tactics throughout the project. The project manager should become an expert at identifying when negative issues need to be addressed and positive behaviors and attitudes need to be praised.

♦ A leader should be a role model to the team - he or she should have complete buy-in to the project and be a walking example of the passion he or she wishes others to demonstrate for the project as well. On the other hand, the leader must know when to take a break and step away from the project, allowing himself to rejuvenate and regain a fresh perspective while maintaining a positive life balance (Moore, 2007). If the leader does not take breaks, continually works late at night, does not take time for lunch, and works as if he or she is on the project 24/7, the other team members will feel an obligation to do the same. This level of work intensity will eventually create resentment and burnout, which can quickly turn a positive environment into a negative one.

If the project leader is someone who feels the need to work through lunch or to put in extra time at night, he or she should address the team and encourage them to take lunches and to leave the workplace at a designated time each evening. The project manager does not want to project their personal obsessive or compulsive work style onto their project team members. Although the spirit and desire to go above and beyond is highly ap-

preciated and beneficial at times, there comes a point when a reprieve is needed. Team members should be able to take breaks and go home at the end of the work day without feeling guilty. In addition, breaks are important to everyone to refresh their minds and bodies to prevent suffering physiological symptoms such as burnout (Moore, 2007).

When it is time for the team members to go home for the day, the leader might consider turning off the lights, closing their door, and taking a twenty minute walk to clear their mind. This will allow the other workers the "emotional freedom" to leave work and go home. After taking a walk, the project leader will return to the office feeling refreshed, and with the other staff gone, can work as late as needed without interruption.

Forcing one's body and mind to go beyond its general capabilities for a significant period of time without getting adequate rest can have a detrimental impact on results. Working excessive late night hours to finish a project can cause fatigue, illnesses, or other physical and emotional breakdowns. It is important for everyone involved, including the project manager, to take adequate breaks to refresh one's physical and emotional capacity. This is in the best interest of the individual, the team, and the project.

♦ The leader should not underestimate the power of humor in the work environment and should consider incorporating some fun into the project when possible. A team who is able to enjoy working on the project will be more likely to bond, develop a better working relationship, and sustain a more energized work environment. Such a culture will help the team maintain focus on the big picture instead of only their portion of the project (Saladis, 2005). Humor can add a lot more to the team than just a chuckle by increasing levels of trust, commitment, and energy among team members which will inevitably have a positive impact on productivity. (Goleman, 2002).

♦ Additional tips for a leader include letting the team know what the goals are and how they are going to be accomplished from the start. This allows each team member be aware of what is expected of each of them, informs the team on how to measure their performance on a regular basis, helps everyone stay positive and praise the achievements that occur, provides the team with the tools they need to succeed, and creates clear indicators which allow opportunities to celebrate achievements (Saladis, 2007b). A team's effectiveness will improve if they know what their role is, where they stand, and are able to celebrate their successes, thus acknowledging a job well done.

♦ The overall role of the leader is to motivate employees to get the job done and provide a positive environment in which this can be accomplished. The leader must possess the technical skills and knowledge as well as the soft skills needed to work with people. The leader must be willing to make decisions that are in the best interest of the team, the project, and the company while striving to maintain a positive environment. This is not to be confused, however, with simply getting everyone to like the leader, which may be beneficial, but it is not always possible. If some people need to be removed from the project, team, or company, it is not likely that person will have positive feelings toward the leader, but the leader must be confident in taking these actions.

Saladis (2007a) provides a relevant quote from General Colin Powell who said "Good leadership involves responsibility to the welfare of the group, which means that some people will get angry at your actions and decisions. Getting everyone to like you is a sign of mediocrity." While great importance is placed on developing and maintaining a positive environment, it should not be done at the expense of productivity and the best interest of the team, project, or company. It may not be possible to get everyone to like you, but they must respect you and the decisions you make; what *is* important and necessary is to get everyone engaged in the process.

ENGAGING EMPLOYEES

The Gallup Organization has developed the Q12 assessment which asks a series of 12 questions to determine employees' level of engagement. Based on the responses, the Gallup Organization concludes whether the employee is engaged, not engaged, or actively disengaged (Davis and Cable, 2006). The definitions of each are as follows:

- **Engaged:** Employees feel a connection to their company and perform their work with a desirable level of energy and passion for what they do. Their performance helps to move the company ahead.
- **Not-engaged:** Employees are basically going through the motions of their daily routine, not putting any extra effort or enthusiasm into their work.
- **Actively disengaged:** Employees are not pleased with their work situation and go a step further to actively show their displeasure (Positive Workplace, 2006).

According to a 2004 Gallup study, only 28% of the United States workforce is actively engaged. The remaining 72% of workers potentially cost an excess of $375 billion in direct costs (Davis and Cable, 2006). The 72% of employees who are not-engaged or actively disengaged present a threat to the positive environment discussed above and can potentially create a negative environment. It is the job of a leader to turn this situation around by creating a positive environment that influences employees towards active engagement. Needless to say, the importance of leadership on a project continues to grow in importance, and it is vital for the project manager to understand his role as a leader who provides the knowledge, motivation, and people-skills needed to effectively lead the team to success. The leader should make every effort to actively engage those on his team. Learning more about the Gallup Q12 assessment process may serve as a guideline for leaders to understand how to get their team members to become more actively engaged on projects and in their regular job functions.

EFFECTS OF THE POSITIVE TEAM ENVIRONMENT

A negative environment can quickly build upon itself, creating a snowball effect as it gains momentum and draws in more people. Maintaining a positive environment is not quite as easy, but the payoff is invaluable.

A team that is composed of the right people doing the right things, has the tools and knowledge to do their tasks, and has the motivation to complete the duties assigned and required of them, is going to be a much higher-performing team than one where negative attitudes and behaviors are tolerated. Workers who do not know how to do what is required of them, people who lack motivation, and employees who waste energy complaining, blaming, and criticizing have a negative impact on the organization's bottom line in regard to increased costs and decreased productivity.

A positive environment is not desirable just because it sounds like fun or because it will make the work more enjoyable. Aside from personal and emotional benefits, a positive environment actually increases productivity as well. One study has shown that companies with a high level of employee engagement and commitment ranked, on average, 36 points higher on "return to shareholders" than did companies with lower engagement scores. According to another study, high levels of employee engagement increased profitability, productivity, sales, customer loyalty and life satisfaction while decreasing theft, safety issues, stress, attrition and absenteeism (Davis and Cable, 2006). Not only did a positive environment improve desirable worker qualities, it decreased undesirable behaviors.

A positive environment will enhance value creation. A positive focus has the potential to

develop many benefits for the company, such as greater market-share, less investment risk, higher quality, increased new product development, better employee morale, and a higher level of retention (Saladis, 2007a). It all begins with effective leadership.

CONCLUSION

A project manager's role on any project goes far beyond task-related deliverables. Although the project manager must be able to effectively manage goals related to time, scope and cost, his or her work does not stop here. The project manager must be able to manage numerous issues and goals, and also be able to influence the people performing them.

A good analogy is to compare a project manager to a basketball coach. The coach must manage the amount of time spent at practice (time), which drills will be performed during that time (scope), as well as the budget for travel, meals, and equipment (cost). The coach can manage these aspects as much as he or she likes, but the members of the team cannot be handled in the same way.

A coach cannot force everyone on the team to make 10 free throws in 3 minutes because that is not a "manageable" task. The coach can, however, lead and encourage the members of the team to accomplish tasks by providing encouragement and guidance regarding their performance. A player who feels supported will be more likely to accomplish the goal than a player who is surrounded by negativity or who lacks the desire to accomplish the task. The leader's support and encouragement helps build the desire for a team's players to accomplish their individual tasks and provides energy and encouragement to push the players to achieve the team's goals. The analogy explains how certain aspects of a project can be managed, yet people must be led, regardless of how well the time, scope and cost are managed. This is the reason why it is so important for a project manager to understand their role of "managing" the tasks at hand and "leading" when it comes to dealing with the people performing the project tasks.

The desired leadership qualities for a project manager are relatively straightforward. However, it may take some time for the project manager to learn and become accustomed to using new skills. Although negative people may be easily identified, dealing with them in a real-world situation may not be so easy. The leader needs to understand, however, that not dealing with negative behavior and attitudes will eventually create greater distress than the discomfort of confronting the situation immediately. The sooner a bad situation is handled, the less damaging it will become.

As the project manager develops his leadership skills and uses them to encourage, motivate, and relate to the members on his team, he can expect to see the emergence of a more positive environment. Not only will such an environment improve job satisfaction and make the overall functioning of the team a smoother process, studies have shown evidence of improved job performance and productivity, as well as a decline in the undesirable qualities that are known to occur on the job. Thus, it seems obvious that time and energy should be spent on developing a positive team atmosphere. The payoff is far greater than the minimal time the project manager has to spend developing leadership skills and the occasional discomfort of dealing with an uncomfortable situation. Upon completion of the project, the project manager/leader will recognize how a positive team environment made a significant difference made in the overall process.

As the project manager reflects with satisfaction, recognizing that the project has been successfully completed and the work environment was positive and productive, he or she can enjoy the satisfaction of a job well done. With the lessons learned as he or she developed into a positive leader, one thing is certain—the project leader can take the knowledge forward to the next project with the understanding that achieving success will involve new strategies and processes. No two projects and teams are ever exactly alike, so new lessons will be learned that can be added to the continuous cycle of leadership, keeping in mind that current knowledge and best practices are not going to be a perfect fit for every project or team environment. However, they can serve as guidelines and "fuel for innovation" for a project manager by providing knowledge and insight for future endeavors (Saladis, 2006).

REFERENCES

Bass, B. M. (1985). *Leadership and performance beyond expectations.* New York: Free Press.

Bennis, W. (2003). *On becoming a leader.* Cambridge, MA: Perseus Publishing.

Canfield, J. (2005). *The success principles: How to get from where you are to where you want to be.* New York: Harper Collins Publishers Inc.

Cohen, M. D., & March, J. G. (1974). *Leadership and ambiguity: The American college president.* Princeton, NJ: The Carnegie Foundation for the Advancement of Training.

Collins, J. (2001). *Good to great.* New York: HarperCollins.

Davis, J., & Cable, J. (2006). *Positive workplace: Enhancing individual and team productivity.* Retrieved July 21, 2007, from http://www.allpm.com/print.php?sid=1634

Goleman, D. (2002). *Primal leadership: Emotional intelligence.* Boston: Harvard Business School Press.

Hersey, P., & Blanchard, K. H. (1984). *Management of organizational behavior* (4th ed.). Englewood Cliffs, NJ: Prentice-Hall.

House, R. J. (1996). Path-goal theory of leadership: Lessons, legacy, and a reformulated theory. *Leadership Quarterly, 7,* 323-352.

Kouzes, J., & Posner, B. (2007). *The leadership challenge.* San Francisco: John Wiley and Sons Publishing.

Levin, G., & Rad, P. (2006). *Successful motivational techniques for virtual teams.* Retrieved July 21, 2007 from http://www.allpm.com/print.php?sid=1637

Moore, L. (2007). *If the sky isn't falling, Why does my head hurt?* Retrieved July 21, 2007, from http://www.allpm.com/print.php?sid=1658

Northouse, P. (2007). *Leadership: Theory and practice.* Thousand Oaks, CA: Sage Publications, Inc.

Project Manager (2007). *Project manager: Manage team performance.* Retrieved August 8, 2007, from http://www.method123.com/articles/2007/05/21/Team-Performance

Rosenthal, R. (1977). The PONS test: Measuring sensitivity to nonverbal cues. In P. McReynolds (Ed.), *Advances in psychological assessment.* San Francisco: Jossey-Bass.

Saladis, F. (2005). *Positive leadership in project management: Leading through laughter.* Retrieved July 21, 2007, from http://www.allpm.com/print.php?sid=1387

Saladis, F. (2006). *Positive leadership in project management: Leadership lessons learned.* Retrieved July 21, 2007, from http://www.allpm.com/print.php?sid=1635

Saladis, F. (2007a). *Positive leadership in project management: Effective project leadership - leading project teams to higher levels of competency and effectiveness.* Retrieved July 21, 2007, from http://www.allpm.com/print.php?sid=1717

Saladis, F. (2007b). *Positive leadership in project management: Establishing the roles of the project team.* Retrieved July 21, 2007, from http://www.allpm.com/print.php?sid=1657

Sanders, D. (2008). *Built to serve.* New York: McGraw-Hill.

Schwalbe, K. (2006). *Introduction to project management.* Boston: Thomson Course Technology.

Turk, W. (2005). *Defense AT&L. Workforce development: Quality management - a primer.* (pp. 30-33).

Yukl, G. A. (2002). *Leadership in organizations.* 4th Ed. Englewood Cliffs, NJ: Prentice-Hall.

KEY TERMS AND DEFINITIONS

Actively Disengaged: Employees are not pleased with their work situation and go a step further to actively show their displeasure.

Aggressor: Criticizes team members and challenges ideas.

Blocker: Provides reasons why ideas will not work (Establishing the Roles, 2007).

Clarifier: Makes sure everyone on the team understands information, decisions, etc.

Devil's Advocate: Challenges ideas and finds fault in suggestions.

Dominator: Manipulates and tries to take control.

Encourager: Supports team members' ideas.

Engaged: Employees feel a connection to their company and perform their work with a desirable level of energy and passion for what they do. Their performance helps to move the company ahead.

Gate Keeper: Keeps team focused and makes sure information stays relevant.

Harmonizer: Creates feelings of unity among team members.

Information Giver: Shares gained knowledge with the team and increases the team's knowledge.

Information Seeker: Desires information to become better informed, looks for resources and supporting information.

Initiator: Looks for new ideas and supports trying different things.

Leadership: The capacity to translate vision into reality (Bennis, 2003).

Leadership: The art of influencing others to their maximum performance to accomplish any task, objective or project (Cohen and March 1974).

Leadership: The process of influencing the activities of an individual or a group in efforts toward goal achievement in a given situation (Hersey and Blanchard, 1984).

Leadership: The ability of an individual to influence, motivate, and enable others to contribute toward the effectiveness and success of the organization (House, 1996).

Leadership: The art of mobilizing others to want to struggle for shared aspirations (Kouzes and Posner, 2007.

Leadership: A process whereby an individual influences a group of individuals to achieve a common goal (Northouse, 2007).

Leadership: The process of influencing others to understand and agree about what needs to be done and how it can be done effectively, and the process of facilitating individual and collective efforts to accomplish shared objectives (Yukl, 2002).

Not-Engaged: Employees are basically going through the motions of their daily routine, not putting any extra effort or enthusiasm into their work.

Recognition Seeker: Argues their position and wants credit for success.

Topic Jumper: Moves from one subject to the next and creates a lack of focus

Withdrawer: Withholds information and does not participate.

Chapter VI
Technology Management by Objectives

Jaby Mohammed
Indiana University-Purdue University Fort Wayne (IPFW), USA

ABSTRACT

This chapter introduces the concept of technology management by objectives. Technology is one of the fastest moving elements in the 21st Century, which could be well explained using the growth theory. The growth theory is defined on the basis of the economic growth from the increasing returns that is associated with the new knowledge. The knowledge has various dimensions in today's world, one of which is the technology. The major portion of any improvement or any development in any sector is due to technology or due to a change in technology. Technology in any organization can improve, sustain, and diminish the business based on the approaches used in the model. The ability to connect technology and gain organization advantage depends upon how efficiently and effectively the technology is managed within the organization. Technology has been managed by different means based on the application of the technology. This chapter would discus how the technology could be management by objectives (TBO). Many approaches have been utilized to integrate individual and team goal with the overall goals of the organization of an enterprise. Each group goal would have a set of objectives and satisfying all these objectives is virtually impossible because many of them contradict to each others. Technology by objectives is a process in which the common goals are identified and would define individually the major area of responsibility in terms of the results and objectives expected in detail. The goals would be jointly established by the administrators and the sub-ordinates and would emphasis on the output variables. Every corporation has different technological goals and visions, so based on the enterprise the goals and objectives are set.

INTRODUCTION

This chapter on technology management by objectives would discuss about the definition and concepts of technology management by objectives. The need and requirements of the TMO is also discussed. Technology management by objectives can be set in all different domains of activities with in organization, right from research, production, sales, service, logistics, human resource, finance, information system etc. Some of the objectives are collective, for the whole enterprise which are called as Global TMO and those objectives that are localized with in the department are called as Local TMO. The objectives for the TMO must be specific, measurable, achievable, relevant, time specific, extendable, and recordable. The objectives for the TMO usually needs quantifying and monitoring which is usually does using a reliable management information system (MIS) that are needed to establish relevant objective and monitor them thorough out the life cycle. MIS is a subset of the overall internal control of a business covering all the aspects of a business there by helping the TMO to reach its goals (Castellano, J. F., Rosenzweig, K., & Harper, A. R., 2004).

TMO is an innovative way to reach the goals but there are limitations with TMO, the use of TMO needs to be carefully aligned with the culture of the organization. While TMO is not as fashionable as it was pre determined, it still has its place in management today. The key difference is that rather than 'set' objectives from a cascade process, objectives are discussed and agreed, based upon a more strategic picture being available to employees. Engagement of employees in the objective setting process is seen as a strategic advantage by many (Handy Understanding Organizations). Another more fundamental and authoritative critique comes from Walter A. Shewhart / W. Edwards Deming, the fathers of Modern Quality Management, for whom TMO is the opposite of their founding Philosophy of Statistical Process Control. TMO aims in increasing the technological performance by aligning the goals and objectives of the enterprise as well as the goals and objectives of the employees thorough out the enterprise. Ideally the employees identify and understand their objectives, the duration to complete the objective, they are also evaluated during different interval of time and finally they get the tracked feedback in the process to reach the objectives. TMO is very similar concept to the Management by Objectives which was first out lines by Peter Drucker in 1954 in his book *'The Practice of Management'*. In the 90s, Peter Drucker himself decreased the significance of this organization management method, when he said: "It's just another tool. It is not the great cure for management inefficiency... Management by Objectives works if you know the objectives, 90% of the time you don't."

DEFINITION AND CONCEPT

There had been many approaches that have been utilized to integrate individual and team goals with overall goals of the organization of an enterprise. Technology management by objectives is basically a strategic process in which the group that works on an objective have a:

- Understand to have a common goal; especially all the members in the group should understand the importance in a big picture.
- Identify the responsibility for each team member in the enterprise, this is also really important because each team member needs to understand how their work would affect the other technology development related to it.
- Use these measures as guides for operating the technology enterprise and accessing the contribution of the team
  - The goals are usually established as a team that work in the in technology

enterprise and agreed upon in advance. The goals are usually emphasized as the output variables (or results) or intervening variables, or a combination of both

o At specific intervals, the TMO performance is reviewed and measured to check with the current goals. The team usually participates in the review and evaluation. The review is done as a team and no arbitrary decisions are made during the meeting.

To conclude Technology Management by Objectives is technology management strategy that implies in managing by properly identifying the objectives of an organization.

TECHNOLOGY MANAGEMENT BY OBJECTIVES (TMO)

The technology management by objectives is an intended goal that prescribes a definite scope and suggests directions to efforts of an enterprise. Technology management is an art of getting things done using technology and people. In today's world when the economy is very competitive its not very easy to get things done unless every individual concerned in the technology management knows what the objectives and targets are and accepts them as being worth attaining.

The basic requirements for the technology management by objectives for to enterprise to work efficiently are as follows:

- Work in the same direction towards achieving company goals
- Vivid communication with in the team
- Objectives must be set such that the can be reasonably attained.
- Review and evaluation at specific intervals

Depending upon the nature of objectives, the technology management by objectives can be identified as:

- **Short term objective:** The objectives that are for a short period of time for example like expediting the works lagging behind the schedule
- **Long term objective:** The objectives that are for a long period of time for example like planning for a diversification
- **Specific objective:** The objectives that are specific for a given task for example like a decision on pricing policies
- **General objectives:** The objectives that are general to the enterprise for example the financial objective or the objective on increasing productivity.
- **Innovative/learning objectives:** These objectives that would improve technology innovation

The technology management by objective is broadly divide in to three base on the types, they are:

1. Broad objectives
2. Major objectives
3. Lesser objectives

Broad objective or corporate objective is a statement of the standing company or enterprise that wishes to achieve, for example

- Provide customers with the technology solutions or services at reasonable or competitive price and at the right time
- Manufacture high end technology products at high quality standards and to strive to make them better at lower costs, etc.

Major objectives are actually a filtered or a shortened version of the broad objectives and they set the tactical areas into which a company wishes to move. For example the major objectives would include the market share, the technology product plan and to plans to extend the technology to different sectors of the customer population.

Lesser objectives are targets, budgets, and department objectives for the technology management, including those governing the performance standards of managers and other members of the enterprise.

STEPS IN SETTING UP TMO

TMO is cyclic processes that strive attain continuous process improvement with in the system. The various steps that are involved in a technology management by objective is shown in the flow chart and is explained below.

The first step is to clarify and to set the common technology goals for the entire organization or enterprise, this step would include meeting with all the upper management people. The outcome of

the first step is to set what they want to achieve.

The second step is to achieve the goals of the technology enterprise, any appropriate changes in the in the enterprise structure are made at this point. One the overall goal of the technology management is set in place next is to list down the objectives that they want to achieve while reaching the goal. Like a change in technology, responsibility for the task, span for the technology, and so forth

Chief technology officers sets the goals for each department and each department heads sets it objectives for its departments and proposes goals for their jobs and select the area in which they must be effective during the company plan, the subordinates also works on the goals and measures for the same. The chief technology officer determines the targets for each of the department and is then sent to the individual department for review.

Both the teams sit together jointly and discuss the objectives to be achieved during the state

Figure 1. TMO cycle

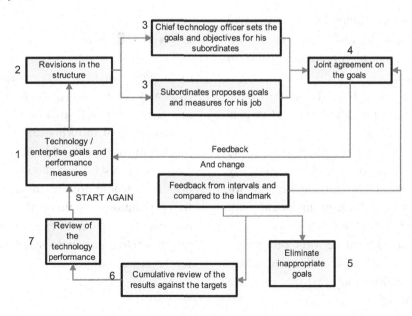

TMO cycle

time period. In other words , the goals are jointly established and agreed upon in advance

During specific intervals, a comparison between the achievable goals and the achieved goals and necessary adjustments are made. Inappropriate goals are eliminated at the earlier stages so that the resources are not necessarily wasted.

The performance are monitored against the TMO plans or targets ad must be formally reviewed at predetermined times of the plan

Finally the accomplishment or the performance of the entire group is evaluated and is reviewed with the objectives with which it was started. If there are any changes between the initial objectives and the results, steps should be taken to overcome the problems responsible for that inaccuracy.

ADVANTAGES OF VARIOUS TMO

As discussed earlier TMO is a systematic and organizational approach that allows and manage the technology to focus on achievable goals and attain the best possible results from available resources. The various advantages of TMO are listed below

- Technology management by objectives may become a powerful tool in gaining mutual commitment and high productivity for an organization
- Technology management by objectives gives the company objectives and targets constantly in view
- TMO gives meaning and direction to people in organization, a common objective is set by the management and individual targets for the group, which all the group would work together to achieve the common goals.
- TMO coordinates the efforts of various departments in of an organization, which makes the entire group feel that they are the vital part of the organization.

- TMO provides motivation to people because they work on objectives decided with their consent
- TMO prevents flittering away of efforts and money, maximizing the resources available and minimizing cost involved in the process.
- TMO offers greater consistency in decision making
- TMO forces management to think ahead in respect of its short term and long term goals, the management sets the short term goals and long term goals based on the market conditions.
- TMO helps the enterprise to focus on the areas where it is vital that management should be effective and isolate the problems preventing progress towards through company objectives
- It assists technology managers in their own self development and leads to an analysis of training requirements if subordinates are to improve their performance in future years
- TMO leads to a better understanding between the various levels in an organization.

CONCLUSION

Technology management working by objectives may follow too rigid a pattern in thinking and action. There is always need for flexibility in management thinking and the provisions of written objectives should not be allowed to affect this adversely. Technology management by objectives would provide transparent objectives for corporations, would be able to keep track on the progress with an efficient feedback system to get back into the track to reach the overall goals for the organization.

REFERENCES

Behn, R. D. (2003). Why measure performance? Different purposes require different measures. *Public Administration Review, 63*(5), 586-606.

Castellano, J. F., Rosenzweig, K., & Harper, A. R. (2004). How corporate culture impacts unethical distortion of financial numbers: Managing by Objectives and Results could be counterproductive and contribute to a climate that may lead to distortion of the system, manipulation of accounting figures, and, ultimately, unethical behavior. *Management accounting quarterly*. Retrieved on 13 November, 2006.

Handy Understanding Organizations (Penguin Business) (3rd Edition) (Paperback)

Khanna, O. (n.d.). *Industrial engineering and management* (2nd edition). Dhanpat rai publications.

Milson, M. A., & Wilemon, D. (2007). *The strategy of managing innovation and technology* (1st Edition). Upper Saddle River, NJ: Prentice Hall Publishing.

Statistical Process Control: the Founders' Way - www.statistical-process-control.org

US Economic Development Administration. (n.d.). *New growth theory, learning and technology.*

Zandin, K. B., & Maynard, H. B. (n.d.). *Maynard's industrial engineering handbook.* 5th ed. McGraw-Hill Professional.

KEY TERMS AND DEFINITIONS

Broad Objective: Broad objective or corporate objective is a statement of the standing company or enterprise that wishes to achieve.

General Objectives: Objectives that are general to the enterprise for example the profit objective or the objective on increasing productivity.

Long Term Objective: Objectives that are for a long period of time for example like planning for a diversification.

Short Term Objective: The objectives that are for a short period of time for example like expediting the works lagging behind the schedule.

Specific Objective: Objectives that are specific for a given task for example like a decision on pricing policies.

Technology Management by Objectives: Technology by objectives is a process in which the common goals are identified and would define the major area of responsibility in terms of the results expected.

Chapter VII
Examining Stakeholders' Roles in Influencing IT Project Cancellation Decisions

Gary Pan
Singapore Management University, Singapore

ABSTRACT

This study adopts a stakeholder analysis to examine stakeholders' roles in influencing organizational decisions to abandon information technology projects. To do so, we adapted from Freeman's (1984) work and developed a theoretical assessment framework to organize and interpret data, and define avenues (five propositions were proposed) for further research into information technology project cancellation. By providing a better understanding of the project stakeholders' perception, expectations and their interrelationship, this study provides practitioners with useful insights to managing project stakeholders during information technology development projects. For researchers, our contribution lies in the development of a project cancellation review model that adds a stakeholder perspective.

INTRODUCTION

Information technology (IT) has been playing an instrumental role in helping organizations to achieve success. However costly IT projects have raised the stakes associated with project failure as IT project cancellation is a widely recognized problem in the software development community (Iacovou and Dexter, 2005; Nelson, 2005). According to a report by *Computing* in 2003 on UK public sector organizations, IT project development emerged as a major problem area encompassing a series of cancellations and delays that incurred a staggering sum of around £1.5 billion. IT experts have attributed the high incidence of failure to the availability of few effective solutions for organizations to prevent project failure (Drummond, 1996) and the failure of organizations to learn from their own experiences (Pan et al., 2007).

While several factors may contribute to IT project failure, the roles played by various project stakeholders during project development may turn out to be vital to the success of project development (Pan and Pan, 2006). Generally, the development of an IT project requires effective participation of diverse stakeholders (Cavaye and Cragg, 1995). Lyytinen and Hirschheim (1987) underline the importance of fulfilling the expectations of relevant stakeholders in an IS development project. Without having proper understanding of stakeholders' roles in projects may cause serious consequences during project development. In some cases, such misunderstanding alone may lead to project failure. Against such a backdrop, we undertook an exploratory research study into an abandoned electronic procurement (e-procurement) system development project. Specifically, the paper *aims to examine stakeholders' roles in influencing IT project cancellation decisions.*

Thechapter is structured as follows: the background and research approach will be discussed. After that, data will be extracted from a case of an abandoned e-procurement project and findings are discussed along with implications and conclusion.

BACKGROUND

IT Project Failure

The dominant stream of research on IT project failure is committed to uncovering factors associated with failure (Nelson, 2005; Barki et al. 1993; Schmidt et al. 2001). These studies worked on the assumption that if factors contributing to project failure are detected, organizations can directly remove these contributing factors. On the other hand, process research on IT project failure has gathered momentum in recent years and has

highlighted a number of themes. The themes are: political (see Drummond, 1996; Bussen and Myers, 1997), technical (see Beynon-Davies, 1995; Wastell and Newman, 1996), strategic (see Mitev, 1994; Sauer and Burton, 1999) and a combination of several factors. Besides all these accounts of IT project failure, other studies have attempted testing process frameworks (e.g. Beynon-Davies, 1995) and proposition of a configurational theory of IT failure (e.g. Sauer et al. 1997). Even though IT project failure has been the focus of many articles in the IT discipline, the subject of IT project cancellation has been largely neglected and under-studied (Ewusi-Mensah, 1997; Oz and Sosik, 2000). Particularly, the lack of progress in understanding stakeholders' roles in influencing IT project cancellation decisions has been highlighted as an important issue awaiting to be addressed (Pan and Pan, 2006).

The concept of stakeholder was first introduced in the early work of system theorists, but it was Freeman (1984) who brought stakeholder theory to the forefront of academic research. Even though the stakeholder concept has been widely accepted among information systems (IS) researchers and practitioners (see Pouloudi and Whitley 1997; Gallivan 2001), very few studies have examined the incompatibilities between stakeholders' perceptions and expectations with the project goal, especially in the case of external stakeholders; and assess the stakeholders' conflicting interrelationship in an IS development project. These are important issues since individual stakeholder cannot be viewed as a single entity in a project. Rather, it is the interrelations among different stakeholders that constitute one of the most appealing mechanisms of stakeholder behaviour (Pouloudi and Whitley, 1997). Therefore, there is urgent need to examine the stakeholders' roles during project development. One way to better understand project stakeholders' roles is through the lens of Freeman (1984)'s stakeholder assessment framework.

Stakeholder Assessment Framework

Freeman's (1984) framework consists of two levels: 'rational' and 'process'. It begins with the 'rational' level where organizations identify project stakeholders by first defining the meaning of stakeholders. This is due to the inconsistency in stakeholder's definitions and uses, which often results in different and conflicting evidence and arguments (Bunn et al. 2002). Next, the project stakeholders are selected according to the stakeholder's identification principles described by Pouloudi and Whitley (1997) and criteria proposed by Lyytinen and Hirschheim (1987).

In the 'process' level, the analysis begins with defining the business objectives and project objectives to guide the information requirements phase of the development process. Then, a contrast analysis is performed to identify the gaps between the project goal and the stakeholders' expectations, since the lack of general agreement on a well-articulated set of project goals and objectives is a major contributing factor to

project success (Ewusi-Mensah, 1997). In order to have a complete understanding of stakeholders' expectations and perceptions, organizations have to be familiar with their interrelationships by assessing the formal and informal organizations (Block, 1983). The main purpose is to identify stakeholders' role conflicts and the formation of any negative networks which could hinder the project development. Finally, organizations should summarize all potential factors that might endanger the success of the project, which could arise from the incompatibilities between the project goal and the stakeholders' expectations; or their conflicting interrelationships or both.

While the stakeholder assessment framework (Figure 1) is not expected to uncover every problem, it is expected to contribute to a more detailed understanding, and assist in developing a set of propositions that could be validated in future research. The framework also helps to develop new factors that might contribute to project abandonment. Thus, our purpose here is limited to illustrating the potential of a stakeholder

Figure 1. The stakeholder assessment framework

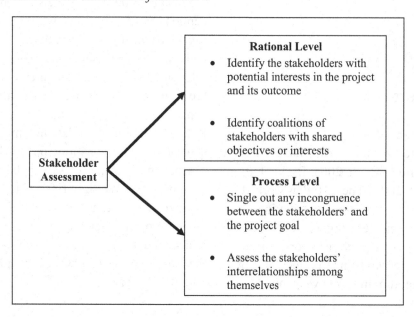

assessment framework for analyzing IS project abandonment situations, and developing propositions that will be useful to both practitioners and researchers.

RESEARCH APPROACH

Our strategy was to undertake research in an organization where the author was an ex-employee of the case organization and as a consequence, obtaining access to the organization turned out to be relatively easy. The main reason why this case was selected for investigation was its complex interrelationships between several groups of stakeholders, both internal and external. Given the exploratory nature, our research employed an interpretative case study approach (Walsham, 1993) as we recognize our belief that reality is socially constructed and much can be learned through the interplay between the subjects and objects of our case study. The study was based on a new e-procurement system development project called E-PRO, in an organization named ElectroCo (a pseudonym). One advantage for using the case study method is its ability to explain what goes on in organizations and it is also particularly good for answering the 'how' and 'why' questions (Yin, 1994).

An eight-month period was spent where data on the abandoned project were collected at ElectroCo. Primarily, eighteen semi-structured interviews were conducted post-hoc and with all the relevant project stakeholders, each lasting one and a half hours. The interviewees were selected based on the types of relationship of the stakeholder to the IS project and also, the direct or indirect 'depth of impact' the stakeholders possess in relation to the project (see Lyytinen and Hirschheim, 1987). The interviewees were allowed to express their views on aspects they considered important. All interviews were taped-recorded and transcribed with the interviewees' permissions. Secondary data such as reports, memos and meeting minutes

were gathered to supplement the information collected through interviews. These documents played a crucial role in establishing triangulation and maintaining the chain of evidence (Patton, 1987).

The transcripts of interviews and observation data were used to create a detailed history of the project displaying the sequence of the events. These data were shown to interviewees to obtain feedback and establish respondent validation (Yin, 1994). To reduce researcher's own bias, both data and investigator triangulation were used (Patton, 1987) to increase the robustness of the results. The next step of the analysis was to determine the set of factors associated with the project stakeholders that seemed to contribute to the eventual cancellation of the project. In the case of the E-PRO, a stakeholder assessment framework based on the two conceptual levels of analysis discussed by Freeman (1984) was used as the basis to identify and organize the factors that seemed to contribute to project cancellation. The case findings were compared against factors found in previous project cancellation literature and new factors were analyzed.

CASE STUDY: ELECTROCO

The case description is presented using the social process model introduced by Newman and Robey (1992). This model explains long periods of stability as episodes that are confronted by major forces of change called encounters. "An episode refers to a set of events that stand apart from others, thus signifying the end of one sequence of activities and the beginnings of another. Encounters mark the beginnings and ends of episodes" (Newman and Robey, 1992, p.253). These confrontations could result in a state of acceptance, rejection, or equivocation by the stakeholders. The model is particularly useful for presenting our case data since it offers a mode of explanation for different actions and decisions taken by the project stakeholders during IS project development process (Newman and Robey, 1992).

ElectroCo was established in 1991 in Singapore as a subsidiary of a Japanese corporation to produce electronic components. The project we studied concerns the development of a proposed electronic procurement system by the procurement department in 1998. Before 1998, the bulk of the procurement activities involved the use of paper-based documents. ElectroCo's relationship with major suppliers, however, turned sour in 1998. This was due to the deadlock in the material price negotiation on key materials, which had been ongoing for a long time. The company had a relatively small supplier base as it depended merely on a single source of supply for most of its production materials. The logic behind such practice was to consolidate their large buying volumes in exchange for cheaper material prices. However, this practice worked against the company in its development of the E-PRO system, which would be illustrated in subsequent events.

Encounter 1: Proposal to Set Up an E-Procurement System and the Initial Reactions from the 'Internal' Stakeholders

In 1998, the procurement manager proposed setting up an E-PRO system to assist the procurement department to reduce the paperwork and to source worldwide for cheaper substitutes in material supply. The IS manager, however, was cautiously supportive towards the project due to the magnitude and the complexity of the new system. Even though, the users expressed scepticism over the new technology attributing to past failures in installing a computerised procurement system, however, the truth was that the users were more concerned with the automation of their daily tasks, which might potentially lead to job cutting. The procurement manager was aware of their fears but did nothing. At this stage, the suppliers were not informed about the IT project.

Episode 1: Acceptance

Although not all internal stakeholders were convinced of the E-PRO system, the project managed to kick off with strong support from the managing director. It was clear at this point that the procurement manager did not investigate what other relevant stakeholders' perceptions towards the project were. He was influenced by the frenzied rush to adopt e-commerce solutions by major organizations within the industry. The wide adoption of e-commerce solutions was, however, fueled by several media reports that heavily publicized the overstated benefits of what e-commerce solutions could provide for businesses.

Encounter 2: Breaking the News to the Suppliers, Faced with Suppliers' Doubts and Suspicions

The procurement manager announced the project in the briefing session with approximately 50 suppliers. He made one-way presentation with little room for discussion and questions. The news threw the suppliers into a state of disarray. Several rumors regarding the project spread among the suppliers with the most disturbing version being reducing the number of existing suppliers. With the prototype almost completed in its development, the procurement manager made no effort to clarify the suppliers' doubts over the objective of E-PRO.

Episode 2: Acceptance

At this stage, the project proceeded as planned. However, the suppliers were upset for not being informed at the project outset and also worried about the entry of new competitors. ElectroCo could bring in new suppliers with this system. One of the key suppliers commented, *"This would make it easier for competitors from other countries that may have similar e-procurement facility to link up."* This episode represented a period of suppliers' secret meetings and planning to interfere with the project development. The procurement manager was totally unaware of the suppliers' activities.

Encounter 3: The Supplier's Appeal to the Procurement Manager, the Procurement Manager Turned Down their Requests

The suppliers had perceived E-PRO as a threat and had decided to act coherently to stop the development project. They requested for the project to be postponed giving reasons such as technical incompatibility with the new system. The procurement manager rejected their request instantly and demanded their full compliance to meet the requirements of the system. The procurement manager responded, *"We have the right to implement any system that deemed beneficial to the company. They must comply with our terms."*

Episode 3: Equivocation

News of the suppliers' objection had affected the project members at ElectroCo. The IS manager was very sympathetic towards the suppliers. The suppliers had also approached the managing director regarding their concerns. The managing director was not informed of the development and was surprised by the gravity of the situation, which he immediately called for a meeting.

Encounter 4: The Final Showdown

In the meeting, discussions were turned into heated arguments. The managing director then decided to consult other project stakeholders. The IS programmers refused to be drawn into this conflict. However, the IS manager changed his stance and spoke on their behalf, *"I think they need more time to upgrade their systems to meet the*

compatibility requirement." The users' opinions were unexpectedly crucial at this stage, *"Several computerization efforts have failed, which has caused distress among us. Therefore, we are also supporting the call to abandon the project".*

Outcome: Project Abandonment

The managing director made the decision to abandon the project. The situation ended with the suppliers *"winning the confrontation,"* as one of the project members described it. In a subsequent interview, the managing director blamed the procurement manager for mishandling the situation. In his opinion, the procurement manager ought to have clarified their doubts, offered them valid explanations and report the matter to top management. The process map for the project at ElectroCo is shown in Figure 2.

FINDINGS AND EMERGING RESEARCH PROPOSITIONS

Using the framework and the case findings, we defined a number of propositions for future investigations and uncovered several factors contributing to project cancellation. The following discussion examines the logic behind the propositions, and draws out a number of supportive findings. Figure 3 below represents a summary model of the factors that contributed to project cancellation decision by using a stakeholder assessment framework in E-PRO. Three new factors have emerged from our findings and reinforced the importance of satisfying the expectations of the stakeholders to ensure project success[1].

Proposition 1 (The Rational Level)

Conducting a stakeholder identification analysis is imperative in establishing a close collaboration, which includes interactions, coordination,

Figure 2. Process map for E-PRO

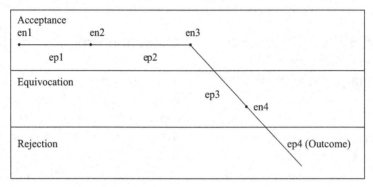

Figure 3. A summary model of factors that contributed to project cancellation through the lens of stake-holder assessment

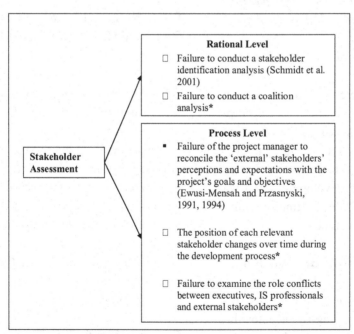

and communication among both 'internal' and 'external' group of project stakeholders.

The key issue associated with the 'rational' level that seemed to contribute to the cancellation of E-PRO, is the failure to conduct a stakeholder identification analysis. As shown in the case, the procurement manager failed to identify the group of suppliers as one of the key project stakeholders who could affect the implementation of E-PRO. He perceived them as outsiders and underestimated their influential role in the project, which subsequently led the project onto a problematic path. This was evident as the managing director also attributed the project failure to his mismanagement of the suppliers. One of the main reasons to why the procurement manager did not conduct a proper stakeholder analysis could be due to the urgent rush to adopt e-commerce solutions. The new technological solution appeared to provide several benefits and most importantly, a quick fix to his problems.

This conclusion is consistent with previous IS project management literature, which stated that IT project managers ought to identify relevant project stakeholders (Schmidt et al. 2001) and devise strategies to counteract anticipated confrontation from actors in the negative networks (Block, 1983). However, one important lesson we have learned is the difficulty of identifying 'external' stakeholders. The question remains as: do we apply the same set of selection criteria for both 'internal' and 'external' group of stakeholders? Or should we explore new dimensions cater to the 'external' group of stakeholders, since existing IS can produce far-fetching impacts with the advent of e-commerce and Internet? Future work should attempt to address this issue by validating the existing stakeholder identification criteria (Lyytinen and Hirschheim, 1987) and principles (Pouloudi and Whitley, 1997) with the emphasis on 'external' stakeholders.

Proposition 2 (The Rational Level)

Identifying and analyzing possible coalitions among stakeholders are important in understanding various groups of stakeholders' shared objectives and beliefs towards the project

Stakeholders, who are governed by their shared motivations, responsibilities, authorities and predispositions, tend to form coalitions when planning a joint initiative. Coalitions have far-reaching impacts on IT project managers during the development process since they could potentially be a source of help or obstruction to project success (Block, 1983). Rowley (1997) reinforces the importance of a coalition as he argues that organizations do not react to each stakeholder independently but focus on the concurrent demands of multiple stakeholders. Previous research has shown that the formation of opposing coalition usually happens in an IT project when stakeholders see their interests threatened by the change initiative and invoke resistance (Robey and Boudreau, 1999).

In the case of E-PRO, the suppliers formed a coalition with a common objective of opposing the development project. Their collective efforts proved to be crucial in the development process, since they successfully overcame the decisions of other stakeholders and generated changes to the original project initiative. The procurement manager failed to identify the existence of the suppliers' coalition and as a result, was not on familiar terms with the common objective and belief shared by the group of suppliers. This information, we believe, would have provided the manager with a more accurate view of why negative project encounters happened and offered predictions on what the coalition was planning to do next.

A review on existing IS literature has shown that coalition analysis has been highlighted as one of the key steps in IT project management (Block, 1983), however it has not been extensively discussed in both IS project failure and cancellation literature (Schmidt et al. 2001; Ewusi-Mensah, 1997). Perhaps, the potential risk to IS projects presented by coalitions has been minimal in previous studies, and hence, a lesser need for scrutinizing their activities during the development process. Nevertheless, we still believe, coalition analysis is useful (Pan and Pan, 2006) and should provide project managers with valuable insights in dealing with groups of stakeholders with common objectives or interests, especially in the case of opposing coalition (Robey and Boudreau, 1999), which we have identified in this study as important for successful project implementation.

Proposition 3 (The Process Level)

The compatibility of the 'external' stakeholder's perceptions and expectations, with the project's goal is often neglected

E-PRO's objective diverged with the suppliers' aim of either expanding or maintaining their current business position with ElectroCo that unavoidably led to the occurrence of conflicts. Efforts were absent from both parties to try to realign their goals, either through negotiation or mediation. The procurement manager failed to even try to ease their doubts or encourage their participation in adopting the new system. Perhaps the undue pressure from the top management to cut cost had eluded his commonsensical judgement of enrolling the suppliers into the project. Furthermore, the expectations of stakeholders were established based on early impressions and understandings of how the proposed changes were to be achieved (Gallivan, 2001). However, the task of dealing with 'external' stakeholders in an IS project can be complicated and demanding. Previous IS research on project implementation focused mostly on managing 'internal' project stakeholders (see Oz and Sosik, 2000) and seldom on the management of 'external' project stakeholders. Perhaps with the burgeoning business-

to-business (B2B) e-commerce systems and the increasing practices of outsourcing of IT services, more insights on 'external' stakeholders' role and their rising influence in IS development projects are needed.

Proposition 4 (The Process Level)

Stakeholders' positional mobility during the project development process depends on their interrelationship.

During IT project development process, stakeholders may change their stance over time (Pouloudi and Whitley, 1997), either on their own accord or through the influence of other stakeholders. In E-PRO, the users and the IS manager only openly withdrew their support towards the project in Episodes 3 and 4. The change was even more dramatic in the managing director's case. He was in full support of the project throughout the first three periods until Encounter 4, where he called for the abandonment of E-PRO. The suppliers' ability to influence the managing director at the later stage of the development process seemed to suggest their close interrelationship. This is an interesting and important finding since no previous IS abandonment literature (Ewusi-Mensah and Przasnyski 1991 & 1995; Oz and Sosik, 2000; Sauer and Burton, 1999; Sauer, 1993) has ever considered the change in the relevant stakeholder's position during the project development process that might contribute to the project cancellation decision. The implication for IS project managers is to track the stakeholders' stance at various encounters during IT project development process. This would help to ensure stakeholders' continued commitment throughout the development process.

Proposition 5 (The Process Level)

Roles and role conflicts between executives, IS professionals and external stakeholders affect stakeholders' interrelationships in IT development projects.

During IT project development process, role conflicts among stakeholders may occur resulting from either their own interactions or through the influence of other stakeholders. In the case of E-PRO, the deteriorating relationship between the suppliers and the procurement manager during the development process initiated the first obstacle to project success. This prompted the suppliers to seek help from the IS manager and the managing director. The suppliers' ability to influence the IS manager and the managing director at the later stages of the IT project development process seemed to suggest their close interrelationships with one another. The newly formed interrelationships among the suppliers, IS manager and the managing director preceded over the original 'trusting' relationship between the managing director and the procurement manager in the midst of the IT development project, which proved to be the turning point in the events leading to the project cancellations decision. Furthermore, the relationship between the IS manager and the procurement manager was questionable as well. One may wonder why did the IS manager not confront the procurement manager or blow the whistle to the managing director right at the beginning of the project since he had serious reservations regarding its implementations? A likely explanation could be that he was miffed at being cut out of the project which led to his unprofessional behavior.

Insights to identifying the more subtle stakeholder conflicts are both interesting and important because very few studies in the IS abandonment area (see Oz and Sosik, 2000; Sauer and Burton, 1999; Sauer, 1993) has examined the roles and interrelationship conflicts among project stakeholders during IT project development process as likely contributing factors leading to a project abandonment decision. Therefore, the implication is for IS project managers to track the stakehold-

ers' interrelationships and avoid the more subtle stakeholder conflicts at various encounters during IT project development process. This would help IS managers to minimize any role conflicts that might arise during IT project development.

IMPLICATIONS FOR RESEARCH AND PRACTICE

The stakeholder analysis conducted in this study has important implications for both research and practice. For researchers, this study is significant in that it represents one of the very few stakeholder analysis case studies of IS project abandonment. While there are other studies involving abandoned IS development projects, previous studies focused on deriving development risk factors (Ewusi-Mensah and Przasnyski, 1991; Oz and Sosik, 2000) rather than stakeholder assessment process. Even though the critical role of the stakeholders in the IS project development has been mentioned in some IT project abandonment studies (Ewusi-Mensah, 1997; Ewusi-Mensah and Przasnyski, 1991), there is no systematic procedure or any guiding framework to analyze the stakeholders' contributions to project abandonment. Our contribution lies in the development of a project abandonment review model that adds a stakeholder perspective. This allows us to combine a range of factors into a more logical framework that can serve as the basis for further investigation. By providing a better understanding of the project stakeholders' perception, expectations and their interrelationship, this study provides IS practitioners with some useful insights to managing stakeholders in IS development projects. In particular, the findings in this study highlight the importance of studying the interests of those promoting particular objectives of transformation and the interests of those opposing them (Robey and Boudreau, 1999).

CONCLUSION AND LIMITATIONS

As there are very few empirical studies on IS project abandonment, this study represents a contribution to knowledge in this subject area. It complements existing studies by offering a new framework to examine the abandonment phenomenon. In this paper, by drawing on a case study of the short-lived E-PRO project experience, the research demonstrated the use of a theoretical framework to explore a number of factors that contribute to IT project abandonment decisions. Five project management propositions were developed for further research. These comprise what stakeholder approach suggests as key issues in IT project management and integrate what our research revealed as essential issues that organizations should be aware of to prevent IT project abandonment situations. The encounters and episodes of the project were mapped in order to demonstrate the changes in stakeholders' perceptions and expectations and their interrelationships at various stages during the IT project development process. This offers valuable insights to what exactly constitutes a change in the project stakeholders' position, which eventually contributed to the decision to abandon E-PRO.

The findings described in this paper are limited in the following: First, the researcher who was an ex-employee of the organization might conjure preconceptions on the project stakeholders and derive biased impressions from prior working experiences, which could have misled the findings. Second, the use of a single case might not be an adequate representation of industries in the general economy. Instead, a study of multiple cases from an assortment of industries should better reflect the elusiveness of IT project management and possibly, unearth more findings on an issue of vast significance to the IS community. Despite the limitations, we are convinced that this study is useful since project cancellation is a common and costly problem among IS development projects, and there can be no question about the importance of a deeper understanding of its nature and avoidance. The stakeholder analysis is especially relevant, given the interorganizational nature of the E-PRO system where managing a range of interests from multiple stakeholders is key to project development success. Finally, the concepts and framework that we discussed could be of great value in terms of guiding IS managers in making decisions throughout the IT project development process, especially with regard to managing relationships with stakeholders.

REFERENCES

Barki, H., Rivard, S., & Talbot, J. (1993). Toward an assessment of software development risk. *Journal of Management Information System*, *10*(2), 203-225.

Beyono-Davies, P. (1995). Information systems 'failure': the case of the London ambulance service's computer aided despatch system. *European Journal of Information Systems, 4,* 171-184.

Bussen, W., & Myers, M. (1997). Executive information system failure: A New Zealand case study. *Journal of Information Technology, 12*, 145-153.

Block, R. (1983). *The Politics of projects*. Yourdon, NY.

Bunn, M., Savage, G., & Holloway, B. (2002). Stakeholder analysis for multi-sector innovations. *Journal of Business & Industrial Marketing, 17*(2/3), 181-203.

Cavaye, A., & Cragg, P. (1995). Factors contributing to the success of customer oriented interorganizational systems. *Journal of Strategic Information Systems, 4*(1), 13-30.

Drummond, H. (1996). The politics of risk: Trials and tribulations of the taurus project. *Journal of Information Technology, 11,* 347-357.

Ewusi-Mensah, K., & Przasnyski, Z. (1991). On Information systems project abandonment: An exploratory study of organizational practices. *MIS Quarterly,* Mar, 67-85.

Ewusi-Mensah, K., & Przasnyski, Z. (1995). Learning from abandoned information systems development projects. *Journal of Information Technology,* (10), 3-14.

Ewusi-Mensah, K. (1997). Critical issues in abandoned information systems development projects. *Communications of the ACM, 40*(9), 74-80.

Freeman, R. (1984). *Strategic management: A stakeholder approach.* Pitman, MA.

Gallivan, M. (2001). Meaning to change: How diverse stakeholders interpret organizational communication about change initiatives. *IEEE Transactions on Professional Communication, 44*(4), 243-266.

Iacovou, C., & Dexter, A. (2005). Surviving IT project cancellations. *Communications of the ACM, 48*(4), 83-86.

Lyttinen, K., & Hirschheim, R. (1987). *Information systems failures- A survey and classification of the empirical literature.* In P. Zorkoczy (Ed.), *Oxford surveys of information technology, 4,* pp. 257-309. UK: Oxford University Press.

Mitev, N. (1994). The business failure of knowledge-based systems. *Journal of Information Technology, 9*(3), 173-184.

Nelson, R. (2005). Project retrospectives: evaluating success, failure and everything in between. *MISQ Executive, 4*(3), 361-372.

Newman, M., & Robey, D. (1992). A social process model of user-analyst relationships. *MIS Quarterly.* June, 249-266.

Oz, E., & Sosik, J. (2000). Why information systems projects are abandoned: A leadership and communication theory and exploratory study. *Journal of Computer Information Systems 41*(1), 66-79.

Pan, G., & Pan, S. (2006). Examining the coalition dynamics in affecting IS project abandonment decision-making. *Decision Support System, 42*(2), 639-655.

Pan, G., Pan, S., & Newman, M. (2007). Information systems project post-mortems: Insights from an attribution perspective. *Journal of the American Society for Information Science and Technology, 58*(14), 2255-2268.

Patton, M. Q. (1987). *Qualitative evaluation and research methods.* Newbury Park, CA: Sage Publications.

Pouloudi, A., & Whitley, E. (1997). Stakeholder identification in inter-organizational systems: gaining insights for drug use management systems. *European Journal of Information Systems,* (6), 1-14.

Robey, D., & Boudreau, M. (1999). Accounting for the contradictory organizational consequences of information technology: Theoretical directions and methodological implications. *Information Systems Research, 10*(2), 167-185.

Rowley, T. (1997). Moving beyond dyadic ties: A network theory of stakeholder influences. *Academy of Management Review, 22,* 887-910.

Sauer, C. (1993). *Partial abandonment as a strategy for avoiding failure.* In D. Avison, J. E. Kendall & J. I. Degross (Eds.), *Human, organizational, and social dimensions of information systems development.* North-Holland, The Netherlands: Elsevier Science Publishers.

Sauer, C., Southon, G., & Dampney, C. (1997). Fit, failure, and the house of horrors: Toward a configurational theory of IS project failure. In *Proceedings of the Eighteenth International Conference on Information Systems*, Georgia, US.

Sauer, C., & Burton, S. (1999). Is there a place for department stores on the Internet? Lessons from an abandoned pilot. *Journal of Information Technology, 14*, 387-398.

Schimidt, R., Lytinnen, K., Keil, M., & Cule, P. (2001). Identifying software project risks: An international delphi study. *Journal of Management Information Systems, 17*(4), 5-36.

Wastell, D., & Newman, M. (1996). Information system design, stress and organizational change in the ambulance services: A tale of two cities. *Accounting, Management and Information Technology, 6*(4), 283-300.

Walsham, G. (1993). *Interpreting information systems in organizations.* Chichester, UK: Wiley.

Yin, R. (1994). *Case study research: Design and methods* (Second Edition). Thousand Oaks, CA: Sage

KEY TERMS AND DEFINITIONS

Case Study: A study of an individual unit, as a person, family, or social group, usually emphasizing developmental issues and relationships with the environment, esp. in order to compare a larger group to the individual unit.

Influence: The capacity or power of persons or things to be a compelling force on or produce effects on the actions, behavior, opinions, etc., of others.

IT Project: A large or major undertaking involving information technology

Project Cancellation: The act of deciding a planned project will not take place.

Project Management: The process of planning, organizing, staffing, directing and controlling the production of a system

Role: A part or character played by an actor.

Stakeholder Analysis: The evaluation of a group that has an interest in the project.

ENDNOTE

[1]   Note: '*' represents new factors that lead to project cancellation which are not found in IT project cancellation literature.

Chapter VIII
Bringing the User into the Project Development Process

Daniel W. Surry
University of South Alabama, USA

ABSTRACT

The goal of any product is to be used. In a very real sense, people judge the success or failure of any product by the extent to which it is used by intended users in their daily practice. Understanding a product from the perspective of the end-user is one of the most important and often overlooked keys to the success of any project. Many products suffer from a lack of widespread utilization because developers and managers often have a deterministic view of the relationship between technology and users. This deterministic view leads to an over reliance on technical specifications as the driving force in the end users' decision to adopt and use a product. However, a wide variety of human, organizational, social, and cultural factors also affect the acceptance and use of any product. Any organization, even those in the most highly technical and advanced fields, is, in reality, a dynamic example of a sociotechnical system in which people and machines interact, negotiate usage, compete for primacy, and generally co-exist. This chapter will provide a broad theoretical overview of the critical role that end-users play in the adoption, implementation, utilization, and institutionalization of any technology. A number of relevant theories will be discussed, including diffusion theory (e.g., Rogers, 1995), technological determinism (e.g., Ellul, 1967), sociotechnical systems (e.g., Volti, 2006), and utopian and dystopian philosophical perspectives (e.g., Rubin, 1996). In addition to a theoretical overview, this chapter will provide practical recommendations for developers and managers who wish to increase the utilization of their products by bringing the user into the development process. The practical recommendations will include a discussion of Ely's (1999) conditions that facilitate the implementation of innovations. These conditions include developing a sense of dissatisfaction with the status quo, providing sufficient time to become familiar with a new technology, and generating meaningful commitment to the project by upper level managers. Also included in the practical recommendations will be a brief discussion of various organizational components that enable the introduction of innovations (Surry, Ensminger, & Haab, 2005). These components include the development and maintenance of an adequate infrastructure of supporting technologies, an emphasis on shared decision making, and ongoing support systems. Other recommendations to be discussed in this chapter will be derived from rapid prototyping models of development (e.g., Tripp & Bichelmeyer, 1990) and recent surveys of user-centered design methods.

THEORETICAL OVERVIEW: END USERS AND PROJECT DEVELOPMENT

Most people would likely agree that understanding the needs, skills, behaviors, and attitudes of end users is a desirable part of the product development process. However, it is also likely that most people do not know the underlying theoretical reasons for understanding the end users. While there are many reasons for understanding the end users, including the refinement of product features and the development of supporting documentation, by far the most important reason is to increase the effective utilization of the product within the desired context of use.

There are many theories about how to increase the utilization of products. Many of these theories focus on the development of highly effective and efficient products as the key to increasing utilization. While no one would argue that the creation of effective and efficient products is an important goal of the development process, it is not sufficient to ensure widespread or effective utilization. In fact, there are many examples of technically superior products that have not found wide use. One of the most interesting historical examples is the case of highly precise methods of mass production in the early years of the Industrial Revolution (Morris, 2005). Even though the use of precision machinery reduced costs, shortened production cycles, and made interchangeability possible, the method was resisted by many, especially in England, because of existing social norms, resistance to innovation,

and opposition from traditional craftsmen and guilds (Morris, 2005).

The preceding example illustrates how technically superior products are not always rapidly or widely adopted by users. It provides anecdotal support for the idea that product developers must have an understanding of how their products will affect users both practically and emotionally. In addition to anecdotal support, there are a number of theoretical and philosophical stances that strongly support the importance of understanding a product from the users' perspective.

Ample theoretical support for including users in the product development process can be found in the cluster of theories related to the diffusion of innovations. For example, diffusion research has shown that users go through a process of fact finding, persuasion, decision, and confirmation before adopting a new product (Rogers, 1995). Because the adoption and use of a new product is a process, not an instant decision, the more time users have to learn about, try out, and interact with a product prior to its introduction, the quicker the product can be adopted and utilized. A key part of this innovation adoption process is re-invention (Rogers, 1995). Re-invention is the phenomenon of user initiated modifications to a product following adoption in response to practical necessities, unique or evolving work conditions, and other factors. If re-invention can take place during the development process, as opposed to post-development, then creative, unique, or desirable features can be included in the initial version of a product and, therefore, enhance adoption and facilitate use.

Innovativeness is another concept from diffusion theory that is relevant to the role of users in the development process. This concept states that different people within a given population will be more or less innovative than others (Rogers, 1995). More innovative people will tend to adopt and use a product earlier than less innovative people. This suggests that the end users of any product are not a homogenous group, but vary widely in their willingness to use a product. However, there is a tendency for highly innovative users to be overrepresented in the development process because they are often more vocal and visible to developers and managers. This overrepresentation skews product development to be more useful and desirable to innovative users while minimizing the needs and opinions of less innovative users. The obvious implication of this is that developers should seek out input from a wide cross section of users, highly innovative and less innovative, and develop products with features that appeal to each group.

Sociotechnical systems theory also provides support for including users in the development process. This theory states that people and technology should not be viewed as separate groups but as parts of a larger sociotechnical system (Pfaffenberger, 1992; Volti, 2006). According to this theory, one must understand the complicated interactions and mutual influences between people and technology in order to fully understand how an organization functions (Cummings, 1978). Traditional product development processes are theoretically flawed because they view products and users as discrete entities and employ fundamentally different strategies for understanding and addressing each entity. For example, the development of a software program is often viewed as a technologically focused activity while the adoption and use of the program is often viewed as a socially focused activity. Understanding how various social and technological factors combine and interact to influence the use of a product can result in not only more effective products, but also increased utilization of those products.

The field of business management also provides theoretical support for the importance of including users in the development process. One of the most commonly cited reasons for the failure of a new product is poor concept (Gruenwald, 1995). Factors that contribute to poor concept include the development of products for which there is no need, or at least no perceived need on the part of end users, products which are overly complex or too innovative, and products which do not provide a meaningful alternative to products currently in use (Gruenwald, 1995). Working with end users during the development process can significantly improve a product's concept and ensure that the product fulfills an important and practical need.

From a more philosophical perspective, technological determinism supports the importance of bringing users into the development process. Technological determinism is the belief that technology has become largely autonomous, beyond direct human control, and the driving force in societal change (Ellul, 1967). While there are certainly many valid criticisms of technological determinism (e.g., Nye, 2006), the theory provides many valuable insights for product developers. The two deterministic ideas most relevant to this discussion are the automation of technical choice and the ever increasing complexity of technology. Ellul believed that as technology became more powerful and played a larger role in society, choices about which technologies to use and how to use them came to be defined not in human or social terms, but in purely technological terms. He also believed that as technology advances, the increasing complexity and interconnectedness of technology makes it impossible for any one person to fully understand, much less control, the impact of technology on a society. This is directly analogous to product development cycles in which development decisions are framed in largely technical, rather than human or organizational, terms and underscores the inability of any one group to understand or anticipate the complex impact a product will have on an organization and its people.

Closely related to technological determinism, philosophical perspectives about the ultimate impact of a new product on an organization often affect how users perceive and use a product. In general, users tend to have either a utopian or dystopian view of technology's impact on an organization (Rubin, 1996). Utopian perspectives see technology as increasing the productivity, efficiency, and capacity of a worksite while reducing stress, errors, and other negative aspects. Utopian perspectives see the advance of technology leading to a gradual improvement of work conditions and, ultimately, to a perfect or, nearly perfect, work environment (Surry & Farquhar, 1997). Conversely, dystopian perspectives see technology as increasing the complexity, frustration, and dehumanization of a worksite while increasing stress and other negative aspects. Dystopian perspectives see the advance of technology as leading to a gradual worsening of work conditions and, ultimately, to a nightmarish work environment (Surry & Farquhar, 1997). There is often a marked difference in the perspective of developers and users in regard to the ultimate impact of technology. Determining the relative philosophical perspectives of the developers and end users and negotiating a shared perspective, if possible, is an important step in creating and implementing an effective product.

It is important for developers of technology to have a broad understanding of the multiple roles that end users play in the lifecycle of a product. Many developers have a narrowly defined view of the user as simply a tool user – someone who employs a product in the manner and purpose for which it was intended (Johnson, 1998). However, the tool user model is not only overly simplistic from a theoretical perspective, it results it flawed decisions during the development process. When developers view the end users merely as passive recipients of technology, they underestimate both the creative, subversive, and adaptive capabilities of the users and the potential of their own products. Johnson (1998) suggests that developers of technology should move from a systems-centered model, which has been the predominate approach, to a user-centered model. In the systems-centered model, developers assume they have adequate understanding of the issues, context, and problems to develop the most appropriate solution. In the user-centered model, the needs and experiences of the user serve as the focus for development and users actively participate in the design and development of the product.

There is a solid theoretical foundation to support the belief that users should be active participants in the product development process. Researchers in a broad range of areas from diffusion of innovations, to management, to philosophy have developed important and influential arguments in favor of including the users. Based on their work, there is little debate that users play a pivotal role in the ultimate success or failure of a product and should, therefore, also play a key role in the development of the product. The only important questions that remain are how to include users in the development process and when to include them. Those important questions will be addressed in the following section.

PRACTICAL RECOMMENDATIONS

Based on theories discussed in the previous section, there is a strong theoretical basis to believe that bringing the end user into the product development process can facilitate implementation and increase utilization. There are a number of practical recommendations which can help to bring the user into the product development process. The first and most important practical recommendation is to carefully identify who the end users are and the contexts in which the product will be used.

Even the smallest, most localized development project will impact multiple user groups who often have competing values and interests. It may also be important to identify and include non-users of a product who can provide valuable insights into reasons for lack of use and competing methods for accomplishing a task (Wyatt, 2005). Developers should also try to identify and consider any possible unintended users who may not be in the target user group but will occasionally use, or at least be impacted by, the product. Representatives from all stakeholder groups should be carefully selected to ensure that all important differences are accounted for and included in development decisions (Gulliksen, Lantz, & Bovie 1999).

A study of user centered design (UCD) techniques used in different business sectors found that user interviews, prototyping, expert evaluation, and usability testing were the most common methods for incorporating the user into the product development lifecycle (Venturi, Troost, & Jokela, 2006). A total of 24 UCD methods were reported in the study including storyboarding, focus groups, and case studies. The authors of that study concluded that UCD methods are being used more frequently, and earlier in the development process, than previously by organizations.

Another survey of UCD practice (Vredenburg, et al., 2002) found that field studies, user requirement analysis, iterative design, and usability evaluation were the most important methods. The authors of that study found that the use of UCD methods, especially when used as part of a multidisciplinary approach, was considered to have resulted in the development of better products. Customer satisfaction, ease of use, and sales were the criteria most commonly cited in the study as measures of the effectiveness of user-centered design methods.

As shown in the surveys of UCD practice, the development and analysis of prototypes is a common method for including the user in the development process. A prototype is a crude or incomplete approximation, or mock up, of a final product. Prototypes are used to facilitate communication and discussion about a product during the development process. Prototypes allow for a more tangible, less conceptual, and increasingly specific discourse between developer and user. Multiple prototypes, developed in a variety of media, can facilitate discussion on different aspects of a product and inform a wide range of development decisions (Gulliksen, Lantz, & Bovie 1999). Tripp and Bichelmeyer (1990) suggest rapid prototyping, in which prototypes are developed quickly and early in the design process and subsequently refined based on input from the users until a final product is created, as an effective, time saving, and less costly method for developing products. They contend that rapid prototyping is an especially effective model in cases where the problem is complex and for which users may have unique or creative solutions.

Ely (1990, 1999) identified eight conditions that facilitate the implementation of a product. The conditions that most closely relate to getting the users involved in the production process are dissatisfaction with the status quo and participation. Dissatisfaction with the status quo refers to understanding the products currently in use and developing a sense of dissatisfaction with those products. To understand the status quo from the users' perspective, developers can conduct site visits, user interviews, and focus groups. Ely's condition of participation refers to including the end users in important decisions related to the development, adoption, and utilization of a product. Active participation on the part of the users creates a sense of ownership and shared purpose which can increase effective utilization. Haab (2007) studied various types of participation and found that team membership was the most preferred method of participation during implementation. This suggests that the development and use of user teams is a useful method to increase participation during development and implementation.

Organizational policies and support systems play an important role in the effective utilization of a product (Surry, Ensminger, & Haab, 2005). The use of any new product will invariably necessitate at least some changes to organizational policies. Large scale products, such as enterprise resource planning systems or Web-based training programs, require fundamental changes to organizational policies, both formal and informal, in order to be successful. Developers can work with users to conduct a document analysis of organizational policies and anticipate changes that may be required or identify unchangeable policies that may affect the development and use of a product. The support systems in place in an organization can also impact the adoption and utilization of a product. In organizations with low levels of support, developers may be required to build higher levels of support into their products or produce more extensive supporting documentation. Techniques such as interviews, focus groups, document analysis, and questionnaires can be used to determine the level of support within an organization as well specific support needed by different user groups.

While the basic premise of this chapter is that it is generally advisable to include the user in the product development process, there are certain times when including the user is especially necessary as well as times when including the user might not be advisable. It is especially important to bring the user into the development process when there is a lack of information among the development team about the end users, the context of use, or competing products. It is also critical to bring users into the development process when there is a need to create shared vision and a sense of ownership among the users. Finally, developers should be certain to include users in the development process when the users possess unique knowledge, insights, or skills related to an organization, a performance problem, a technology, or a process.

There are times when including the end user in the development process might not be advisable. For example, the most commonly cited disadvantages of user-centered design are that the process can be more costly and take longer than traditional development methods (Abras, Maloney-Krichmar, & Preece, 2004). When additional costs and time can not be justified, developers may be forced to rely on a more abbreviated or superficial level of user input. In addition, there is a danger that users will provide input that is flawed, outdated, or incompatible with other organizational priorities (Beale, 2007). There are also a number of potential organizational problems that could preclude bringing users into the development process including competition between departments, lack of shared vision, and incompatible organizational culture (Gulliksen, Lantz, & Bovie 1999). Other instances when including the user in the development process might not be advisable include times when doing so would result in loss of focus, loss of status among the development team, or the potential loss of propriety information.

One final note, while this chapter has focused on the importance of users to the product development process, users should be given opportunities for input after development as well. Users of a product can provide valuable information about the effectiveness, appeal, advantages, and disadvantages of a product in actual use. This information can be used to improve subsequent versions of the product or in the development of other similar products. The information can also be valuable in re-designing the development process or identifying potential new markets and is essential in maintaining a positive relationship with customers.

SUMMARY

The effective utilization of a product by intended users is the ultimate goal of the product development process. The best way to increase effective utilization is to understand the needs, opinions, concerns, and perspectives of the end users of the product. While many organizations are increasing the use of user-centered design and other methods for accounting for end users, much development is still conducted with little, if any, meaningful user input. Traditional mindsets, rigid design models, tight development timelines, and cost considerations are likely reasons why users are still often excluded from development. However, this chapter has shown that there is a solid theoretical basis to believe that including the users in the development process can have a profoundly positive impact on the effective use and widespread adoption of a product. Even in those rare instances when including the user in an ongoing basis might not be advisable, developers can benefit from an increased understanding of the context of use and user characteristics. There are a wide number of methods that developers can use to incorporate users in the development process including interviews, observation, prototyping, usability testing, and questionnaires. Perhaps the most important recommendation is to value the insights, knowledge, and perspectives of end users and to aggressively seek out ways to include them in the development process whenever possible.

REFERENCES

Abras, C., Maloney-Krichmar, D., & Preece, J. (2004). User-centered design. In B. W. Sims (Ed.), *Berkshire encyclopedia of human-computer interaction*, (pp. 763-767). Great Barrington, MA: Berkshire Publishing Group.

Beale, R. (2007). Slanty design. *Communications of the ACM, 50*(1), 21-24.

Cummings, T. G. (1978). Self-regulating work groups: A socio-technical synthesis. *The Academy of Management Review, 3*(3), 625-634.

Ellul, J. (1967). *The technological society*. New York: Knopf.

Ely, D. P. (1990). Conditions that facilitate the implementation of educational technology in-novations. *Journal of Research on Computing in Education, 23*(2), 298-305.

Ely, D. P. (1999). Conditions that facilitate the implementation of educational technology innova-tions. *Educational Technology, 34*(6), 23-27.

Gruenwald, G. (1995). *New product develop-ment* (2nd ed.). Lincolnwood, IL: NTC Business Books.

Gulliksen, J., Lantz, A., & Bovie, I. (1999). User centered design – Problems and possibilities. *SIGCHI Bulletin, 31*(2), 25-25.

Haab, M. (2007). Relationship between modes of participation and satisfaction of implementation of enterprise resource planning systems in higher education. *Dissertation Abstracts International*, 68/11, May 2008.

Johnson, R. R. (1998). *User-centered technol-ogy: A rhetorical theory for computers and other mundane artifacts*. Albany, NY: State University of New York Press.

Morris, C. R. (2005). *The tycoons: How Andrew Carnegie, John D. Rockefeller, Jay Gould, and J. P. Morgan invented the American supereconomy*. New York: Times Books.

Nye, D. E. (2005). *Technology matter: Questions to live with*. Cambridge, MA: The MIT Press.

Pfaffenberger, B. (1992). Social anthropology of technology. *Annual Review of Anthropology, 21*(1), 491-516.

Rogers, E. M. (1995). *Diffusion of innovations* (4th ed.). New York: The Free Press.

Rubin, J. S. (1996). And another thing…Utopia or Dystopia? *LOGOS, 7*(3), 242-244.

Oudshoorn, N., & Pinch, T. (2005). Introduction: How users and non-users matter. In N. Oudshoorn & T. Pinch (Eds.), *How users matter: The co-construction of users and technology* (pp. 1-25). Cambridge, MA: MIT Press.

Surry, D. W., Ensminger, D. C., & Haab, M. (2005). *A Model for Integrating Instructional Technology into Higher Education. British Journal of Educational Technology, 36*(2) 327-329.

Surry, D. W., & Farquhar, J. D. (1997). Diffusion theory and instructional technology. *Journal of Instructional Science and Technology, 2*(1) [online].

Tripp, S., & Bichelmeyer, B. (1990). Rapid prototyping: An alternative instructional design strategy. *Educational Technology Research & Development, 38*(1), 31-44.

Venturi, G, Troost, J., & Jokela, T. (2006). People, organizations, and processes: An inquiry into the adoption of user-centered design in industry. *International Journal of Human-Computer Interaction, 21*(2), 219-238.

Vredenburg, K., Mao, J., Smith, P. W., & Carey, T. (2002). A survey of user-centered design practice. *CHI Letters, 4*(1), 471-478.

Volti, R. (2006). *Society and technological change* (5th ed.). New York: Worth.

Wyatt, S. (2005). Non-users also matter: The construction of users and non-users of the internet. In N. Oudshoorn & T. Pinch (Eds.), *How users matter: The co-construction of users and technology.* (pp. 67-79). Cambridge, MA: The MIT Press.

KEY TERMS AND DEFINITIONS

Context of Use: The conditions under which a product is used by intended users in the performance of a task. This includes not only the technical environment but also all of the social, organizational, and personal characteristics of the performance site. Understanding context of use can assist developers in creating products that are practical, useable, and desirable to end users.

Diffusion: The process by which a product is introduced and disseminated throughout an organization or social system. The diffusion process begins after the initial decision to adopt a product and continues until the product is either abandoned or becomes institutionalized within the organization.

End User: Any person who employs a product to complete a task. End users can be intended or unintended. However, it is more common to identify and consider intended end users during the development process as unintended end users can be difficult to anticipate.

Implementation: The process of facilitating the effective utilization of a product by end users in an organization or social system. Implementation commonly focuses on identifying potential barriers to the use of a product at a worksite and planning for the removal of those barriers.

Institutionalization: The point at which a product ceases to be considered new or innovative as a result of widespread, ongoing, and substantive utilization by members of an organization or social system. Institutionalization is often seen as the ultimate goal of the adoption/implementation/diffusion process.

Sociotechnical Systems: A theory that views people and technologies not as separate and discrete entities but as parts of a larger system. Sociotechnical systems theory states that a full understanding of any organization or social system can not be attained without understanding both how societal issues shape the development and use of technology and how technology shapes the capabilities, desires, and beliefs of society.

Technological Determinism: A philosophical stance that, in its most extreme form, views technology as and autonomous force and the primary driver of change in the modern world. Technological determinists believe that technological considerations tend to minimize or eliminate social, human, and organizational factors during the development and diffusion of a product.

Utilization: The manner and method that a product is actually employed by end users in the context of use. Studying the utilization of a product can provide valuable information about the product, its features, its effectiveness, and potential upgrades and revisions.

Chapter IX
Information Technology Projects System Development Life Cycles:
Comparative Study

Evon M. O. Abu-Taieh
The Arab Academy for Banking and Financial Sciences, Jordan

Asim A. El Sheikh
The Arab Academy for Banking and Financial Sciences, Jordan

Jeihan M. Abu-Tayeh
World Bank, USAID, Jordan

Maha T. El-Mahied
Institute of Traditional Islamic Art and Architecture, Jordan

ABSTRACT

This chapter will discuss more than 20 system development life cycles (SDLC) found in the Information Technology project management arena, whereby, a comprehensive overview of the SDLCs history as well as the trigger that instigated its development would be laid out. Subsequently, the chapter will discuss the advantages and disadvantages of using SDLC, whereby the chapter will explain where and when to use which SDLC. As such, the chapter will classify the different SDLCs into three non-exclusive categories: Traditional methodologies, agile methodologies, spiral methodologies and other types of methodologies that used in IT project Management.

INTRODUCTION

System development life cycle (SDLC) engulfs the whole system life cycle. Not only spanning over the feasibility study, analysis, specification, design, development; but also encompassing the aspects resonating in the operations, maintenance and enhancement, which would take place only after the system has been accepted by the end user.

Additionally, Project encapsulates the management environment set up, whereby ensuring delivery of specifically tailored business product to cater to a pre-defined business case. As such, Project does not cover all stages of system life cycle and covers mostly the technical deliverables.

Within this context, System development life cycle would be also denoted system process in software engineering as an integral part of IT project management. Highlighting the fact that many system development life cycles are developed to enable project managers to manage their project and overcome many constraints, *inter alia*: Money, Time, effort and Human resources. However, in view that two elements affect the project management apt choice of the SDLC; Familiarity of the project and the size of the project, whereas the authors use familiarity when referring to how familiar the project cadre is with the technology implemented in the project and the culture of the project, while the authors use the size of the project when referring to the time needed for project accomplishment, cost of the project, project people (users and development team), and the area of the project.

Accordingly, this chapter will discuss more than twenty SDLCs found in the IT project management arena, whereby, a comprehensive overview of the SDLCs history as well as the trigger that instigated its development would be laid out. Subsequently, the chapter will discuss the advantages and disadvantages of using SDLC, whereby the chapter will explain where and when to use which SDLC. As such, the chapter will classify the different SDLCs into three non-exclusive categories: Traditional methodologies, agile methodologies and spiral methodologies, of which the chapter will attempt to discuss some models as stipulated in Figure 1.

TRADITIONAL SDLC

This section discusses nine renowned SDLCs: Waterfall, Incremental, V Model, b Model, Fountain Model, Prototyping, Relay Race Methodology (RRM), and Structured Systems Analysis and Design Method (SSADM).

In this regard, certain properties can be attributed to traditional SDLC; First, traditional SDLC is comprised of discrete phase. Second, each phase has a deliverable product at the end. As such, traditional SDLCs are usually used in large projects where the familiarity element is very high.

Waterfall Model

The Waterfall SDLC was first introduced by Dr. Wiston Royce in 1970. Royce's intention was to modify the waterfall model to an iterative model. Albeit, this model offered discrete phase with an emphasis on deadlines, documentation while specifying what each phase entails. Yet this model had many disadvantages, including; lack of user involvement as well as a mistake that was made in the earlier phase and cannot be rectified.

In addition, although this model had many flavors, however, it fell back on the logical thinking process; first, the problem should be defined by collecting the requirements. Second, the solution should be designed in manner that is acceptable to the client. Third, the implementation and execution of the designed solution should be properly planned. Finally, the validation and verification of the implemented solution should be conducted, in order to ensure that the designed solution is efficient and up to the standards of the client.

Figure 1. System development life cycle taxonomy

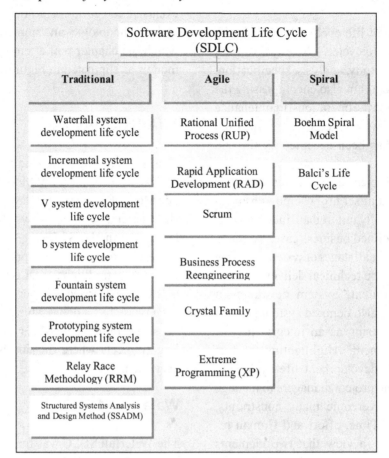

Figure 2. System development life cycle taxonomy (Adapted from Hoffer et al, 2005)

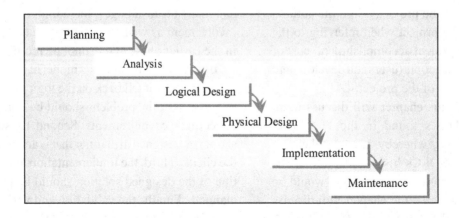

As aforementioned, the chapter will discuss the three known flavors of the waterfall model: The first, which was suggested by Hoffer et al (2005) and articulated in Figure 1; whereby the SDLC commences with planning for the software project, in which the initiation of the project is embedded, followed by the analysis, in which the requirement collection is embedded, after that the two phases of logical and physical design, to be followed by the implementation phase, which includes coding, and testing, concluding by the maintenance, which Hoffer et al (2005) claims to represent more than 30% of the project life span.

The second flavor of the waterfall SDLC, seen in Figure 3, whereby SDLC sets off with the first phase, denoted initiation, while the rest of the phases remain similar to that of traditional waterfall SDLC, except that the sequence of the phases is not emphasized by the arrow.

The third flavor of the waterfall model, seen in Figure 4, which differs from the aforementioned two flavors in two things; (1) this model of SDLC is iterative and (2) provides a mechanism for Validation and Verification (V&V), in this regard, it is worthwhile to differentiate between V&V; where Validation stands for asking the question *are we building the right product?*, whereas verification stands for asking the question *are we building the product right?*

Nevertheless, the third flavor of the waterfall model starts with a phase denoted as system feasibility, after that the model suggests the phase of planning and requirement collection, to be followed by Product design, which includes the logical and physical design phases of the previously mentioned two models. Next the model suggests the Coding phase, which entails unit testing as a method, after that the Integration phase of the code, which entails product verification, to be followed by the Implementation phase, which entails another testing as a test for the whole system, then the model concludes with operation and maintenance.

In retrospect, the waterfall model, along with its flavors, has advantages and disadvantages, stipulated as follows:

The major advantages are: (1) the activities are sequentially listed in the model, which helps in optimally organizing and processing the work; (2) validation and verification, being an important issue, is continuously addressed within the model; (3) configuration management, by benchmarking at the end of each stage, is addressed within the model. However, the model exhibits a major drawback, in view that it has no explicit means of exercising management control, i.e. risk management and risk mitigation are not covered.

As such, waterfall models are best used when requirements are well understood and the business

Figure 3. Another flavour of the waterfall model (Adapted from Hoffer et al, 2005)

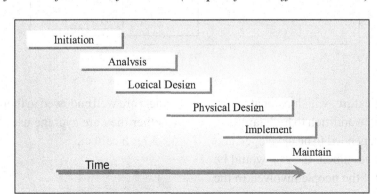

Figure 4. Waterfall Model with feedback option and designated V&V (Adapted from Boehm, 1988)

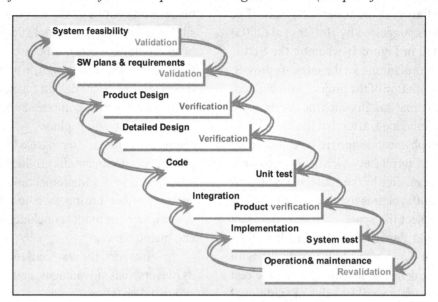

Figure 5. The phased-release model (Adapted from Cadle & Yeates, 2004)

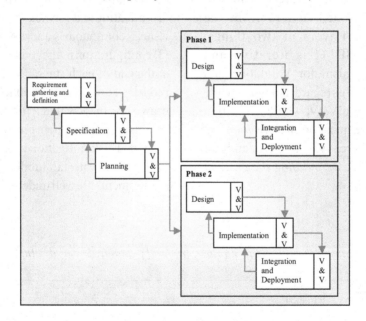

is of mainstream in nature, which resonates low risk (risk mitigation) in addition to high familiarity of the application needed to be developed and technology being used, albeit, the risk would be relatively mitigated if the people involved in the project are well endowed in their area of expertise whether they are average users, technical users, or of high caliber.

The Incremental Model

The incremental model was first introduced as *the phased-release model*, as stipulated in Figure 5, resonating the philosophy "Divide and Conquer", whereby the software to be developed is broken into two or more subsystems, provided careful consideration, planning, and design. After that each subsystem is designed in tail, then coded, tested and integrated. As demonstrated in Figure 6, the life cycle is similar to that of the waterfall; in addition another flavor of the incremental model can be seen in Figure 7.

Figure 6. Incremental model #1 (Adapted from Cadle & Yeates, 2004)

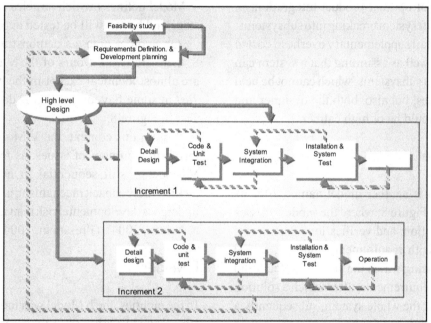

Figure 7. Incremental model #2 (Adapted from Pressman, 2004)

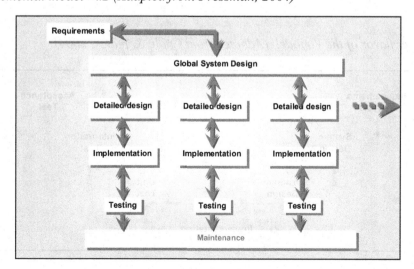

Accordingly, such models are commonly used when the project scope is clearly defined. Retrospectively, the model offers the advantage of the totality (all in one) function of a system to be delivered in phases over a period of time, which makes delivery and testing more manageable (Cadel & Yeates, 2004), as can be seen in Figure 7, in view that the model delivery is in small units, which involves prompt feedback and tests thereby improving the model.

However, not only does the model introduce the difficulty of optimal product integration, in addition to swift system breaking into subsystems; which may entail supplementary overhead cost to the project as well as assuming that a system can be divided into subsystems, which cannot be held true at all times, but also, both the designer and the analyst should be of high caliber.

The V-Model

The V Model is another model named after its shape as seen Figure 8, where the model stresses testing, validation, and verification. The model commences with requirements analysis, as the first phase, during which the analyst collects and analyzes the requirements, after which a solution is designed for the whole system, subsequently a detailed Design is put forth, where more broken down solutions would be designed, after that the model concludes in implementation as the final phase. In this regard, it is worthwhile to note that for each phase there is a corresponding testing phase, whereby the requirement analysis phase is corresponded with an acceptance test, the system design is matched up with the integration test phase, and the detailed design phase is corresponded with Module/unit test phase, accordingly, the model improves on the testing strategy, particularly in view that for each counterpart in the project there are sub contractors, whereby the V-Model defines the deliverables of each phase/stage and how it will be tested and validated.

On another note, as demonstrated in Figure 8, there are two flavours of the V model, which are almost identical except in the phase *Module Test* in some flavours, which is denoted as *Unit Test* in Figure 8.

Within this context, the V-Model is like waterfall in a number of issues, as follows: (1) the V-Model is still sequential in nature, thereby lacking the feedback mechanism; and (2) V-model undergoes developmental risk management (Cadle & Yeates, 2004), (Pressman, 2004).

b Model

In the eighties, the b Model was introduced by N. Birrell and M. Ould (1985), which was denoted the letter "b" because of its shape, seen in the Figure

Figure 8. Another flavor of the V model (Adapted from Cadle & Yeates, 2004)

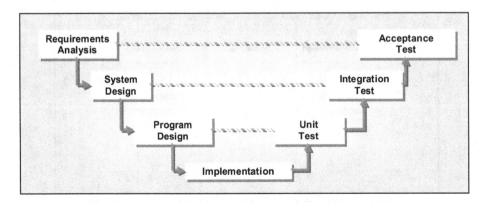

9. Although this model has been characterized an iterative model, yet, Birrel and Ould claimed that the maintenance phase in the waterfall takes about 70% of cost and time of the SDLC, as such, the b model was suggested as follows:

The b model sets off with an inception, denoted as an initiation for a need, consequently, such a need is analyzed and a solution is designed, upon which the design is produced during the Production phase, to be followed by the acceptance phase. After that, the solution goes into Operation, to be evaluated later. Taking into account that since during the latter phase some needs may rise due to many reasons, accordingly, another inception is proposed and the life cycle iterates again by the same phase sequential Analysis, Design, and Production.

Fountain Model

Fountain Model is used for a typical Iterative Object Oriented system development, as shown in Figure 10, noting that the model uses metaphorically the water fountain, whereby the water rises up from the middle of the pool and falls back on itself, and as the water falls back into the pool, some of the water will again be thrown up again while some of it will fall back into the pool. In this context, the model follows similar terms to this metaphor, in the process of developing a software system (Henderson-Sellers & Edwards, 1990) and (Pillai, 1996).

Accordingly, there a number of characteristics attributed to the Fountain Model, *inter alia*: (1) phases overlapping, and (2) iterative, given that both criteria do exist in real life development of the software. In this regard, many flavors for the Fountain Model have been referred to in (Henderson-Sellers & Edwards, 1990), (Pillai, 1996), (Graham et al., 1997), and (Henderson-Sellers, 2007).

Figure 9. The b model (Adapted from Cadle & Yeates, 2004)

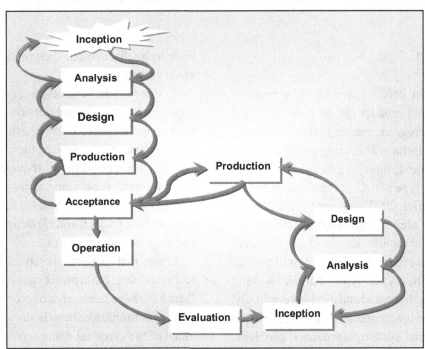

Figure 10. Fountain model (Adapted from Graham et al., 1997)

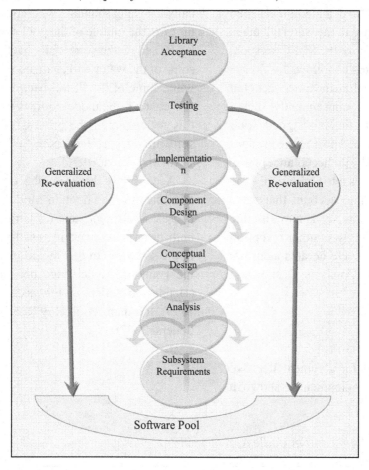

Prototyping

Prototype is an iterative development process, whereby the end product can be either a model or a working program, noting that the former is used as a requirement collecting process.

In this context, there are many models and flavors of prototype SDLC, as stipulated in Figure 11, where (Hoffer, 2005) suggests the following phases: First, identify the problem, based on which the initial requirements will be produced, in view that these initial requirements will be used to develop a prototype. After that the working prototype is implemented and used. Accordingly, if the prototype is acceptable, then it is converted to an operational system, however, if problems

were to be discovered, then the prototype is revised and enhanced.

In this manner, prototyping quickly converts requirements to working version of a system. As such, once the user observes the requirements being converted to system, then actually modifications and/or additional requests may evolve. Nevertheless, prototyping is mostly used in the case of (1) unclear requests, (2) few users are involved in the project, and (3) designs are complex and require concrete form.

Given that many tools have been developed and available to build prototypes rather easily, and there have been relatively no recording of analyst-user miscommunication history, nevertheless, much of the essential documentation is missing,

Figure 11. The prototype methodology (Adapted from Hoffer, et al, 2005)

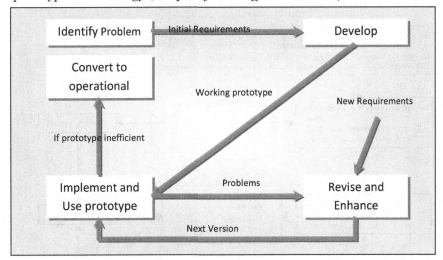

and many of the checks in the traditional SDLC are bypassed (Hoffer et al, 2005).

Relay Race Methodology (RRM)

Relay Race Methodology (RRM) is based on the fundamentals of the Relay Race. In every phase a core team must attend, where the core team is always composed of Analyst, Programmer, Statistician, and User, and in every phase, two of the quad-core team from previous phase must attend the subsequent phase. Although the idea of the relay race is apparent, yet the reason is that some of the accumulated knowledge of the project team members cannot be all documented. Additionally, the shared (itinerant) team members will be held liable and thereby responsible for defending; explaining, and/or accepting changes suggested in subsequent phases, in this regard Figure 12 illustrates the aforementioned phases.

Within this context, use of case tools; i.e. planning toolkit, analysis toolkit, design toolkit, and coding toolkit are essential in RRM. In addition, JAD sessions are highly encouraged, since part of their job is to clarify any ambiguity that may rise.

Some of the drawbacks of RRM are the following: (1) RRM relies heavily on highly skilled and experienced team members, as such; user commitment is needed for final product, while considering that simulation systems projects are long. (2) RRM relies heavily on the use of case tools *Rational Rose* and *Designer 2000,* although such a fact is not really a drawback, since case tools actually save much needed time and effort in simulation system project. (3) RRM enfolds the resources, which is translated to cost, yet such accusation can be defended, when considering the cost incurred of finding the error before or after the end of the simulation system project.

Nevertheless, RRM is flexible, in terms that shared (itinerant) team members may relocate from any phase to the previous one. Moreover, RRM has open channels of communication, which is considered essential to produce a correct simulation system. Likewise, user involvement is a basic ingredient in RRM. Additionally, RRM uses diagrammatic documentation; i.e. graphic based documentation.

Furthermore, there is initial business case or defined acceptance criteria, which facilitates the measurement of success/failure. In addition, RRM

Figure 12. Relay race methodology (RRM) (Adapted from Abu-Taieh et al, 2008)

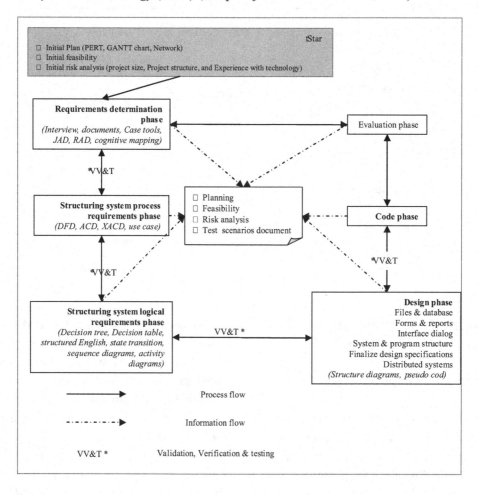

has discrete stages & defined structure; thereby the quality management issues are addressed through Validation and Verification, as well as covering the risk analysis issue.

Structured Systems Analysis and Design Method (SSADM)

Structured Systems Analysis and Design Method (SSADM) is highly structured SDLC described to the smallest detail. SSADM is best described as "Cook book" or industry standardization of SDLC enforced by the UK government through Central Computing and Telecommunications Agency in

the 1980s. The SSADM life cycle encompasses of the following:

- Feasibility study
- Requirements analysis
- Requirement specification
- Logical system specification
- Physical Design

Within this context, SSADM uses the modelling notation of Data Flow Diagram (DFD) and Logical Data Modelling, and Event\Entity Relationship diagram (ER) to put forth three points of view regarding the intended project, in this regard, the SSADM is best described by Cadle & Yeates (2004).

In the same manner, SSADM takes over traditional methods. While, SSADM is characterized by: User involvement, Emphasis on data, Diagrammatic documentation, Defined structure, however, when using SSADM, the following must be taken into account: (1) Comprehensive training on reading and understanding the necessary documentation should be in place for user, analyst/developer, thereby the time devoted on part of the user will increase, however, its rebuttal is that user commitment is needed for end product. (2) The level of documentation is relatively increased thereby a major criticism involving red tape and bureaucracy. (3) SSADM can be adopted blindly, yet it should be noted that the analyst and not the method that is doing the work.

AGILE SDLC

Agile SDLCs came to life due to pressure of delivering systems swiftly and fast, particularly since the market cannot wait long for an Information System to be delivered, noting that part of the delay in delivering systems in a timely manner and according to the market demand can be attributed to the bureaucratic nature of the traditional SDLCs. As the name suggests, the main characteristics in agile SDLCs are speed, light weight, iterative, and incremental. Following is a thorough discussion of seven SDLCs namely; Rational Unified Process (RUP, Rapid Application Development (RAD), Scrum, Business Process Re-engineering, Crystal Family, and Extreme Programming (XP).

Rational Unified Process (RUP)

Rational Unified Process (RUP) is one of the Object Oriented Development Methodologies that appeared in 1980s, which involves an iterative, incremental approach to systems development. In this regard, object oriented approach is more natural and more organic reflections of the real world, of which the basic concepts revolve around the fact that the software contains data (variables)

Figure 13. Phases OOSAD-based development (Adapted from Hoffer et al, 2005)

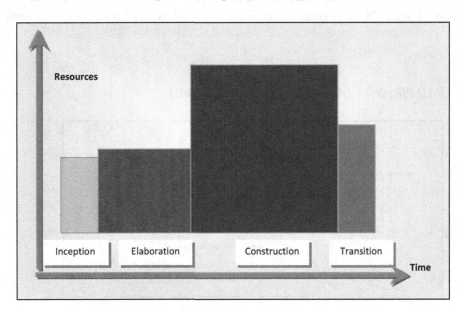

and process (methods), whereby objects can be grouped in classes, which are used to build hierarchy. Retrospectively, object oriented project has emerged with the following:

- **Unified Modeling Language (UML):** Supplies visual language for Object Oriented projects
- **Unified Process (UP):** Supplies Process Model, within which the phases include: Inception, Elaboration, Construction and Transition.

Rapid Application Development (RAD) Model

James Martin brought Rapid Application Development (RAD) to prominence in his book, *Rapid Application Development* (Howard, 2002). According to Howard (2002) and Hoffer et al (2005), the goal of this methodology is to decrease the time allocated for design and implementation, whereby, the methodology involves using prototyping, Joint Application Development sessions, CASE tools as well as code generators.

Generally, RAD is based on quick application development, in this context, many models for RAD have been in existence, see Figure 14. Nevertheless, Howard (2002) pointed out an important issue raised in RAD: Quality and Time; while some consider RAD as anti-quality since speed is an essential part of RAD, whereas, others consider it as a way to cut through the bureaucracy and red tape of other SDLC.

Scrum

Scrum is an agile and adaptive system development life cycle, based on the Scrum in the game of rugby, which was introduced by "H. Takeuchi and I. Nonaka in their article, "The New Product Development Game" (Harvard Business Review, Jan.–Feb. 1986)" (Poppendieck, 2002), and later explained by Ken Schwaber and Mike Beedle in their book *Agile Software Development With Scrum* (Prentice Hall, 2001).

The following simple description best describes how Scrum works:

A Scrum project collects stakeholder input in a feature list called "the backlog." Each month, the development team starts at the top of the backlog and selects as many of the top-priority features as they think can be developed in the next 30 days. The team is then left alone for the month, at the end of which time; the result is demonstrated to the stakeholders. This provides a basis for rethinking the backlog features and priorities. The

Figure 14. RAD life cycle (Adapted from Hoffer et al, 2005)

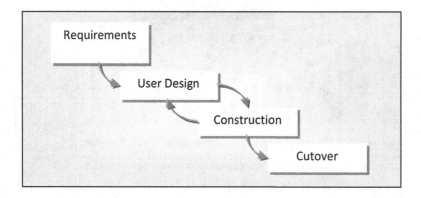

stakeholders are allowed to modify and reprioritize the backlog, after which the team selects its next month's work from the top of the list.

Scrum is adaptive and "allows the development team to make regular progress, even if their problem is not well understood" (Poppendieck, 2002). In addition, Scrum ", it offers a method for stakeholders to discuss the problem and reach consensus, creating a way for solutions to emerge, as is necessary for wicked problem resolution" (Poppendieck, 2002).

Nevertheless, Scrum is not without faults, particularly since many wonder if scrum made up for problem understanding on the account of time, thereby loss of productivity and market share can be attributed to resulting delays.

Business Process Reengineering (BPR)

Business process reengineering (BPR) is the analysis and redesign of workflow within and between enterprises, (Davenport & Short, 1990), whereby efficient analysis and radical redesign of business processes using objective, quantitative methods and tools and management systems, in order to accomplish change and/or performance improvement (Davenport, 1993). BPR is denoted as Re-Engineering, Reengineering, Process Reengineering, Process Quality Management, Process Innovation, Process Improvement, and Business Process Engineering, was formerly introduced in 1990 by Davenport & Short and reached higher when Michael Hammer and James Champy published their best-selling book, "Reengineering the Corporation".

According to Hoffer et. al. (2005), BPR encompasses of seven major steps:

1. Organize around outcomes, not tasks.
2. Identify all the processes in an organization and prioritize them in order of redesign urgency.
3. Integrate information processing work into the real work, which would produce the information.

Figure 15. Scrum life cycle (Adapted from Poppendieck, 2002)

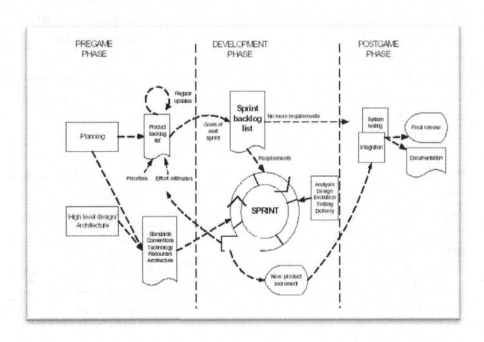

4. Treat geographically dispersed resources as though they were centralized.
5. Link parallel activities in the workflow instead of just integrating their results.
6. Put the decision point where the work is performed, and build control into the process.
7. Capture information once and at the source.

As such, many software tools have been developed for the sake of BPR, Table 1 cites their internet address.

While "Approximately 70% of BPR Projects fail" (Grant, 2002), nevertheless, the following can be considered as the major incentives for BPR, namely; (1) Increase accountability of the workers, (2) Enhance clarity of work procedure, (3) Improve visibility of decision making, (4) Save money, (5) React quicker to competition.

Crystal Family Methodology

Developed by Alistair Cockburn to reflect that different projects demand and necessitate different methodologies, highlighting that "one size fits all" idea does not work. Accordingly, Alistair Cockburn took into account elements that make projects differ from each other: People, project

Table 1. BPR software packages

Software name	Website address
Apache ,	www.eil.utoronto.ca/tool/list/Apache.html
Bonapart ,	www.eil.utoronto.ca/tool/list/ Bonapart.html
Business Design Facility,	www.eil.utoronto.ca/tool/list/ BDF.html
Business Improvement Facility,	www.eil.utoronto.ca/tool/list/ BIF.html
Caddie	www.eil.utoronto.ca/tool/list/ Caddie ..html
Ithink ,	www.eil.utoronto.ca/tool/list/ithink.html
Vensim ,	www.eil.utoronto.ca/tool/list/vensim.html
METIS,	www.metis.no/Homepage.html
DPA ,	www.eil.utoronto.ca/tool/list/DPA.html
CTAVe Process Manager ,	www.metabpr.com/index.htm
Logic Works' BPwin,	www.logicworks.com
Gensym's ReThink ,	www.gensym.com/products/rethink.html
Clear Process ,	www.clearsoft.com/software/process/
Optima! and Optima! Express	www.advanedge.com/
Extend+BPR ,	www.imaginthatinc.com
Cosmo ,	www.eil.utoronto.ca/tool/list/osmo.html
Workflow Analyser ,	www.eil.utoronto.ca/tool/list/orkflow_analyzer.html
FirstSTEP,	www.interfacing.com
Process Charter,	www.scitor.com/pc/pc_page.htm
Business Resource Software ,	www.brs-inc.com/
DTIC,	www.dtic.mil/bpr-helpdesk
CROSSFLOW ,	www.mcc.com/projects/crossflow/crossflow.html
ETC ,	www.world-wide.com/etc/default.htm
The Workflow Factory ,	www.delphigroup.com/bprtools/bprtools.htm

size, project criticality, and priority of project. Alistair Cockburn developed a matrix of different dimensions that would enable project managers choose the most suitable methodology to follow in compliance with the project needs, based on the four aforementioned elements. Alistair Cockburn authored many books like "Crystal Clear: A Human-Powered Methodology for Small Teams" and developed his own Website (http://alistair. cockburn.us/) that is dedicated to explaining the idea of Crystal Family.

Extreme Programming (XP)

Extreme Programming (XP) was developed by Kent Beck and Ward Cunningham in early 1990s, and was put to the test when Beck was working for DaimlerChrysler in 1996 (XP, 2007). XP is agile, light weight methodology specially developed for the purpose of agility and small size projects.

"Communication, Simplicity, Feedback, and Courage are the four values sought out by XP programmers" (XP, 2007). The process of XP is best seen in an interactive environment as on the Website (extremeprogramming.org), as such, (Hoffer et al, 2005) distinguished some characteristics of XP, namely; (a) Short, incremental development cycles, (b) Automated tests, (c) Two-person programming teams, and (d) Coding and testing operate together.

In this manner, the user (always available) writes a story, usually a problem with help of one of the development team, and then if the user story is complex, it would be broken down, in view that the stories are used to estimate the required amount of work and to create acceptance tests. After that, a *release plan* is devised, in order to determine which stories will be available in which release, noting that each release is preceded by a release planning meeting, and each day starts with a stand-up meeting.

Within this context, the advantages of XP lies in the amount of communication between developers, high level of productivity, and high-

quality code. Although XP assumes things like "user is always available" which unrealistic in real life, yet, as explained earlier, XP is for light weight project, as such; the user availability is not an issue.

SPIRAL SDLC

This section discusses two SDLCs: Boehm's Spiral Model and Balci's Life cycle for simulation. The spiral SDLC family is distinguished by evolution and iterations, in view that such life cycles best fit for IS that the end result of it is vaguely defined and the solution methodology is not well defined. In this regard, and in order to build Human resources application typically the team leader knows that such an application must be based on Database. As such, the venues for the solution are clear. Whereas, in order to build a simulation model for nuclear explosion or a simulation model for a hurricane, many variables in the application are neither known nor understood. Therefore, the team leader must learn as the project is evolving.

The Spiral SDLCs the phases are not discrete and the output of each phase is not well defined, accordingly, with spiral models, the problem is understood while working on the solution, which is best termed as wicked problem.

Boehm's Spiral Model

The Spiral Model is an iterative model that was originally developed by Professor Barry Boehm in 1988. Other iterative models evolved from Boehm's Spiral model. The model has four major phases that comprises of different sub-phases based on the time frame. As stipulated in Figure 16 the four major phases are:

First, the project objectives, alternative solution, and constrains are determined. Second, the PM evaluates and identifies the alternatives while resolving and mitigating the risks. Third, the PM develops and verifies the next-phase product. Fourth, encapsulates planning for the next phase.

The most interesting element in Boehm Spiral Model is the risk analysis, whereby the life cycle goes on while the PM measures and analyzes the risk. Accordingly, such model is best used when many elements in the project are not known i.e. simulation projects.

Another flavor of Boehm's Spiral model can be seen in Figure 17, which is comprised of six iterative cycles of project phases:

1. Requirements definition
2. Risk analysis
3. Prototyping
4. Simulate, benchmark
5. Design, implement, test
6. Plan next cycle (if any)

Both models are famous for treating the Risk factor in the IT project. One of the Risk elements is that the difficulty of setting the project scope. The task of setting and defining the project scope is not well understood at the outset. Such phenomenon is called "Wicked problem" which is "problems that are fully understood only after they are solved the first time" (Rittell and Webber, 1973). The presence of wickedness is what makes the iterative/incremental approaches most appealing.

In light of the aforementioned, it can be concluded that in such models there are no end date. Distinctively from the waterfall model, the spiral

Figure 16. Boehm's spiral model (Adapted from Boehm, 1988)

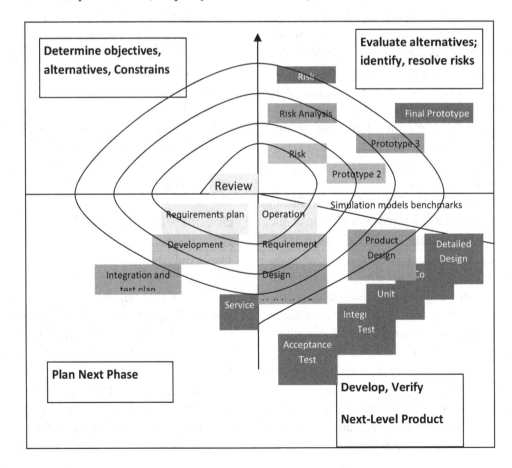

model treats the Risk management on the account of time. The phases are not clear in respect to start and end time. Moreover, the phases are not broken down into tasks where jobs being carried are defined and clear. The end product of each phase is not described either.

Balci's Methodology

Osman Balci, a well known simulation scientist, proposed many development life cycles which handle the process of building simulation programs. Thereby, defining Simulation in its broadest aspect as embodying a certain model to represent the behavior of a system, whether that may be an economic or an engineering one, with which conducting experiments is attainable. Such a technique enables the management, when studying models currently used, to take appropriate measures and make fitting decisions that would further complement today's growth sustainability efforts, apart

from cost decrease, as well as service delivery assurance. As such, the Computer Simulation technique contributed in cost decline; depicting the "cause & effect", pinpointing task-oriented needs or service delivery assurance, exploring possible alternatives, identifying problems, as well as, proposing streamlined measurable deliverable solutions, providing the platform for change strategy introduction, introducing potential prudent investment opportunities, and finally providing safety net when conducting training courses. Yet, the simulation development process is hindered due to many reasons.

Like a rose, Computer Simulation technique, does not exist without thorns; of which the length, as well as, the communication during the development life cycle. Simulation reflects real life problems; hence, it addresses numerous scenarios with handful of variables. Not only is it costly, as well as, liable for human judgment, but also, the results are complicated and can be misinterpreted.

Figure 17. Spiral model (Adapted from Boehm, 1988)

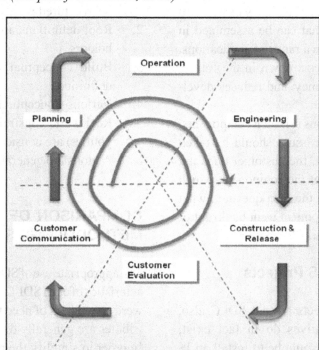

In many of his papers (1994, 1995, 1997, 2003), Balci suggested the life cycle described in his research. Each time Balci concentrated on one aspect or another in SDLC: development, validation and verification, and accreditation.

OTHER METHODOLOGIES

Some methodologies belong as a subset to other methodologies. This section groups these SDLCs namely: Component-based system, package based systems, soft system methodology. The first two methodologies may best be used when practicing RAD or BPR or other agile methodologies. On the other hand the third methodology is sometimes used when applying BPR on knowledge based organization.

Component-Based System

Component-based system is not a SDLC per say, however, such an approach to build IT applications and systems should be discussed, whereby the objective is to develop a large library of standard software components that can be assembled in various ways to produce a range of applications. Such approach drives cost down in the future, creates greater consistency, and reduces development time.

Some IT organizations sell such components; thereby two significant issues should be taken into consideration: first, the customer does not know the source code of the component, which subsequently brings up the next question, what if the developer of component went bankrupt or disappears from the market?

Packaged-Based IS Projects

Package-based IS projects are not SDLC also, however, such alternatives do in fact exist, whereby the objective would be to install an IS package, in which case there is no need to start from scratch.

On one hand, the advantages of such approach are less time, lower cost, and support/enhancements are readily available. On the other hand many drawbacks may appear: first, the package may not be a perfect fit to solve the problem, which crystallizes the subsequent drawback: changes to package are in the hands of vendor.

Soft System Methodology (SSM)

Soft System Methodology (SSM) originated in 1970s and 1980s by Professor Peter Checkland, whose philosophy was based on the "World System", which insinuates that in the real world problem definition is rarely well defined and structured. In this manner, and although SSM is not an IT approach, yet it is used since it follows the logical thinking, as such, this methodology is best described in Checkland's book "Soft Systems Methodology in Action" written in 1999, whereby Checkland suggested the following steps (Checkland & Scholes, 1999):

1. Problem situation is stated but perhaps in unstructured way.
2. Root definitions are collected from stakeholders
3. Build conceptual models based on root definitions
4. Various Conceptual models are discussed
5. Real world constrains (time, cost, culture, politics) are considered
6. Actions are generated.

COMPARISON OF THE METHODOLOGIES

The appropriate use of SDLC depends on the characteristics of each SDLC, yet, in view that SDLCs were created out of need then the comparison attributes are generally different from each other. In order to simplify the matter, however, Hoffer et al (2005) compared the agile, traditional, and spiral SDLC based on size, criticality, dynamism, personnel, and culture as stipulated in Table 2. In this regard, the following will discuss the SDLCs most suitable circumstances and uses:

In regards to the waterfall SDLC, which is best used when all input and end-products are well known and defined, the size attribute (time, money, people, area) are large, and the familiarity in technology being used and culture are both high.

Vis-à-vis the incremental SDLC, which is best used when there is a time constraint, the development team members are of low capacity, noting that the team leader (project manager) must have the expertise to compensate for the need of accurate design.

In respect to the V-Model, which is mainly used when validation, verification, and testing are essential and considered an integral part of the software being developed, thereby concluding that the V-model is another picture of the Boehm's spiral model, while highlighting that in so many cases there will be validation, verification, and testing although the point of what is being done exactly would be vague.

With regard to the b-model SDLC, which is best used when many inceptions are expected, considering that inceptions are usually rectifying orders issued by the customer to project manager, where the customer issues such orders because of two reasons, namely; first, the customer did not know what s/he wanted, and/or the requirements are not clear, and second, the customer discovered new needs as s/he learns as the project progresses.

A propos the Fountain model SDLC, which depicts the real life picture of the system growing and expanding. Information systems projects are not of the type said-and-done, as IS projects usually keep on going and by the time they are implemented many of the requirements changed and technology changed. In other words fountain model depicts the ever-changing and ever-growing nature of IS projects.

In respect of the prototype SDLC, which is best used to collect requirements and to educate the customer, more straightforwardly, it is a way of communication.

Vis-à-vis the Relay Race Methodology (RRM), which is an SDLC that demands expertise and knowledge transfer throughout the IS project, in order to build an airplane simulator, for example, the development team needs to learn how to fly an airplane, which is not practical to say the least. Taking into account that the development team cannot just change during the duration of the project, as such, part of the knowledge acquired by the development team can be transferred easier from one team member to another (designer to programmer) rather than re-learning the whole idea from the pilot.

Regarding Structured Systems Analysis and Design Method (SSADM), which is mainly used when standardization is needed. SSADM is used in the UK to standardize the governmental work.

With respect to Rational Unified Process (RUP), which is used for Object –oriented environment and when there is a lack of time. The RUP is not used without using tools like Rational Rose and Designer 2000 both packages generate code.

A propos Rapid Application Development (RAD) Model, of which the goal is to decrease design as well as implementation time, according to Howard (2002) and Hoffer et al (2005). The methodology involves using prototyping, Joint Application Development sessions, and using CASE tools in addition to code generators.

In respect of Scrum SDLC, which is best used when the environment is object oriented and the requirement are not clear, noting that there is a need to produce the end-product and deliver to the customer.

In regards to Business Process Reengineering (BPR), which is best used when there is need to start clean-slate, the BPR is an agile methodology but is conversant with failure and mistakes. In

Table 2. Factors distinguishing agile and traditional system development (Hoffer et al, 2005)

	Agile	Traditional	Spiral
Size	Smaller	Larger	**Complex**
Criticality	Better for low critical	Better for highly critical	
Dynamism	High dynamism	High stability	**High dynamism**
Personnel	Experts needed throughout	Experts only needed earlier	**Experts needed throughout**
Culture	High degree of freedom	Well-established procedures	**High degree of freedom**

addition, BPR is radical in nature used as a last resort methodology.

With respect to Crystal Family Methodology, which, as the name suggests, is a family of SDLCs, whereby each SDLC is used based on a number of attributes.

Concerning Extreme Programming (XP), which is best used in case of small amendments to existing system where there is lack of time and urgent need for quick delivery. In addition to when there are many requests for many amendments but no radical changes in the system. Still with such methodology there is a need to keep the latest version of the software and to keep track of the changes made.

In connection with Boehm's Spiral Model, which is mainly used when requirements and end-product are neither well defined nor clear, as such, the risk analysis of the project is an integral part of the life cycle. Such SDLC is used in wicked problem type of situation. Relating to simulation projects that fall in the category of wicked problems, Balci developed his own methodology for computer simulation.

CONCLUSION

This chapter discussed more than twenty SDLCs found in the IT project management arena, whereby, a comprehensive overview of the SDLCs

history as well as the trigger that instigated their development have been laid out. Subsequently, the chapter discussed the advantages and disadvantages of using SDLC, where the chapter explained the *where* and *when* to use which SDLC. As such, the chapter classified the different SDLCs into three non-exclusive categories: Traditional methodologies, agile methodologies and spiral methodologies, some of which the chapter had discussed.

As stipulated in the first section, in which nine well known traditional SDLCs had been discussed: Waterfall, Incremental, V Model, b Model, Fountain Model, Prototyping, Relay Race Methodology (RRM), and Structured Systems Analysis and Design Method (SSADM).

Subsequently, the second section discussed seven Agile SDLCs namely: Rational Unified Process (RUP, Rapid Application Development (RAD), Scrum, Business Process Re-engineering, Crystal Family, and Extreme Programming (XP).

Consequently, the third section discussed two Spiral SDLCs: Boehm's Spiral Model and Balci's Life cycle for simulation. The spiral SDLC family is distinguished by evolution and iterations. Such life cycles best fit for IS that the end result of it is vaguely defined and the solution methodology is not well defined. In conclusion, the last section compared all SDLCs their uses and when to be used.

REFERENCES

Abu-Taieh, E. El-Sheikh A., Abu-Tayeh, J. (2008). Methodologies and approaches in discrete event simulation relay race methodology (RRM): An enhanced life cycle for simulation system development. In *Simulation and modeling: Current technologies and applications*. Hershey, PA: IGI Global.

Balci, O. (1994). Validation, verification, and testing techniques throughout the life cycle of a simulation study. *Annals of operations research, 53*, 215-220

Balci, O. (1995). Principles and techniques of simulation validation, verification, and testing. In C. Alexopoulos, K. Kang, W. R. Lilegdon, & D. Goldsman, (Eds.), *Proceedings of the 1995 Winter Simulation Conference*. (pp. 147-154). New York: ACM Press.

Balci, O. (1997, December 7-10). Verification, validation and accreditation of simulation models. In S. Andradóttir, K. J. Healy, D. H. Withers, & B. L. Nelson (Eds.), *Proceedings of the Winter Simulation Conference* (pp. 135-141), Atlanta, Georgia, USA.

Balci, O. (2003). Verification, validation, and certification of modeling and simulation applications. *ACM Transactions on Modeling and Computer Simulation, 11*(4), 352–377.

Birrell, N. D., & Ould, M. A. (1985). *A practical handbook for software development*. UK: Cambridge University Press.

Boehm , B. (1988). A spiral model of software development and enhancement. *IEEE, May*.

Cadle J., & Yeates D. (2004). *Project management for information systems*, 4/E. NJ: Prentice Hall.

Checkland, P., & Scholes, J. (1999). *Soft systems methodology in action*. John Wiley & Sons.

Davenport, T. H., & Short, J. E. (1990). The new industrial engineering: Information technology and business process redesign. *Sloan Management Review*, 11-27.

Davenport, T. H. (1993). *Process innovation: Reengineering work through information technology*. Boston: Harvard Business School Press.

Graham, I., Henderson-Sellers, B., & Younessi, H. (1997). *The OPEN process specification*. ACM Press/Addison-Wesley Publishing Co.

Grant, D. (2002). A wider view of business process reengineering. *Communications Of The ACM, 45*(1).

Henderson-Sellers, B., & Edwards, J. M. (1990). The object-oriented systems life cycle. *Commun. ACM, 33*(9), 142-159. DOI= http://doi.acm.org/10.1145/83880.84529

Henderson-Sellers, B., France, R., Georg, G., & Reddy, R. (2007). A method engineering approach to developing aspect-oriented modelling processes based on the OPEN process framework. *Inf. Softw. Technol. 49*(7), 761-773. DOI= http://dx.doi.org/10.1016/j.infsof.2006.08.003

J. Hoffer, J., George, J., & Valacich, J. (2005). *Modern systems analysis & Design*, 4th edition. NJ: Prentice Hall

Howard, A. (2002). Rapid application development: Rough and dirty or value-for-money engineering? *Communications of the ACM, 45*(10).

Meredith, J., & Mantel, S. (2002). *Project management: A managerial approach*, 5th Edition. NY: John Wiley. ISBN: 0-471-07323-7.

Pillai, K. (1996). The fountain model and its impact on project schedule. *SIGSOFT Softw. Eng. Notes, 21*(2), 32-38. DOI= http://doi.acm.org/10.1145/227531.227536

Poppendieck, M. (2002). *Wicked Problems, Software Development Magazine*. http://www.

sdmagazine.com/documents/s=7134/sdm0205g/ sdonline/authors.html#mpoppendieck, [Accessed 2002]

Pressman, R. S. (2004). *Software engineering: A practitioner's approach.* The McGraw-Hill Companies. ISBN: 007301933X

Rittel, H., & Webber, M. (1973). Dilemmas in a general theory of planning, (pp. 155-169). *Policy Sciences, 4.* Amsterdam: Elsevier Scientific Publishing Company, Inc.

Sommerville I. (2004). *Software engineering*,7th Edition. Addison-Wesley Publishing Company, USA

XP (2007). http://www.extremeprogramming. org/Kent.html, [accessed 2007]

KEY TERMS AND DEFINITIONS

Agile SDLC: Are SDLCs that were developed to apply on light IT projects.

Information Technology Projects (ITP): Project that involve the development of Information systems.

Spiral SDLC: SDLCs that are have beginning date but the end of date is not really known. Such SDLCs are used when the project of research nature.

System Development Life Cycle: A process to develop computer information systems. The process is composed of discrete phases, each phase must have a begin /end date and a result or end product.

Traditional SDLC: Are generally the SDLC that were borrowed from different sciences like Civil Engineering and applied in IT projects. Mainly these types of SDLC are rigid in applying deadlines.

Validation: Is asking the question *are we building the right product?*

Verification: Is asking the question *are we building the product right?*

Chapter X
Analyzing Diffusion and Value Creation Dimensions of a Business Case of Replacing Enterprise Systems

Francisco Chia Cua
University of Otago, New Zealand

Tony C. Garrett
Korea University, Republic of Korea

ABSTRACT

This chapter uses the Diffusion of Innovations (DOI) theory and examines a business case, highlighting certain gaps in the theory. First, confusion can be present between the innovation construct (in this instance, replacing the enterprise systems) and the diffusion construct (that is, selling that innovation to upper management). Second, the business case has never been examined in diffusion research. Research about business cases generally focuses on techniques such as Discounted Cash Flows and Total Cost of Ownership. Third, although a good business case can lead to successful innovation, it should not influence upper management to be overly positive or too cautious. One extreme leads to over-commitment. The other extreme leads to under-commitment or upper management's inability to commit. Both extremes have unexpected and undesirable consequences. This single-case study examined a business case. The data included in the triangulation are observations, in-depth interviews, and archival documents. The analysis of a business case document was done with the ATLAS.ti v5.0 software. It is hoped that understanding a "real world" business case will give the academics insights on the relationship between the innovation and its diffusion as well as teach the practitioners the caveats of a business case.

INTRODUCTION

The consequences of a bad business case are certainly disastrous. Two business cases, one presented to the upper management of FoxMeyer (United States) and the other one to that of Fonterra (New Zealand), are good examples. The former company went bankrupt. The latter incurred a huge sunk cost of about NZ$ 260 million. The Diffusion of Innovations (DOI) theory enhances the understanding of the business case development (process), the business case document (product), and the message conveyed (diffusion) to the upper management by the executive sponsor (adopters and social networks). Business case matters in walking the innovation. It is a form of diffusion that comes with consequences.

A business case is generally ambitious. It has to be and it should be. Radical innovation with regards to replacing enterprise systems poses big risks to big organizations like FoxMeyer (USA) and Fonterra (NZ). Without great expectations, the projects of FoxMeyer and Fonterra would not have started in the first place. FoxMeyer did not succeed in its Project Delta III which bundled with the SAP R/3 and the Pinnacle warehouse-automation. In Chapter 11 (of the Bankruptcy Code), its gatekeepers claimed that their implementation of the enterprise systems drove them to bankruptcy (Caldwell, 6 July 1998; O'Leary, 2000; Stein, 31 Aug 1998; SAP and Deloitte Sued by FoxMeyer, 27 Aug 1998). They sued SAP and Andersen Consulting for a total of US$1 billion dollars. The dairy giant Fonterra put on hold its global SAP ERP project called Project Jedi (Foreman, 2007). Project Jedi is supposed to standardise its disparate manufacturing systems in line with its new business model of "One Team, One Way of Working" (Jackson, 2006; Ministry of Economic Development, Feb 2004). Fonterra justified the suspension of the project: first to reduce further capital spending and second to provide its farmer-shareholders slightly higher dividends (Jackson, 2006). It did not escalate Project Jedi despite of

the huge sunk costs of about NZ$ 260 million from 2004 to 2006.

The Fonterra experience is a good example of conflict between shorter-term stability and longer-term change to sustain and manage growth (Burrell & Morgan, 2005; Dettmer, 2003; Trompenaars & Prud'homme, 2004). Fonterra attempted to simplify the business processes, shrink the distance of its "food" chain, and deliver the value proposition of "quality and reliability at the right price" (Ministry of Economic Development, Feb 2004). Because this vision has the capacity to sustain growth, it outweighs the risks of Project Jedi and the substantial cash flows required to finance it. Fonterra managed its longer-term change through Project Jedi, which constituted a radical innovation. However, it suspended that project to manage its shorter-term stability in the form of dividends (cash flows) to its shareholders. There could be other actual behind-the-scene reasons for the suspension.

The undesirable unexpected consequences experienced by FoxMeyer and Fonterra highlight a concern in the business case. In large organizations, upper management generally makes accept-reject decision on the basis of a business case. It is a matter of corporate governance to impose a business case for capital expenditures. The innovation could be strategic to a vision or reactive to a crisis. Their executive sponsor explores all options that best fit the strategic or reactive intentions and then develops a business case for submission to the upper management for approval and funding. The business case "sells" the innovation. It attempts to diffuse that innovation to the upper management to make favorable accept-reject decision (aka, adoption decision). Project Delta III and Project Jedi would not have started if their business cases were not convincing. Good business cases sell. The spectacular ones make the upper management over-commit. This is a reality. A business case influences upper management to be cautious, positive, or overly positive. At one extreme of the continuum is upper management's inability to commitment or under-commitment. At the other extreme is an over-commitment. Both extremes in the continuum result to undesirable unexpected consequences. A successful diffusion, that is a good business case, is not necessarily good.

Despite of the high popularity and exposure of the Diffusion of Innovations (DOI) theory, it has two major gaps. The extensive literature review conducted includes the five editions of *"Diffusion of Innovations"* by Everett M Rogers (2003), the diffusion research in the disciplines of information systems, marketing, communications, and health care, and the meta-analyses of Damapour (1991, 1992), Granados *et al.* (1997), Greenhalgh *et al.* (2004), Meyers *et al.* (1999), Tornatsky & Klein (1982), Wejnert (2002), and Wolfe (1994). Yet there is no diffusion research about the business case. A recent search (10th of February, 2008) in ScienceDirect, Ebsco, Proquest 5000, Proquest Dissertation and Theses databases still showed no evidence of diffusion research on the business case, particularly in the context of enterprise systems. Yet real world cases—such as those of FoxMeyer and Fonterra—have highlighted a need to understand the business case in the innovation process. The DOI theory has overlooked the business case as a construct. Likewise, it has overlooked "visioning" (or a view of the future) as a crucial element in walking the innovation. Rogers (2003, p. 420) mentions that organizations generally react to problems and thereafter perceives the need for innovation. His two process models clearly indicate that walking the innovation is reactive to a problem and not strategic to a vision. That reactive intention probably leads to an oversight of strategic intention. For a radical innovation such as that of replacing enterprise systems, vision is particularly crucial.

How should the application of DOI theory be practiced in the context of the business case of replacing enterprise systems? This research problem effectively asks: What should the relation between the DOI theory and its application to the practice be in that context? Some practitioners have given their relatively simple answers. They would rather have solutions than the high sounding theories which, sometimes, they do not and cannot understand. For example, they want a simple framework of a business case that they can use. Theorists such as Burrell & Morgan (2005), Dettmer (2003), Hammer (1996), Trompenaars & Prud'homme (2004) give fundamental assumptions to the application of theory in practice. Replacing enterprise systems is about balancing long-term and short-term achievements, ultimately sustaining growth in the end. It is a problem-solving intervention that fosters seamless alignment (Hammer, 1996). It is possible to learn business processes, complex interactions, shared meanings, and defensive mindsets all at once from hard and soft knowledges. The archival documents, in-depth interviews, and observations give rich contextual, empirical, and experiential evidences. The contribution to knowledge of the research will therefore depend on understanding, interpreting, and evaluating the perceived value and other evidences. There can be, and should be, a tight integration of the mindset with regards to the antecedents, the innovation process, and the consequences of the innovation under study. That mindset could be illogical or irrational behaviours in disguise. Between the concrete and specific demands of the practitioners and the abstract and philosophical interests of the academics is the teleology of a theory. A theory is a tool to practice. Clegg, Kornberger, and Rhodes (March 2004) argue that a theory should not be simply a tool to understand the practice. Instead, it should be a tool that is used to create disturbance on that practice so that the organization can transform itself through the relationship between theory and practice.

Utilising the DOI theory as a research problem theory and replacing enterprise systems as a context, this paper explores a business case. A business case is *likely* a form of diffusion of that innovation. In a risk-averse organization, walking that innovation inevitably demands a business case to facilitate upper management to make an accept-reject decision. The executive sponsor submits the business case to convey the rigour of examining that innovation and its options. He intends to sell that innovation and justify his beliefs of the benefits and attributes of the innovation. Preceding the accept-reject decision of the upper management is a matchmaking stage of the innovation process. That stage provides a wider lens for triangulation while the research focuses on the business case as a process, a product, and a message of diffusion. The research gathers the chain of evidences that convey those underlying justified beliefs. The argument takes into account a diagram in Figure 3 (Hample, 1992; Toulmin, 1969). Please see Box 1.

This chapter is written with the academics and the practitioners in mind. The academics would like to look at the relationships of DOI constructs that have relevance to the business case. The prac-titioners, on the other hand, would like to know more about the business case, taking the caveat that a good business case is not necessarily good to the organization. The next section undertakes a review of diffusion of justified beliefs which the executive sponsor uses to convey his message in the business case. That review continues with the innovation process. Developing a business case is a crucial stage in the initial phase of an innovation process. Because walking an innovation involves shaping the future of the organization, reviewing the projection of that future is needed. The third section discusses the big picture of a business case. Understanding a macro viewpoint helps to identify research questions in order to understand more thoroughly that innovation. The fourth section presents an argument and explores a claim that a business case is *likely* a form of diffusion. The argumentation utilizes an

Box 1.

An exploratory single-case study of a business case of replacing enterprise systems

This single-case study research analyzed a business case document and validated the evidences in that document using other archival documents such as the Request for Information (RFI), Request for Proposal (RFP), the responses to RFI and RFP, the weighting scorecards, and attachments to that business case document. Other methods of triangulations included observations during the workshops on business process redesign and in-depth interviews with the executive sponsor, financial analyst, external change agent, incumbent software vendor, and the two short-listed vendors who did not or declined to participate in the RFP.

The University of Australasia (name disguised) is a large public sector research organization that had a 400% increase in total revenue and assets in the period of 1990 to 2005. During the same period, the Financial Services Division (FSD; name disguised) introduced a number of initiatives such as budgeting, accounting of the research funding, and monthly reporting. Craig (name disguised), the Director of the FSD, submitted a business case to replace the old financial management information systems to the Board of Directors on the 25th of July 2006. He had prioritised the replacement when he joined the organization in April 2005.

Taking ownership of the RFI and RFP, the third party agent from Providence Consulting released the RFI on the 3rd of November 2005 via the government electronic tendering service and also advertised it in a newspaper. More than 150 individuals downloaded the document. He received twenty (20) formal responses covering thirteen (13) different software products two weeks later. The four short-listed vendors received the RFP on the 1st of December 2005. Vendors of System E5 and System P12 (eg, Vendor E System 5; disguised) submitted their proposals. Vendors of System K9 and System L10 did not participate.

After exploring all available options and having considered the two strongest candidates at hand, Craig went on with the RFP process. A six-person evaluation team took charge of determining the weights of the important attributes, scoring the proposals, managing the vendor presentations, getting inputs from the participants, conducting reference site visits, and doing other follow-up activities.

The business case, dated 4 July 2006, consisted of eight sections and is supported by 6 other documents (APPENDIX A). To reflect the rigour of walking the innovation as well as the thinking involved in making the decision, Craig revised the project definition he submitted a year before. He presented his recommended option (System E5) and mentioned the other three options explored. The project definition summarised the expected consequences and the options required to achieving them. It included a project strategic evaluation form and four risk assessments (one risk assessment for each option).

---

inductive approach and therefore that claim is at best not definitive. The fifth section interprets the DOI theory in a context. That interpretation consists of three steps. It involves clarifying an assertion that a business case takes into account a view of the future, the vision, into the relationship between innovation and diffusion. Another step is articulating interrelated components and concepts. A further step is the portrayal of the structure by accurately reconstructing the interrelating thoughts. These three steps, which are not sequential nor discrete, are the three steps of reasoning (that is, interpretation) of Scriven (1976). The last two sections discuss future trends and give a conclusion.

BACKGROUND

Diffusion

Rogers (1962, 2003) defines diffusion as a communication process through certain channels over time among the members of a social system. Diffusion sells a new idea—the innovation—and its attributes so that the audience will buy that idea. Take the new idea, replacing the enterprise systems, as an illustration. If a business case is a form of diffusion, then it should be able to sell that new idea to the upper management (the audience) hoping that they will agree to commit financial and other resources for the executive sponsor to replace the enterprise systems.

Therefore, diffusion could be regarded as a pre-requisite of an innovation. To explain and understand this concept of diffusion in the context of replacing enterprise systems, the classical attributes of an innovation is not sufficient. Replacement of enterprise systems is an economic decision. This innovation should take into account both the classical diffusion and economic attributes of that innovation.

. The classical perceived attributes of innovation is a crucial concept in DOI (Hurt and Hubbard,

1987; Kwon & Zmud, 1987; Moore & Benbasat, 1991; Rogers, 2003; Tornatzky and Klein, 1982; Van de Ven, 1993). These attributes can be real or imaginary strengths (positives) and weaknesses (negatives) of an innovation. The key word of that concept is perception. Before perception becomes present, there must be awareness. After the existence of perception comes a personal bias. What matters most in perception is belief. Simply put, the perceived attributes of an innovation result in favorable or unfavorable biases regardless of real or imaginary strengths or weaknesses.

Justified Beliefs in Diffusion

The message in a business case is a form of knowledge.

Epistemology, a processed knowledge, comes from the Greek words *episteme* (knowledge) and *logos* (reasoning or argumentation). The observation of a phenomenon and the process of conducting an in-depth interview are forms of *episteme*. However, both are not *epistemology*. Instead they simply illustrate methods of the knowledge-gathering process (Grix, 2002) where the outcome of that process is assumed to contribute to epistemology. A knowledge-gathering process is epistemology only if it has reasoning.

That knowledge-gathering process consists of three essential components: access, reflection and argumentation. Kant (1934) argues that the individuals must first gain access to the reality which is a form of knowledge. At the same time, they must have the faculties for reflecting on and structuring their experiences. That access is a fundamental premise that relates ontology (reality) to epistemology (processed knowledge).

A true knowledge is, in effect, consensual knowledge. What exists in reality or is perceived to exist can be known (Blaikie, 2000). Nevertheless the concept of absolute truth cannot apply (Wyssusek & Schwartz, 2003). Instead, the concept of consensus is more appropriate. It is through consensus that a reality becomes a true knowledge

(Wyssusek & Schwartz, 2003). Absolute true knowledge simply does not exist.

Plato imposes a further condition. A true knowledge cannot be processed knowledge unless it is a justified true belief (Myles, 1990). Two conditions must be present. A first condition is justification. It is a form of reasoning. A second condition is belief. Fact is not a condition. Neither is reality. Therefore, a statement is processed true knowledge if reasoning makes that statement true and if the community believes that that statement is true. Likewise, a statement is processed false knowledge if a community falsifies it as being false.

There are many types and sources of knowledge. Verified true knowledge and falsified false knowledge are types of processed knowledge. They can also be considered as propositional knowledge. Another type of knowledge is the experiential knowledge of the participants in a case study research. The narrations and situational descriptions in a case study report convey the evidences and experiences of the observers and participants. They enhance the readers and their experiences when they study the case (Stake, 2005, 454). Effectively, there is a transfer of knowledge from the participants to the observers and from the observers to the readers. Empiricists and rationalists have conflicting opinions about those sources of knowledge. To the empiricists, empirical evidences and experiences are sources of knowledge (Wyssusek & Schwartz, 2003). The empirical evidences are the objective components while the experiences are the subjective components of the same reality. Rationalists regard reasoning as a source of knowledge.

Plato compares epistemology and the knowledge-gathering process to a journey through a dark cave, walking through the long tunnel and coming out into the open to view objects under the bright light of day (Melling, 1987; Santas, 2006). The individuals inside the cave can only see the illusions on the wall. They are ignorant of the reality outside the cave. If they successfully walk out into the open and expose themselves to the sun for the first time, they will realise the reality outside the cave. They will be enlightened. They will discover a *higher realm* of reality through a long challenging intellectual journey while probing inside the cave. The reality outside the cave as well as the illusions that they have experienced inside the cave are both their sources of knowledge. Those realities, one inside the cave and the other one outside the cave, are sources of knowledge and make the processed knowledge better. For instance, in a case study, Stake (2005) suggests drawing all the information from multiple sources at the same time to learn about the case and to answer the epistemological questions of the case.

Justified Perceived Attributes of the Innovation

Classical Diffusion Attributes of the Innovation

Which set of classical diffusion attributed to the same innovation is more important given that there are two sets of stakeholders (gatekeepers and users) and there is one final accept-reject decision to make? Set 1 concerns the gatekeepers (Rogers, 2003; Rogers & Shoemaker, 1971). Set 2 concerns the users. Sometimes, the conflict between these two sets is unavoidable (Hurt and Hubbard, 1987). For instance, the gatekeepers might find an option to have better attributes in Set 1 while the users might find that same option to possess worse attributes in Set 2.

Differentiating those two sets is important when justifying an innovation (Downs Jr & Mohr, 1976; Moore & Benbasat, 1991). In Set 1, the perceived attributes of Rogers (1962, 1983, 1995, 2003; Rogers & Shoemaker, 1971) consists of relative advantage, compatibility, complexity, trialability, and observability. With the exception of complexity that correlates negatively, the other four attributes correlate positively to the accept-reject decision and the speed in making that decision. Moore & Benbasat (1991) add image, visibility, and voluntariness. Set 2 emphasizes users' acceptance of technology. The perceived usefulness (similar to relative advantage) and perceived ease of use (opposite of complexity) have positive correlation to accepting and using the innovation (Davis, 1986).

Relative advantage offers certain advantages over competing innovations. It includes the notions of image (the social status mentioned by Tornatzky and Klein), economic value, total cost of ownership, and change of vision (Cua & Theivananthampillai, 2006; Moore & Benbasat, 1991; Rogers, 1962, 2003; Tornatzky and Klein, 1982). Image connotes adopting an innovation to gain social status (Rogers, 2003; Tornatzky and Klein, 1982). Another notion is the economic value. The gatekeepers make accept-reject decision knowing that the relative advantages and other perceived attributes will have impact on their decision (Drucker, 1995; Essinger & Gay, 2000). Not necessarily the lowest cost (Paquette, 2003), the relative advantage and other perceived positive attributes include direct, indirect and intangible benefits and the total cost of ownership. The concept of value becomes relevant when the cost of ownership is integrated with the change of vision (Cua & Theivananthampillai, 2006) in relation to specific time frames: short term (one to three years), medium term (three to ten years), and long term (ten to fifty years). Tornatzky and Klein (1982) separate image from relative advantage because their effects could be different. Using a similar logic, the value, total cost of ownership, and change of vision may likewise warrant a differentiation.

Aside from relative advantage, two other attributes relevant across a broad range of innovations are **compatibility** and **complexity** (Tornatzky and Klein, 1982). Compatibility refers to the degree to which an innovation is perceived to be consistent with the required functionalities and needs of the gatekeepers; other rules of thumb to assess compatibility includes orientation, values, and experiences (Chin & Gopal, 1995; Kozar, 1989; Kwon & Zmud, 1987; Moore & Benbasat, 1991; Mustonen-Ollila & Lyytinen, 2003; Prescott & Conger, 1995; Rogers, 1962, 2003; Tornatzky and Klein, 1982). Complexity is the perceived ease of use (Chin & Gopal, 1995; Davis, 1986; Moore & Benbasat, 1991; Mustonen-Ollila & Lyytinen, 2003). It is the degree to which an innovation is perceived to be easy or difficult to understand and use.

The two remaining classical attributes of innovation are **trialability** and **observability**. Trialability is the ability to experiment and try an innovation with minimal commitment of resources (Fichman & Kemerer, 1993; Kozar, 1989; Rogers, 1962, 2003). Observability is similar to demonstrability and visibility. It is the ability to observe and communicate the benefits and results of adopting the innovation (Fichman & Kemerer, 1993; Kozar, 1989; Rogers, 1962, 2003; Zajonc & Markus, Sept. 1982).

Economic Attributes

The concept of Total Cost of Ownership (TCO) is an economic approach of diffusion. It appears to be unbiased. The calculation can be substantiated by the presence of a worksheet. This mindset puts TCO at risk unless the innovation is integrated with other drivers of total value holistically (Cua & Theivananthampillai, 2006). TCO evolves from a traditional concept of cost[1]. In the case of the new enterprise systems, the initial cash outflows include software, hardware, installations, modification, training and supports, and consulting. Other ongoing cash outflows are for maintenance, subsequent training requirements, modifications, fine-tuning, other supports, and upgrades. Many of these expenditures are hidden costs which can be substantial when they are accounted for in the long term (Schweitzer, Sept 2003).

TCO has a basic assumption. It equates the value of an innovation to the total benefits minus the total cost of ownership (Best, 2004). That formula is simple and easy. However, how does an executive sponsor translate those benefits to something quantitative? How does he estimate the value of the brand? Service? Product? How does he calculate all the costs relevant to the ownership? In short, TCO is at best an estimate.

A Value Approach: Diffusion and Economic Attributes

The concept of value is a means of assessing whether a business case adds economic value in the medium term and long term (Copeland *et al.*, 2000; Morin & Jarrell, 2001; Rappaport, 1986; ten Have *et al*, 2003). But what constitutes value? How do enterprise systems help an organization to create value? How does an executive sponsor sell that value to the upper management?

What constitutes value to an organization? It is easier to understand this concept of value through the lens of Porter's sustainable competitive advantage (Porter, 1980, 1985, 1991). This concept of competitive advantage is rooted in the logic of value creation and distribution (Feeny *et al.*, 2003). An organization achieves sustainable competitive advantage when the value it creates in an economic exchange is greater than the value that could be created if the organization did not participate in that exchange (Brandenburger & Stuart, 1996). That sustainable competitive advantage is the value derived from its value chain of suppliers, distributors, customers, and other stakeholders, says Porter. All business processes, even if some of them are discrete, could be interrelated to create that value (Porter, 1991) and to sustain growth in the end. In short, value *ala* Porter emphasizes the value chain which is tantamount to the integration of all business processes and operational excellence to foster excellent customer services. The key drivers of that value, therefore, are the perception of the highest value by the customers, operational excellence, and relationship management (aka, value chain or relationship

marketing), stated Treacy & Wiersema (1996). It is only through the integration of innovation toward maximising customer value, fostering operational excellence, and establishing intimate relationships and value chain with stakeholders can organizations be sustainable in the long term (Kaplan & Norton, 1996a, 1996b, 2001, 2004; Niven, 2002; ten Have *et al.*, 2003).

How do enterprise systems help an organization to create value? With the understanding of the significance of that value to an organization, it is then possible to understand how enterprise systems can enable the organization to create that value. The value that the enterprise systems provide is the seamless integration (Hammer, 1996) of possibly all interrelated as well as discrete business processes (Porter, 1991). The four principles of Hammer (1996) clarify that seamless integration. To satisfy the needs of customers (Principle 1), the organization must put together all processes to achieve that mission (Principle 2). Superior process performance is a requirement (Principle 3) and its pre-requisite is to undertake process design or process redesign in order to foster an environment that inspires people to work productively (Principle 4). Briefly, the value of enterprise systems is an application of the way the organization does its business (Luftman & Koeller, 2003).

How does an executive sponsor sell the value of the enterprise systems to the upper management? The third question concerns justifying his belief of the benefits that could be derived by replacing the enterprise systems and the perceived diffusion and economic attributes of the innovation. Nevertheless, what constitute justified beliefs?

Developing a Business Case

Walking the innovation roughly follows certain steps (Figure 1): being aware of an idea, forming an attitude toward it, making accept-reject decision, implementing the innovation, and lastly,

Figure 1. In Everett M Rogers' model, the innovation process passes through five stages. It starts with the knowledge (stage i) and proceeds to the persuasion (stage ii), the decision stage (iii), and the implementation (stage iv). It ends with the confirmation (stage v).

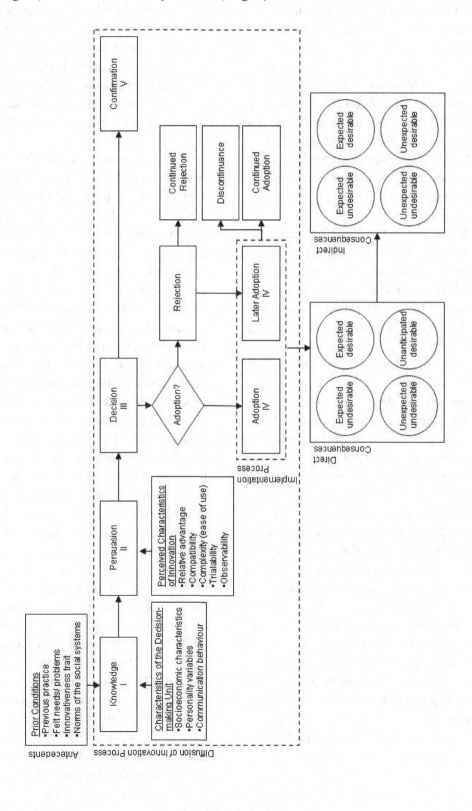

evaluating the decision. These five generic steps compose the innovation-decision process model of Rogers (2003). An individual or a decision-making unit is involved. That individual may be an executive sponsor, an opinion leader, or a change agent.

- In the knowledge stage (stage 1), the executive sponsor becomes aware of the innovation. This awareness can lead to the perception of needs or vice versa (Rogers, 2003, p. 172). He will attempt to learn more about it, what it does, and how it works. Diffusion in this stage is about favorable first-impression awareness.
- In the persuasion stage (stage 2), the executive sponsor (the gatekeeper) is more thorough with his knowledge of the innovation. He is able to perceive the positive and negative attributes of the innovation. Perception is tricky though. An object may be perfect but if an individual perceives it to be defective, then that object is defective. What is in the mind (the subjective bias) becomes more important than the evidence (the objective fact) that contradicts that perception. In that game of persuasion, an individual has free assent to believe or not to believe it at all. Diffusion likewise becomes crucial in this second stage. It demands more explicitness to the needs, the view of the future (vision), and/or the expected consequences. At the end of this second stage, the decision-making unit or the executive sponsor develops an inclination that moves toward or away from the innovation.
- The decision stage (stage 3) includes all activities leading to an accept-reject decision. Therefore, in this third stage there are two possibilities: adoption or rejection. There is a third possibility: to delay making the decision.
- The implementation stage (stage 4) represents the walking of the innovation.

- The confirmation stage (stage 5) involves searching for evidence to determine that the adoption, rejection, or status quo decision is right. That last stage may occur after the third stage. Sometimes, the third stage may lead to abandoning the innovation when the messages are in conflict. The implementation stage however may lead to discontinuing the innovation. Ambiguity and uncertainty are more of a norm than certainty.

The second process model of Rogers consists of two phases[2]. The initiation phase (phase 1) drives the implementation phase (phase 2). First, the executive sponsor perceives a gap and sets his agenda (stage 1). Then the matchmaking (e.g., matching) stage (stage 2) follows. In a risk-averse organization, the matchmaking stage is generally formal. It consists of Requests for Information (RFI), Request for Proposal (RFP), and the Business Case (BC). These are structured components, the standard operating procedures, to ensure that there is a perfect match between the proposed strategic investment and the project vision. In phase 1, the executive sponsor seeks information, interacts with external and internal stakeholders, identifies available options, and develops a business case, taking into account the total cost of ownership (TCO), benefits, and risk. That phase eventually culminates to an accept-reject decision. This decision is not for the executive sponsor to make. Rather, it is elevated to the upper management who controls the resource and gives permission to the innovation. In the same context of deploying enterprise systems, phase 2 encompasses the pre-production stage (stage 4), the production stage (the enterprise systems going live; stage 5), and the never-ending post-production stage (maintenance and upgrades; stage 6). The stages in phase 2 are somewhat consistent with the redefining/restructuring stage (stage 4), the clarifying stage (stage 5), and the routinizing stage (stage 6). The accept-reject decision, represented by the dotted-line, makes phase 1 to be an antecedent of phase 2.

Other authorities break down the innovation process differently. Walking the innovation is akin to escaping from an island prison (Ross & Vitale, 2000)[3]. Van de Ven *et al.*, (1999, pp. 23-25) uses the metaphor of an innovation journey of twelve stages in three phases[4]. In general, these are variants that are more or less similar to the two process models of Rogers (Cooper & Zmud, 1990; Daft, 1978; Ettlie, 1980; Meyer & Goes, 1988; Ross & Vitale, 2000; Tornatsky & Fleishcher, 1990; Van de Ven *et al.*, 1999; Zaltman *et al.*, 1973). The innovation process is without doubt ambiguous and uncertain.

A process model is deceiving. The stages in the innovation process are identifiable. The innovation process seems to be simple and linear. But, it is certainly complex, not linear, and iterative (36-Tornatzky & Fleishher, 1990). Van de Ven *et al.* (1999, p. 16) describe the innovation journey as "messy (p. 16)," "highly ambiguous (p. 65)," "often uncontrollable (p. 65)," and *"a nonlinear cycle of divergent and convergent activities that may repeat over time and at different organizational levels if resources are obtained to renew the cycle."* The stages that involve external stakeholders are generally defined in expected order while those, which originate within the organization or which are more complex, tend to muddle and overlap (Rogers, 2003). The accept-reject decision in the process model of Rogers further illustrates this confusion. Is there really a "dotted line" between the initiation phase and the implementation phase of the innovation process (Rogers, 2003)? A diffusion research that focuses on that "dotted line" decision has weaknesses (Wolfe, 1994).

A View of the Future in a Business Case

The outcome of the adoption, capital investment, and implementation of enterprise systems can be a strategic success or a colossal failure. Enterprise systems can empower or constrain an organization. To understand these issues, practitioners would fare well to understand the conflicts, pressures, and processes including the management of change and innovation. By doing so, the outcome of success or failure can be understood more clearly.

It is always necessary for organization to adapt to the ever-changing external environments. To adapt is to change radically. Change disrupts. Therefore, in the process of adapting and changing itself, the organization should be stable enough to sustain the many impacts brought about by that change. Being able to maintain stability in the short term in order to afford change in the long term is inherently contradictory (Burrell & Morgan, 2005; Dettmer, 2003; Trompenaars & Prud'homme, 2004). One illustration of the external pressures compelling radical change is that of an airline company. Air New Zealand outsourced the maintenance of its wide-bodied jets Boeing overseas. More than six hundred engineers were affected by the job cuts ("Air NZ has no option: Norris", 22-23 Oct. 2005; Dearnaley, 2005). This change (the innovation) was an attempt to reduce costs and improve profit. Air New Zealand has attempted to manage its profitability and cash flows in the short term and innovation in the long term to be able to sustain itself in the end.

What should the change be? How should it be implemented? Of these two crucial questions at the broadest level of change and innovation (Nadler and Tushman, 2004; Trompenaars & Prud-homme, 2004), the former concerns a change in vision. The second question concerns walking the change. It presupposes that the change fits the vision and that it is good for the organization. This vision comes with references to time and future. Just as people are bound to their self-conscious *image of the future* (Polak, 1973), organizational change can also be bound by the corporate vision. Radical innovation at the broadest level concern a vision, an innovation that fits that vision, and an innovation process.

A "vision" is a view of the future. The term and the "future" are not in the index section of the book entitled Diffusion of Innovations written by Rogers (2003). However, "uncertainty" is in that section. So is "time". Rogers has mentioned "vision" and "future" in the discussion of the innovation-development process (Rogers, 2003, pp. 136-167), the birth of the laptop computer at Toshiba (Abetti, 1997; Rogers, 2003, p. 145), and the fumbling the future at Xerox PARC (Rogers, 2003, p. 153). Although vision is a crucial element in walking the innovation, that vision is a missing construct in the DOI theory.

A BIG PICTURE OF A BUSINESS CASE

Walking a radical innovation (F in Figure 2) fosters longer-term success (B) where the achievement of growth and sustainability is the endpoint (A). This requires adequate cash flows (G) which are generally derived from the profitability earned during the shorter-term (C). In fact, cash flows together with profitability represent the lifeblood of the organization. Without the cash flows, it is not possible to walk the innovation and sustain growth in the end. Radical change and stability

are therefore always in conflict. Whereas cash flows and profitability are crucial elements of stability, uncertainty, risk management, and governance are crucial elements of radical change (that is, walking the innovation). The organization cannot walk the innovation effectively unless it manages uncertainty, mitigates the risks related to that uncertainty, and governs the innovation process. Walking the innovation inevitably disrupts stability.

A business case (H) should not only manage uncertainty, mitigate risks, and govern innovation process. It should also resolve the many assumptions (D), especially the hidden ones, that affect the innovation (change), stability, and their conflict. One assumption is the role of innovation. It is a means (a tool) of achieving an end, which as Figure 2 indicates sustains growth. Another assumption is the innovation process. Walking the innovation is a problem-solving intervention with expected consequences in mind. Those expectations include a view of the future and the undesirable consequence(s) to avoid. The third assumption concerns the potential functionalities and reporting capabilities of the new enterprise systems to satisfy the needs of the various departments and

Figure 2. A business case should emphasize a vision of the future (eg, growth and sustainability) Adopted from Cua & Garrett (in press)

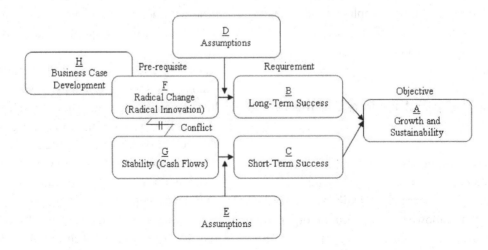

thereafter to eliminate existing feral systems or to avoid developing new ones. Whether there are new demands that warrant new feral systems remain to be seen. Only time will tell how long that third assumption will hold.

The big picture of a business case of replacing enterprise systems takes into account a view of the future (e.g., growth and sustainability), the conflict between stability and the radical change, its resolution, and the explicit and/or hidden assumptions that concerns it: expected desirable consequences to achieve, expected undesirable consequences to avoid, required and desired functionalities and reporting capabilities. Changing and improving business processes constitute the big picture—real value—of deploying the enterprise systems.

A BUSINESS CASE IS *LIKELY* A FORM OF DIFFUSION

Because replacing enterprise systems is a problem-solving intervention, the executive sponsor and upper management impose logic and reason in their decision-making. A business case of replacing enterprise systems is not only a form of corporate governance. It is *likely* a form of diffusion and conveys that radical innovation as a means to sustain growth. The schematic diagram in Figure 3 outlines an argumentation. It can be used as a warrant by relying on the evidences gathered. That inference (the right arrow ⇨), from the evidence box to the claim box, is inductive. Whereas a claim in a deductive inference is definite, a claim in an inductive inference is not definite. Because a business case is *likely* a form of diffusion, the evidences gathered and interpreted from analyzing a business case should support that claim.

There are critical evidences to look for in a business case in order to determine if it can be constituted as a diffusion (Rogers, 2003). A business case should sell the new idea through certain channels over time among the members of a social system. It means that a business case document should (1) introduce a felt need (a gap), (2) examine an innovation to resolve that gap, (3) explore the options of that innovation, (4)

Figure 3. Claim #1 – A business case is likely a form of diffusion

Warrant
A business case communicates the underlying beliefs beyond the surface of the written and spoken words.

⇩

Evidences		Claim
The evidences to support the argument may be written words or images that convey underlying beliefs to achieve the expected desirable consequences and to avoid undesirable consequence. Those evidences may not be necessary logical or reasonable.	⇨	A business case is *likely* a form of diffusion to examine the innovation and its options with a view of the future and other expected desirable and undesirable consequences in mind. It attempts to sell (diffuse) the innovation through its perceived attributes.

articulate at least a view of the future for which that innovation becomes a means to achieve that view, (5) identify desirable expectations, and (6) highlight undesirable expectation(s) to avoid. (7) It should also identifying positive attributes of the innovation and the preferred option in order to help sell the innovation to the upper management. These are the seven critical components in a diffusion. Using a complete set of labels (a super set of Appendix B) and coding the main business case document using ATLAST.ti version 5, the analysis revealed that the business case document contains these critical components. In this case, coding is used as a form of analyzing the business case. The business case document and its attachments in Appendix A provide some forms of triangulation.

Evidence 1

In context of replacing enterprise systems by a large public sector organization, the business case proposes a new idea with at least seven components of the concept of diffusion:

- A current state (a felt need or a gap)
- The solution (the innovation) to resolve that gap
- Alternative options
- A future state (a view of the future)
- Desirable expectations (desirable expected consequences) to achieve
- Undesirable expectations (undesirable expected consequences) to avoid
- Positive attributes of the innovation and its options

Evidence 2

The executive sponsor writes the business case to get approval from upper management.

The executive sponsor utilized at least seven components to convey his perception of the current state and sell the innovation. He presented a screen shot of the DOS-based systems installed in the 1990s. That picture spoke more loudly than words. Feedbacks were even louder. "Get rid of Counterbalance and get something that is user friendly." "A new financial system is badly in order. Counterbalance is so out of date and useless, it isn't funny." By using an image (a screen shot) and emotional comments, the executive sponsor painted a current state and justified a need for a change toward a future state. Appendix B and Here is a contradiction. Was that radical innovation of replacing enterprise systems strategic to the corporate vision or reactive to a problem at hand? Was that innovation a strategic innovation or a reactive innovation? What are the evidences from the business case document and its attachments (Appendix A)? The executive summary mentioned a consistency with strategy. The project is consistent with the Strategic Direction to 2012, particularly the imperative of building and sustaining capability. It stated that "the current financial systems falls well short of 'excellence' due to its age…, poor reporting capability, difficulty of use and general limited functionality." It highlighted a risk. "A major consideration is the probability that the support of the existing system by the [incumbent] vendor will cease. The number of organizations using the system is small and falling, and it seems inevitable [underline emphasized] that this will lead to a decision by the vendor to cease support in the next few years." Section 6 of the business case reiterated the two undesirable consequences to avoid: "The current system is likely to go unsupported in the medium term and the cost of maintaining the current infrastructure is likely to increase."

Table 1 present details and tabulate those seven and other components.

Evidence 3

The business case under study uses image and opinions (comments) as evidences to convey underlying beliefs of a current state.

In the business case, the executive sponsor presented four alternative courses of action. Option 1 was given a higher score when it came to user friendliness and reporting capability. The perception of better user interface and reporting capability was based on the feedbacks given by the participants when the respective vendors provided a demonstration of their products. Option 3 involved having a joint venture with the other universities in the country and sharing the same software package in Option 2 with them. It would seem that there was more to Option 2 (and Option 3) on the surface. Otherwise Option 3 would not be an alternative. The last (fourth) option was doing nothing.

Evidence 4

The business case explores alternative options, namely:

- The preferred option (Option 1)
- The option of maintaining status quo (doing nothing, Option 4)
- Other options (Option 2 and Option 3)

Evidence 5

The business case explores two options (the second and the third option) that involve the same enterprise systems. The third option concerns a "joint venture" of managing the enterprise systems with other universities.

Evidence 6

The business case identified six attributes to score the options, namely:

- Modern, user friendly system
- Long term support by vendor
- Integrated system
- Excellent reporting capability
- Accounts for entire University group
- Assists with Budgeting

Evidence 7

The option of doing nothing (Option 4) scores low in all the attributes.

Evidence 8

The executive sponsor gave Option 1 a higher score than Option 2 (and Option 3) for user interface and reporting capability.

Evidence 9

Although an option may score higher in an attribute, all these attributes are likely positive attributes for all the options except the last option of doing nothing. There seems to be no negative attributes in the list, as believed by the executive sponsor.

Evidence 10

Although Option 2 (and likewise Option 3) scores 4 for user interface and 4 for reporting capability while Option 1 scores 5 for those two attributes, there is likely more beyond the surface of those scores for Option 2 otherwise Option 3 will not be considered as an option.

Evidence 11

Except Option 4, all the first three options are likely to satisfy the requirements. This implicates a challenge of comparing the three options (e.g., oranges and apples).

Other than the six attributes used to compare the options, the executive sponsor had linked his case to certain desirable expected consequences to achieve and undesirable expected consequences to avoid. Those desirable expectations were typically high-level project outcomes or key performance indicators. To illustrate, modern systems (label 4avii in Appendix B) indicate operational excellence. User friendly (label 4ax) means "internal marketing" or making the employees happy. He gave a warning. If the innovation was not implemented (Option 4), the incumbent software vendor would likely cease to support the "old" enterprise systems (label 6b).

Attached to the business case document was a project strategic evaluation (attachment 2 in Appendix A). It was Capex Form 3 that established linkages of the project to the university and divisional strategies. The three sources were the university charter, the university strategic direction to 2012, and the Financial Services division plan. The university charter imposes excellence in administration, support services, and technologies and the contribution to the country and tertiary sector through the provision of infrastructure and support services and the building of managerial capability. The same charter also mandates governance and management which encompasses financial accountability and financial reporting. The replacement of the enterprise systems would ensure that the University would be capable of maintaining that excellence. A strategic direction to 2012 mandates that the University would be able to build and sustain its capability. Financial accountability and financial reporting are responsibilities of Financial Service Division. Craig warned that his division would not be able meet those responsibilities if the incumbent vendor had ceased to support the old systems.

Evidence 12

Corporate governance in UoA dictates the evaluation of a capital expenditure project as strategy. The evaluation articulates the strategies and how the project responses to these strategies.

Evidence 13

Although the business case has established a link of the proposed innovation to certain views of the future, it has highlighted the undesirable consequences to avoid if the innovation has not taken place.

Appendix B and Table 1 present details and tabulate those seven and other components.

Evidence 14

Replacing the enterprise systems by UoA is likely a reactive innovation rather than a strategic innovation.

Evidence 15

Linking this innovation to corporate-wide and divisional strategies likely conveys a layer of reasons for an urgent agenda.

Evidence 16

Gatekeepers are likely to impose reasons as part of a problem-solving intervention by linking their intention of walking the innovation to the shared belief and view of the future.

By grouping the total cost of ownership (10.42%), risk assessment (4.17%), and perceived positive attributes of innovation (8.33%) together, the business case conveys a message about the classical diffusion and economic attributes of the innovation (a total of 22.92% in Table 1). What are the classical attributes that the executive sponsor was looking for? First is the perceived ease of use (that is, the friendly user interface) that belongs to Set 2. Then there is the relative advantage in the form of functionality (modules), reporting capability, and the integration of these modular functionalities. Complexity is a double-edged knife. It could likely affect the user interface. But the same complexity could provide the required functionalities, reporting capabilities, and integration. For the economic attributes, the concept of total cost of ownership makes the analysis seemingly unbiased as a form of risk assessment.

The business case justifies the need to replace the old systems with ongoing vendor support, requirements of internal users, feral systems, functional reporting, and integration requirements. These justifications are predominantly the benefits expected from the new financial systems.

Evidence 17

The business case gives three major reasons to replace the enterprise systems: (1) Ongoing sup-

Table 1. Critical messages in a business case document of replacing enterprise systems

1. A felt need	2. The innovation	3. The options explored	4. A view of the future	5. Desirable expectations	6. Undesirable expectations	7. Positive attributes	8. Others		
				✓				29.17%	Expected desirable consequences
✓	✓	✓						22.92%	The innovation and its options
					✓			2.08%	Undesirable consequence, a risk, to avoid
			✓					2.08%	A vision of the future
								56.25%	*Sub-total*
							✓	12.50%	The social systems
						✓		10.42%	Total cost of ownership
						✓		8.33%	Perceived positive attributes of innovation including software image
							✓	8.33%	The innovation process
						✓		4.17%	Risk assessment
								43.75%	*Sub-total*
								100.00%	*Overall total*

port, (2) user interface, functionality, reporting, and integration, (3) feral systems.

Evidence 18

The business case gives two major benefits of the new financial systems: (1) Ongoing support and (2) user interface, functionality, reporting, and integration.

Evidence 19

The business case does not state that minimizing or eliminating feral systems is a benefit.

Evidence 20

The executive sponsor could assume that the new enterprise systems will satisfy all informational and reporting requirements and therefore feral systems will likely reduce in the end.

Evidence 11 implicates a challenge. How does one compare oranges and apples? With the exception of Option 4, all the first three options are likely to satisfy the requirements. This implicates a challenge of comparing the three options (e.g., comparing oranges and apples). The solution is presented in Figure 4. It takes into account all the six qualitative attributes, assigns a weight (Weight A) and a score (Score B) for each attribute and multiplies the weight to the score in order to determine the weighted score (A x B), compute the total cost of ownership for each option, assign a risk (the beta) index to each option, and use a

Figure 4. Qualitative benefits, economic costs (total cost of ownership), and risk

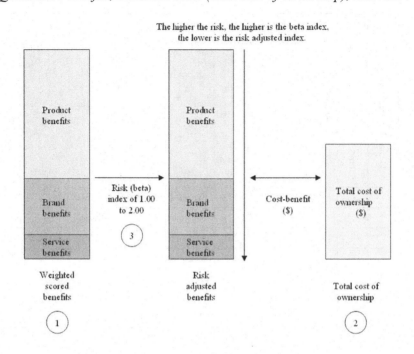

formula to calculate the risk-adjusted benefits. The risk index for the four options were 1.00, 1.00, 1.30, and 2 respectively. The cost per risk-adjusted benefit were $29,000, $38,000, $50,000, and $155,000.

Evidence 21

That total cost of ownership embodies shared meaning and defensive reasoning for analyzing cost versus benefits.

Evidence 22

A business case of replacing enterprise systems is likely to delimit the examination of positive diffusion and economic attributes.

DOI THEORY IN A CONTEXT

In this section, a model of the Diffusion of Innovations theory is interpreted. The interpretation involves (1) clarifying an assertion that a business case takes into account a view of the future, the vision, into the relationship between innovation and diffusion, (2) articulating interrelated components and concepts, and (3) reconstructing accurately those components and concepts into a whole.

In his seminal book entitled *Diffusion of Innovations*, Everett M Rogers (1962, 2003) describes the innovation process, its antecedents, and consequences with greater clarity than the diffusion that is embedded into it (❶ in Figure 5). He explains diffusion in terms of how, why, and at what rate new ideas and technology is spread through the social systems. His discussion on those aspects are thorough. The expected consequences and perceived attributes of innovation are antecedents (❷) of the innovation process. An important aspect affecting the spread of innovation is the social networks. The S curve, the early adopters, the early majority are some lenses through which Rogers discusses the diffusion. Overlooked is the business case stage that precedes the accept-reject decision. Diffusion is not possible without the innovation. This is the essence of the term "diffusion of innovations." Innovation is about an idea, practice, or object that is perceived to be new to the entity (individual or organization) adopting it or intending to adopt it. It is a requirement of diffusion (that is, innovation ⇨ diffusion). Diffusion infuses the innovation into the minds of the audience being communicated. Naturally, innovation comes first. Diffusion follows (❸). But, successful diffusion is a requirement of successful innovation (Baskerville & Pries-Heje, 2001), or diffusion ⇨ innovation (❹). By putting together these two statements, the relationship between innovation and its diffusion can therefore be defined as two directional (that is, innovation ⇔ diffusion). There is an alternate view, however. Diffusion is a requirement of a successful innovation process (that is, diffusion ⇨ innovation process) that ultimately leads to a successful innovation (that is, innovation process ⇨ innovation). This makes the relationship of innovation ⇨ diffusion ⇨ innovation process ⇨ innovation circular (❺) rather than two directional.

Even if there is innovation, diffusion is still not possible unless the social networks (❻), such as the entity, act as a conduit in which diffusion will pass through. Prior to the publication of the

Diffusion of Innovations in 1962, Elihu Katz (1956, 1961, 1962) has talked about the widening of communication over time for the new idea to permeate through the social networks. Clearly, the social networks represent a pre-requisite of diffusion of innovation (that is, social networks ⇨ (innovation ⇔ diffusion)). A requirement of innovation consist of the social networks, specifically the targeted audience. The audience is a requirement of the innovation (❼) while the innovation is a requirement of diffusion (❸). Both the social networks and innovation are antecedents of diffusion. To clarify, the audience is the upper management for the diffusion through a business case. In effect, either (social networks ⇨ (innovation ⇔ diffusion)) or (social networks ⇨ (innovation ⇨ diffusion ⇨ innovation process ⇨ innovation)) depicts the relationships that involve people and their complex interactions.

Although diffusion is embedded into the innovation process, it is most crucial in the initiation phase (❽). The process model of Rogers has an arrow from the perceived attributes of innovation to the matchmaking stage of the initiation phase (❾; Chapter 2). That arrow means that diffusion bears the expected consequences in mind and communicates the perceived attributes as the

Figure 5. Interrelating concepts of Diffusion of Innovations theory

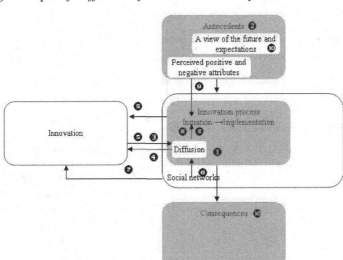

selling points of the innovation (❾). The executive sponsor uses the business case document to sell the innovation to the upper management. The opinion leaders likewise sell the innovation with their participation. In the former instance, diffusion is explicit. In the latter instance, it is implicit.

Confusions with terminologies are inevitable. First, diffusion and communication are quite similar and can cause some confusion. Rogers (1962) appears to have encountered this dilemma with his book. After giving the first edition the title, *Diffusion of Innovations*, the second edition was entitled *Communication of Innovations: A Cross-Cultural Approach* (Rogers & Shoemaker, 1971). The change from diffusion to communication could be due to the presence of a coauthor. If that was the reason, the name *Diffusion of Innovations: A Cross-Cultural Approach* (2nd ed.) would dis-

tinguish it from *Diffusion of Innovations* (1st ed.). The 3rd, the 4th, and the 5th edition reverted to *Diffusion of Innovations* (Rogers, 1983, 1995, 2003). Apparently, the term diffusion is more appropriate for describing the dispersion of a new idea (the innovation) than the term, communication which is more applicable to describing new or old idea alike. The second confusion concerns expectations and consequences. Expected consequences that are similar to perceived attributes of innovation, are the antecedents and not the consequences while the actual consequences are those that may be desirable or undesirable (❿).

Figure 5 and Figure 6 reconstruct the relationships of key constructs and concepts of the DOI theory and give greater clarity to the existing DOI theory. The difference between the two diagrams is the level of generalisation that is applicable to each. Figure 5 is applicable to all types of in-

Figure 6. Interrelating the concepts of the Diffusion of Innovations theory in the context of an entity that demands a business case document to make an accept-reject decision

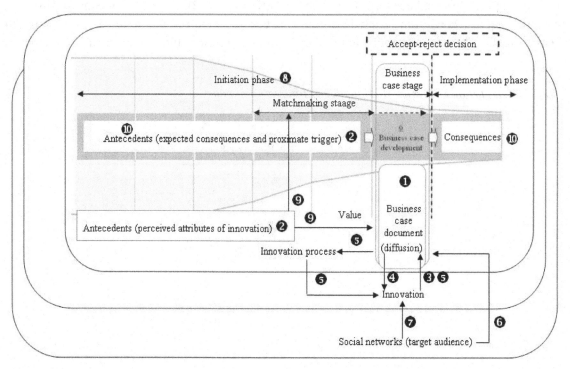

novation. Figure 6 applies to an innovation that requires a business case. It is generally applicable to a risk-averse entity. A point of emphasis is the value derived from the expectations and perceived attributes of innovation. The value represents the selling points examined in the business case. Diffusion interrelates with perceived attributes through the innovation process and influences the accept-reject decision at the end of the initiation phase of the innovation process. A business case document is a means of selling (diffusing) the value of the innovation. The role of the business case is twofold. One is the business case development (a process). The other is the business case document (a product of that process). There are other implications. The newness has to convey value in order for the innovation to really matter. The innovation ought to have the attributes perceived to be of value to the entity individually or collectively. Successful diffusion ultimately influences the accept-reject decision favorably.

FUTURE TRENDS

The Diffusion of Innovations theory takes into account the antecedents (❶ in Figure 7) which includes the conditions, the expected consequences, and the perceived attributes (❹)of the innovation,

the process which consists of the decision points in that process (❷), and the consequences (❸). An objective of future research is to examine the decision points in the process, particularly those decision points in the matchmaking stage and the business case stage, and to understand the impact of those decision points in terms of performance metrics, control systems, and their implications.

The co-creation of the total value requires management to understand the full implications of the enterprise systems to all strategic and ethically critical stakeholders. The diffusion of an innovation to the stakeholders fosters value creation, their interactions, and relationships. Reflecting on that value, a diffusion research on business case development (process) and/or business case document (outcome) should consider these questions:

1. What are the vision and objectives of the organization?
2. On the bases of those vision and objectives, what constitutes value to the organization?
3. What is the change of the business process and how does it help to achieve that value?

Figure 7. A theoretical framework for a diffusion research on business case

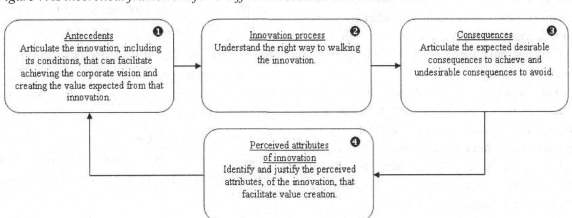

157

4. What are the relevant information technologies that will enable the expected radical change to bring in the value?

5. How should the organization walk the innovation in order to be able to leverage the information technologies?

6. What are the benefits expected from that radical innovation?

7. How do those benefits align with the vision, objectives, and value (eg, total value of ownership)?

A mode of analysis is to regard the business case process as a hermeneutic process. It is an interpretive approach to understanding the way the executive sponsor and the upper management make the adoption decision meaningful (Boland Jr, 2002). Hermeneutics is an interpretative study used to understand a text where the portion of text is considered in relation to the complete text as a whole.

CONCLUSION

This chapter has provided an overarching framework and reinterpretation of the Diffusion of Innovations theory to understand the business case construct. It has integrated the total cost of ownership and other economic attributes into the Diffusion of Innovations theory. It further integrates the innovation with operational excellence and marketing. In this manner, a richer and more comprehensive framework can be understood and leveraged to build capacity and to be sustainable in the long term.

The Diffusion of Innovations (DOI) theory is used as an *a priori* framework to study how an executive sponsor with the aim of seeking approval to commit significant amounts of resources to implement the replacement diffused his business case of replacing old enterprise information systems.

A question that this study attempts to answer concerns how the innovation (that is, the replacement of old enterprise information systems) relates to its diffusion (that is, the selling of the idea) to the upper management. Diffusion authorities argue that innovation is not possible without diffusion and likewise, diffusion is not possible without innovation. As the case has revealed, gatekeepers in risk-adverse organizations set the innovation agenda as a reaction to a perceived threat, which in this instance is the cessation of support by the incumbent vendor, and decide to adopt an innovation because of the perceived value. Although there are perceived attributes that are classical to the diffusion theory, the total cost of ownership and the number of organizations using the software and supported by the vendor are economic in nature. Whether the attributes are classical diffusion (marketing) or economic, the relationship between the innovation and its diffusion concerns value. Therefore it is possible to extend the statement that innovation is not possible without diffusion and diffusion is not possible without value.

REFERENCES

Abetti, P. A. (1997). Birth and growth of Toshiba's laptop and notebook computers: A case study in Japanese corporate venturing. *Journal of Business Venturing, 12*, 507-529.

Air NZ has no option: Norris. (22-23 Oct 2005). *Otago Daily Times.*

Baskerville, R. L., & Pries-Heje, J. (2001). A multiple-theory analysis of a diffusion of information technology case. *Information Systems Journal, 11*, 181-212.

Best, R. J. (2004). *Market-based management: Strategies for growing customer value and profitability.* Upper Saddle River, NJ: Pearson Education Inc.

Blaikie, N. (2000). *Designing social research.* Cambridge: Polity.

Boland Jr., R. J. (2002). In M. D. Myers & D. Avison (Eds.), *Qualitative research in information systems: A reader* (pp. 225-240). London: Sage Publications.

Brandenburger, A. M., & Stuart, H. W. (1996). Value-based business strategy. *Journal of Economics and Management Strategy, 5*(1), 5-24.

Burrell, G., & Morgan, G. (2005). *Sociological paradigms and organisational analysis: Elements of the sociology of corporate life.* Ardershot: Ashgate Publishing Limited.

Caldwell, B. (6 July 1998). Andersen sued on R/3. *InformationWeek.*

Chin, W. W., & Gopal, A. (1995). Adoption intention in GSS: Relative importance of beliefs. *The Data Base for Advances in Information Systems, 26*(2 & 3), 42-64.

Clayton, M. J. (Dec 1997). Delphi: A technique to harness expert opinion for critical decision-making tasks in education. *Eduational Psychology, 17*(4), 373-386.

Clegg, S. R., Kornberger, M., & Rhodes, C. (Mar 2004). Noise, parasites and translation: Theory and practice in management consulting. *Management Learning, 35*(1), 31-44.

Cooper, R. B. & Zmud, R. W. (1990). Information technology implementation research: a technological diffusion approach. *Management Science, 36*(2), 123-139.

Copeland, T., Koller, T., & Murrin, J. (2000). *valuation: Measuring and managing the value of companies* (3rd ed.). New York: John Wiley & Sons.

Cua, F. C., & Garrett, T. C. (in press). The role of business case development in the Diffusion of Innovations theory for enterprise information systems. In B. Cameron & P. Weaver (Eds.), *En-cyclopedia of information technology, accounting, and finance.* Hershey, PA: IGI Publishing.

Cua, F. C., & Theivananthampillai, P. (2006, 29 Jun - 2 Jul 2006). *Value management of sourcing decisions: The cost of ownership in performance management systems.* Paper presented at the Pacific Asian Consortium for International Business Education & Research (PACIBER) 2006, Cebu, Philippines.

Daft, R. L. (1978). A dual-core model of organizational innovation. *Academy of Management Journal, 21*, 193-210.

Damanpour, F. (1991). Organisational innovations: A meta-analysis of effects of determinants and moderators. *Academy of Management Journal, 34*, 555-590.

Damanpour, F. (1992). Organisation size and innovation. *Organization Studies, 13*, 375-402.

Davis, F. D. (1986). *A technology acceptance model for empirically testing new end-user information systems: Theory and results.* Unpublished Doctoral dissertation, Massachusetts Institute of Technology.

Dearnaley, M. (2005). Air NZ engineers plead for their jobs. *The New Zeland Herald.*

Dettmer, H. W. (2003). *Strategic navigation: A systems approach to business strategy.* Milwaukee, WI: ASQ Quality Press.

Downs Jr, G. W., & Mohr, L. B. (1976). Conceptual issues in the study of innovation. *Administrative Science Quarterly, 21*(4), 700-714.

Drucker, P. F. (1995). *Managing in a time of great change.* Oxford, UK: Butterworth-Heinemann.

Essinger, J., & Gay, C. L. (2000). *Inside outsourcing.* London: Nicholas Brealey.

Ettlie, J. E. (1980). Adequacy of stage models for decision on adoption of innovation. *Psychological Reports, 46*, 991-995.

Feeny, D., Ives, B., & Piccoli, G. (2003). Creating and sustaining IT-enabled competitive advantage. In J. N. Luftman (Ed.), *Competing in the Information Age* (2nd ed., pp. 107-136). UK: Oxford University Press.

Fichman, R. G., & Kemerer, C. F. (1993). Adoption of software engineering process innovations: The case of object orientation. *Sloan Management Review, 34*, 7-12.

Foreman, M. (2007). *Fonterra to offshore IT jobs to India?* Retrieved 19 Nov 2007, from http://www.zdnet.com.au/news/software/soa/Fonterra-to-offshore-IT-jobs-to-India-/0,130061733,339274389,00.htm

Gitman, L. J. (2003). *Principles of managerial finance, brief edition* (3rd ed.). Boston: Addison-Wesley.

Greenhalgh, T., Robert, G., MacFarlane, F., Bate, P., & Kyriakidou, O. (2004). Diffusion of innovations in service organizations: Systematic review and recommendations. *The Milbank Quarterly, 82*(4), 581-629.

Grix, J. (2002). Introducing students to the generic terminology of social research. *Politics, 22*(3), 175-186.

Hammer, M. (1996). *Beyond reengineering: How the process-centered organization is changing our work and our lives.* New York: HarperCollins Publishers, Inc.

Hample, D. (1992). The Toulmin model and the syllogism. In W. L. Benoit, D. Hample & P. J. Benoit (Eds.), *Readings in argumentation: Pragmatics and discourse analysis* (pp. 225-237). Berlin: Foris Publications.

Hurt, H. T. & Hubbard, R. (May, 1987). *The systematic measurement of the perceived characteristics of information technologies: Microcomputers as innovations.* Paper presented at the ICA Annual Conference, Montreal, Quebec.

Jackson, R. (2006). *Fonterra puts SAP project on ice.* Retrieved 5 Oct 2006, from http://computerworld.co.nz/news.nsf/news/3C182BBD1B82A2C1CC2571F80016AEF1?Opendocument&HighLight=2,fonterra

Kant, I. (1934). *The critique of pure reason* (J. M. D. Meiklejohn, Trans.). London: J M Dent.

Kaplan, R. S., & Norton, D. P. (1996a). *The balanced scorecard: Translating srategy into action.* Boston: Harvard Business School Press.

Kaplan, R. S., & Norton, D. P. (1996b). Using the balanced scorecard as a strategic management system. *Harvard Business Review, 76*(5), 134-142.

Kaplan, R. S., & Norton, D. P. (2001). *The strategy-focused organisation: How balanced scorecard companies thrive in the new business environment.* Boston: Harvard Business School Press.

Kaplan, R. S., & Norton, D. P. (2004). *Strategy maps: Converting intangible assets into tangible outcomes.* Boston:Harvard Business School Press.

Katz, E. (1962). The social itinerary of social change: two studies on the diffusion of innovation. *Human Organization, 20*, 70-82.

Katz, E. (Ed.). (1961). *The social itinerary of social change: Two studies on the diffusion of innovation.* CA: Institute for Communication Research, Stanford University.

Kozar, K. A. (1989). Adopting systems development methods: An exploratory study. *Journal of Management Information Systems, 5*(4), 73-86.

Kwon, T. H., & Zmud, R. W. (1987). Unifying the fragmented models information systems implementation. In R. J. Boland Jr. & R. J. Hirschheim (Eds.), *Critical issues in information systems research* (pp. 227-251). New York: John Wiley & Sons.

Luftman, J., & Koeller, C. T. (2003). Assessing the value of IT. In J. N. Luftman (Ed.), *Competing in the information age: Align in the sand* (2nd ed., pp. 77-106). UK: Oxford University Press.

MacKenzie, D., & Wajcman, J. (Eds.). (1999). *The social shaping of technology* (2nd ed.). Buckingham, UK: Open University Press.

Melling, D. (1987). *Understanding Plato*. New York: Oxford University Press.

Meyer, A. D. & Goes, J. B. (1988). Organizational assimilation of innovations: A multilevel contextual analysis. *Academy of Management Journal, 31*, 897-923.

Meyers, P. W., Sivakumar, K., & Nakata, C. (1999). Implementation of industrial process innovations: Factors, effects, and marketing implications. *Journal of Product Innovation Management, 16*(3), 295-311.

Ministry of Economic Development. (Feb 2004). *Restructuring to accommodate the "new" model.*

Moore, G. C., & Benbasat, I. (1991). Development of an instrument to measure the perceptions of adopting an information technology innovation. *Information Systems Research, 2*(3), 192-222.

Morin, R. A., & Jarrell, S. L. (2001). *Driving shareholder value*. New York: McGraw-Hill.

Mustonen-Ollila, E., & Lyytinen, K. (2003). Why organizations adopt information system process innovations: a longitudinal study using diffusion of innovation theory. *Information Systems Journal, 13*, 275-297.

Myles, B. (1990). *The Theaetetus of Plato* (M. J. Levett & M. Burnyeat, Trans.). Indianapolis, IN: Hackett Publishing Company, Inc.

Nadler, D. A. & Tushman, M. L. (2004). Implementing new design: Managing organizational change. In M. L. Tushman & P. Andersen (Eds.),

Managing strategic innovation and change: A collection of readings (2nd ed.). UK: Oxford University Press.

Niven, P. R. (2002). *Balanced scorecard step-by-step*. New York: John Wiley & Sons, Inc.

O'Leary, D. E. (2000). *Enterprise resource planning systems: Systems, life cycle, electronic commerce, and risk*. New York: Cambridge University Press.

Orwell, G. (1949). *Nineteen eighty-four*. London: Secker.

Paquette, L. (2003). *The sourcing solution: A step-by-step guide to creating a successful purchasing program*. New York: American Management Association.

Polak, F. L. (1973). *The image of the future*. Amsterdam: Elsevier.

Porter, M. E. (1980). *Competitive strategy: Techniques for analyzing industries and competitors*. New York: The Free Press.

Porter, M. E. (1985). *Competitive advantage: Creating and sustaining superior performance*. New York: The Free Press.

Porter, M. E. (1991). Towards a dynamic theory of strategy. *Strategic Management Theory, 12*(1), 95-117.

Prescott, M. B. & Conger, S. A. (1995). Information technology innovations: A classification by IT locus of impact and research approach. *The Data Base for Advances in Information Systems, 26*, 20-41.

Rappaport, A. (1986). *Creating shareholder value: A guide for managers and investors*. New York: The Free Press.

Rogers, E. M. (1983). *Diffusion of innovations* (3rd ed.). New York: The Free Press. (Original work published 1962).

Rogers, E. M. (1995). *Diffusion of innovations* (4th ed.). New York: Free Press.

Rogers, E. M. (2003). *Diffusion of innovations* (5th ed.). New York: Free Press/Simon & Schuster, Inc.

Rogers, E. M., & Shoemaker, F. F. (1971). *Communication of innovations: A cross-cultural approach* (2nd ed.). New York: The Free Press.

Ross, J. W., & Vitale, M. R. (2000). The ERP revolution: Surviving vs thriving. *Information Systems Frontiers, 2*(2), 233-241.

Santas, G. X. (Ed.). (2006). *The Blackwell guide to Plato's Republic*. Malden, MA: Blackwell Publishing Ltd.

SAP and Deloitte Sued by FoxMeyer. (27 Aug 1998). The New York Times Retrieved 17 Feb 2007, from http://query.nytimes.com/gst/fullpage.html?res=9A05E7D7123CF934A1575BC0A96E958260

Schweitzer, D. (Sept 2003). Track the true TCO: Watch out for hidden costs over the long term. *Processor, 25*(39).

Scriven, M. (1976). *Reasoning*. New York: McGraw-Hill.

Stake, R. E. (2005). Qualitative case studies. In N. K. Denzin & Y. S. Lincoln (Eds.), *The Sage handbook of qualitative research* (3rd ed., pp. 443-466).

Stein, T. (31 Aug 1998). SAP sued over R/3. *InformationWeek*.

ten Have, S., ten Have, W., Stevens, F., van der Elst, M., & Pol-Coyne, F. (2003). *Key management models: The management tools and practices that will improve your business*. Harlow, Essex: Financial Times Prentice Hall/Pearson Education Limited.

Tornatzky, L. G. & Fleishcher, M. (1990). *The process of technological innovation*. Lexington, MA: Lexington Books.

Tornatzky, L. G. & Klein, K. J. (1982). Innovation characteristics and innovation adoption-implementation: A meta-analysis of findings. *IEEE Transactions on Engineering Management, 29*, 28-45.

Toulmin, S. (1969). *The uses of argument*. UK: Cambridge University Press.

Treacy, M. & Wiersema, F. (1996). *Discipline of market leaders: Choose your customers, narrow your focus, dominate your market*. London: HarperCollins.

Trompenaars, F. & Prud'homme, P. (2004). *Managing change across corporate cultures*. Chichester, UK: Capstone.

Van de Ven, A. H., Polley, D. E., Garud, R., & Venkataraman, S. (1999). *The innovation journey*. New York: Oxford University Press.

Wejnert, B. (2002). Integrating models of diffusion of innovations: A conceptual framework. *Annual Review of Sociology, 28*, 297-326.

Wiek, J. (2007). *Parasites are the agents of progress: Interview with Michel Serres*. Retrieved 2 May 2008, from http://www.philippwente.com/daten/philippwente_200708_hpc_serres_artikel.pdf

Wolfe, R. A. (1994). Organizational innovation: Review, critique and suggested research directions. *Journal of Management Studies, 31*(3), 405-431.

Wyssusek, B. & Schwartz, M. (2003). *Towards a sociopragmatic-constructivist understanding of information systems*. Hershey, PA: IRM Press.

Zajonc, R. B. & Markus, H. (Sept 1982). Affective and cognitive factors in preferences. *Journal of Consumer Research, 9*, 123-131.

Zaltman, G., Duncan, R., & Holbek, J. (1973). *Innovations and organizations*. New York: John Wiley and Sons.

KEY TERMS AND DEFINITIONS

Business Case: Is used both to describe a process and a document. Corporate governance generally compels a business case document as a tool to justify a capital investment (a radical innovation). In this report, the exploitation of an agenda by an executive sponsor is considered a form of diffusion. A completed business case document is a formal written document that argues a course of action, which contains a point-by-point analysis that leads to a decision after considering a set of alternative courses of action to accomplish a specific goal. A business case process walks through the initiation phase of the innovation.

Business Case Stream of Diffusion Research: Embraces a plurality view of visualising, mapping, and realising future consequences. It permits an attempt to understand the perceived needs (the current state), the solution (aka, the innovation), its alternatives (objects of innovation), the preferred choice, a view of the future (the future state), the desirable expected consequences to achieve, the undesirable expected consequences to avoid, and the perceived positive attributes required.

Diffusion: Essentially the communication of a new idea (aka, the innovation) within a social system (such as an organisation) with the intention of convincing the audience to adopt or use the innovation.

Diffusion of Innovations (DOI) Theory: A theory of Everett M Rogers (1962) that concerns the study of communicating a new idea to individuals or organisations. It can be defined as the study of how, why, and at what rate the new idea (the innovation) diffuses and its adoption takes place.

Innovation: Represents a product, a service, or an idea that is perceived or should be perceived by the audience or the market in which this innovation is intended to be new and of value.

Implementation Phase: Proceeds after the initiation phase of "walking an innovation." For enterprise systems, this phase consists of pre-production, production, and post-production (also known as upgrade and maintenance). Refer to innovation process.

Initiation Phase: Consists of awareness stage and matchmaking stage, which ends with an accept-reject decision. This phase is the first phase of the innovation process. The second phase that follows is the implementation phase. Refer to innovation process.

Innovation Process: Starts with an initiation phase through which the individuals or decision-making units move from identifying and understanding the innovation, to forming an attitude toward that innovation. This subsequently leads to the decision to accept or reject it. The awareness stage is an agenda setting stage. The attitude formation stage is the matchmaking stage in which the executive sponsor attempts to match the attributes of the innovation to the requirement. The accept-reject decision terminates the initiation phase. An accept decision continues the innovation process toward the implementation phase, which consists of the pre-production, production, post-production, and confirmation stages.

Perceived Attributes of an Innovation: The Set 1 positive or negative biases that the decision makers have. These attributes may be real or imaginary. However, it is the perception of their presence that matters.

Perceived Attributes of Using an Innovation: The Set 2 positive or negative biases that the users have. Similar to the perceived attributes of an innovation (Set 1), what matters is the perception regardless of whether the attributes (eg, perceived usefulness and perceived ease of use) are real or imaginary.

Risk: Connotes a possible negative impact to something of value. It symbolises the probability of a loss.

Risk Assessment: An approach that measures the magnitude of the risk and the probability of its occurrence.

Total Cost of Ownership: Also known as TCO, is a rigorous and holistic methodology, which helps in estimating how much an investment will cost to operate over its lifetime. It takes into account all direct and indirect costs. The indirect costs are generally insignificant individually. However, they become very substantial when accumulated over time.

ENDNOTES

[1] Costing considers the money paid, directly or indirectly, in exchange for future economic benefits (value) over a certain period. It consists of direct and indirect cost. It consists of capital expenditure and operating expenditure. A capital expenditure demands cash outflows for a long period of time. It, therefore, involves cash forecasting and decision techniques such as the Return on Investment, Payback Period, Discounted Cash Flows, Net Present Value, and Internal Rate of Returns (Gitman, 2003, p 305; Luftman & Koeller, 2003). These traditional financial techniques, however, have shortcomings (Luftman & Koeller, 2003).

[2] A third process model of Rogers is an innovation-development process with six stages (Rogers, 2003, pp 137-139), namely: Needs/problems (stage 1), basic and applied research (stage 2), development (stage 3), commercialisation (stage 4), diffusion and adoption (stage 5), and consequences (stage 6).

[3] In the design stage, a prisoner executes a plan, carefully considers if he should go through his intentions (vision and expected consequences), and maps out the path to take at the same time. Then, in the implementation stage that follows, he takes a dive off a cliff and toward the bottom of the sea. The third stage is stability. Before running out of breath, he attempts to resurface, hoping that he would not be shot. The fourth stage is improvement. He starts to swim to freedom. The last stage is transformation. If he succeeds, he transforms himself into a free man.

[4] The initiation phase consist of the gestation (stage a), the shocks (stage b), and the planning (stage c). The planning stage is tantamount to the business case stage in which a plan (eg, the business case) is submitted to the top management (the resource controller) to obtain the resources needed to move on to the next phase. In the development phase, one can find the stages of proliferation (stage d), setbacks and mistakes (stage e), changing of goal post (stage f), fluid team composition (stage g), getting continuous support from the top management (stage h), building interorganizational relationships (alliances; stage i), and involving network externalities (stage j). The third phase is implementation phase composing of constant adoption and re-adaptation of old to new (stage k) and visible cultural change (stage l).

APPENDIX A: BUSINESS CASE AND ATTACHMENTS

The business case document consists of eight sections (1 to 8) and six attachments (a to f).
Sections in the business case document:

1. **The executive summary**
    The summary requested a funding of $2.8 million for a preferred option (Systems E5) and high-lighted the University's Strategic Direction to 2012 which involves "invest(ing) in the staff and the physical and information technology resources required to achieve excellence." The current financial management information system fell short of that excellence. A major consideration for the replacement was the risk of ongoing support that would cease from the incumbent vendor.

2. **The evaluation process**
    That process involved visiting several sites and discussing the issue with the Chief Financial Of-ficers of several Australasian universities. The departments in UoA provided their requirements. A third- party change agent took charge of the RFI and RFP. He was responsible for the team review of responses and the short listing of vendors. The selection process that followed was participative and reflected a common opinion that favored System E5 because of its user-friendly interface and low operation costs. Craig then conducted several meetings with the vendor of System E5.

3. **Why is a new finance system needed?**
    The justification of replacing the enterprise systems considered the risk of losing ongoing support from the incumbent vendor. There remained twelve organizations in the country using the old system. The section also mentioned the unfriendly DOS-based and the inadequacy to satisfy the requirements of the users. Other justifications included the significant increase of feral systems and their undesirable consequences, the inefficiencies and errors in preparing the reports, and the need for functionalities such as integrated budgeting, grants/research module, integrated fixed assets, procurement, and others.

4. **Benefits of a new financial system**
    Above justifications were somewhat reiterated and considered as benefits. Not mentioned as a benefit was the expected decrease of using and maintaining the feral systems.

5. **What is the recommended solution?**
    There were many reasons for recommending System E5 such as significantly lower on-going costs and a better user interface. Other factors included the references from existing clienteles using it, the presence in the tertiary sector, on-going support, required functional fit, and higher overall weighing scores than System P12.

6. **What will happen if a new financial system is not implemented?**
    This section touched on the dreadful status quo. The incumbent vendor might stop supporting the old enterprise systems in the medium term, causing an increase in maintenance costs.

continued on following page

APPENDIX A. CONTINUED

7. **Proposed time frame**

   The tentative timeframe specified a start date (September/October 2006) and the go live dates (May/June 2007 for the core functions and September 2007 for the other functions).

8. **What resources will be required?**

   Although the initial capital cost of System E5 ($2,800,000) was greater than that of System P12 ($2,600,000) by $200,000, the annual ongoing costs of System E5 ($188,500) was significantly lower than System P12 ($344,000).

Attachments

a. **Project definition (2 pages)**

   Craig submitted a project definition that contained a detailed description of the project. He revised this attachment on 22nd of May 2006. The replacement of financial system was classified as a strategically justifiable project. Its indicative cost was $2.8 million for Systems E5 and $2.6 million for System P12. Its annual on-going costs were estimated respectively at $188,500 and $344,500. The expected outcomes of the short-listed systems include improved reporting, information, and vendor's long-term support. In the project definition, the performance metrics first included (1) user friendliness, (2) ability to meet the needs of the FSD's clients, (3) improved reporting capability, (4) assistance with departmental budgeting, (5) integration of other necessary financial modules, and (6) discouragement of the use of feral systems. Later on, it included (7) the ability to account for the entire University Group on a single system and simplify reporting, reconciliation, and budgeting procedures. The long-term support by vendor, a performance metrics specified in the cost benefit analysis (attachment #5) was not included.

b. **Project strategic evaluation**

   Dated 22 May 2006, the project strategic evaluation form linked the project to the university wide and divisional strategic linkages. Craig identified three sources (the university charter, strategic direction to 2012, and divisional plan) that triggered his agenda and stated how the project would respond to them.

c. **Project risk assessments of the 4 options (4 pages)**

   Four project risk assessments, dated 22 May 2006, analyzed the risk of each of the four options that included purchasing System E5, purchasing System P12, sharing service with other universities using System P12 and doing nothing. The beta score for each option ranged from 1.00 to 2.00. System E5 and System P12 had the lowest risk (1.00). The requirements to establish the facility and the entity to run the system on behalf of the member universities increased the beta index of Option 3 to 1.30. Option 4 had a very high beta of 2.00.

d. **Cost summary**

   The sum of the present value of the initial costs and annual ongoing costs for ten years constituted the total cost of ownership (TCO). The TCO for Option 1 (System E5) amounted to $4,120,000

continued on following page

APPENDIX A. CONTINUED

and that of Option 2 (System P12), to $5,020,000. Costing for Option 3 was estimated, but not calculated, at $5,000,000. The discounted present value of Option 4 assumed that Option 1 would become essential in three years.

e. **Cost benefit analysis**

The cost benefit analysis utilized a spreadsheet template and calculated the cost per unit of risk-adjusted benefit. To illustrate, Option 1 had a total benefit score of 141. It means that Option 1 had 141 benefits. There were six benefits expected from each option (column 1). Each benefit had a maximum weighing score (column 2). The total benefit score could be derived by multiplying the weighting score (column A) and the assigned score (column B) and then adding its scores. Given that Option 1 had a beta index of 1.00, therefore the risk-adjusted benefit was derived by dividing the total benefit score of 141 by the beta index of 1.00. The answer was still 141, meaning that there were 141 benefits for Option 1. If its beta index was 2.00, the risk-adjusted benefits would be lower (70.50). A higher risk made the beta index higher. A higher beta index made the number of risk-adjusted benefits lower. Given that total cost of ownership was roughly about $4,120,000 and that there were 141 benefits accrued from Option 1, the average cost per one benefit was calculated by dividing the first figure by the second figure. The cost per benefit of Option 1 was $29,220. Each option was then ranked by the cost per benefit.

f. **Memorandum – Project summary (evidence not made available)**

APPENDIX B: LABELS USED IN CONTENT ANALYSIS

Total – 12	**Innovation**
Sub-total 3	1. The new idea (ie, project definition or name): The replacement of enterprise systems.
Sub-total 8	2. The innovation objects including options and their images or screen shots
1	a. Recommended option
1	b. Unrealistic option
6	c. List of options (including short-listed software packages from the RFP, the new innovation objects considered in the business case, or the options considered)
Sub-total 1	3. Type of innovation (the notion of medium term or long term is under change vision)
1	a. Anticipatory (strategic) innovation or reactive (tactical) innovation
Total - 26	**Antecedents**
Sub-total - 14	4. Expected consequences consists of the higher level change vision (refer to 4), high level project outcomes, or measurable results.
	a. Breakdown of either high-level project outcomes or KPIs
1	i. Avoidance of data reconciliation
1	ii. Consolidation of accounts
3	iii. Efficiency in business process (eg, bank reconciliation or organizational or department budgeting)
2	iv. Functionality (modular) and integration (include user requirements and usability)
1	v. Improved financial information management which includes easier or minimized development of customized interface with external systems
2	vi. Improved reporting capability or simplified reporting process
1	vii. Modern systems
1	viii. On-going support by respected vendor in long-term
1	ix. Reduction of feral systems
1	x. User friendly (user-interface, navigation, intuitive, mouse capable)
Sub-total - 3	5. Perceived attributes about the innovation are real or imaginary bias in favor or against the innovation object or specific options.
	a. Perceived high functional fit is a relative advantage that concerns the availability of functional modules and the integration of modules.
1	i. Fixed asset module
2	ii. Other functional fit factors (eg, modern and more advance)
Sub-total - 5	b. Total cost of ownership (TCO) or price is another relative advantage
1	i. Total cost of ownership also includes the notion of expensive or cheap.
2	ii. Capital expenditure
1	iii. Operating expenditure (on-going costs) which includes annual license fee, estimated upgrade costs, and estimated support for upgrade
1	iv. Source of or seeking for funding
Sub-total – 1	c. Image - software
1	i. No of universities in the region or country
Sub-total 3	6. Risk assessment
1	a. Medium-term or long-term risk
2	b. Ceasing to support the software (the undesirable consequence to avoid)
Total - 4	**Process**
Sub-total - 3	7. Matchmaking stage
1	a. Tendering process such as RFI, evaluation of responses to RFI and short-listing, RFP, and evaluation of responses to RFP
1	b. Site visits (to several universities in Australasia)
1	c. Consultation with University departments about their requirements (independent scoping requirements and survey of the current state)
Sub-total - 1	8. Business case stage
1	a. Document date
Total - 6	**Organization, social systems, and others**
Sub-total - 6	9. Social systems
1	a. The organization including the corporate culture
4	b. Stakeholders (eg, the business unit, departments)
1	c. Value chain

Chapter XI
IT Project Planning Based on Business Value Generation

Otavio Prospero Sanchez
Sao Paulo Methodist University & Fundacao Getulio Vargas FGV/EAESP, Brazil

Alberto Luiz Albertin
Fundacao Getulio Vargas FGV/EAESP, Brazil

ABSTRACT

This chapter introduces the Firm-Level Value Creation Model as a means of planning Information Systems projects based on their potential for generating business value. It presents a review of economic literature on firm-level value creation based on the premise that ex-ante economic inefficiencies embedded in the firm processes are the key enabler of effectiveness in IT project implementations. After presenting a detailed case study in the banking industry to discuss the argument, the chapter describes how to implement a practical assessment of the potential effectiveness of any IT project. By presenting the underlying theoretical foundations of the business value generation mechanism, the author intends to contribute to the academy by bringing the economic theories to the center of the analysis of IT value generation. On the other hand, the chapter also assists practitioners by presenting a tool that can identify projects more likely to deliver value.

INTRODUCTION

Achieving effectiveness in Information Technology (IT) projects is becoming increasingly important for organizations as market competition changes and poses threats to value creation at the firm level (Kohli & Devaraj, 2003). Recent literature has emphasized how IT deployment can improve firms' strategic positions based on the difficulty of imitation of the combination of IT and organizational resources (Wade & Hulland, 2004); it has also underscored how rare IT resources can allow a firm to reach a sustainable position of competitive advantage (Melville, Kraemer, & Gurbaxani, 2004).

Many works have shown that the amount invested in IT has reached over 50% of the total of firms' investments. In addition, the proportion of IT investments to net income has increased as business complexity has increased. While it is argued that the use of IT is becoming more expensive to firms as businesses' environmental conditions increase in complexity, other streams of research have argued that it is difficult to evaluate the firm-level benefits of IT uses given the intangibility of many of those benefits.

These intangible benefits are usually associated with the business side of the firm, mainly related to market aspects, geographical presence, and customer satisfaction, among other things. In this sense, IT investment decision prioritization skills tends to become part of the job description of business executives rather than that of IT executives (Bassellier, Benbasat, & Reich, 2003; Tallon, Kraemer, & Gurbaxani, 2000).

Nevertheless, decisions about IT investment have been seen as complex and risky. In an attempt to cope with this complexity and risk, a myriad of interdisciplinary financial and non-financial techniques and methods have been used to support the prioritization processes. These include ROI, Payback, EVA, BSC, cost/benefit, transaction costs, gap analysis, etc. (Schniederjans, Hamaker, & Schniederjans, 2004). In practice, however, organizations usually deal with a number of simultaneous IT projects in a situation in which the costs tend to be more easily identified than the benefits.

Consequently, the ability of executives to identify the benefits of any specific future IT deployment is an important determinant of better investments prioritization, which constrains the possibility of delivering value and business performance. Therefore, shared knowledge between business managers and IT professionals is an important enabler of the alignment of business and IT objectives (Reich & Benbasat,

2000). Based on the above, we have observed two tendencies:

a. Business executives are required to be more involved in IT decisions because they are in a better position to evaluate an intangible, business-related parcel of benefits and,

b. IT executives are demanded to be more involved in business aspects, lowering the emphasis on exclusively technical issues (Bassellier *et al.*, 2003).

However, executives' perceptions of the business value generated by IT deployment is limited (Simon, 1978) because both business and IT executives lack the personal skills necessary to produce an appropriate analysis that encompasses two such diverse domains, with very different rationales (Bassellier *et al.*, 2003; Tallon *et al.*, 2000). Additionally, the success or failure of a firm using IT in business is only partially dependent on how deeply the executives understand the aspects involved. There are some emblematic cases of failure or even unexpectedly sound success in using IT that still require explanation. Some inconsistencies remain unexplained when the best practices are applied, but even so, there has been no IT investment effectiveness observed (Santhanam & Hartono, 2003).

This chapter posits an explanation for those cases through a conceptual framework that supports an understanding of the determinants of the business value that IT generates, revealing situations where potential value is not identified by the methods of analysis currently available. This framework is supported by the *Ex-ante Economic Inefficiency Hypothesis* (*EEIH*), borrowed from the body of economic theories. This proposition poses that informational inefficiencies may be found inside the economic relationship of two agents and lead to sub-optimal allocations of resources—the inadequate uses of the resources involved—which then yield results inferior to the ones that would be possible if those inefficiencies didn't exist (Hunt, 1997; Milgrom & Roberts, 1992; Varian, 1999).

We have applied the *EEIH* to the circumstance of IT deployment and found that *ex-ante* economic inefficiencies *are antecedents of the effectiveness of IT investments in projects that solve them*. In other words, if there is no economic inefficiency to be solved by implementing any specific IT, this investment will not deliver business value—will be not effective—thus resulting in a non-effective investment. Considering a project portfolio decision, one may use EEIH to find out what are the projects most likely to produce business value, and define the project prioritization based on this.

In order to explain how *EEIH* can be used to identify the circumstances where business value can be generated by applying IT, we first present the theoretical background for the hypothesis, which is build on transaction costs theory (Williamson, 1979), neoclassic economic theory (Williamson, 1986), and organizational design economics (Milgrom & Roberts, 1992), among others (Michel Benaroch, 2001; Clemons & Hitt, 2004; Mayer & Salomon, 2006; Orlikowski, 2002; Varian, 1999; Wade & Hulland, 2004).

Then, we present an embedded case study that illustrates how EEIH can be applied in order to prioritize projects in portfolio management. We discuss the reasons that led to the choice of case study and the techniques applied in collecting and analyzing the data. After presenting a general description of the cases, we analyze and present the framework usage and show how the results are achieved. Finally, we discuss the contributions that the theory thus developed brings to the managerial practice and to future research.

FIRM-LEVEL VALUE CREATION

Firm Model

From economic theory, we define firm management as a set of deliberate actions intended to de-

liver value. They involve relationships with other economic agents (Varian, 1999) and an adequate combination of resources and capacities both internal and external to the firm (Mayer & Salomon, 2006; Penrose, 1997). The proper combination of those resources and capacities, along with business strategy, enables the firm to generate and capture part of this value. The firm's management is considered as having made effective choices if the economic value generated and captured is higher then through other viable alternatives and at similar overall risk (Bodie, Kane, & Marcus, 1999; Milgrom & Roberts, 1992).

As an economic agent in the market, the firm's fundamental relationship is established with *Customers*, and the relationship attribute is *Utility*. Hence, *Clients* agree to get into business relationships with the firm depending upon their expectation that they will receive compensation in terms of *Utility*. For this reason, firms develop internal processes based on their internal resources and capacities and, quite possibly, establish new external relationships to get access to required resources and capacities, as long as the integration costs are higher then those of obtaining them outside their boundaries (Williamson, 1986). Often the ability to create value depends on the appropriateness of the strategy in combining internal and external resources and capabilities. This concept, known as *Complementarity*, is described in *Resource-Based View - RBV* literature (Penrose, 1997; Wade & Hulland, 2004). Among other resources and capacities, IT is becoming a fundamental tool for the creation of business value—a change that has accelerated since the emergence of the information economy (Teece, 1992), in which the goods and services utility value is becoming predominantly informational (Evans & Wurster, 2000; Varian & Shapiro, 1999).

Not all resources and capacities that are needed are internally available. Consequently, firm-level value creation depends upon its ability to develop *Cooperation* with *Partners* and *Suppliers*, which contribute materials or pieces of the process that allow the firm to focus on its own internal specialized capabilities (Clemons & Row, 1992; Prahalad & Hamel, 1990) targeted to benefit from scale and scope economies (A. D. Jr. Chandler, 1997).

In order to decide about investing in a specific activity, the firm compares the returns and risks of each product and services portfolio, along with the possibilities of internalizing the required resources and capacities, and compares them with other viable alternatives (Bodie *et al.*, 1999). Essentially, this analysis requires *Information* and the constant monitoring of the business environment (Clemons & Hitt, 2004).

To summarize, as shown in Figure 1, the model guide to the effective management of a firm involves adequately dealing with external relationships with *Customers* and *Partners/ Suppliers*, targeting them to achieve *Complementarities* with regard to a set of *Resources* and *Capacities*, both internal and external, which are intended to generate superior *Economic Value* under a given *Risk*.

Ex-Ante Economic Inefficiency Hypothesis (EEIH)

The argument that economically efficient markets deliver value to the agents is classical within economic literature (Pindyck & Rubinfeld, 2006; Williamson, 1975). The economics literature states that inefficiency within economic agents' relationships is due to imperfect market organization, which leads to sub-optimal overall generated value. It means that once those inefficiencies are solved, the ex-post result is better than the ex-ante, allowing the economic agents to benefit from the value generated (Varian, 1999).

Considering that businesses are essentially relationships performed between agents, and since such relationships are in most part informational, it is possible to admit the hypothesis that economic inefficiencies on those processes might be associated to a lack of capability to conduct informational processes. A number of researchers have developed this argument based

Figure 1. Firm-level value creation model

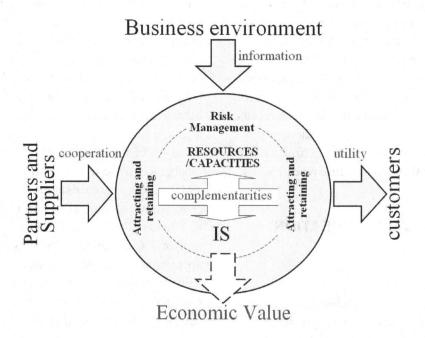

on economic theories, yet their works are spread over different areas such as economics and Information Technology (Bailey & Bakos, 1997; Barua, Kriebel, & Mukhopadhyay, 1995; Brynjolfsson, 1993; Brynjolfsson & Hitt, 2003; Casson, 1994; Clemons & Hitt, 2004; Kohli & Devaraj, 2003; Mayer & Salomon, 2006; Melville *et al.*, 2004; Porter, 2001; Shapiro & Katz, 1986; Teece, 1992; Varian & Shapiro, 1999).

Table 1 presents a non-exhaustive set of literature references in this area, classified in accordance with the five dimensions represented in the model shown in Figure 1, and configures the ex-ante research construct of this work (Eisenhardt, 1989).

Because the IT deployment can mitigate preexisting informational economic inefficiency between agents, identifying the possible causes of the previous inefficiencies may help one to better decide about the prioritization of IT projects that have the potential to solve them. This chapter uses the *EEIH* as a conceptual framework to support the view that a firm can generate value by solving previous economic inefficiencies present inside

its relationships with other economic agents, leading to better IT investment and prioritization decisions.

Investment Decision Process and Value Perception

Almost all methods for guiding IT investment decisions assume the supposition that positive net value will be generated by the deployment of IT. However, it is difficult to determine precisely the cost-benefit relation of each investment project, as the costs are usually more easily expressed in financial terms than are the benefits. There are many forms of intangible benefits to be considered in any assessment of IT investment described by the literature, and the decision-maker perception is of fundamental importance (Gardner, 2000; Schniederjans *et al.*, 2004).

In the time domain of an IT project's implementation, there are two kinds of value perception recognized by the literature: (a) *Potential Value*, which expresses the maximum value that can be generated by an IT utilization, assessed before

Table 1. Dimensions, economic concepts and literature references

Model Dimensions	Main Economic Concepts	Economic Theory References
UTILITY (Customer relationship)	Localization, Substitution e Transaction Costs; Coordination; Standardization; Reputation/Warranties; Moral Hazard, Adverse Selection	(Bailey & Bakos, 1997; Evans & Wurster, 2000; Melville *et al.*, 2004; Milgrom & Roberts, 1992; Porter, 2001; Varian, 1999; Venkatraman & Henderson, 1998; Williamson, 1979)
COOPERATION (Partner and Suppliers relationship)	Co-specialization; Transaction volume and frequency; Reputation/ Warranties; Externalities; Concentration; Coordination; Complementarities	(Casson, 1994; A. D. Jr. Chandler, 1997; Milgrom & Roberts, 1992; Porter, 2001; Shapiro & Katz, 1986; Stalk, Evans, & Shulman, 1992; Teece, 1992; Varian & Shapiro, 1999; Venkatraman & Henderson, 1998; Williamson, 1986, 1996)
COMPLEMENTARITIES (Capacities and Resources relationship)	Complementarities (internal and external); Technical substitution of the factor; Opportunity costs	(Barua *et al.*, 1995; Brynjolfsson & Hitt, 2003; A. D. Jr Chandler, 1990; A. D. Jr. Chandler, 1997; Penrose, 1997; Porter, 2001; Powell & Micallef, 1997; Prahalad & Hamel, 1990; Stalk *et al.*, 1992; Teece, 1987, 1992; Varian, 1999; Wade & Hulland, 2004)
RISK (Environment relationship)	Information Asymmetry; Real options; Technological advances; Networks externalities; Lock-in	(M. Benaroch & Kauffman, 1999; Bodie *et al.*, 1999; Casson, 1994; Simon, 1978; Teece, 1992; Varian, 1999; Venkatraman & Henderson, 1998; Williamson, 1996)
ECONOMIC VALUE	Scope and Scale economies; Transaction costs; Coordination costs	(Brynjolfsson, 1993; Brynjolfsson & Hitt, 1996; Hunt, 1997; Kaplan & Norton, 1996; Melville *et al.*, 2004; Williamson, 1996)

the implementation (*ex-ante perceived value*); and (b) *Realized Value*, the value derived from the implementation (*ex-post perceived value*) (Davern & Kauffman, 2000). The actual *ex-post* achievement of the *Potential Value* depends on a number of possible barriers being overcome, which are found during the implementation process—such as the lack of managerial and technical skills, budget limitations, time restrictions etc., as illustrated in Figure 2.

Success or Failure of IT Projects

Executives frequently have a limited ability to perceive the business value of IT. This is due to a lack of specific skill at understanding a set of complex circumstances related to very different domains of knowledge, like business and technology management and strategies (Bassellier *et al.*, 2003; Simon, 1978; Tallon *et al.*, 2000). An executive's lack of understanding of the rationales related to these different areas may cause him or her to undervalue a project's Potential Value, which may lead to a limitation of resources or even eliminate viable projects, which are thereby deemed not valuable enough. Yet, Potential Value may be also overvalued, and this is what misleads those executives who tend to over-invest in low-potential projects. Both circumstances can contribute to the low firm-level overall effectiveness of an IT investment portfolio: they can either underem-

phasize (or even eliminate) good IT investment options or overemphasize bad projects, wasting resources, as illustrated in Figure 3 .

We may define the effectiveness of an IT investment as the relation between the potential value that the IT project may ideally deliver to the business and the value that a firm actually achieves by using it.

$$IS\_Investment\_effectiveness = \frac{Potential\_Value}{Realized\_Value}$$

However, executives present a lack of value perception that is much more influential in the planning phase than after implementation has ended. The reason is that executives have limited skill at connecting and applying the knowledge within both areas—business and technology—which is required during the planning phase. After the IT implementation has ended, the resulting business value can be more easily assessed than during the previous stages, as executives can observe it directly or by means of consequent business variables such as market share, brand image, customer satisfaction, etc. In order to effectively guide the use of firm resources, executives should better understand how technology might generate business value during the previous steps of the analysis of portfolio management.

We introduced the concept of "Idealized Potential Value" in the model previously offered

Figure 2. Implementation barriers to firm-level value realization

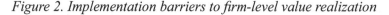

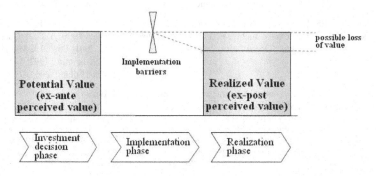

by Davern and Kauffman (Davern & Kauffman, 2000) to illustrate the influence of the executive's lack of perception during the earlier stages of the IT deployment, as shown in Figure 3. Since the misunderstanding of how IT contributes to business value is a source of the low effectiveness of IT investment projects, executives should improve their skill at determining Idealized Potential Value.

Admittedly, EEIH is the underlying principle that explains Idealized Potential Value. Economic value is generated by applying IT in business situations where previous economic inefficiencies exist, as long the IT implementations solve them. Following this assumption, we conducted this research to verify how useful EEIH is in assessing Idealized Potential Value, how skilled executives are in identifying the EEIH attributes, and how effective executives' investment decisions actually are.

METHODOLOGY

We adopted the case study research strategy because it is considered adequate for the investigation of contemporary phenomena, especially the ones where the context and the boundaries of the phenomenon are not evident (Yin, 2002). The case study is a particularly recommended research strategy when its intent is to build a theory that answers questions about *what* and *how* something happens, by means of the observation of the phenomenon in its natural environment, allowing one to understand the relationship between and complexity of its elements (Benbasat, Goldstein, & Mead, 1987; Eisenhardt, 1989).

The case study adopted an explanatory perspective and was conducted with extreme cases. By extreme cases, we mean occurrences of either failure or surprising success with IT implementations within IT skilled companies. These cases were analyzed from the point of view of the EEIH hypothesis and in accordance with the methodological procedure described in this section.

Sample Definition

The sample was intentionally defined (Eisenhardt, 1989; Yin, 2002) considering the following requirements:

a. The firms should be identified as leaders in the economic sector and should be information-intensive. The firms should also be proficient in the use of IT and have shown significant annual investment in IT implementations for at least five years. These conditions, combined, were considered as *a proxy* for the wisdom in using IT that is gained through access to best-practices for

Figure 3. Executive's lack of perception and consequences on IT investments effectiveness

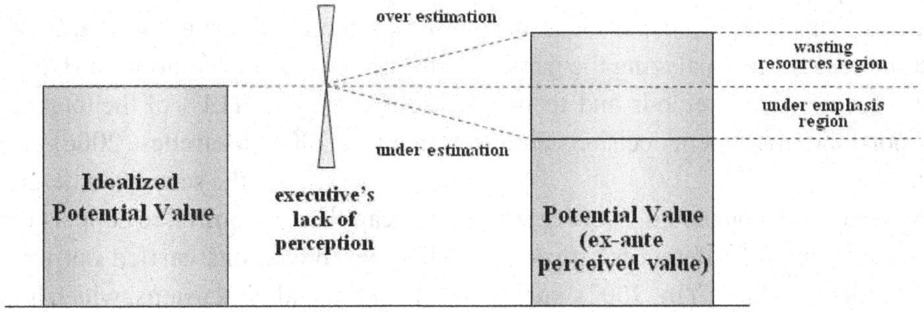

IT deployment, as well as for business and IT strategies combination;

b. They should have implemented a significant number of IT projects during the last five years, with "significant" defined at the level of at least 500 projects per year;

c. They should present business relationships with business partners as skilled in IT implementations as they are. Having fulfilled all the conditions above, the firms should also present similarities to one another in order to allow for theoretical replication between the cases (Eisenhardt, 1989) (Yin, 2002). We considered similar banks that presented almost the same net incomes, numbers of employees and organizational structures.

The underlying logic that oriented the research was the study of cases where IT implementation was considered either a failure or a surprising success, and where—in either case—available methods of IT portfolio decision-making could not explain the outcomes. We adopted the relation between *Realized Value* and *Perceived Value* as a definition of success. So, cases of low *Realized Value* compared to relatively high *Perceived Value* were considered cases of failure, cases of high *Realized Value* compared to relatively low *Perceived Value* were considered cases of success.

We considered the condition of IT proficiency a key to the study because we wanted to focus attention on previous economic inefficiencies as antecedents of *Perceived Value*, rather than considering any other circumstance derived from a lack of ability or knowledge with regard to managing IT implementation issues. In other words, IT-skilled firms were the ideal locus in which to find the cases fit for analyzing the gaps presented by the up-to-date methods and techniques for IT portfolio investment decisions and management.

Hence, the study was conducted in order to avoid other possible causes of differences between Potential and Realized values (Yin, 2002), such as the inability of firm executives to manage the process of implementation, any misalignment between IT and business strategies, team inadequacies, resources limitations, guidance pitfalls, project management failures, etc.

We adopted the strategy of selecting organizations in a wealthy information-intensive sector of the economy because these organizations were more likely to be skilled in the up-to-date methods and techniques of IT decision prioritization. Equally important was to find organizations with a proven history of intensive use of IT, showing a significant number of IT implementations during a long period.

Moreover, in the chosen firms, the IT usage had to be seen as key to business value creation. Accordingly to this requirement, our decision was to select firms that are leaders in a competitive information-intensive sector of the economy (a *proxy* for skill in extracting business value from IT) and seen by the market as leaders in IT usage (a *proxy* for skill in IT and project management).

We selected the Brazilian banking sector because it is considered a mature, worldwide-competitive information-intensive sector of the economy, one that is building a vigorous financial market after decades of IT implementations of fast and flexible systems that were required in the old hyper-inflation environment. Nowadays, from the point of view of the quality of the IT skills thereby developed, this heritage of hyperinflation can be considered positive. The players have learnt many lessons and can now exhibit years of experience in banking technological innovation at a worldwide competition level. For example, the total expended in IT by the sector was equivalent to US$ 5.5 billion during the year 2004, according to the Brazilian Federation of Banks (Febraban, 2006), reaching 11.1% of the total net income in the year 2005 (Meirelles, 2006). The IT adoption maturity in the sector can be exemplified by the capillarity required to support the volume of banking operations carried out in this country of continental dimensions, which has around 8.5

millions of square kilometers, and by the sheer number of electronic transactions, as shown in Table 2.

In order to identify a representative sample of the sector, we selected the major banks in Brazil from a list of banks ordered by total assets and provided by the Brazilian Central Bank (Banco Central do Brasil, 2006), as shown in Table 3. The criteria for selecting banks in terms of IT usage proficiency were based on IT magazines. The procedure involved selecting from IT-specialized magazines that have a regular process for electing the best cases of IT implementation. Thus, we prepared a second list of firms that were so distinguished at least twice in five years in the sector of financial and banking services.

A final list of eight institutions emerged when we compared the two lists against each other. After identifying the target institutions, we evaluated each one for the degree of possible access to information, since we aimed to conduct an in-depth search for evidence and many interviews would be needed within many different departments. The purpose of this strategy was to collect evidence intended for data triangulation (Eisenhardt, 1989; Yin, 2002).

Is this phase, we used phone calls and emails to the main executives at the institutions. We created and followed a standard letter explaining to the executives the objectives and procedures of the research; we included a clause guaranteeing the secrecy of the study to executives who might so desire it. After making the initial contacts, we focused on three financial institutions that granted enough access to information within the various branches of the organization structure. The three institutions belong to the Brazilian private financial sector and have similar customer profiles and operations covering the whole country. They are among the Top 7 private banks in the Brazilian banking market: they hold 22% of the assets in the banking sector, as well as 28% of the total equity, and manage more than 20% of the country's deposits, counting 4,000+ agencies in March of 2005 according to the Brazilian Central Bank (Banco Central do Brasil, 2006). Below, we summarize the profiles of the cases.

Case 1: Bank A is one of the major international private capital banks in the Brazilian market. It is also present in 70 countries and takes part in a nationwide conglomerate of financial companies

Table 2. Brazilian banking sector - electronic automation increment (Source: FEBRABAN, 2006, p.4)

(Millions of Transactions)	*2002*	*2003*	*2004*	*2004/2003*
Automatic debts, payroll etc	599	610	667	9.4%
Automatic taxes and others	3,893	6,758	7,514	11.2%
Auto-services, deposits, checks, clearing	6,094	7,585	9,891	30.4%
Home and Office Banking	970	1,174	1,862	58.6%
Internet Banking	1,139	1,457	2,045	40.4%
POS	549	581	1,002	72.5%
Branches transactions	4,463	4,451	3,609	- 8.9%
Compensated checks	2,397	2,246	2,107	-6.2%
Call Centers w/ attendant	380	321	301	-6.3%
Call Centers w/o attendant (AAU)	1,133	994	850	- 4.5%
Banking correspondents	-	125	187	49.6%
TOTAL	*21,617*	*26,302*	*30,035*	*14.2%*

that reached an equity value of over US$ 6 billion in 2005 as well as an assets volume of over US$ 30 billion, according to the Brazilian Central Bank (2006). Bank A has more than 12 million clients and 28,000 workers supported by a complex information system that processes around 150 million transactions per month. In real time, the system network integrates 6,000 points of sale, over 1,900 branches and 600 Automatic Teller Machines (ATMs) that operate 4 million cash accounts and 1.9 million low-income financial applications all over the country. The academic and professional profiles of Case 1 interviewees show the organization's emphasis on the professionalism of the team. Many of them hold both business and technical top international-level scholarly degrees. In particular, the vice-president of technology is a very well-known professional in the IT community. The focus of the IT team management has been to shift the executive's predominant technical-skilled profile to a more business-like profile. The interviewees hold the following positions in the organizational structure: Vice-president of Technology; IT director; Executive Superintendent of Retail Solutions; Executive Superintendent of Internet; Execu-tive Superintendent of Intelligence Solutions; and Executive Superintendent of Services and Operations.

Case 2: Bank B is a major private bank in the Brazilian market with a minor foreign share. It belongs to a financial conglomerate with US$ 4 billion of equity value, assets valued at over US$ 36 billion, and around 23,000 workers, according to the Brazilian Central Bank (Banco Central do Brasil, 2006). Its countrywide banking services network interconnects 17,000 points of sale, as well as a financial transaction capture network of 900 branches, 350 branches with affiliated company partners and 2,700 ATMs. These facilities oper-ate 13 million in currency accounts and low-tier financial applications. Bank B implements 500 IT projects every year on average. The organi-zational structure is highly professional and the IT staff focuses in bridging business areas and fulfilling their demands. Bank B interviewees hold the following positions in the organizational structure: Executive Director of IT; Superinten-dent of Business Support Architecture; and IT investments Manager.

Table 3. Brazilian banking sector, as March, 2005 (Source: BANCO CENTRAL DO BRASIL, 2006)

Pos	Institution	Total Asset (US$ 1000)	Equity (US$ 1000)	Net Income (US$ 1000)	currency deposits (US$ 1000)	Number of workers
1	Banco do Brasil	122,231,522	7,429,302	479,891	59,749,499	103,965
2	Caixa E. Federal	77,867,402	3,471,381	236,275	48,352,257	104,435
3	Bradesco	77,015,512	8,231,370	599,815	35,554,496	67,531
4	Itau	69,741,843	8,343,191	644,900	22,005,894	47,918
5	Unibanco	37,528,398	4,283,472	206,449	17,845,824	23,282
6	Santander Banespa	35,785,166	4,123,618	151,233	11,751,657	21,380
7	ABN AMRO	32,380,627	4,543,578	105,040	16,749,746	28,297
8	HSBC	20,837,363	1,400,672	72,555	12,893,253	25,942
9	Safra	19,177,576	1,841,389	69,416	4,782,880	4,786
10	Nossa Caixa	15,427,446	1,115,984	44,225	10,932,850	14,316

Case 3: Bank C is a Top 3 private bank in the Brazilian market, owning 20,000 access points that span every geographic region of the country. It has a structure of 48,000 workers that supports 20 million clients and processes 12 million transactions per day. Bank C is part of a financial conglomerate with US$ 8 billion of equity value and over US$ 70 billion in assets, according to the Brazilian Central Bank (Banco Central do Brasil, 2006). Its network interconnects more than 20,000 points of sale and branches operating over 35 million currency and small applications accounts. The transaction capture network counts on more than 22,000 ATMs, making Bank C a worldwide standard in banking services automation. The Internet banking services systems provide operations to more than 5 million frequent users. In the year 2005 alone, 400 million Internet banking transactions were completed. The Bank C interviewees hold the following positions in the organizational structure: Vice President of Operations, IT Executive Director, and Superintendent of Budget & Control.

Data Gathered

The data was collected by way of direct interviews and direct observation during one six-month period, from October 2005 to March 2006. The sole interviewer produced a case study protocol to guide the interviews and observations. After specialists assessed the protocol, we tested it in a pilot case, selected from among the three institutions identified. The interviewees were selected from within the organizational structure by means of a questionnaire designed to map the current IT investment decision structure and processes as well as the main *stakeholders* of the projects.

Each team decided what IT projects should be assessed after the researcher explained the need to find extreme situations (Eisenhardt, 1989; Yin, 2002) in which the *Realized Value* would be very different from the *Perceived Value*. We verified that this criterion was met independent of any bias of the team during the interview process, using additional evidence, control questions, individual interview sections, and material evidence (Davis *et al.*, 1992; Yin, 2002).

Researchers have used three types of interview analysis to interpret the meaning of an interviewee's narrative: hermeneutics, narrative, and semiotics (Davis *et al.*, 1992). These techniques were particularly useful in this case as the interviewees recreated the rationale for their decisions (usually made some time before the interview was conducted), tending to interpret the past in ways that were more favorable to themselves, especially when they had been agents of the decisions or their implementation (Avison & Myers, 1995).

Table 4. Perception of project failure/success

Bank		Project	Initial Assessment		Final Assessment	
A	1	Customer relationship management		Very promising	Failure	
	2	Correspondent agent facility	Promising		Success (ongoing)	
	3	Home broker	Less promising			Very successful
B	4	Call center	Promising		Success	
	5	Cost allocation system		Very promising	Failure	
	6	Extract emitter	Promising		Failure	
C	7	Payment receipt emitter	Less promising			Very successful
	8	Currency logistics planner	Promising			Very successful

*Table 5. Evaluation and argument example for **UTILITY** dimension*

Bank		Project	Potential of business value generation	Argument example
A	1	Customer relationship management	(+) potential	"...initially we found this tool as very important for identifying the customer needs along all the Bank segments, but that actually didn't happened ..."
	2	Correspondent agent facility	Very high	"...the value comes from the reduction of customer's difficulties to find the alternative of product that fits well. So, the customers now have access to the correct product offer through the right channel since a capillary access was achieved..."
	3	Home broker	Very high	"...the broker now provides a service that otherwise should be provided by a phone call, passing through an operator. Using the system, the customer no longer needs to wait for counseling, but goes straight to the solution wanted.... Many of them(customers) don't need counseling and see the operator as a barrier to be overcame, not exactly a facilitation ..."
B	4	Call center	No	"...The operation already exists. It is only an internal automation..."
	5	Cost allocation system	(+) potential	"...and we thought it would result in better cost structure identification which ultimately would result in cost reductions..."
	6	Extract emitter	(- -) Utility reduction	"...this project eliminated an important not formal channel of communication with the customers, and afterwards they became to find it very hard to get the information they need..."
	7	Payment receipt emitter	Existent, but hidden	"...we never expected that. Actually, the customers were keen to receive information about the check liquidation that we didn't think before. Once the solution was online, many customers realized that the old process was very bureaucratic and became heavy users of the system..."
C	8	Currency logistics planner	No	"...This is a kind of internal automation which has no direct impact to customers, but to overall currency logistics optimization..."

RESULTS AND DISCUSSION

As shown in Table 4, the results of the assessment are revealing. There are a number of situations where unexpected discrepancies between initial and final assessments are revealed. Even in a very skilled, information intensive industry that is able to acquire best-practices for producing good investment decisions, one may definitely observe the interesting existence of these unbalanced perceptions.

There are substantial gaps between initial perceptions of business value and the final perceptions of the value actually created. The interviewees judged three of eight projects as failing to deliver the initially expected business value, while other three projects were found surprisingly successful and yet suffered budget limitations during their implementation. It is valuable to note that this proportion does not represent the banks' figures overall, as we intentionally selected the extreme cases.

The data collection procedure involves identifying the possible presence of inefficiencies situations as defined by *EEIH* following the literature predictions as shown in Figure 1 and Table 1. The embedded cases (specific IT projects) were assessed in terms of their potential for solving the inefficiencies found in the theoretical referential listed in

Table 1. For example, consider the possibility of a *Home Broker* application that, once implemented, diminishes the customer's need for information and eases the process of finding of any required product or service. According to the model in Figure 1 and the theoretical framework in

Table 1, this application would be evaluated as positive in terms of its potential to generate value because, if it were deployed, it would contribute to reducing the localization costs customers incur.

The same procedure was executed for each dimension and IT project as we looked to find the inefficiencies that could be present in each relationship. We defined the intensity of the *Potential Value* of a specific project based on the existence of economic inefficiencies as foreseen in Figure 1. The researcher and the interviewees assessed the impact of these inefficiencies depending upon the overall strategy of the bank. For example, if the institution's overall strategy is to capture market share by delivering value to low-end customers, capillary access to these customers is a very important feature. In this case, an IT application that allows the bank to reach customers, lowering the localization costs that customers incur, thereby contributes to *Potential Value*. The researcher worked as a group facilitator in meetings designed for this purpose. One major aim was to keep the researcher from over-influencing the interviewees' interpretations.

The group considered each dimension of the framework, analyzing each project for any possibility of economic inefficiencies and their possible impact on business value, given the overall institution strategy. Table 6 illustrates the results of the assessment of the five dimensions for the eight projects.

The column *"Economic Inefficiencies Solved and Contribution to Potential Value"* presents the consensus of the group about the value the project could generate once implemented, given the existence of the economic inefficiency observed (if any). The *Revised Potential Value* category, shown in column five, tabulates these contributions for each project. On the other hand, *Previously Perceived Potential Value,* in the same column, shows previous perceptions of Potential Value made using all available tools and techniques except *EEIH*. Differences arise when one compares both values for each project, leading to the

recommendation found in column 6 of Table 6. When comparing *Revised Potential Value* with *Previously Perceived Potential Value*, we find that the expectations are to be kept only for Projects 2 and 4, while the expectations for the other six projects should be revised. When comparing the results shown in Table 6 with the content of Table 4, we can conclude that there is a complete match. The "Significantly Decrease" recommendation in Table 6 is applicable to Projects 1, 5 and 6, and failure is the perceived result for the same projects, as shown in Table 4. This perfect match also happens for the successful projects: Projects 3, 7 and 8. This perfect match indicates that it is valid to generalize from the results found using the *EEIH* concept in order to improve executives' perception of value, as recommended by Eisenhardt (Eisenhardt, 1989).

Together with the results above, we identified some important aspects of the perception of Potential Value:

a. The decision process has to be well-structured. It requires the complete identification of the executives responsible for the information and demands that the criteria be established before the decision-making process starts;

b. Those of the executives' abilities that are required in order to identify economic inefficiencies should be improved; it is not currently a structured process, yet it is also not difficult to implement.

The structure of the decision-making process: This is an important consideration. The role of the decision structure is essential in the organization in facilitating the perception of value. Usually, economic inefficiencies happen on the borders of the functional areas inside the companies where executives are not completely aware of the details involved in business relationships. Consequently, the possible economic inefficiency observed becomes an issue to be solved by two

*Table 6. Revision of the potential value by using the concepts of **EEIH***

Bank		Project	Business strategy attribute	Economic Inefficiencies Solved and Contribution to Potential Value (+ or -)	Revised Potential Value X Previously Perceived Potential Value	After-Assessment Expectation Correction (-) (+)
A	1	Customer relationship management	Customer value	Utility (+, potential)	Potential Value / Perceived Value	Significantly Decrease
	2	Correspondent agent facility	Market share	Cooperation (+ +) Utility (+ +) Risk management (-)	Potential Value / Perceived Value	Maintain
	3	Home broker	Assets utilization	Utility (++) Complementarities (++)	Potential Value / Perceived Value	Significantly Increase
B	4	Call center	Assets utilization	Complementarities (+) cooperation (+)	Potential Value / Perceived Value	Maintain
	5	Cost allocation system	Cost structure optimization (potential)	Complementarities (- -) risk management (- -) utility (+, potential)	Potential Value / Perceived Value	Significantly Decrease
	6	Extract emitter	Cost structure optimization	Utility (- -)	Potential Value / Perceived Value	Significantly Decrease
	7	Payment receipt emitter	Customer value	Utility (+ +) Complementarities (+)	Potential Value / Perceived Value	Significantly Increase
C	8	Currency logistics planner	Assets utilization	Cooperation (+)	Potential Value / Perceived Value	Increase

or more executives. None of them is completely focused on it, as the responsibility on the border is not well-defined. For example, a decision about a system ultimately intended to create value for the customer may involve, among others, such multiple objectives as technological risk, organiza-tional impacts, the existence of complementarities with other internal resources, and economies of scale and scope. In this case, the problem is how to structure the decision-making process within the organization in order to emphasize these important aspects, with their perception usually not assigned to the unilateral authority of a specific executive but rather distributed within the organization as illustrated in Figure 1.

Executive's abilities: The concept of EEIH is not always present in the mindset of the executives who make decisions about IT investments. During our research, we found that the ability to understand pertinent concepts is present in the organizations, but not in an organized way. It is not a structured skill, it is hardly perceived, and it is not regularly used in these organizations-especially for IT investment decisions.

HOW TO IMPLEMENT THE PROJECT PRIORITIZATION BASED ON *EEIH*

The main consideration is that *EEIH*, when combined with the multidimensional model shown in Figure 1, also results in a multidimensional variable. Executives have to analyze this overall result based on the strategic propositions of the firm. The question is how to properly evaluate the potential value given that it is produced in four different dimensions.

There are a number of possibilities for fulfilling the analysis. First, the executives may define scores for the four dimensions, considering their relative importance for business strategy. For example, one might consider a firm as strongly dependent on the supply chain, based on its market segment, competitors' strategies, and consumer requirements. This hypothetical situation could

produce the scores for the four dimensions as shown in Table 7.

A number of tools may be applied to produce the executive group consensus shown in Table 7. In our studies, we used the AHP—Analytic Hierarchy Process (Saaty, 1990)—to determine the dimensions' scores for each firm researched. After having established the relative scores for the dimensions based on the strategic propositions of the firm, we ranked the projects based on the grades attributed to them considering the *EEIH* as described earlier. We adopted a 5-degree scale for evaluating each dimension with reference to each project, as listed in Table 8 . The scale we have adopted had negative numbers (-2; -1) attributed to the projects that would create economic inefficiency with respect to the correspondent dimension evaluated. For example, Project 2 as shown in Table 8 poses a risk increase to the firm because its technology is considered new and not compatible with firm standards (-2 grade). The inverse was also applied, as the scale shows positive scores (+1; +2) attributed to projects that contribute to the elimination of the economic inefficiencies previously found in the firm. For example, in Table 8, Project 1 reduces the localization costs imposed on the customers who find it difficult to locate better service solutions for their needs, earning a grade of 2 in the UTILITY dimension.

The full list of projects may be properly ranked by combining the scores presented in Table 7 and Table 8.

However, executives may consider it difficult to translate the firm strategy into the terms shown in

Table 7. Example of a hypothetic firm strategic score

Dimension	Score
UTILITY (Customer relationship)	10%
COOPERATION (Partner and Suppliers relationship)	50%
COMPLEMENTARITIES (Capacities and Resources relationship)	20%
RISK (Environment relationship)	20%

*Table 8. Example of a project portfolio prioritization based on **EEIH***

Dimension	Project 1	Project 2	Project 3	...	Project n
UTILITY (Customer relationship)	2	1	0	...	-2
COOPERATION (Partner and Suppliers relationship)	-1	-1	1	...	-1
COMPLEMENTARITIES (Capacities and Resources relationship)	0	-1	-1	...	0
RISK (Environment relationship)	2	-2	1	...	2

Figure 4. Four-dimension IT project potential value

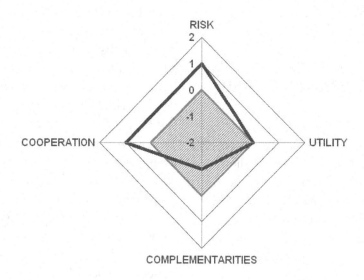

Table 7 for a number of reasons. In this case, the IT project prioritization can be based on a more "qualitative" perspective, as shown in Figure 4, produced with only the data in an assessment similar to the one illustrated in Table 8. Without having to establish a precise strategic score, one may assess the absolute impact of the project on business value based on EEIH. Figure 4 illustrates the IT project example identified as Project 3 in Table 8. Based on the data provided, this project shows positive contributions to *Potential Value* with reference to RISK and COOPERATION while demonstrating a negative impact in terms of COMPLEMENTARITIES.

The projects can then be ranked based on the observed area outside the shaded area in Figure

4, which is proportional to the executive's perception of the IT project's Potential Value based on *EEIH*.

CONCLUSION

Considering that IT is a strategic and expensive resource, firms have been looking forward to finding new ways of better managing this resource. Many specialists have recognized that important parts of the benefits of using IT are intangible—and, therefore, difficulty to measure.

However, in trying to evaluate any IT project portfolio, executives need to correctly evaluate the intangible benefits in order to make better decisions about investments and project prioritization. Firms have been involving business executives in this task because they usually present the most well-developed profile for understanding the business benefits of using IT. The decision is frequently made through a comparison between costs and benefits. Costs often are measurable, at least in aggregated form. For example, many organizations use the zero-based budget technique, where the costs are centralized and afterwards shared among the business areas based on any specific allocation criteria, such as hours of development or others. The business areas are ultimately responsible for business results and so have to decide why, when, where, and how IT should be implemented in order to better add value to business. However, neither IT executives nor business executives are completely aware of the intricacies of this process because it requires knowledge from very different areas and supported by very diverse rationales.

Some sectors of the economy, mainly those that are information-intensive, demand that successful firms use IT extensively in order to compete. In certain sectors—such as the banking industry, for example—the use of IT is absolutely mandatory. In consequence, firms in this sector have developed very good skills over the years: they successfully deploy and capture value through IT projects. Still, it is amusing to see how, despite having access to best-practices regarding how to implement IT projects, executives often display low effectiveness in IT investments. Executives are interested in improving their ability to better decide about IT investments and prioritize IT projects, as IT is a strategic and expensive resource.

The best-practices and available knowledge used by firms in order to avoid issues of low effectiveness are not good enough. Even in applying them, firms have faced uncertain situations because some projects have presented unexpected results. In many cases, executives fail to get the expected results from projects that were previously intended to deliver high business value. In some other cases, executives face unexpectedly high value delivered by projects they did not predict would do so.

The methods and theories currently available for project portfolio prioritization are not sufficient to predict the success or failure of IT investments. There is an underlying cause, exposed only by the use of the *EEIH*, which can shed light on the cases where IT projects failed. The latent economic inefficiency in the context where the IT project is intended to be deployed is revealed as the real cause of such dissonant results found in the market. In applying the concepts of the *EEIH*, we find that IT deployment in business situations where previous economic inefficiencies have not been observed delivers no business value. In contrast, it is reasonable to expect that a high degree of business value be generated if IT is harnessed in order to solve economic inefficiencies inside business relationships. Of course, the intensity of the *Potential Value* of a specific IT project will depend upon the specific business strategy.

This chapter shows how and why the *EEIH* is found to be an underlying cause of business value generated by IT implementation. The set of techniques presented here can help executives to better identify the *Potential Value* of a specific IT implementation and therefore prioritize the overall portfolio.

Furthermore, our analysis has clarified that executives' skill in identifying previous economic inefficiencies determines the effectiveness of IT investments. Even in very skilled firms, however, the use of this skill is still not usually structured; it is not routinely activated by managers and not universally utilized during IT investment decisions, even though best-practices and methods may be widely available.

REFERENCES

Avison, D. E., & Myers, M. D. (1995). Information technology and anthropology: An anthropological perspective on IT and organizational culture. *Information Technology & People, 8*(3), 43-57.

Bailey, J. P., & Bakos, J. Y. (1997). An exploratory study of the emerging role of electronic intermediaries. *International Journal of Electronic Commerce, 1*(3), 7-21.

Banco Central do Brasil (2006). Evolution of accountable values of financial institutions in Brazil. Retrieved jun, 13, 2006, from http://www.bcb.gov.br/fis/TOP50/port/Top502005030P.asp

Barua, A., Kriebel, C. H., & Mukhopadhyay, T. (1995). Information technologies and business value: An analytic and empirical investigation. *Information Technology Research, 6*(1), 3-24.

Bassellier, G., Benbasat, I., & Reich, B. H. (2003). The influence of business managers' IT competence on championing. *Information Technology Research, 14*(4), 317-337.

Benaroch, M. (2001). Option-based management of technology investment risk. *IEEE Transactions on Engineering Management, 48*(4), 428-445.

Benaroch, M., & Kauffman, R. (1999). A case for using real options pricing analysis to evaluate information technology project investments. *Information Technology Research, 10*(1), 70-87.

Benbasat, I., Goldstein, D. K., & Mead, M. (1987). The case research strategy in studies of information technology. *MIT Quarterly, 5*(4), 369-386.

Bodie, Z., Kane, A., & Marcus, A. J. (1999). *Investments* (4th ed.). Irwin / McGraw-Hill.

Brynjolfsson, E. (1993). The productivity paradox of information technology. *Communications of the ACM, 35*(12), 66-78.

Brynjolfsson, E., & Hitt, L. M. (1996). Productivity, business profitability and consumer surplus: Three different measures of information technology value. *MIT Quarterly.*

Brynjolfsson, E., & Hitt, L. M. (2003). Computing productivity: Firm level evidence. *Review of Economics & Statistics, 85*(4), 793-809.

Casson, M. C. (1994). Why are firms hierarchical? *Journal of Economics of Business, 1*(1), 47-77.

Chandler, A. D. J. (1990). *Sale and scope - The dynamics of industrial capitalism.* London: Harvard University Press.

Chandler, A. D. J. (1997). Strategy and structure - Chapters in the history of the industrial enterprise. In N. J. Foss (Ed.), *Resourses firms and strategies* (pp. 40-51). New York: Oxford University Press.

Clemons, E. K., & Hitt, L. M. (2004). Poaching and the misappropriation of information: Transaction risks of information exchange. *Journal of Management Information Technology, 21*(2), 87-108.

Clemons, E. K., & Row, M. C. I. (1992). Information technology and industrial cooperation: The changing economics of coordination and ownership. *Journal of Management Information Technology, 9*(2), 9-29.

Davern, M. J., & Kauffman, R. J. (2000). Discovering potential and realizing value from information technology investments. *Journal of Management Information Technology, 16*(4), 121-144.

Davis, G. B., Lee, A. S., Nickles, K. R., Chatterjee, S., Hartung, R., & Wu, Y. (1992). Diagnosis of an information system failure: A framework and interpretive process. *Information & Management, 23*(5), 293-319.

Eisenhardt, K. M. (1989). Building theories from case study research. *Academy of Management Review, 14*(4), 532-550.

Evans, P. B., & Wurster, T. S. (2000). *Blown to bits - How the economics of information transforms strategy.* Boston: Harvard Business School Press.

Febraban, F. d. B. B.-. (2006). *Asset ranking of Brazilian banks*. Retrieved June, 13, from http://www.febraban.org.br/Arquivo/Servicos/Dados-dosetor/2006/item13.asp

Gardner, C. (2000). *The valuation of information technology*. New York: John Wiley & Sons.

Hunt, S. D. (1997). Evolutionary economics, endogenous growth models, and resource-advantage theory. *Eastern Economic Journal, 23*(4).

Kaplan, R. S., & Norton, D. P. (1996). *The balanced scorecard: Translating strategy into action*. Boston: Harvard Business School Press.

Kohli, R., & Devaraj, S. (2003). Measuring information technology payoff: A meta-analysis of structural variables in firm-level empirical research. *Information Technology Research, 14*(2), 127-146.

Mayer, K. J., & Salomon, R. M. (2006). Capabilities, contractual hazards, and governance: Integrating resource-based and transaction cost perspectives. *Academy of Management Journal, 49*(5), 942-960.

Meirelles, F. S. (2006). *Administração de Recursos de Informática*. Pesquisa Anual. São Paulo: Centro de Tecnologia da Informação Aplicada - CIA, FGV-EAESP.

Melville, N., Kraemer, K., & Gurbaxani, V. (2004). Review: IT and organizational performance: An integrative model of IT business value. *MIT Quarterly, 28*(2), 283-323.

Milgrom, P., & Roberts, J. (1992). *Economics, organization and management*. Upper Side River NJ: Prentice Hall.

Orlikowski, W. J. (2002). Knowing in practice: Enacting a collective capability in distributed organizing. *Organization Science, 13*(3), 249-274.

Penrose, E. (1997). The theory of the growth of the firm. In N. J. Foss (Ed.), *Resourses, firms and strategies* (pp. 13). New York: Oxford University Press.

Pindyck, R. S., & Rubinfeld, D. L. (2006). *Microeconomia* (6ª ed.). São Paulo: Prentice Hall.

Porter, M. E. (2001). Strategy and the Internet. *Harvard Business Review*, 61-79.

Powell, T. C., & Micallef, A. D. (1997). Information technology as competitive advantage: The role of human, business and technology resources. *Strategic Management Journal, 18*(5), 375-406.

Prahalad, C. K., & Hamel, G.-. (1990). The core competence of the corporation. *Harvard Business Review, to be verified*(May/Jun), 79-92.

Reich, B. H., & Benbasat, I. (2000). Factors that influence the social dimension of alignment between business and information technology objectives. *MIT Quarterly, 24*(1), 81-112.

Saaty, T. L. (1990). How to make a decision: The analytic hierarchy process. *European Journal of Operational Research, 48*(1), 9-26.

Santhanam, R., & Hartono, E. (2003). Issues in linking information technology capability to firm performance. *MIT Quarterly, 27*(1), 125-153.

Schniederjans, M. J., Hamaker, J. L., & Schniederjans, A. M. (2004). *Information technology investment*. New Jersey: World Scientific.

Shapiro, C., & Katz, M. L. (1986). Technology adoption in the presence of network externalities. *Journal of Political Economy, 94*(4), 822-842.

Simon, H. A. (1978). Rationality as process and as product of thought. *The American Economic Review, 68*(2), 1-17.

Stalk, G., Evans, P. B., & Shulman, L. E. (1992). Competing on capabilities: The new rules of corporate strategy. *Harvard Business Review, {to be verified}Mar/Abr*, 57-69.

Tallon, P. P., Kraemer, K. L., & Gurbaxani, V. (2000). Executive's perceptions of business values of information technology: A process-oriented aproach. *Journal of Management Information Technology, 16*(4), 145-174.

Teece, D. J. (1987). Profiting from technological innovation: Implications for integration, collaboration, licensing and public policy. In D. J. Teece (Ed.), *The competitive challenge*. New York: Harper & Row.

Teece, D. J. (1992). Competition, cooperation, and innovation: Organizational arrangements for regimes of rapid technological progress. *Journal of Economic Behavior and Organizations, 18*(1), 1-26.

Varian, H. R. (1999). *Intermediate microeconomics* (5th ed.). New York: W.W. Norton & Company.

Varian, H. R., & Shapiro, C. (1999). *Information rules - A strategic guide to the network economy*. Boston: Harvard Business School Press.

Venkatraman, N., & Henderson, J. (1998). Real strategies for virtual organizing. *Sloan Management Review, 40*(1).

Wade, M., & Hulland, J. (2004). Review: Resource-based view of IT research. *MIT Quarterly, 28*(1), 107-143.

Williamson, O. E. (1975). *Markets and hierarchies*. New York: Free Press.

Williamson, O. E. (1979). Transaction cost economics: The governance of contractual relations. *Journal of Law and Economics, 22*(2), 233-262.

Williamson, O. E. (1986). *Economic organization - Firms, markets and policy control*. New York University Press.

Williamson, O. E. (1996). *The mechanisms of governance*. UK: Oxford University Press.

Yin, R. K. (2002). *Case study research: Design and methods* (3rd ed.). Newbury Park, CA: Sage Publications.

KEY TERMS AND DEFINITIONS

Business Value: Value generated and captured by the firm based on its operations.

EEIH (Ex-Ante Economic Inefficiency Hipotesys): The pre-existent condition for the business value generation of the IT implementation.

IT Payoff: The extent in which a specific project generates benefits comparison to the amount invested.

IT Project Effectiveness: The relationship between actual value generated by the implementation and the ex-ante potential value.

Chapter XII
Managing ICT Based Service Innovation

Bendik Bygstad
Norwegian School of IT, Norway

Gjermund Lanestedt
Lanestedt Consulting, Norway

ABSTRACT

In this chapter the authors investigate the management of service innovation projects; can ICT based service innovation be facilitated by traditional project management thinking? Or should the initiators strive for more interaction with users and other stakeholders, thus organizing the initiatives much looser than what the traditional project work method allows for? Building on a large survey, the authors found that ICT based service innovation was not associated with a tightly run project – focused on cost, time and quality; nor with the presence of a professional project manager. Rather, successful service innovation was found in projects where the service providing organization and the users of the forthcoming services were well integrated in the project. They discuss three alternatives to the traditional project work form model, called Integrated Classic Structure, Mutual Adaptation and TQM, and assess their potential strengths and weaknesses in service innovation, as an agenda for further experimentation and empirical research.

INTRODUCTION

The point of departure and the subject to our investigation is the question of to what extent ICT based service innovation can be successfully facilitated by traditional project management methods. Today, services constitute the dominant part of Western economies, and the innovation of new services is recognized as an important strategy in the global competition (Tidd & Hull,

2003). A particularly interesting strategy is ICT based service innovation, which – combined with the general liberalization of services in the 1990s – has transformed our financial services, telecom and IT, media and several other industries. In the start of the new millennium, we now witness the rapid transformation of even more sectors, as the music industry and e-government.

The management of the service innovation processes is a basic matter of concern here; should service innovation initiatives be organized the same way as high-tech product innovation, i.e. with expert teams in well structured projects? Or should they be organized in some looser fashion, with more interaction with users and other stakeholders? The innovation research communities—both the service innovation and the project management research—are divided on this question. A key issue is the classic trade-off between integration and differentiation known from sociological and project management research, i.e. to what degree should the project be isolated from its mother organization?

BACKGROUND

A project in its classic form is the set-up of a temporary separate organization with a single aim. This allows for a strong focus, but as documented in the thorny relationship between projects and organizations, the same trade-off between differentiation and integration applies here. A number of more or less sophisticated mechanisms to handle this issue, such as steering groups and user representation, are well known to the project communities.

The project management research community has certainly acknowledged this tension between integration and separation. In the *PMI Guide to the Project Management Body of Knowledge* (PMI, 2000) a key issue in Project Management is defined as the management of *scope:* To decide the amount of work to be done and to demarcate

against the work that should not be done. This constitutes the rationale for a planned and manageable project, where the performed activities deliver the business purpose.

Researchers have challenged this classic model as they point out that an increasing share of projects has a wider scope than producing a technical solution. These projects are often termed *business projects,* aiming at organizational innovation and change (Winter, Andersen, Elvin, & Levene, 2006). Other researchers have found that there is a difficult choice between separation and integration: A well-run separate project, with its own identity, rationality and specific results, is not suited to implement its own results back to its mother organization. Correspondingly, the results from projects that are tightly integrated with the organization (but less innovative!) are much easier to implement. This means that project owners and managers actually face the dilemma either to accomplish innovation or to prioritize implementation (Johansson, Löfström, & Ohlsson, 2007).

Do these findings imply that service innovation should *not* be organized as projects? We think there is no easy answer to this, and for certainty there is a need for more knowledge on the topic. We note, as a point of departure, that the overall picture is that the "hard" and "separate" paradigm, as represented in the PMI Guide to the Project Management Body of Knowledge, is predominant. There may be sound reasons for this. One may easily argue that the phenomenal success of the project management discipline the past 60 years rests on the parsimonious clarity of the project concept, which allows the project manager to concentrate on his objectives.

Service Innovation

Innovation research does not agree whether the innovation of services is fundamentally different from the innovation of products (Drejer, 2004). A service is commonly defined as the non-material equivalent of a good. One strand of research, however, has documented empirically that the service innovation *process* often differs from the innovation of products. There are at least two important differences (Tidd & Hull, 2003); first, services are usually developed in close interaction with the customers; second, services are usually innovated in networks rather than in labs.

Further, an ICT based service innovation presents another challenge; it usually redefines the roles of the service provider and the users. An illustrative and very successful example is the Web bank. The real innovation of Internet banking is not the Web software, but the *redefinition of roles*: The bank clerks traditionally conducted most of the actual work, included, of course, the transactions. On Internet, the bank provides the technological infrastructure, the technology is made available 24/7, and the customers are doing the transactions themselves. The actual innovation is the interplay between the providing organization, the new technology and the users (Tidd & Hull, 2003).

This has important bearings for the success of ICT based innovation: it is more dependent on the acceptance of the redefined roles rather than the actual provision of the service. The crucial question in our research context is therefore: Will traditional project management methods support this kind of innovation, where stakeholder behaviour is essential?

A much cited contribution is Atkinson's critique of the "iron triangle" (Atkinson, 1999). His main argument is that the traditional project success criteria of time, cost and quality may conflict with the perceived stakeholder benefits. Steven Alter (Alter, 2000) has showed that these differences in perception relate to a fundamental question of the *scope* of the project: For the software developers success is an attribute of the software produced; for the external stakeholder success can only be measured by business indicators, such as more efficient business processes. A key implication of this research is that it—at least for ICT projects—is essential to differentiate between the *success of the project* (in terms of time, cost and product quality) and the *organizational impact* (in terms of user behaviour and business benefits). As Atkinson argues, the link between project success and organizational impact may be weaker than generally assumed. Thus, to understand ICT based service innovation it is necessary to understand both project success and organizational impact. Specifically, it is important to understand how different project attributes influence on organizational impact of the project results.

Hypotheses

To investigate the relationship between project attributes and the actual service innovation outcome we chose to study a portfolio of public ICT projects where an exploitation of broadband communication was part of the scope. Broadband infrastructure is indeed a powerful enabler of digital services. Therefore, we assumed that these projects offered an interesting opportunity to study technology based service innovation. Our empirical basis was a large, governmental broadband program in Norway, organizing several hundreds of small-scaled, ICT based service innovation projects in the public sector.

Based on our research review three hypotheses were developed. First, we investigated whether the traditional project success criteria were associated with the organizational impact. *Hypothesis A: Successful organizational impact is associated with projects that are completed on time, on budget and with satisfying quality.* This hypothesis builds on the basic theoretical assumption in project management; that the planned activities in a project deliver the business objective (PMI, 2000).

Second, we asked whether the attributes of the project manager were associated with the organizational impact. *Hypothesis B: Successful organizational impact is associated with the use of professional project managers.* This hypothesis also builds on the general assumptions from project management theory (PMI, 2000) and from Information Systems Project theory (Cadle & Yeates, 2004) emphasizing the importance of the ability of the project manager.

Third, we studied whether an integrated project design was associated with organizational impact. This hypothesis was derived from the more general literature on IS implementation success (Markus & Keil, 1994). It also builds on earlier research on the importance of external stakeholders (Alter, 2000; Coakes & Elliman, 1999). *Hypothesis C: Successful organizational impact is associated with projects containing a detailed project plan over the desired organizational effects.* The assumption here was that a project that has assessed and actually planned for the organizational implementation and realisation of benefits, must be considered to be well integrated.

METHOD

To investigate our hypotheses we chose a positivist research approach, focusing on quantitative data (Straub, Gefen, & Boudreau, 2005). In addition, a minor qualitative analysis was done. The quantitative survey was conducted within the frames of a high-profile broadband initiative, the Hoykom program (Norwegian_Research_Council., 2007). It is run by the Norwegian Government, as an important part of their action plan – *eNorway 2009 The Digital Leap* – for modernization of the public sector. The program was initiated in 1999, initially for a period of three years (1999 - 2001), but successively prolonged. Its third and current period of operation runs from 2005 to 2008. The Hoykom program plays an important role in the modernization efforts by supporting public sector organizations that wish to establish broadband intensive e-government services – within the scope of a time limited project. More than 500 ICT projects have been accomplished so far. A majority of them conducted by local

authorities, but the portfolio also includes projects implementing e-services and digital cooperation at central governmental level. The program has also been an important instrument in financing and supporting central and regional e-government policies and related initiatives. Accordingly, it serves as a provider of examples of successful e-government implementations and projects that are candidates for extensive roll out.

The Hoykom projects had a traditional structure of publicly funded projects. The initiators had described their plans in extensive proposals to the financing body, and every proposal was closely examined by experts, the program administration and a program board. Usually, the proposer was a public sector body, representing a consortium of several public sector organizations, planning to cooperate in developing a new service. Some consortia also included research institutions, ICT consultants or ICT vendors.

More than 50 percent of the proposals to the program were rejected due to poor quality or lack of resources. Accordingly, only the very best (with respect to project and proposal quality, and to what degree program objectives are addressed) projects were funded. Further; the program only covered 35 to 50 percent of actual costs – leaving the rest to be financed by the applicants. This mechanism had its main purpose to ensure the commitment from the initiators and stakeholders. Most of the projects were relatively small, 67 percent having a budget less than USD 350.000. Some examples of Hoykom projects were:

- Telemedicine pilots in Northern Norway
- A National Digital Database of Films
- Four rural municipalities sharing a Learning Management System for their primary schools
- A Web portal for tourism and sports in a mountain region

The main focus of the Hoykom program has been to disseminate and exploit broadband communication throughout the public sector. The approximately USD 20 Million a year financial support scheme, combined with an extensive e-government agenda, would boost the demand for broadband infrastructure throughout the country (were local authorities, schools, hospitals and other public bodies are located). This demand would in turn stimulate investments by the market players, pushing forward the establishment of broadband services also in more remote areas.

According to this, the Hoykom proposals typically had a predominant 'technical' point of departure. Even so, the project plans followed a mandatory, traditional formal structure, describing time frames, budget, responsibilities, risk factors, planned deliverables and project outcome in terms of e-government related services. The proposal form explicitly asked the applicants to give an account for costs and financing (from others), and for the degree of commitment from the stakeholders to the project's objectives. In about half of the projects the initiator hired a professional project manager; otherwise they appointed as project manager a line manager or a key stakeholder from within the organization or from one of the project partners.

Data Collection and Analysis

A questionnaire with 38 questions was designed, on the basis of the three hypotheses described above. Initially, a pilot survey was undertaken in order to determine the suitability and clarity of the questions. The Web based questionnaire was emailed to 352 Hoykom project managers and project owners of accomplished projects. The questions focused on project attributes and organizational impact. Organizational impact was defined as service innovations: new or improved services, or improved processes to produce the already established services. Of the 352 persons addressed, 130 responded, which is 37 percent. Non-response bias was investigated in respect of project size, geographic distribution and type of project manager, but not found to be significant.

A descriptive statistical analysis was performed, generating frequencies and cross-tabulations, to document the perceived degree of success on projects and organizational impact. The results are shown below. Second, a correlation analysis focusing on the relationships between various project attributes and organizational impact was deployed, to measure the degree of co-variation between the variables. To supplement the quantitative analysis a minor qualitative analysis was undertaken. Two projects that appeared particularly successful (in the survey), and one failure, were analyzed in detail, using the Hoykom administrative project database as the source. This analysis included the assessment of the original application documentation and the final reports from the projects.

The distribution is shown in Table 1, confirming the general view that Hoykom indeed is a successful program. Actually, most projects achieved their objectives within time, budget and quality. Only 22 percent (17+5) of the projects did not meet these criteria.

Table 1. Project success in Hoykom

Project success	Percentage
High degree of success	54%
Medium high degree of success	24%
Medium low degree of success	17%
Low degree of success	5%
Total	*100%*

Regarding organizational impact the figures were somewhat less impressive, as shown in table 2. The majority of projects were judged to have a medium low (57 percent) or low (20 percent) organizational impact. This illustrates an important point discussed earlier in this paper; that is, service innovation is dependent on more factors than project success. It also reveals that the relationship between project success and organizational impact is more complex than often is assumed. A correlation analysis was deployed to investigate this aspect.

To test our three hypotheses, we conducted a correlation analysis. The result is shown in table 3. There was some support for the first hypothesis and no support for the second. For the third hypothesis there was relatively strong support in the collected data. These results are somewhat surprising, because they contradict the general assumptions on project management, described in a previous section. They are, however, consistent with current research on service innovation, as reviewed earlier. We discuss these issues in the next section.

DISCUSSION

In the above, our research approach is based on the analytical distinction between a successful project and its organizational impact. Broadband based service innovation is seen as a two-step process; first, a technologically oriented project, followed by an organizational implementation. This sequence is well known from traditional IS implementation research. Project success is the responsibility of the project manager, who is assessed on his ability to reach the target on time, on budget and on quality. The main focus for the project manager is the availability of the new service. In contrast, the organizational impact is the responsibility of the CEO or line manager. The success criteria are the acceptance and use of the service by the user community.

This distinction is even more important in service innovation than in product innovation, because an unused product may still have some value, while an unused service does not.

Table 2. Organizational impact of projects in Hoykom

Organizational impact	Percentage
High organizational impact	3%
Medium high organizational impact	20%
Medium low organizational impact	57%
Low organizational impact	20%
Total	*100%*

Table 3. Results of correlation analysis

Hypothesis	Results
A. Successful organizational impact is associated with projects that are completed on time, on budget and with satisfying quality.	Some support
B. Successful organizational impact is associated with the use of professional Project Managers.	No support
D. Successful organizational impact is associated with projects with a detailed project plan over the desired organizational effects.	Strong support

Returning to our hypotheses, we will now assess the findings presented in the analysis section.

The first hypothesis assumed that *successful organizational impact is associated with ICT projects that are completed on time, on budget and with satisfying quality.* Our findings did indicate some support for this hypothesis, but the association was not very strong. Rather, the result gives some support to Atkinson's (1999) argument that was reviewed in the beginning of this chapter: some projects may be successful, but their organizational impact is low. Vice versa, unsuccessful projects (in terms of cost, time and quality) may actually lead to successful service innovations.

The second hypothesis assumed that *successful organizational impact is associated with the use of professional project managers.* Our findings did not support this hypothesis. Successful service innovation could not be explained by the use of an external professional project manager, and neither by the use of an internal project manager. What makes the external project manager a professional is his/her ability to deliver the project on time, cost and quality. However, the success criterion of service innovations is the acceptance and actual use of the service. The external project manager does not possess any particular skill to achieve this; rather it can be argued that a lack of local knowledge and authority may represent a barrier in this capacity.

The third hypothesis assumed: *Successful organizational impact is associated with ICT projects that have a detailed project plan over the desired organizational effects.* This hypothesis was strongly supported. How should we interpret this finding? Does it suggest that if you plan for organizational success you will achieve it?

Two Successful Cases

To discuss the finding above in more depth, we conducted a small qualitative analysis on the two projects having maximum score on both organizational success (impact) and on organizational change. Both projects were from the west coast of Norway. The first was a project named "Community network of the Nordfiord district – Regional broadband dissemination based on cooperation among seven municipalities". The objectives was to implement digital public services (i.e. video casts from the municipalities' executive board meetings, GIS- and map services, interactive library services) in all of the seven municipalities – based on a secure common infrastructure and a model of cooperation and mutual ICT service hosting. The second project was the set-up of a joint 24/7 medical service facility, based on tele-medicine solutions, for several small communities in the coastal part of the county of Hordaland, not very far from the city of Bergen in western Norway.

Analyzing the plans of the two projects more in detail, we found that both projects obviously had been given much attention from their respective stakeholders, regarding the problems to be tackled, the actual project plans, goals and ambitions. This included involvement from local politicians, employees as well as users. Both projects had formulated very clear objectives, as they were (according to the initiators) responses to resource shortage challenges (competence and money) – forcing small communities in rural districts to cooperate to uphold the mandatory public services. The project plans addressed these issues explicitly.

Further, they focused on:

- Organizational and contextual matters, without compromising on technology issues
- The involvement of users and all stakeholders in preparatory phases, in strategy processes and important decision points
- The actual organizational impact of the technology, not just in general but in detail (i.e. impact on established work routines,

work flow and necessary service process redesign)

- Risk factors concerning organizational matters (like competence demands, need of systematic usability tests of services)

In our view, these two projects clearly demonstrate the importance of integration. The projects had a strong focus on organizational matters, and were tightly linked to their mother organizations and the stakeholder's needs. And they succeeded; the results of the projects made a difference for the involved communities.

Summarized, our findings indicate that successful ICT based service innovation in the public sector is dependent on an integrated project structure. Organizational impact is neither associated with a tightly run project nor a professional project manager, but with a strong integration with the mother organization and its business environment – that means the service providing organization, its internal users and its external users (customers). Planning for organizational success presupposes that the project manager is able to build alliances with these key stakeholders in order to ensure that the service is successfully adopted. Key stakeholders are certainly the users, but in our public broadband context they also include line managers, cooperative municipalities and other government agencies.

The findings do not support the notion of a trade-off between innovation and implementation; that integration will constitute a barrier to innovation (Johansson et al., 2007). Rather, we find that the integrated service innovation projects are quite successful. However, this success does not come for free. From our qualitative study of two of the successful projects we do find clear indications that this integration greatly increases the complexity of the projects. Thus, the job of the project manager will be quite demanding, requiring local knowledge and the ability to build alliances with central stakeholders.

Implications for Research and Practice

Our findings in this research indicate that the traditional project management focus on cost, time and quality (PMI, 2000) is not effective, and may be even harmful, to technology based service innovation in the public sector. The success of service innovation was found to be dependent on the understanding of a complex range of organizational issues, and of the enrolment of key stakeholders. This is hardly congruent with a strict project schedule, and project owners and initiators should seek other mechanisms for controlling the implementation of new services.

Does this imply that the traditional project organization is an inappropriate tool for technology based service innovation? We think the answer is yes, if traditional project organization means a clear isolation of the project in relation to its environments. We do, however, believe that project management may be successfully applied, on two conditions. First, the project organization should be more integrated with the service provider organization and users than is traditionally perceived as effective. We return, in the next section, to the question on how this can be designed. Second, the project manager should not be assessed on his/her ability to deliver on time, cost and quality. Rather, since the success criteria are related to the capacity to plan and manage organizational change, the project manager should have a well developed understanding of the actual line organization, the stakeholder's needs and the business environments.

FUTURE TRENDS

Considering our findings, we think particularly the public sector could benefit from experimenting with alternative methods and approaches in their modernization and service innovation efforts. Although the project is well-established and non-questionable as the working form in most recent service innovation initiatives in the public sector, it should be of every manager's concern to sometimes question even the non-questionable. It is of everyone's interest that innovations, service improvements and change are managed in the most efficient manner. In our opinion, the key issues here is to prevent the project to lose the mother organization out of sight, and to ensure the commitment of line managers and ownership by line users as well as end users in the innovation process.

So, what would be the reasonable solution to these challenges? For the sake of argument, we discuss three alternative models, in addition to the traditional project management model. The classic project structure assumes that the project organization concentrates on building the solution, in our case, the ICT solution constituting the actual e-government service. When completed, the solution is handed over to the mother or client organization, which takes care of the implementation and necessary training of users. We have, in this paper, demonstrated that this model is not well suited for service innovations, and suggest three alternative models.

The Integrated Classic Structure

First, we think that the classic project model can be improved by a redefinition of responsibilities. In the second model, called "*Integrated classic structure*", we suggest that the line organization plan both the project and the implementation as one single integrated plan.

Using the term "PSO (People, System, Organisation) development" Winter et al., (2006) argue that business projects concerned with organizational change must have a certain breadth, thus reflecting that successful change processes is a matter of "changing several things in the organization at the same time". Our two detailed success cases, described earlier, are examples of this approach, where stakeholders influence

strongly on the process, and where the project is more integrated in the line organization than in the classic model. The advantage of this model is the strong integration with the line organization, ensuring a successful implementation. The obvious challenge for the integrated or PSO project model is the potentially great number of dependencies this approach tends to create for the project. In line with the arguments of Johansson et al., (2007), one may also argue that this model may be a barrier to innovation, because it presupposes that the line organization is able to specify the innovation before the start of the project.

Mutual Adaptation

This presupposition is not supported by much modern innovation research; service innovations are not always specified, rather they are often the result of more emergent processes (Leonard-Barton, 1988; Tidd & Hull, 2003). Therefore, one may take yet another path, allowing for more innovation through mutual adaptation. In this (third) model the project organization and the line organization run two parallel processes; a technical innovation process and an organizational change process. These two processes *interact over time*, in the sense that they influence directly on each other though learning and adaptation (Bygstad, 2005; Leonard-Barton, 1988). When the project is completed, the solution is already implemented in the organization. This mutual adaptation model allows for innovation, but it increases the complexity of the project, making it difficult to control. Such lack of control must indeed be assumed to be a challenge especially for public sector bodies, as their budget policies normally offers very little flexibility when it comes to financing of project activities.

Total Quality Management

A fourth model is the approach known as TQM or Total Quality Management (Juran & Godfrey,

1998), where permanent improvement initiatives, for example quality groups, continuously acts on ideas (and customer complaints etc) to innovate new services. In TQM, the awareness of quality is embedded in all organizational processes. Members of the organization are all "tuned in" to continuous process improvements. Based on the participation of all members of an organization, and aiming at long-term success through customer (user) satisfaction and benefits to all members of the organization, we think TQM has an adequate focus on organizational change and adaptation to user needs.

In the 1990s the TQM approach was criticized for focusing too much on improving existing processes; thus conserving old structures (Giroux & Landry, 1998). The crucial question is to what degree the TQM approach would support the innovative processes necessary for radical, technology based change and redesign of processes. As the work of Stacey and other Complexity Theory influenced thinkers show, it is imperative for the knowledge creation and innovation that individuals interact creatively within groups and project organizations (Stacey, 1996). This also includes creating new knowledge. In line with this, we suggest the Continuous Improvement concept still to be a viable approach for service innovation. Especially, we think the TQM model applies well in the public sector, with its normally rather rigid decision structures and the need of a systematic and controllable framework for the innovation and organizational change processes.

The alternative models highlighted above share some attributes that are important for service innovation. They emphasize the managerial obligation and commitment to service innovation; it cannot be outsourced to a vendor. They also include the involvement of users and other stakeholders in both the strategic and technical aspects of the innovation process.

Further issues include the role of vendors and budget policies. Traditionally, vendors are chosen solely on price criteria and their ability to deliver the technology. Considering our findings we suggest that the vendor is more involved in the innovation process. Further, vendors should also be selected on organization development and change management skills, and on long term partnership – rather than solely price criteria. As we have learned from the Hoykom projects in our study, external financing is often crucial for fuelling innovation initiatives. For public sector bodies, governmental financing schemes like Hoykom offer financial flexibility and independence from their own budget practices. The drawback of such external funding opportunities is, of course, the possible reduced commitment and involvement among the actual stakeholders – as long as their own money isn't really at stake. Anyhow, we think a more flexible budget policy could support and strengthen the innovative capacity in the public sector. Budget policies and cost-benefit analysis should reflect the non-linear structure of innovation; too harsh practices tend to strangle service innovation.

CONCLUSION

Our concern is how organizations can manage service innovation in an efficient way. In this paper we asked: *Can ICT based service innovation be facilitated by traditional project management thinking?* The question is relevant because successful ICT based service innovation is more dependent on the acceptance of the redefined roles rather than on the actual provision of the service. This dependency gives sound reasons to question the adequacy of the project work form when it comes to organizations planning or conducting digitisation of their services.

Based on a survey of a large number of public sector broadband projects in Norway our conclusions are:

- Successful ICT based service innovation is not associated with a tightly run project (focused on cost time and quality) nor with the presence of a professional project manager.

- Rather, successful service innovation is found in projects with a strong integration with the service providing organization and the external users of the services.
- Planning for organizational success presupposes that the project manager is able to build alliances with key stakeholders in order to ensure that the service is successfully adopted.
- Thus, successful service innovation should not be sequenced in first a tightly run technical project followed by an organizational implementation, because this is a barrier to innovation.

Predominantly, public sector bodies use the project work form as framework for their efforts to develop the organization, adapt to new technologies, or to redesign or redefine internal work processes as well as their services to the public. Our study indicates that this strong reliance on the traditional project work method is questionable. Our findings imply that the public sector should experiment with alternative project models to achieve ICT based service innovation. We have discussed three such models, called *Integrated Classic Structure, Mutual Adaptation* and *TQM,* and discussed their potential strengths and weaknesses in service innovation, as an agenda for further experimentation and empirical research.

REFERENCES

Alter, S. (2000). Same words, different meanings: Are basic IS/IT concepts our self-imposed Tower of Babel? *Communications of the Association for Information Systems, 3*(April), 2-87.

Atkinson, R. (1999). Project management: cost, time and quality, two best guesses and a phenomenon, it's time to accept other success criteria. *International Journal of Project Management, 17*(6), 337-342.

Bygstad, B. (2005). Managing the dynamics of mutual adaptation of technology and organisation in IS development projects. *Software Process: Improvement and Practice (SPIP), 10*(3), 341-353.

Cadle, J., & Yeates, D. (2004). *Project Management for Information Systems.* Harlow: Prentice-Hall.

Coakes, E., & Elliman, T. (1999). The role of stakeholders in managing change. *Communications of the AIS, 2*(4).

Drejer, I. (2004). Identifying innovation in surveys of services: A Schumpeterian perspective. *Research Policy, 33*(3), 551-562.

Giroux, H., & Landry, S. (1998). Schools of thought in and against total quality. *Journal of Managerial Issues, 10*(2), 183-202.

Johansson, S., Löfström, M., & Ohlsson, Ö. (2007). Separation or integration? A dilemma when organizing development projects *International Journal of Project Management, 25*(5), 457-464.

Juran, J. M., & Godfrey, A. B. (1998). *Juran's quality handbook.* . New York: McGraw-Hill.

Leonard-Barton, D. (1988). Implementation as mutual adaptation of technology and organization. *Research Policy, 17:5*, 251-267.

Markus, M. L., & Keil, M. (1994). If we build it, they will come: Designing information systems that people want to use. *Sloan Management Review, 35*(4).

Norwegian_Research_Council. (2007). Høykom. from http://www.hoykom.no

PMI. (2000). *A Guide to the project management body of knowledge.* PA: Project Management Institute.

Stacey, R. (1996). *Complexity and creativity in organizations*. San Francisco: Berrett-Koehler.

Straub, D., Gefen, D., & Boudreau, M.-C. (2005). The IS World quantitative, positivist research methods Website, (Ed.) D. Galletta. Retrieved from http://www.dstraub.cis.gsu.edu:88/quant

Tidd, J., & Hull, F. M. (2003). *Service innovation. Organizational responses to technological opportunities & market imperatives.* London: Imperial College Press.

Winter, M., Andersen, E. S., Elvin, R., & Levene, R. (2006). Focusing on business projects as an area for future research: An exploratory discussion of four different perspectives. *International Journal of Project Management, 24*(8), 699-709.

KEY TERMS AND DEFINITIONS

ICT-Based Service Innovation: The provision of new services on the Internet, based on a redefinition of roles between the service provider and the customer.

Integrated Classic Structure: A project structure where technical development and organisational implementation is conducted as an integrated process.

Mutual Adaptation: A project structure where the development of new services and organizational change is conducted as two parallel, but interactive processes.

Total Quality Management: An innovation strategy based on step-wise improvement and experimentation.

Chapter XIII
Employee Preparation, Participation, and Performance

Katy E. Ellis
Northeastern State University, Oklahoma, USA

ABSTRACT

This chapter provides a framework for technology project implementation in systems where the human is an integral element of the completed project. Unlike logically devised software codes and performance tested hardware components, human responses can be unpredictable when faced with the combined stressors of technological and organizational change, which occur when management dictates a technological upgrade. As such, the human interface is a dynamic system component that has the ability to degrade or disable system performance in ways unlike other subsystems. This leads to the idea that integrating employee preparation and participation into the design process from concept development through system deployment improves technology adoption and thereby overall system performance and acceptance of the technological enhancements. An analysis of peer-reviewed literature combined with the author's industrial experience provides a ten-step process for converting an existing manual system to an automated or computerized version with emphasis on integrating the human element.

EMPLOYEE PREPARATION PARTICIPATION AND PERFORMANCE

Replacement of a firm's existing manual systems with a computerized version necessitates address- ing employee concerns as well as the mechanics of the replacement task itself. In this case, computerization refers to the activity of facilitating or automating procedures or activities by means of electronic computer (Webster's, 1986). Management may desire to update the existing system because there is a belief that long-term productivity and efficiency gains will outweigh the effort and cost associated with the introduction of new technology. However, if employees resist the change and refuse to use the new system, or continually bypass it in favor of familiar work routines, then it does not matter how well one designs the system or plans the system implementation, productivity gains will not occur, if the employees will not use the system (Shneiderman, 1986).

In considering the adoption of new workplace technology, employee preparation and participation in the change process may greatly enhance the performance of the new system (Lippert & Davis, 2006). With this approach, the process begins by addressing employee concerns first and then, instigates a structured approach that systematically progresses through the various design phases taking into consideration issues related to the adequacy of existing facility infrastructure, compatibility with existing computer systems, and proposed system functionality, as well as other technical nuances of the process. Therefore, this chapter addresses the problem of converting an existing manual system to a computerized system by first addressing personnel issues and second by addressing the mechanics of the conversion process highlighting opportunities for human integration.

BACKGROUND

There are many schools of thought regarding the most critical design functions necessary for successfully deploying new technology in the workplace. It is not difficult to discern the bias presented in arguments made by hardware engineers versus software engineers or even operations managers. However, this writer agrees with Pulat's (1997) assessment of system priorities. Pulat proposed that, any complex system that includes humans as part of the system interface must address the inefficiencies of the humans by

augmenting their capabilities with technology designed to overcome their inherent limitations. In other words, improvements in system efficiency gained through technology adoption will be limited at the junctures of human-machine interface. Managers that desire to maximize production efficiency can only achieve limited improvement, if they do not also address the need to optimize human performance as well.

Due to the impact that the human element can have on technology deployment and its eventual performance, the reader will note that this chapter presents a human-biased approach to the problem of replacing an existing manual system with a computerized version. The subject is introduced with a discussion on the human response to change, particularly technology driven change, but even in the detailed task-structure emphasis is given to areas that significantly impact the user interface in terms of learning time, performance speed, error rate, and user satisfaction.

ANTICIPATING AND MITIGATING EMPLOYEE CONCERNS

Management's announcement that a new and efficient computerized system will soon replace the old manual system is likely to garner less employee enthusiasm than what is hoped for. Never mind that employees have complained for years about the inherent problems of the old system, the typical human response to management change initiatives is one of employee resistance resulting in performance degradation (Elrod & Tippett, 2002). Knowing this, management can anticipate employee response and structure the introduction of the change so that employees are less likely to reject it.

Employee resistance manifests itself in a variety of symptomatic behaviors. The evaluative study conducted by Elrod and Tippett (2002) cited behavior that ranged from a refusal to acknowledge that change was immanent up to and including outright criticism or sabotage of the change initiative. Davidson (2006) believed that management must strive to understand the employee perspective in order to realize positive outcomes from not only the change initiative, but also for the successful adoption of the technology itself.

Davidson's (2006) perception that the introduction of automation to previously manual processes creates two change initiatives that employees must internalize is a critical point. The first change proposal is subtle in that it would exist whether management was shifting the process to a computerized system or if they were simply altering the existing manual system. From the employee perspective, it is a change that they must incorporate. The second change proposal that Davidson refered to is that of introducing the technology. The fact that there are actually two change proposals for employees to accept and internalize increases the degree and variety of potential negative employee responses that management must address. Managers may be tempted to use coercive power to overcome this employee resistance, but modern management philosophies such as those presented by Senge, Kleiner, Roberts, Ross, Roth, and Smith (1999) suggest a less confrontational approach that has its basis in understanding and addressing the true cause of employee resistance versus attacking the behavior that is representative of it.

Harvey (1990) proposed that the individual's perception of loss directly relates to the negative behavioral response. Harvey reasoned that all forms of change result in a loss of some type for the person who must do the changing. Both Harvey's assessment and Davidson's (2006) perception of dual change initiatives apply in the context of computerizing an existing manual system. Some perceived losses could be attributed to the fact that change is occurring whereas others are directly attributable to the technology aspect of the change.

Anxiety and fear of the unknown can be representative responses to any suggested change.

Alcorn (1986) wrote that the feelings of anxiety and the fear of the unknown result in homeostasis, a type of resistance demonstrated by efforts to retain the status quo. Employees may perceive changes in the familiar rhythm and flow of work as the loss of opportunities to socialize with peers (McGinn, 1991). Changes dictated by others can be perceived as a loss of control over one's life. Often, a person's sense of self interweaves closely with their daily work. Management changes that disrupt the pattern of daily work can upset the individual's perception of self (Elrod & Tippett, 2002).

Technology driven change manifests a different set of employee concerns. Individuals may fear a lack of personal competency and the appearance of looking uneducated (McGinn, 1991). They may fear that efficiency gains from computerization may eliminate their jobs (Dainoff & Dainoff, 1986). They may believe that the technology will eliminate opportunities for social interaction and result in alienation (Alcorn, 1986).

It is important to prepare employees emotionally for the change proposal in order to increase the probability of employees adopting and internalizing the new technology (Lippert & Davis, 2006). Managers need to develop a strategy that addresses both aspects of the change initiative. Emotional preparedness for the change should address the fundamental employee concerns that manifest resistive behavior regardless of whether those concerns derive from the idea that change is occurring, or the idea that the change relates to technology implementation.

People respond differently to self-initiated change versus mandated change. Wagner and Hollenbeck (2005) proposed that the difference in response ties to perceptions of control. For example, a person who voluntarily attends night school in order to qualify for a promotion to a new job does not resist or necessarily fear the changes that will occur in his or her work environment when the promotion occurs. However, when management proposes changes in the work environment, employees often feel they have no control over the issue or its impact on them personally. This feeling of helplessness leads to various forms of resistance as individuals strive to regain a sense of control over their work lives.

It is logical to mitigate the negative response by encouraging a participatory change effort (Senge et al., 1999). Instead of issuing a management directive that mandates computerization, executives can communicate to employees the necessity of improvements in system efficiency and solicit employee ideas. Wood (2007) believed strategic initiatives are more likely to succeed when managers offer vague goals and then allow employees to engineer the mechanisms for achieving the goals. McGreevy (2003) also supported this theory by suggesting that, the more employees are involved in determining the future outcome of change initiatives, the greater their level of commitment and support for the change will be because participation restores some level of control. Therefore, this writer believes the initial step in preparing employees emotionally to adopt new technology is to first prepare them for the idea that things are changing by openly communicating about the change and increasing their participation in the process.

Senge et al. (1999) described a type of employee referred to as a network leader. This person's strength is their ability to move through the organization unencumbered by hierarchical authority and develop networks of alliances with those who have similar ideology. This writer suggests that early buy in and acceptance of the change by these individuals can be critical to the success of the project because of the network leader's ability to persuade others.

In addition to involving network leaders, management may want to identify employees who have been vocal about the existing system's inadequacies as well as those who have made previous suggestions for process improvement that had successful outcomes. Individuals belonging to these groups may feel a kinship for, or have

a stake in supporting the change initiative and therefore might make good candidates for acting as both advocates for the proposed change as well as communication conduits for managers who want to increase employee involvement.

The literature offers several techniques for increasing employee participation and feelings of ownership relative to change proposals. Suggestions include informal brown-bag lunches as venues for brainstorming ideas, formal surveys, establishing committees, providing monetary incentives for suggestions, or simply asking employees to assess the current situation and propose alternative solutions (McGreevy, 2003). In addition to facilitating the transition, employee participation can provide valuable insights into the functional requirements for the computerized version of the new system (Symon & Clegg, 2005). Managers may believe that they understand how the existing system works, but employees know how and why it works like it does because of their day-to-day manipulation of it.

One cannot over stress the criticality of emotional preparedness of employees to accept and internalize the change proposal. Lippert and Davis (2006) suggested that failing to prepare employees psychologically for changes that will result in the introduction of new technology risks having employees reject the technology. Shneiderman (1986) stated it most clearly and his message is worth repeating. If employees will not use the new technology, then it does not matter how well designed it is or how well planned its implementation, management objectives will not be met.

SYSTEM DEVELOPMENT

Employee acceptance and buy in to the change initiative can facilitate system optimization of the computerized version by increasing user participation in the selection or development of the new system while at the same time developing a sense of ownership for the new system that may work to negate opportunities for resistance. In addition, active employee participation provides the advantages of lessons learned from existing operations as well as creative insight about what might work better (Bailey, 1989). After ensuring that employees are emotionally prepared to accept the change and agreeable to orchestrating it, the next step in converting an existing manual system to a computerized version is to outline the tasks that will accomplish the transition.

Depending on the level of detail one is interested in presenting, an outline of tasking necessary to convert manual operations to computerized ones could have as few as three or even hundreds of individual tasks listed, but many authors provide a list of approximately twelve high-level tasks. The following outline is a synthesis of progressive tasking developed from the writer's own experience as well as guidelines suggested by Bailey (1989), Niebel and Freivalds (1999), Pulat (1997), and Shneiderman (1986). Task presentation appears sequential, progressing in a linear manner; however, in reality there is typically overlap in some areas while others lend themselves to simultaneous development:

1. Conduct needs assessment
2. Perform task analysis
3. Ensure compatibility with existing systems
4. Determine reliability performance criteria
5. Conduct tradeoff studies
6. Initiate system acquisition
7. Perform system tests
8. Conduct user training
9. Deploy system
10. Monitor system performance

Needs Assessment

The needs assessment is an activity that takes place during the early stages of the system development life cycle (SDLC) that attempts to discover and make known the explicit needs of the business owner (customer) as well as those who will operate (users) the new computerized system (Russell & Yilmaz, 2006). The set of needs that the computerized solution satisfies must synchronize with the customer and users' actual needs for the solution to be considered successful. Customers are concerned with the business results such as cost, efficiency, productivity improvement, etc. that the system delivers. Users focus on accomplishing their daily tasks with ease and minimal opportunity for error (Bailey, 1989).

One cannot over emphasize the importance of performing an accurate and detailed needs assessment. Russell and Yilmaz (2006) stressed this as well when they wrote, "The development effort will be a failure if the users are not able or willing to use the system" to perform their daily tasking (¶ 8). The firm that hopes to win the development contract must accurately assess and address two sets of criteria: The customer's and the users' in order to provide system functionality that will ensure productivity improvements.

The needs assessment and the task analysis have areas of commonality and at first glance, may seem to be the same activity. However, there is a difference. The needs assessment is a higher-level assessment with a more concentrated effort expended on detailing the customer, or business owner's needs with some consideration for user or operator requirements. Task analysis is opposite of this. There is recognition that the user must function within the context of stated business objectives, but the greater effort of designers during the task analysis phase is to identify all of the tasks and sub-tasks performed by users (Shneiderman, 1986). Both the needs assessment phase and the task analysis phase are ripe with opportunities to solicit employee involvement. Encouraging this involvement helps employees develop ownership of the change process and thereby increase their feelings of control and level of acceptance of the change.

Task Analysis

One can equate the identification of user tasks with system functionality. Adequate functionality must include identification of frequent tasks, occasional tasks, and emergency or repair situations that may require infrequent yet critical user input or interface. Frequent user tasks are typically easy to discover through observation of existing operations. However, infrequent, or emergency tasks are not always discernable by this process. Therefore, the involvement of end users in the process of task development is justified (Russell & Yilmaz, 2006).

Shneiderman (1986) also advocated user involvement in task analysis activities. He argued that user involvement provides more accurate descriptions and details of tasking and performance objectives. In addition, Shneiderman pointed out that user participation during the task analysis phase creates a "sense of participation that builds ego investment in successful implementation and the potential for increased user acceptance of the final system" (p. 393). Shneiderman's statement supports the argument presented previously that advocates a need to address the human behavioral response to change in order to ensure technology adoption.

According to Symon and Clegg's (2005) evaluation of current literature, not everyone is in favor of having user participation in system design. Arguments against too much user participation include cost and negative impact on implementation schedules due to time-consuming meetings, increased user antagonism from those users who are not involved or whose ideas are rejected, as well as the possibility of design compromises based on maintaining a civil working relationship between users and designers. Symon and Clegg believed there are two major issues that contribute to these problems. The first is selecting the most effective strategy or level of user participation and the second is selecting the right users to participate. While Symon and Clegg's work provides a

counterpoint to the argument for user involvement, the majority of scholars advocate strong support for user involvement throughout the SDLC, but particularly during the task analysis phase.

System Compatibility

System developers need to consider whether their proposed solution will be compatible with existing computer and non-computer systems. The SDLC phase that assesses compatibility with existing systems traditionally considers facility infrastructure, existing technology interfaces, and the impact of environmental conditions on proposed hardware solutions. A human-centered approach adds the elements of existing skill levels, training, and educational achievement of the workforce to the equation.

Minor differences between existing and proposed systems can cause annoying and possibly dangerous errors, if the system is a life-critical system such as those operated in some hospitals or by aircraft control towers (Shneiderman, 1986). Operator errors in life-critical systems can result in major system damage or significant loss of life. Substantial differences between existing and proposed systems may require costly retraining (Bailey, 1989). Incompatible hardware and software creates a burden for system maintainers and contributes to overall lifecycle costs related to spare part management and the number and variety of necessary test equipments (Orsburn, 1991). Incompatibility between system operational requirements and the current skill sets of operators can also lead to technology rejection.

The firm may find that their existing facility infrastructure i.e. electrical supply and distribution or air conditioning system is inadequate to support the new computerized system's needs. When this occurs, management readily supports budget and schedule adjustments necessary to upgrade these elements. Similarly, in the area of compatibility with existing features of the operation, management accepts expenditures related to environmental and operational conditions that dictate equipment constraints specifying ruggedized equipment, waterproof equipment, shielding from electromagnetic interference, etc. However, technology upgrades do not operate in isolation from their human companions.

The human is as much a part of successful system operation as any other system critical component and deserves the same level of consideration and expenditure when considering system compatibilities. It seems logical that if facility upgrades are necessary expenditures, then so too are employee skill set upgrades. The traditional solution is to hire new employees with compatible skill sets. Possibly, this is where the employee perception equating loss of employment with technology upgrades stems from. Consider instead upgrading the skill sets and knowledge base of existing employees. Existing employees are already familiar with operations and objectives, have proven themselves to be good workers, and in many cases will develop both increased company loyalty and a keener insight into the benefits of the technology upgrade. They can become advocates for change.

Reliability Requirements

Reliability performance criteria relates to system operational availability, mean time to repair equipment or recover from errors, and mean time between failures of the system or system components (Locks, 1973). Different types of businesses may have different system availability and operational reliability requirements. For instance, some organizations are in businesses that could have a direct and detrimental impact on human life if there was a failure or critical anomaly in their computerized system. As previously explained, a system is considered life-critical if people's lives depend on the system being not only operational, but also reliable in terms of accurately performing tasks (Shneiderman, 1986).

Examples of life-critical systems include some hospital systems, power utility systems, nuclear reactor systems, and jet aircraft environmental controls. From the firm's perspective, if the proposed computerized system replaces an existing manual system that controls or performs a core business function, then the firm may consider the new system to be life-critical relative to keeping the business alive (Locks, 1973). The firm may impose more stringent operational reliability requirements on designers.

A firm that converts its existing manual order processing function to a computerized system can sustain significant economic impacts when the system is unavailable or when it incorrectly processes customer orders. Likewise, the firm that converts manual production processes to computer-controlled processes can experience significant financial loss associated with a disabled system or one that incorrectly mixes or manufactures products that do not meet minimum quality standards (Locks, 1973).

The reliability performance criteria must support business needs, but a system that is 100% available and reliable may not be technologically feasible, or if it is feasible, it may be cost prohibitive to design and deploy (Patton, 1994). The firm will have to assess reliability requirements in terms of its tolerance for risk related to the system being unavailable or introducing errors.

Users have a slightly different perspective on system reliability. User expectations include system availability and error free or minimal error introduction with ease of recovery. A reliable system from the user perspective generates feelings of success, competency, and clarity in the user population (Shneiderman, 1986). As observed by Lippert and Davis (2006), technology trust, the perception that the technology can be depended on to correctly accomplish the user's tasking, is crucial to user adoption of technology-based change initiatives. The user's level of technology trust is not only directly dependent on the reliability of the system's hardware and software, but also dependant on the user's skill set as developed through training and hands-on manipulation of the technology.

Management decisions relative to reliability performance criteria affect system life cycle cost i.e. the cost to maintain the system over the course of its expected useful life. High-reliability hardware components equate to reduced maintenance costs because these components extend the mean time between failures and maintenance intervention activities occur less frequently (Patton, 1994). The costs associated with managing and maintaining the spare parts inventory decreases when the system exhibits high levels of reliability (Orsburn, 1991). Management tradeoff analyses will determine the correct level of inherent system reliability based on risk tolerance, cost, schedule, and possibly other criteria.

Tradeoff Studies

Once management has determined what the system needs are and performed assessments of user tasks, evaluated compatibility with existing systems, and defined reliability constraints, tradeoff studies are likely to be required. In a perfect world, all business needs, user tasking, compatibility and reliability issues could be addressed within budget and schedule constraints without necessitating compromise between system features. However, satisfying all of these requirements may not be technologically feasible, or the cost of meeting them may make the endeavor uneconomical to pursue (Patton, 1994).

Shneiderman (1986) contrasted tradeoff considerations for life critical systems against those that may apply to systems designed for industrial or commercial uses. He explains that in the life-critical system, one expects high costs, but these costs pay for increased system reliability and effectiveness, rapid error-free operations justify long training times, and low user satisfaction is mitigated because users are well-motivated and

compensated. However, the industrial or commercial system's development is often cost-driven versus reliability-driven so lower costs may be more important than high reliability. If a significant number of employees will require expensive training, this may be offset by a requirement to focus on ease of learning for the new system (Shneiderman).

There are no concrete rules that dictate which system elements are candidates for tradeoff analyses, except those generated or agreed to by the business owner who funds the computerization project. Different industries and even different companies within the same industry have varying competitive strategies and resources available for developing their technology initiatives. As such, the contributing or constraining factors and tolerance for risk that reside within each organization will play an important role in dictating the results of any tradeoff analysis.

Steps 1 through 4 of the task outline to move the firm from a manual to a computerized system generate a wish list of everything that the customer, user, and deployment environment define as essential system elements. Step 5, the tradeoff analysis, represents a reality check. Rarely does an organization have the luxury of acquiescing to the needs of all system stakeholders. The tradeoff process results in a more realistic set of system requirements refined by the constraints of reality. It is from this position that executives can then focus on questions specific to the system acquisition.

System Acquisition

The initial question addressed by the system acquisition phase is that of make or buy. Should the firm custom build a system, or purchase a commercial-off-the-shelf (COTS) application? One finds extensive arguments both for and against each approach in the literature, but Bajaj (2006) condenses these into a manageable summary descriptive of the historical debate as well as inclusive of current trends.

Bajaj (2006) describes the make or buy argument as one that has come full circle in response to the various evolutions in hardware and software technology. Initially, firms in need of large-scale information technology (IT) systems developed these systems in-house. However, Bajaj reports that many of today's systems are COTS products purchased with the belief that COTS would eliminate problematic and time consuming development efforts. He also reported perceptions of reduced costs attributed to the COTS developer's ability to gain economies of scale by distributing the fixed development costs to multiple customers, and the potential to lower an organization's risk by employing a system already known to work in other organizations. These arguments appear reasonable when one contrasts these features with the shortcomings of existing legacy systems.

The firm may believe that developing another in-house computerized system may lead to fragmentation of existing business practices, if the new system is not compatible with existing systems. Never mind that these customized systems may provide fantastic support for individual business functions within the organization, if the systems cannot communicate with each other, there are likely to be detrimental results for business productivity and performance (Simchi-Levi, Kaminsky, & Simchi-Levi, 2003).

Perceived disadvantages to selecting a COTS solution exist as well. Bajaj (2006) cites future increases in costs as vendors upgrade the software, the inability to customize because of the frequent upgrades, and time and budget overruns during implementation, as negative aspects of a COTS solution. In addition, one should consider that his or her firm would have to align their existing practices to conform to the model offered by the COTS vendor. This may result in a loss of competitive advantage or differentiation, if the firm's competitors have adopted the same COTS solution.

Bajaj (2006) mentions an emerging trend that may present a viable third alternative for the firm considering a large IT project. He suggests a hybrid solution that involves some COTS application tools used to support development of custom features. Bajaj believed that the right mix of interface development tools such as Visual Basic®, Visual Café®, or Oracle Developer® combined with low-cost outsourcing of custom code features might provide the least risk and greatest opportunity for some firms.

In addition to these high-level concerns, there are many lower-level functions to consider that may affect a firm's system acquisition decision. Users must receive training to operate the new system. A decision to build the new system in-house may also be a decision to develop the training material as well. Does the firm possess the necessary skill sets in its labor force, or will hiring of training staff be a factor to consider. A similar consideration arises regarding system life cycle costs. Patton (1994) described the operational portion of a systems lifecycle as potentially more expensive than the entire development phase when one considers the facility needs for the maintenance staff, their salaries, test equipment, spare parts inventory, etc. Does the firm have the ability to maintain a system that it has developed, or would the organization be better off to acquire a COTS solution complete with training packages and warranty services? Regardless of the final decision, buy or make, or create some hybrid solution, the system put in place will require testing.

System Tests

System tests ensure that the adopted solution meets the functional and operational needs of the users and customer. The process for moving the firm's manual systems to a computerized system is presented here as a mostly linear activity. However, decision makers may find that an iterative process that involves early prototype testing and revisions based on user feedback results in a more successful deployment (Shneiderman, 1986). In addition to infrastructure testing to ensure hardware and facility interfaces are acceptable, testing may require that selected users manipulate software systems, view screen layouts and menu selections, and suggest improvements. User participation at this level enhances the probability that technology adoption by employees will occur upon deployment (Bailey, 1989).

It is not easy to separate development from testing because development leads to testing which often leads to more development efforts (Bailey, 1989). However, once all of the components are tested and approved, system-level tests to ensure acceptable levels of performance provide documentation of contract compliance for COTS applications, or in the case of in-house development, ensure that project objectives have been met.

Those who are familiar with contract law suggest that explicit acceptance criteria should be written into both the requirements document and the contract offer (Whelan, 1985). The contract or requirements document should state the criteria for system acceptance or rejection in measurable terms so there is no opportunity for subjective interpretation of test results.

User Training

Training entails the systematic development of user skills, knowledge, and attitudes. When the training is for a computer system, the training should, "ensure that terminal-use skills are developed, that a general knowledge about the system is provided, and that users' attitudes about the new system change be positive" (Bailey, 1989, p. 387).

Training users to employ a computerized system representative of an existing manual system offers both disadvantages and advantages. If the new system procedures and work flow differ greatly from the old manual system, users will have to unlearn what might amount to years of experience (Pulat, 1997). Mistakes and errors may be frequent causing user frustration

and eventual rejection of the system (McGinn, 1991). Conversely, mimicking existing process flows and terminology and even recreating existing paper forms as electronic input screens can greatly reduce training time and error rates while contributing to overall user acceptance of the new system (Pulat).

McGinn (1991) wrote that many users feel uncomfortable with new technology because they fear that their ignorance of the operational nuances will cause them to make embarrassing mistakes that may negatively affect how they are viewed by coworkers. It is therefore important that the training environment be conducive to system experimentation that encourages and supports user efforts to explore error recovery techniques. As proposed by the Lippert and Davis (2006) model, an environment of trust is necessary for successful technology adoption and this environment includes the training environment as well as the overall organizational culture.

The basic approach to training, as presented by Bailey (1989) involves analyzing functions, tasks, and work modules, developing training objectives and training materials, and testing to ensure training was effective in terms of meeting objectives. However, one might also recognize that the training period is an optimal time to reinforce user buy in to the new technology by creating a sense of excitement and anticipation regarding system deployment and the immediate benefits that users will realize. Recall the earlier statement that users must be prepared emotionally as well as intellectually for the system deployment to be effective.

System Deployment

System deployment can be a phased activity or it can occur all at once. For some organizations, a phased approach wherein the existing manual system operates in tandem with the new computerized system provides risk mitigation in the event that system anomalies occur. Other firms may believe that the weekend provides ample downtime to install the new system and remove remnants of the past so that employees can immediately begin work with the new system on Monday morning. If it will not adversely affect operations, decision makers might consider asking the employees which approach they would prefer. This method might serve to increase employee ownership by providing another venue for participatory change (Senge et al., 1999).

By the time the new system is ready for deployment, some managers may feel that the time and expense involved in creating it justifies an attitude of disregard for the employees who must work with the new system. This is unfortunate because, even if the firm has done all of the right things to encourage user acceptance, users can still sabotage the system deployment with activities that involve resistive behavior such as refusal to input data in a timely manner, intentional error production, and by-passing the new system by continuing to use the old one (Shneiderman, 1986).

Realistically, the deployment of the new system at this point is likely a done deal. It will happen. However, it does not have to be a painful ordeal for management or the employees. Executives acting as facilitators can do much to alleviate employee concerns and encourage acceptance of the new system if, as stated earlier, they understand the sources of employees' resistive behavior and address those issues directly.

McGreevy (2003) suggested that organizations undergoing an extensive change, such as that which occurs when the deployment of computerized systems negates existing manual systems, rejoice in their past, even consider throwing a party. He suggested that executives not disparage the past, because many employees may still feel ownership for it. Managers need to vocalize the good things from the past while recognizing that the past is past and the time has come to adapt to the present and future focus of the organization.

For the deployment to have a chance of success McGreevy (2003) believed that mangers should listen to their employees' concerns and involve them by inviting their input because he perceived that this will encourage commitment of staff to the change initiative. In addition, establishing a culture of employee ownership that includes an environment of trust in which employees feel comfortable vocalizing system problems may facilitate obtaining the objectives outlined in the system-monitoring phase.

Performance Monitoring

Initial system performance monitoring assures management that the adopted solution actually meets the firm's needs. Continued monitoring and feedback leads to system enhancements that may increase productivity and efficiency. System performance monitoring is necessary for both continued employee buy in to the new technology as well as to achieve maximum profitability from the technology initiative (Niebel & Freivalds (1999).

The deployment stage is also a good time to remind employees that the effort is not complete. There will be changes made to the new system after deployment and employee critiques and input will be the likely source for those changes. It is important, so that employees do not become disgruntled or frustrated with the new system, to ensure that they know in advance that operations might not be as smooth as expected. Despite due diligence and their support to the design effort, day-to-day operations are likely to reveal system deficiencies, or at least areas that need improvement.

Assuring employees that their opinion is valued and needed to ensure system success reinforces user feelings of ownership and circumvents the efforts of those who resist the change by complaining about the inadequacies of the deployed system (Senge et al., 1999). Complainers should be encouraged to document the problem and suggest improvements. When complaints are legitimate, this process will actually work to improve system performance by correcting for inadvertently neglected design parameters (Niebel & Freivalds, 1999).

In addition to correcting anomalies and fine turning aspects of the computerized process, the monitoring function assures that labor, supervision, and management are following and supporting the new work methods (Niebel & Freivalds, 1999). The goal of post-deployment performance monitoring is one of continuous process improvement as well as one of increasing feelings of employee ownership and control over the new system.

CONCLUSION

Replacement of a firm's existing manual systems with a computerized version necessitates addressing employee concerns as well as the mechanics of the replacement task itself. Depending on the size of the system and its functional specifications, one might outline hundreds of discrete tasks necessary to convert to a computerized system. However, one can logically allocate most of these tasks to one of the ten primary tasks listed in this chapter. System designers may debate the task sequence or even the level of importance assigned to each task, however in almost every instance of system deployment, regardless of the type or size of the system, it will have to interface with humans.

Unlike other subsystems that constitute the computerized system, the human interface is a dynamic system component that has the ability to degrade or disable system performance in ways unlike other subsystems (Shneiderman, 1986). An otherwise brilliantly engineered and meticulously deployed technology initiative has a high probability of not succeeding if employees are not emotionally and intellectually prepared

to deal with the changes it brings (Lippert & Davis, 2006).

The most cited human response to management dictated change proposals is one of resistive behavior predicated on fears about how the change will impact the individual on a personal level as well as negative feelings associated with a loss of control (Senge et al., 1999). The resistive behavior is a symptom of the underlying emotional turmoil the employee is experiencing. Managers should recognize this propensity and respond proactively to address not the symptom, but the underlying cause of it (Senge et al.). Creating a culture of trust in the work environment entails open dialog with employees about their concerns to prepare them emotionally for the change. Participation in the change process allows employees to regain their feelings of control over the work environment and develops feelings of ownership relative to the change that are likely to increase the chances of its successful deployment (Bailey, 1989). This leads to the idea that employee preparation and participation improve performance when converting an existing manual system to a computerized version.

REFERENCES

Alcorn, P. A. (1986). *Social issues in technology: A format for investigation*. Englewood Cliffs, NJ: Prentice-Hall, Inc.

Bailey, R. W. (1989). *Human performance engineering: Using human factors/ergonomics to achieve computer system usability* (2nd ed.). Englewood Cliffs, NJ: Prentice-Hall, Inc.

Bajaj, A. (2006, Fall). Large scale requirements modeling: An industry analysis, a model and a teaching case. *Journal of Information Systems Education, 17*(3), 327-339. Retrieved September 21, 2007, from Proquest database.

Dainoff, M. J., & Dainoff, M. H. (1986). *People and productivity*. Toronto, Ont: Holt, Rinehart, and Winston of Canada, Limited.

Davidson, E. (2006, March). A technological frames perspective on information technology and organizational change. *The Journal of Applied Behavioral Science, 42*(1), 23-40. [Electronic version] Retrieved September 10, 2007, from Proquest database.

Elrod, P. D., & Tippett, D. D. (2002). The "death valley" of change. *Journal of Organizational Change Management, 15*(3), 273-291. Retrieved September 8, 2007, from Proquest database.

Harvey, T. R. (1990). *Checklist for change: A pragmatic approach for creating and controlling change*. Boston: Allyn and Bacon.

Lippert, S. K., & Davis, M. (2006, October). A conceptual model integrating trust into planned change activities to enhance technology adoption behavior. *Journal of Information Science, 32*(5), 434. Retrieved September 9, 2007, from Proquest database.

Locks, M. O. (1973). *Reliability, maintainability, and availability assessment*. Rochelle Park, NJ: Hayden Book Company, Inc.

McGinn, R. E. (1991). *Science, technology, and society*. Englewood Cliffs, NJ: Prentice Hall.

McGreevy, M. (2003). Managing the transition. *Industrial and Commercial Training, 35*(6/7), 241-246. Retrieved September 9, 2007, from Proquest database.

Niebel, B. W., & Freivalds, A. (1999). *Methods, standards, and work design* (10th ed.). Boston: WCB/McGraw-Hill.

Orsburn, D. K. (1991). *Spares management handbook*. Boston: McGraw-Hill.

Patton, J. D., Jr. (1994). *Maintainability and maintenance management* (3rd ed.). Research Triangle Park, NC: Instrument Society of America.

Pulat, B. M. (1997). *Fundamentals of industrial ergonomics*. Prospect Heights, IL: Waveland Press, Inc.

Russell, B. D. & Yilmaz, M. R. (2006, Fall). Using gap analysis to improve system acceptance. *Information Systems Management, 23*(4), 37-42. Retrieved September 19, 2007, from Proquest database.

Senge, P., Kleiner, A., Roberts, C., Ross, R., Roth, G., & Smith, B. (1999). *The dance of change: The challenges to sustaining momentum in a learning organization*. New York: Doubleday.

Shneiderman, B. (1986). *Designing the user interface: Strategies for effective human-computer interaction*. Reading, MA: Addison-Wesley Publishing Company.

Simchi-Levi, D., Kaminsky, P., & Simchi-Levi, E. (2003). *Designing and managing the supply chain: Concepts, strategies, and case studies* (2nd ed.). Boston: McGraw-Hill Irwin.

Symon, G., & Clegg, C. (2005, September). Constructing identity and participation during technological change. *Human Relations, 58*(9), 1141-1167. Retrieved September 20, 2007, from Proquest database.

Wagner, J. A., & Hollenbeck, J. R. (2005). *Organizational behavior: Securing competitive advantage* (5th ed.). Mason, OH: Thomson South-Western.

Webster's new world dictionary (3rd college ed.). (1988). New York: Webster's New World.

Whelan, J. W. (1985). *Cases and materials on federal government contracts*. Mineola, NY: The Foundation Press, Inc.

Wood, R. C. (2007). How strategic innovation really gets started. *Strategy & Leadership, 35*(1), 21. Retrieved September 9, 2007, from Proquest database.

KEY TERMS AND DEFINITIONS

Computerization: The activity of facilitating or automating procedures or activities by means of electronic computer.

COTS: An acronym for Commercial Off the Shelf – used in reference to original hardware and software purchased from a commercial vendor and installed into an operational system without first undergoing modification by the purchaser.

Needs Assessment: An activity that takes place during the early stages of the system development life cycle and that attempts to discover and make known the explicit needs of the business owner (customer) as well as those who will operate (users) the new computerized system.

Participatory Change: Change initiatives in which the individuals who will experience the change are invited to contribute their thoughts and ideas to the nature, scope, and timing of the change proposal.

System Optimization: The activity of enhancing system capabilities and integration of subsystem elements to the extent that all components operate at or above user expectations.

Task Analysis: A high-level assessment with a concentrated effort expended on detailing all of the tasks and sub-tasks performed by system users. Not only routine tasking, but also sporadic event tasking and emergency event tasking is included.

Technology Trust: The perception that the technology can be depended on to correctly accomplish the user's tasking and that any errors or malfunctions that do occur are easily recovered from and will not have catastrophic consequences.

Section III
Project Quality and
Risk Management

Chapter XIV
Quality Assurance with Project Management

Jaby Mohammed
Indiana University-Purdue University Fort Wayne (IPFW), USA

Ali Alavizadeh
Morehead State University, USA

ABSTRACT

Project management is a carefully planned, organized effort to manage the resources in order to successfully accomplish specific project goals and objectives. It involves the entire life cycle of a project right from the feasibility study of the project, project planning, implementation, evaluation, support, and maintenance of the project. Each phase of the project is a vast topic within project management. The topic of interest for this chapter is quality assurance and its relationship project management. By defining quality and situating the concept within the frame of project management, the authors' scope and understanding of project completion will be improved.

INTRODUCTION

Project management is carefully planned, organized effort to manage the resources in order to successfully accomplish specific project goals and objectives. Project management covers the entire life cycle of a project right from the feasibility study of the project, project planning, implementation, evaluation, support, and maintenance of the project. Each phases of the project is a vast topic within project management. The topic of interest here is the quality assurance in project management.

Although it seems that there is not a unique definition for the tern quality, in general, quality is referred to as the degree to which the customer is satisfied with the service/product provided. In this regard, Quality Assurance (QA) is an important portion in any business organization and is a universal term which includes the quality policy, quality management, and quality control functions. The quality assurance is the assurance that is given to the client that the product or the services is delivered at the right condition, right time, and also the ability to satisfy the given needs. QA can be considered as a part of Total Quality Management (TQM) philosophy which is geared towards the excellence of the entire organization.

WHAT IS QUALITY?

When the term "quality" is used, one often thinks about excellent performance of a product or service. In general, when the product/service exceed one's expectations, he/she consider that quality (Besterfield, 2004). Therefore, one may define quality as:

$$Q = \frac{P}{E}$$

Where P is performance and E is expectations. P and E may not be necessarily quantitative variables. In addition, these are most likely to be based on perception; the customers determine expectation while the organizations determine performance. Quality and quality tools, such as statistical tools, are often considered as a par of a bigger, more general concept, called *Total Quality Management* (TQM). TQM is simply the application of quantitative methods and human resources to improve all the processes within an organization to meet and/or exceed customer needs now and in the future ((Besterfield, Besterfield-Michna, & Besterfield-Sacre, 2003)

QUALITY AND DESIGN

Product design and design methodologies have a direct impact on the quality of the product. The design process historically has been implemented in isolation from other functions of the enterprise such as manufacturing, sales, etc. There are some disadvantages in this form of implementation in terms of longer cycle time, higher costs, and products designs not being optimal. For instance, due to the sequential nature of traditional design practices, the manufacturing engineers do not have a voice in the conceptualization phase where as much as 90% of the production cost may have already been specified (Chang, Wysk, & Wang, 1998).

Companies are challenged to increase their product quality and shorten the lead time for developing new products, while lowering their production costs, all of which are rooted in the quality and timeliness of the design solutions (Suh, 2001). Singh (1996) states that several studies have suggested that most of a product's cost become fixed in its early life cycle stage before the original design cycle is completed. A typical characteristic curve that indicates the cost incurred and committed during the product life cycle is shown in Figure 1 (Singh, 1996, p. 106).

As seen in Figure 1, the majority of the product development cost occurs in the conceptual and detailed design phase. Also, the overall design change is easier in the earlier phases.

Poor design practices lead to higher production cost and longer lead time due to extensive use of materials and parts as compared to well-designed products and, furthermore, poorly designed products are more difficult to manufacture and maintain (Suh, 2001). Therefore, considering the fact that approximately 40% of the sale price is the manufacturing cost (DeGarmo, Black, & Kosher, 1999), it seems that the design stage is the most significant stage of product development. Quality Function Deployment, Taguchi Method, Design for Six Sigma, and Design for Manufacturing are

Figure 1. The cost incurred and committed characteristics within the life cycle of a product

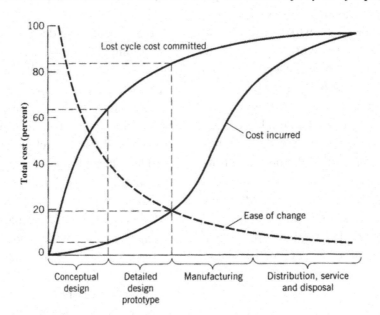

Table 1. The dimensions of quality (Besterfield, 2004)

Dimensions	Meaning
Performance	Primary product/service characteristics, such as weight
Features	Secondary characteristics, added features, such as remote control
Conformance	Meeting industry standards or product/service specifications
Reliability	Consistency of performance over time
Durability	Useful life including repair
Service	Problem/complaint resolution, easy to repair
Response	Human-to-human interface
Aesthetics	Sensory characteristics such as color
Reputation	Past performance such as being ranked first

some examples of design methodologies geared toward quality improvement and enhancement.

Quality has nine dimensions as shown in Table 1. These are in general independent, though there may be some overlapping. Moreover, a product/service may not be excellent in all on them but just a few. For example, In the 70's Japanese automobile manufacturers were known for high-quality cars based on reliability, aesthetics, and conformance (Besterfield, 2004). Therefore, quality product/service can be determined by just a few of these dimensions.

PROJECT MANAGEMENT

Briefly speaking, project management is a set of tools, techniques, and knowledge that, when applied, helps one produce better outcomes for the project (Martin & Tate, 2001). Trying to manage a project without project management is similar to coach a team without a game plan. With investment in planning ahead of time, one can save time and resources, as shown in Figure 2 (Martin, & Tate, 2001). This will contribute to the quality of the product at the end of the project.

Project management provides one with a process that can be followed, a series of moves/actions that help one address some basic questions before starting the project. The questions can include, but not limited to, what is/are the final product(s)? Who is going to do it? What are the customer needs? How long will the project take to finish? How much will the project cost? And so on. Questions are addressed up front so that the work can proceed smoothly and efficiently (Martin & Tate, 2001).

QUALITY AND PROJECT MANAGEMENT

Project management includes managing for quality, and managing for completing the project in a timely manner (Cleland & King, 1988, P. 513). Completing a project on time and within cost loses importance, if the quality of outcomes is not met. It is essential therefore, to embed quality considerations in project management from the beginning.

COST CONSIDERATIONS

Costs include the money and resources required to finish the project. It includes equipment, people, and materials. Usually, the customer wants the project at the lowest cost possible. Plus, the budget for the project is approved based on the scope and schedule (Richman, 2002).

The cost of the project is influenced by the following factors:

* Specifications of the end products, such as quality, levels of performance, and reliability.
* Compliance with institutional, internal standards, or governmental.
* Technical requirements such as upgrade computer software/hardware and administrative needs such as an organization's financial policies (Richman, 2002).

Figure 2. A comparison of a planned and not-planned project from time and resource consumption viewpoints

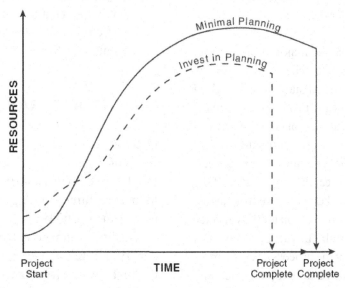

PROJECT QUALITY MANAGEMENT

Project quality management encompasses all the activities of an organization that determine quality objectives, policy, and responsibilities so the project will satisfy the needs for which it was defined (A guideline to the project management, 2000). It includes:

- **Quality planning:** Identifying the relevant standards to the project and the ways to satisfy them.
- **Perform quality assurance:** Applying the planned activities to ensure that the project will employ all the necessary actions to meet its requirements.
- **Perform quality control:** Monitoring specific project outcomes to see whether they meet relevant quality standards and to identify to eliminate causes responsible for unsatisfactory outcomes.

The outcome of quality control and quality management will be an improvement to the product/service. Initial attempts at improving the practice of project management originated from experiences obtained from individual projects. Typically, there are three steps in project improvement practices (Wysocki, 2001):

a. **Project reviews:** At major project milestones, meetings are scheduled to review and assess the general status and health of an ongoing project and to offer get well plans as appropriate. They also provide opportunities to discuss the use of documented project management processes and other practices. These discussions can be very useful. If the project team has taken variance from an established process, the reason for the variance should be discussed. The variance may exist due to the fact that the process does not meet the specific needs of the project. The variance might also be due to the existence of an alternative process brought up by the team that it believes is better than the established process. In addition, the variance may be due to ignorance on the part of the project team. In all of these cases there is valuable intelligence to be collected. The intelligence can lead to improvements practice of process and/or the process itself.

b. **Best practices:** Project managers can pick up good ideas, practices, and processes by reading, attending conferences, and talking with project managers at other companies or those recently-hired project managers in their company. Project managers have an opportunity to use what they have learned in their projects. If there is a process in place to transfer that knowledge to the company in a useful form, all future projects can benefit from it.

c. **Lessons learned:** Through a post-implementation audit, project managers should to pass on what they have learned about process/practice to other project teams that follow them. They should have learned new approaches and new strategies for improving their own project management that will be valuable to others to follow. In addition, they might discover approaches that simply do not work. That information should also be passed forward so other project managers would use them.

QUALITY ASSURANCE

Quality Assurance (QA) is the application of a series of systematic, planned activities to insure that the project will use all the necessary processes to meet requirement (A guideline to the project management, 2004).

Quality assurance is the process of building quality into the project process—doing it right the first time—and is an important method of cost avoidance. But further, quality assurance is the integral aspect of project processes that create a safe and reliable product. For instance, the imposition of reliability testing in a product is a good indicator of the internalization of quality assurance into the design and production process. QA is not an external concept; it is the total integration of procedures and processes that test, validate, and verify the functionality of the product according to customer needs. Quality assurance is scheduled early in the project in the form of a set of quality assurance tasks, e.g., design reviews that examine how initial design tasks were performed and whether those processes were consistent with professional design standards. New design software in the engineering field now provide for these tests and ensure that computer-aided design work is performed right the first time (Barkley, 2008).

Usually a quality department, division, etc. oversees quality assurance activities in an organization. Its support may provide to a variety or people or sub-division within the organization such as the project team, the management, and the stakeholders. It provides an umbrella under which other quality activities such as quality control and continues quality improvement are implemented.

Figure 3 depicts various steps in performing QA (A guideline to the project management, 2000).

Each of these steps is explained briefly as follows:

- **Input:**
  o *Quality management plan:* A description of how the project management team will implement the quality policy developed in the organization.
  o *Quality metrics:* A set of operational definitions that specifically describe what things are how the quality control process would measure them.
  o *Steps for analyzing the steps used to identify none-value adding processes:*
  o *Work performance information:* This information includes the status of the project activities being performed.
  o *Approved change request:* They are the documented, authorized changes used to expand the scope of the project in hand. An approved change can modify various items such as cost or budget, procedures, project management plan, and so on.

Figure 3. QA steps (A guideline to the project management, 2000, P. 188)

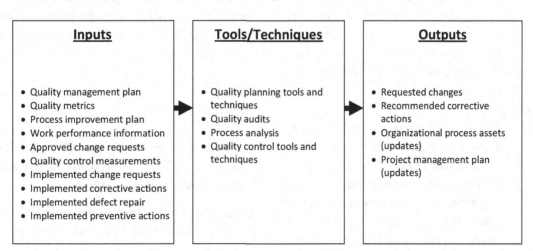

Inputs	Tools/Techniques	Outputs
• Quality management plan • Quality metrics • Process improvement plan • Work performance information • Approved change requests • Quality control measurements • Implemented change requests • Implemented corrective actions • Implemented defect repair • Implemented preventive actions	• Quality planning tools and techniques • Quality audits • Process analysis • Quality control tools and techniques	• Requested changes • Recommended corrective actions • Organizational process assets (updates) • Project management plan (updates)

o *Quality control measurements:* These measures are the results of quality control activities and, are sent back to the QA for use in re-evaluating the quality standards.

- **Tools/Techniques:**

o *Quality planning tools and techniques:* There are various tools used to promote quality in projects and plans. Some of these tools include cost-benefit analysis, benchmarking, Design of Experiments (DOE), and Cost of Quality (COQ).

o *Quality audits:* This is an structured, independent review to see whether it comply with the organizational and project policies, procedures, and processes. The audits may be done randomly or based on an schedule. Plus, either trained, in-house inspectors or external ones can carry on the audit.

o *Process analysis:* The purpose is to identify areas of improvement from an organizational and technical standpoint. In addition, this process examines any problems and constraints, non-value-adding activities identified during process operation.

o *Quality control tools and techniques:* These techniques include cause and effect diagram, control charts, run chart, flowcharts, Pareto diagram, histograms, scatter diagram, statistical sampling, inspection, and defect repair review.

- **Outputs:**

o *Requested changes:* It includes taking actions to increase the effectiveness and efficiency of the policies and procedures of the organization

o *Recommended corrective actions:* Corrective actions, which come as results of quality assurance activity, are recommended to the organization.

o *Organizational process assets (updates):* Organizational process assets include any process-related asset that has influence on the success of the project. These assets can even be from other organizations involving in the project. Updating the quality standards will provide validation of the efficiency and effectiveness of the organization's quality standards.

o *Project management plan (updates):* This plan will be updated which can include incorporation of processes that have been gone through improvement.

CONCLUSION

Project management encompasses the entire life cycle of a project, including such aspects as feasibility study of the project, project planning, implementation, evaluation, support, and maintenance of the project. Quality must be an embedded part of any project and one therefore, needs to insure that the project is finished on time and within cost range and with the desired quality. In this regard, Quality assurance is the process of building quality into the project process—doing it right the first time. QA includes three steps: input (i.e. quality management plan, etc.), tools/techniques (i.e. quality audit, etc.), and output (i.e. requested change, etc.).

REFERENCES

A guideline to the project management body of knowledge (2004). (3rd ed.). *An American national standard* (ANSI/PMI 99-001-200).

Barkley, B. (2008). *Project management in new product development.* New York: McGraw-Hill.

Besterfield, H. D. (2004). *Quality control,* 7th ed. Upper Saddle River, NJ: Prentice Hall.

Besterfield, D. H., Besterfield-Michna, C. B., & Besterfield-Sacre, M. (2003). *Total quality management* (3rd ed.). Upper Saddle River, NJ: Pearson Prentice Hall.

Chang, T., Wysk, R. A., & Wang, H. (1998). *Computer-aided manufacturing* (2nd ed.). Upper Saddle River, NJ: Prentice Hall.

Cleland, D. I., & King, W. R. (Ed.), (1988). *Project management handbook* (2nd Ed.). John Wiley.

DeGarmo, E. P., Black, J. T., & Kohser, R. A. (1999). *Materials and processes in manufacturing* (8th ed.). New York: John Wiley & Sons

Martin, P. K., & Tate, K. (2001). *Getting started in project management.* New York: John Wiley & Sons.

Richman, L. (2002). *Project management step-by-step.* New York: Amacon.

Singh, N. (1996). *Systems approach to computer-integrated design and manufacturing.* New York: John Wiley & Sons.

Suh, N. P. (1998). Axiomatic design theory for systems. *Research in Engineering Design., 10,* 189-209.

Wysocki, R. K. (2004). *Project management process improvement.* Artech House Publishers.

KEY TERMS AND DEFINITIONS

Cost Considerations: The money and resources required to finish the project. This includes equipment, people, and materials. Usually, the customer wants the project at the lowest cost possible. Plus, the budget for the project is approved based on the scope and schedule.

Project Management: Project management is carefully planned, organized effort to manage the resources in order to successfully accomplish specific project goals and objectives. Project management covers the entire life cycle of a project right from the feasibility study of the project, project planning, implementation, evaluation, support, and maintenance of the project. Each phases of the project is a vast topic within project management. The topic of interest here is the quality assurance in project management.

Project Quality Management: All the activities of an organization that determine quality objectives, policy, and responsibilities so the project will satisfy the needs for which it was defined.

Project Review: Project milestones meetings that are scheduled to review and assess the general status and health of an ongoing project and to offer get well plans as appropriate.

Quality: Excellent performance of a product or service.

Quality Assurance: The application of a series of systematic planned activities to insure that the project will use all the necessary processes to meet requirement.

Total Quality Management (TQM): The application of quantitative methods and human resources to improve all the processes within an organization to meet and/or exceed customer needs now and in the future.

Chapter XV
Quality Management, Control, and Assurance:
Tools and Techniques

Sohail Anwar
The Pennsylvania State University, Altoona College, USA

ABSTRACT

This chapter provides a fundamental yet comprehensive coverage of quality management. Bringing managers and engineers the most up-to-date quality management tools, research, and theory, this chapter shows readers how to plan for quality and achieve quality control. Broad in scope and inclusive in methodology, the material covered in this chapter will be useful for anyone concerned with quality management and control in business and industry. Topics covered include planning and organizing for quality, total quality management, quality improvement, statistical quality control, and ISO 9000. The chapter begins with an introduction to the concept of quality. Next, the quality management philosophies developed by Deming, Juran, and Crosby are presented. The principles of total quality management (TQM) are described next. The major steps in planning and organizing for quality are addressed in this chapter. Next, the quality improvement process, approaches to problem solving, and tools for quality improvement are presented. The concepts and techniques of statistical quality control are also covered in this chapter. Finally, the ISO 9000 and ISO 14000 quality standards are described.

INTRODUCTION

During the past two decades, there has been a revolution in quality. Significant improvements have occurred not only in the quality of products and services, but also in the leadership quality and business management quality. The demand for higher levels of quality appears to be customer driven. People want to produce and use quality products and services.

The prevailing view of quality is that it is everyone's responsibility. According to Besterfield (2001), "The responsibility for quality begins when marketing determines the customer's quality requirements and continues until the product is received by a satisfied customer" (p.5).

Most organizations view quality more as a continuously improving process than a product. It is a process where lessons learned are used to improve future products and services. Therefore, present emphasis is on the development of quality improvement processes which constitute an important component of the strategic planning process.

The quality management system of an organization consists of collective plans, activities, and events that are provided to ensure that a product or a service will satisfy given needs. To be effective, the quality management system needs coordination and compatibility of its component processes and an understanding of their interfaces. The elements of a quality management system may include teamwork, strategic integration, continuous improvement, customer focus, and structured problem solving.

DEFINITIONS OF QUALITY

While the importance of quality is now generally recognized, there is no single generally accepted definition of "quality". Some of the definitions provided by Pyzdek (1996) are as follows:

1. **Transcendent definition:** "Quality cannot be defined, you know what it is". (Persig 1974, p. 213)
2. **User-based definition:** "Quality consists of the ability to satisfy wants". (Edwards 1968, p. 37) "Quality is fitness for use". (Juran 1974m, p. 2-2)

3. **Manufacturing-based definition:** "Quality is the degree to which a specific product conforms to a design or specification". (Gilmore 1974, p. 16)
4. **Value-based definition:** "Quality is the degree of excellence at an acceptable price and the control of variability at an acceptable cost". (Broh 1982, p. 3)

In addition, Besterfield (2001) quantifies the definition of quality as follows:

$$Q = P/E$$

Where

Q = quality
P = performance
E = expectations

The ISO 9000 definition of quality is provided by Kerzner (2006) as "the totality of features and characteristics of a product or service that bears on its ability to satisfy stated or implied needs" (p. 834)

Nine different dimensions of quality are described by Garvin (1988). They are:

1. **Performance:** Primary operating characteristic of a product.
2. **Features:** Secondary characteristics of a product.
3. **Conformance:** The extent to which physical and performance characteristics of a product meet specifications.
4. **Reliability:** Consistency of performance over time.
5. **Durability:** Useful life of a product.
6. **Serviceability:** Resolution of problems and complaints, competence, and ease of repair.
7. **Response:** Human-to-human interface.
8. **Aesthetics:** Sensory characteristics of a product.

9. **Perceived quality:** Past performance and other intangibles.

QUALITY MANAGEMENT PHILOSOPHIES

Three individuals, W. Edwards Deming, Joseph Juran, and Philip Crosby, have emerged as major quality "gurus". They have developed distinct philosophies on how to measure, manage, and improve quality. Their quality management philosophies are presented in this section of the chapter.

Deming's 14 Points for Management are listed in Table 1.

Deming's quality philosophy emphasizes the improvement of product and service conformance to specifications by reducing variability in the design and manufacturing process. Deming believes that variation is the main cause of poor quality. Although variations cannot be completely eliminated, one can learn more about them and eventually reduce them.

Juran's 10 steps to Quality Improvement are listed in Table 2.

Juran believes that the manufacturer's view of quality is conformance to specifications, whereas the customer's view of quality is fitness for use. Juran defines five attributes of quality. They are:

1. **Quality of design:** Focuses on market research, the product concept, and the design
2. **Quality of conformance:** Focuses on manpower, management, and technology

Table 1.

Deming's 14 Points for Management
1. Create constancy of purpose for improvement of products and services.
2. Learn the new philosophy.
3. Cease dependence on inspection to achieve quality.
4. End the practice of awarding business on the basis of price tag alone.
5. Improve constantly and forever every process for planning, production, and service.
6. Institute training.
7. Adopt and institute leadership.
8. Drive out fear and create trust.
9. Break down barriers between staff areas.
10. Eliminate exhortations and targets for the work force.
11. Eliminate numerical quotas for production.
12. Remove barriers that rob people of pride of workmanship.
13. Institute a vigorous program of education and self-improvement for everyone.
14. Everyone in the organization should work to accomplish the transformation.

Table 2.

Juran's 10 steps to Quality Improvement
1. Develop an awareness of the need and opportunity for improvement.
2. Set goals for improvement.
3. Organize to achieve the goals.
4. Institute training.
5. Solve problems.
6. Report progress.
7. Give recognition.
8. Communicate results.
9. Keep score.
10. Make annual improvement a part of the regular processes and systems of the organization.

3. **Availability:** Focuses on reliability, maintainability, and logistical support
4. **Safety:** Focuses on the potential hazards of product use
5. **Field use:** How the product will be used by the customer

Crosby's 14 Steps to Quality Improvement are listed in Table 3.

Crosby's Four Absolutes of Quality are as follows:

1. Quality means conformance to requirements, not elegance.
2. Quality comes from prevention
3. The only performance standard is "zero defects".
4. Quality is measured by the cost of nonconformance.

Unlike Juran and Deming, Crosby's quality philosophy is primarily behavioral. His approach focuses more on management and organizational processes for changing corporate culture than on the use of statistical techniques. However, Crosby's focus is on managerial thinking than on organizational systems. His philosophy fits well within existing organizational structures

TOTAL QUALITY MANAGEMENT (TQM)

Total quality management (TQM) is the process of building quality into goods and services from the beginning. TQM makes quality everyone's responsibility since it is an integrative management concept for continuously improving the quality of goods and services. TQM requires the following basic concepts:

1. A committed and involved management.
2. A focus on customers.
3. Effective involvement of all the employees.
4. Continuous improvement of all the business and manufacturing processes,
5. Development of effective partnerships with suppliers.
6. Establishment of performance measurement systems for all the business and manufacturing processes.

TQM integrates basic management techniques, continuous improvement efforts, and technical tools under a disciplined approach. The primary purpose of TQM is to provide a quality product or service to customers, which will, in turn, result in

Table 3.

Crosby's 14 Steps to Quality Improvement
1. Management should demonstrate its commitment to quality.
2. Establish quality improvement teams with representation from each department in the organization.
3. Find out where current and potential quality problems lie.
4. Determine the cost of quality and explain its use as a management tool.
5. Raise the quality awareness of everyone in the organization.
6. Take appropriate actions to correct quality problems.
7. Set up a committee for the zero-defect program.
8. Properly train supervisory personnel to effectively play their role in the quality improvement program.
9. In order to let everyone in the organization realize that a change has been made, organize a "zero-defects day" event.
10. Encourage everyone in the organization to establish improvement goals for himself/herself.
11. Encourage employees to communicate to management regarding the difficulties they face in achieving their improvement goals.
12. Establish a system of recognition.
13. Set up quality councils to communicate regularly.
14. Do it all over again to demonstrate that quality improvement is a never ending process.

an increased productivity and lower costs. Some of the benefits of TQM are as follows:

1. Improves customer satisfaction.
2. Enhances the quality of products and services.
3. Reduces waste and inventory, resulting in lower costs.
4. Increases productivity.
5. Reduces product development time.
6. Improves customer service and delivery times.
7. Results in a better utilization of human resources.

The TQM program in an organization consists of the following elements:

1. **Quality policy:** A document that is typically developed by quality experts. It is fully supported by the top management. The quality policy of an organization provides information regarding the quality objectives, the level of quality acceptable to the organization, and the responsibility of the organization's members for implementing the policy.
2. **Quality objectives:** Are a part of an organization's quality policy. They should be achievable, clearly stated, define specific goals, and state specific time frame for their completion.
3. **Quality assurance:** A collective term for the activities carried out to ensure that products and services meet the required quality level.
4. **Quality control:** A collective term for activities, within the process, that are intended to produce specific quality characteristics. Such activities include continuous monitoring of processes, identification and elimination of problem causes, and use of statistical process control to reduce process variations.

5. **Quality audit:** An independent assessment conducted by qualified personnel to ensure that the project is meeting the quality requirements and that the established quality procedures are being followed.
6. **Quality plan:** A roadmap to deliver a quality product or service. Identifies all the customers and causes the organization to be responsive to customer's needs.

Successful implementation of TQM will depend on a number of factors. They include the following:

1. **Long-term vision:** Improvements do not take place instantly. The planning and organization of quality improvement process takes time and needs a major commitment from everyone in the organization.
2. **Focus on customers:** Quality is driven by and defined by the customers. A variety of methods should be used to understand customer needs and values.
3. **Top management commitment:** Top management must demonstrate a firm and highly visible commitment to quality improvement.
4. **Training and tools:** Everyone in the organization needs training in TQM concepts and techniques. Training must be viewed as a continuous effort and not as a one-time project.
5. **Involvement:** Everyone in the organization must get involved in the quality improvement efforts. All the employees must be empowered to make decisions that impact quality.
6. **Evaluation and reporting:** Appropriate measures must be established to assess quality improvement efforts. Reporting of information must be timely and accurate.
7. **Communication:** Improved communications within the organization support the TQM efforts.

8. **Strong leadership:** Top management must function as organization's TQM leaders.

Several international awards have been established to recognize the successful quality efforts made by organizations all over the world. Two notable awards are the Deming Prize and the Malcolm Baldrige National Quality Award. The Deming Prize was established in 1951 by the Union of Japanese Scientists and Engineers (JUSE) in recognition of Edward Deming's superior achievements in statistical quality control. The Deming Prize is awarded to those companies which meet a high standard in the application of organization-wide quality control based on statistical quality control. The Deming Prize has several categories, including prizes for individuals, factories, and small companies. There are only a small number of awards that are given each year. One of the objectives of the Deming Prize is to ensure that an organization has so effectively established a quality process that it will continue to improve long after a prize is awarded.

The other notable quality award is the Malcolm Baldrige National Quality Award. In the USA, the need to recognize the outstanding quality improvement efforts made by companies was realized through the establishment of the Malcolm Baldrige National Quality Award. This highly prestigious award is given to those organizations that have achieved a level of world-class competition through their quality management efforts. The criteria for the award include the following categories:

1. Leadership
2. Strategic planning
3. Customer and market focus strategy
4. Information and analysis
5. Human resource development and management
6. Process management
7. Business results

In accordance with the award guidelines, up to two organizations can win a Baldrige Award in each category of manufacturing, small business, and service. Since 1988, when the first Malcolm Baldrige Award was presented, there have been a few winners. This indicates the high standard of quality management which the companies need to achieve in order to win this award.

PLANNING AND ORGANIZING FOR QUALITY

Planning is the process by which goals and objectives are defined and actions are selected to obtain desired results. Planning for quality requires that one determines goal or objective and then selects the actions needed to achieve the desired result. Indeed, planning is the starting point for ensuring that a total quality concept is developed.

Elements of the Quality Planning Process are as follows:

1. **Develop a vision statement:** "Vision" for an organization consists of the guiding principles and the direction of expected growth of an organization. The vision statement is generally developed by key managers.
2. **Determine the purpose (TQM):** Focused organizations state their purpose in terms of customer satisfaction and commitment to quality.
3. **Determine the organizational mission:** The mission of an organization is a broad statement describing the direction in which the organization will be moving. It is generally stated in terms of the products that the company intends to produce.
4. **Conduct environmental survey:** The environmental survey is conducted to develop knowledge about all the internal and external activities which impact the mission of the organization. Examples of such activities

include customer requirements, competitive conditions, and resource constraints.

5. **Develop specific and measurable objectives:** These objectives must be in agreement with the overall organizational goals.

6. **Determine and schedule action steps:** Decision must be made regarding the action steps to be taken in order to meet objectives. In doing so, one must consider the assumptions made regarding the future and the restrictions that limit the choice of actions.

7. **Evaluate the plan:** The evaluation of a proposed quality plan must be done in light of financial constraints. As such, adjustments to budgets may be required.

8. **Establish a control mechanism:** Methods for measuring results in light of objectives must be developed. One possible way to monitor a quality program is through use of quality audits. A quality assurance audit is a periodic and systematic review of the documented requirements of a quality assurance program.

According to Pyzdek (1996), the following questions need to be answered during the development of effective quality plans:

1. What specific quality work is to be done?
2. When, during the product development, production, and service cycles does each work activity has to be completed?
3. How is it to be done? What method or device will be used?
4. Who does it? What is his/her position in the organization?
5. Where is it to be done? At what location?
6. What tools or equipment to be used?
7. What are the inputs to the work?
8. What are the outputs of the work to be performed?
9. Is any record of the action to be made? If so, what is the form of data needed?

10. What are the other alternative actions?
11. What are the criteria for those alternative actions?
12. What is the time limit on the work to be performed?

All quality planning must be customer-driven. Customer requirements must be determined, translated into product specifications, and realized through production. Quality Function Deployment (QFD) is a technique used to ensure that the customer's voice is carried through the product design and production process. The key planning document used in QFD is called the House of Quality which provides a planning structure for relating customers' requirements to technical specifications. The House of Quality ensures that the key technical specifications are identified and deployed throughout the production process. In a simple graphical format, the House of Quality relates customer requirements, product characteristics, and competitive analysis. Building the House of Quality involves the following steps:

1. Identity customer attributes.
2. Identify counterpart characteristics
3. Determine the relationship between the customer attributes to the counterpart characteristics.
4. Conduct an evaluation of competing products.
5. Evaluate counterpart characteristics and develop target values.
6. Find out which counterpart characteristics need to be deployed in the remainder of the product process.

Organizing is the process of assigning work and responsibilities to appropriate functions and individuals along with the proper delegation of authority. Thus, organizing establishes lines of authority, improves efficiency and quality of work, and enhances communication.

The key steps of organizing are:

1. Identify the tasks to be performed.
2. Assign responsibility for these tasks.
3. Assign work to individuals to accomplish these tasks.

Evans and Lindsay (1993) list the four key considerations in structuring the quality control component of an organization. These considerations are:

1. Keep levels of supervision to a minimum so that the lines of communication can be kept as short as possible.
2. Keep spans of supervision as broad as possible. The span of supervision is a term that
   refers to the number of individuals reporting directly to a supervisor.
3. Place similar work components into a similar work package that can be handled by an individual.
4. Ensure that the highest reporting level of the quality organization is high enough to indicate the importance of the quality function.

The major components of a quality organization are new design control, incoming material control, manufacturing quality assurance, special process studies, and general management. Extra planning and lead time need to be built into the design phase of any product development process.

Incoming material control is a key component of the quality function. Costs must be incurred to test and inspect incoming materials, maintain tools and equipment, and visit suppliers to audit their quality systems and processes. Acceptance sampling techniques are often applied to the incoming material control.

Manufacturing quality assurance requires that measurement, control, and quality improvement activities are carried out in timely and cost-effective ways. Also, the appraisal activity must be carried out in the areas of inspection, testing, development of procedures and guidelines, training of operators, maintenance of test equipment, and reporting of quality levels and results.

The most important type of special process study is to determine the capability of most important processes in an organization. The improvement study is another type of special process study. It often requires a team approach.

General management includes finance and marketing groups within an organization. It has the overall responsibility for planning and implementing the quality assurance program. Also, general management has the responsibility for obtaining customer feedback, analyzing complaints, and initiating corrective actions when needed.

PROBLEM SOLVING PROCESS

Evans and Lindsay (1993) define problem solving as the activity associated with changing the state of what is actually happening to what should be happening. According to Besterfield (2001), the problem solving approach as applied to process improvement has the following phases:

1. Identify the opportunity for improvement.
2. Analyze the current process.
3. Determine the optimal solution.
4. Implement the optimal solution.
5. Analyze the results.
6. Standardize the solution.
7. Develop a plan for the future.

As stated above, the Phase 1 of the problem solving process leads to problems that have the greatest potential for process improvement. There are several ways to identify problems:

1. Pareto analysis.

2. Proposals/suggestions from people inside the organization.
3. Assessment of customers' needs.
4. Research data on performance of products versus competitors.
5. Findings of government regulatory agencies.
6. Employee surveys.
7. Brainstorming by work groups.

Problems offer opportunities for improvement. For a situation to qualify as a problem, it must meet the following criteria:

1. Is the problem important? Why?
2. Will solving this problem result in the achievement of goals?
3. Is it possible to quantify the problem?

The Phase 2 of the problem solving approach requires an understanding and an analysis of the current state of performance of the process under consideration. The major activities to be conducted during this phase include the following:

1. Determine the measurements needed to analyze the process under consideration
2. Gather data.
3. Define the process boundaries.
4. Define the process outputs and the customers.
5. Define the process inputs and the suppliers.
6. Determine the process flow.
7. Identify root causes of the problem.
8. Determine levels of customer satisfaction.

During the Phase 3 of the problem solving process, possible solutions are determined and the optimal solution is recommended. All the possible solutions for the problem under consideration are determined first. Then the evaluation or testing of the solutions is done. The evaluation or testing determines which of the possible solutions have the greatest potential for success. During this phase, the brainstorming is the key technique used.

During the phase 4, the optimal solution selected during Phase 3 is implemented. During this phase, the following steps are completed:

1. Prepare the implementation plan.
2. Obtain approval for the plan.
3. Implement the process improvements.
4. Study the results.

During the phase 5, the results are studied. In order to do so, measurements need to be taken. Measurement tools include run charts, control charts, Pareto charts, histograms, and check sheets.

During the phase 6, the solution is standardized by positive control of the process, process certification, and the operator certification

During the phase 7, appropriate systems are established by management to identify areas for future improvement and to track performance with respect to internal and external customers.

QUALITY MANAGEMENT: QUANTITATIVE TOOLS AND TECHNIQUES

The quantitative tools of total quality management include statistical process control (SPC), acceptance sampling, reliability, design of experiments (DOE), and the failure mode and effect analysis (FMEA).

SPC consists of seven tools:

1. Pareto Analysis.
2. Cause and Effect Diagrams
3. Check Sheets.
4. Flow Charts.
5. Scatter Diagrams.
6. Histograms.
7. Control Charts

Pareto analysis is the process of ranking opportunities to determine which of the several potential opportunities need to be pursued first. It separates the "vital few" from the "trivial many". There are three types of Pareto analysis:

1. **Basic Pareto analysis:** Identifies the vital few contributors to the quality problems.
2. **Comparative Pareto analysis:** Focuses on any number of program actions.
3. **Weighted Pareto analysis:** Gives a measure of significance to factors that may not look significant initially.

Pareto analysis should be used at various stages in a quality improvement process to determine which step to take next. Being a powerful quality improvement tool, Pareto analysis is applicable both to problem identification and the measurement of progress.

To perform a Pareto Analysis, Pyzdek (1996) lists the following step-by-step method:

1. Determine the classifications (Pareto categories) for the graph. If the desired information does not exist, obtain it by designing checksheets and logsheets.
2. Select a time interval for analysis. The interval should be long enough to be representative of typical performance.
3. Determine the total occurrences (i.e., cost, defect counts, etc.) for each category. Also determine the grand total. If there are several categories which account for only a small part of the total, group these into a category called "other."
4. Compute the percentage for each category by dividing the category total by the grand total and multiplying by 100.
5. Rank-order the categories from the largest total occurrences to the smallest.
6. Compute the "cumulative percentage" by adding the percentage for each category to that of any preceding categories.

7. Construct a chart with the left vertical axis scaled from 0 to at least the grand total. Put an appropriate label on the axis. Scale the right vertical axis from 0 to 100%, with 100% on the right side being the same height as the grand total on the left side.
8. Label the horizontal axis with the category names. The leftmost category should be the largest, second largest next, and so on.
9. Draw in bars representing the amount of each category. The height of the bar is determined by the left vertical axis.
10. Draw a line that shows the cumulative percentage column of the Pareto analysis table. The cumulative percentage line is determined by the right vertical axis.

Cause-and-Effect Analysis uses diagramming techniques to represent a meaningful relationship between an effect and its causes. It was developed by Dr. Ishikawa in 1943. Cause-and-effect diagrams are also known as fishbone diagrams. The cause-and-effect analysis requires the following six steps:

1. **Identify the problem:** This step often involves use of other SPC tools, such as Pareto analysis, control charts, and histograms. The completion of this step leads to a clear and concise problem statement.
2. **Select an interdisciplinary brainstorming team:** An interdisciplinary team covering several knowledge areas is needed to determine causes of the problem.
3. **Draw problem box and prime arrow:** The problem box contains the problem statement. The prime arrow provides the foundation for the major categories of the problem causes.
4. **List major categories:** The major categories contributing to the problem are identified. The basic categories for the primary causes of a problem are most often personnel,

method, materials, machinery, measurements, and environment.

5. **Identify defect causes:** After listing the major causes contributing to the problem stated in the problem box, the causes related to each of the major categories need to be identified.

6. **Identify corrective action:** The corrective action analysis is conducted in the same way as the cause-and-effect analysis. The cause-and-effect diagram is now reversed

A check sheet is used to ensure that the data are collected carefully and accurately by the operators. Data should be presented in such a form that it can be easily and quickly used and analyzed. Whenever possible, it should include information on time and location. Data collection for such a check sheet is accomplished by placing an "X" in the appropriate square of the sheet. Figure 1 shows a check sheet for a 9-cavity plastic mold. This check sheet shows that there are quality problems at the upper corners of the mold.

A flow chart is a useful graphical tool to show the inputs, actions, and the outputs of a given process. Inputs include the factors of production, such as, land, materials, labor, equipment, and management. Actions represent the ways in which the inputs are manipulated to create value. Actions include procedures, handling, storage, transportation, and processing. Outputs are the products or services which result from actions. Outputs are delivered to the customers. Outputs also include undesirable forms such as scrap and rework.

A scatter diagram is the simplest way to find out if a cause-and-effect relationship exists between two variables. A scatter diagram is plotted as a simple graph with X and Y coordinates showing the relationship between the two variables. This relationship falls into four basic categories:

1. **No correlation:** The data points are widely scattered resulting in the absence of a pattern.

2. **Negative correlation:** It has a downward or a negative slope.

3. **Positive correlation:** It has an upward or positive slope.

4. **Curvilinear correlation:** It is demonstrated by a somewhat U-shaped curve.

A Histogram is a pictorial representation of a set of data created by grouping the measurements into cells.

Histograms help determine the shape of a data set. A histogram makes it easy to see the dispersion and central tendency. The construction of a histogram involves the following steps:

1. Find the largest value and the smallest value in a set of data.

2. Determine the range of the given set of data by subtracting the smallest value from the largest.

3. Choose a number of cells for the histogram. The following guidelines may be used for the determination of the number of histogram cells:

    a. If the sample size is 100 or less, the number of histogram cells should be 7 to 10.

    b. If the sample size is 101 – 200, the number of histogram cells should be 11 to 15.

Figure 1. Check sheet for plastic mold nonconformities

XXXX XXX	XX	XXXX XX
	X	
	XX	X

c. If the sample size is 201 or more, the number of histogram cells should be 13 to 20.

d. Find the width of each cell using the equation

$$W = \frac{Range}{Number\ of\ Cells}$$

where W is the cell width.

e. Determine the cell boundaries. The low boundary of the first histogram cell must be less than the smallest value in the data set. Other cell boundaries are determined by adding the cell

f. width W to the previous cell boundary. Continue doing so until the upper boundary exceeds the largest value in the data set.

g. Review the raw data and determine which histogram cell each value falls.

h. Count the number of raw values which fall in each cell. This count is also called the frequency.

i. Construct a graph from the frequency table. The vertical axis of the graph will show the frequency in each cell. The horizontal axis represents cell boundaries.

j. Construct bars to represent the cell frequencies. The bars should all be of the same width. The height of a bar corresponds to the frequency of the corresponding histogram cell.

Control charts are a very valuable tool for the process quality improvement. The use of control chart focuses on the prevention of defects, rather than their detection. When a control chart is first introduced, the process is generally unstable. When the assignable causes for out-of-control conditions are identified and the corrective action has been taken, the process becomes stable.

The analysis of a control chart reveals if the inherent process variability and the process average are at stable levels, whether one or both are unstable or whether appropriate corrective action should be taken. The control charts are also used to distinguish between common cause variation and the special cause variation.

Common cause variation is a source of random variation which is present in any process. It is inherent in a process. The cause of this variation can be corrected only by a management decision.

Special cause variation can be controlled at the local level. A special cause is indicated either by a point on the control chart that is beyond the upper or the lower control limit or by a trend. When a process goes out of control, special causes exist. Thus, corrective action must be taken.

Two types of control charts are as follows:

1. **Variable control charts:** They are used when measurements from a process are variable. Examples of variable data are the diameter of a bearing, the thickness of a clutch plate, or the electrical output from a transducer.

2. **Attribute control charts:** They are used for attribute data. Attributes have only two values, such as, conforming/non conforming, go/no-go, and present/absent.

The variable control charts have the following basic types:

1. $\bar{X}$ **and R charts:** Used to study changes in the mean and range of a process.

2. $\bar{X}$ **and s charts:** Used to study changes in the mean and the standard deviation of a process.

The attributes charts have the following types:

1. **ρ chart:** Used for the fraction of attributes nonconforming or defective in a sample of varying size.
2. **nρ chart:** Used for the number of attributes non conforming or defective in a sample of constant size
3. **c chart:** Used for the number of attributes non conforming or defects in a single item within a subgroup or a lot.
4. **u chart:** Used for the number of attributes non conforming or defects in a single item within a subgroup or a lot.

All control charts have certain common features. Each control chart has a centerline, statistical control limits, and the control data. The two statistical control limits consist of an upper control limit for values greater than the mean and a lower control limit for values less than the mean.

Specification limits are used when specific parametric requirements exist for a process or a product. They differ from statistical control limits in that they are specified for a process, rather than resulting from the process measurements. Two specification limits exist, the Upper Specification Limit (USL) and the Lower Specification Limit (LSL).

Process capability is the ability to produce a product that meets design specifications. An indicator of the process capability is expressed as "$C\rho$" which is given as:

$$C\rho = \frac{USL - LSL}{6\sigma}$$

where "σ" is the standard deviation. The generally accepted rules for "$C\rho$" are:

i. $C\rho > 1.33$ which means that the process is well within the customer's specifications.
ii. $1.33 \geq C\rho \geq 1.0$ which means that the process is marginally acceptable. Improvements in process control are needed.
iii. $C\rho \leq 1.0$ which means that the process is unacceptable as is. Improvements in process control are mandatory.

Besides the above mentioned seven tools of statistical process control (SPC), there are other quantitative tools of total quality management (TQM) which will be described now. Acceptance Sampling is one of the quantitative tools of TQM.

Lot-by-lot acceptance sampling is the most commonly used type of sampling. A predetermined number of samples from each lot is inspected by attributes. If the number of non conforming units is less than the prescribed minimum, the lot is accepted; otherwise, the lot is rejected.

Acceptance sampling is most frequently used in one of the following situations:

1. When the destructive testing is being performed.
2. When the cost of 100% inspection is higher compared to the cost of passing a non conforming unit.
3. When there are many similar units to be inspected.
4. When information such as a variable control chart or an attributes control chart or process capability index $C\rho$ is unavailable.
5. When automated inspection is not available.

The acceptance sampling has the following advantages

1. Since the emphasis is shifted from inspection, rapid improvement in the process is possible.
2. It is more economical because of fewer inspections.
3. Can be used with destructive testing.

The acceptance sampling has the following disadvantages:

1. More time and effort must be devoted to planning and documentation.
2. There is no assurance that the entire lot conforms to specifications.

Reliability is another TQM tool. It is the ability of a product to perform its intended function over a period of time. The four factors that are associated with reliability include the numerical value, the intended function, life, and the environmental conditions. The numerical value is the probability that a product will function satisfactory during a particular period of time. Intended life of a product refers to the length of time it will last.

Design of Experiments (DOE) is another TQM tool used to determine those variables in a process or product that are the critical parameters and their target values. Changes to the process or product are introduced by means of carefully designed experiments. Design of Experiments should actually precede SPC in many situations since it is used to identify the critical parameters and their target values.

Yet another TQM tool, Failure Mode and Effect Analysis (FMEA), is a group of activities intended to:

1. Evaluate the potential failure of a product or process.
2. Identify actions that could reduce or eliminate the chance of the occurrence of the potential failures.
3. Document the process.

QUALITY MANAGEMENT: NON-QUANTITATIVE TOOLS

The non quantitative tools of TQM include ISO 9000, ISO 14000, and QS 9000.

The ISO 9000 series is a standard Quality Management System (QMS) that has been approved by many countries (Sower, Savoie, & Renick, 1999).

The term ISO stands for International Organization for Standards.

ISO 9000 is applicable to almost all the organizations including manufacturers, developers of software, producers of processed materials, and service providers. In 2000, the ISO 9000 standards were revised significantly so that their structure more closely resembles the way organizations are managed. The eight key principles built into the ISO 9000: 2000 standards are as follows:

1. Involvement of people
2. Leadership
3. Focus on customers
4. Process approach
5. Continuous improvement
6. System approach to management
7. Factual approach to decision making
8. Mutually beneficial relationships with suppliers

The ISO 9000: 2000 series consists of three areas:

1. ISO 9000: 2000 – Covers fundamentals and vocabulary
2. ISO 9001: 2000 – Comprises the Quality Management System requirements/
3. ISO 9004: 2000 – Provides guidance for performance improvement.

The first area in the series ISO 9000: 2000, provides information about the concepts and vocabulary used in the other two standards. This area serves as a reference to support the interpretation of ISO 9001: 2000

The requirements listed in ISO 9001:2000 constitute the criteria for an acceptable Quality Management System (QMS). The four clauses of the QMS are as follows:

1. **Management responsibility:** This clause consists of subclauses associated with customer requirements, legal requirements,

quality policy, planning, system requirements, and management review. A quality policy is developed in order to meet the needs of the organization and its customers as well as meeting requirements. The planning process consists of the identification of the quality characteristics at all stages, verification activities, acceptability criteria, and the quality records. System requirements are developed as a means of meeting the quality objectives and conformance to customer requirements. Management review is needed to make sure that the QMS remains effective.

2. **Resource management:** This clause consists of subclauses which deal with human resources, information, infrastructure, and work environment. Effective resource management is needed to make sure that the organization can determine and provide the required resources for the establishment and maintenance of the Quality Management System

3. **Product/service realization:** This clause includes subclauses which deal with customer related processes, design and development, purchasing, production and service operations, and control of measuring equipment. The organization ensures that these processes function under controlled conditions and their outputs meet customer requirements.

The ISO 9004: 2000 standard provides guidelines for organizations planning to go beyond ISO 9001: 2000 and establish a quality management system that not only meets customer requirements but also emphasizes performance improvement. ISO 9004: 2000 is not a requirement and does not lead to certification. ISO 9004 provides a continuous improvement model.

The major automotive manufacturers, such as General Motors, Ford, and Chrysler, worked together in 1990s to develop a quality system that has its foundations in ISO 9000. This compre-

hensive standard, titled QS 9000, was intended to develop fundamental quality systems that provide for quality improvement. The QS 9000 standard emphasizes defect prevention as well as the reduction of variation and waste. The two key components of QS 9000 are ISO 9001 and the Customer Specific Requirements. Automotive supplier must be ISO 9001 certified. The Customer Specific Requirements include statistical process control techniques, Production Part Approval Process, Failure Modes and Effects Analysis, Measurement Systems Analysis, and Quality System Assessment.

The Environmental Management Standard (ISO 14000) encourages environmental protection and the prevention of pollution while taking into consideration the economic needs of society (Summers, 2006). A company complying with ISO 14000 standards is better positioned to meet its legal and policy requirements. The ISO 14000 standards enable a company to improve environmental management voluntarily. The standards do not establish product or performance standards. Also, they do not establish mandates for emissions or pollutant levels. Often, companies complying with ISO 14000 incur significant savings through more efficient resource management and waste reduction.

NEW DIRECTIONS IN QUALITY MANAGEMENT

In many cases, the quality management systems did not deliver their promise. There are several problems in the prevalent quality management approaches (Antilla, 2004; 2006; 2007). These problems include:

1. Management is not committed
2. Communication between business managers and quality experts is not effective
3. Quality initiatives are not business-centered

4. There are numerous different, distinct, and competing quality methodologies

5. Several other specialized managerial initiatives compete with quality management

6. Quality initiatives in many organizations are focused on certification and not on the business performance improvement

7. Often quality related actions are reactive and not proactive

8. Formal documentation is emphasized instead of a comprehensive management strategy

The above mentioned problems have led to a great deal of confusion regarding the quality related initiatives in many organizations. Some of the traditional quality management tools have not been adequately flexible to accommodate the needs of modern business environment. Thus, innovative quality management approaches are needed in today's market driven business environment. Some of the innovative principles, tools, and infrastructures for quality management in the modern business environment include:

1. Recognizing business performance excellence instead of a narrow quality thinking

2. Striving for flexible realization of quality of management and leadership instead of distinct and vague quality management (i.e. management of quality)

3. Adopting organizational learning instead of continual improvement

4. Applying the "systematicity" (systematic approach) of the quality of management and leadership instead of formal and distinct quality systems

5. Using business-related principles and actions of the quality of management instead of formal and general quality assurance requirements only

6. Setting stretched business objectives for quality of management instead of minimum standard requirements

7. Aiming at innovative and unique solutions instead of stereotyped systems

8. Getting advantage of tacit knowledge and collaborative learning instead of only records of explicit data and information

9. Having genuine impacts on the organization's quality approach and success by the behavior of the top management

CONCLUSION

Traditional basic concepts of quality and quality management are still valid in the modern business environment. However, these concepts must be understood and applied using an integrative approach. Integration implies:

- Implementing effective and efficient quality principles and methodology embedded into the normal strategic and operational business management activities.
- Enhancing business performance in a systematic way.
- Avoiding build up of formal and distinct "quality systems".
- Adopting organizational learning instead of continual improvement.
- Taking advantage of tacit knowledge and collaborative learning.

All quality initiatives and measures should strive for enhancing overall operational performance. Quality management is primarily based on the beneficial use of business related data, information, and knowledge. Methodologies, tools, and practices of managing knowledge should be used in the context of professional quality applications.

REFERENCES

Antilla, J. (2004). *Tacit knowledge as a crucial factor in organizations' quality management*. Paper presented at the Quality Conference, Ostrava, Czech Republic.

Antilla, J. (2006). *Modern approach of information society to knowledge work environment for management.* Paper presented at the IEEE International Conference on Industrial Technology (ICTT 2006), Mumbai, India.

Antilla, J., Savola, K., Kajava, J., & Lindfors, J. (2007) *Fulfilling the needs for information security awareness and learning in information society.* Paper presented at The 6th Annual Security Conference, Las Vegas.

Besterfield, D. H. (2002). *Quality control,* 6th Edition. Upper Saddle River, NJ: Prentice Hall.

Broh, R. A. (1982). *Managing quality for higher profits.* New York: McGraw-Hill.

Edwards, C. D. (1968). The meaning of quality. *Quality Progress,* October 1968.

Evans, J. R., & Lindsay, W. M. (1993). *The management and control of quality.* St. Paul, MN: West Publishing Company.

Garvin, D. A. (1988). *Managing quality.* New York: The Free Press.

Gilmore, H. L. (1974). Product conformance cost. *Quality Progress,* June 1974.

Juran, J. M. (Ed.). (1974). *Quality control handbook,* 3rd edition. New York: McGraw-Hill.

Kerzner, H. (2006). *Project management: A systems approach to planning, scheduling, and controlling.* Hoboken, NJ: John Wiley & Sons.

Persig, R. M. (1994). *Zen and the art of motorcycle maintenance.* New York: Bantam Books.

Pyzdek, T. (1996) *The complete guide to the CQE.* Tucson, AZ: Quality Publishing.

Sower, V. E. Savoie, M. J., & Renick, S. (1999). *An introduction to quality management and engineering.* Upper Saddle River, NJ: Prentice Hall.

Summers, D. C. (2006). *Quality,* 4th edition. Upper Saddle River, NJ: Pearson/Prentice Hall.

KEY TERMS AND DEFINITIONS

Cause-and-Effect Diagram: A tool for analyzing process dispersion.

Continuous Improvement: The ongoing improvement of products, services, or processes through incremental and breakthrough improvements.

Control Chart: A chart with upper and lower control limits on which values of some statistical measure for a series of samples or subgroups are plotted.

ISO 9000 Series Standards: A set of international standards on quality management and quality assurance developed to help companies effectively document the quality system elements to be implemented to maintain an efficient quality system.

Pareto Chart: A graphical tool for ranking causes from most significant to least significant.

Process Control: Using statistical process control to measure and regulate a process.

QS 9000: A quality standard utilized by the automotive industry to ensure the quality of its and its supplier's components, subsystems, and finished products.

Quality: A subjective term for which each person has his or her own definition. In technical usage, quality can have two meanings: (1) the characteristics of a product or service that bear on its ability to satisfy stated or implied needs and (2) a product or service free of deficiencies.

Quality Management (QM): The application of a quality management system in managing a process to achieve maximum customer satisfaction at the lowest overall cost to the organization while continuing to improve the process.

Total Quality Management (TQM): It is a management approach to long-term success through customer satisfaction. TQM is based on the participation of all members of an organization in improving processes, products, services, and the culture they work in.

Chapter XVI
Software Quality Assurance

Dawn M. Owens
University of Nebraska at Omaha, USA

Deepak Khazanchi
University of Nebraska at Omaha, USA

ABSTRACT

Successful implementation of IT (information technology) projects is a critical strategic and competitive necessity for firms in all industrial sectors today. However, due to cost overruns, schedule delays, unfilled requirements and poor quality, it is reported that less than 30% of IT projects are perceived to be successful. Much has been written about causes of project failure and many have provided best practices and critical success factors for effective management projects, yet projects still continue to fail. As a first step to overcome systemic causes of project failure we propose a unified definition of software quality assurance (SQA). We use this definition to develop and present an approach to SQA that focuses on controlling risks and provide a framework for assuring the development and project management life cycles.

INTRODUCTION

Successful implementation of IT (information technology) projects is a critical strategic and competitive necessity for firms in all industrial sectors today. This is even more important in times of scarce resources needed for other competing strategic initiatives important to a firm. However, it is well established that a significant numbers of software and infrastructure projects still fail to deliver on time and within target costs and specifications (The Royal Academy of Engineering, 2004). Due to cost overruns, schedule delays, unfilled requirements and poor quality, less than 30% of IT projects are perceived to be successful (Glass, 2006).

Companies spend billions of dollars on IT projects each year, with the average spending at 4 to 5 percent of annual revenue on IT (Charette, 2005). In 2005, organizations spent an estimated $1 trillion on IT hardware, software, and services worldwide (Charette, 2005). Project failures have cost the US economy at least $25 billion and maybe as much as $75 billion (Charette, 2005). Based on the current project failure statistics, companies are faced with billions of wasted dollars on IT projects alone.

Many have written about the causes of project failure and have provided suggestions and critical success factors for effective management of projects. This chapter takes a different approach by examining how *software quality assurance practices* can impact project outcomes. It is the authors' contention that **software quality assurance (SQA)** plays a critical role in the software development lifecycle (SDLC) and can impact a project's overall success. Failure to pay attention to SQA can result in budget overruns, schedule delays, failure to meet project objectives and poor customer satisfaction (Chow, 1985). In fact, quality is considered a vital requirement of software products, a business essential, a competitive necessity, and even a survival issue for the software industry (Murugesan, 1994). Strong quality focus is emerging in all phases of the software development lifecycle with increasing emphasis on product quality, process maturity, and continual process improvements (Murugesan, 1994).

No matter how advanced the tools and techniques – all will come to nothing and the project will fail if the quality management system is not effective (Gill, 2005). The term SQA is often misunderstood, being viewed strictly in terms of software testing activities. However, in our view, SQA is a much broader concept. As we will present in this chapter, SQA is a set of assurance processes that are implemented across all phases of the project and software development lifecycles. Using this definition, we propose in this chapter a comprehensive SQA process. The

SQA phases presented will provide IT professionals with a framework for software practitioners and managers to analyze their quality assurance practices and determine where to initiate changes that will reduce and/or prevent causes of project failure. The rest of the chapter is organized around four main objectives: (1) Discuss the reasons for project failure, (2) Define software quality assurance, (3) Propose a software quality assurance process and discuss how it can be used to assure quality, and (4) Discuss implications for research and practice.

REASONS FOR PROJECT MANAGEMENT FAILURES

The statistics on project management success are dismal and probably not surprising to most IT professionals. When a project fails it can jeopardize an organization's reputation with its customers and its name in the marketplace (Charette, 2005). In addition, project failures can be costly to organizations in terms of wasted dollars and resources. The bottom line is that projects continue to fail for many reasons.

It is generally accepted that software project failures predominantly occur due to cost or schedule overruns and quality control problems. Table 1 summarizes the most common reasons for project failure documented from published literature.

Many projects fail due to a combination of the factors listed in Table 1 (Charette, 2005). Complicating matters is the fact that there are a number of unique challenges related to software development itself, such as, technology, the development process, scope and complexity of projects, and risk of projects (Reel, 1999). However, since most causes of software failures are predictable and avoidable, premeditated planning and inclusion of proper controls and processes can result in diminishing of these concerns, resulting in project success. Project success requires carefully

Table 1. Common reasons for project failure

	Reasons for Failure	Citations
1	*Planning* - Insufficient planning	[Nelson, 2007]; [Brown et al, 2007]; [Murugesan, 1994]
2	*Scope* - Poorly defined requirements and scope	[Nelson, 2007]; [Charette, 2005]; [Baker, 2001]; [Reel, 1999]
3	*Stakeholder* - Ineffective stakeholder management	[Nelson, 2007]
4	*Commitment* - Lack of executive support or project sponsorship	[Nelson, 2007]; [Brown et al, 2007]; [Reel, 1999]; [Murugesan, 1994]
5	*Time* - Poor estimation and/or scheduling; unrealistic deadlines	[Nelson, 2007]; [Galin, 2004]
6	*Cost* - Unrealistic budget	[Galin, 2004]
7	*Quality and Testing*- Shortened or elimination of quality assurance practices; inadequate testing or reduction of testing time within the software development lifecycle;	[Nelson, 2007]; [Murugesan, 1994]
8	*Resources* – Insufficient qualified resources	[Nelson, 2007]; [Galin, 2004]; [Charette, 2005]; [Murugesan, 1994] ; [Reel, 1999]
9	*Communication* - Poor or ineffective communication	[Brown et al, 2007]; [Charette, 2005]; [Wong and Tein, 2004];
10	*Risk* - Insufficient risk planning and risk management	[Nelson, 2007]; [Charette, 2005]
11	*Politics* - Stakeholder politics; user politics; corporate politics	[Nelson, 2007]; [Charette, 2005]; [Reel, 1999]
12	*Stakeholder* - Lack of user and stakeholder involvement	[Nelson, 2007]; [Brown et al, 2007]; [Murugesan, 1994]
13	*Project manager* - Poor project management or project manager	[Charette, 2005]
14	*Process* - Undefined development processes or lack of adherence to process standards (Sloppy development practices); failure to implement best practices and lessons learned	[Charette, 2005]; [Reel, 1999]
15	*Product* - Speed to market, desire for innovation; deliver now and correct errors later	[Murugesan, 1994]
16.	*Project Goals* - Unrealistic or unarticulated project goals	[Charette, 2005]; [Wong and Tein,2004]
17	*Change Control* - Poorly managed change control	[Reel, 1999]
18	*Technology* – changes in technology	[Reel, 1999]

followed processes that assure quality at every phase of the project and development lifecycles. Quality assurance practices can minimize project failures by providing checks throughout this process. Many people associate quality assurance with testing and most people think about testing once development is complete. However, developers and managers need to consider SQA and testing as being integral to every phase of the project lifecycle.

DEFINING SOFTWARE QUALITY ASSURANCE (SQA)

In this section we develop a unified definition for SQA. There are many different definitions of software quality assurance found in the literature (refer to Table 2).

These definitions are built on the premise that SQA is a process or set of activities that assures adherence to standards as well as assuring that the stated software requirements are met.

Table 2. Definitions of SQA

Definitions of Software Quality Assurance	
SQA is the planned and systematic approach to the evaluation of the quality of and adherence to software product standards, processes and procedures. It includes the process of assuring that standards and procedures are followed throughout the software lifecycle.	Agarwal et al., 2007
Quality assurance is providing assurance and credibility that the product works correctly.	Feldman, 2005
A set of actions necessary to provide confidence that the software development or maintenance process of a software system product conforms to established requirements while staying within the schedule and budget confines.	Galin, 2004
Software quality assurance is an umbrella activity applied to each step in the software process. It involves mapping managerial precepts and design disciplines of quality assurance onto the space of software engineering.	Gill, 2005
Conformance to functional and performance requirements, documented development standards, and implicit characteristics that are expected of all professionally developed software.	Pressman, 2005
A planned and systematic pattern of actions necessary to provide confidence that the product conforms to established requirements.	IEEE Std 730-1998
The purpose of SQA is to provide management with appropriate visibility into the software process being use and of the software product being built. It involves reviewing and auditing software products and activities to verify they conform to procedures and standards (Schulmeyer & McManus, 1999).	CMM
ISO9000 defines the requirements for a quality management system in order to produce higher quality products (Pressman, 2005). Quality is the totality of features and characteristics of a product that impact its ability to satisfy stated or implied needs (Stockman et al, 1990).	ISO9000

Another approach to defining SQA is to consider "*assurance as a set of services or a set of activities that inspire confidence and certainty*" (Merriam Webster, 2008). In this vein, Khazanchi and Sutton (2001) discuss assurance services and its impact on assuring quality specifically in business to business (B2B) electronic commerce related business practices. They define assurance services as a set of activities conducted by trusted, independent organizations to certify and/or validate business transactions between business partners by reviewing internal control mechanisms with the fundamental objectives to reduce risk, assess internal controls, and improve quality (Khazanchi & Sutton, 2001). Premeditated assurance against project failures can potentially be achieved through the establishment of controls. We think of controls as a *system of procedures, mechanisms or policies that could proactively prevent and detect software project failures.* A software quality assurance process should incorporate control mechanisms to assure conformity with an organization's policies, procedures, and standards.

Software quality assessment is difficult due to the uniqueness of software products (Rosqvist et al., 2003); therefore a well defined repeatable process is necessary in order to deal with the unique challenges. Repeatable processes such as CMMI have shown to result in higher levels of quality and project performance (Subramaniam, et al, 2007). Any such SQA process must also address schedule and budget constraints. Projects continue to fail because they do not meet stated time or cost constraints. It is important that the implementation of such a process does not negatively affect the ability to deliver on time and within budget.

Gill (2005), describes SQA as an umbrella activity that is applied to each step of the software process. We believe that this umbrella activity should apply not only to the software development lifecycle, but also the project management lifecycle. Based on the above discussion, we define software quality assurance as follows.

Software Quality Assurance (SQA)

SQA *is a well defined, repeatable process that is integrated with project management and the software development lifecycles to review internal control mechanisms and assure adherence to software standards and procedures. The objective of the process is to assure conformance to requirements, reduce risk, assess internal controls and improve quality while conforming to the stated schedule and budget constraints.*

As stated earlier, the SQA process needs to be well integrated with other lifecycle processes. Therefore, SQA cannot occur late in the lifecycle as a last attempt to add quality at the end of development activity (Voas, 2003). The next section provides a more in depth discussion of the SQA process.

THE SQA PROCESS AND ROLE OF SQA TEAMS

Many developers and managers continue to believe that quality is something to think about after the code has been compiled. Although this might be the reality, it should not be the practice. The SQA process is a *continuous assessment* mechanism deployed throughout the project and development lifecycles with specific controls and documentation requirements (Thayer & Fairley, 1999). The process should be used to control and assure the software development process, assure a quality outcome (e.g., zero defects) and assure project success (e.g., on-time within budget delivery). The activities in the SQA process may include formal reviews, testing, control of documentation, measurement, and reporting (Pressman, 2005). At a high level, the function of SQA is to perform the following (Galin, 2004):

- **Assure software project planning has taken place:** Quality practices should be planned well in advance so that there is time for them to be implemented.
- **Assure user requirements:** Requirements should be reviewed from beginning to end to assure conformance to established standards and conformance to user needs.
- **Assure the design process:** Provide guarantee that methodologies are followed and requirements are met by the design.
- **Assure coding practices:** Coding standards, practices, and guidelines must first be established, and then adhered to.
- **Assure software integration and testing has taken place:** Software integration and testing should be planned, implemented, and executed accordingly
- **Conduct random and scheduled audits:** Perform SQA audits to assure the necessary controls are in place.

The SQA process consists of a variety of phases with specific activities. These activities should be performed by a group such as an SQA team that is independent of the project participants. The software engineers should have responsibility for performing the technical work while the SQA group is responsible for software quality assurance planning, analysis, and reporting (Pressman, 2005). SQA is most effective when it reports up through a separate management team so they can remain committed to the process and remain objective to the deliverable. The teams should consist of appropriately skilled professionals (Godbole, 2004). The responsibilities of the SQA team include review of documentation (development plans, testing plans, project plan) for completeness and adherence to standards, participation in inspections, review of test results, and periodic audits of controls (Godbole, 2004). The SQA team should document any plans or processes that do not reflect adherence to standards and best practices. The SQA team should also conduct all design reviews and audits that regulate the software development and project management activities.

The functions performed by the SQA team are similar to that of IT auditors. Both are concerned with the existence of standards, adherence to standards, and documenting deviations (Weber, 1999). The existence of an SQA team can change how both internal and external auditors perform their work. SQA personnel are dedicated to quality assurance; therefore, the SQA team will likely undertake more comprehensive checking of controls than auditors (Weber, 1999). However, in the absence of an SQA team, auditors will perform many of the checks that the SQA team would perform.

Once a SQA process has been fully implemented it can help eliminate defects and prevent ambiguous and changing requirements resulting in improved customer satisfaction (Schulmeyer & McManus, 1999). The cost to find and repair defects or problems increases significantly as a project progresses through the requirements

phase to the implementation phase. Implementing an integrated SQA process has the potential for generating cost savings in the long run.

THE SQA PROCESS EXPLORED

The SQA process has its own lifecycle and covers all facets of a software project. It typically requires careful planning and gathering of data in the form of various snapshots of artifacts (Feldman, 2005). For example the SQA plan, project management plan, and project metrics are potential artifacts that could be found in the project document repository. SQA is not a single process, but an approach that provides assurance and credibility throughout the project management and development lifecycle processes (Feldman, 2005). Figure 1 represents the SQA process and shows how it encompasses the project management and development processes.

The combined project management life cycle (PMLC) and systems development life cycle

Figure 1. Software quality assurance (SQA) process integrated with PMLC and SDLC

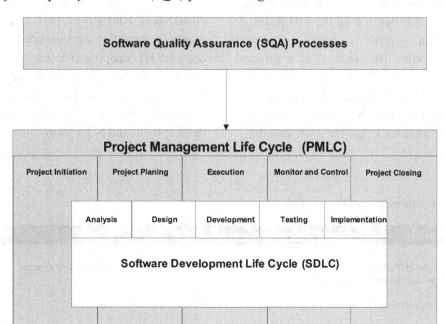

(SDLC) consists of eight unique phases – initiation, planning, analysis, design, development, testing, implementation, and closing. For each one of these phases there is a corresponding SQA process – SQA initiation, SQA planning, requirements assurance, design assurance, development assurance, testing assurance, implementation assurance, and SQA closing. Each SQA phase contains a feedback loop to the corresponding PMLC or SDLC phase. The purpose of the feedback loop is to provide input regarding issues or problems found during SQA activities and to ensure continuous improvement. Figure 2 denotes each of the SQA phases aligned with each of the eight combined PMLC or SDLC phases and the feedback loop. Each SQA phase has specific outputs which provide quality controls and documentation throughout the life of the project.

SQA LIFECYCLE PHASES

The following section discusses each of the phases in the combined project and development lifecycles along with the corresponding SQA activity. We provide a formal definition of each phase and list the inputs, outputs, and controls associated with that phase. We will begin with the first phase – project initiation.

Project initiation (see Box 1) is a project management function. This phase is the official start or formal kickoff of a project. The project manager is assigned and they begin working on the necessary initiation steps. The corresponding

SQA phase, SQA initiation is intended to notify the SQA team that a new project is being initiated. One of the key outcomes of this phase is to define the quality control and audit processes for the project and to ensure that the proper controls are in place.

- **Inputs**
  - o Feasibility Analysis
  - o Business Case Document
- **Outputs**
  - o Project Charter
  - o Preliminary Scope Statement
- **Controls**
  - o Verify the appropriate outputs have been completed.
  - o Check the content of the outputs for correctness, consistency, and completeness (3 Cs)[1].

During project initiation the project charter is completed, which identifies the project sponsor, stakeholders, project objectives, and preliminary scope statement.

The controls in this phase include assuring that the proper outputs have been completed. The project charter document should be verified for correctness, consistency, and completeness. For example, the following questions need to be addressed: Has the project manager been identified and have the key stakeholders been identified? Have the project team members been informed? Have the stakeholders been engaged? Have the development and SQA teams been engaged?

Box 1. Project Initiation ⇒ SQA Initiation

Definition
Project Initiation: The launching of a process that can result in a new authorized project with a formal scope definition (PMBOK, 2004).
SQA Initiation: The launching of SQA activities after a project has been authorized.

Figure 2. Combined PMLC, SDLC, and SQA process

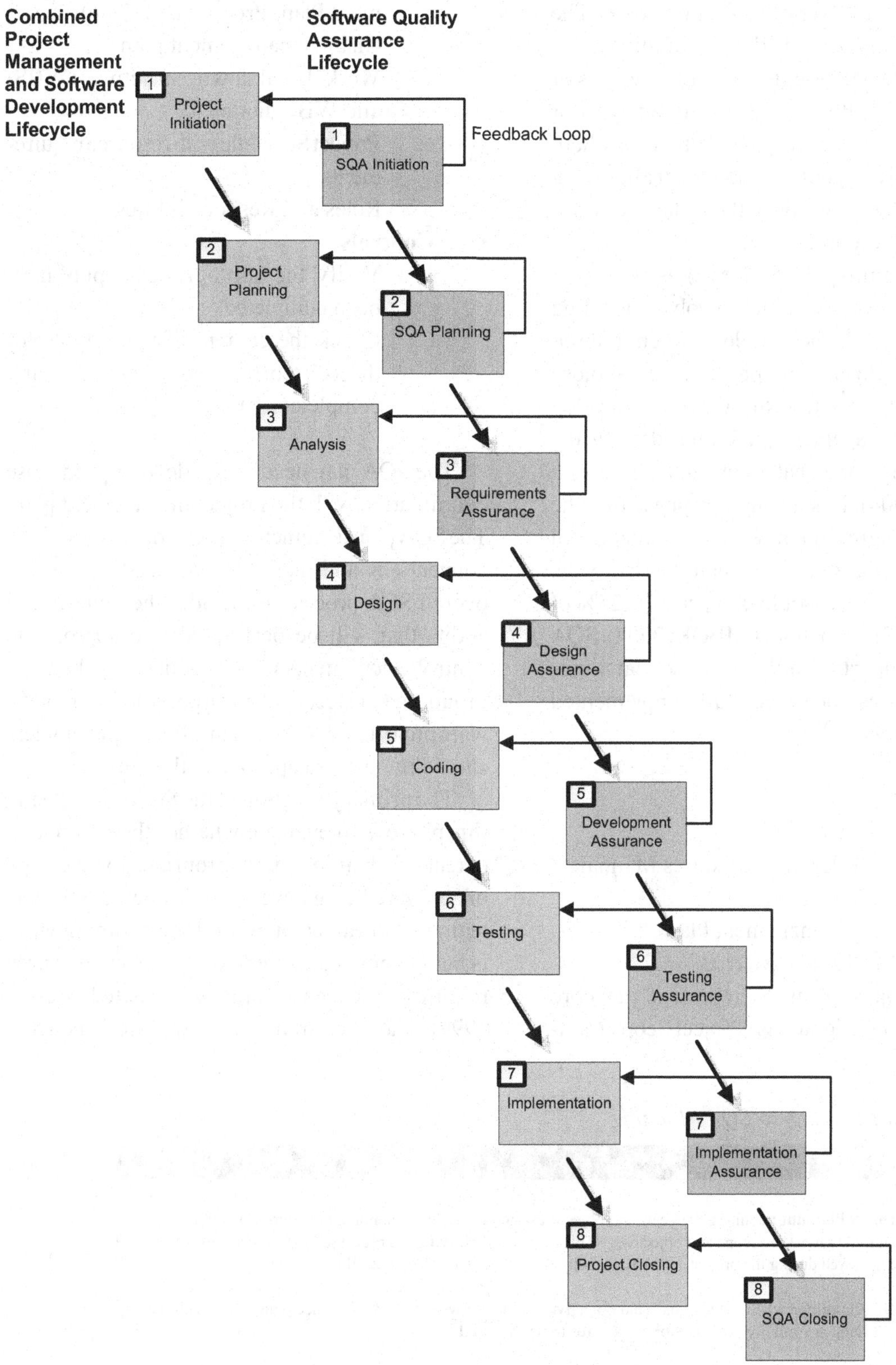

Combined Project Management and Software Development Lifecycle

Software Quality Assurance Lifecycle

1 Project Initiation

1 SQA Initiation

Feedback Loop

2 Project Planning

2 SQA Planning

3 Analysis

3 Requirements Assurance

4 Design

4 Design Assurance

5 Coding

5 Development Assurance

6 Testing

6 Testing Assurance

7 Implementation

7 Implementation Assurance

8 Project Closing

8 SQA Closing

The potential risks at this phase of the project are low, however, if not identified can be detrimental to the overall project outcome. The major risk in this phase is the risk of initiating a project without a thorough feasibility analysis or business case. Without a feasibility analysis or business case, projects may be initiated without formal executive signoff, without clear alignment of strategic objectives, or without the necessary technological resources.

Project planning (see Box 2) is a project management function which involves deciding in advance what do, how to do it, when to do it, and who will do it. This phase includes those processes performed to define the scope, develop the project management plan, and identify the schedule and activities that occur within the project (PMBOK, 2004). It is during this phase that the team should agree upon which organizational processes will be used throughout the lifecycle. The planning phase should comprise 20-25% of the overall project timeline (PMBOK, 2004). SQA planning is important at this stage so that assurance practices can be successfully implemented (Godbole, 2004).

- **Inputs**
  - Project Charter
  - Standards and Procedures Manual
- **Outputs**
  - Project Management Plan
  - SQA Plan and Metrics
  - Project plans to represent the core knowledge areas (Project Scope Management Plan, Cost Management Plan, Communication Plan, Risk Management Plan, Procurement Plan)
  - Change management plan
  - Work Breakdown Structure (WBS) and WBS dictionary
  - Project Schedule with resource requirements
  - Roles and Responsibilities
- **Controls**
  - Verify the appropriate outputs have been completed.
  - Check the content of the outputs for the 3 Cs (correctness, consistency, and completeness).

The SQA plan needs to be developed in close coordination with the project management plan. The SQA plan documents the standards, practices, conventions and metrics to be used during the overall SQA process. It includes the reviews and audits that will be performed, the appropriate controls, documents to be produced by the SQA group, and the feedback to be provided to the software project team (Pressman, 2005). Stakeholders should review and approve both plans.

The primary function of the SQA team during this phase is to evaluate whether the nature and extent of planning are appropriate for the type of software being developed (Weber, 1999). The team must evaluate how well the planning work is being completed – for example, have resource requirements been accurately estimated (Weber, 1999). These assurance activities are conducted

Box 2. Project Planning ⇒ SQA Planning

Definition
Project Planning: defining the goals and objectives for a project and planning the course of action required to meet the scope and objectives. This includes specifying the processes and procedures that will be followed during the project. (PMBOK, 2004; Christensen & Thayer, 2001).
SQA Planning: defining the goals and objectives of the software quality assurance plan which includes specifying any quality processes or procedures to be followed.

via interviews, observations, and reviews of documentation (Weber, 1999).

The potential risks at this phase of the project can be critical. A major challenge in many software development projects is incorrect schedules, incorrect cost estimates, inadequate project accountability procedures, and imprecise goals and success criteria – all products of the planning and analysis phases (Godbole, 2004). Not all of these risks can be prevented, but the key is to mitigate and control the risks by monitoring and ensuring that outputs include all facets that are relevant. For example, it is important to assure that the project schedule accounts for potential known risks.

Analysis (see Box 3) is an SDLC phase in which the project team gathers and documents formal user requirements. The software requirements are the foundation for subsequent phases (Pressman, 2005). The major steps in this phase include defining, reviewing, approving and base lining the requirements. Lack of confidence in requirements leads to lack of quality, therefore, it is important that the appropriate controls to ensure quality are implemented at this stage. During this phase the requirements are validated and the SQA team assures that the appropriate documents have been created.

- **Inputs**
  - Standards and Procedures Manual
- **Outputs**
  - Requirements Definition and Baseline
  - Requirements Traceability Matrix
  - Software Development Plan
  - High Level Design Plan
- **Controls**
  - Software Requirements Review
  - Preliminary Design Review
  - Verify the appropriate outputs have been completed.
  - Check the content of the outputs for the 3 Cs (correctness, consistency, and completeness).
  - Verify the requirements to ensure testability and feasibility.

Requirements verification includes a review of the requirements to ensure conformance to established standards. It also includes examining the specifications to ensure that all requirements have been stated unambiguously and to ensure testability (Pressman, 2005). If a requirement cannot be tested, it has not been stated clearly. After the requirements have been reviewed they should be approved by the major stakeholders. Once approved, a baseline is established. This baseline is used to track changes to the requirements in order to improve processes along the way and provide an audit trail of which requirements were changed.

Additional outputs in this phase include a requirements traceability matrix, a software development plan, and a high level design plan (Pressman, 2005; Galin 2004). A requirements traceability matrix is used in future phases to map the requirements back to specific functionality. It is a two-dimensional grid that lists out the require-

Box 3. Analysis ⇒ Requirements Assurance

Definition
Analysis: defining exactly what must be done to solve the problem by gathering and analyzing requirements and creating the initial software system model (Davis and Yen, 1999; Galin, 2004).
Requirements Assurance: providing assurance that requirements are testable and complete.

ments on one side and the functionalities on the other. This matrix is used in both development and testing. (Godbole, 2004). It can be used to determine how a change in one requirement will affect changes to other requirements or functionality. A software development plan determines how the software will be developed and includes a description of the processes and standards that will be used in development. A high level design (HLD) plan may also be created. According to IEEE standard 730.1 1995, the HLD should state which standards, practices, conventions and metrics will be used for specifying the internal structure of each program (IEEE Std730, 1998).

Due to its importance, the analysis phase of software development needs careful consideration in terms of risk. If the proper controls are not in place there is the potential for poor project outcomes. Incorrect, incomplete, unclear or inconsistent requirements can lead to risks such as poor customer satisfaction, not meeting customer expectations, or poor scope management. (Godbole, 2004). It is very important that the scope statement is managed and controlled in order to prevent scope creep, which can result in schedule delays or cost overruns. It is at this point that scope changes need to be documented, verified and approved.

In the design phase (see Box 4), the information from the analysis phase is translated into a blueprint that can be used for developing the software (Pressman, 2005). Lack of quality during design can invalidate good requirements

(Godbole, 2004). During the design process, it is determined which standards will be used as well as the design process that the software team will use to perform the work (Pressman, 2005). Standards also address matters such as naming conventions and use of program design language (IEEE Std 730, 1998). If those standards are not followed, the end result is a product with poor quality (Pressman, 2005).

The objective of design assurance is to assure the processes being used to create the design conform to standards and that design is verified against the established requirements. Once a design process (i.e., waterfall, iterative, or prototyping) is chosen by the software design team, the SQA team reviews the selected design process in order to ensure compliance with organizational policies, internal software standards, or externally imposed standards such as ISO9000 (Pressman, 2005). Product and process metrics can be used to measure design coverage and complexity. Examples of process metrics used to measure the development process include development time and average level of developer experience (Godbole, 2004). Examples of product metrics include lines of code to measure size and number of integrated modules to measure complexity (Godbole, 2004). Quality metrics include lines of code and test case coverage (Godbole, 2004). It is important to identify metrics during the analysis and design phases to ensure that the proper measures are put in place.

Box 4. Design ⇒ Design Assurance

Definition
Design: an iterative process where requirements are translated into an architecture or blueprint for developing the software and the inputs, outputs and processing procedures of the system are defined (Pressman, 2005; Galin, 2004).
Design Assurance: executing the appropriate controls to assure design has been completed according to stated policies and standards as well as assuring the necessary outputs have been completed.

- **Inputs**
  - o Requirements Definition and Baseline
  - o Software Development Plan
  - o High Level Design Plan
  - o Requirements Traceability Matrix
- **Outputs**
  - o Detailed Design Plan and Design Process
  - o Metrics Definitions to be used in the process (Product Metrics, Process Metrics, and Quality Metrics)
- **Controls**
  - o Design walkthrough and inspection
  - o Evaluation of the design process to ensure planned methodologies are followed
  - o Check the design process for adherence to organizational policies and standards.
  - o Verify the appropriate outputs have been completed.
  - o Check the content of the outputs for the 3 Cs (correctness, consistency, and completeness).

SQA controls in this phase are implemented to assure adherence to the defined process and to assure a completed design. The SQA team is primarily concerned with determining whether the programmers used a systematic approach to the design of the software (Weber, 1999). For example, the team should utilize design practices that support a design plan and modular reusable code. The team can obtain evidence of design practices by conducting interviews, observations of programmers at work, and review of documentation (Weber, 1999).

Design walkthroughs and inspections are effective for providing traceability of requirements back to design, identifying potential defects, increasing programming quality, and increasing effectiveness of testing activities (Schulmeyer & McManus, 1999). Best practice suggests that for every hour of design a software engineer should spend .59 hours in design review and for every hour of coding they should spend an average of .64 hours of code review (Humphreys, 2004).

During development (see Box 5), design is translated into code. At this stage test plans and test cases are developed so that when the software is implemented testing can be done. The SQA team works on assuring that the design process is of high quality and that testing plans are appropriate for the implementation.

- **Inputs**
  - o Standards and Procedures Manual
  - o Software Development Plan
  - o Detailed Design Plan
- **Outputs**
  - o Code (testable software product)
  - o Test Plan and Test Cases
  - o Metrics
- **Controls**
  - o Verify unit testing
  - o Conduct random audits through code walkthroughs, inspections, and peer reviews

Box 5. Development ⇒ Development Assurance

Definition
Development: code is generated, reviewed, compiled and tested (Pressman, 2005).
Development Assurance: assure that the development team is following the stated development process and coding standards.

o   Audit Test Plan

o   Check the code to ensure adherence to standards

o   Verify the development process for adherence to organizational policies and standards.

o   Verify the appropriate outputs have been completed.

o   Check the content of the outputs for the 3 Cs (correctness, consistency, and completeness).

The objective of writing test cases is to detect undiscovered errors, not to show that the product functions correctly (Godbole, 2004). As the testing team reviews the requirements and design documents to create the test plans, they should document any problems they encounter with the design. If the requirements document is incomplete or unavailable, the ability to detect defects is compromised (Baker, 2001). Therefore, this is one of the reasons why controls for complete requirements are necessary. It is much less expensive to catch these problems earlier, before the code has been completely developed.

The controls in this phase are designed to review the code to catch defects, even before testing begins and to capture metrics that were defined during the planning and design phases. The controls are also used to verify development processes and standards were followed. Unit testing and code walkthroughs are the two methods used to catch defects. The SQA team should evaluate how well unit testing has been

performed by evaluating whether a systematic approach to unit testing has been chosen (Weber, 1999). Random code walkthroughs, inspections, and peer reviews are very effective tools to address the basic question whether the design has been correctly converted to the target coding language (Schulmeyer & McManus, 1999). Additional issues to consider are: Does the code meet the specified requirements? Have the programmers followed established programming conventions (Weber, 1999)? Is there any erroneous, ineffective, or inefficient code (Weber, 1999)? Random inspections conducted by the SQA team can help uncover defects early, before they become costly or before they become so deep-rooted in the system that it is impractical to remove them (Grady, 1993; Boehm, 2001).

One of the biggest risks is developing a product that does not meet the stated requirements or developing a product full of defects. The development controls and assurance activities are necessary to mitigate these risks and detect defects early and the risks associated with software development are diminished.

The goal of testing in SDLC (see Box 6) is to find and document defects. A defect is something that detracts from the products ability to meet the stated requirements (Humphreys, 2004). Testing activities include integration testing, automated testing, regression testing, and performance testing. The SQA team needs to work closely with the testers and developers to ensure testing procedures are of the highest quality (Weber, 1999).

Box 6. Testing ⇒ Testing Assurance

Definition
Testing: the goal is to uncover as many software errors as possible in order to achieve an acceptable level of quality assurance (Galin, 2004).
Testing Assurance: providing assurance that adequate testing has been completed and defects have been tracked and recorded.

- **Inputs**
  - Test Plan and Test Cases
- **Outputs**
  - Test Summary Report
  - Implementation Plan
  - Metrics
- **Controls**
  - Review Test Summary Report
  - Review Testing procedures (Test data, test environment, automated testing)
  - Review Implementation Plan
  - Verify the appropriate outputs have been completed.
  - Check the content of the outputs for the 3 Cs (correctness, consistency, and completeness).

The foundations of software testing include defining test processes, test cases and test plans, testing techniques, methodologies, tools, standards, and testers (Murugesan, 1994). Once testing is completed, the test results should be documented in a test summary report and reviewed with the developers and stakeholders. This important step is necessary before making a decision on whether or not to proceed with implementation. The test summary report should also provide a list of the documented risks of moving forward with the known defects.

The purpose of the controls in this phase is to review the testing results to ensure complete and rigorous testing procedures were followed and to assure metrics have been captured. Metrics are important for measuring performance and to provide useful measures for future projects. If these controls are not implemented correctly, there is risk in deploying a product that has many defects.

Once the project team has been given the okay to move forward, the implementation team (see Box 7) will install the product into production. The implementation team should carefully review the implementation plan including the change management and conversion strategy. The SQA team should conduct a post release review and ensure that production testing of the software is complete and satisfactory to the users.

- **Inputs**
  - Implementation Plan
- **Outputs**
  - Implemented Software
- **Controls**
  - Product Release Review
  - Verify the appropriate outputs have been completed.
  - Check the content of the outputs for the 3 Cs (correctness, consistency, and completeness).

The primary control in this phase is the product release review. The product release review is necessary in order to assure there are no new defects present once the software is in production.

Both the project team and the SQA team should wrap up any project activities together including finalizing the project documentation

Box 7. Implementation ⇒ Implementation Assurance

Definition
Implementation: after the software system has been approved, the software is installed into the target production environment (Galin, 2004).
Implementation Assurance: providing assurance that the necessary implementation steps have been completed prior to and after implementation.

and notifying the stakeholders and sponsors of project completion (see Box 8).

- **Inputs**
  - o Metrics
  - o Documentation from prior phases
- **Outputs**
  - o SQA Summary Report
  - o Post Project Review (lessons learned)
  - o Metrics
- **Controls**
  - o Verify the appropriate outputs have been completed and delivered.
  - o Check the content of the outputs for the 3 Cs (correctness, consistency, and completeness).

During this phase there should be a formal documentation of lessons learned through a post project review. It is necessary to take the time to understand what went right and what went wrong so as not to repeat the same mistakes. It is also important to gather all the metrics that have been collected during the project. These metrics can help identify trends and best practices for future projects.

IMPLICATIONS FOR PRACTICE

Based on our experience and anecdotal evidence, we believe that using a well defined SQA process can substantially improve the chance of project success. Our proposed SQA framework provides an overarching framework for practitioners to develop an integrated assurance process to mitigate potential risks associated with project management and software development.

Implementing a SQA process is not easy. It takes commitment and executive support. The term process has a negative reputation in the world of IT development. People think of a process as slowing down the delivery of software and as a result there is a reluctance to consider new processes. However, once the value of SQA has been shown, IT personnel are more likely to embrace it. Clearly, any SQA process needs to include metrics and concrete deliverables in order to measure its value and help provide support for the future improved development of software products.

Project managers educated about the importance of the SQA process can champion its inclusion at the beginning of a project and not as an afterthought. Clear communication on the expectation of SQA is also important. All stakeholders need to understand and agree upon the role of the SQA process and team.

Organizations should have a dedicated SQA staff. This staff needs to be educated on risks, organizational standards, and policies and procedures relating to software development. Quality should be part of everyone's job and not just the responsibility of top management (Gill, 2005). Having management support for implementing SQA processes in all software development projects can go a long way to ameliorating risks and reducing software defects.

Box 8. Project Closing ⇒ SQA Closing

Definition
Project Closing: the processes performed to end all activities of a project, transfer the completed project, or close a cancelled project (PMBOK, 2004).
SQA Closing: completing all the assurance process which includes making sure the necessary project closing activities have been completed.

IMPLICATIONS FOR RESEARCH

Clearly there is consensus from research about why projects fail. However, little effort has been made in proposing processes that can integrate development with software quality assurance. This chapter proposes one approach for achieving this goal. Further research needs to be conducted on whether incorporating such a process leads to greater project success. In addition, research needs to be conducted to better understand the nature of risks in each phase of software development and the types of controls necessary. Finally, it would be also interesting to study how such controls are used and whether other factors need to be included.

CONCLUSION

In this chapter, we have discussed the reasons why projects fail and made a case for why a software quality assurance process is necessary to mitigate risk of failure and reduce failure rates. We have proposed a consolidated definition of SQA and developed a process for assuring software quality that encompasses the whole software development and project management life cycles.

REFERENCES

Agarwal, R. Nayak, P., Manickam, M., Suresh, P., & Modi, N. (2007). Virtual quality assurance facilitation model. *IEEE International Conference on Global Software Engineering (ICGSE 2007),* IEEE Computer Society.

Baker, E. R. (2001). Which way, SQA? *IEEE Software,* January/February 2001, 16-18.

Boehm, B., & Basili, V. R. (2001). Software defect reduction top 10 list. *Computer, 34*(1), 135-137.

Brown, S. A., Chervany, N., L., & Reinicke, B. A. (2007). What matters when introducing new information technology. *Communications of the ACM, 50*(9), 91-96

Charette, R. N. (2005). Why software fails. *IEEE Spectrum,* September, 2005, *42.*

Chow, T. W. (1985). *Software quality assurance: A practical approach.* Silver Spring, MD: IEEE Computer Society Press.

Christensen, M. J., & Thayer, R. H. (2001). *The project manager's guide to software engineering best practices.* Los Alamitos, CA: IEEE Computer Society.

Davis, W. S., & Yen, D. C. (1999). *The information system consultant's handbook: System analysis and design.* Boca Raton, FL: CRC Press.

Feldman, S. (2005). Quality Assurance: Much More than Testing. *ACM Queue,* February 2005, (pp. 27-29).

Galin, D. (2004). *Software quality assurance: From theory to implementation.* Harlow, UK: Pearson Education Limited.

Gill, N. S. (2005). Factors affecting effective software quality management revisited. *ACM Sigsoft Software Engineering Notes, 30*(2), 1-4.

Godbole, N. S. (2004). *Software quality assurance: Principles and practice.* Pnagbourne, U.K.: Alpha Science.

Grady, R. B. (1993). Practical results from measuring software quality. *Communications of the ACM, 36*(11), 62-68.

Humphreys, W. S. (2004). *The software quality profile,* Retrieved September 12, 2004, from http://www.sei.cmu.edu/publications/articles/quality-profile/index.html

IEEE Std730 (1998). IEEE standard for software quality assurance plans Std 730-1998. *IEEE standards software engineering,* Vol. Two, Process Standards, 1999 Edition, IEEE, (pp. 1-16).

IEEE Std1012 (1998). IEEE standard for software verification and validation. IEEE standards Software Engineering, Vol. Two, Process Standards, 1999 Edition, IEEE

Khazanchi, D., & Sutton, S. (2001). Assurance services for business-to-business electronic commerce: A framework in implications. *Journal of the Association for Information Systems, 1*(11).

Merriam Webster (2008). *Merriam Webster online: Assurance.* Retrieved March 17, 2008, from http://www.merriam-webster.com/dictionary/assurance

Murugesan, S. (1994, Dec. 21-22). Attitude towards testing: A key contributor to software quality. *IEEE's Proceedings of 1st International Conference on Software Testing, Reliability and Quality Assurance,* (pp. 111-115).

Nelson, R. R. (2007). IT project management: Infamous failures, classic mistakes, and best practices, *MIS Quarterly Executive, 6*(2), June 2007, 67-78.

PMBOK (3rd Ed) (2004). *A guide to the project management body of knowledge.* Newton Square, PA: Project Management Institute.

Pressman, R. S. (6th Ed.) (2005). *Software engineering: A practitioner's approach,* Boston: McGraw Hill.

Rosqvist, T., Koskela, M., & Harju, H. (2003). Software quality evaluation based on expert judgment. *Software Quality Journal, 11*(1), 39-55.

The Royal Academy of Engineering (2004). The challenges of complex IT projects. *The Royal Academy of Engineering and the British Computer Society.* Retrieved April 08, 2008, from www.bcs.org/server.php?show=conWebDoc.1167

Reel, J. S. (1999). Critical cuccess factors in software projects. *IEEE Software*, May/June, 18-23.

Schulmeyer, G. G., & McManus, J. I. (3rd Ed) (1999). *Handbook of software quality assurance.* Upper Saddle River, NJ: Prentice Hall.

Glass, R. L. (2006). The Standish report: Does it really describe a software crisis? *Communications of the ACM, 49*(8), 15-16.

Stockman, S. G., Todd, A. R, & Robinson, G. A. (1990). A framework for software quality measurement. *IEEE Journal on Selected Areas in Communications, 8*(2), February, 224-233.

Subramaniam, G. H., Jiang, J., & Klein, G. (2006). Software quality and IS project performance improvements from software development process maturity and IS implementation strategies. *The Journal of Systems and Software, 80,* 616-627.

Thayer, R. H., & Fairley, R. E. (2nd Ed.) (1999). software engineering project management: The silver bullets of software engineering. *Software Engineering Project Management,* (pp. 503-504). Los Alamitos, CA: IEEE Computer Society,.

Voas, J. (2003). Assuring software quality assurance. *IEEE Software,* May/June, 48-49.

Weber, R. (1999). *Information systems control and audit.* Upper Saddle River, NJ: Prentice-Hall, Inc.

Wong, B., & Tein, D. (2004). Critical success factors for enterprise resource planning projects. *Journal of the Australian Institute of Project Management, 24*(1), 28-31.

KEY TERMS AND DEFINITIONS

Design Assurance: Executing the appropriate controls to assure design has been completed according to stated policies and standards as well as assuring the necessary outputs have been completed.

Development Assurance: Assure that the development team is following the stated development process and coding standards.

Implementation Assurance: Providing assurance that the necessary implementation steps have been completed prior to and after implementation.

Requirements Assurance: Providing assurance that requirements are testable and complete.

Software Quality Assurance: A well defined, repeatable process that is integrated with the project management and the software development lifecycles to review internal control mechanisms and assure adherence to software standards and procedures. The objective of the process is to assure conformance to requirements, reduce risk, assess internal controls and improve quality while conforming to the stated schedule and budget constraints.

SQA Closing: Completing all the assurance process which includes making sure the necessary project closing activities have been completed.

SQA Initiation: The launching of SQA activities after a project has been authorized.

SQA Planning: Defining the goals and objectives of the software quality assurance plan which includes specifying any quality processes or procedures to be followed.

Testing Assurance: Providing assurance that adequate testing has been completed and defects have been tracked and recorded.

ENDNOTE

[1]   IEEE Std 1012-1998 (IEEE Standard for Software Verification and Validation) uses the 3 Cs for V&V (Verification and Validation). The 3 Cs consist of correctness, consistency, and completeness.

APPENDIX A: SQA CHECKLISTS

PMLC and SDLC Phases	SQA Lifecycle Checklist Inputs	Outputs	Controls
1. Project Initiation	☐ Feasibility Analysis ☐ Business Case	☐ Project Charter ☐ Scope Statement	☐ Verification ☐ Check 3 Cs
1. Project Planning	☐ Project Charter ☐ Standards/Procedures Manual	☐ PM Plan ☐ SQA Plan & Metrics ☐ PM plans for core knowledge areas ☐ CM Plan ☐ WBS & dictionary ☐ Project Schedule & resource requirements ☐ Roles & responsibilities	☐ Verification ☐ Check 3 Cs
2. Analysis	☐ Standards/Procedures Manual	☐ Requirements definition & baseline ☐ Requirements traceability matrix ☐ Software development plan ☐ High level design plan	☐ Software requirements review ☐ Preliminary design review ☐ Verification ☐ Check 3 Cs ☐ Verify for testability and feasibility
3. Design	☐ Requirements definition & baseline ☐ Software development plan ☐ High level design plan ☐ Requirements traceability matrix	☐ Detailed design plan and design process ☐ Metrics	☐ Design walkthrough and inspection ☐ Evaluation of processes ☐ Check for adherence to process ☐ Verification ☐ Check 3 Cs
4. Development	☐ Standards/Procedures Manual ☐ Software development plan ☐ Detailed design plan	☐ Code ☐ Test plan & test cases ☐ Metrics	☐ Unit testing ☐ Code walkthroughs, inspections, and peer reviews ☐ Check code for adherence to process ☐ Verification ☐ Check 3 Cs
5. Testing	☐ Test plan & test cases	☐ Test summary report ☐ Implementation Plan ☐ Metrics	☐ Review test summary report ☐ Review testing procedures ☐ Review implementation plan ☐ Verification ☐ Check 3 Cs
6. Implementation	☐ Implementation Plan	☐ Implemented software	☐ Product release review ☐ Verification ☐ Check 3 Cs
7. Project Closing	☐ Metrics ☐ Documentation from prior phases	☐ SQA summary report ☐ Post project review (lessons learned) ☐ Metrics	☐ Verification ☐ Check 3 Cs

Chapter XVII
The Integrated Project Risk Model:
A Risk–Based Model for Managing Information Technology Projects

Fayez Ahmad Albadri
ADMA-OPCO, Abu Dhabi, UAE

ABSTRACT

An overwhelming number of Information Technology (IT) projects experience persistent problems and failures. This chapter reflects on some of the important aspects of IT Project Management as applied to the implementation and post-implementation of Enterprise Information Systems and ERP applications. The proposition is based on the author's professional experience as a system consultant, a manager and an educator. It also echoes some of the important findings of a major action research undertaken by the author over seven years, where he had a dual role as a project resource and a researcher, allowing him a first hand experience of enterprise applications issues and problems, culminating in a clear insight to why IT projects fail and how to overcome persisting inadequacies that lead to project failures. By investigating 25 major IT projects and analysing the variables that influence project performance, the research has successfully developed, tested and refined a hypothesised risk-based management model. With its components, processes, metrics and tools clearly defined and characterised, the Integrated Project-Risk Management (IPRM) model and system are presented as viable alternatives to conventional project management approaches and tools.

INTRODUCTION

There is no doubt that huge investment funds have been committed as a result of rapid corporate business increasing acceptance of enterprise information systems since the early 1990s. This has created unprecedented levels of synergy and momentum within organizations to implement new enterprise systems and replace outdated legacy systems. Unfortunately, by large the outcomes of such projects were less than satisfactory, and many project failure cases were widely publicized in the literature.

From traditional project management viewpoint the majority of projects have suffered from deadly schedule and delivery delays, cost over-runs and compromised quality of the delivered products. Nevertheless, the investigation of reported failures have opened practitioners' eyes to important non-traditional issues such as change management problems and users' acceptance dilemmas among other things.

Although investigations of IT projects' unfavorable outcomes linked to the deployment and assimilation of enterprise systems have resulted in new approaches and methodologies as proposed recipes for success, a close examination of the offerings indicate that the majority seem to be merely re-packaged versions of the traditional project management model.

While some of the proposed models offer minor improvements by targeting best-of-practice in conventional time-based project management processes; others incorporate additional components (add-ons) such as quality, risk and configuration. Nevertheless, there is no substantial proof that these approaches were based on a deep understanding of the causes and symptoms of failures, the specific IT environment and issues, and the complex interaction between the technology, business and human resources. When these new models and implementation methodologies were put to the test in many different applications the outcomes were less than impressive, and the failure of projects have persisted.

RESEARCH BACKGROUND

To establish a clear context of the research on hand and to prepare for a clear definition of the research question, scope and objectives was only possible through a comprehensive literature review of the relevant issues, the outcome of which is summarized as follows:

Information Technology is clearly an important industry and discipline, with far-reaching impact on all aspects of life. The discipline has accomplished milestones in terms of technology development, and indications are that its importance and widespread applicability will continue to expand, with increased IT investment in areas such as hardware infrastructure projects, software development and enterprise applications implementations. The literature emphasises the persisting issues of coping with the change associated with technology adoption and the definition of the role of IT in business and in relation to other disciplines.

The mishandling and mismanagement of IT projects is one of the main themes of the research. IT Projects are the vehicles for adopting, deploying, implementing or upgrading IT, and yet they are different from those of other disciplines, because of their environment, technical complexity, dynamic nature, relative uniqueness, strong impact on business processes, strong impact on business culture and users attitudes, varying stakeholders expectations and acceptability, interrelationships with other disciplines, and unproven return on investment (Anderson et al., 2002, Yeo 2002, Niazi et al., 2003, Westerveld 2003, Peterson et al., 2002; Ross 2003).

The literature has highlighted the unsatisfactory record of IT projects in terms of failure to be delivered on time and within budget, or to meet satisfactory scope and quality of deliverables (Flowers, 1996; Glass, 1997; Sauer, 1999; Cunningham, 1999; KPMG, 2002; Johnson et al., 2001; Standish 1995; Standish, 1998; Standish, 2004; Lemon et al., 2002). Many projects suffer from poor technical performance, system bugs, and data and security problems, and fail to improve the business or even to realise the sought benefits or returns on investment (McManus and Wood-Harper, 2003). Overall, IT projects are important, different, risky, and generally perceived as failures.

IT Project Management has evolved over time into a formal discipline. As a vehicle for supporting other disciplines, it uses a number of different approaches, standards, best practices and vendor-developed methodologies. The literature has illustrated aspects of the failure of project management models, methodologies and practices, and their practicality, inadequacy, suitability, effectiveness, and control (Kliem and Ludin 1999; Goldratt 1997; Evaristo and van Fenema, 1999).

The concepts and applications of risk are still in many cases perceived abstractly, used reluctantly and applied ineffectively by many professionals and project managers, especially in a field as critical and risky as IT Project Management. Nevertheless, the promotion and evolution of the Risk Management applications in the management of software development and IT projects has been enhanced by a number of outstanding contributions: Boehm's pioneering work on project risk management (PRM) and the definition of processes (Boehm, 1991), Fairley's seven-step PRM processes (Fairley, 1994), the Australian–New Zealand Standards for Risk Management (Standards Australia, 1995, 1999), *The Risk Management Guide* by US Defense Systems Management College (DSMC, 1989), ADCMS Project Risk Management Guidelines (DCAMS, 1996), The Central Computer and Communication Agency's PRINCE 2 Project Management methodology (CCTA, 1995, 1997,

1999, 2000, 2001), The Software Engineering Institute's CMM the Capability Maturity Model for Software development (SEI, 1993, 1994, 1995,1997), and the CRAMM methodology (Sokratis Katikas, 1998).

It is almost three decades since risk management was applied firstly to software development and later to IT. Many individuals and organisations have contributed to this progress, but the following contributions are particularly significant in the advance of IT risk management: Nolan (1979), McFarlan (1981), Alter and Ginzberg (1978), Davis (1982), Boehm (1981, 1987, 1988, 1989 & 1991), Charette (1989), Saarinen (1996), Chittiser and Haimes (1993), Berny and Townsend (1993), Sisti and Joseph (1994), Hall (1995), Karolak (1996), Michales (1996), Hefner (1996), Kansala (1997), Kitchenham and Linkman (1997), Madcahy (1997), Foo and Muruganantham (2000), Department of Defense (DoD, 1988), Institute of Electrical and Electronics Engineers (IEEE, 1987, 1992), Institute of Standards Office (ISO, 1991), Standards Australia (1995, 1999), and the Software Engineering Institute (SEI, 1993, 1994, 1995, 1997).

Lately, the term 'Implementation Methodology' has been widely used in the literature and in practice to describe the process of managing IT projects, and Enterprise Resource Planning (ERP) systems in particular. Increasingly, an implementation methodology is synonymous with a structured project road map, which is designed to ensure the successful delivery, on time, to plan and within budget (the three sides of the golden triangle) derived from the software quality assurance discipline (Wallmueller, 2004). Many software vendors, implementation partners and management consulting firms have developed their own methodologies, but vendors have used these methodologies mainly as marketing tools to alleviate customers' fears and perceived risks in relation to investing in new applications. However, ERP methodologies have now acquired recognition as vital project management tools and roadmaps.

Based on the above, in a field as critical, risky and important as IT project management, a comprehensive review of the suitability and effectiveness of the current approaches, practices and tools, including the utilisation of risk management, is essential to address the persisting IT project failures and to overcome their associated problems and causes. (Raz and Michael 2001; Yates and Arne 2004). The numerous attempts by different researchers and studies to cope with this problem indicate the scale, importance and urgency of the problem, and justify the need for further investigation to understand the causes and suggest solutions, the purpose of the current research.

RESEARCH QUESTION

Traditional project management practices and tools have been relatively successful in simpler, more certain, less dynamic projects in a wide range of business areas from marketing and education to engineering and construction (Stewart et al., 2002). However, conventional models and tools are not necessarily ideal for IT projects, which can entail the implementation of corporate enterprise information systems such as ERP, EAM, CMMS or the deployment of technology solutions in association with e-commerce and web-based applications.

The research question is concerned mainly with the development and testing of a new risk-based model for managing IT projects, that is more suitable, more effective, more relevant, more practical, more flexible and certainly more user-friendly than other models and approaches that are currently used for managing technology projects.

The thesis reflects the development process and the characterisation of the final model as a result of investigating the suitability and effectiveness of the project management practices and tools currently being used in the new complex IT environment. In particular, in terms of examining whether traditional management practices can adequately cope with the specific IT environment and issues, and provide the necessary tools to successfully implement the computer systems and business applications, or whether more dynamic and flexible project management models and tools are required.

The main aim of the research is to contribute to the resolution of the persisting high rate of IT project failures by suggesting IPRM model as an alternative with the potential to maximise the likelihood of success and minimise the likelihood of failure.

RESEARCH SCOPE AND OBJECTIVES

This study analysed data from several IT projects, and used the results to assess and investigate those factors likely to contribute to a project's performance outcomes and its success or failure in delivering its set goals. In addition, the study aimed to improve the understanding of IT projects, in terms of the environment, practices, parties, strengths and weaknesses, and issues relevant to any particular project. The analysis results and the increased understanding of issues peculiar to IT were then applied to building and refining an alternative model, more effective for managing IT projects than the various outdated and unsuitable models and methodologies currently being used.

The research project focused primarily on the implementation phase and the eventual delivery of the project objectives, on time and on budget. In practice, however, the implementation and post-implementation phases cannot be viewed in isolation. Therefore, issues related to the user's acceptability of the system, the organisation's perception of the strategic (business) value of the delivered solution, and the technical status of the delivered systems also had to be included in the investigations.

The main objectives of the research are summarized as follows:

1. To gradually build and refine the Researcher's Knowledge-Set (RKS) through acquiring a deeper understanding of IT projects' environment, vulnerabilities, issues and specifics, leading to an insight into why IT projects fail to achieve their goals and plans

2. To examine the suitability and effectiveness of conventional project and risk management paradigms and practices currently used in system implementation and technology adoption

3. To gradually construct, and iteratively refine, a model based on lessons learned through experience, results of earlier investigations, hypotheses testing and the analysis of selected variables that influence project performance outcomes

4. To propose a practical method and provide a set of guides and supporting tools for the improved management of IT projects

5. To provide the main system features and functional specifications for future development of the Integrated Project Risk Management System, an enhanced collaborative IT project-risk management solution that complements the IPRM model

6. To suggest a mechanism for continual refinement of the research findings and the output model through future research.

RESEARCH STRATEGY AND TECHNIQUES

The practical nature of the research question warranted a reliable, vigorous, hands-on approach to support the underlying theory. The researcher's professional experience in system implementation consulting and IT project management allowed direct observation of the problems and risks from within the projects, rather than simply relying on others' experiences through interviews. This is a major advantage that has led to a deeper understanding of the relevant issues and lent credibility to the research findings.

The need to adopt a full project life-cycle approach that covers all the project phases from project kick-off to project rollout has influenced the scope and length of the research (nearly seven years), the number of model iterations, and the number of IT projects involved. Testing and refining selective features of the proposed model using project data required special arrangements with stakeholders and project managers, who consented to the researcher gathering project data through either 'Observations' or 'Observations and Interventions'. Most IT projects managers viewed the researcher's role positively; other more conservative, security-conscious managers were cautious and less enthusiastic. The researcher worked closely with parties involved in the decision-making process, in order to observe, analyse and critique management's attitude and behavior in leading, managing and controlling projects through different stages. The researcher also participated in routine project progress meetings, project checks and health reviews.

To ensure that the selected research strategies and techniques are appropriate, a structured and controlled evaluation and validation process was used in the pre-research phase. Different techniques and tools were reviewed in practices standards and the literature, were tested and evaluated for suitability to the research objectives, and were modified where needed based on the contributions of focus groups. The main consideration in the selection of the research techniques and tools was the goal of building an investigation framework and assessment criteria that could reliably measure project variables to use in a comparative analysis. It is, however, important to emphasise that the relative values or ratings (rather than the absolute values of the variables) were used to compare the project health, suitability of adopted practices, and performance outcome of the participating projects.

Some features of the research approach resemble longitudinal research, in that successive model refinements occurred throughout the research period. In other aspects the research can be viewed as adopting the 'participant-observation' method, reflecting the researcher's dual roles as a member of the project team and an observer, allowing him to collect research data by observation as well as direct participation.

Overall, the analysis techniques were either directly influenced by concepts in the literature, such as performance management and benchmarking, or based on standard qualitative methods, such as perspective analysis, SWOT analysis (Horn, 1994; Bplans, 2006) and balanced scoreboards

techniques that are used to evaluate IT projects (Milis and Mercken, 2004).

RESEARCH PHASES

The development and refinement of the initial hypothesised model was completed over six research phases (Figure 1). Each phase comprised a set of four research activities or research functions integrated within the adopted research framework: Information, Investigation, Analysis and Evaluation functions. The Information function included activities such as observation and data collection, and was followed by the Investigation function, involving selected tests of the adopted practices. The practices were then subject to different types of analysis in the Analysis function, leading to proposing and introducing adjustments to the input

Figure 1. Research map outlining research phases and involved projects

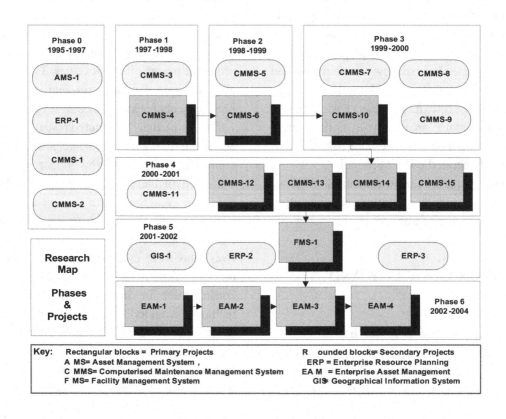

model during the Evaluation function.

The research map in the figure below shows that 25 projects were investigated, of which 12 were Research-Participant projects involving direct collection of data by the researcher (rectangular blocks in Figure 1), and 13 were secondary projects where data were collected indirectly through interviews (rounded blocks). The IT projects investigated included the implementation of different enterprise state-of-the-art applications and systems that support different business processes and functions; the deployment of appropriate network and hardware infrastructure, data preparation and migration; and end-user training and help desk support.

The naming convention for the projects indicates the type of implemented system or solution. For instance, ERP is an implementation of an Enterprise Resource Planning ERP system, AMS is Asset Management System, CMMS is a Computerised Maintenance Management Systems, EAM is an Enterprise Asset Management application, GIS is a Geographical Information System and FMS is a Facility Management System.

RESEARCH FINDINGS

The key aim of the research was to address the important question of 'Why do IT projects fail?' The increasing level of understanding throughout the research as to the causes and contributing factors of IT project failure led to proposing a new model that is focused on maximizing opportunities for success and minimizing risks of failures. The research has shown that persisting and frequent project issues, concerns, problems and threats (ICPT) that are linked to unfavorable project performance outcomes are related to:

- Project governance defectiveness
- Manager's (oversight) incompetence
- Project management practices inadequacy

- Risk management practices misuse
- Project control shortfalls
- Lack of integration between processes and functions
- Ineffectiveness of used software tools

These links and relationships were observed consistently throughout the research, and were validated by further investigating practices suitability and effectiveness (PSE) applied to the relevant areas. These investigations confirmed the identified areas as the most vulnerable and so they were, in turn, incorporated into building the Integrated Project-Risk Management (IPRM) model and defining its components and attributes.

The PSE investigations were crucial to validating the findings from the ICPT analysis, and to consolidating the acquired knowledge-set to give an insight into why projects fail. This increase in understanding throughout the research contributed to gradually building the IPRM model around the theme of maximizing success opportunities and minimizing failures threats. This aim is achieved by prescribing proven suitable and effective integrated management and control practices, promoting good project governance, ensuring oversight competences and efficient usage and utilization of metrics and software tools. The research identified the weaknesses and strengths of the practices associated with the existing methodologies and the time-based paradigm, confirming the validity of some practices and/or highlighting inadequacies that need to be addressed to prevent causes of failure, mitigate identified threats and utilize opportunities.

The research approach provided the mechanism for translating the outcomes of the investigations and hypothesis testing into building and refining the proposed IPRM model. Therefore, the growing understanding of why IT projects fail was ultimately complemented by the development of the IPRM model that answers the question 'How can IT project failures be prevented?' and adopting a holistic ERP Life-Cycle Management (ELCM) approach that ensures appropriate 'Usage' an 'Utilization' leading to the realization of sought benefits and Return on Investment (ROI).

A detailed analysis was performed at the end of each of the six research phases, using observations and data collected directly or indirectly from the projects involved. The results from several pre-defined and phase-specific investigations and tests were consolidated to represent the main findings of the phase investigations. The pre-defined research techniques provided the framework to define the scope and objectives of the research, and guided the progression of the research at three distinct levels: project level, phase level and research level:

1. Investigations at the project level

Investigations at this level were intended to maximise the benefits and lessons learned from each participating project as an independent entity with its own specific profile, management approach, environment, tools, resources and performance. The domain of these investigations included 25 major IT projects, of which 12 were primary projects, where data were accessed and collected directly by the researcher in his dual roles as a project resource and researcher. Thirteen secondary projects provided additional data that were collected indirectly through interviews and other means.

The investigations at this level have included the following perspectives:

- **ICPT perspective:** The investigations of projects' 'Issues, Concerns, Problems and Threats' (ICPT) commonly used in different system implementation methodologies and IT projects

- **PPO perspective:** The investigations of Project Performance Outcome (PPO), used in this research as a measure of the projects' final performance and also indicate the relative success or failure of projects to achieve their goals incorporating the fol-

lowing indicators: Quality, Cost, Time, User Acceptance, Technical Status and Business Value.

- **PSE perspective:** The examination of Practices Suitability and Effectiveness (PSE) to evaluate the appropriateness of the main systems and components proposed for the IPRM model, namely, Management System (MS) including the PM and RM components, the Control System (CS) representing PC project control and monitoring and the assessment of Manager's Oversight (MO) competences and evaluate Project Governance (PG).

- **PHI perspective:** The measurement of selected project health indicators (PHI) that combine four attributes of the project: Project Performance, Project Vulnerability, Project Cohesiveness and Project Continuity.

2. Investigations at the phase level

The aim of this level of investigation was to consolidate the findings from the projects within each research phase and translate them into a meaningful, tangible increase in knowledge. Each of the six phases, of 6–12 months' duration, focused on one of the main components of the proposed IPRM model: Project management (PM), Risk Management (RM), Project Control (PC), Manager's Oversight (MO), Project Governance (PG) and Project Metrics and Tools. Each phase contributed to confirming, validating, enhancing and/or adding to the Researcher's Knowledge-Set (RKS). This increased understanding provided the basis for introducing modifications to the evolving IPRM model.

3. Investigations at the research level

At the research level, the investigations were intended to link and integrate the separate research phase outcomes, by having the output of each phase acting as the input to the following phase throughout the six iterations of model development.

THE BUILDING OF IPRM

The development of a model such as IPRM model, which is the prime objective of this research, may belong to the 'design science' which has its own definitions, approaches and guidelines for defining the process by which the framework is developed and the final product architecture is characterized (Hevener et al., 2004; March and Smith, 1995; Walls et al., 1992). Nevertheless, despite that the selected approach in this research was tailored to suit the environment in which it was conducted, it has successfully delivered on both the process and the product.

IPRM, the Integrated Project Risk Management model, is the main outcome of this research. The initial hypothesised model was gradually constructed and iteratively refined, based on hypothesis testing and practical investigation in major system implementations and IT projects, and by identifying and analysing variables with potential impact on the performance outcome of these projects.

The research objectives were realised by investigating Issues-Concerns-Problems-Threats (ICPT) items, and by examining practice suitability and effectiveness (PSE) of commonly employed management and control practices. These practices are typically linked to the conventional project management paradigm, and several of its offspring implementation methodologies. Most importantly, however, the objectives were achieved by building up the knowledge needed to understand why IT projects fail.

The model developed from a simple improvement proposition to a comprehensive offering, a process that extended over seven years as the increased knowledge base gained from project investigations during successive research phases contributed to the increasing complexity of the model.

THE ARCHITECTURE OF IPRM-7

The systematic development and structured refinement process of the IPRM model over the six phases of investigations and explorations culminated in a well defined, refined and tested model, which can also be viewed as a framework, a road map and a guide for managing IT projects.

Figure 2 presents IPRM-7 as a structured configuration of integrated systems and functions. The PM and RM components are seamlessly integrated within the core management system. The project control system is integrated to the management system on one side and is interfaced with MO-PG, the oversight-governance joint functions, on the other side.

The main processes associated with each of the model's components have also been identified, investigated and built into the model structure. This was made possible by the longitudinal approach adopted for the refinement and testing of the model, and the iterative adjustments introduced to the model as a result of increasing knowledge, results of investigations such as ICPT and PSE, and relevant literature review and validation.

The characterisation of appropriate project 'Metrics' and 'Tools' to support the management and control processes and aid management decision making was incorporated and built into the model offering. The model departs from the current use of isolated metrics and tools with limited benefits and questionable interpretation; instead it adopts a comprehensive structured grid of meaningful measurements and supporting tools that serve specific predefined objectives within the overall project management and control processes, while also being of critical value to management decision-making and project governance.

Considering that the final proposed model is the end product of the gradual development process, IPRM-7 is well defined in terms of structure and details of its constituent systems, components, processes and functions and their interrelationships, attributes, metrics and tools. It comprehensively

Figure 2. IPRM-7 Model

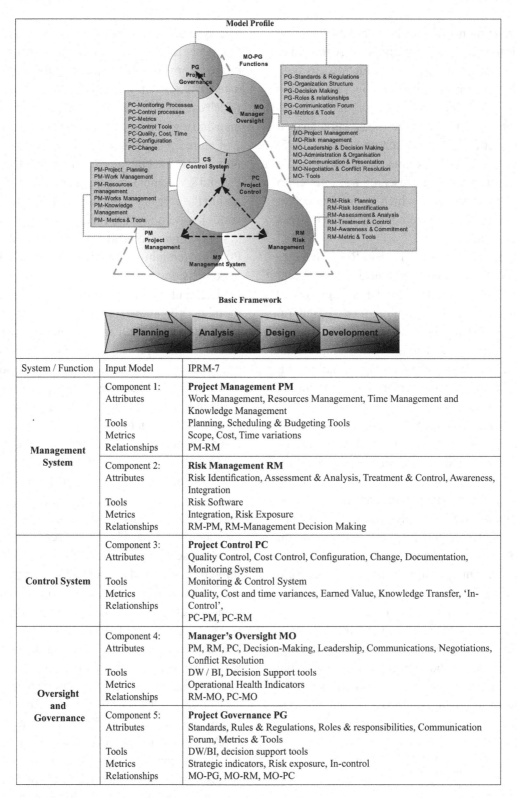

System / Function	Input Model	IPRM-7
Management System	Component 1: Attributes Tools Metrics Relationships	**Project Management PM** Work Management, Resources Management, Time Management and Knowledge Management Planning, Scheduling & Budgeting Tools Scope, Cost, Time variations PM-RM
	Component 2: Attributes Tools Metrics Relationships	**Risk Management RM** Risk Identification, Assessment & Analysis, Treatment & Control, Awareness, Integration Risk Software Integration, Risk Exposure RM-PM, RM-Management Decision Making
Control System	Component 3: Attributes Tools Metrics Relationships	**Project Control PC** Quality Control, Cost Control, Configuration, Change, Documentation, Monitoring System Monitoring & Control System Quality, Cost and time variances, Earned Value, Knowledge Transfer, 'In-Control', PC-PM, PC-RM
Oversight and Governance	Component 4: Attributes Tools Metrics Relationships	**Manager's Oversight MO** PM, RM, PC, Decision-Making, Leadership, Communications, Negotiations, Conflict Resolution DW / BI, Decision Support tools Operational Health Indicators RM-MO, PC-MO
	Component 5: Attributes Tools Metrics Relationships	**Project Governance PG** Standards, Rules & Regulations, Roles & responsibilities, Communication Forum, Metrics & Tools DW/BI, decision support tools Strategic indicators, Risk exposure, In-control MO-PG, MO-RM, MO-PC

covers all activities to be planned, performed or managed through the project life cycle, and the implementation phases of planning, analysis, design, and development.

AT one level, IPRM-7 is conceptually limited to two distinct sets: a system of management and control processes, and the oversight–governance function. For practical purposes, the model should be viewed as an assembly of five components belonging to three functional groups:

1. A Management System (MS) that encompasses two tightly integrated management components:
   i. Project Management (PM), corresponding to all project activities within the certainty domain
   ii. Risk Management (RM), representing all activities within the uncertainty domain.
2. A Control System (CS) that encompasses the processes and activities that belong to a multidimensional integrated monitoring and control system.
3. The Oversight-Governance integrated function that assimilates the attributes of the two components, Manager's Oversight (MO) and Project Governance (PG).

THE IMPLEMENTATION OF IPRM

The IPRM model can be flexibly used as a guide, either fully or partially, subject to the discretion of IT project stakeholders and managers. It is beneficial for managing IT projects and system implementations because it reflects management priorities. It emphasises suitability and effectiveness tests, with commonly used traditional concepts and practices re-defined and re-packaged within the IPRM components, but it also includes new proven concepts based on practical experience of real issues, concerns, problems and threats in actual IT projects and system implementation.

The model is complemented by several add-ons that can contribute to enhancing the practices and improving project performance outcome. These include the Cockpit Control Model (CCM), through which management can, at any time during a project, verify its health status by measuring system supported, built-in Project Health Indicators (PHI) associated with project performance, vulnerability, cohesiveness, and continuity; these were shown to correlate with the final Project Performance Outcome (PPO) during the research investigations. The novel view adapted by IPRM in regard to the role of Tools and Metrics offers an important opportunity for improvement, particularly by effectively using new technologies such as relational databases, KPI dashboards, analytical reporting, knowledge management, business intelligence, decision support tools and data warehousing.

The flexibility and simplicity of the IPRM offering allows it to be used fully or partially as a guide to managers who may be committed to other approaches or methodologies in their projects. In such cases, managers may seek to use IPRM for improvement in specific areas. These could include the effective handling of non-traditional project management issues, the effective integration of risk management into the main project main stream processes, the effective implementation of a multidimensional control and monitoring system, to proactively attending to matters associated with the oversight and governance functions, or even by taking advantage of the model's novel use of tools and metrics to help achieve goals and objectives. Nevertheless, one of the strengths of IPRM is its integrated nature and its structured approach, and thus for maximum benefit and efficiency the recommendation would be to adopt IPRM as a package. This might include attending an appropriate IPRM modular training program, and the development and use of IPRMS, the Integrated Project Risk Management System to support the bulk of IT project management processes and activities proposed by the IPRM model. Managing IT projects and implementing systems using the IPRM model as a guide typically extends over the project life cycle and includes critical tasks in the pre-implementation phase, the implementation phase and post implementation phase.

The development of the IPRM model employed types and causes of failure for reviewing the effectiveness and suitability of management and control practices, failure-proof measures and risk mitigating strategies. Therefore the definition of the IPRM systems and functions, their attributes, metrics, tools and interrelationships provide the main guides to be followed. Furthermore, IPRM can be used as either a manual guide or in conjunction with an automated Integrated Project Management System (IPRMS), which reflects the features of the model and the requirements associated with the model's proposed enhanced practice.

IPRM: Implementation Guide

The effective use of IPRM as a guide to managing IT projects generally, and system implementations in particular, depends on the implementers' ability to formulate a meaningful understanding the model's offering within the project success-failure context in which it was developed, and to project its guiding themes onto conventional management and control practices. This section describes the basic model themes to which the project's planning, management and control activities are linked:

IPRM context: The model was developed as a result of investigating IT project failures, and it has been structured to capture proven, suitable and effective practices and tools that have been identified to have the potential to maximise the likelihood of success and minimise the likelihood of failure.

Project performance (success/failure): The adopted project success/failure context goes beyond the common definition based on plan deviations and variances of budget, schedule and scope, to a more comprehensive scope that includes the following project performance outcome dimensions: cost, time quality, user, technical, business and strategic.

Project life-cycle: Although the main focus of the research is on the implementation phase, the project life cycle approach adopted suggests that the model will be most useful and effective when used throughout an integrated project life that includes pre-implementation, implementation and post-implementation phases, and treats each as a sub project.

IPRM and project outcome: The model's offering reflects the model's components, attributes and features. Project Performance Outcome, either the project's success or its failure, is a combined function of Project Governance, Manager's Oversight, and the Integrated Management and Control Systems defined by IPRM. Positive correlations were identified between project performance outcome (PPO) and each of the established inputs. As the main objective sought from the research developed model is to maximise PPO (project success), it follows that each of the inputs (PG, MO, PM, RM and PC) also needs to be maximised.

IPRM and project health: The combined project health indicators (PHI), including performance, vulnerability and continuity, have been confirmed by the research as good predictors of the performance outcome of a project and its potential for success or failure. Therefore, when IPRM is used as a guide, a main component is to employ PHI in conjunction with the monitoring and control system and as key feeders into management decision making.

IPRM guiding mechanism: The proposed mechanism for using the IPRM model as a guide to managing IT projects requires that each of the

Figure 3. IPRM practical guide

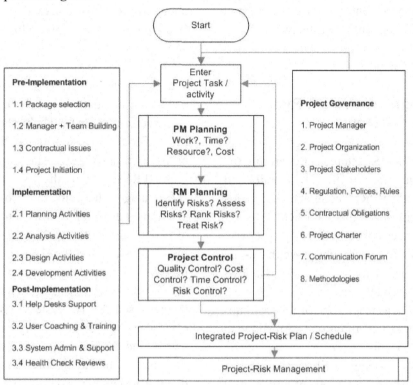

input variables (model components) be projected onto the planning, management and control activities within each of the project phases. The process entails the following steps:

1. Promote and apply IPRM guiding themes throughout the project life, including pre-implementation tasks (such as package selection, manager selection, team building, contract award and project initiation), implementation phase activities (planning, design, analysis and development), and post-implementation activities (help desk support, training and coaching, and system administration). The main IPRM guiding themes are:

    ○ Efficient → Project → Governance (Function)

    ○ Competent → Manager → Oversight (Function)

    ○ Integrated → Project-Risk Management → Practices (System)

    ○ Effective → Project Control → Practices (System)

    ○ Suitable → Implementation → Software (Tools)

2. Build the basic project's work breakdown structure guided by the IPRM definition of project, phases, activities and deliverables, and convert it to a basic project plan.

3. Develop multi-perspective profiling based on IPRM components (PG, MO, RM, PM and PC) at activity, phase and project levels in the planning, management and control aspects of the project. Each project task and activity needs to be investigated and processed

against the IPRM proposed attributes of the project management, risk management and project control, within a framework that is defined through the project governance and oversight function.

IPRMS: Integrated Project-Risk Management System

The proposed IPRMS system is built around the offering and requirements of the IPRM model, and will complement the IPRM model achieved in this research. It is envisaged that the IPRMS system will be an enhanced collaborative IT project-risk management solution, combining proven back-end relational databases with user friendly window-like front-end user interface, through which users can access and navigate a variety of core and support modules and applications that correspond to the IPRM components (Table 1).

The proposed system will automate the planning, scheduling, management and control processes, and will be packaged with a library of templates and wizards to guide project team members in executing their different activities. The system is expected to have intelligent features based on the consolidation of experiences from many different projects; these will be communicated to users in the form of hints or stated facts and figures.

The IPRMS system will enjoy functionality and user-friendly features such as GUI, security, audit trail, navigation, collaboration, hyperlink, on-screen query, on field help, shortcuts and data filters. For effective adoption of the IPRM model proposition, and the efficient usage and utilisation of the IPRMS system, the project team members and managers need to undergo an appropriate pre-implementation training program composed of two components, the IPRM guide to managing IT projects, and the IPRMS system training modules.

The following figures show sample screens of the proposed IPRMS system. The screens show clearly that the system design is based on the IPRM model components, attributes and tools. It also reflects the key features and functionalities that this research has shown to enhance practice and minimise risk of failure. The main menu screen (Figure 4) shows that the system includes the following modules: Project Management, Risk Management, Project Controls, Project Governance and Manager's Oversight.

Table 1. IPRMS modules and applications

IPRMS Module	Applications
Governance & Oversight	1. Project Contract, 2.Rules & Regulations, 3.Organisation, 4. Oversight
Project Management	1.Project Planning, 2.Work Management, 3.Project Costing, 4.Project Resources, 5.Project Reports
Risk Management	1. Risk Planning, 2.Risk assessment, 3.ICPT & Risk Register, 5. Risk Control, 6. Risk Reports
Project Control	1. Monitoring, 2.Quality Control, 3.Cost Control, 4.Change Control, 5.Document Control, 6.Control Panel
Support Module	1.Database Administration, 2.Configuration Tools, 3.Reports, 4.KPI & Metrics, 5.Workflow Engine, 6.Document Management, 7.Signature Security, 8.Help

Figure 4. IPRMS main menu screen

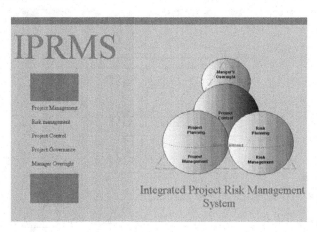

Figure 5. IPRMS PM application (main screen)

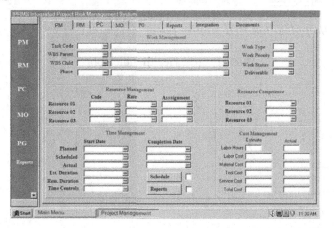

Figure 5 shows the PM main application reflecting relevant IPRM PM attributes such as Work management, Time, Resources, and Cost.

Figure 6 shows the main screen of the RM application reflecting risk attributes and processes, including the ICPT and Risk registers and tools to support risk identification, analysis, assessment and control.

Figure 7 shows a typical control panel used in the IPRMS MO application. This control panel provides an oversight window to standard real time project health indicators, or to other indicators that can be selected by the manager and configured in the system. These indicators will be based on measurement and parameter definitions in the system's PC application, to be viewed by selected parties involved in project control and decision making.

Figure 8 shows a typical project chart. IPRMS provides multiple perspective views of project activities, including conventional PM project progress based on time cost and quality; risk exposure profile at activity-phase-project levels; 'In-Control' status and other views that can be flexibly selected by the manager and configured in the system.

When developed, the IPRMS system will provide IT project managers and team members with an automated version of the IPRM-7 model. The

Figure 6. IPRMS RM application (main screen)

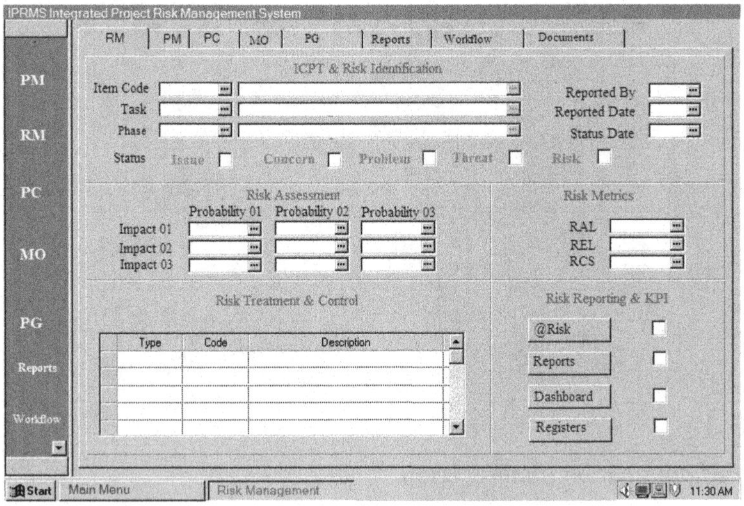

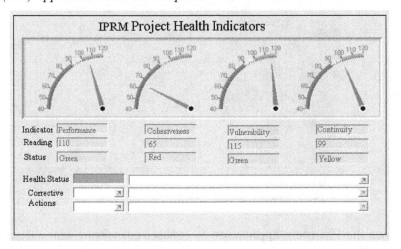

Figure 7. IPRMS (MO) application PHI control panel

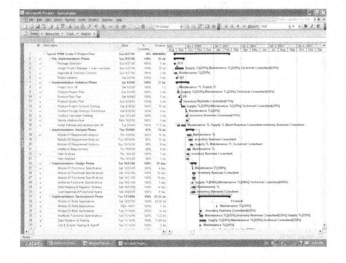

Figure 8. Typical project schedule

system will incorporate features of the model—the definition of the systems, practices, processes, function, attributes, metrics and tools—shown by the research to represent a major improvement to traditional practices, and which is expected to substantially reduce project failures caused by inadequate practices.

A major improvement to the practices will result, in particular, from integrating risk management and project management processes into a unified Management System and from systematically implementing a control system. In addition, adopting IPRM-7 and its MO-PG functions guide and procedures will reduce failures related to inefficient management and governance.

The IPRMS system provides the opportunity to automate IPRM processes using the appropriate tools, and to make available suitable databases, applications, tools, registers, workflow engines, analytical reporting, document management, and a communication forum for project managers, team members and project stakeholders.

CONCLUSION

Why IT Projects Fail?

The key aim of the research was to address the important question of **'Why do IT projects fail?'** The increasing level of understanding throughout the research as to the causes and contributing factors of IT project failure led to proposing a new model that is focused on maximising opportunities for success and minimising risks of failures. The research has shown that persisting and frequent project issues, concerns, problems and threats that are linked to unfavourable project performance outcomes are related to:

- Project governance defectiveness
- Manager's (oversight) incompetence
- Project management practices inadequacy

- Risk management practices misuse
- Project control shortfalls
- Lack of integration between processes and functions
- Ineffectiveness of used software tools.

These links and relationships were observed consistently throughout the research, and were validated by further investigating practices suitability and effectiveness (PSE) applied to the relevant areas. These investigations confirmed the identified areas as the most vulnerable and so they were, in turn, incorporated into building the IPRM model and defining its components and attributes.

The PSE investigations were crucial to validating the findings from the ICPT analysis, and to consolidating the acquired knowledge-set to give an insight into why projects fail. This increase in understanding throughout the research contributed to gradually building the IPRM model around the theme of maximising success opportunities and minimising failures threats. This aim is achieved by prescribing proven suitable and effective integrated management and control practices, promoting good project governance, ensuring oversight competences and efficient usage and utilisation of metrics and software tools. The research identified the weaknesses and strengths of the practices associated with the existing methodologies and the time-based paradigm, confirming the validity of some practices and/or highlighting inadequacies that need to be addressed to prevent causes of failure, mitigate identified threats and utilise opportunities.

The research approach provided the mechanism for translating the outcomes of the investigations and hypothesis testing into building and refining the proposed IPRM model. Therefore, the growing understanding of why IT projects fail was ultimately complemented by the development of a model that answers the question **'How can IT project failures be prevented?'**

Research Contributions

The following contributions of this research are linked to the introduction of the IPRM model as an alternative to conventional project management approaches:

1. The research has provided a deeper understanding of IT issues, problems and practices that are linked to unfavourable negative outcomes.
2. The research has developed and tested the IPRM (integrated project risk management) model on the basis of encountering important project outcome-related issues in real project scenarios, identifying and re-defining the main components, processes, attributes, metrics and relationships.
3. The research has formulated and introduced new concepts, such as 'Project Health Profile', 'Cockpit Control', 'Knowledge Intelligence' and 'Manager's Competence' that can have a substantial impact on the way projects are planned, managed and controlled.
4. The research has introduced the IPRM practical guide to managing IT projects and systems implementations.
5. The research has introduced the main features of a proposed integrated project risk management system IPRMS, with relevant modules, applications and functionalities that reflect the IPRM model offering, and that can be used as the platform for managing IT projects.

How IPRM is Different

With special emphasis on minimising risk of project failure and maximising opportunities of success, the IPRM model adopts a comprehensive project life-cycle approach that integrates risk management principles and practices with time-based project planning and management.

IPRM is also packaged with a number of tools and metrics that serve each of its components in a systematically structured framework, to guide project managers and team members in efficiently executing their tasks in a controlled environment.

However, it is important to emphasise that the model's contribution and relevance is derived from, and linked to, its suitability and effectiveness for the IT environment and the unique characteristics of IT. Most significantly, it was conceived and developed specifically for IT, and not for manufacturing, construction or any other industry.

The rationale behind the model is ascertaining the quality of deliverables and containing risk levels within acceptable bounds. The model achieves this by promoting well-informed, proactive risk management concepts and techniques in a controlled project environment. The final packaged version of the model is expected to provide a major contribution to successful project implementation. IPRM will provide immunity against an important category of project failure threats where existing methodologies and practices have drastically failed.

The model differs from other methodologies and practices in that it reflects real issues, problems and threats; it addresses and overcomes weaknesses rather than evading them. To those accustomed to the traditional time-based project management paradigm, IPRM may appear as a rebellion against the status quo, or it may be prejudged as another new, fancy, valueless trend. However, those IT managers and professionals who have wrestled with the limitations and irrelevance of current implementation methodologies will certainly view IPRM positively as a serious practical attempt to fill the gap with a guide that is more suitable, more effective, more relevant, more practical, more flexible and certainly more user-friendly.

One of the challenges of this research has been to cross conceptual boundaries and make the

IPRM model useful and practical. To ensure that the model is a viable alternative to conventional approaches in managing IT projects and implementing information systems, it is well defined through the characterisation of its components, processes, metric and tools.

IPRM: Future Outlook

Further improvements to IPRM could include the following:

- Continued improvement of the IPRM model by using it in real implementations under different conditions. Such action could identify and overcome any weaknesses and limitations, and refine the model's offering by introducing enhancements to the features, tools, and associated systems, such as a library of templates and How-To guides.
- Development of the Integrated Project-Risk Management System IPRMS, packaged with relevant modules, applications, tools and features that reflect the IPRM model offering. This system could be used as a platform to effectively and efficiently manage IT projects.
- Preparation of relevant system documentation including a users' manual, implementation guide and training manuals.
- Exploration of innovative concepts and new technologies to support the IPRM model components and system, particularly by investigating a means of integrating project and risk management, and improving the planning, scheduling and control processes, team collaboration, decision making, and business intelligence. These concepts can play a role in introducing badly-needed tools to improve the practice of project management, especially in relation to managing IT projects.

In view of the continuing high failure rate of IT projects, it is anticipated that the results of this research will substantially improve management practices by providing the tools to ensure smooth healthy running of projects, and thus will help minimise project failures and maximise successful outcomes.

REFERENCES

Alter, S., & Ginzberg, M. (1978). Managing uncertainty in MIS implementation. *Sloan Management Review, 20*(1), 23-31.

Anderson, E. S., Dyrhaug, Q. X., & Jessen, S. A. (2002). Evaluation of Chinese projects and comparison with Norwegian projects. *International Journal of Project Management* 20, 601-609.

Berny, J., & Townsend, P. R. (1993). Macrosimulation of project risks–A practical way forward. *International Journal of Project Management, 11*(4), 201-208.

Boehm, B. W. (1991). Software risk management: Principle and practices. *IEEE Software, 8*(1), 32-41.

Bplans (2006). *Performing a SWOT analysis.* Retrieved January 12, 2006, from http://www.bplans.com/ma/swotanalysis.cfm

CCTA (1995). *An introduction to managing project risk.* London: HMSO.

CCTA (1997). *The management of risk.* Central Computer and Communications Agency. Retrieved November 13, 1997, from http://www.open.gov.uk/ccta/pubcat/riskkey.htm

CCTA (1999). *Managing successful projects with PRINCE 2* (Central Computer and Telecommunication Agency). London: The Stationary Office.

CCTA (2000). *Managing successful projects with PRINCE 2.* Norwich, UK: The Stationary Office:

CCTA (2001). *Managing successful projects with PRINCE2.* Central Computer and Communication Agency, UK.

Charette, R. N. (1989). *Software engineering risk analysis and management.* New York: McGraw-Hill.

Chittiser, C., & Haimes, Y. (1993). Risk associated with software development: A holistic framework for assessment and management. *IEEE Transactions on Systems, Man and Cybernetics, 23*(3), 701-723.

Cunningham, M. (1999). It's all about the business. *Information, 13*(3), 83.

Davis, G. (1982). Strategies for information requirements determination. *IBM Systems Journal, 2*(1), 4-29.

DCAMS (1996). *Strategic asset management: Project risk management guidelines, risk management section.* Department of Contract and Management Services, Western Australia.

DoD (1988). *Military standard, defense system software development.* DoD-STD-2167A. Washington, DC: Department of Defense.

DSMC (1989). Risk management, concepts and guidance. FT. Belvoir, VA: Defense Systems Management College.

Evaristo, R., & van Fenema, P. C. (1999). A typology of project management: Emergence and evolution of new forms. *International Journal of Project Management, 17*(5), 275-281.

Fairley, R. E. (1994). Risk management for software projects. *IEEE Software, 11*(May), 57-67.

Flowers, S. (1996). *Software failure: Management failure.* Chichester, UK: John Wiley.

Foo, S. W., & Muruganantham, A. (2000, November 12-15). Software risk assessment model. In *Proceedings of IEEE ICMIT 2000 International Conference on Management of Innovation,* (pp. 536-544).Singapore.

Glass, R. L. (1997). *The software runaways.* NJ: Prentice Hall and Yourdon Press

Goldratt E. (1997). *Critical chain great barrington.* MA: North River Press.

Hall, E. M. (1995). *Proactive risk management methods for software engineering excellence.* Florida Institute of Technology..

Hefner, R. (1994). Experience with applying SEI's risk taxonomy. In *Proceedings of 3rd SEI Conference on Software Risk Management.* Pittsburgh, PA: SEI.

Hevner, A., March, S., Park, J., & Ram, S. (2004). Design science in information systems research. *MIS Quarterly 28*(1), 75-105.

Horn, L. (1994). *SWOT analysis and strategic Planning - A manual.* Hamburg, Germany: GFA.

IEEE (1987). *IEEE standards for software project management plans,* Std 1058.1-1987. New York: IEEE.

IEEE (1992). *IEEE standards for software quality metrics methodology.* IEEE Std 1061-1992. NY: IEEE.

ISO (1991). *Information technology software life cycle processes* ISO/IEC (JTC1)-SC7.Geneva, Switzerland: ISO.

Johnson, J., Boucher, K. D., Connors, K., & Robinson, J. (2001). The criteria for success. *Software magazine, 21*(1), 3-11.

Kansala, K. (1997). Integrating risk assessment with cost estimation. *IEEE Software* (May/June), 61-67.

Karolak, D. W. (1996). *Software engineering risk management.* Los Alamitos, CA: IEEE Computer Society Press.

Kitchenham, B., & Linkman, S. (1997). Estimates, uncertainty, and risk. *IEEE Software, 14*(3), 69-74.

Kliem, R. L., & Ludin, I. S. (1999). *Tools and tips for today's project manager*. Pennsylvania: PMI Project Management Institute.

KPMG (2002). *Programme management survey*. Retrieved February 13, 2003. from http://www.theregister.co.uk/2002/11/26/it_project_failure_is_rampant/

Lemon, W. Leibowitz, J. Burn, J., & Hackney, R. (2002). Information systems project failure: A comparative study of two companies. *Journal of Global Information Management, 10*(2), 28-39.

Madachy, R. J. (1997). Heuristic risk assessment using cost factors. *IEEE Software, 14*(3), 51-59.

March, S. T., & Smith, G. F. (1995). Design and natural science research on information technology. *Decision Support Systems*, (15), 251-266.

McFarlan, W. (1981). Portfolio approach to information systems. *Harvard Business Review*, 65, 68-74.

McManus, J., & Wood-Harper, T. (2003). Information systems project management: The price of failure. *Management Services, 47*(5), ABI/INFORM Global, 16.-19.

Michales, J. V. (1996). *Technical risk management*. Upper Saddle River, NJ: Prentice Hall.

Milis, K., & Mercken, R. (2004). The use of balanced scoreboard for the evaluation of information and communication technology projects. *International Journal of Project Management, 22*, 87-97.

Niazi, M., Wislon, D., & Zowghi, D. (2003, November). Critical success factors and critical barriers for software process improvement: An analysis of literature. In *Proceedings of 14th Australasian Conference on Information Systems*, (pp. 26-28).Perth Western Australia.

Nolan, R. (1979). Managing the crisis in data processing. *Harvard Business Review* March/April, 115-126.

Peterson, D. K., Kim, C., Kim, J. H., & Tamura, T. (2002). The perceptions of information systems designers from the United States, Japan, and Korea on success and failure factors. *International Journal of Information Management, 22*, 421-439.

Raz, T., & Michael, E. (2001). Use and benefits of tools for project risk management. *International Journal of Project Management, 19*(1), 9-17.

Ross, J. (2003, November). The importance of political influence in explaining project management success factors. In *Proceedings of 14th Australasian Conference on Information Systems*, (pp. 26-28). Perth, Western Australia.

Saarinen, T. (1996). An expanded instrument for evaluating information system success. *Information and Management, 31*, 103–118.

Sauer, C. (1999). Deciding the future for IS failure: Not the choice you might think. In Currie & Galliers, *Rethinking management information systems: An introductory perspective*. UK: Oxford University Press.

SEI (1993). *Key practices of the capability maturity model*. Pittsburgh, PA: Software Engineering Institute, Carnegie Mellon University.

SEI (1994). *Proceedings of 3rd SEI Conference on Software Risk Management*. Pittsburgh PA: Software Engineering Institute.

SEI (1995). *Proceedings of 4th SEI Conference on Software Risk Management*. Pittsburgh PA: Software Engineering Institute.

SEI (1997). *Proceedings of 5th SEI Conference on Software Risk Management*. Pittsburgh PA: Software Engineering Institute.

Sisti, F. J., & Joseph, S. (1994) *Software risk evaluation method*. Pittsburgh PA: Software Engineering Institute.

Sokratis Katsikas (1998). *Risk analysis and risk management CRAMM methodology*. University of Aegean S Navy. Retrieved September 13,

1998, from http://epic.onion.it/workshops/w08/slides13/

Standards Australia (1995). *AS/NZS 4360:1995 risk management standards*. Homebush, NSW Australia.

Standards Australia (1999). *AS/NZS43660:1999 Risk management standards*. Melbourne, Australia.

Standish Group (1994). *The CHAOS report*. Retrieved March 1, 2004, from http://www.standishgroup.com/sample_research/chos_1994_1.php

Standish Group (1995). *The scope of software development project failures, CHAOS Report*. Retrieved March 15, 1997, from http://www.standishgroup.com/chaos.html

Standish Group (1998). *CHAOS '98: A summary review*. A Standish Group Research Note. The Standish Group, USA.

Stewart, R., Sherif, M., & Daet, R. (2002). Strategic implementation of IT/IS projects in construction: a case study. *Automation in Construction, 11*(6), 681-694.

Wallmueller, E. (2004). *Software quality assurance - A practical approach*. NJ: Prentice Hall.

Walls, J. G., Widmeyer, G., & El Sawy, O. A. (1992). Building an information system design theory for vigilant EIS. *Information Systems Research, 3*(1), 36-59.

Westerveld, E. (2003). The project excellence model: Linking success criteria and critical success factors. *International Journal of Project Management, 21*, 411-418.

Yates, J. C., & Arne, P. H. (2004). Balancing the scales: Managing risks in IT projects. The *Computer & Internet Lawyer Journal, 21*(8), 1-6.

Yeo, K. T. (2002). Critical failure factors in information system projects. *International Journal of Project Management, 20*, 241-246.

KEY TERMS AND DEFINITIONS

Project Health Indicator (PHI): The measurement of selected project health indicators (PHI) that combine four attributes of the project: Project Performance, Project Vulnerability, Project Cohesiveness and Project Continuity.

Term 01-Practice Suitability and Effectiveness (PSE): The examination of Practices Suitability and Effectiveness (PSE) to evaluate the appropriateness of the main systems and components proposed for the IPRM model.

Term 02-Issues-Concerns-Problems-Threats (ICPT): The investigations of projects' 'Issues, Concerns, Problems and Threats' (ICPT) commonly used in different system implementation methodologies and IT projects

Term 03-Project Performance Outcome (PPO): The investigations of Project Performance Outcome (PPO), used in the research as a measure of the projects' final performance and also indicate the relative success or failure of projects to achieve their goals incorporating the following indicators: Quality, Cost, Time, User Acceptance, Technical Status and Business Value.

Chapter XVIII
Technical Risk Management

Pete Hylton
Indiana University Purdue University Indianapolis, USA

ABSTRACT

In today's highly competitive industrial environment, many high-tech businesses are using Technical Risk Management (TRM) in their engineering design programs as a means of improving the chances of success. TRM allows program mangers to pinpoint potential failure modes of a project early in the process, so that corrective actions can be taken in the most effective manner. TRM also allows managers to appropriately prioritize program tasks so as to achieve optimum use of available technical resources. TRM requires that a methodology of practices and processes be implemented on an ongoing basis. These processes identify, evaluate, mitigate, and manage technical risks affecting program success. This chapter will discuss implementation of the TRM process and provide a simple example to show how the process works.

INTRODUCTION

Technical Risk Management (TRM) is a process by which the technical risks that can negatively impact program success are identified, ranked, and addressed so as to decrease the chances of project failure. Recently, many high-tech industries have included TRM as a part of their new technology programs. Modarres (2006) notes, "engineering systems are becoming more complex and demand for risk analysis is greater than ever." (p. 3) He continues, "recently, many legislators including U.S. Congress have advocated greater reliance on the use of risk information." (p. 3) The United States Department of Defense has instituted a requirement that risk management procedures be defined at the proposal stage for many new programs and that any major technical reviews include a status update on the management of all identified risks. Even where TRM is not required by contract, many businesses are implementing their own internal requirements for a technical risk management process to be in place.

A TRM process forces the design team into critical problem solving mode early in the program, thus avoiding last minute panics. It also facilitates the most intelligent ordering of task priorities and the most efficient allocation of available resources. For these reasons it is becoming popular with program managers as a means of reducing the risk of program failure and simultaneously helping them manage their programs with the leanest possible staffing resources.

BACKGROUND

A recent risk analysis survey, conducted in the aerospace industry, stated, "Increasingly, Government customers and Industry contractors seek better methods to identify and manage technical, schedule, and cost risk." (Black, 2001, p. 1) The survey documented that 39% of industry representatives surveyed expect their technical staff to play the major role in risk management, whereas 33% placed responsibility for risk management on the cost estimators, 14% on management and 14% elsewhere. Clearly the technical staff in aerospace firms is expected to participate heavily in the management of technical risks. The medical device industry is another industry with this expectation. Kaye and Crowley (2000) have described the use of TRM in that industry, saying "Risk Management is a systematic application of policies, procedures, and practices to the analysis, evaluation, and mitigation of risks. It is a key component of quality management systems, and is a central requirement of the implementation of design controls in the Quality Systems Regulation." (p. 8) Software development engineering is

yet another arena where the importance of managing risk has been recognized. Kendall (2007) has stated that at least 25% of software design projects are cancelled before completion and 89% overrun budget. Based on this, the report goes on to say "It is no surprise, then, that one of the drivers in the evolution of software engineering, as a discipline, has been the desire to indentify reliable, quantifiable ways to manage software development risks." (p. 1)

For U.S. Department of Defense programs, guidelines for estimating the probability of occurrence and the magnitude of failure impact are published as part of military standard MIL-STD-882, System Safety Program Requirements, which states "A formal safety program that stresses early hazard identification and elimination or reduction of associated risk to a level acceptable to the managing activity is the principle contribution to effective system safety." (U.S. DoD, 1984, p. 2) The TRM concept is required for virtually all new military contracts. Plans are frequently subject to monthly tracking by program-wide risk review boards comprised of members of the technical staff of both the vendor and the contracting agency. Additional government agencies are adopting this practice and many commercial customers contracting for new designs in high-tech industries are instituting internal requirements for TRM to be part of every program.

Branscomb (2000) described the impact of a failure to effectively manage technical risk, in the forward to a government sponsored paper entitled *Managing Technical Risk*, when he said "The risks associated with science based commercial innovations are real and often hard to quantify and circumscribe. These risks contribute to business failures, but more importantly to underinvestment in the early stages of research and to opportunities foregone." (p. 2) Today's new engineering and technology college graduates would benefit from inclusion of TRM concepts into the curriculum. In fact, a national survey of faculty involved in collegiate engineering and technology capstone design courses, as reported by Conrad and Sireli, (2005) indicated that the least successful performance area for university students was the "ability to foresee potential risks involving the project and create contingency plans." Instructors rated this skill as between "moderate" and "poor" for their students, making it the lowest score of any skill set on the survey. (p. 3)

TECHNICAL RISK MANAGEMENT

The TRM process that will be discussed here, consists of four phases. They are: Risk Identification, Risk Ranking, Risk Reduction Planning, and Risk Tracking. The first phase, Risk Identification, causes the project team to take a serious look at the design they are working on. This must be done with particular attention paid to possible failure modes that could impact program success. The second phase, Risk Ranking, requires the project team to assess which of the identified failure modes present the biggest threat to the success of the project. This step allows the program manager to use the assessment of his technical staff and appropriately prioritize the analyses and design efforts necessary to improve the likelihood of success. This phase has the effect of driving proper scheduling of tasks and allocation of resources.

In the third phase, the Risk Reduction Plan, the technical staff must define the design, analysis, or testing steps that they plan to take in order to avoid, or at least minimize, the project risk for each of the failure modes which were identified in the first step and ranked in the second step. This phase requires the design team to enter into critical problem solving mode early in the program. This avoids last minute panics which usually result in programs running over budget and late relative to schedule. The fourth and final step of the TRM process is Risk Tracking. This step is an ongoing activity that actually covers the longest period of time because it involves following through on the Risk Reduction Plan. The project team must

ensure that all of the steps from phase three are completed, so that the risk is actually reduced as intended. It is important to understand that unless the plan is properly followed through to completion, the time spent on the first three steps was wasted effort.

Risk Identification

There is no such thing as identifying a potential risk too early in a design project. Earlier is always better than later, because reaction and response times are shorter earlier in the program. Thus early identification of risks maximizes the team's ability to appropriately address and resolve them with minimal shifting of resources. This provides the best opportunity to reach a solution without impacting overall program cost and schedule. The design team should perform its first risk identification soon after the initial concept is formulated. This identification session may even parallel the brainstorming session that usually is the first step in formulating a design. In fact, paying attention to possible project risks may actually help narrow the field of brainstormed ideas. Every member of the team should try to step back and look at all possible failure modes for the design.

All possible failures that are seen as a potential risk by any member of the team should be considered a valid risk to the project. No effort should be made to determine relative importance of the risks at this time. There should also be no attempt to define design solutions to eliminate potential risks. That comes later. If a team comes up with only one or two risk items, then the members are not being realistic in their identification. There are always things that can go wrong, and team members should keep an open mind, so as to capture all potential risks.

Even after the initial risk identification is completed, the project team should continue to be alert for new risks that may arise as the project proceeds. These could occur because the effort put in during the detailed design or analysis phase

285

raises new potential issues. Such new risks should be added to the list of identified risks whenever they arise. This is almost certain to occur as a design evolves and changes. In fact, a design team which does not uncover new risks as it moves through the design process is probably not taking a truly objective view of its efforts.

Risk Ranking

The first step, which forced the team to step back and consider possible failure modes of their design, is an important step on its own. However, the next step involves determining which of these risks is the greatest threat, and should therefore be addressed first. The TRM process described here provides a mechanism that supports the determination of optimum task prioritization and allocation of resources. In order to do this, a Risk Ranking, or scoring system, is needed. Schmidt (2001) points out that quantifying the risks associated with a technology project requires finding a way to evaluate "the product of uncertainty associated with project risks times some measure of the magnitude of the consequences." (p. 6)

The team must address every risk that was listed in the Risk Identification phase. The likelihood of its occurrence and its potential consequence, or impact, if it does occur, must be evaluated. Likelihood is a measure of the probability that a failure identified in the first step will actually occur. Such probabilities could be quantitative and actually come from probabilistic design calculations. However, at least early in the program, they will have to come from educated estimates based on the preliminary design work being done by the team, because exacting calculations are simply not possible. Realistically, there are risk aspects of the project that can never be accurately quantified by a numerical probability. For this reason, qualitative assessments based on the judgment by the technical staff will have to suffice.

Kumamoto and Henley (1996) present a thorough mathematical treatment of probabilistic risk. They say that each risk should preferably be "expressed as an objective probability, percentage or density per action or unit time, or during a specified time interval." But they go on to acknowledge, "Unfortunately, the likelihood is not always exact; probability, percentage, frequency, and ratios may be based on subjective evaluation. Verbal probabilities such as *rare, possible, plausible, and frequent* are also used." (p. 2) For purposes of this discussion, we will use three subjective graduations; low probability, medium probability, and high probability.

Next, the consequence of such a failure actually occurring must be assessed. Failure consequences are even more difficult to quantify, and Kumamoto and Henley (1996) say that "verbal and ambiguous terms such as *catastrophic, severe, and minor* may be used instead of quantitative measures." They also point out that consequences need to be tailored to the particular project because significance depends on intangibles such as "cultural attributes, ethics, emotion, reconciliation, media coverage, context, or litigability," as well as the fact that "people estimate the outcome significance differently when population risk is involved in addition to individual risk." (p. 22) For example, the consequences of the failure in a rocket ship design are inherently different than the consequences in the design of a new and improved concrete building block. The point is, however, to realized that there are consequences to the occurrence of a failure in any program. This simply points out that the method used to score a risk should be tailored to the needs of each individual program. Again, for purposes of this discussion, we will designate the consequences to be low impact, medium impact, and high impact. Consequences associated with program risk generally fall into the following types:

- **Budget impact:** How much money does the program stand to lose if the failure occurs? This could result from lost income because the failed product does not sell. It could result from increased expense to fix the problem through redesign and additional analysis and testing. Or, it could result from liability claims from others who received injury or damage due to the failure. A combination of all three is, naturally, a possibility as well. What constitutes a budget impact of low versus moderate, versus high, consequence must be tailored for each individual program.

- **Schedule impact:** Schedule impact also varies from one project to another. On some programs a delay of three months may be considered "high impact," but a few weeks is manageable. On other programs, a three week delay may have a detrimental impact. This is particularly true if the contract with the customer has stipulated financial penalties for late delivery. Time management is proving to be one of the most critical responsibilities of today's project management team. (Horenstein, 2005, p. 86)

- **Technical impact:** The technical impact is a function of how much redesign effort is required to correct the problem associated with a particular failure mode. This impact would include the required redirection of

both manpower resources and supporting resources associated with rectifying the failure.

Once the probabilities and consequences have been evaluated, each individual risk item can be assigned a Risk Score. One means of doing this is via a scoring matrix like the one shown in Figure 1. This matrix can also be tailored to specific projects. For example, if higher refinement is required, a five-by-five or larger matrix could be used, featuring new and more refined graduations of probability and consequence. In general, risks with both high probability and high consequence receive the highest overall risk score. The scoring matrix accomplishes two things. First, it quantifies the risks, giving them a score which is based on a combination of probability and of consequence. This makes it easy for them to be prioritized. Second, it allows them to be categorized into three simple and easily comprehensible levels. These levels are usually color coded, red, yellow, and green. Although simplistic, this color coding method provides a means of quickly and clearly highlighting which risks are the biggest concerns. To the engineer this might seem an oversimplification of a complex issue. But as

Figure 1. A typical Risk Scoring matrix is displayed

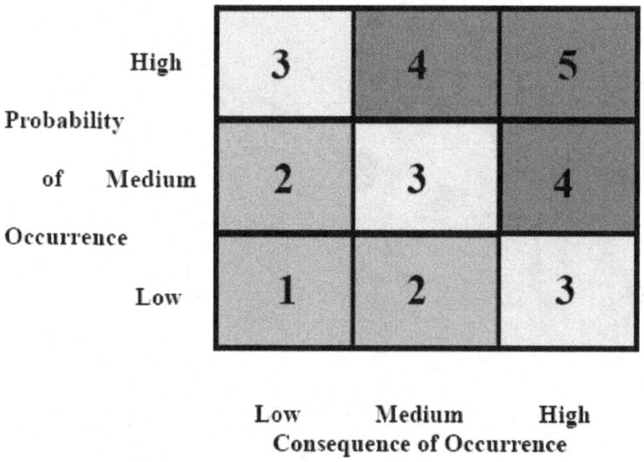

Jarrett (2000) explains, the corporate executive is the member of the organization which deals ultimately with risk decisions, and "even if it were possible to develop complex representations of risk accurately, it is difficult for the executive to deal with them. Instead, the executive is able to deal with a few scenarios and possible cases, and only with three general levels of conceptual risk associated with them: High Risk, Medium Risk, and Low Risk." (p. 77).

It can be seen that the scoring matrix in Figure 1 applies equal weight to both probability and consequence. This need not be the case, however. This is another instance where the process can be tailored to meet the specific needs of a particular program. The scoring matrix can be skewed slightly toward the consequence axis to better account for the impact of potential failures, or vice versa.

Risk Reduction Plan

In many ways, the most useful part of TRM process is the third phase, which involves developing a Risk Reduction Plan. The objective is to define a list of steps that will attack each item that has been assessed as having an unacceptably high risk. These steps may involve redesign of existing aspects of the project, analysis of parts that have been designed, testing, or addition of new aspects of the project that lower the possible impact of a failure if it occurs. The project team must use their knowledge, skills, and resources to schedule a series of risk reduction steps that will reduce the high risk scores to low risk scores, by planning a course of action that reduces each red or yellow risk item to green.

Risk Tracking

The fourth and final stage of the TRM process is the execution of the Risk Reduction Plan. This stage cannot be effectively described in any detail, because its details are actually in the plan. This management oriented phase covers the longest time period and is the most important of the four steps because it involves the team actually performing the steps outlined in the plan, ensuring that each step is completed and the risk is actually reduced. Identifying, assessing, and mitigation planning are all pointless unless the plan is followed.

Figure 2. This figure presents an assembly drawing of a winch for use in a TRM example

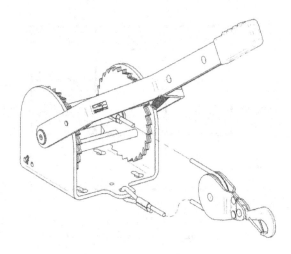

Example

Perhaps the easiest way to understand how this process can work is by using a fairly simple example. For purposes of the example, let's look at a design project somewhere between the rocket ship and the concrete block on the technology scale. By picking something that almost anyone will recognize and understand, the example can have meaning to anyone. Let us consider ourselves on a team that is tasked with designing and prototyping a new hand operated winch. This is a fairly straightforward mechanical apparatus, as shown in Figure 2. Yet it has enough components which carry some level of loading that it gives us something to consider. We must begin by identifying potential risks to our program. These include not only possible failures of mechanical components

due to loading, but also related technical problems that could impact our objectives. We might come up with a list of failure modes, like that shown in the list in Table A.

Now we need to determine a ranking order for the identified risks. This needs to be done in terms of both probability of occurrence and impact of occurrence. Begin with the first item on the list. Prior to any analysis being performed, the random selection of a cable size would not take into account the loading on the cable. Therefore, we could consider the probability of cable failure on the order of 50%. So let's assign the likelihood of occurrence as medium. If the device were being used to winch a car onto a trailer, a typical use for such a mechanism, the car will suddenly be released and roll backwards. This would create the potential for damage or injury to anything

Table A. Risks identified by the example design team for the Winch Project

1.	Failure of the cable
2.	Failure of the handle/lever which the user pushes on
3.	Failure of the drum onto which the cable is wrapped
4.	Failure of the shaft the drum spins on
5.	Failure of the ratcheting gear
6.	Failure of the latch which prevents ratchet from unwinding
7.	Failure of the bolts mounting the winch to the trailer
8.	Failure of vendor to supply components for assembly on time
9.	Failure of fabrication shop to meet schedule

Table B. Risk probabilities and consequences assigned for the Winch Project

Failure Mode	Probability	Consequence
1. Failure of the cable	Medium	High
2. Failure of the handle	Medium	Low
3. Failure of the drum	Low	Medium
4. Failure of the shaft	Medium	Medium
5. Failure of the gear	Low	High
6. Failure of the latch	High	High
7. Failure of the bolts	Medium	High
8. Failure of vendor supply	Low	High
9. Failure of fab. shop	Medium	High

or anyone which might be behind the trailer at the time. This might well be assumed as a high consequence. Following a similar process for all of the identified risks, we would create a series of assessments like those shown in Table B.

Using the ranking matrix from Figure 1, we would use the probabilities and impacts from Table B to generate the risk scores shown in Table C. From this, it becomes obvious which risks deserve to receive attention first and which risks can be dealt with later in the program, or possibly ignored if the risk is adequately low. At this point we have turned qualitative assessments of the likelihoods and impacts for the potential risks into a quantitative assessment that gives project management direction as to which issues to address first, and thereby, where program resources should be directed.

The next step is to design a Risk Reduction Plan for all relevant items. After the Risk Ranking stage, the biggest issue was determined to be the ratcheting latch which keeps the ratcheting gear from allowing the drum to spin backwards. The latch is a heavily loaded piece which prevents the winch from releasing its load. Let us consider a Risk Reduction Plan for this component.

- **Step 1**. Determine how much load is on the latch, based on the design specifications for the device.

- **Step 2**. Step 1 did not reduce the risk. But, using the information, we can perform hand stress calculations on the latch, which gives a much better assessment of the acceptability of the risk, or allows for the latch design to be improved to accommodate the load.

- **Step 3**. Create a three dimensional model of the latch, suitable for both manufacturing and analysis

- **Step 4**. Using the model from Step 3, apply finite element analysis techniques to predict the stresses in the latch. Compare predicted loads to material properties. This will either confirm acceptability and thus further reduce the likelihood of failure, or it will lead to improving the strength of the latch design.

- **Step 5**. Enhancing the design reduces the impact of latch failure. For example, incorporation of an inertia catch, intended to stop the winch drum if it begins to spool too quickly (as it would after a latch failure) lowers the consequence of a latch failure.

Figure 3 shows the anticipated effect of the Risk Reduction Plan on the Risk Ranking. The fourth and final phase of the TRM process would involve tracking the design through to completion of the project.

Table C. Risks scored by the example design team for the Winch Project

Failure Mode	Probability	Consequence	Risk Score
1. Failure of the cable	Medium	High	4
2. Failure of the handle	Medium	Low	2
3. Failure of the drum	Low	Medium	2
4. Failure of the shaft	Medium	Medium	3
5. Failure of the gear	Low	High	3
6. Failure of the latch	High	High	5
7. Failure of the bolts	Medium	High	4
8. Failure of vendor supply	Low	High	3
9. Failure of fab. shop	Medium	High	4

Figure 3. This figure shows the effect of the Risk Reduction Plan on the example design

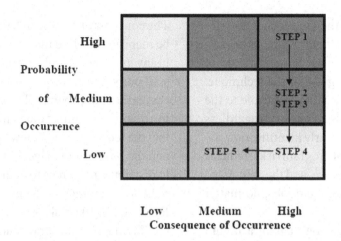

Figure 4. This figure shows an example of a non-symmetric Risk Ranking matrix

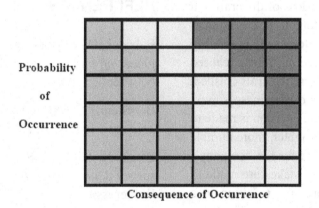

Let us now consider another example that will help explain why the Risk Ranking matrix might be set up to be skewed rather than symmetric. Assume that we are working for an aerospace company, somewhere in the American midwest, on a new prototype airplane which is part of a highly schedule driven program. One occurrence that could impact schedule is the possibility of a mid-winter blizzard which could shut the plant down for up to a week. If our plant is located in the snow-belt, then there is a very real possibility of losing a week due to weather. Thus we would consider this a high probability. However, with the ability to communicate from remote locations and correspond by emails from home, the staff will not fall as far behind as they might have a few years ago. There also is the likelihood of working overtime as soon as the weather clears, to help catch up. So the impact is probably low. Compare this to a potential failure mode in one of the aero control surfaces. Perhaps the likelihood is low, but if loss of airplane could result, impact would be high. Should these two risks, both with one high and one low assessment, end up generating an equal risk score? Quite probably not. For this reason, the matrix, especially if it uses more graduations, might well be skewed to something more like what is shown in Figure 4.

FUTURE TRENDS

Although it tended to be the high-tech industries that first began to implement TRM processes, more industries, producing a broader range of products, are now making use of the technique. The benefits should be equally applicable to the program management of any industry, regardless of the level of technology. Early identification, assessment, and reduction of program risks, reduces the chance of program failure, and the associated loss of revenue, reputation, and jobs, no matter what the program.

Using the previous analogy again, a failure that results in the loss of a rocket ship has the potential for large financial impact on a company, due both to the immediate loss of the craft and its payload, and from the long term loss of business. That does not even address the possibility that there may have been external damage caused depending on how and where the craft crashed. But consider a company whose business is making concrete blocks, and the decision is made to develop a newer, stronger, lighter, more durable block. This should be great for the company's future. However, what if mistakes are made in the design of the new product, resulting in a block that is subject to failure when used in heavy construction? Such a failure can just as easily bankrupt a small, low-tech firm, which makes it catastrophic in its own right. Therefore, there is merit in using the principles of TRM in any business regardless of the technology level. In support of the applicability of risk management practices, which play a role in all aspects of life, Bernstein comments, "Risk Management guides us over a vast range of decision-making, from allocating wealth to safeguarding public health, from waging war to planning a family, from paying insurance premiums to wearing a seatbelt, from planting corn, to marketing cornflakes." (1998, p.2)

CONCLUSION

The concepts of Technical Risk Management can be incorporated into the technical design process in any industry. The advantage is that the technical staff pinpoints the technical risks to program success early in the program. These risks are evaluated in a manner that ranks them in order of priority, so that the technical staff knows what to attack first, and the program manager can best evaluate how to distribute resources to address the appropriate risks. Developing and then implementing a plan for mitigating the risks will significantly improve the likelihood of program success

REFERENCES

Babcock, D., & Morse, L. (2007). *Managing engineering and technology.* Upper Saddle River, NJ: Prentice Hall.

Bernstein, P. (1998). *Against the gods: The remarkable story of risk.* New York: John Wiley.

Black, H. (2001). U.S. aerospace risk analysis survey. *Journal of Cost Analysis & Management*, Winter issue.

Branscomb, L. (2000). *Managing technical risk.* US Department of Commerce, NIST GCR 00-787.

Conrad, J., & Sirel, Y. (2005, October). Learning project management skills in senior design courses. In *Proceedings of the 35th ASEE/IEEE Frontiers in Education Conference,* Indianapolis, Indiana.

Horenstein, M. (2005). *Design concepts for engineers,* 3rd edition. Upper Saddle River, NJ: Prentice Hall

Hylton, P. (2006). Technical risk management as the connectivity in a capstone design course. *ASEE Journal of Mechanical Engineering Technology, 23*(1), 48-53.

Jarrett, E. (2000). Effect of technical elements of business risk on decision making. *Managing technical risk*. US Department of Commerce, NIST GCR 00-787.

Kaye, R., & Crowley, J. (2000). Medical device use-safety: Incorporating human factors engineering into risk management. *U.S. Dept. of Health and Human Services Guidance for Industry and FDA Premarket and Design Control Reviewers*. U.S. Dept. of Health and Human Services, Washington D.C.

Kendall, R., Post, D., Carver, J., Henderson, D., & Fisher, D. (2007). A proposed taxonomy for software development risks for high-performance computing (HPC) scientific/engineering applications. *Software Engineering Institute* (Technical Note CMU/SEI-2006-TN-039).

Kumamoto, H., & Henley, E. (1996). *Probabilistic tisk assessment and management for engineers and scientists*. New York: IEEE Press.

Marcus, M., & Winters, D. (2004). Team problem solving strategies with a survey of these methods used by faculty members in engineering technology. *Journal of STEM Education, 5*(1,2), 24.

Modarres, M. (2006). *Risk analysis in engineering*. New York: Taylor and Francis.

Schmidt, R. (2001). Identifying project risks: An international Delphi study. *Journal of Management Information Systems, 17*(4), 5-36.

US Department of Defense (1984). *MIL-STD-882B, system safety program requirements*. Washington D.C., AMSC F3329.

KEY TERMS AND DEFINITIONS

Consequence of Occurrence: A measure of the negative result associated with the occurrence of a failure mode identified in a risk analysis study.

Impact of Occurrence: The quantitative or qualitative measurement of the consequence occurring when a failure mode is realized.

Probabilistic Design Analysis: A design approach which attempts to assign numerical, quantitative probabilities to the likelihood of a failure occurring. This process uses the theories of statistical analysis and the variance of statistically quantifiable terms to calculate such numeric probabilities.

Probability of Occurrence: A value assigned to the likelihood that a particular failure will occur. This may be quantitatively assigned using approaches like those from probabilistic design analysis, or may be qualitative based on the instincts and experience of a design team.

Risk Identification: The phase of a risk management process where identification is made of all possible risks which could potentially impact the result of a program.

Risk Management: A process to identify and quantify sources of technical risks and their program impacts and find ways to avoid or control them. (Babcock, 2007, p. 217)

Risk Ranking: The phase of a risk management process where all identified risks are assessed either quantitatively or qualitatively, to ascertain which ones have the highest likelihood of occurrence and which ones have the greatest consequence of occurrence so as to rank the risks in overall order of importance.

Risk Reduction Plan: A plan, created as part of a risk management process, wherein steps are determined which will address a particular program risk so as to reduce either its likelihood of occurrence, or the consequence of its occurrence, or both, such that there is a reduction in its potential impact to the program.

Technical Risk: Any occurrence which could negatively impact the result of a program which could be mitigated by application of technical skills resulting in an improved design of a component, system, or process, thereby reducing the potential impact on the program.

Section IV
Project Planning and Assessment

Chapter XIX
Early, Often, and Repeat:
Assessment and Evaluation Methods for Ensuring Stakeholder Satisfaction with Information Technology Projects

Lauren Fancher
University System of Georgia, USA

ABSTRACT

IT projects across all sectors are relying on more iterative methodologies that can employ early and frequent assessment and evaluation processes in order to ensure that project deliverables are satisfactory. This chapter provides a practical overview of assessment and evaluation processes and how they can be built into any of the various project management and development models. Methods discussed include: audience and needs assessment; approaches for maintaining engagement with stakeholder audiences; requirements and feedback-gathering methods including focus groups, surveys, and other communications; and evaluation and review methods such as usability testing and user acceptance testing. Iterative cycles of assessment, prototyping, evaluation, and implementation will be demonstrated through examples and process model flow diagrams.

FAILURE AND SUCCESS: INTRODUCTION AND BACKGROUND

Ask any project manager: How many ways can a project fail? They will list many paths to failure, from doomed objectives to overdrawn budgets to implementation that is delivered just as core technologies become obsolete. Ask how many ways can a project succeed? Many project managers will say "by delivering the desired functionality on time and within budget." But the visionary project manager, the tuned-in project manager, the flexible and proactive project manager? They will tell you that success must be achieved in the eye of the stakeholder. Just as the tree falling alone in the forest makes no sound, without stakeholders to perceive success, there is no success. Three propositions regarding stakeholder satisfaction with IT projects synthesize the practices of project management, stakeholder analysis, and evaluation and form the foundation of this chapter.

Proposition One: *The perception of success is subjective and requires stakeholders.*

The practice of managing projects has produced a number of different popular formulaic approaches, which may differ in emphasis but typically share some common elements related to planning, managing, controlling, communicating about, and learning from projects. Often the emphasis in managing information technology (IT) projects is placed on controlling the schedule, coordination and supply of staff resources, and implementation costs (Schwalbe, 2000). In many environments, the service or system to be delivered impacts multiple audiences that exist in organizational or customer spaces that are isolated from each other as well as from those involved in the project deployment. The definition of "stakeholder" is in itself often overly limited to members of executive management or other higher-ups. As a result, key stakeholders are not identified ahead of time, critical inputs are missed, and misplaced assumptions regarding priorities result in great unhappiness amongst all of the potential stakeholders, in spite of a project that has been delivered on time, within budget, and matching the requirements that have been provided to the project team (Drummond & Hodgson, 2003). While timely and frequent communication with stakeholders is often noted as a key to project success, early identification of and engagement with all stakeholder audiences is even more fundamental (Pinto & Kharbanda, 1996). Stakeholders can be defined in multiple ways and may vary based on the context and project. A primary first step for any project is

to identify the stakeholders and determine how best to engage and manage their participation (Umbach, 2006).

Stakeholder analysis is a practice within the fields of business and management that seeks to identify and manage stakeholders within an organization. (Mayer, 2008). Research and theory regarding stakeholders and how to define and manage them has proliferated since the early 1990's. Motivations for broadening the definition of "stakeholder" within an organization can include both social responsibility and profit. The stakes that are held may be weighted with according difference (Mitchell, Angle, & Wood, 1997). In either case, the goal of attending to stakeholder interests for the purpose of achieving success has been well documented (Van Grembergen, 2002).

Project management has become a commonplace tool for success in multiple fields, from construction, architecture, and engineering, to business, technology, health, and increasingly, higher education environments. The practice of inclusion and attendance to stakeholders in these fields varies, but IT project management does recognize some aspects of both the role of the stakeholder, primarily in the form of communications, and the role of evaluation, primarily in the form of testing (Schwalbe, 2000). However, a more comprehensive assessment and evaluation methodology is needed within IT projects in order to account for an unusual multiplicity of audiences. For example, a typical information system's stakeholders may include the system administrator that supports the machine on which the application resides, the application administrator who supports the administrative users of the application, the administrative user who provides customer support and service for the application, the customer who receives services from the application, and the management team who reviews performance and makes decisions based on metrics and customer feedback regarding the application. All too often, one or more of these key audiences is overlooked, with the result that delivered IT functions and services don't match critical needs and requirements (Schwalbe, 2000).

When one looks to the sources of this omission, it is sometimes simply that the IT folks don't interact with the stakeholders directly, whether as users or as managers, and so have limited understanding of who might actually be impacted by a particular project (Fowler & Gilfillan, 2003). The isolation of the IT functions within (or increasingly, outside) many organizations is not, however, the sole responsibility or obligation of the IT staff to address. All too often, business process owners are reluctant to commit resources, time, or political capitol to implementations with significant IT components, preferring instead to let the IT staff wiggle on the hook of unpopular opinion. Increasingly, governance processes are defined for IT projects to include all affected areas of the organization (Weill & Ross, 2005). We just need to accept the fact that for any IT project, stakeholder analysis is an important foundation for success. Consensus is key to success, but as we will see, balancing opinions among diverse stakeholders is also necessary. We will define success as: keeping most stakeholders satisfied with most of the project outcomes.

In truth, all endeavors of man have planning, communication, and stakeholders, and all endeavors benefit from asking stakeholders what they think about this or that plan and being responsive to the answers.

Proposition Two: *Objectively managing the subjective inputs of stakeholders can help to achieve the perception of success on the part of stakeholders.*

The language of project management has some universal elements, but the literature often reflects the particular culture of the authors while seeming ignorant of equivalent approaches in unrelated fields of knowledge. These semantic differences become more important as the "science"

of project management seeps into more and more workplaces, many of which have always had planning and execution processes that are in fact very similar to the universals of project management, but may follow a local practice or a particular model related to their field. The terminology and methods of project management often arrive into an IT or other workplace setting bundled together with a big enterprise system implementation and in themselves become a front of culture clash that undermines project success (Black & Dehoney, 2008; Fowler & Gilfillan, 2003). For this reason, IT project managers have to communicate for multiple stakeholder audiences with sensitivity to their particular culture, needs, and concerns throughout all aspects of their project (Kliniotou, 2004).

Assessment and evaluation are really just particular types of communication. In many projects, a matrixed communication plan would map these activities as types of communication along with all of the others routine to managing the project, such as status reports, action minutes, and meetings. Unfortunately, in the IT fields (information technology and instructional technology) failure and success are often discovered in post-mortem review sessions to be attributable to missed opportunities to conduct stakeholder-inclusive processes, including project definition processes such as needs assessment and feasibility reviews, and requirements-gathering; project evaluation processes such as phase reviews, usability reviews, and user acceptance testing; and project closure processes such as post-mortem reviews themselves (Pinto & Kharbanda, 1996; Hefner & Malcolm, 2002; Van Grembergen, 2002).

Evaluation is a field in the social sciences that provides a framework for collecting both subjective and objective inputs in an objective process. The American Evaluation Association has developed guiding principles for evaluators that address the values, competencies, and ethical practices for evaluation of programs, products, personnel, and policy (AEA, 2004). Objectivity is essential for weighting competing perspectives and building trust in a process. According to Van Grembergen:

An IT evaluation program, structured in terms that all stakeholders are comfortable with, helps bridge the communication gap between the different stakeholders and helps manage the complexity of IT in an organization. It is therefore aimed at all stakeholders; it replaces opinion with fact; and it directs towards substantial, measurable improvements (2002, p. 285)."

Proposition Three: *Assessment and evaluation methods can help IT projects objectively respond to stakeholders in order to ensure their satisfaction.*

In order to achieve this outcome, we need to know who these stakeholders are, what they want, how they want to have input into the process, and how their input will be considered in balance with other stakeholders. Others have addressed the science of stakeholder analysis at length; here we will look more specifically at the role of stakeholders in needs assessment and evaluation processes that will help ensure that (as much as possible) project objectives are identified through consensus and validated with objectivity. While methods are available for mapping the personalities and interests at play in the stakeholder groups, science alone cannot create consensus -- the project manager must use a touch of intuitive magic mixed with common sense and the personal touch to be truly successful. To assist with this, we will look at the following:

- Guiding words for IT project assessment and evaluation: *Early, Inclusive, Objective, Transparent, Genuine, Independent, Responsive, Regenerative*
- Approaches to fostering stakeholder engagement in project assessment and evaluation
- Practical, common-sense, and adaptable

assessment and evaluation methods that anyone can employ

- Iterative approaches that can be employed across the spectrum of project management (PM) and software/system development life cycle (SDLC) models, with some attempt to show appropriate interventions at key stages

SANTA CLAUS AND BLUEBERRIES: GETTING TO KNOW YOUR STAKEHOLDERS

Guiding Words: EARLY and INCLUSIVE

When Santa Claus is planning his annual gift giving project, he starts with a list of everyone in the whole world, he checks it twice, and he finds out who is deserving (nice) and who isn't (naughty). If you look over the wealth of literature about stakeholder analysis and mapping, you will find that most models employ some variation of this strategy. While instead of "nice," stakeholders might be labeled "supportive," or instead of "naughty", they might be "time bombs," all of the models suggest sorting stakeholders by different characteristics (Savage, Nix, Whitehead, & Blair, 1991; Simon & Murray-Webster, 2005). You will need to do this as well through the following steps.

1. Review

As soon as possible in the project initiation, you will want to consider the areas of interest relative to your project, both internal and external to your organization. According to Pinto and Kharbanda (1996), stakeholders can include "any group, internal or external to the company, that has an active stake in the project's development. They include clients, the overall marketplace, internal functional departments, top management, the project team, and external groups [...]." Fowler and Gilfillan (2003) also mention consultants and vendors. A simple first step is to review the organization chart and circle those areas that might be impacted by or interested in the project. Umbach (2006) points out that it may be more practical to have a single individual represent an entire group. Consider the following points: Within those organizational groups, is there a particular manager or subject matter expert that would make a good contact? Is there someone who can influence the project for better or worse? Next, consider the external groups that might be impacted by or interested in the project and ask the same questions.

Make a list of every possible stakeholder, and then share it with your sponsor or core team for review and revision. You may wish to consider groups such as senior managers, project resource managers, customers, business process owners, administrative users, subject matter experts, analysts, system administrators, application administrators, interface designers, developers, instructional designers, employees, and support or customer service groups. At this point, you want to be sure that you identify each stakeholder area and possible representatives for each stakeholder area. The longer your list, the more likely it is that you will need to have some way of sorting stakeholders. The shorter your list, the more likely it is that you have forgotten someone.

Like blueberries, each stakeholder is unique and care should be taken while picking them as possible representatives in project processes. A blueberry that looks perfect may taste sour and one that looks soft on one side can taste delicious. For example, a long-term administrative user may be resistant to change and have the potential to throw up roadblocks, but may also possess considerable wisdom and knowledge about business processes. Consider how the stakeholders will work together over the course of the project — after all, it's the blend of blueberries that makes a pie. Ultimately, this list will form the foundation

of the evaluation plan that will demonstrate how each of these stakeholders will be consulted and considered throughout the project.

2. Sort

Santa has it easy – he's just sorting known people into two categories. Most stakeholder mapping models provide for some greater degree of complexity. Mitchell, Agle, and Wood (1997) summarize all the different models of stakeholder identification from 1963 to 1995, putting the models into groups based on various relationships between power, influence, legitimacy, claims, and risks. They propose a theory in which the salience, or priority, of particular stakeholder claims, is mutable based on the particular issue at hand, and can "be identified based upon the possession, or the attributed possession, of one, two, or all three of the attributes: power, legitimacy, and urgency" (pp. 853-854).

These strategies can help identify those users with the greatest potential for positive and negative influence. (The project manager will want to be sure to plan how to connect on both formal and informal bases with these VIP (very influential person) stakeholders.) Sort the list of stakeholders into groups of common interests. Examples of interest groups might be: staff resource planning, user experience, project metrics, customer impacts, and system architecture. An individual may be a stakeholder in more than one group.

3. Develop a Stakeholder Matrix

Once you have sorted your stakeholders through some mapping process, you need to develop a matrix of how each of them will be engaged in the evaluation process. What roles will they play? How will their feedback be objectively gathered? As mentioned above, stakeholder analysis affects multiple project planning areas. This stakeholder matrix will provide a foundation or overlap with the development of the project plan, communication plan, and other project initiation efforts, as well as provide an input into the evaluation plan.

4. Collect Feedback

Remember that Santa doesn't actually tell people whether they are naughty or nice, he lets the gifts speak for themselves. Once you are sure that you have found positive ways to include all VIP stakeholders, share the stakeholder matrix with key internal stakeholders for review and feedback. Once it is revised, you should incorporate as appropriate into the project initiation processes so that the stakeholders overall have a chance to respond and clarify their interests. This can be done as part of the scope or charter documents, project kick-off processes, or focus group. The point is to get stakeholders themselves to agree that they have been properly identified. As Kliniotou points out,

It is important to identify the project stakeholders at the project outset. Through open discussions or one-to-one interviews the facilitator identifies the

professional, organizational and, in some cases, personal values with which stakeholders judge the project, their level of project interest, power and influence (2004, p. 371).

AVOIDING PIE IN THE FACE: EVALUATION PLANNING

Guiding Words: OBJECTIVE and TRANSPARENT

The stakeholder matrix is used as a foundation for developing an evaluation plan, which will provide a framework for objectively establishing project goals and objectives, achieving consensus on requirements, collecting feedback on prototypes, responding with appropriate change mechanisms, affirming usability, gaining acceptance from users, and regenerating lessons learned into the next project cycle. While all of these things sound terrific, significant barriers to incorporation of evaluation into IT projects abound, including resistance to terminology (just as some resist the project management terminology), resistance to

Figure 1. Example of stakeholder analysis matrix

Stakeholder Type	Organizational Affiliation and Role	Areas of Interest	Project Roles	Feedback Channels
Executive Sponsor	Internal Head, Information Systems Division	• Project Metrics • System Architecture	Sponsor	• Project Initiation Processes • Core Team • Phase Reviews • Project Closure Processes
Customer	External President, Universal Business Solutions	• Project Metrics • System Architecture • User Experience	Requirements Review	• Requirements Focus Group • Prototype Review Focus Group
Developer	Internal Staff, Information Systems Division	• System Architecture • User Experience	Designer	• Project Initiation Processes • Implementation Team • Phase Reviews • Project Closure Processes

additional planning or allocation of resources, and, as Reeves and Hedberg point out, resistance to "asking certain questions or addressing certain issues" (2003, p. 70). Planned evaluation will not prevent predetermined and secret organizational agendas. However, providing objective and transparent evaluation processes can help to offset those behaviors.

Reeves and Hedberg provide an excellent template of an overall evaluation plan for interactive learning systems design, including descriptions of what each component should address and why: introduction, background, purposes, audiences, decisions, questions, methods, sample, instrumentation, limitations, logistics, timeline and budget (p. 71). For evaluation planning, the questions to investigate and methods of investigation are key. Ultimately, your evaluation plan will also need to include details about instruments that will be used in each of your activities, and it will also need to be reviewed with appropriate audiences.

EDSELS, WEBSITES, AND ERP: BEST APPROACHES FOR GATHERING STAKEHOLDER FEEDBACK AND VALIDATING PROJECT OUTCOMES

Guiding Words: GENUINE, INDEPENDENT, RESPONSIVE

The goal of the evaluation plan is to gather stakeholder feedback at optimal times, provide a mechanism for response, and gain validation of project outcomes. Activities can be grouped into three evaluation stages that conform to the project initiation, design and implementation, and validation and closure phases (Reeves & Hedberg, 2003; Schwalbe, 2000).

- **Preliminary (project initiation):** Example activities include feasibility review, audience and needs assessment, benchmark analysis,

Figure 2. Example of questions and methods evaluation matrix for new Web-based information service

Stakeholder Community	Assessment Method	Assessment Objective / Questions
Internal Staff User Group Committee Steering Committee	Internal stakeholder web-based review	1. What problems or issues with the proposed prototype are revealed (if any)? 2. What suggestions for improvement are made? 3. What content is missing (if any)?
Casual User *Student/K-12/Lifelong Learner *Information Seeker/Hobbyist *Scholar/Researcher Government/Business Community	Usability testing using think-aloud protocol (*These users have the most critical usability needs and should be the focus for the testing effort.)	4. When users are tested with scenarios based on the most commonly expected tasks, what problems or issues revealed (if any)? 5. What suggestions for improvement are made? 6. What content is missing (if any)?
Information Providers External Subject Matter Experts Educators	External stakeholder focus group review	7. What problems or issues with the proposed prototype are revealed (if any)? 8. What suggestions for improvement are made? 9. What content is missing (if any)?

literature review, predecessor interview, focus groups, survey

- **Formative (design and implementation):** Example activities include focus groups, survey, web discussion forums, prototype review, usability testing, expert or heuristic review, phase review
- **Summative (validation and closure):** Example activities include focus groups, user acceptance testing, lessons learned, survey

As you can see, some of these activities can occur at multiple points in the project, and others are typically at one particular stage. Key methods include:

- **Focus groups:** The techniques for working with a focus group can be applicable in multiple group work contexts. An independent facilitator is ideal. A product manager can also serve effectively in some situations. Five is a good size for one smaller group, but a larger group can be used very creatively. Include a mix of people with different backgrounds, statuses, and opinions to afford the greatest opportunity for stakeholders to learn from each other. Prepare questions or prompts in advance to keep discussion focused and ensure that objectives are met. Brainstorm with the whole group using nominative group technique (round robin) or in subgroups that are tasked with specific problems to discuss and report findings. Engage stakeholders as much as possible in talking directly to each other and capturing their own feedback for reporting back to the group and compilation into the captured findings. Engage stakeholders as much as possible in the review, re-grouping, and prioritization of feedback. Provide follow-up in the form of a report or other artifact. Agile Project Management (Highsmith, 2004) emphasizes the importance of direct communication with the development team through mixed stakeholder/project team focus groups in order to enhance requirements gathering. However, Highsmith also cautions that it is important that developers not get involved in discussing feasibility of suggestions in these settings. Other caveats include avoiding the Edsel phenomenon, in which including everything that everybody suggests results in mediocrity (Neil, 2007; Carlson, 2007).

- **Audience and needs assessment:** The purpose of an audience and needs assessment evaluation is to identify the audiences for a particular product or service, determine each audience members' primary needs, characteristics, and tasks, and produce a comprehensive audience profile. Analysis of which users have the most typical characteristics will reveal which users and tasks are benchmarks that can then be the focus for development of features and of testing protocols.

An audience and needs assessment process can be conducted using focus groups, surveys, or other feedback collection approaches such as the BaseCamp collaboration and project management web forum (http://www.basecamphq.com/) or wikis (Hammond, 2007). Involving stakeholders in the audience and needs assessment processes helps ensure that the needs of the primary user drives the development and prioritization of requirements and change requests.

- **Survey:** The power of surveys is the ability to collect large amounts of feedback from geographically scattered people at the same time, with a common format for ease of compilation, and the possibility of providing anonymous response for optimal honesty. Frame questions as neutrally as possible, using Likert Scale or other neutral scoring method. Offer at least one open-ended ques-

Figure 3. Example audience profile for k12 information system

Typical Tasks Matrixed Trend Analysis Benchmark Users and Benchmark Tasks Bordered in Bold	K-5 Student-Regular Education	6-8 Student Regular Education	9-12 Student Regular Education	9-12 Advanced Placement	Virtual Student	Home-Schooled Student	Differentiated Instruction Student	K-5 Gifted	6-8 Magnet and Gifted	ELL Students K-5	ELL Students 6-8	ELL Students 9-12	Student teachers/Grad Students of Education	School Teacher-Librarians (Media Specialists)	Educators	Parents	Administrators	Support Staff
Simple research – answering basic questions	X	X	X	X	X	X	X	X	X	X	X	X	X	X	X	X	X	X
Current events	X	X	X	X	X	X	X	X	X	X	X	X	X	X	X	X	X	X
Homework	X	X	X	X	X	X	X	X	X	X	X	X	X	X	X	X		
Science fair activities		X		X	X			X						X	X	X	X	
Supporting children with their assignments														X	X	X		X
Coordination with state curriculum and Department of Education														X	X		X	
Assignments from their administrators																		X

tion. Keep surveys short in order to avoid survey fatigue. Offer an incentive such as the chance to win a prize in a random drawing. Use web-based survey software such as Survey Monkey (http://www.surveymonkey.com/) for optimal ease of reporting.

- **Usability testing:** Jakob Nielsen (1993) developed the standard for usability testing with actual users, clarifying that usability testing should be centered on what users actually do, not what designers want them to do. An audience profile can be used as the foundation for a usability testing task-based protocol. Nielsen states that usability testing can be conducted effectively with a small group of 3-5 users. Users should work through tasks on their own, with no intervention from the observer/facilitator. Users

should be encouraged to use the "think-aloud protocol" which reveals why they are making particular decisions. Observations should be recorded of user decisions and problems that are encountered. Recordings can be through technologies such as video cameras or usability testing labs, or through writing. Problem areas require re-development. Iterative development processes will conduct usability testing on paper, semi-functional, or fully functional prototypes.

- **User acceptance testing (UAT):** Standard in implementation of Enterprise Resource Planning Systems (ERP), User Acceptance Testing is a validation method to ensure that stakeholders sign off on the delivered functionality. InfoTech notes that "User

Acceptance Testing is not usability testing" (2008, p. 2), adding that:

"User acceptance test cases are developed from user requirements and are validated in conjunction with actual stakeholders of the system. With stakeholders executing test cases, the experience is more focused on the business needs and helps to uncover bugs in the integration of the application with business processes (p. 2)."

- **Lessons learned or post-mortem review:** Conducted as part of the project closure processes, this type of evaluation can include both internal and external participants, or separate processes can be conducted for these stakeholders. Hoffman (2005) notes that the project manager does not typically conduct the effort.

While some of these processes can be managed appropriately by the Project Manager, often the person in that role is perceived as having a particular agenda, so the use of an independent evaluator and/or facilitator can help ensure the greatest participation and development of trust from and with stakeholders. In lieu of an independent evaluator, a small team composed of diverse stakeholders can provide some measure of objectivity and conduct the evaluation activities themselves. Evaluators will work closely with project managers to develop protocols and communications, document and code findings, and draft reports.

Evaluation allows project teams to learn from the project processes and inputs and respond flexibly, which makes it an ideal partner to iterative design processes. As noted by Jones and Wicks (1999), learning and responsiveness are processes that can create problems with change management, project plans, and the mental well being of team members, but when managed effectively can produce better products and better long-term stakeholder relationships.

A NOTE ABOUT STAKEHOLDER (DIS)ENGAGEMENT

We have been going along describing different approaches and methods as if every stakeholder wants nothing more than to sit in a focus group or review a document or answer questions. The truth is that it is not always easy to make a claim on the time and attention of stakeholders, especially those that are geographically dispersed or in high-level positions. Web conferencing, online surveys, project collaboration forums, listservs, newsletters, and websites are all ways of keeping in touch with stakeholders that don't require them to be physically present. Even so, with the volume of email and other technologically-delivered communications, stakeholders often have a hard time focusing on specific or complex information and the project manager may need to conduct some behind-the-scenes outreach to re-engage the stakeholder. In some cases, ensuring that higher-ups have clearly communicated the expectations regarding participation is helpful. As Kerr (2006, p. 44) notes in his Ten Commandments,

Thou Shalt Require Full-Time Business Participation:
To ensure that the desired results are delivered, the business perspective must be represented on a full-time basis. Moreover, if business leaders want the best and brightest from IT working on their initiatives, they need to provide the same form the business side. By committing full-time resources to every project, business leaders confirm that project work is important."

A CORNUCOPIA OF DEVELOPMENT MODELS

Guiding Words: REGENERATIVE

Many processes that are routinely employed in IT projects are designed to be repeatable and regenerative. Ideally, formative evaluation processes roll new inputs into the revisions of project deliverables and summative evaluation processes roll new inputs into the next project. Iterative development models include the Software/System Development Life Cycle (SDLC) model for software and system development, Agile (Highsmith, 2004) and Agile with SCRUM (Schwaber, 2004) models for project management, and the ADDIE (Analysis, Design, Development, Implementation, and Evaluation) model (Visscher-Voerman & Gustafson, 2004) for instructional systems design. The methods for evaluation that we have reviewed are all equally applicable to these models. The figure below demonstrates which of these evaluation processes might fall into the general phases for each of these models.

THE FUTURE: NOW OR LATER

As Jawahar and McLaughlin (2001) describe, in addition to the cycles of project work, development work, and evaluation, the organization itself is going through a life cycle of growth, maturity,

and decline. We are in a period of uncertainty with technology and the role of internal technology service providers, changes to which will have significant impacts on internal business processes. We are also in a period where usability and user-centered design is accepted and expected. Websites have become much more usable and standardized in their usability.

The role of testing is changing in some IT environments. A recent article in the Times (Markoff, 2008) reported on the changes to development processes that have arisen as part of the boom in open-source and user-created software, where testing is actually a function of the community of interest and not necessarily driven through ownership of process.

While it may be that in the future of evaluation becomes more like a community review forum, such as the product and book reviews in Amazon, or the slam lists in MySpace, in the short term project managers will still need to grapple with the needs and opinions of stakeholders. Remembering the guidewords for project management will help to begin processes EARLY, be as INCLUSIVE as

Figure 4. Evaluation processes

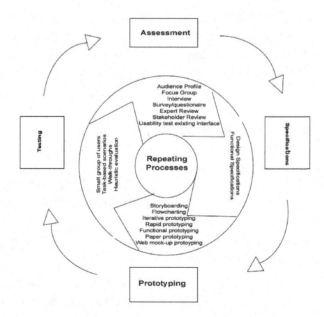

possible with participants, be OBJECTIVE when gathering data, share documents and plans so that they are TRANSPARENT to everyone, make a GENUINE effort to conduct meaningful processes, use an INDEPENDENT evaluator when possible, be RESPONSIVE to stakeholder issues, and maintain REGENERATIVE processes. Following these guidewords will help to keep most stakeholders satisfied with most of the project outcomes, which translates into success.

ACKNOWLEDGMENT

The author would like to gratefully acknowledge the influence of Dr. Thomas Reeves of the University of Georgia College of Education on the development of her evaluation practices.

REFERENCES

American Evaluation Association. (2004, July) *Guiding principles for evaluators*. Retrieved April 1, 2008, from http://www.eval.org/Publications/GuidingPrinciples.asp

BaseCamp. http://www.basecamphq.com/

Black, E., & Dehoney, J. (2008, January). *Opening the door: Academic Technology and Library Collaborations at Ohio State*. Paper presented at the annual meeting of the Educause Learning Initiative (ELI), San Antonio, TX.

Carlson, P. (2007, September 4). The flop heard round the world. *Washington Post* (p. C01). Retrieved March 29, 2008, from http://www.washingtonpost.com/wp-dyn/content/article/2007/09/03/AR2007090301419.html?sub=new

Drummond, H., & Hodgson, J. (2003, September). The chimpanzees' tea party: A new metaphor for project managers. *Journal of Information Technology, 18*(3), 151. Routledge, Ltd. [Electronic version] Retrieved March 29, 2008, from Academic Search Complete database.

Fowler, A., & Gilfillan, M. (2003, December). A framework for stakeholder integration in higher education information systems projects. *Technology Analysis & Strategic Management, 15*(4), 467-489. [Electronic version] Retrieved February 5, 2008, from Academic Search Complete database.

Hammond, R. (2007, September). Party lines, Wikis, and project management. *Online, 31*(5), 30-33. [Electronic version] Retrieved March 18, 2008, from Professional Development Collection database.

Hefner, D., & Malcolm, C. (2002, February). 15 essential steps of IT project management. Healthcare financial management. *Journal of The Healthcare Financial Management Association, 56*(2), 76-78. [Electronic version] Retrieved March 18, 2008, from MEDLINE with full text database.

Hoffman, T. (2005, July 11). After THE Fact. *Computerworld, 39*(28), 39-40. [Electronic version] Retrieved March 29, 2008, from Academic Search Complete database.

InfoTech Group. (2008, March 18.) Ensure user satisfaction with user acceptance testing. *Research Notes*.

Jawahar, I., & McLaughlin, G. (2001, July). Toward a descriptive stakeholder theory: An organizational life cycle approach. *Academy of Management Review, 26*(3), 397-414. [Electronic version] Retrieved March 30, 2008, from Business Source Complete database.

Jones, T., & Wicks, A. (1999, April). Convergent stakeholder theory. *Academy of Management Review, 24*(2), 206-221. [Electronic version] Retrieved April 10, 2008, from Business Source Complete database.

Kerr, J. (2006, October 2). The ten commandments of project management. *Computerworld, 40*(40),

44-44. [Electronic version] Retrieved March 18, 2008, from Computer Source database.

Kliniotou, M. (2004, September). Identifying, measuring and monitoring value during project development. *European Journal of Engineering Education, 29*(3), 367-376. [Electronic version] Retrieved April 8, 2008, from Academic Search Complete database.

Markoff, J. (2008, February 10). Mashups are breaking the mold at Microsoft. *New York Times Online.* [Electronic version] Retrieved March 29, 2008, from http://www.nytimes.com/2008/02/10/business/10slipstream.html?em&ex=1202878800&en=96a368de807a0923&ei=5087%0A#

Mayer, D. (n.d.). Stakeholder theory. *Encyclopedia of Business,* 2nd ed. [Electronic version] Retrieved March 29, 2008, http://www.referenceforbusiness.com/encyclopedia/Sel-Str/Stakeholder-Theory.html

Mitchell, R., Agle, B., & Wood, D. (1997, October). Toward a theory of stakeholder identification and salience: Defining the principle of who and what really counts. *Academy of Management Review, 22*(4), 853-886. [Electronic version] Retrieved April 10, 2008, from Business Source Complete database.

Neil, D. (2007, September 17). Edsel Agonistes. *Time,* (p. 28). [Electronic version] Retrieved February 26, 2008, from Academic Search Complete database.

Nielsen, J. (1993). *Usability engineering.* Boston: Academic Press.

Pinto, J., & Kharbanda, O. (1996, July). How to fail in project management (without really trying). *Business Horizons, 39*(4), 45. [Electronic version] Retrieved March 18, 2008, from Business Source Complete database.

Reeves, T., & Hedberg, J. (2003). *Interactive learning systems evaluation.* Englewood Cliffs, NJ: Educational Technology Publications.

Savage, G., Nix, T., Whitehead, C., & Blair, J. (1991, May). Strategies for assessing and managing organizational stakeholders. *Academy of Management Executive, 5*(2), 61-75. [Electronic version] Retrieved April 10, 2008, from Business Source Complete database.

Schwalbe, K. (2000). *Information technology project management.* Cambridge, MA: Course Technology, Thomson Learning.

Schweber, K. (2004). *Agile project management with scrum.* Redmond, WA: Microsoft Press.

Simon, P., & Murray-Webster, R. (2005, December). Making sense of stakeholder mapping. *Project Manager Today, 8.* [Electronic version] Retrieved April 8, 2008 from Project Manager Today journal Web site.

Survey Monkey. http://www.surveymonkey.com/

Umbach, J. (2006). Working with stakeholders: How to avoid the traps. *Feliciter, 52*(2), 47-47. [Electronic version] Retrieved March 30, 2008, from Academic Search Complete database.

Van Grembergen, W. (Editor) (2002). *Information systems evaluation management,* (p. 285). Hershey, PA: IGI Global Publishing. [Electronic version] Retrieved March 7, 2008, from eBrary database.

Visscher-Voerman, I., & Gustafson, K. (2004). Paradigms in the theory and practice of education and training design. *Educational Technology Research & Development, 52*(2), 69-89. [Electronic version] Retrieved April 1, 2008, from Academic Search Complete database.

Weill, P., & Ross, J. (2005, Winter). A matrixed approach to designing IT governance. *MIT Sloan Management Review, 46*(2), 26-34. [Electronic version] Retrieved April.

KEY TERMS AND DEFINITIONS

Agile: A form of project management that emphasizes small teams, close interaction between developers and customers, and rapid development cycles

ADDIE: An instructional design and development model consisting of iterative steps: Analysis, Design, Development, and Implementation.

Benchmark: The best or most fitting example of its kind.

Communication Plan: A chart of stakeholders and the communication methods that will be used to gather feedback and to keep them informed about the project status.

Evaluation: A process for gathering information about a thing for the purposes of making decisions.

Focus Group: A small group discussion that is focused on a particular topic.

Heuristics: Best practice benchmarks against which something can be evaluated.

Stakeholder: Someone who has an interest or concern in the outcome of a particular endeavor.

Stakeholder Analysis: Understanding everything there is to discover about stakeholders and sorting them into categories.

Stakeholder Matrix: A chart of stakeholders, their interests, organizational affiliations, roles on the project, and input channels.

Usability Testing: An evaluation procedure in which actual users conduct tasks according to a protocol and whose performance can indicate design problems.

Chapter XX
A Needle in a Haystack:
Choosing the Right Development Methodology for IT Projects

Chad J. Cray
Capella University, USA

ABSTRACT

Considering the high failure rate of information technology (IT) projects over the last 40 years, project managers should use all the tools at their disposal in order to make their project a success; however, more than half of all project managers fail to use a powerful tool that is readily available – a development methodology. A development methodology provides structure to a project, which facilitates communication, establishes expectations, enhances quality and promotes consistency. One potential reason project managers do not employ a development methodology is that selecting the correct methodology from among the hundreds available can be an overwhelming task. For this reason, understanding the decision-making process, and identifying those factors that influence it, is a worthwhile endeavor. While empirical research in this area is lacking, a review of the extant literature reveals several factors that are important when choosing a development methodology. In this chapter, many of these factors are identified, a model for categorizing them is proposed, and a model for selecting a methodology is presented.

INTRODUCTION

Information technology (IT) projects are notoriously difficult to complete on time, under budget and within scope. In fact, over the last decade IT projects faced a 20 to 30 percent chance of being canceled and a 50 to 70 percent chance of exceeding their schedule or budget (Ewusi-Mensah,

1997; Kappelman, McKeeman, & Zhang, 2006). With over 50 years of research and experience in developing information systems, why are these projects so difficult to complete? One potential answer—which has received insufficient research—is that project managers use the wrong system development methodology or they fail to use one at all. As Ewusi-Mensah pointed out, projects needed "some structure [to] be imposed on the development effort to help guide the system to successful completion" (p. 76). A lack of imposed structure, or an inappropriate one, can hinder the development process and contribute to the failure of the project.

Aside from providing structure for the information system project, using a development methodology can provides other significant advantages. One such advantage is that "a quality process will result in a quality product" (Khalifa & Verner, 2000, p. 366). Development methodologies, which are a type of quality process, can instill a certain amount of rigor within the development effort. By forcing the project team to follow each step of the process, it is possible to ensure all critical tasks are completed and, perhaps more importantly, it can be used to recreate the team's success on future projects. A successfully implemented methodology can be used as the framework on which future systems are developed. In other words, it enables the team to develop systems consistently.

Hopelain and Loesh (1985) provided yet another reason for using a development methodology; it built trust among the primary stakeholders – developers, users and management. The argument made by Hopelain and Loesh was that each of the stakeholder groups had to trust each other in order to work together to complete the project. Without this cooperation, success was unlikely. A methodology agreed on by the stakeholders facilitated cooperation since it would "more likely occur if there is a procedure in place which each group understands and believes will produce a system that meets its particular needs" (p. 43).

It would appear that the benefits of using a development methodology are prodigious, but research conducted by Fitzgerald (1998) turned up interesting and alarming statistics about the frequency with which methodologies were used in organizations. According to Fitzgerald's research, only 40% of the organizations surveyed were using a methodology and less than 10% were using one consistently. In addition, of those not using a methodology, only 21% were considering the use of one.

Based on the complexity of organizations, information system development projects and implementing processes within an organization, it is likely that many factors contribute to the dearth of organizations using development methodologies. A potential factor is the complexity of selecting a methodology from among the hundreds of options. Guntamukkala, Wen, and Tarn (2006) noted that "project managers often face a daunting task of selecting the most appropriate software life cycle model [or development methodology] for a given project" (p. 266). A review of the extant literature identified those factors that influenced the selection of a development methodology for use within an organization. From this, a framework can be developed to facilitate the classification of those factors and a model can be constructed that illustrates how project managers can choose a development methodology that is right for their organizations.

BACKGROUND

An Overview of Methodologies

Before exploring the process of selecting a development methodology, it is important to understand what is meant by the term. A concise definition of "methodology" was presented by Hopelain and Loesh (1985) as "[a] coherent, disciplined... approach to the development of integrated software and database systems" (p. 43). This definition was in keeping with that used in other research; Siau and Tan (2005) added specificity to the definition by describing a development methodology as "[r]ecommended phases, procedures, tools, and techniques" (p. 862) used to create an information system. For this chapter, the working definition of development methodology will be an amalgamation of these two definitions: a logical and disciplined use of phases, processes, and techniques used to create information systems.

One of the earliest, and most well known, development methodologies—the waterfall model—consisted of six iterative steps: requirements collection, analysis, design, build, test and field (Boehm, 2006; Guntamukkala *et al.*, 2006). Each step should follow sequentially, and presumably, completion of all steps would result in a functioning system. The waterfall model was simple but provided the coherent and disciplined approach inherent in all methodologies.

Despite its widespread use in the early eras of software engineering and information system development, the waterfall model was far from perfect and was not compatible with all development projects (Boehm, 2006; Guntamukkala *et al.*, 2006). In order to overcome these deficiencies, new methodologies were developed and it is estimated that there were between 100 and 1000 different methodologies as of 2005 (Siau & Tan). Some of these methodologies were slight variants of the waterfall methodology, while others were drastic departures from this seminal model. For example, the throwaway prototyping model, described by Bersoff and Davis (1991), followed the waterfall model with the addition of prototypes occurring at the requirements gathering and design stages. On the other hand, the SCRUM methodology had three phases: pre-sprint, sprint, and post sprint (Guntamukkala *et al.*, 2006). While these three phases incorporated virtually all of the activities described in the waterfall model, they were done frequently and rapidly.

The number and variety of methodologies can be overwhelming for a project manager who must select one for his or her team. Differences between methodologies can range from the seemingly insignificant to the drastically diverse. To make things more complicated, the nuances of each methodology can be difficult to grasp, thereby, making the selection of a single one that much more difficult. For example, who could tell the difference between throwaway prototyping and evolutionary prototyping (Bersoff & Davis, 1991)? How does a project manager choose between these two similar methodologies? These types of questions are at the core of this chapter, but before delving into them further, it is useful to note that there are critics of development methodologies.

Are Development Methodologies Really that Useful?

As prominent critics of the usefulness of development methodologies, Nandhakumar and Avison (1999) conducted a study that led them to the following conclusion:

[T]raditional IS [information system] development methodologies are treated primarily as a necessary fiction to present an image of control or to provide a symbolic status, and are too mechanistic to be of much use in the detailed, day-to-day organization of systems developers' activities. (p. 176)

Nandhakumar's and Avison's assertion appeared to be a direct contradiction to a significant body of research on development methodologies (Ewusi-Mensah, 1997; Hopelain & Loesh, 1985; Khalifa & Verner, 2000; Milner, 1985; Nord & Tomayko, 2006; Punter & Lemmen, 1996). A cursory review of the development methodology research literature revealed a general acceptance that methodologies were important to system development and a realization that many of them failed to provide all the benefits that were promised. The research by Nandhakumar and Avison highlighted this dichotomy.

It is important to note, however, that the research conducted by Nandhakumar and Avison (1999) employed an ethnographic approach that focused entirely on one organization that was using a specific development methodology. As such, it was difficult to determine if their research identified that methodologies are "a necessary fiction to present an image of control" (p. 176) or if they found an organization that was employing the wrong methodology. It is possible that Nandhakumar and Avison found a significant problem with methodologies in general but it is equally possible that they discovered what happened when an organization used the wrong development methodology. Similarly, it could be that the problem found by the researchers was that of a poorly implemented methodology. What they did find, however, is an area that needs more research.

SELECTING A METHODOLOGY: WHICH FACTORS MATTER?

In their research, Nandhakumar and Avison (1999) identified a gap in the body of knowledge about development methodologies and their use. In this, they were not alone. The majority of articles reviewed for this chapter identified a need for more research pertaining to development methodologies. For example, Khalifa and Verner (2000) noted that research had been conducted to identify various factors that affected the adoption of specific methodologies but "the relationships among [the factors] have not been explored" (p. 360). While Khalifa and Verner identified specific research needs, Vessey, Ramesh, and Glass (2002) found in their study that research about development methodologies was conspicuously underrepresented in

the major information system journals. Iivari and Huisman (2007) highlighted this knowledge gap when they stated, "[u]ntil recently, there has not been much research into actual use of systems development methods" (p. 36).

Despite the apparent shortage of empirical studies concerning development methodologies, there were several articles published about methodologies and factors that should be considered before selecting one for use within an organization. Furthermore, other articles were available about those factors that influenced the implementation of methodologies within organizations. The remainder of this section will review the available literature in order to identify specific factors that influence the selection of development methodologies. These factors will then be used to construct a generic framework for a model that depicts , in general, those items and issues that influence the methodology selection process.

Three Requirements for a Methodology

According to Catchpole (1986), a good methodology should have the following characteristics: it effectively used the available information; it provided a means for adequate communication among the stakeholders; and it encompassed all the activities needed to develop a system. In other words, a good methodology needs to be able to take the available data, use it to create a system and then communicate the details about this system to the various stakeholders. In order for this process to be successful, the methodology needs to have a scope that encompasses the entirety of the project. Catchpole's suggestions, modified slightly, provided three factors important to the selection of a development methodology. These factors were scope, communicability and information use.

Expert Identified Categories for Evaluating Development Methodologies

In their study, Siau and Tan (2005) enlisted the aid of 28 "experienced researchers and practitioners in systems analysis and design" (p. 865). These researchers and practitioners were asked to participate in a brainstorming activity designed to identify which criteria should be used for evaluating a methodology. After the brainstorming session was completed, Sia and Tan were able to identify three categories of criteria that were important in assessing a methodology. These categories were: "methodology design, methodology use, and methodology deliverables" (p. 868).

Given that these three categories have been identified as central to effectively evaluating methodologies, it makes sense that they should also be included in a model for selecting a methodology. Interestingly enough, there is significant overlap between the results of this study and the factors derived from Catchpole's (1986) article – scope, communicability, and information use. In fact, scope, communicability, and information use appear to be subsets of methodology design.

Lightweight, Middleweight, and Heavyweight Methodologies

One way to classify development methodologies, as presented by Guntamukkala *et al.* (2006), was by the degree to which they were flexible and responsive to change. Highly flexible methodologies—such as extreme programming, SCRUM, and Dynamic Systems Development Method—would be considered lightweight. Inflexible methodologies, on the other hand, were considered heavyweight (a classic example being the waterfall model). Middleweight methodologies were between these two extremes with most prototyping methodologies considered as middleweight.

In their article, Guntamukkala *et al.* (2006) focused on flexibility as a primary factor in selecting a methodology. As it turned out, flexibility was a key criterion in evaluating methodologies as identified by Siau and Tan (2005); as such, it could be considered a subset of the methodology use category identified in Siau and Tan's research. However, Guntamukkala *et al.* mentioned several other factors that were of some importance in selecting a methodology. In discussing which type of methodology to use, Guntamukkala *et al.* suggested that project size, uncertainty, risk and outward signs of progress were all factors to be considered.

On closer examination, Guntamukkala *et al.*'s (2006) suggestions fell into two categories that were factors influencing the selection of a methodology – the internal and external environment. The internal environment consists of project size and uncertainty (e.g., how firm the requirements are and how well the technology is understood). The external environment is comprised of risks to the project (e.g., lack of management support, deadlines, and budget constraints) and customer/user perception of the project. The environment in which a system is being developed will have a significant impact on which methodology is selected. For example, Guntamukkala *et al.* suggested that large projects with low risk and well-known requirements were best suited for the heavyweight methodologies. On the other hand, small projects with high levels of uncertainty and risk were best suited for lightweight methodologies.

Will They Use It?

Choosing a methodology is important but only to the extent that it is used by the development team. With this in mind, it is important to select a methodology that will not be rejected by the team. For this reason, intent to use the methodology should be considered as a possible factor for methodology selection.

Based on research by Khalifa and Verner (2000), the intent of employees to use a methodology consisted of facilitating conditions and perceived consequences. They described facilitating conditions as "objective factors in the environment that facilitate the performance of an act" (p. 362). Perceived consequences were defined as the likelihood that the methodology would lead to increased product quality or increased process quality. In their research, however, it was found that only the perceived increase in process quality was significant. Of course, this research was not all inclusive, so perceived consequences could be left as a subcategory despite the findings of Khalifa and Verner's study.

Intent to use the methodology shares certain characteristics with the internal environment discussed previously. For instance, the organizational structure of the development team would be one aspect of the organization's environment and it would also be considered a facilitating condition. It is for this reason that intent to use is considered a subset of the internal environment and both facilitating conditions and perceived consequences are considered subsets of intent to use.

Employee intent to use a methodology was studied by Kautz, Hansen, and Jacobsen (2004) and they identified five factors that influenced the use of development methodologies. Of these five factors, confidence and experience were the only two not already accounted for in previously discussed research. As Kautz, Hansen, and Jacobsen (2004) noted, "developers explicated a need to feel confident about the progress of their work" (p. 14). If the methodology being used enhanced the developers' confidence in their work and the progress of the development effort, they were more inclined to use the methodology. On the other hand, experienced developers may be less likely to follow a methodology, especially if it is one with which they are not familiar or one with which they disagree. In both cases, however, these factors can be considered a part of the facilitating conditions discussed above because they are correlated with the developers' intent to use the methodology.

Yet another component of employees' intent to use a development methodology is their perception of the efficacy of the methodology; if employees feel the methodology is burdensome or worthless, they are likely to circumvent its use. Additionally, as Huisman and Iivari (2006) discovered, perception about the usefulness of a development methodology could vary widely between employees and their supervisors, which could complicate matters significantly. Ideally, the selected methodology should be perceived as useful by all employees, not just by one subgroup.

The Right Culture for the Right Methodology

The last factor that will be considered in this literature review is that of organizational culture. Iivari and Huisman (2007) conducted a study that examined the relationship between an organization's culture and its use of development methodologies. They found that an organization with "a hierarchical culture that is oriented toward security, order, and routinization" (p. 35) was more likely to employ a development methodology. Although this research clearly linked organizational culture to the use of a development methodology, there was much about the relationship that still needed to be researched. For example, does the use of a methodology impose on the organization a certain sense of order and routinization? In other words, there is a relationship between culture and methodology use but it is unclear if it is a cause-effect relationship. Despite the dearth of research in this area, Iivari and Huisman's research demonstrated a significant relationship between culture and methodology use; therefore, a model depicting the factors surrounding the selection of a development methodology would be remiss if it failed to include organizational culture.

MODELS OF METHODOLOGY SELECTION FACTORS

Categorizing the Factors

In the previous sections, many factors that influence—or should influence—the selection of a development methodology were identified by extracting them from the current body of literature. In an attempt to consolidate these factors and make it possible to categorize them, a hierarchical classification model is suggested (see Figure 1). In the model the three primary categories are Internal Environment, External Environment and Methodology; the next level down on the model is, in most cases, specific categories that can be used to classify individual factors. For example, Uncertainty is a category that contains two specific factors: the novelty of the technology and the state of the requirements. In other words, both the technology being employed and the fluidity of the requirements can be used to define the state of uncertainty within the project.

There is one other aspect of this model that needs further elaboration and that is the Intent to Use category. Based on the available research literature, this was an important category consisting of two sub-categories: Consequences and Facilitating Conditions. Neither of these sub-categories is specific enough to be a measurable factor but they can be used to categorize individual factors. For instance, an employee's perception of the usefulness of the methodology can be measured and it is an indicator of the facilitating conditions within the organization.

Using the model shown in Figure 1, factors that influence the selection of a development methodology can be categorized as follows:

- **Internal Environment**
  - Project Characteristics
  - Uncertainty
  - Intent to Use: Consequences
  - Intent to Use: Facilitating Conditions

Figure 1. A hierarchical classification model

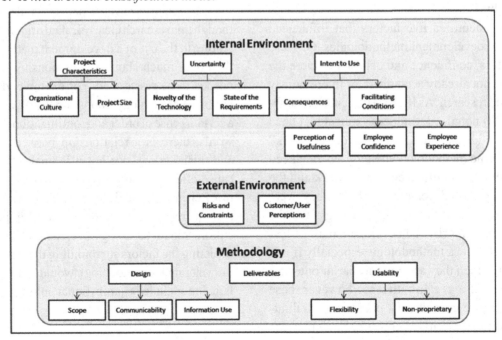

- **External Environment**
  - Risks and Constraints
  - Customer/User Perceptions
- **Methodology**
  - Design
  - Deliverables
  - Usability

A Model for the Development Methodology Selection Process

In the previous section, a method for classifying the various factors that influenced the development methodology selection process was proposed. Based on this taxonomy, it is possible to create a basic model of the selection process (see Figure 2). It is important to note, however, that this model is intended to be prescriptive in nature rather than descriptive. It is equally important to note that this model has not been tested to determine its efficacy but is based on ratiocination that will be elaborated on in the following paragraphs.

By following the process illustrated in Figure 2, project managers should be able to select the methodology that is right for their organization. In essence, a large number of available development methodologies are reduced to a single methodology by employing a filtering technique. The first step in this process is to determine which methodologies are excluded from consideration based on the organization's external environment. The reason for this is that the external environment is the one over which management has the least control. As an example, consider a project team working for a customer that wants to see incremental builds of the system being developed so that they can better refine the requirements. Immediately, the number of potential methodologies is reduced only to those that allow for prototyping or similar incremental builds of the system. The project team is unlikely to alter the customer's decision, and as a consequence, the choice of methodology is restricted. This should make choosing a methodology easier for the project team.

The next step is to filter methodologies based on the organization's internal environment. Those methodologies that do not fit the organization's

Figure 2. The development methodology selection process

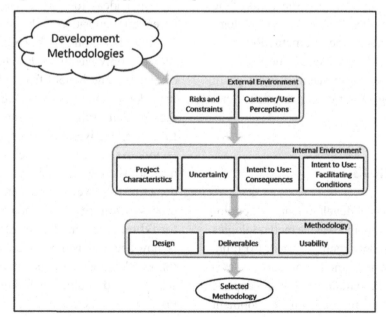

level of uncertainty, project characteristics or facilitating conditions should be rejected. However, this process may not be as straightforward as it would appear. One complication is that a methodology might be well suited for projects that are constantly changing but not appropriate for a large project team. If the project is large and rapidly changing, should this methodology be discarded since it does not meet both requirements? Answering this question may be difficult, especially if no single methodology fits all the requirements imposed by the organization's internal environment. If there are no methodologies that meet all the requirements, there are two options. First, use a weighted scorecard approach to rank the methodologies and select only the highest ranking ones. Second, modify the methodology so that it better meets the organization's needs.

The final step in the selection process is to evaluate the methodologies based on their individual characteristics; of course, this is assuming that, at this stage in the process, there are still multiple methodologies to choose from. Each methodology still being considered should be examined in detail and all of its factors considered in the context of the organization. For example, do the methodologies' deliverables (e.g., Data Flow Diagrams, prototypes, etc.) meet the needs of the organization? Does the scope of the methodology cover the entire project? Does the methodology allow for incremental design stages? Questions like these will allow the project manager to ascertain which methodology has the characteristics that best fit the project.

FUTURE TRENDS

To date, discussions of development methodologies centered on the nuances of the methodologies and how to implement them. It was also quite popular to devise new methodologies, as evidenced by their overabundance. It would appear, however, that future research on development methodologies would benefit from focusing on the decision making process that leads to selecting a methodology. Understanding this process might help managers to avoid known pitfalls in the selection process; this knowledge would better prepare project managers who face the difficult task of selecting a development methodology for their team. It is hoped that this avenue of research will be explored in the near future.

Another area in need of research, and mentioned in multiple articles, was how organizations actually employed the development methodologies they selected (Iivari & Maansaari, 1998; Kautz et al., 2004). For example, many studies examined what types of methodologies were used, which organizations used them and which factors facilitated the implementation of a methodology. What was not addressed, however, was how each organization used its selected methodology. Did they use it exactly as it was described in the literature or was it adapted for use within their organization? Did everyone use the methodology, or were there employees who refused? Did all the employees have a thorough understanding of the methodology and how it should influence their work? These questions and others have yet to be answered by research.

Other ideas for future research become apparent after considering the classification system illustrated in Figure 1. The External Environment category only has two sub-categories, which indicates it could benefit from additional research in order to identify more sub-categories and factors that influence methodology selection. Likewise, Deliverables does not have specific factors assigned to it, which could indicate the need for further research. In addition, the model depicting the development methodology selection process in Figure 2 raises many questions suitable for future research. The most obvious question is: how accurate is the model? If an organization follows the model, are they more or less likely to select a methodology that suits their organization? While this model is based on the available literature and deductive reasoning, it has yet to be validated empirically. Furthermore, this model is intended to be prescriptive in nature but it could be altered in order to describe the process by which organizations select a methodology. The list of questions is nearly limitless, which highlights the need for research on this topic.

CONCLUSION

In this chapter, two different models were proposed: one model used to classify those factors that influenced the development methodology selection process and the other used to suggest a process by which organizations can select the methodology most appropriate for them. Due to the lack of research in this area, both models can be used to highlight knowledge gaps in the area of development methodology selection. As research in this field continues, it is expected that each of these models can be enhanced and modified.

At present, however, the development methodology selection process illustrated in Figure 2 provides a good starting point for a project manager attempting to select the proper methodology from among the numerous alternatives. Similarly, the classification system outlined in Figure 1 can be used by researchers to categorize factors as they are discovered. While the model needs to have more details added – especially in the External Environment category – the next step in refining the model is to depict how each factor influences the selection process. For example, project size is known to be an important factor in selecting a methodology but it is uncertain how it influences the selection process. Similarly, projects of a certain size may be prone not to use a development methodology. It is also possible that project size may influence which type of methodology will be used. None of these suppositions have been tested, but doing so would make it possible to add this information to the model. This, in turn, will facilitate a general understanding of the process,

and it is the accumulation of knowledge like this that will lower the exorbitantly high project failure rate that has plagued project managers over the last several decades.

REFERENCES

Bersoff, E., & Davis, M. A. (1991). Impact of life cycle models on software. *Communication of the Association for Computing Machinery, 34*, 104-117.

Boehm, B. (2006). *A view of 20th and 21st century software engineering*. Paper presented at the International Conference on Software Engineering.

Catchpole, P. (1986). Requirements for a successful methodology in information systems design. *Data Processing, 28*(4), 207.

Ewusi-Mensah, K. (1997). Critical issues in abandoned information systems development projects. *Communications of the Association for Computing Machinery, 40*(9), 74-80.

Fitzgerald, B. (1998). An empirical investigation into the adoption of systems development methodologies. *Information & Management, 34*(6), 317.

Guntamukkala, V., Wen, H. J., & Tarn, J. M. (2006). An empirical study of selecting software development life cycle models. *Human Systems Management, 25*(4), 265-278.

Hopelain, D., & Loesh, B. (1985). Automated development methodologies: Overview and conclusions. *Data Processing, 27*(2), 43.

Huisman, M., & Iivari, J. (2006). Deployment of systems development methodologies: Perceptual congruence between IS managers and systems developers. *Information & Management, 43*(1), 29-49.

Iivari, J., & Huisman, M. (2007). The relationship between organizational culture and the deployment of systems development methodologies. *MIS Quarterly, 31*(1), 35-58.

Iivari, J., & Maansaari, J. (1998). The usage of systems development method: Are we stuck to old practices? *Information & Software Technology, 40*(9), 501.

Kappelman, L., McKeeman, R., & Zhang, L. (2006). Early warning signs of IT project failure: The dominant dozen. *Information Systems Management, 23*(4), 31-36.

Kautz, K., Hansen, B., & Jacobsen, D. (2004). The utilization of information systems development methodologies in practice. *Journal of Information Technology Cases and Applications, 6*(4), 1.

Khalifa, M., & Verner, J. M. (2000). Drivers for software development method usage. *IEEE Transactions on Engineering Management, 47*(3), 360.

Milner, D. (1985). An integrated approach to systems development. *Data Processing, 27*(3), 13.

Nandhakumar, J., & Avison, J. (1999). The fiction of methodological development: A field study of information systems development. *Information Technology & People, 12*, 176-191.

Nord, R. L., & Tomayko, J. E. (2006). Software architecture-centric methods and agile development. *IEEE Software, 23*(2), 47.

Punter, T., & Lemmen, K. (1996). The MEMA-model: Towards a new approach for method engineering. *Information and Software Technology, 38*(4), 295.

Siau, K., & Tan, X. (2005). Special theme of research in information systems analysis and design - IV Evaluation criteria for information systems development methodologies. *Communications of AIS, 2005*(16), 860-876.

Vessey, I., Ramesh, V., & Glass, R. L. (2002). Research in information systems: An empirical study of diversity in the discipline and its journals. *Journal of Management Information Systems, 19*(2), 129-174.

KEY TERMS AND DEFINITIONS

Agile Development: A development methodology that favors speed, flexibility, and iterative development. Although this methodology is often employed in software development projects, it can be used in system development projects as well.

Information System: An amalgamation of human, hardware, software, and firmware components used to process data within organizations.

Information Technology: The computer-based components of an information system.

Prototype: In the context of information systems development, a prototype is a model of the system and is typically used to refine the final design of the system.

Systems Development Life Cycle (SDLC): Similar to systems development methodology but extends to the maintenance and support of the system.

Systems Development Methodology: A logical and disciplined use of phases, processes and techniques used to create information systems.

Weighted Scorecard: A method for comparing multiple choices along various factors. Each factor is given a numerical weight in order to give it more or less importance in the final comparison.

Chapter XXI
Project Management Assessment Methods

Mysore Narayanan
Miami University, USA

ABSTRACT

In this chapter, the author describes how one can implement and incorporate creative techniques to design, develop, document and disseminate a systematic process for conducting assessment, whether it be in a multinational corporation or it be in a small business environment. The author accomplishes this by providing models, samples and established guidelines for effectively using assessment results for continuous quality improvement. The author focuses on the importance of adopting modern techniques and stresses that technology should not be viewed just as a growing trend. The author shows how technology can be intelligently implemented as an invaluable assessment tool that can quickly identify areas for improvement so that a given corporation can continue to climb the ladder of success in a competitive global market of the 21st Century.

INTRODUCTION

Assessment, by itself, in simple terms and in principle, may apply to a wide variety of disciplines and can be interpreted in multiple ways. For example, one may discuss *performance assessment* of an individual employee assigned to manage a specific technology project. On the other hand, the long term strategic planning process and operational methodology of a senior executive in a multinational corporation can be *assessed*. A team of police officers, paramedics, fire marshals and rescue officials may visit the site of an accident and *assess* the situation. Another example may be taken from educational establishments and accreditation agencies. For educators, assessment of student learning is a highly structured process that involves recording, reviewing, reflecting and reporting essential results for purposes of continuous quality improvement.

Assessment is *not* just procurement of data. Meaningful data must be methodically collected, correctly correlated and instinctively interpreted. Properly tabulated and viewed, assessment data will provide important information that can further be used to significantly improve the existing situation, whether it be project management, long term planning, marketing analysis, customer support, clientele interaction or student learning. The primary of objective of *assessment* must be to promote overall growth and enhance professional development. Executives, Employers, Educators and Administrators are therefore able to obtain valuable insight from analyzing gathered data in a systematic and scientific manner.

Assessment is essential for the successful operation of all types of ventures, whether they be small businesses, commercial establishments, large companies, retail outlets, industrial conglomerates or multinational corporations. Active assessment techniques provide useful feedback that can be fruitful in increased productivity, improved efficiency, reduced costs and boosted morale. It has to be recognized that assessment is not just a 'rehash' of the company's annual report, rather must be viewed as a quality improvement tool that is embedded in the governance document of the corporation. Assessment should be at the 'heart' of an industrial environment should encompass everything from pre-manufacturing market analysis surveys all the way to post-sales customer support. This obviously implies that a corporation must assess *market research* separately from *manufacturing*. They need to assess *engineering design* separately from *customer support*. Regardless all these separate assessment data have to be effectively consolidated to provide one 'big-picture' that can be representative of the industrial conglomerate's assessment efforts. It is further recognized that large volumes of data are being collected that need to be standardized, streamlined and systematized for sound, judicial interpretation.

The ultimate objective of assessment practices in an educational establishment should be to examine and determine whether or not the current curriculum of their college is meeting the needs of their designated clientele. Assessment methods should emphasize entire programs and treat the student body as a complete group and document their overall educational accomplishments. It must be observed that assessment in educational establishments is normally classified into two major areas. First is identified as *Formative Assessment* and is normally administered during the *lifetime* of a chosen program. This type of assessment is expected to provide immediate feedback as to how the program can be improved, the next time it is implemented. Many instructors consider *formative assessment* to be a part of routine instructional methodology. The second is known as *Summative Assessment* and is administered after the program has been *in place* for some time. The results of summative assessment may help decide whether or not activities pertaining to the selected program should be continued. Some administrators view *summative assessment* as a measure of accountability. In this chapter the author outlines some techniques for documenting and analyzing assessment data.

While the example chosen by the author may focus on a particular discipline, the reader should recognize the fact the philosophy of assessment methodology can be easily modified and adapted to meet the needs of the individual situation. Some assessment techniques may choose a scale similar to *Likert Scale* for analyzing the data they have collected.

Appendix A briefly outlines the *Likert Scale*.

ASSESSMENT BASICS

Marchese considered to be among higher education's 25 most influential leaders. According to Marchese *"Assessment is the systematic collection, review, and use of information about educational programs undertaken for the purpose of improving student learning and development."* (Marchese, 1987). While it is well known that Marchese was referring to educational establishments, one can easily visualize a similar definition that can encompass other disciplines, small businesses, large companies, industrial conglomerates and multinational corporations. Learning to work efficiently and effectively in a corporation that appreciates increased productivity at lower costs involves investment in valuable time and requires strenuous effort. The strong support of the management completely depends on the sound knowledge that their efforts are indeed being rewarded and the employees are actually generating the results that were expected. This data alone enables the corporation to increase its management effectiveness. It is interesting to observe that Assessment should not be just *covering* the issues, rather be indeed *uncovering* the issues. Needless to add that the share holders, community, customer base, clientele, suppliers and sub-contractors expect documented evidence that the corporation is indeed moving successfully towards accomplishing its goals and objectives effectively.

Accomplishing these basic goals requires that a selected corporation to follow a systematic scientific approach.

1. In many companies, goals and objectives of an assessment process may be implicit. These criteria must be made explicit so that the employees of the corporation clearly understand what is expected of them.

2. It is important to discuss and document procedures with the employees and section heads. Furthermore, the senior management officials should outline the methodology adopted for successfully attaining the specified goals and objectives.

3. Whenever possible, clarify and communicate how each and every item is reviewed and evaluated for the overall welfare of the employees as well as the corporation and the community as a whole.

4. Be prepared to accept and apply necessary improvement procedures to successfully implement a gradual change in accordance with company policies and governance documents.

5. Finally, research and review the actions frequently, twice a year at least, to determine if instituted changes have indeed yielded the results expected. Share the results with selected group leaders and invite them to provide you with constructive feedback.

6. One has to keep in focus that the ultimate objective is to help in developing a corporate-wide culture wherein evidence is explored, carefully collected, repeatedly reviewed for establishing a steady and continuous improvement process.

In order to fulfill the above requirements it is therefore essential to establish a set of *rubrics* in the form of a template. There are many advantages of *rubrics* and some of these benefits are outlined in *Appendix B*.

ASSESSMENT RUBRICS

A *rubric* is a matrix that is considered to provide clear guidelines for carrying out a task successfully based on a full range of criteria. It is like a scoring guide that can be used to evaluate the performance of an employee. A rubric can be holistic or analytic and is to be treated as a working guide that should be made available to the employee before the assessment is carried out. This helps the employee to get to think and act about the criteria his/her work performance will be judged and assessed. Dozens, perhaps hundreds of different kinds of Rubrics are readily available and one can easily modify one of these *ready-made* rubrics to meet their specific needs. One can create rubrics for one's project-based activities using *RubiStar*.

RubiStar is a free tool that is available on line at http://rubistar.4teachers.org/index.php

A rubric is indeed a real authentic assessment tool that addresses real life situations and is considered as a formative type of assessment. It should be an integral part of employee's daily routine and activity. It would be advantageous if the rubrics are designed in consultation and cooperation with the employees or their representatives. Such an involvement helps in *empowering* the employee and consequently generates interest is in the assessment process. Authentic assessment should therefore considered to be a two-way street wherein the employee and the employer work together to determine what has been happening and how it can be improved.

Rubrics must address three categories specifically:

1. **Objective:** Rubrics should concentrate on measuring a stated level of quality of performance of a given employee.
2. **Range:** Rubrics should describe a reasonable range over which the performance is to be rated.
3. **Degree:** Rubrics should provide guidance as to what degree of level, a particular performance characteristic has been attained.

Experts are of the opinion that rubrics always provide an outlet for improving employee's morale which would ultimately result in improved end products. Experienced managers, employees, supervisors and administrators know implicitly what, when, how and why an outstanding final result can be accomplished successfully. Rubrics provide a means of communication between the employee and the employer. The employees know, beforehand how their performance will be evaluated and this helps them to adjust their work ethics accordingly. A well designed and creatively created assessment grid provides a ladder necessary for the employees to progress towards better accomplishments each time.

Appendix C briefly outlines a set of *Rubrics for conducting Performance Analysis.*

ASSESSMENT CYCLE

A Poem by Rudyard Kipling following the story *"Elephant's Child"* in *"Just So Stories"* goes like this:

I keep six honest serving men
They taught me all I knew:
Their names are
What and Why and When
and How and Where and Who.

An assessment cycle when judiciously implemented, is expected to addresses the above cited six questions:

- What are we trying to accomplish by conducting this *Assessment?*
- Why are we spending time and effort to document these painstakingly?
- When and how frequently are we supposed to perform this task?
- How do we know and how well do we know that our methodology is correct?
- Where and which manner will we use the information for improvement?
- Who will be responsible for gathering, interpreting and disseminating the data?

The assessment cycle is a process that is continuous. It identifies and documents:

1. **Strengths:** What are the good aspects and how that has been beneficial to the corporation, its employees, the clientele and the community.
2. **Weaknesses:** What areas the company should focus on working in order to improve its image, its efficiency and its productivity.
3. **Needs:** What items the company should to procure so that it can meet its commitment to continue to improve its strengths further and correct its weaknesses.
4. **Improvements:** How to institute the changes that dynamic and prove to be essential to eliminate the corporation's weak points and accentuate its strong points.
5. **Future plans:** What precautions can be taken so that, in future, weak points are identified immediately for corrective action.

An example of an Assessment Cycle is shown in *Appendix D.*

ASSESSMENT PRINCIPLES

Assessment should be considered as a vehicle for establishing effective communication between the employer and the employee. Assessment Principle, in reality begins with and enacts a vision of the kinds of environment the corporation values most for its employees.

1. There is absolutely no need to involve each and every employee in the complete and detailed process of conducting assessment. However, each and employee shall contribute towards providing essential and appropriate data that may be necessary to the respective assessment teams.

2. Vital evidence can be extracted and reorganized from a pool of data that may be already available and can be obtained from the respective division. Duplication of data collection must be avoided to prevent employee resentment.
3. Project assessment should primarily focus on the effectiveness of project implementation, economic impact, and the overall success of the project but it should not concentrate on the performance of the individual employees or the respective project leaders.
4. Realistic, attainable goals must be established when implementing an assessment plan. Sometime assessing half-a-dozen goals may be adequate for a specific project. Having an unnecessarily large number of goals may result in the gathering voluminous data, which may be difficult to interpret properly. Care must also be taken to avoid redundant and repetitive data.
5. It is extremely essential to identify multiple sources for gathering data. Evidence must be collected from independent sources and *not* inter-dependent sources. Some of the ideas for identifying multiple *sources* may be obtained from Appendix E wherein "*Possible Venues*" are listed.
6. Furthermore, data must be gathered using both quantitative methods and qualitative methods. The methods employed should be within the expertise of the division and of the assessment team.
7. Selected portion of the results of assessment must be properly disseminated to all the employees in some manner or the other. If this is ignored, it will be difficult to carry out future assessment projects and institute changes. The workforce will fail to respond with honesty.
8. Employees must be made aware of the fact that the process of assessment will have a definite impact on their workplace environ-

ment. Only when the implemented changes have worked, the employees recognize that they have a voice in the overall welfare and organization of the corporation.

9. Senior administration officials should clearly outline what they hope to accomplish by making the employees effectively participate in the assessment process. They should also indicate how the process helps the entire corporation evaluate and monitor its own progress.

10. Upper management should also be candid in explaining to its employees how effective and how successful they have been in their efforts to institute change for the better of their employees, customers, community and the corporation. They must also indicate how they are planning to utilize the knowledge gained to benefit overall improvement.

Governance documents of a corporation should therefore indicate not only *what* they want to assess but also *how* they want to assess. Assessment should not be a routine exercise in measuring what is already obvious and easy, rather should become a creative and intelligent process that strives at improving what the corporation really values and cares about.

A partial list of Assessment Tools can be found in *Appendix E*.

ASSESSMENT MATRIX

Many corporations may benefit from the use of an *Assessment Matrix* to provide them with sufficient data from multiple sources, so that the upper management can institute intelligent improvements and make informed decisions. This type of tool is highly advantageous because the performance of the employee is studied and *assessed* not just by his/her supervisor but by different divisions and departments of the entire corporation. While an employee may not be the ideal one in the eyes of the supervisor, the rest of the departments in the company may have completely different opinions and this can *stand out* when an *assessment matrix* is filled out with diligence and honesty. In other words, it is possible to obtain the *big picture* when an *Assessment Matrix* is put in place properly. Sometimes feedback from such a system provides constructive recommendations for upper management. Based on the feedback received, the upper management may conclude that the talents of the individual in question could be much more productive in a different sector of the corporation. This may eventually help in moving the employee to a different division or department in the company. In large corporations, there may exist a need for the development of multiple styles of *assessment matrices*. A single matrix may not be adequate to address the different ideologies, multitude of responsibilities and varied targets.

Again, it is extremely important to emphasize how the *goals* are written and identified. Furthermore, it is essential that only the appropriate department shall be authorized to address the specified goal. It is necessary to identify whose responsibility it is to provide a certain specified feedback or input.

An example of *Assessment Matrix* is shown in Appendix F.

ASSESSMENT MEASURES

There are three types of assessment measures.

*   **Direct measures:** This is considered to be the best one because it is based on hard data collected and analyzed in a scientific manner. An example could be professional licensure or required certification that an employee has obtained a in a specific discipline. Another example could be the external expert evaluation of a company employee on the success of a chosen performance project portfolio.
*   **Indirect measures:** This is considered to be

good enough but not the ideal one. Mostly indirect measures may utilize surveys and needless to say that surveys may be skewed depending on the individual. Feedback from customers and clientele is important and valuable however, one may have to take this with a grain of salt.

- **Inferential measures:** This is considered to be of limited value because it is based on judgment. For example questionnaires that describe employee participation, morale, outlook etc. are nice to have but the submissions must be viewed very carefully. Two committees may review the document with two different viewpoints and arrive two different conclusions.

One of the most common terminologies used by a variety of scholars is *Authentic Assessment*. Here, the employee is assigned a task to perform and complete during a specific period of time. Later, a rubric is utilized to evaluate how well the employee has performed on the assigned task. This is totally different from *Traditional Assessment* such as, for example, review of employee's annual report. It should be emphasized that *Authentic Assessment* always complements *Traditional Assessment*. In other words, an employee must demonstrate that he/she has a strong foundation and a broad knowledge base that is essential for maintaining the technical competitiveness and supremacy of the corporation. This may be recognized by traditional assessment techniques. But, it is also equally important to document that the employee can *apply* that huge wealth of knowledge to real world situations and support the corporation in its business ventures. It is extremely important to mention here that *Authentic Assessment* is sometimes referred to as *Direct Assessment* or *Alternative Assessment* or *Performance Assessment*.

A brief comparison of Authentic Assessment vs. Traditional Assessment is outlined in Appendix G.

ASSESSMENT STRUCTURE

Assessment structure should closely follow the corporate structure so that all the procured data can be streamlined and easily consolidated electronically to provide the big picture that is essential to make sound, informed, intelligent decisions. For example, consider a multinational corporation that has 5 plants in 4 different countries. Imagine that each plant has 6 major divisions and each major division is responsible for 20 different project cells. This means that the entire corporation has data coming in from 2400 units. It is extremely difficult to process voluminous data like this unless the assessment consolidation structure is highly methodical. Meaningful interpretation of data will not be possible if there exists no proper, systematic and organized structure in place. Crucial data may be lost in compilation and accomplishments may not be appreciated and highlighted. It is also obvious that important signals may not be read correctly to indicate where immediate action may be needed and moreover, significant improvement is warranted. A very highly structured system should be effectively instituted place so that the electronic data base can almost automatically identify a problem area by raising a red flag immediately.

The assessment data collected by each project cell should be electronically compatible so that a given division can quickly compile a consolidated assessment report for the division, without spending much more time or effort. Similarly, the consolidated assessment report for a given division should be fully compatible with the other divisions and so on. When such an assessment structure is properly implemented it can also be easily reversed. A top-down approach from the senior management can easily identify a particular project cell that may be exemplary in its performance and use its technique as a model for other divisions that may be looking for opportunities for improvement.

An example of how *Assessment Structure* can be arranged and organized is outlined in *Appendix H.*

ASSESSMENT PROTOCOL

It is a common practice to have documented, written assessment protocols when it becomes absolutely necessary to consistently determine whether or not a specified goal or criteria is being met and is serving its designated purpose. These existing protocols should be reviewed annually by upper administration officials and external agencies whenever possible. Protocols should also be updated as new and improved assessment tools and approaches become available for use. The *Monitoring and Assessment* section of a selected division in the corporation may be in charge of developing the guidelines for preparing the detailed protocol to serve the cited need and purpose. A protocol should basically outline a definite clear cut pathway that a committee of members can follow to arrive at some judicial conclusions and prepare a set of positive recommendations. Whenever possible, the protocol should provide the committee with a step-by-step procedure as to how the specified task is to be completed. Protocols may sometime describe advantages and disadvantages that the committee may encounter. It may also provide indications as to the *pitfalls* the committee may have to guard against.

Appendix I briefly outlines a sample of such an Assessment Protocol.

ASSESSMENT TECHNOLOGY

Researchers have shown that systematic use of technology actually helps employers address perceptual dimensions of their employees' learning capabilities. It is important to acknowledge that employees understand the needs of a specific project better when alternative modes of information processing are made available at businesses and commercial establishments. Technology should not be viewed just as a growing trend; rather it must be intelligently implemented as a valuable instructional tool that can accommodate diverse learning styles of 21st century workforce. (Watkins, 2005). Dr. Walter B. Barbe, a nationally known authority in the fields of reading and learning disabilities has shown that perceptual modality styles provides an indication of an individual's dominant learning mode. The degree of processing speed, accuracy and retention that an individual is able to accomplish when encountering information depends upon to what extent the medium in which information presented matches his or her learning style. (Barbe & Milone 1980 and 1981).

The officer in charge of assessment must first complete the fundamental task of articulating the goals and objectives pertaining to a chosen project, topic, course, curriculum or program. For example, information may have to be gathered at multiple levels: Corporation-wide, Plant-wide, Division-wide or Section-wide. In an educational establishment it may be at institution-level, college-level and department-level. Once these are set in place, it is now necessary to choose the correct approach and an appropriate method that can provide the needed data in a useable format. An intelligently designed and carefully planned rubric is totally indispensable while interpreting the data collected in an accurate manner.

A table that can be used to correlate components of assessment is outlined in *Appendix J.*

ASSESSMENT TRIO

Three of the most common terminologies that are encountered in the area of assessment are: *ABC, PTA and SSS.*

ABC stands for Assessment of Basic Components and this is one of the areas that receives attention first and foremost. In a large multinational corporation there are multitude of operations that are constantly in progress and as a consequence one can assess a number of different aspects. It is therefore necessary to pin point the exact items pertaining to a given project that one must specifically assess in order to obtain qualitative and quantitative data. Essential elements that are crucial to the productivity and progress of the corporation are to be identified first. Once these basic components have been listed, it is now necessary to develop the procedures for assessing these basic components. This can be carried out in the form of a table and Appendix K provides a brief guideline as to how such a table can be created.

PTA is an abbreviation for Primary Trait Analysis is sometimes defined in academic circles as the methodology employed for identifying selected major characteristics or *traits* that are to be expected in a student's work. A similar definition can be developed for companies and corporations wherein the *primary traits* expected of an employee can be conveniently categorized, analyzed and assessed. This involves identifying and defining precise criteria with different levels of performance standards for each specified trait. Obviously each and every project may require different skills thereby creating a new matrix of primary traits.

SSS stands for Scrutinize, Synthesize and Summarize. It is of fundamental importance that the data collected has to be first, scrutinized for integrity, accuracy, consistency, reliability and regularity. The next step would be to synthesize the data collected and understand what the data is telling us. This has to be done with care because an inexperienced group of individuals may interpret a given set of data incorrectly and arrive at erroneous conclusions. Once the data has been correctly synthesized, the final step would be to generate a summary. The summary should highlight the salient features of the process completed and should be precise to the point. Upper

management may not have the time to look in to the detailed process and as such the summarized version of assessment should clearly outline all the necessary focal points, whether they be bouquets or brickbats. A good summary should immediately indicate all the positive aspects as well as provide recommendations for eliminating the negative aspects.

ABC, PTA and SSS have always yielded impressive and valuable results when the data is collected scientifically has been examined with care and analyzed with diligence. Several scholars have made significant contributions in these areas and multiple formats have been recommended in each case for assessment documentation. However, *Washington State University's Critical Thinking Project* has provided all of us with massive ideas and multiple venues for documenting assessment data in a methodical manner. Even though it primarily focuses on an educational setting, one can easily extract extremely useful literature out of the project report. The practice and techniques of assessment become much more streamlined when *WSU's CT* project ideas are implemented in a systematic manner.

Appendix L briefly outlines how PTA can be scored using *Likert Scale.*

ASSESSMENT DIMENSIONS

This is a very important first step. This guides the entire assessment process and the dimensions must be carefully chosen to meet the necessary goals and objectives of the corporation. It's what distinguishes the assessment process from a traditional, routine report. When a summative evaluation is being generated one has to select about 4 – 6 dimensions. When a formative or diagnostic assessment is being carried out one may select more than 6, perhaps 8 – 10 dimensions.

Assessment dimensions are normally determined once ABC and PTA are finalized. Once the *Basic Components* are agreed upon, the assessment team can then focus on the depth to which they want to examine a given component. For example one may want to assess the *Communication Skills* of an employee. The next question to ask is what type of *communication skill?* One may arrive at three different possibilities. *Verbal, Vocal* and *Visual*. Verbal is also sometimes referred to as *Written Communication Skills*. Vocal is sometimes referred to as *Oral or Speech Communication Skills*. In each case, one can probe in to further details as to how many *dimensions* are to be assessed. Again, it is important to emphasize that the assessment team, the employees and supervisors should not be overwhelmed by the amount of data they collect.

An example of how to determine *Assessment Dimensions* is shown *Appendix M*.

ASSESSMENT PEDAGOGY

Provost David L. Potter of George Mason University chaired a joint task force and presented a report entitled *"Powerful Partnerships: A Shared Responsibility for Learning"* in June 1998. It begins with a statement of the insights gained through the scholarly study of learning and their implications for pedagogy, curricula, learning environments, and assessment. The main goal is to make a difference in the *quality* of student learning. Further, it is important to *assess* this difference and document it (Potter, 1998). It is important to recognize the fact that assessment practices throughout the country are in a state of rapid transition. There is a need for implementing revised ideas that are designed and geared so that the desired competency is documented in an organized portfolio. It is necessary to make these revised assessment practices to be more authentic. The goal should be to involve students and document the dynamics in the actual or simulated performance of a task (Linn, Baker, & Dunbar, 1991).

The question is: *"How can we continuously assess the performance of our individual students?"* Student performance measures should include skills that clearly show their progress through a sequence of preservice professional development activities and, thus, demonstrate growth. The process of developing a method for assessing this continuous growth requires thoughtful planning and careful implementation (Greenwood & Maheady, 1997). In an industrial setting, of course, the question can be easily re-phrased: : *"How can we continuously assess the performance of our individual employees?"*

Assessments of learning typically document students' knowledge but do not examine how classroom practices contribute to learning outcomes. Traditional methods for evaluating teaching examine instructional practices but often ignore how those practices influence students' learning, thinking, and development. The literature supports our intuitive belief that education in a new learning paradigm will prepare students for the work ahead of them (Cox, Grasha and Richlin, 1997). This principle can easily be modified to suit commercial establishments as well as modern multinational corporations.

According to guidelines proposed by the American Association for Higher Education (AAHE, 1992), assessment requires attention to outcomes but also and equally to the *experiences* that lead to those outcomes. Information about outcomes is of high importance; where students "end up" matters greatly. *Similarly, in an industrial setting one has to examine how assessment data gathered can be used benefit the overall growth of the corporation as well as its employees.*

But to improve outcomes, we need to know about student experience along the way. One needs to learn about the curricula, teaching, and the kind of student effort that lead to particular outcomes. Assessment can help us understand which students learn best under what conditions; with such knowledge comes the capacity to improve the whole of learning (Cerbin, 1993). One of the most critical connections in students' education-the link between teaching and learning-is often overlooked in assessment practices. Assessment focuses on either learning or teaching but not on the interplay between the two. In many cases Assessment of learning may typically document students' knowledge but may not examine how classroom practices have contributed to learning outcomes (Cerbin, 1994).

Even portfolio assessment approaches, which document teaching and learning more fully, do not necessarily examine the interplay between the two. Teaching portfolios may contain evidence of students' learning, but such information is optional, and when included, it may be only one of many pieces of material (Edgerton, Hutchings, & Quinlan, 1991; Seldin, 1991). Student portfolios, which document learning in more detail, seldom reveal how teaching contributes to students' progress (Forrest, 1990). Traditional methods of assessment certainly contribute to the improvement of education. However, practices that separate teaching from learning increase the chances that faculty members will perceive both types of assessment as irrelevant to their day-to-day classroom work. *Similarly, in an industrial environment, an employee's annual performance review may not be providing adequate assessment data as to the contribution of the employee to the welfare of the company or employee's professional growth.*

Assessment can also be conducted by utilizing certain principles and established models. The *Concept Mapping Model* utilizes the principles of a learning paradigm. (Tagg, 2003). The principle is to select an appropriate learning paradigm approach and preferably categorize and assign the needed information into the various components of that chosen paradigm. A model for knowledge acquisition and content delivery can be suggested however, this is normally accomplished utilizing well established and standardized building blocks of a learning paradigm (Barr and Tagg, 1995).

The *Structured Content Model* may be chosen as an alternative when the instructor finds that the *Concept Mapping Model* may not be suitable. Here subject matter content can be created independent of presentation format or delivery methodology. Regardless, this is not completely open ended and is mainly dictated by the educational objectives and course outcomes. (Gardner, 1993, 2000).

An example of how a *Project Report* can be assessed is outlined in *Appendix N*.

ASSESSMENT IMPACT

Decades ago, a book: *The Impact of College on Students* had made a dramatic impact in higher education circles (Feldman and Newcomb, 1969). University of Iowa Professor Ernest Pascarella and Pennsylvania State University Professor Patrick T. Terenzini took up where Feldman and Newcomb left off and systematically analyzed research data collected over decades. Their research focuses on impact of college on students and issues in assessing student educational outcomes. In their famous book: *How College Affects Students,* Pascarella and Terenzini say: *"We need a new standard of quality, one based on the quality of our results in producing student development."* Concluding their massive review of research on the development of students in college, Pascarella and Terenzini (1991), call for a *"shift in the decision-making orientation"* of administrators toward *"learning-centered management."*

Although *Pascarella and Terenzini's* research focused on the college campus one can easily extract very useful information that would be beneficial to the large multinational corporations, expanding business ventures and industry conglomerates. In the book, it is said: *"Despite large differences in size, selectivity, resources, prestige, type of governance, or curricular emphasis, large differences in outcomes disappeared once students' characteristics upon entry were accounted for."* Similarly, multinational corporations have to work with diverse workforce with different cultures to meet desired objectives and successfully complete multitude of tasks. It is therefore important to observe that assessment methods adopted will have a profound effect on the end results. Assessment analysis should be designed, developed and implemented so that they are completely independent of above mentioned variable characteristics such as race, gender, ethnicity, etc.

A simple method to Measure and Document Assessment Impact is outlined in *Appendix O.*

ASSESSMENT ARTICULATION

It is always admirable to articulate assessment process as an instrument that incorporates intricate details which could benefit the employees as well as the corporation. One can easily observe that *Assessment* can help in promoting a constructive dialogue among all its participants, upper management, division heads, project leaders and participating employees. Assessment helps the corporation determine and document its accomplished progress towards aspirations. It also helps in enhancing the expertise of its employees for contributing to the community.

Nevertheless, one has to admit that there will be lots of resistance and one has to skillfully articulate the situation to overcome lack of interest or participation from the employees. The perception that *assessment* is an additional task that takes too much of time must be completely eliminated. On the contrary it should be made clear that *assessment* actually provides a venue to create shared perspectives and a common language to describe accomplishments. Furthermore assessment always clarifies purposes and goals of the individual as well as the corporation. It also documents the effectiveness of the corporate leadership and procedural governance. While the employees may already be accomplishing intellectual development in their own personalized

way, assessment puts a *team approach* perspective to the environment that already exists. It should also be emphasized that it is possible to precisely determine success and effectiveness when proper assessment procedures are practiced. Assessment also addresses community concerns as to whether or not the available resources are being used effectively and efficiently. Furthermore, assessment offers a proactive strategy that permits the company to exercise *self control,* demonstrating institutional integrity and corporate accountability before being forcibly asked to document a certain process by an outside body or an external agency.

ASSESSMENT AUDIT

Here, the corporation takes its initial steps outlining the importance of assessment, whether it be for internal use or for submission to an external agency. An *Assessment Audit* is like a preliminary task inventory that is fairly comprehensive and sets the tone for future action plans. Mostly a committee of senior executives in co-operation with the research and development department create this list that will be known as *Assessment Audit* list. An example of an *Assessment Audit* may look like this.

Collect information on corporation-wide measures that provide guidance towards purposeful assessment procedures and data collection.

Plant-wide action-items that are specific to the location involved should then be put in place to support the measures provided corporation-wide.

Each division should be asked to provide information in an appropriate format so that pant-wide action-items are implemented successfully.

Every project cell supervisor contributes the details about their accomplishments and help the respective division consolidate and prepare a comprehensive document that can be quickly analyzed .

These divisional documents should always specify plans for further improvement and should pave the path for future expansion.

The divisional documents should primarily correlate to previous year's documents. They should indicate what measures were taken and how they have led to increased productivity, safer workplace environment, boosting employee morale, etc.

Written documentation should also include how the assessment data and information consolidated will be used in future to benefit the employees of the corporation.

Recommendations should also be made for improvement in the assessment procedure itself. For example, the *assessment team* of the corporation may be required to actively participate in a workshop training session where new ideas can be brainstormed.

The *assessment team* of a corporation must be a *dynamic* team and bring in *new talent* whenever feasible and deemed appropriate.

ASSESSMENT STRATEGIES

It is of utmost importance that the upper management emphasizes the fact that corporate assessment strategies actually enhance employee morale and promote active participation in the day-to-day running of the company. Assessment in reality does not take time away from the employee productivity; on the contrary, properly instituted assessment strategies themselves can be very productive and fruitful for everyone. The primary aim of assessment strategy is to provide a *big pic*ture for the employees. The strategy is to promote participants' productive skills that will be beneficial to the employees, not only at present, but also throughout the rest of their career, even outside the limits of the corporation.

An example of tabulating assessment strategies is outlined in *Appendix P*.

ASSESSMENT RESOURCES

A wide variety of textbooks, web sites and multitude of other resources are available in the area of *Assessment*. Given below is only a very small list of assessment related books. Many may refer to assessment in an educational environment. However, it is important to recognize that the principles can be modified and adapted to a corporate setting or a commercial scenario or a business venture.

Palomba, Catherina A. & Banta, Trudy W. (1999). *Assessment essentials.* San Francisco: Jossey-Bass Publishers.

Angelo, Thomas A., & Cross, Patricia K., (1993). *Classroom assessment techniques* (2nd ed.). San Francisco: Jossey-Bass Publishers 1993.

Huba, Mary E., & Freed, Jann E. (2000). *Learner-centered assessment on college campuses.* Needham Heights, MA: Allyn & Bacon Publishers.

Cambridge, Barbara L. & Williams, Anne C. (1998). *Portfolio learning.* Englewood Cliffs, NJ: Prentice Hall Publishers.

Smith, Brenda, Brown, Sally, & Race, Phil (2000). *500 tips on assessment.* London: Kogan Page Publishers.

Nichols, James O., & Nichols, Karen W. (2001). *The Nichols guide to assessment.* Flemington, NJ: Agathon Press.

Sharan, Shlomo (Ed.) (1994). *Handbook of cooperative learning methods.* Westport, CT: Greenwood Press.

Schwartz, Peter, & Webb, Graham (2002). *Assessment: Case studies.* Herndon, VA: Stylus Publishing.

Walvoord, Barbara E., & Anderson, Virginia Johnson (1998). *Effective grading: A tool for learning and assessment.* San Francisco: Jossey-Bass Publishers,

ASSESSMENT CONFERENCES

A wide variety of conferences take place throughout the United States and around the world, which focus on the area of *Assessment*. Given below is only a very short list.

The Assessment Institute organized and directed by Dr. Trudy Banta, Senior Advisor to the Chancellor, IUPUI, Indianapolis, Indiana is the largest and oldest conference dedicated to *Assessment*. The institute, which started in 1992 has steadily grown and attracts more than 1200 participants from all over the world. It is normally conducted during the last week of October or first week of November of every year at the Westin Indianapolis, Indiana.

Steven G. Mihaylo College of Business and Economics at California State University, Fullerton has been conducting an *Annual Western Assessment Conference* since 1996, during mid-march.

Texas A & M Assessment Conference is held at College Station, Texas during the 3rd or 4th week in February. This is conference started in the year 2000.

NC State Undergraduate Assessment Symposium is held during March – April at Cary, North Carolina.

REFERENCES

AAHE Assessment Forum. (1992). *Principles for good practice for assessing students' learning.* Washington, DC: American Association for Higher Education.

Barr, R. B., & Tagg, J. (1995, November/December). *From teaching to learning: A new paradigm for undergraduate education.* Change, (pp. 13-24).

Cox, M. D., Grasha, A., & Richlin, L. (1997, March). *Town meeting. Between teaching model and learning model: Adapting and adopting bit by bit.* Lilly Atlantic Regional Conference.

Tagg, J. (2003). *The learning paradigm college.* Bolton, MA: Anker.

Cerbin, W. (1994). The course portfolio as a tool for continuous improvement of teaching and learning. *Journal on Excellence in College Teaching, 5*(1), 95-105.

Cerbin, W. (1993). Fostering a culture of teaching as scholarship. *The Teaching Professor, 7*(3), 1-2.

Edgerton, R., Hutchings, P., & Quinlan, P. (1991). *The teaching portfolio: Capturing the scholarship in teaching.* Washington, DC: American Association for Higher Education.

Feldman, K. A., & Newcomb, T. M. (1969). *Impact of college on students.* San Francisco: Jossey-Bass.

Forrest, A. (1990). *Time will tell: Portfolio-assisted assessment of general education.* Washington, DC: American Association for Higher Education.

Greenwood, C., & Maheady, L. (1997). Measurable change in student performance : Forgotten standard in teacher preparation? *Teacher Education and Special Education, 20*(3), 265-275.

Gardner, H. (1993). *Multiple intelligences: The theory in practice.* New York: Basic.

Gardner, H. (2000). *Intelligence reframed: Multiple intelligences for the 21st century.* New York: Basic.

Linn, R., Baker, E., & Dunbar, S. (1991). Complex, performance-based assessment: Expectations and validation criteria. *Educational Researcher, 20*(8), 15-21.

Marchese, T. J.(1987). Third down, ten years to go. *AAHE Bulletin, 40*, 3-8.

Pascarella, E. T., & Terenzini, P. T. (1991). *How college affects students: Findings and insights from twenty years of research.* San Francisco: Jossey-Bass.

Potter, D. L. (June, 1998) *Powerful partnerships: A shared responsibility for learning.* A Joint Report: American Association for Higher Education, American College Personnel Association & National Association of Student Personnel Administrators.

Watkins, A. F. (2005). Using learning styles in college teaching. *Journal on Excellence in College Teaching, 16*(3), 83-101.

IMPORTANT WEBSITES FOR FURTHER READING

Fleming, N. D. & Mills, C. (1992).*VARK a guide to learning styles.* http://www.vark-learn.com/English/index.asp

http://telr.osu.edu

http://wsuctproject.wsu.edu/ctr.htm

http://www.pz.harvard.edu/PIs/HG.htm

http://www.icbl.hw.ac.uk/ltdi/cookbook/info_likert_scale/

Heidi Goodrich Andrade. "Understanding Rubrics." [Online] Retrieved October 22, 2001. <http://www.middleweb.com/rubricsHG.html>

Teachervision.com (2001). *The advantages of Rubrics: Part one in a five-part series.* [Online] Retrieved October 22, 2001, <http://www.teachervision.com/lesson-plans/lesson-4522.html>

Nancy Pickett and Bernie Dodge. "Rubrics for Web Lessons." [Online] Retrieved October 22, 2001. <http://edweb.sdsu.edu/webquest/rubrics/weblessons.htm>.

KEY TERMS AND DEFINITIONS

Critical Thinking: Michael Scriven and Richard Paul defined Critical Thinking at the 8th Annual International Conference on Critical Thinking and Education Reform, Summer 1987. According to these Scriven and Paul:

Critical thinking is the intellectually disciplined process of actively and skillfully conceptualizing, applying, analyzing, synthesizing, and/or evaluating information gathered from, or generated by, observation, experience, reflection, reasoning, or communication, as a guide to belief and action. In its exemplary form, it is based on universal intellectual values that transcend subject matter divisions: clarity, accuracy, precision, consistency, relevance, sound evidence, good reasons, depth, breadth, and fairness.

Diversity: The term *diversity* is used in a different context in this chapter. One is not referring to gender diversity or racial diversity. Diversity of *talents* and diversity in the form of *growth marketing strategy* is of great importance to a multinational corporation. The objective is to increase the volume of sales by creating new products aimed at different markets. One is generally looking to enter in to promising business ventures that offer to establish new market share, presently not available.

Learning Outcomes: These are statements that outline what employees will acquire as a result of a given activity. They may acquire a certain skill or establish a foundation knowledge base or develop a new attitude or attain a desired condition. *Learning Outcomes* are supposed to serve as guidelines for assessment and evaluation.

Portfolio: Portfolios aim at the documentation of work accomplishments and skills acquired. They are also used to monitor professional development. They are not just two-page resumes. Portfolios document an employee's capabilities and open a window for his/her future potential.

Protocol: A *Protocol* is an agreed-upon format for performing a given task. The task may be, for example, assessment, and then the *Assessment Protocol* defines and determines how assessment is to be conducted and is expected to provide clear guidelines pertaining to the exact procedure that needs to be followed.

Rubrics: Rubrics provide guidelines for rating employee performance. It is created in the form of a table or a matrix and provides the officer in charge of assessment with a tool to judge the performance of an employee.

Teamwork: Teamwork in a multinational corporation aims at aligning the employee's mindset to develop the concept of a group of people working in cooperation with each other. It is very important to identify that what may actually appear as teamwork for an outsider, may not necessarily be genuine teamwork for the inside group of people.

APPENDIX A.

LIKERT SCALE: A Brief Overview

Likert scale is named after Rensis Likert, an American social scientist (1903 – 1981) who is also well known for introducing the concept of participatory management. Likert scale is a unidimensional scaling method wherein a statement is presented to a respondent and the respondent is asked to provide feedback on a five point scale. The respondent indicates if he/she

- Strongly Agrees with the statement. (A *Likert Scale* score of 5)
- Agrees with the statement. (A *Likert Scale* score of 4)
- Undecided or remains neutral. (A *Likert Scale* score of 3)
- Disagrees with the statement. (A *Likert Scale* score of 2)
- Strongly Disagrees with the statement. (A *Likert Scale* score of 1)

It is important to observe that the data collected are ordinal. They have to follow a sequence and there exists an inherent order built-in. The difference between *Strongly Agreeing* and *Agreeing* may be *1* on a Likert Scale. The difference between *Disagreeing* and *Undecided* may also be *1* on a Likert Scale. But these two *1s* are *not* the same.

Therefore one can *not* calculate the *mean* when one is analyzing data collected using *Likert Scale*. The only logical way is to summarize the data collected using *mode*. Furthermore, the distribution of the data analyzed must the displayed as a bar chart. Again, it should be emphasized that the data procured is *not continuous* and therefore a histogram is totally invalid.

It should be pointed out here that some researchers recommend the use of a seven point scale instead of a five point scale. Some scholars also recommend using *median* to analyze *Likert Scale* data. Others *modify* the structure like this:

- Outstanding. (A score of 6)
- Very good. (A score of 5)
- Good. (A score of 4)
- Fair. (A score of 3)
- Acceptable. (A score of 2)
- Needs improvement. (A score of 1)
- Unacceptable. (A score of 0)

However, the author strongly disagrees with these ideas and believes that these are blatant violations of the principles on which Rensis Likert established the famous Likert Scale.

APPENDIX B. ADVANTAGES OF RUBRICS

1	Rubrics indicate what is expected of the employee and how the employee's work will be evaluated.
2	The amount of time spent by the evaluator is greatly reduced once rubrics are instituted properly.
3	Productive feedback can be obtained by the proper use of rubrics regarding administrative effectiveness.
4	Informative feedback can also be given to employees about their strengths and their weaknesses, using rubrics.
5	Rubrics cut a clear path and places a demand on the supervisor to clarify his/her criteria for evaluation.
6	Employees become significantly better judges of their own work performance with the help of a *Rubrics Template*.
7	Rubrics permit the person who conducts the assessment to be strictly objective constantly consistent.
8	A creative set of rubrics easy to use and will be welcomed both by the employer and the employee.
9	It is almost impossible to effectively handle today's' diverse workforce without the help of creative rubrics.
10	Rubrics have been shown to improve employee performance and management effectiveness.

APPENDIX C.

Inspired by: http://wsuctproject.wsu.edu/index.htm

Recommended Rubrics for conducting Performance Analysis

↓   ←

Likert Scale Score	**PERFORMANCE ANALYSIS**
5 Has demonstrated excellence. Has provided documentation. Evidence of critical thinking skills. Very good performance	Has analyzed important data precisely. Has answered key questions correctly. Has addressed problems effectively. Has evaluated material with proper insight. Has used deductive reasoning skills. Has used inductive reasoning skills. Has employed problem solving skills. Has discussed consequences of decisions. Has been consistent with inference.

continued on following page

APPENDIX C. CONTINUED

3

Has demonstrated competency.

Adequate documentation.

Critical thinking ability exists.

Acceptable performance.

Data analysis can be improved.

More effort to address key questions.

Need to address problems effectively.

Expand on evaluating material.

Improve deductive reasoning skills.

Improve inductive reasoning skills.

Problem solving skills need honing.

Must discuss consequences of decisions.

Has been vague with inference.

1

Poor, unacceptable performance.

Lacks ability to think critically.

Absence of analytical skills.

Answers questions incorrectly.

Addresses problems superficially.

Lacks documentation.

Inability to evaluate material.

Shows no deductive reasoning power.

Inductive reasoning power nonexistent.

Poor problem solving skills

Unaware of consequences of decisions.

Unable to draw conclusions.

APPENDIX D. AN EXAMPLE OF AN ASSESSMENT CYCLE

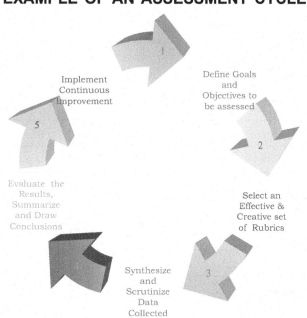

APPENDIX E. ASSESSMENT DOCUMENTATION

Technology Project Management

Possible venues for documenting assessment

A partial list of assessment tools

that may help an employer assess

the success of a chosen project.

Assessment Tool ↓ Likert Scale Score →	5	4	3	2	1
Feedback from customers					
Supervisor's comments					
Interaction with colleagues					
Professional development					
Currency in technology					
Meeting crucial deadlines					
Presentation of material					
Completion of project					
Project competitiveness					
Participation & group dynamics					
Innovation and Intuitiveness					
Report writing style					
Appeal to clientele					
Effective use of technology					
Timeliness & punctuality					
Descriptive journal reports					
Portfolio documentation					
Poster preparation & presentation					
Individual's project success					
Visual aids, graphs & pictures					
Vocal, Verbal and Visual Communication					

APPENDIX F. AN EXAMPLE OF ASSESSMENT MATRIX

Goals and Objectives

Goal # 1: *Intellectual Growth:* Demonstrates the efficient and effective monitoring of one's own success in intellectual growth and professional development.

Goal # 2: *Customer Welfare:* Understands the key concepts of company policy and philosophy towards customer welfare and needs of the clientele.

Goal # 3: *Technology Integration:* Intelligently integrates technology for the benefit of company's success in satisfying the demands of a challenging and competitive field.

Goal # 4: *Teamwork & Diversity:* Demonstrates commitment to values, supports productive team work, understands diversity and appreciates multicultural perspectives.

Goal # 5: *Ethics & Environment:* Shows respect for the environment, strongly supports ethical decision making processes and a commitment to justice.

Goal # 6: *Critical Thinking:* Promotes critical thinking, engages fellow employees in an exciting dialogue and takes up responsibility in a purposeful inquiry for meeting company's goals and objectives.

√ = Responsible Departments	Goal # 1: Intellectual Growth	Goal # 2: Customer Welfare	Goal # 3: Technology Integration	Goal # 4: Teamwork & Diversity	Goal # 5: Ethics & Environment	Goal # 6: Critical Thinking	Recommendations for Improvement
Employee's Annual Report	√					√	
Customer Service		√					
I.T. Department Officer			√				
Project Supervisor	√			√	√		
Feedback from co-workers				√	√		
Human Resources		√			√		
O.S.H.A. Division				√			

APPENDIX G. COMPARISON OF TRADITIONAL ASSESSMENT AND AUTHENTIC ASSESSMENT

Traditional Assessment	Authentic Assessment
Determines if the employee is fulfilling the needs outlined in *job description.*	Examines the overall performance appraisal of an assigned task, successfully completed.
May be *contrived:* Can the employee successfully handle hypothetical situations.	Document proficiency by actually negotiating to perform an assigned task efficiently.
Recall and Recognize: Examining the fundamental knowledge base and depth of understanding by the employee.	Synthesize and apply the knowledge base to create productivity in a substantive manner beneficial to the corporation.
Almost always uniform throughout the Company and is Corporate-wide and is traditionally structured.	Structured to meet the needs of the individual and the project jointly by the Employee and Supervisor.
Indirect Evidence: One has to infer that the employee can handle a given task because of his/her educational background and experience.	Direct Evidence: Judicial construction and implementation of knowledge for meaningful applications in complex real-world situations.

APPENDIX H. ASSESSMENT STRUCTURE

Partial List. Project Cell # 1

	Exceeds Expectations. State-of-the Art. **GRADE A**	Meets Minimum Standards. Acceptable Level. **GRADE B**	Needs Improvement. Update Essential. **GRADE C**	Immediate Action Required. Unacceptable. **FAIL F**	Recommendations
Innovative Engineering and Product Design	√				
Shop Floor Effectiveness, Production Supervision		√			
Precision Instruments and Quality Planning & Control			√		
Maintenance of Equipment and Up-keep of Grounds		√			
Employee Safety and Work Place Security			√		
Environment, Ethics, O.S.H.A. Compliance			√		
Structured Sales and Intelligent Marketing				√	
Product Promotions and Public Relations			√		
Clientele Interaction & Customer Support				√	
Human Relations Employee Welfare		√			

continued on following page

APPENDIX H. ASSESSMENT STRUCTURE CONTINUED

Overall Summary for One Division with 8 Project Cells

	Project Cell # 1	Project Cell # 2	Project Cell # 3	Project Cell # 4	Project Cell # 5	Project Cell # 6	Project Cell # 7	Project Cell # 8	Overall Summary
Innovative Engineering and Product Design	A	B	A	A	A	B	A	A	6 A , 2 B
Shop Floor Effectiveness, Production Supervision	B	B	B	B	B	A	B	B	1 A , 7 B
Precision Instruments and Quality Machine Tools	C	B	B	B	B	B	B	C	6 B , 2 C
Maintenance of Equipment and Up-keep of Grounds	B	A	B	A	B	A	B	A	4 A , 4 B
Employee Safety and Work Place Security	C	F	C	F	F	F	C	F	3 C , 5 F
Environment, Ethics, O.S.H.A. Compliance	C	B	B	B	B	B	B	C	6 B , 2 C
Structured Sales and Intelligent Marketing	F	C	F	F	C	C	C	C	5 C , 3 F
Product Promotions and Public Relations	C	B	B	C	C	B	B	C	4 B , 4 C
Clientele Interaction & Customer Support	F	C	C	C	C	F	F	F	4 C , 4 F
Human Relations Employee Welfare	B	B	B	B	A	B	B	B	1 A , 7 B

continued on following page

APPENDIX H. ASSESSMENT STRUCTURE (CONTINUED)

Consolidated Summary for One Unit with 3 Divisions

	Division # 1	Division # 2	Division # 3	Consolidated Summary
Innovative Engineering	6 A	7 A	5 A	18 A , 6 B
and Product Design	2 B	1 B	3 B	
Shop Floor Effectiveness,	1 A	3 A	4 A	8 A , 16 B
Production Supervision	7 B	5 B	4 B	
Precision Instruments,	6 B	5 B	7 B	18 B , 6 C
Quality Planning & Control	2 C	3 C	1 C	
Maintenance of Equipment	4 A	5 A	6 A	15 A , 9 B
and Up-keep of Grounds	4 B	3 B	2 B	
Employee Safety and	3 C	4 C	2 C	9 C , 15 F
Work Place Security	5 F	4 F	6 F	
Environment, Ethics,	6 B	6 B	5 B	17 B , 7 C
O.S.H.A. Compliance	2 C	2 C	3 C	
Structured Sales and	5 C	6 C	4 C	15 C , 9 F
Intelligent Marketing	3 F	2 F	4 F	
Product Promotions and	4 B	6 B	4 B	14 B , 10 C
Public Relations	4 C	2 C	4 C	
Clientele Interaction &	4 C	5 C	1 C	10 C , 14 F
Customer Support	4 F	3 F	7 F	
Human Relations	1 A	2 A	3 A	6 A , 18 B
Employee Welfare	7 B	6 B	5 B	

continued on following page

APPENDIX H. ASSESSMENT STRUCTURE(CONTINUED)

Column Graph for 1 Unit with 3 Divisions, each division with 8 Project Cells

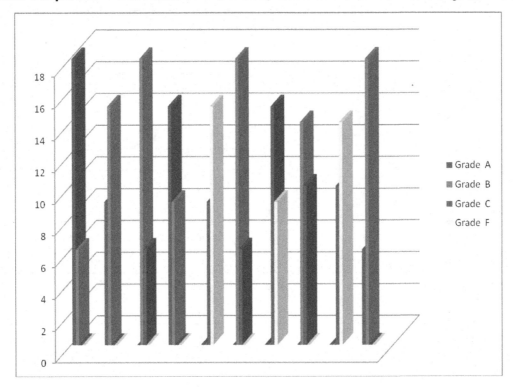

Analysis of the Column Graph:

The above column graph represents consolidated data for one unit with three divisions and each division with eight project cells. Comprehensive data collected from 24 project cells is displayed above.   The x-axis represents (from left to right) the ten components that are being assessed. The y-axis represents the score recorded (Out of a maximum possible 24). Many record A's and B's and these may be ranked *acceptable*. Some others record C's and F's and these need to be looked in to. Of particular interest are three areas that recorded lowest scores are:

- Employee Safety and Work Place Security (15 F's)
- Structured Sales and Intelligent Marketing (9 F's)
- Clientele Interaction & Customer Support (14 F's)

The corporation has to take immediate action, so that these F's are completely eliminated.

Corporate assessment structure should be streamlined like this so that consolidated summary can be generated with minimum most effort. The above mentioned philosophy can be extended to a plant that has for example four units and for a corporation that has five plants in seven different countries.

APPENDIX I. A SAMPLE *ASSESSMENT PROTOCOL*

An Example	Assessment Protocol
Overview of the document	This document details the procedure for completing a specified training Program titled *"Needs Assessment."*
Objectives of this document	The objectives of this document is to Recommend guidelines for narrowing the gap that exists between the corporation and its employees.
Definition of *Needs Assessment*	*Needs Assessment* should not be confused with a *wish list*. *Need* is the gap between: "what it is now" and "what it should be in future."
Procedure # 1	The chosen committee will first conduct an initial survey using a 20-item questionnaire to examine the situation at present.
Procedure # 2	The committee will then conduct interviews with selected groups that represent various divisions and different classifications of employees. The group interview is limited to 1 hour max.
Procedure # 3, 4, 5, etc.	………
Final Report	………

APPENDIX J. COMPONENTS OF ASSESSMENT CORRELATED

Correlating Assessment

Project Cell # 1 Employee # →	A	B	C	.	.	.	.	X	Y	Z	MEDIAN	MODE	AVG.

LIKERT SCALE WEIGHT DISTRIBUTION :
(1 : Strongly Disagree; 5 : Strongly Agree)

		A	B	C	.	.	.	.	X	Y	Z		MODE	
1	Has fundamental knowledge and is professionally competent	4	4	3	.	.	.	.	4	3	3		5	
2	Ability to identify and determine salient features of a given task	3	4	5	.	.	.	.	5	5	5		4	
3	Follows systematic methodologies and uses Creative problem solving techniques	5	4	3	.	.	.	.	3	4	5		4	
4	Structured analysis of needs and necessities, essential for the project	3	3	5	.	.	.	.	4	3	4		3	
5	Effective team player and excellent group dynamics	3	3	5	.	.	.	.	5	4	4		5	
6	Capable of demonstrating leadership qualities when needed	4	4	5	.	.	.	.	5	4	5		4	
7	Strong communication skills: Visual, Verbal and Vocal	4	3	4	.	.	.	.	3	4	3		5	

A *Bar Chart* based on *Mode* is shown on the following page.

continued on following page

APPENDIX J.

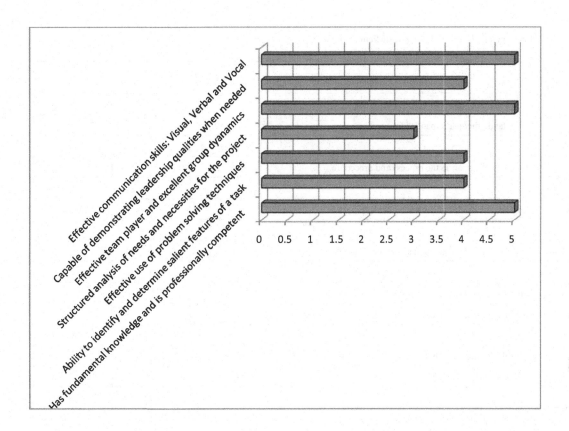

Analysis of the Bar Chart:

From the above bar chart it is easily observed that almost all the employees in *"Project Cell # 1"* are professionally competent, communicate very well and are team players. The above three categories display a Likert Scale score of **5** each.

However, these group of employees have to work on improving and understanding the *"Structured analysis of needs and necessities, essential for the project."* This category recorded the lowest score, **3.**

There are three other categories that have shown a Likert Scale score of **4.** While this may be considered adequate, however the aspiration should be to attain a Likert Scale score of **5** on all the categories listed. While one may criticize that it too ambitious, one should remember the famous adage: *"Reach for the sky and you'll touch the ceiling."*

APPENDIX K. PRIMARY TRAITS EXAMPLE (GROUP DYNAMICS / TEAMWORK)

Primary Traits ↓ Likert Scale Score →	5	4	3	2	1
1 Puts in genuine efforts to listen, admire and understand other participant's ideas and input.					
2 Takes an active part in the process and procedure.					
3 Supplements useful information when appropriate.					
4 Contributes to the discussion and makes it lively.					
5 Is dynamic and takes a leadership role in his/her area of expertise, when called for.					
6 Skillfully challenges other viewpoints effectively by presenting factual data.					
7 Is observant and is alert to indicate when and where contradiction may exist.					
8 Is prepared to revise or modify his/her opinion when provided with substantive facts and figures.					
9 Convincingly explains his/her own view points.					
10 Artfully promotes interesting arguments.					
11 Clearly outlines the rationale for his/her actions.					
12 Provides a concise summary of the proposed solutions.					
14 Exhibits creativity by describing alternative paths that can be taken.					
15 Instinctively intervenes to offer corrections when a Discussion steers *off track*.					

APPENDIX L. ORAL PRESENTATION RUBRICS (LIKERT SCALE)

Project Presentation To Upper Management

A sample of how assessment can be administered
Assessment Recorded by: One Selected Manager
Assessment for the entire PROJECT CELL # 1 and not an individual employee.

Vocal & Visual Communication Skills					
Assessment of an Audio-visual Presentation	5	4	3	2	1
Project Cell # 1	Strongly Agree	Agree	Undecided	Disagree	Strongly Disagree

		5	4	3	2	1
1	Problem statement, definition and specifications of constraints	√				
2	Literature survey, feasibility studies, evaluation of hypothesis		√			
3	Documentation of the use of engineering methodologies		√			
4	Modeling, application of engineering science and mathematics			√		
5	Technical expertise, Utilization of resources and knowledge		√			
6	Gantt charts, Fishbone diagrams, Statistical data, Graphs	√				
7	Relationship to other departments, overall company needs			√		
8	Cost-benefit analysis, consideration of different solutions	√				
9	Data analysis, calculations, assessment and conclusions		√			
10	Group dynamics, brainstorming sessions, teamwork	√				
11	Suggestions for future work, outline of ideas for other projects			√		
12	Presentation clarity, etiquette, visual aids and professionalism	√				

Consolidated Summary of Assessment.
Summarized feedback from different managers, section supervisors, peers, external reviewers, etc.
Assessment for the entire PROJECT CELL # 1 and not an individual employee.

continued on following page

APPENDIX L. ORAL PRESENTATION RUBRICS (CONTINUED)

Oral Project Presentation To Upper Management

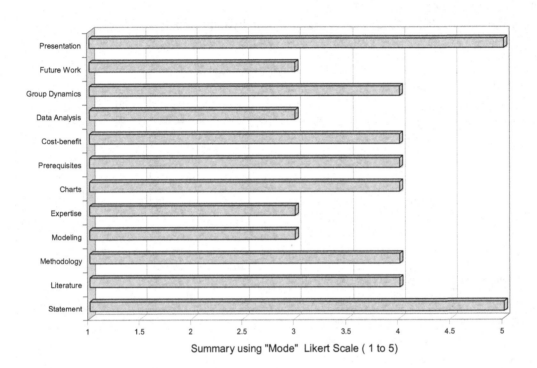

Analysis of the Bar Chart:

From the above bar chart it is easily observed that almost all the employees in *"Project Cell # 1"* clearly understand what needs to be done in the project. This is supported by a Likert Scale score of **5** for the category: *"Problem statement, definition and specifications of constraints"* Furthermore, when they present the project, their *"Presentation clarity, etiquette, visual aids and professionalism"* are excellent. This is again documented in the bar chart with a Likert Scale score of **5.**

However, these group of employees have to work on improving and understanding four other categories that have recorded the lowest Likert Scale score, **3.**

There are six other categories that have shown a Likert Scale score of **4.** While this may be considered adequate, for the time being, one should aspire to bring this Likert Scale score to the maximum possible score of **5.**

APPENDIX M. ASSESSMENT DIMENSIONS (LIKERT SCALE ANALYSIS EXAMPLE)

Task Assessed	Dimensions of Assessment	5	4	3	2	1
Vocal Presentation	Clarity and diction					
	Pronunciation					
	Organization of ideas					
	Voice projection					
	Body language					
	Business Attire					
Visual Presentation	Technical Content					
	Quality of slides					
	Visual clarity					
	Systematic organization					
	Absence of clutter					
	Readability of material					
Verbal Presentation	Grammar and structure					
	Chapter organization					
	Good *'flow'*					
	Sequence of topics					
	Absence of vagueness					
	Creative formatting					
Product Design	Creativity in design					
	Competitiveness					
	Economic impact					
	Strong Justification					
	Sound judgment					
	Methodical Approach					

APPENDIX N.

Project Report Analysis Rubric (Likert Scale)

Reviewer indicates the score (between 5 & 1) in the middle column.

		Exemplary	Reviewer's Score	Poor
		5		1
1	Introduction	Excellent introduction provides a logical *lead-in* to the contents of the report.		Introduction lacks clarity and does not indicate what to expect in the report.
2	Research & Development	Thorough, up-to-date and precise to the point. Utilizes State-of-the art knowledge.		Inadequate and does not know what is "out there."
3	Project Needs and Description	Clearly addresses the project needs based on documented research findings.		Haphazard approach, extremely vague in addressing the problem needs.
4	Procedure and Planning	Presents a detailed easy-to-follow step-by-step procedure.		Fails to follow a systematic, methodical approach. Absence of planning.
5	Documentation of Results & Data Analysis	Accurately analyzes and documents the data using established techniques.		Records the data incorrectly which has led to misleading conclusions.
6	Graphical Representation	Generates creative useful graphs that highlight the salient features of the project		Graphs generated do not represent needed documentation and have no bearing on the project needs.
7	Summary and Conclusions	Summarizes the results correctly and provides a logical explanation for findings and addresses the needs.		Does not provide a useful concise summary and important questions remain unanswered.
8	Mechanics	Grammatically correct and presents a good *flow*.		Many grammatical errors. Difficult to read.

APPENDIX O. ASSESSMENT IMPACT (LIKERT SCALE ANALYSIS EXAMPLE)

Measuring Assessment Impact (Likert Scale)
Reviewer indicates the score (between 5 & 1) in the middle column.

Previous Year to Present Year Comparison	Has had a profound and positive effect on the employee workforce and has boosted corporate image	Perceived Score	Not observed / Not recorded / Unable to comment/ Lack of available data / Very little impact
	5		1
1	Freshly formed *Discussion Groups* and their feedback		
2	New procedures for conducting performance review of the employees		
3	Modifications and Changes Instituted in Operations and Safety Procedures		
4	Effectiveness and Operation of New Security Systems Installed		
5	Revised Guidelines for Shop Floor Supervisor		
6	New Brochures for Publicity and Promotions		

APPENDIX P: ASSESSMENT STRATEGIES

		Implemented	In the Planning Stage	Need to work on
	APPENDIX P: ASSESSMENT STRATEGIES			
1	Have employees write, discuss, document and communicate their creative ideas.			
2	Utilize proven rubrics to make standards and evaluation criteria explicitly clear.			
3	Get employees working in groups, on substantive tasks, in and out of corporate environment.			
4	Provide prompt and productive feedback frequently to employees about their progress and accomplishments.			
5	Establish and communicate high expectations, both for the supervisors and for the employees.			
6	Create opportunities and help employees to achieve those expectations and criteria.			
7	Focus on helping the employees successfully attain their goals and objectives, with enthusiasm.			
8	Promote Critical Thinking and support creativity. Respect diversity and admire individual's talents.			
9	Appreciate multitude ways of reason, logic and pave a path for problem solving methodologies.			
10	Encourage supervisor-employee interaction, in and out of the industrial establishment circles.			

continued on following page

APPENDIX P. ASSESSMENT STRATEGIES (CONTINUED)

	Assessment What Is The Myth ?		Assessment What Does Research Say?
1	Employees should *blindly* follow orders.		They should not. Employees prefer *Involvement*.
2	Supervisors can not provide all this *'latitude'* to the employees.		Good supervisors tend to *listen* to what the employees say.
3	You can't do this *'assessment stuff'* in large corporations		If the method of *approach* is correct, anything is possible.
4	It takes too much effort, lots of time and resources.		Not if proper documents are already in place.
5	Employee resentment is very high if the supervisor is too demanding		Creativity in communication can always provide an outlet for compromise.
6	All these documentation : Is this really necessary? Is this of any use?		Absolutely YES. This helps the corporation remain competitive in the field.

Chapter XXII
Static and Dynamic Determinants of Earned Value Based Time Forecast Accuracy

Mario Vanhoucke
Ghent University, Belgium & Vlerick Leuven Gent Management School, Belgium

ABSTRACT

It is well-known that well managed and controlled projects are more likely to be delivered on time and within budget. The construction of a (resource-feasible) baseline schedule and the follow-up during execution are primary contributors to the success or failure of a project. Earned value management systems have been set up to deal with the complex task of controlling and adjusting the baseline project schedule during execution. Although earned value systems have been proven to provide reliable estimates for the follow-up of cost performance, they often fail to predict the total duration of the project. In this chapter, results of a large simulation study to evaluate the forecast accuracy of earned value based predictive metrics are presented. No detailed mathematical calculations are presented in the chapter, but instead an overview from a project life cycle point-of-view is presented. Details can be found at the end of the chapter (key terms and definitions) or in the references cited throughout this chapter.

INTRODUCTION

Typically, a project goes through a number of different phases, which is often referred to as the *project life cycle*. This cycle has been described extensively by many authors (see e.g.,the Project Management Body of Knowledge (PMBOK, 2004)) and consists of a project conception phase, a project definition phase, a phase in which the project has to be scheduled, the execution of the project, the project control phase which monitors the current performance of the project and the termination and/or evaluation of the project. Figure 1 displays a 6 phased example project life cycle that will be used throughout this chapter.

The simulation research study deals with the control phase of the project life cycle, and the corresponding performance measurement feedback loop (see figure 1) from project control to the planning/scheduling phase. More precisely, the focus is on a reactive scheduling and performance measurement system using Earned Value Management (EVM). Although EVM has been set up to follow-up both time and cost, the majority of the research has been focused on the cost aspect (for a general overview of earned value, the reader is referred to Fleming and Koppelman (2005)). Recently, different sources in literature show that the 'classic' earned value metrics fail in predicting the total project duration in an accurate way (see e.g., Lipke (2003)). In this chapter, the accuracy of various earned value predictive methods is tested to measure and forecast the final duration (i.e., time focus, not a cost focus) of a project in order to look for determinants that affect the accuracy of these predictive methods.

The outline of this chapter is given along the following lines. The section "An overview of predictive EVM measures" presents a brief review of three earned value based predictive methods that will be used in the simulation study. Section "Determinants of forecast accuracy" presents static (i.e., before the start of the project) as well as dynamic (i.e., during project execution) determinants that affect the forecast accuracy of the predictions. In section "simulation results", an objective comparison between the various state-of-the-art EVM based methods is presented that predict a project's final duration. Section "Earned schedule project tracking in software" briefly introduces the reader to a software tool that is able to rerun the simulation tests presented in the chapter. The final section ends with overall conclusions and highlights possible avenues for future research.

AN OVERVIEW OF PREDICTIVE EVM MEASURES

The terminology used throughout this chapter is based on the overview paper written by Vandevoorde and Vanhoucke (2006). Three project duration forecasting methods have been presented in literature, referred to in this chapter as the *Planned Value Method* (PVM, Anbari (2003)), the *Earned Duration Method* (EDM, Jacob (2003)) and the *Earned Schedule Method* (ESM, Lipke (2003)).

Both the planned value method and the earned duration method rely on the traditional schedule performance index $SPI = EV/PV$ used to measure the current time performance and to predict the project's final duration. However, the classic SPI indicator has been shown to report an unreliable performance estimate at the end of the project since it always tends to go to 1 (indicating a 100% perfect performance) when $EV = PV$ (which is always the case at the end of the project, regardless of its performance!). The earned schedule method has been developed to overcome this quirky behavior

Figure 1. The project life cycle (PLC) with a reactive scheduling approach

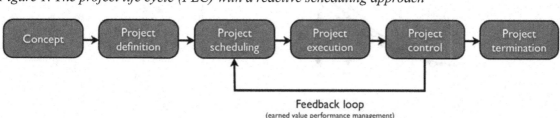

Feedback loop
(earned value performance management)

and has presented a novel SPI(t) indicator based on the earned schedule (ES) metric presented by Lipke (2003). The earned schedule metric measures the time point at which the earned value should have been accrued. It allows the calculation of the SPI(t) indicator as ES / AT which, unlike the SPI, measures the correct project status along the life of the project[1].

Table 1 gives a brief overview of the main characteristics of each predictive method and a short description of the formulas used to predict the final project duration. An extensive overview of the terminology is outside the scope of this chapter and can be found in Vandevoorde and Vanhoucke (2006). The abbreviation EAC(t) is

used to denote the final duration forecast of each method (Expected At Completion (Time dimension)) and each predictive method assumes that the future expected performance is in line with the current time performance (measured by the current SPI or SPI(t) trend). Details about all other abbreviations can be found at the end of the chapter (key terms and their definitions).

Figure 2 displays an example graph with the three input metrics, the planned value PV, the actual cost AC and the earned value EV, and shows the current status at the actual time point AT as well as the forecast project duration EAC(t) at the end of the project. The cumulative ES metric is displayed as ES < AT indicating a current project performance behind schedule at the current time

Table 1. The basic characteristics of the three EVM based time forecasting methods

EAC(t) method	Main characteristics	Formulas
Planned Value Method	Time is expressed in monetary terms and the SPI indicator shows a quirky behavior at the end of the project (always equal to 100%, even for late projects)	SPI = EV / PV and EAC(t) = PD / SPI
Earned Duration Method	Time is expressed in time units instead of monetary terms but the SPI indicator is still unreliable at the end of the project (always equal to 100%)	ED = AT * SPI and SPI = EV / PV EAC(t) = AT + (ED - AT) / SPI = max(PD,AT) / SPI
Earned Schedule Method	Time is expressed in time units and the new SPI(t) indicator reflects real time performance until the end of the project	ES is projection of EV on PV line SPI(t) = ES / AT EAC(t) = AT + (PD - ES) / SPI(t)

Figure 2. The three EVM metrics (PV, AC and EV) and the earned schedule (ES) for a project behind schedule at current time AT and the final project duration forecast EAC(t)

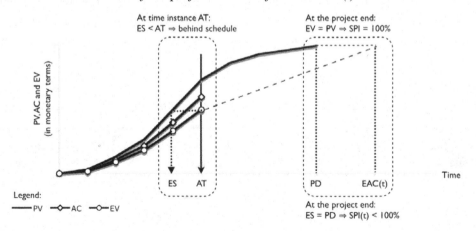

AT. The figure also shows that the SPI indicator will be equal to 100% at the project end, although the project is forecast to be late, while the SPI(t) indicator will report a value lower than 100%, expressing the real project delay.

DETERMINANTS OF FORECAST ACCURACY

In this section, the simulation results are analyzed in search of determinant factors that influence the accuracy of earned value based predictive methods to forecast a project's final duration. A distinction is made between *static* determinants, which can be calculated before the start of the project (i.e., during definition and scheduling phase) and *dynamic* determinants, which can by calculated during the project's execution phase. Figure 3 gives an overview of the four determinants along the life of the project that will be discussed in the next subsections.

At the beginning, in the so-called *conceptual phase*, an organization identifies the need for a project or receives a request from a customer.

In the *definition phase* the organization defines the project objectives, the project specifications and requirements and the organization of the whole project. In doing so, the organization decides on how it is going to achieve these objectives. Based on this information, the organization can start with the estimation of the duration and cost of the activities, the resource requirements and availabilities and the precedence relations between the activities. The next step is the *scheduling phase* in order to present a timetable for the project activities resulting in a (resource-feasible) baseline schedule. In the next section, static determinants (referring to periods before the start of the project, i.e., the definition and scheduling phase) will be discussed to search for factors that influence the predictive power of earned based methods to forecast a project's final duration during the execution phase.

During the *execution phase* and the *control phase* the project has to be executed, monitored and controlled to detect whether it is performed according to the existing schedule. If deviations occur, corrective actions have to be taken which results in a reactive feedback loop to bring the project back on track. The second subsection 3.2 refers to dynamic determinants during the life of the project that affect the quality of the earned value based predictive methods.

The *termination phase* involves the completion and a critical evaluation of the project. This

Figure 3. Static and dynamic determinants of EVM accuracy

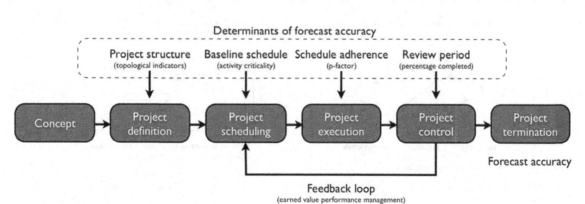

information can then be used during the project life cycle of future, similar projects since the specifications of a project, the estimates of the durations and costs and many things more are often determined on the basis of averages of past performances.

Static Determinants of Forecast Accuracy

The static determinants during the preparation phases of the project (i.e., definition and scheduling) have been displayed in Figure 4, and will be summarized along the following lines of the section.

Definition phase: The topological structure of a project network, defined by the number and distribution of the activities and their precedence relations, can be easily measured through the use of often simple mathematical calculations of indicators that distinguish between various structures

of project networks (see the information box). In doing so, these indicators serve as measures of diversity able to detect project networks that differ substantially from each other from a topological structure point-of-view. The use of topological network indicators is not new in literature. Research has revealed that the topological structure of a project network heavily influences the constructed schedule (Patterson, 1976), the risk for delays (Tavares et al., 1999), the criticality of a network (Tavares et al., 2004) or the computational effort an algorithm needs to schedule a project (Elmaghraby and Herroelen, 1980). The current chapter will test the influence of a serial/parallel topological indicator SP on the accuracy of EVM predictive methods. The indicator measures the closeness of a network to a complete serial or complete parallel network. Mathematical details are outside the scope of this chapter, and hence, the information box attached to this chapter serves as a non-exhaustive illustration of the intuitive meaning of four indicators (among which the SP

Figure 4. Static determinants of EVM accuracy during project definition and scheduling phase

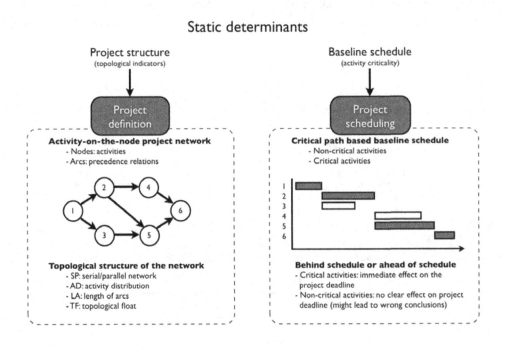

indicator) to measure the topological structure of a project network. The first hypothesis can be formulated as follows:

H₁: *The topological structure of a project network has an influence on the accuracy of EVM duration forecast measures.*

Scheduling phase: Project scheduling aims at the construction of a baseline schedule where each activity is sequenced subject to the precedence constraints (known as the critical path method) and possible resource constraints (known as the resource-constrained critical chain method). Traditional forward pass calculations result in the presence of a critical path (or alternatively, a critical chain when resources are present). The activity criticality heavily determines the accuracy of earned value based metrics, since changes (delays or accelerations) in critical activities have an immediate effect on the project duration, while changes in non-critical activities might have no effect at all on the final duration of the project. It is exactly for this very reason that Jacob and Kane (2004) argue that the well-known EVM performance measures (SPI, SPI(t), ...) are true indicators for project performance as long as they are used on the activity level, and not on the control account level or higher Work Breakdown Structure (WBS) levels. As an example, a delay in a non-critical activity might give a warning signal that the project is in danger, while there is no problem at all when the activity only consumes part of its slack. When the performance measures are calculated on the project level, this will lead to a false warning signal and hence, wrong corrective actions could be taken.

In the simulation study of this chapter, these performance measures are calculated on the project level, and not on the level of each individual activity, for very pragmatic reasons. It is recognized that effects (delays) of non-performing activities can be neutralized by well performing activities (ahead of schedule) at higher WBS levels,

which might result in masking potential problems, but it is common belief that this is the only approach that can be easily taken by practitioners (see e.g., the note given in the paper by Lipke et al., (2008)). The earned value metrics are set-up as early warning signals to detect in an easy and efficient way (i.e., at the cost account level, or even higher), rather than a simple replacement of the critical-path based scheduling tools. This early warning signal, if analyzed properly, defines the need to eventually "drill-down" into lower WBS levels. In conjunction with the project schedule, it allows to take corrective actions on those activities which are in trouble (especially those tasks which are on the critical path). The second hypothesis can be formulated as follows:

H₂: *The activity criticality reported by a project's baseline schedule has an influence on the accuracy of EVM duration forecast measures.*

Dynamic Determinants of Forecast Accuracy

Figure 5 gives an overview of the dynamic determinants of EVM forecast accuracy during the life of the project. The adherence of the original baseline schedule (execution phase) as well as the choice of the length of the review period between the start and the end of the project provide dynamic information about the accuracy of the project schedule performance. Details of these two sources of dynamic information parameters are described along the following lines.

Execution phase: During the execution of the project, the original activity timetable can be disrupted due to numerous reasons leading to a project execution that is not in congruence with the original baseline schedule. This lack of schedule adherence can be dynamically measured through the use of the p-factor initially proposed by Lipke (2004). The p-factor value is a simple measure based on the calculation of the traditional

Figure 5. Dynamic determinants of EVM accuracy during project execution and control phase

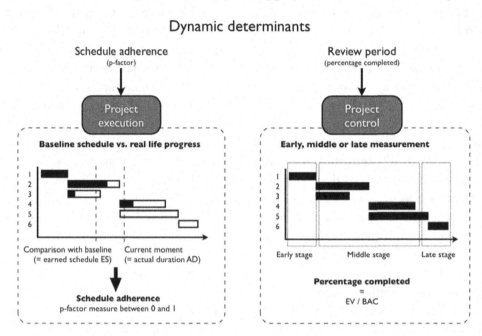

EVM metrics (AC, PV and EV) and measures the portion of the work that is done in congruence with the original baseline schedule. While the ES metric measures the current duration performance compared to the baseline schedule and indicates whether the project is ahead or behind schedule, the p-factor measures the performance of the project relative to this ES metric, and hence, measures the degree of schedule adherence given its current (good or bad) performance up-to-date.

The lack of schedule adherence can be contributed to numerous factors, among which activity overlapping (out-of-sequence execution of activities), deviations from the original baseline activity estimates (in terms of time and cost) or nonlinear EV accrue have been tested by Vanhoucke (2008). The third hypothesis tested in this chapter can be described as follows:

H₃: *The degree of schedule adherence has an influence on the accuracy of EVM duration forecast measures.*

Control phase: During the control phase, the decision maker (i.e., the project manager) has to determine the length of the review periods as well as the interval in which EVM based predictive metrics might produce reliable results. A crucial assumption of EVM based forecasting is that the prediction of the future is based on information on performance from the past, and hence, unreliable data from the past might give false predictions to the future. It is therefore of crucial importance to determine the time window in which the EVM metrics produce more or less reliable result. Undoubtedly, the accuracy of forecasts depends on the completion stage of the project. Obviously, the EVM metrics measured at the very beginning of the project are often very unreliable due to the lack of sufficient data to assume that future performance will follow the current performance up-to-date. Moreover, the classic schedule indicators (SV and SPI) have been shown to be unreliable as project duration forecasting indicators since they show a strange and unreliable behavior over the final third of the project. This observation has led to the development of the earned schedule concept by Lipke (2003) which behaves correctly over the complete project horizon.

For these reasons, the accuracy of index-based time forecasts is measured as a function of the completion stage of the project, given by the percentage completed EV / BAC. The average accuracy of these predictions made in the early, middle and late stages of the project execution phase is determined, both for projects ahead of schedule or for projects with a delay. The early stage is defined as the first 30% of the project completion, the middle stage is defined as the interval between 30% and 70% completion and the late stage equals the last 30% completion of the project. A last hypothesis can be written as follows:

H$_4$: *The earned schedule method is more reliable than the traditional earned value methods in all stages of the project.*

SIMULATION RESULTS

This section gives a summary of results of a large experiment using Monte Carlo simulation, initially setup by Vanhoucke and Vandevoorde (2007a,b, 2008). 4,100 project networks have been generated under a controlled design (i.e., under a controlled combination of topological structure indicator values (see information box) to guarantee project diversity). Each project network is linked to a baseline schedule constructed using the straightforward critical path based calculations. During the simulation, the generated execution phase differs from the original baseline schedule, leading to deviations between earned value and planned value. Each simulation run consists of 100 generated real-life executions, resulting in 4,100 * 100 = 410,000 simulated project executions. During project execution (i.e., simulation) the earned value metrics are calculated and the

final project duration EAC(t) is estimated at each review point in time. After each simulation, the real project duration is compared with its baseline planned duration, and the forecast accuracy is measured as the absolute or relative percentage deviation between all the predictions along the life of the project and the final project duration. The settings of each simulation run differ among the hypotheses and will be described for each individual hypothesis hereunder.

Hypothesis 1. Topological Network Structure

In order to test hypothesis 1, two types of simulations have been run: early project and late project simulations. Figure 6 displays the average percentage deviation between the real project duration and the duration of the baseline schedule, with positive (negative) values denoting an average overestimation (underestimation) of the EVM metrics along the life of the project.

The results have been split up for three different topological structures: a parallel, a serial/parallel and a serial network set containing networks with SP values of 0.2 (close to a complete parallel network), 0.5 (in-between a serial and parallel network) and 0.8 (close to a complete serial network). The results show that the topological structure of a project network has a clear influence on the accuracy of EVM duration forecast measures. The more the project resembles a serial network, the higher the accuracy of the predictive measures. The results also show that the earned schedule method produces more accurate forecasts than the planned value and earned duration methods.

Hypothesis 2. Activity Criticality

Figure 7 displays the relation between the average criticality of a project and the absolute forecast accuracy of the earned schedule method (ESM). Each project network has been simulated under the presence of random variation with a symmet-

Figure 6. The EVM forecast accuracy for projects with a different topological structure (H₁)

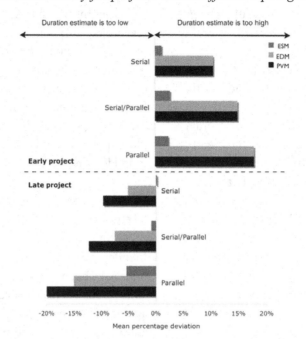

Figure 7. The influence of the average activity on the forecast accuracy (H₂)

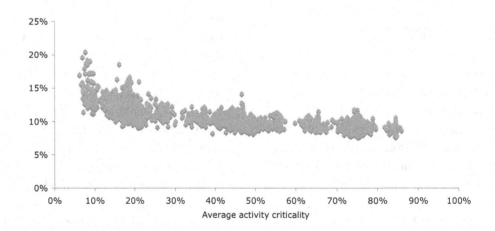

ric triangular distribution (i.e., with a minimum/maximum real duration restriction equal to 0.4/1.6 times the original baseline duration). Consequently, the simulations contain projects ahead of schedule (early projects), projects behind schedule (late projects) and projects on schedule, for which no distinction has been made in the figure.

Figure 7 clearly confirms the second hypothesis and shows that the average activity criticality has a clear influence on the accuracy of the predictive methods as follows: the higher the activity criticality, the better the accuracy of the forecasts. Obviously, a lower activity criticality means a lower probability of being on the critical path, and hence, the more likely a delay (within the activity slack) reported by the SPI indicators has no effect on the final project deadline. Consequently, the number of critical activities observed in the baseline schedule gives a first rough indication on the accuracy of the future EVM tracking performance measures.

Hypothesis 3. Schedule Adherence

While the constructed baseline schedule provides a static determinant of the future forecast accuracy before the start of the project, the evaluation of the accuracy of the forecasts during the execution of the project might provide a more dynamic measure of validity of the current performance measures and predictive metrics. Indeed, many things change during project execution (e.g., deviations in durations and costs, overlaps between activities, etc.) which not necessarily lead to a low project performance. These deviations result in a deviation from the original baseline schedule (referred to as a lack of schedule adherence) which might affect the quality of the forecasting measures.

The p-factor has originally been proposed by Lipke (2004) and further investigated by

Vanhoucke (2008) and measures the adherence of project execution to the baseline schedule relative to its current performance. A p-factor of 100% indicates perfect schedule adherence while lower p-values give indications of a certain degree of lack of schedule adherence. The simulation setting of this hypothesis equals the settings of hypothesis 2.

Figure 8 shows the relation between the average p-factor and the forecast accuracy of the earned schedule method. The scatterplot shows a negative relation between the average p-factor and the forecast accuracy, i.e., lower p-factor values denoting a certain lack of schedule adherence often result in less accurate forecasts. Hence, the p-factor, which can be dynamically measured during a review of the project (i.e., project tracking) based on the traditional EVM metrics, can be considered as a dynamic warning signal of the duration forecast accuracy.

Hypothesis 4. Stage of Completion

Hypothesis 4 tests the relevance of the new schedule performance indicator SPI(t) used in the earned schedule method. More precisely, the test

Figure 8. The influence of schedule adherence of the forecast accuracy (H_3)

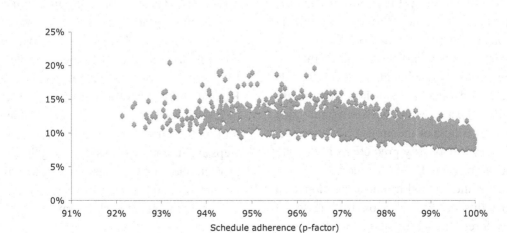

Schedule adherence (p-factor)

Figure 9. The EVM accuracy for early and late project along the early, middle and late execution stage (H_4)

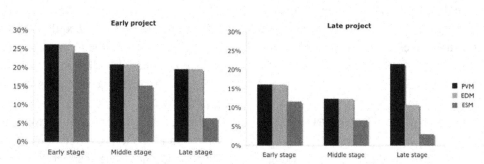

has been setup to investigate whether the more reliable behavior of the SPI(t) indicator (which, unlike the traditional SPI measures the real time performance until the end of the project) also leads to better time predictions during the different stages of the project. Figure 9 displays results for early/late project simulations similar to hypothesis 1 and reports results for the forecast accuracy for the early stage (i.e., percentage completed PC ≤ 30%), the middle stage (30% < PC < 70%) and the late stage (PC ≥ 70%).

The results from the figure confirm the previously found results and show that the earned schedule method outperforms, on average, the other forecasting methods in all stages of the project execution phase (i.e., confirmation of hypothesis 4). The results also illustrate the quirky behavior of the SPI indicator (used in the planned value and earned duration methods) at the late stage of the project. Indeed, the late stage forecast accuracy is much better for the ES method compared to the PV and ED methods. The results for the planned value method show that the use of the SPI indicator, which goes to a final value of 100%, regardless of the project performance, leads to very low quality predictions at the late stage of the project. The SPI(t) indicator of the earned schedule method has been developed to overcome this quirky behavior, leading to an improved forecast accuracy at the end of the proj-

ect. Obviously, measuring project performance and predicting future performance based on the resulting data leads to the lowest accuracy at the early stages of the project execution phase.

EARNED SCHEDULE PROJECT TRACKING IN SOFTWARE

ProTrack (acronym for Project Tracking software) is a novel software tool that combines project scheduling with earned value simulation and forecast accuracy measurement. The software combines project scheduling and tracking with earned value management and allows the calculation of a project's time duration forecast using the three EVM methods mentioned earlier. On top of that, a project generation, a simulation and a time forecasting engine can be added to randomly generate project networks and simulate the execution phase in order to test a baseline schedule's sensitivity (this is known as schedule risk analysis, see Hulett (1996)) as well as to measure the accuracy of EVM based predictive methods (which is the topic of the current chapter). The project tracking steps are automatically saved along the life of the project, allowing to measure the accuracy of the predictions and to review the current status of the project at a moment back in time.

The four hypotheses discussed in the current manuscript are built in the software and are accessible to the user through different optional engines. A *project generation engine* allows the creation of fictive projects with a controlled structure (hypothesis 1). A *simulation engine* allows the simulation of activity duration and cost variations and measures the criticality of individual project activities (hypothesis 2). Earned value/earned schedule metrics are automatically calculated during project tracking (the more traditional EVM methods as well as the earned schedule metrics including the p-factor) (hypothesis 3). The *time forecasting engine* measures the accuracy of project duration forecasts along various stages of the project life cycle (hypothesis 4). Details can be found on www.protrack.be.

CONCLUSION AND FUTURE RESEARCH AVENUES

The simulation study described in this chapter measures the accuracy of three forecasting methods based on the traditional earned value metrics to predict the final duration of a project.

Exhibit 1.

Information box:

Vanhoucke et al. (2008) have defined four indicators that measure the design and structure of an activity-on-the-node project network containing activities and precedences between these activities. These four indicators have been rescaled and lie between 0 and 1, inclusive, denoting the two extreme structures. The logic behind each indicator is straightforward, as follows.

- The serial/parallel indicator SP measures the closeness of a network to a serial or parallel network. More precisely, when SP = 0 then all activities are in parallel, and when SP = 1 then the project is represented by a complete serial network. Between these two extreme values, networks can be generated close to a serial or parallel network. The SP indicator determines the maximal number of 'levels' of the network, defined as the longest chain (in terms of the number of serial activities) in the network.

- The activity distribution indicator AD measures the distribution of project activities along the levels of the project, and hence, the 'width' of the network. When AD = 0, all levels contain a similar number of activities, and the number of activities are uniformly distributed over all levels. When AD = 1, there is one level with a maximal number of activities, and all other levels contain a single activity.

- The length of arcs indicator LA measures the length of each precedence relation (i, j) in the network as the difference between the level of the end activity j and the level of the start activity i. When LA equals 0, the network has many precedence relations between two activities on levels far from each other such that the activity can be shifted further in the network. When LA equals 1, many precedence relations have a length of one, resulting in activities with immediate successors on the next level of the network, and with little freedom to shift.

- The topological float indicator TF measures the topological float of a precedence relation as the number of levels each activity can shift without violating the maximal level of the network (as defined by SP). TF = 0 when the network structure is 100% dense and no activities can be shifted within its structure with a given SP value. A network with TF = 1 consists of one chain of activities without topological float (they define the maximal level and, consequently, the SP value) while the remaining activities have a maximal float value (which equals the maximal level, defined by SP, minus 1).

Mathematical details can be found in Vanhoucke et al. (2008). For a more detailed discussion of the network characteristics used in this chapter, the reader is referred to Vanhoucke and Vandevoorde (2007a,b).

The research questions in this study tackle both static and dynamic determinants that affect the quality of the forecast.

Our future research intentions are threefold. Our first intention is an ongoing search to real-life data to confirm or reject the simulated results and to detect which project characteristics/sectors/etc... drive these results. Secondly, we plan to continue the accuracy research and apply a more thorough statistical analysis to investigate whether CHAID regression tree analysis as well as statistical process control can contribute to the performance measurement of projects. Our last and obviously ultimate research intention is to use the information generated by the simulation experiments to improve the forecasting accuracy and to support the project manager in the interpretation of the data and the necessary corrective actions that should be taken in order to bring the project back on track. In this respect, the ProTrack software will allow the user to generate random project data and/or to measure the accuracy of the various duration predictive methods under various scenarios and hence, can be used as a tool to test and redo all experiments described in this chapter.

REFERENCES

Anbari, F. (2003). Earned Value Method and Extensions. *Project Management Journal, 34*(4), 12-23.

Elmaghraby, S. E., & Herroelen, W. S. (1980). On the measurement of complexity in activity networks. *European Journal of Operational Research, 5,* 223-234.

Fleming, Q., & Koppelman, J. (2005). *Earned value project management,* 3rd Edition. Newtowns Square, PA: Project Management Institute.

Hulett, D. T. (1996). Schedule risk analysis simplified. *PM Network,* (pp. 23-30).

Jacob, D. (2003). Forecasting Project Schedule Completion with Earned Value Metrics. *The Measurable News, 1,* 7-9.

Jacob, D. S., & Kane, M. (2004). Forecasting schedule completion using earned value metrics revisited. *The Measurable News, 1,* 11-17.

Lipke, W. (2003). Schedule is different. *The Measurable News,* (pp. 31-34).

Lipke, W. (2004). Connecting earned value to the schedule. *The Measurable News, Winter, 1,* 6-16.

Lipke, W., Zwikael, O., Henderson, K., & Anbari, F. (2008). Prediction of project outcome: the application of statistical methods to earned value management and earned schedule performance indexes. *To appear in the International Journal of Project Management.*

Patterson, J. H. (1976). Project scheduling: the effects of problem structure on heuristic scheduling. *Naval Research Logistics, 23,* 95-123.

PMBOK (2004). *A Guide to the Project Management Body of Knowledge,* 3rd Edition. Newtown Square, PA: Project Management Institute, Inc.

Tavares, L. V., Ferreira, J. A., & Coelho, J. S. (1999). The risk of delay of a project in terms of the morphology of its network. *European Journal of Operational Research, 119,* 510-537.

Tavares, L. V., Ferreira, J. A., & Coelho, J. S. (2004). A surrogate indicator of criticality for stochastic networks. *International Transactions in Operational Research, 11,* 193-202.

Vandevoorde, S., & Vanhoucke, M. (2006). A comparison of different project duration forecasting methods using earned value metrics. *International Journal of Project Management, 24,* 289-302.

Vanhoucke, M. S. (2008). *The effect of rework in a project's activities on the forecasting accuracy of earned value metrics.* Working paper, under review.

Vanhoucke, M., Coelho, J. S., Debels, D., Maenhout, B., & Tavares, L. V. (2008). An evaluation of the adequacy of project network generators with systematically sampled networks. *European Journal of Operational Research, 187*, 511-524.

Vanhoucke, M., & Vandevoorde, S. (2007a). A simulation and evaluation of earned value metrics to forecast the project duration. *Journal of the Operational Research Society, 58*, 1361–1374.

Vanhoucke, M., & Vandevoorde, S. (2007b). Measuring the accuracy of earned value/earned schedule forecasting predictors. *The Measurable News*, Winter, (pp. 26-30).

Vanhoucke, M., & Vandevoorde, S. (2008). Earned value forecast accuracy and activity criticality. *The Measurable News*, Summer, (pp. 13-16).

KEY TERMS AND DEFINITIONS

Earned value key parameters:

PV: Planned Value (resulting from the baseline schedule)

EV: Earned Value

AC: Actual Cost

AT: Actual Time (i.e., the current time instance during project tracking)
= often referred to as actual duration

ES: Earned Schedule
$= t + (EV - PV_t) / (PV_{t+1} - PV_t)$ with t the time point where $EV \geq PV_t$ and $EV < PV_{t+1}$

ED: Earned Duration (= AT * SPI)

Earned value performance measures:

SV: Schedule Variance (PV - EV) expressed in monetary terms

SPI: Schedule Performance Index (PV / EV) used in the traditional EVM calculations

SV(t): Alternative Schedule Variance (ES - AT) expressed in a time dimension

SPI(t): Alternative Schedule Performance Index (ES / AT)

CPI: Cost Performance Index

Earned value predictive methods:

EAC(t): Expected Time At Completion (i.e., a project's duration forecast)

PVM: Planned Value Method

EDM: Earned Duration Method

ESM: Earned Schedule Method

Schedule adherence:

p-factor: dynamically measures to what degree the EV is accrued according to the baseline schedule
$= sum_i(PV_{i,ES}, EV_{i,AT}) / sum_i(PV_{i,ES})$ with sum_i the sum over all activities i.

ENDNOTE

[1] Since EV equals PV at the end of the project, the SPI indicator is always equal to 100%, regardless of the final status (ahead or late) of the project. Since ES is always equal to the planned duration PD at the end of the project, the SPI(t) indicator measures the real status of the project (ahead of schedule (AT < ES and SPI(t) > 100%), on schedule (AT = ES and SPI(t) = 100%) or behind schedule (AT > ES and SPI(t) < 100%)).

Section V
Case Study Examples in Technology Project Management, Planning, and Operations

Chapter XXIII
Technology Exploration:
From Ideas to New Services

Michele De Lorenzi
ETH Zurich, Switzerland

ABSTRACT

This chapter presents a technology exploration process designed to support service innovation for information and communication technologies in a university environment. The mission of the technology exploration is to highlight possible applications of new technologies on the basis of prototypes which, following an evaluation phase, are used to develop new services. The exploration process is composed of several stages. In the first stage a number of proposals are generated beginning with the analysis of users' expectations, best practices and technology developments. In the next stage prototypes for selected proposals are implemented. Only the most viable prototypes are then further developed to maturity, providing a reliable service. This chapter is based on the experience gathered by our team over a period of 18 months. During this period six prototypes have been developed, three of which have been further developed to full maturity. The introduction of a voice over IP service for all the university members illustrates the exploration process.

INTRODUCTION

Rapid development of information and communication technologies has a direct impact on all areas of education and research. The amount of knowledge and information that is available is growing exponentially. Radically new models of cooperation, networking and knowledge exchange are emerging. A well developed and solid Information and Communication Technology (ICT) infrastructure is thus indispensable to support education and research and has become an increasingly important advantage in the global competition among universities.

The presented technology exploration process was part of ETH World (http://www.ethworld.ethz. ch), a program for the development and introduction of technologies to enhance communication and cooperation at ETH Zurich. ETH World was responsible for the evaluation of technological, pedagogical and organizational ICT developments inside and outside the University and for the support testing of promising new technological developments within ETH Zurich. Especially its role was to take the lead in identifying potentially new technological developments. ETH World ran for six years from 2000 to 2005.

The initial innovation process at ETH World was based on a bottom-up approach. On a regular basis ETH World requested proposals. All ETH Zurich units could propose projects to be implemented. After about three years an external peer review (Bates, Bobrow, Ernst, & Hutch, 2003) pointed out some shortcomings of this bottom-up process:

While producing many innovative projects and tools, a number of these projects have been too inward-looking and were not always aware of relevant developments elsewhere. [...] It is important to differentiate between technology invention/ development and innovation in teaching. The attraction of inventing/developing technology inside ETH has obviously been a strong pull on many of ETH's engineering spirits but may have distracted from a closer look at technological developments and models of good technology-based teaching practice outside ETH. For instance, it is just as innovative to take already existing technological products and apply them in a new way to teaching and learning. This is less of an economic risk than re-inventing the wheel and developing new technology, which in most cases will require substantial investment and commercial partners if it is to be successful.

On the basis of these findings, the peers proposed the following measures:

ETH World should be encouraged to continuously evaluate technological, pedagogical and organizational ICT developments outside the institution while supporting the testing of promising developments within ETH.

ETH World should take a leadership role in identifying potentially new technological developments in broad consultation across the university. For example, regarding future calls for proposals, ETH World should include a pre-proposal phase to be able to prioritize two or three areas of technological developments.

ETH World should strengthen the external focus of the ETH World program and the individual projects through partnerships, cooperation, technology exploration and transfer.

The management of ETH World reacted to the suggestions with the creation of a new position for technology exploration. In this chapter we summarize the experience we have gained in this position in the last 18 months of the duration of ETH World.

Because of the limited available time, we decided to pursue a very pragmatic approach for the definition of the exploration process and in the daily work. The goal was to come up with results within few months. The resulting process for technology exploration has proved itself and can be used as starting point for similar initiatives.

TECHNOLOGY EXPLORATION

The mission of the *Technology Exploration* is to verify that a given prototype will fulfill its intended task as a new technological application when fully developed. Following an evaluation phase the prototypes are used as a starting point for the development of new services. The exploration process is represented in Figure 1 like a funnel (from left to right). In the *Early Stage* a number of proposals are generated starting from the analysis of the user expectations, best practices and the technology developments. In the *Prototype Stage* prototypes are created for selected proposals. These prototypes are evaluated again and only the promising ones are then further developed to full services. The transition from the technology exploration to the service provision is supported by a *Transformation* step.

The whole process is described in the following sections, starting from the early stage and ending with the final transformation.

The Early Stage

The goal of the *Early Stage* is to develop proposals for new services. The integration of users, the analysis of best practices and the monitoring of technologies have demonstrated to be an important starting point in the search for new ideas.

User Integration

In order to obtain an added value in the process of technology exploration, it is important to un-

derstand the requirements of the university users. This is the task of the *User Integration* process, which is conducted by interviewing representatives of different university stakeholders. The analysis of the business and IT strategies of the university can also be understood as being part of the User Integration process.

Best Practices

The evaluation of *Best Practices* provides an insight into the services of other universities, and highlights currently used technologies and trends. Furthermore, external experience is used to gain insights into risks and opportunities of different technologies and services.

At ETH World we organized an excursion (De Lorenzi, Report – ETH Zurich Study Tour, 2004) of 15 representatives from different units of ETH Zurich (central services and research departments) to USA and Canada. During the excursion we visited a variety of organizations: universities, foundations, start-ups and established companies.

Figure 1. The technology exploration process

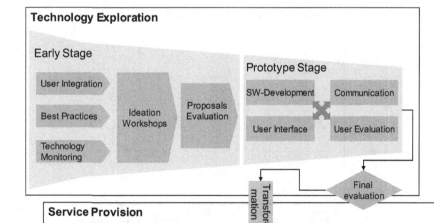

Technology Monitoring

During the *Technology Monitoring* phase relevant technologies are identified to support innovative services. Technology Monitoring can gather a large amount of information from sources like technical journals, conferences, Web searches or personal relationships with R&D departments.

A first selection is drawn from the large number of available technologies and their varied applications by checking their visibility in the marketplace. The typical visibility pattern of a technology in the marketplace is called "Hype-Cycle" (Gartner, 2008) and is represented in Figure 2. The phase relevant for the technology exploration is highlighted in grey. The technology is not very young anymore and has already reached some technical maturity. At the same time the technology is not yet part of a product which can be bought "off-the-shelf".

Ideation Workshops

Proposals for new services are developed in *Ideation Workshops*. In these workshops the user needs, the best practices and the available technologies are analyzed. The goal is to develop innovative services which could be useful for some university members.

At ETH World we had workshops in small informal work groups. We used "Wikis" to document and work on the proposals. The refinement of a proposal could last several months. During this phase small prototypes were developed to test the new technologies in a real environment with real users. This made it possible to continue the discussion and to formulate more precise proposals.

Evaluation of the Proposals

In the *Proposals Evaluation* phase certain proposals are selected to be further advanced into prototypes. The evaluation is based on formal and non formal criteria like:

- The proposal must provide an added value for the end user, i.e., it should address an existing requirement or offer new applications.
- The new service should be relevant for a large number of people in the university.

Figure 2. Technologies relevant to the exploration process according to the Hype Cycle curve

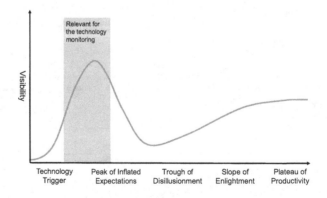

- The used technologies should be mature enough to be deployed in an operational system within one or two years. The technology exploration process ought to contribute to the development of a new technology but should not aim to create new technologies. This remark is especially relevant in a university where members are expected to develop new technologies as part of their research projects.
- Finally the exploration team must have adequate skills and interests to develop a prototype (hardware and software).

A prototype should only start once the support of one or more external project partners can be secured. These partners would provide the operational service in case of success. They should have a positive attitude towards the project, will serve as sparring-partners, and will be invited to special project meetings. However, no additional funding on their behalf is to be expected.

The requirements for the prototypes and their potential applications are defined together with the project partners. These specifications are non-binding. New findings during the development of a prototype can lead to modifications of the requirements and of the use cases.

The Prototype Stage

During the *Prototype Stage* the proposals are developed into prototypes. The final decision on whether to introduce a new service will be based on the experience gained in this process. The prototype should provide a good insight into the future service: functionality, user interfaces, technical architecture. The goal of the prototype is not only to create an application. It is also crucial to advance the initial idea with all of its different opportunities. The prototype is best developed by an interdisciplinary team, based on a variety of different skills.

For the development of the prototype the functional specification and the schedule are only roughly defined. It is important to maintain flexibility to assure that unexpected aspects are fully analyzed and advanced further. The implementation and execution of a prototype should not exceed 6 months of work by one full time equivalent.

In the following subsections the most important processes of the Prototype Stage are described. All processes should be addressed in parallel and should interact with each other.

Software and Hardware Development

The technical infrastructure of the prototype is created with the process *Software and Hardware Development*. Concerns regarding operations and the embedding of the prototype into the existing infrastructure of the university have to be addressed already in the development phase of the prototypes. This can be crucial for the introduction of a new service, i.e., the integration of the new service into the existing user identification and authorization infrastructure.

User Interface

All elements which are related to the perception of the service are developed as part of the *User Interface* process, like an appealing name, a logo, a graphical user interface or Web pages. The goal is to provide a most realistic impression of the new service.

The existing guidelines for Corporate Design, Web-Design, Accessibility, Internet rules and Corporate Language of the university should be obeyed already in the prototype phase.

Communication

Although the prototype will not necessarily lead to a new service, the results of the prototype should be communicated within the university. This can be useful for different purposes:

- Inform the members of the university about new trends and opportunities for new services.
- Increase the attention and create a dialogue on new technologies and their possible impact on teaching, research and infrastructure services.
- Inform about the technology exploration process.

A communication concept coordinating the work of different project partners and specifying, what and when has to be communicated, ought to be defined as well. The concept can be extended to support a seamless communication in case the prototype is developed to an operational service.

User Evaluation

The success or failure of a new service is tightly tied to the reaction of the end users. A prototype offers a great opportunity to let users to evaluate the proposed service. As a basis for the evaluation we propose to use the reference model depicted in Figure 3.

According to this model the users are asked to name their requirements and expectations of the new service (1). The users interact with the prototype and have a first impression of the new service (2). Furthermore, the users are asked about their experience (3) and finally, the initial expectations are compared to the provided services (4).

Final Evaluation

At the end of the technology exploration process, the project team analyses the results of the prototype in a *Final Evaluation*. The key findings are summarized in a final report: Service overview, description of the prototype, results of the user evaluation and final recommendations. All interest groups within the university get a copy of the report. The results may also be presented to the general public or the media.

The final report should serve as a basis for the discussion with potential service providers. In the discussion it is decided whether to continue the development of a new service or not. At this stage it is important to have the liberty not to implement the proposed service. The prototype ought to show where the limits of the initial proposal are and whether it is worth to invest further resources in the development of a new service.

Figure 3. Framework for the user evaluation

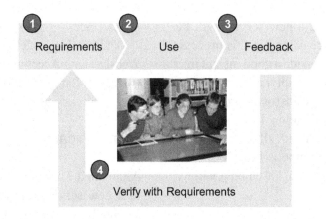

Transformation, Service Development and Service Operation

The *Transformation* step is only started if a sponsor for the new service is found willing to introduce the new service, starting with the prototype. The term "transformation" suggests that the results of the exploration process are used as a guideline to specify the new service. All aspects may be reconsidered based on the learned lessons during the prototype phase. The outcome of the transformation process is typically a detailed specification of the new service. During this step the exploration team may consult the future service provider.

The new service provider is responsible for the *Service Development* and the subsequent *Service Operation* processes. The exploration team may be further involved in the knowledge transfer as external project advisor.

RESULTS OF THE TECHNOLOGY EXPLORATION AT ETH WORLD

In the context of the technology exploration at ETH World we have been able to develop the following prototypes:

- "sipETH" (De Lorenzi & Baur, 2005) – A prototype for a service, which allows all members of the university to communicate via audio, video and instant messaging. This service is based on the Session Initiation Protocol (SIP). The central IT services of ETH Zurich decided to develop sipETH into a full service called PolyPhone (http://www. polyphone.ethz.ch). In an industry cooperation ETH Zurich and Logitech (Fremont USA) also developed a SIP software client for PolyPhone. In addition we participated in the SIP.edu (http:// www.Internet2.edu/ sip.edu) initiative: ETH Zurich has been the fifth university worldwide that made the existing campus PBX accessible via SIP. In the next chapter we will describe in more detail the exploration process for PolyPhone as a case study.

- "Webcam Platform" (http://www.webcam. ethz.ch) – A prototype for a platform for the management of Webcams deployed at ETH Zurich. The platform provides useful functions for the provider and the end users, like directories of the available cameras, creation of fast motions or making a camera accessible to selected users. Starting from the prototype, the corporate communications division of ETH Zurich developed a new service for the university. All persons using a Webcam on the campus can now register their cam on the platform.

- "blogs" (http://www.blogs.ethz.ch) – Prototype of a Web log (blog) application with the goal to support asynchronous communication and the building of communities within the university. On the basis of the gained experience, the didactic center of ETH Zurich created a service based on a WordPress (http://wordpress.org/).

- "tRoom: Collaboration Space for Teams" (De Lorenzi & Wunden, 2006) – tRoom supports small teams that work together while using laptops. The prototype allows different users in the same room to display their screen content on a common screen or beamer. The video content is transmitted wirelessly and it is very easy to switch between different laptops.

- "Web Services" (De Lorenzi & Baur, 2005) – Prototype of a UDDI server (Universal Description Discovery and Integration) for the management of Web services at ETH Zurich. The goal is to make a list of the Web services at ETH Zurich available and to support the reuse of software components.

- "Internet live broadcast of the Venus transit in front of the Sun" (De Lorenzi & Baur, 2004) – An interdisciplinary project with the goal to retransmit live over Internet the astronomical event of the planet Venus transiting in front of the Sun and to show the work of a research group during this event. More than 40'000 persons accessed the live stream within a few hours (http://helene. ethz.ch/archive/venustransit/live.html).

The first three of these six projects have led to the development of a new service. This is equivalent to a success rate of 50%, i.e., a new service every six months.

There are several reasons why the last three prototypes did not lead to a new service. Even if the interest in tRoom was high, no interested partner could be found to develop and deploy an operational service. The Web Services prototype demonstrated that this service first had to be addressed at the IT architecture level and only later a new service could be introduced. The broadcast of the Venus transit was a show case demonstrating how a natural phenomenon can be broadcasted to a broader public. The creation of a new service was not addressed.

In addition to the realized prototypes, we also created further ideas for new services which could be addressed when additional resources are available and a project sponsor can be found.

The process of the technology exploration will be described in more detail by the prototype for PolyPhone.

CASE STUDY: POLYPHONE

PolyPhone is the result of a close cooperation between ETH World and the division of computing services of ETH Zurich. ETH World explored how new technologies for audio and video communication over the Internet can support the cooperation and the communication across the university. The division of computing services developed a new service, starting with the results of the Technology Exploration process.

The processes of the Technology Exploration and the Service Development are represented in Figure 4. It took two years from the start of the exploration process in May 2004 until the final deployment of PolyPhone: 6 month for the technology exploration and additional 18 months to develop the operational service.

The Technology Exploration

The Early Stage

In the mid of 2004 ETH World analyzed the technology trends in the telecommunication domain. In particular there were a lot of activities in the field of the voice communication over the Internet, Voice over IP (VoIP). At the same time a growing number of broadband connections for private users were observed, both for students and the employees of ETH Zurich. As a consequence, an ever increasing number of users was always online, transferring large amounts of data. For the first time it was possible to offer telecommunication services over the Internet in sufficient quality.

During the Early Stage we analyzed the needs of the university by interviewing the computing services of ETH Zurich. As the operator of the existing telephone infrastructure, they were interested to find out what new telecommunication services they could offer to the university: not only as a replacement of the existing infrastructure but as new services offering additional qualities.

As a result of the early stage, ETH World and the computing services together defined the goal of the prototype as to verify how the communication inside the ETH community could be improved by using the SIP technology. The end-users should be able, independent of their location (at one of the two ETH campuses, at home, on the way, at another university) to easily communicate with each other. Finally, the new technology had to run as an integral part of the existing telephone infrastructure.

Figure 4. The milestones of the Technology Exploration process for PolyPhone

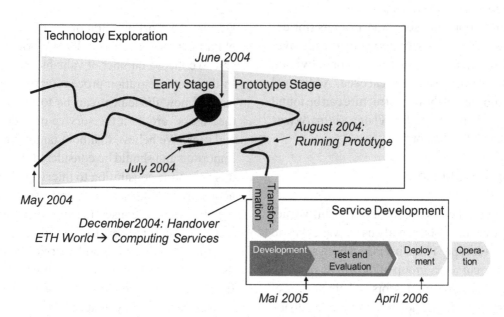

The Prototype Stage

The prototype for PolyPhone has been developed in the second half of 2004. The prototype was built on a flexible infrastructure allowing the testing of different usages. In a first step the scope of the new services has been iteratively refined and implemented. In the previous figure this phase is represented by a curve moving between the early stage and the prototype phase. This is to express the seeking and refinement of the initial project idea.

Already in the prototype stage we tried to get an idea how the final service could look like. So we defined a temporary name for the service and a logo. We created Web pages with information about the service and with the necessary masks to control the application. We also paid attention to operational aspects like the integration in the central user authorization system of ETH Zurich.

Service Development

By the end of 2004 we summarized the results of the exploration project in a vision for a new service. In a further step, the telephony group of the department of computing services transferred this vision into a corresponding service. The exploration team supported this process as an external advisor to ensure the continuity of the project.

Development

The infrastructure of PolyPhone has been developed during the year 2005. Special attention was given to the integration of PolyPhone into the existing infrastructure, and in increasing the number of users which could be supported. In addition, the availability of the service has been increased by the addition of redundant systems. Most of the infrastructure has been built on an open platform. At the center of this infrastructure is the "SIP Proxy Registrar", where all the registered users are managed. On the basis of this information, all user authorizations (for example if they can make international calls over the traditional phone infrastructure) or individual phone forwarding rules are checked. Additional information about the infrastructure can be found on the Web pages of PolyPhone (http://www.polyphone.ethz.ch/about).

Test and Evaluation

In parallel to the development of the infrastructure, a group of about 70 early users was asked to test the prototype. These users had been selected from different users group of the university, like students, assistants, professors and employees of the internal services. The users provided feedback about the acceptance of the service, reported on system errors and provided input for additional requirements.

The early users were also asked to participate in an evaluation of PolyPhone. The goal was to obtain their opinion on the new system and to assess the service.

Deployment

In April 2006 PolyPhone was finally introduced at ETH Zurich as a new service for all members of the university. For the introduction a communication plan had been defined. A press release has been sent to the media, an article about PolyPhone was been published via the internal newspaper of ETH Zurich in printed and online form. The echo to the information campaign has been amazing: A number of print-media in Switzerland and in Germany reported on the service. Two weeks after the kick off more than 1'600 persons (of a community of about 18'000 persons) registered for PolyPhone.

LESSONS LEARNED

Despite the short duration of the technology exploration process as part of ETH World, we were able to collect a number of valuable experiences. In the user integration process (early stage), we learned how difficult it can be to identify who the "users" are. Is it the service provider or the end user? We believe that both target groups are important and should be considered. In practice, it is very time consuming to interview heterogeneous groups like students, professors and staff members. As a consequence, we preferred to interview only the service providers, assuming that they already had a good overview of the end-user needs. In any case, the end users have to be involved during the User Evaluation process. A service cannot be evaluated just by the service providers themselves.

During the Ideation Workshop and the Proposals Evaluation phases we were missing reference goals. This would have helped us in setting priorities and focus on our work. As a consequence, we initiated a project to develop an institutional strategy for the use of Information and Communication Technologies (ICT) in education, research and services at the ETH Zurich.

The support of the "Transformation" and the "Service Development Processes" has been an important duty of the exploration team. This task guaranteed the knowledge transfer from the exploration phase. For the members of the exploration team, this task created new interesting professional perspectives, possibly being able to secure a position in the team of the service provider. Or vice versa: Employees from service provision groups could change for a sabbatical into the exploration team.

To conduct the technology exploration, ETH World employed a team of two full time equivalents over 18 months. Three new services were introduced. We supervised three term projects and half a dozen of external presentations about our work and the results of the exploration process.

Thanks to the projects "PolyPhone" and "Venus transit" we achieved large media coverage.

The initial goal to generate a new service out of the exploration process every six months was met. Since in the exploration phase the vision and the range of required services were iteratively verified and adjusted, the resulting project proposals were easily and clearly expressed. The exploration process also reduced the project risks because each proposal was evaluated twice, at the end of the Early Stage (Proposals Evaluation) and in the Prototype Stage (Final Evaluation). The user evaluation has also helped as well as an external review of the project.

REFERENCES

Bates, A. W., Bobrow, D. G., Ernst, R., & Hutch, D. (2003). *Intermediate evaluation of the ETH world programme: Report of the peer review committee submitted to the executive board of the ETH Zurich.*

De Lorenzi, M. (2004). *Report – ETH Zurich Study Tour.* Retrieved from ETH World Web site: http://www.ethworld.ethz.ch/events/explore/study_trip/Report_Study_Tour_ETHZ_050207.pdf

De Lorenzi, M., & Baur, M. (2004). *Live broadcasts.* Retrieved from ETH World Web pages: http://www.ethworld.ethz.ch/technologies/live_broadcast

De Lorenzi, M., & Baur, M. (2005). *sipETH: Internet telefonie for the ETH Zurich.* Retrieved from ETH World: http://www.ethworld.ethz.ch/technologies/sipeth

De Lorenzi, M., & Baur, M. (2005). *Web Services an der ETH Zürich.* Retrieved from ETH World Web pages: http://www.ethworld.ethz.ch/technologies/web_services

De Lorenzi, M., & Wunden, T. (2006). *tRoom - Collaboration space for team.* Retrieved from ETH World Web Pages: http://www.ethworld.ethz.ch/technologies/tRoom

Gartner. (2008). *Understanding hype cycles.* Retrieved from Gartner Web pages: http://www.gartner.com/pages/story.php.id.8795.s.8.jsp

KEY TERMS AND DEFINITIONS

Early Stage of the Technology Exploration Process: The Early Stage of the Exploration Process develops and assess proposals for new services starting from the analysis of best practices, the monitoring of technologies and by integrating the users in the development of innovative applications for the new technologies.

Prototype Stage (of the Technology Exploration Process): The goal of the Prototype Stage is to develop a service proposal and to verify if the new service has a real chance to be adopted by the organization. The prototype should provide a good insight into the future service: functionality, user interfaces, and technical architecture.

Technology Exploration: The ultimate goal of the *Technology Exploration* is to develop innovative services based on new information and communication technologies. The traditional service development starts from the user requirements to create new services. The Technology Exploration starts from new available technologies and invites the users to create ideas for innovative services

Technology Exploration Process: The Technology Exploration Process defines the steps leading from the monitoring of new technologies to the development of a new service.

Technology Monitoring: During the *Technology Monitoring* relevant technologies are identified to support innovative services. Technology Monitoring can gather a large amount of information from sources like technical journals, conferences, Web searches or personal relationships with R&D departments.

Transformation (of a Prototype): In the *Transformation* step the results of the exploration process are used as a guideline to specify a new service. All aspects may be reconsidered based on the lessons learned during the prototype phase. The outcome of the transformation process is typically a detailed specification of the new service.

Chapter XXIV
Planning for Technology Integration

Henryk R. Marcinkiewicz
Aramco Services Company, USA

ABSTRACT

Three models structure the planning for technology integration into instruction. Institutional needs are assessed for three dimensions suggested in Gilbert's, "Model of Human Competence." The areas needing addressing are typically within instruction; therefore, the process steps of a generic instructional design model are used. Within designing for instruction, Bransford's, "variables affecting learning," are the focal points organizational planners need to consider in planning instruction. Instruction is framed as "faculty-as-learner centered instruction." The variables are also a significant aspect of the content of instruction for faculty because faculty will use them in planning their own instruction integrated with technology.

INTRODUCTION

The work of integrating technology into instruction at an institution may be daunting, particularly in the absence of a plan. To support technology integration, a plan is described with the goal of competence in the area of teaching. The plan calls for assessing the co-requisite conditions of an institution and their influences on the goal. The underlying model is Thomas Gilbert's model of human competence (Chevalier, 2003; Gilbert, 1978). The institutional needs assessment is combined with the general process of an instructional design model. The latter is used because a typical institutional condition needing intervention is the need for instruction among personnel. In practice, the entire process is best organized as a series of

questions. The discussion is outlined according to that logic. The process flow will be familiar to instructional technologists and organizational planners and it will appeal to their sense of a systemic approach to problem solution.

In the first part of the plan, technology is identified, and needs are assessed. The next two steps are instructional planning based on three reasons. First, most work in technology integration has a training need—personnel need to understand institutional information, or how, why, and when to use the target technology. Second, instructional planning models may be fairly wide-ranging and are flexible enough to apply to organizational systems—they work well for that purpose. Third, it is useful to consider faculty as the benefactors of learner-centered instruction, it may be considered as, "faculty-as-learner centered instruction."

There are several strategies for the integration process that are based on research in the adoption of instructional technology. They are meeting subjective norms, which is akin to peer pressure, and the management of institutional expectations. The dimension for deciding the use of either strategy is the relative novelty or newness of a technology to an institution.

In summary, the process is workable, practical, and effective; that is, if followed it does help one to achieve technology integration at an institution. This ought to offer a strong measure of reassurance to those professionals undertaking the task. The challenge, as often happens, is in the actual implementation.

THE PLAN

Which technology is needed?

This is a wide-ranging question with conceptual as well as practical answers. For the purposes of institutional planning, the latter are more important; there are several notions of what technology is and which technology is wanted. Begin by considering the materials, tools, and processes that are useful for instruction. The technology used in instruction typically refers to computers or the software applications for computers.

The kinds of technology most institutional planners deal with include communication systems such as e-mail or messaging, and software applications for administrative use including student auditing systems. They also include instructional technologies that encompass software and hardware to facilitate learning. These include online learning management systems, individual audio devices, and online virtual worlds.

The purpose of identifying technology is to focus your work and to select that with which you will work. The result of this process is an answer to the question of which technology you want faculty to use in instruction. You know what is needed in general. Specify what is needed and set that as a standard expectation.

Part A: Assess the Institution Conceptual Model

1. Define Competence

A standard expectation has been established that faculty will use the given technology. (The working example in this chapter will be that faculty will use a learning management system (LMS) in instruction.) Express the expectation into operational terms—faculty will be competent in integrating an LMS in instruction. There may be other expectations, but for whichever expectation is decided, the criterion for it is competence. Identifying the expectation thus allows for using Thomas Gilbert's model of human competence to structure this phase of the overall process (Chevalier, 2003; Gilbert, 1978).

The model suggests three co-requisite dimensions addressed from two areas of the institution. The dimensions are information, instrumentation, and motivation. The two areas are the external and the internal. The external refers to the institution. Typically, it includes the administration and its

Exhibit 1. Gilbert's model of human competence

Environmental Supports (Institution)	Information	Instrumentation	Incentives
Repertory of Behavior (Faculty Member)	Knowledge	Capacity	Motives

members who support and provide the conditions for the success of an individual faculty member. Because it does not include faculty, it is external to the individual faculty member. The internal refers to individual faculty members. The emphases for the dimensions vary as appropriate for each area and are depicted in the matrix shown in Exhibit 1.

For the external area—Information:
Information refers to the expectations of the institution expressed as vision, mission, and goal statements and includes institutional philosophy. It is the body of information about the institution that must be communicated to employees generally and specifically. It is likely that some parts will differ by institutional organization. There may be different expectations for faculty than there are for residential life staff, for example. The role of the external area including all levels of administration and support is to communicate the expectations for competence towards the faculty. This means that the provost as well as a librarian or a student activities staff member know that faculty are expected to use an LMS in instruction.

For the internal area—Knowledge:
To achieve competence in using an LMS for instruction, a faculty member must be aware of the information from the institution. A faculty member must also know, understand, and especially, accept the expectations for competence. The three dimensions are co-requisite meaning that all of them must be successful in order to

achieve the goal of competence for individuals. It is obvious how if a faculty member does not accept the expectation, meeting competence is thwarted.

For the external area—Instrumentation:
Instrumentation refers to the tools and resources necessary to complete the competent behavior. For LMS use it includes computers, connection to a network, LMS software, support software, etc. The responsibilities of the institution are to ensure that the necessary resources are available and functioning at the expected level of quality, the availability is communicated, and use of the resources is possible. The institution is also responsible for providing education and training to learn how to use the technological resources.

For the internal area—Capacity:
Instrumentation for a faculty member refers to the ability or capacity, the interest or inclination towards, the scheduling allowing, or the selection of personnel for using LMS technology. Levels of individual instrumentation vary and the degrees of variation determine the quantity and quality of instruction or other remediation. Faculty may understand how to use LMS technology but do not have a preference for it, or vice versa.

For the external area—Motivation—Incentive:
The provision of incentives properly states the contributing role that an institution has towards a faculty member in regards to motivation. It is the responsibility of the institution to provide

incentives for achieving competence by integrating LMS technology into instruction. There are a variety of incentives including salary, awards or other recognition such as the recognition for the use of technology in instruction towards tenure and promotion. Motivation does not occur if the intended recipient does not accept the incentive. It is the responsibility of the institution to provide the appropriate incentives for faculty.

For the internal area—Motivation—Motives:

Faculty need to communicate their expectations for incentives. It is not accurately stated as a responsibility of faculty but rather as a natural consequence that if the appropriate incentives are made available, faculty will be motivated to achieve competence. For the purposes of this process, Gilbert's model is a useful structure. It is not entirely all-encompassing as an example, for much of faculty competence in using an LMS may be prompted by internal incentives such as personal or professional satisfaction. A knowledgeable institution will be aware of that, understand it, and foster it among faculty by making the conditions necessary for internal incentives to occur.

2. Assess Whether all Conditions are Met for Competence.

Consider the three dimensions of the model of human competence. Use the model of competence to structure the assessment of an institution to determine which parts of the institution are providing the conditions necessary for competence to occur. Recall that the premise is that the competence is being sought. Specifically, competence in the integration of technology in instruction is being sought. The working example is the integration of Learning Management Systems (LMS) in instruction.

Here is what to do:

External Information

Assess the institution's information. Recall that the external area refers to those parts of the institution that contribute to the work conditions of the target employee, which is in this case an individual faculty member. Following are samples of assessment questions germane to the target of competence.

Message Communicated
- What is the institution's vision?
- Does it refer to the integration of technology? To what level of specificity?
- What is the institution's philosophy?
- Does it refer to the integration of technology? To what level of specificity?
- What are the goals of the institution?
- Do they refer to the integration of technology? To what level of specificity?
- Assess the layers of administration for the above questions beginning with the entire institution to the next level which may be a college, school or department, etc.

Communication Process
- How is the message communicated? It could be in an annual presidential or other executive address. It could also be in the institutional catalogue or other prominent publication.
- To whom is the message communicated? Is it for the general public? Is there an expectation that the message be received? How is that expectation operationalized? Is there an executive order directing all managers to announce the messages? Is it expected to be received by virtue of the fact that it is part of the primary point of contact for the institution, such as a Web site may be?
- Is there an expectation that the messages be accepted as well as being received and understood? How is that expectation operationalized? Is there an order from the executive or other level of administration

directing the faculty to acknowledge and accept the messages?

- In summary, it needs to be established
  - o Whether relevant communications are being made
  - o Whether relevant communications are being made via appropriate channels
  - o Whether the institution expects faculty to receive, understand, and accept the messages.

Internal Information

Assess faculty members' responses to the institution's information about competent behavior in the integration of technology in instruction—the use of an LMS.

Following are samples of assessment questions:

- Do the faculty know that the institution at some level of administration has a target of competence in the use of an LMS?
- Do the faculty know that competence in the use of an LMS is expected?
- Do the faculty understand the institutional target? Do they know what an LMS is? Do they know which is being used by the institution? Do they know what the implementation plans for such a system are?
- Do the faculty understand the institution's intentions?
- Do the faculty understand the institution's expectations?
- Do the faculty accept the institution's intentions?
- Do the faculty accept the institution's expectations?
- Will the faculty act on the institution's intentions and expectations?
- In summary, it needs to be established
  - o Whether relevant communications about the expectations of competence are being received

- o Whether relevant communications are being understood, and
- o Whether relevant communications are being accepted by faculty.

External Instrumentation: Resources

Assess the institution's resources. In the discussion above about the conceptual model, an assumption was made that it was the responsibility of the institution—the area external to the target of competent behavior, the faculty member—to provide the necessary resources in all its connotations. These include hardware, software, and spaces for the instrumentation to be used such as laboratories, classrooms, or offices. The connotations include reasonable availability to the instrumentation in its various locations. Reasonable accessibility needs to be provided, also. Importantly, either instruction in the use of the instrumentation needs to be provided or means for the instruction need to be provided. The institution may conduct faculty development programming or faculty may participate in such instruction externally.

Following are samples of assessment questions:

- Is the appropriate kind of hardware provided?
- Is the appropriate kind of software provided?
- Is there enough instrumentation or are there enough opportunities to use it?
- Is the instrumentation functional, current, reliable, and in good working order?
- To what degree of accommodation must faculty submit in order to use the instrumentation? Is it within proximity? Is the schedule for the use of it reasonable?
- Is instruction for the competent behavior, using an LMS, provided?
- Is the necessary instrumentation accessible? (Can it be readily accessed?)

- Is instruction relevant to the needs of the students, that is, the faculty?
- Is instruction scheduled to meet the widely heterogeneous schedules of faculty?
- In summary, it needs to be established
    - o Whether there is appropriate instrumentation
    - o Whether the instrumentation is available, there is enough of it
    - o Whether the instrumentation is operational
    - o Whether the instrumentation is accessible, the distance to it is reasonable and the schedule for access is reasonable
    - o Whether there is appropriate training.

Internal Instrumentation: Capacity

Assess faculty members' responses to the instrumentation. Following are samples of assessment questions:

- Do the faculty know which resources are needed?
- Do the faculty know when the resources are available?
- Do the faculty know where the resources are available?
- Do the faculty know how to get access to the resources, that is, locations, log in, passwords, etc.?
- Do the faculty schedules allow for accessing the resources?
- Do the faculty know how to use the resources?
- Do the faculty know how to access instruction for the use of the resources?
- Do the faculty learn from the instruction?
- In summary, it needs to be established
    - o Whether the faculty know what resources are needed
    - o Whether the faculty know how the resources are available

- o Whether the faculty know how to access the resources
- o Whether the faculty can accommodate the expected use of the resources per their schedule
- o Whether the faculty know that training is available
- o Whether the faculty make use of available training
- o Whether the faculty learn from the training.

External Motivation: Incentives

Assess the institution's use of incentives for faculty to reward competence in the use of an LMS. Recall that the institution's contribution to motivation is in the provision of incentives. Following are samples of assessment questions:

- Are there incentives for the use of an LMS?
- Which incentives are there for the use of an LMS?
- Do the incentives match the needs and expectations of faculty?
- Are the incentives material, such as salary or other compensation?
- Are the incentives symbolic, such as awards?
- Do the incentives acknowledge the professionalism of the faculty?
- Does competence in LMS use contribute to faculty promotion and tenure?
- Are conditions made available that promote faculty members' internal motivation for the pursuit of competence?
- In summary, it needs to be established
    - o Whether incentives are available to faculty for LMS use
    - o Whether the incentives are appropriate.

Internal Motivation

Assess the faculty members' responses to incentives rewarding competence in the use an LMS. Recall that it is characteristic of human nature that an appropriate incentive be given in order for a person to accept it.

Following are samples of assessment questions:

* Are the incentives appropriate, that is, do they motivate the faculty to pursue competence in using the LMS?
* Is internal motivation encouraged?
  In summary, it needs to be established
  o Whether faculty respond to the incentives.

3. Repair the Areas of Deficiency

Communication Deficiency

The model suggests the most important dimensions that contribute to competence. Once they have been defined and identified in an organization, the next step is to determine the status of whether the dimensions are meeting the expectations for competence. If, for instance, the institution has formulated a statement about the use of an LMS but demonstrates limited communication of it as evidenced by the absence of principal communication media for the campus such as its Web site, internal e-mail or print publication, communication through the chain of command, etc. and if a survey of employees, particularly the faculty, reveals that there is a little awareness of the institutional view, then there is a deficit of some sort. From this deficit it can be inferred that there may not be enough communication, or that the media are ineffective, or that the intended audience, the faculty, does not respond to the media. It is impossible to expect that there would be action taken or understanding of a communication if attention is not paid to it. The action of identifying deficits in expectations and then correcting them is the essential process for enabling the conditions necessary for competence in the use of an LMS.

Instrumentation Deficiency

The institutional assessment may reveal that there is an LMS license, but few of the faculty have been exposed to it or have been instructed in its use. Deficiencies in this case are the lack of familiarity with and knowledge and skill in the use of the LMS for instruction. The need to be addressed would be the understanding and the skill sets of the faculty.

Motivation Deficiency

The institutional assessment may reveal that there are not any incentives provided to encourage and maintain the use of the LMS. The faculty members who have integrated it into instruction are largely early adopters who respond to their own personal incentives who would attempt to use the LMS regardless of an institutional common plan.

The examples of deficits are generalized and there will be nuanced versions of them in the organizational assessment. Predictable deficiencies are in the areas of faculty capacity and knowledge and in institutional incentives in respect of the integration of technology. Because these two areas of deficiency are the most likely to occur, strategies for addressing them are suggested.

Part B: Professional Development—Provide Instruction

When your organizational assessment reveals that the area of deficiency is capacity, it may be that training for professional development is appropriate. Consider the technology that you are targeting, LMS in a matrix of two dimensions: degree of importance and level of skill among faculty.

See Exhibit 2. The quadrant of interest is the intersection of high importance and low skills. This may be evidence for the need for instruction.

Exhibit 2. A need for training indicated

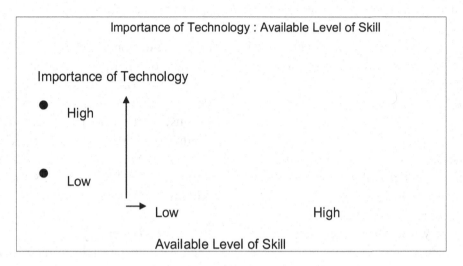

If there were high importance and high related skills, then it is unlikely that instruction would satisfy the deficit determined by the organizational assessment.

The deficiency between the importance of the skills needed and the actual skills available illustrates a situation predicted by Rossett's (1987) initiators of training needs assessments—the use of an LMS may be a "new system or technology" for those faculty with low skills in the integration of the highly important use of LMS. When there is a need for instruction, follow an instructional design model even though the learners are faculty members. In this case, you can develop "faculty-as-learner centered instruction."

An Instructional Design Model

Consider preparation for teaching faculty as planning for instruction—follow an instructional design model to guide your instructional planning. ADDIE is a model with most of the elements which are found in other instructional design models as well as in research and planning models. The acronym stands for Assessment, Design, Develop, Implement, and Evaluate (Molenda, 2003; Schrock, 1991)

Assessment

How do you know instruction is needed?

The organizational assessment that was done within the parameters of the model of human competence resulted in the identification of deficiencies such as the need for instruction among faculty. The assessment should also have revealed the level of instruction needed.

Design Instruction

What do the faculty need to learn? What are your expected outcomes for the instruction?

Understand your students and their needs and plan to meet them. Plan "faculty-as-learner centered" instruction: What do you need to know about your faculty-students?

To guide your design process focus on the factors affecting learning suggested by Bransford (1979). These factors will be used twice in your planning; once for planning the instruction of your students. The second time will be as the content of the instruction your faculty-students will learn. The factors are the learners' characteristics; the media of instruction, the method of instruction, and assessment of learning.

Learner Characteristics

Who are faculty?

What are their needs?

How do they respond to technology?

Some characteristics of academic faculty include the love of and the pursuit of learning and recognition for one's intellect. Find other traits that would be relevant to your instruction of them. Faculty response to the use of technology may not be the same as the general public because faculty members are increasingly confronted with technology in their work. As a result, they would have more opportunities and direct experience to form opinions about technology.

Media

Which media are appropriate?

Because one of the subjects being taught would be the use of an LMS, the system itself ought to be used directly in instruction. Faculty as highly intelligent, adult learners ought to respond well to the medium of instruction being the same as the subject of instruction. There is a double lesson in this instruction in that if the media are used well to demonstrate how technology can facilitate media, then the point needs to be made that that is the eventual goal.

Method

What will the learners need to do during instruction?

In the basis for Bransford's original work, the term used was orienting task. This refers to the activity that the learner performed in order to learn the point of the instruction. This could be a method. Would the presentation and practice of information be orchestrated for the learners' discovery or would it be provided by the instructor or other source of information? For this group of adult learners, experience has shown that non-embarrassing actual or "hands on" practice in very small groups is appreciated.

Assessment

How will you and the students know they are learning?

Are your faculty-students learning what you and they expected? Is your instruction successful? A much used and useful assessment of your instruction is the Small Group Instructional Diagnosis (Clark & Redmond, 1982).

There are three questions:

1. What did you like about the instruction?
2. What should have been excluded from the instruction?
3. What should have been included in the instruction?

Content

What will they learn?

The subject of the instruction for the faculty is the knowledge and skills necessary for using the LMS. In order to achieve integration of the LMS, the faculty-students also need to learn about the factors affecting learning to help plan their instruction. Just as the planner for technology integration follows an instructional design model and the factors affecting learning, faculty need to know about the factors affecting learning for their students. They need to know the characteristics of their students, the ones that will cause them to modify or target their instruction such as students' reading ability. There may be needs to keep in mind such as the familiarity with the native language of instruction.

The faculty-students need to know which media work well with the subjects they are teaching and with the needs of their students. They need to know which methods work well with their students and with the media they use. They also need to know which assessments are informative and instructive.

Part C: Motivation—Select a Strategy

It is necessary to create the conditions for which technology can be integrated. To select your strategy, determine the relative novelty for technology use at the institution. The assessment of the institution using the competence model ought to reveal the relative novelty of the technology being integrated. Is the use of an LMS something new and unfamiliar or is it common knowledge and there is much experience in the use of it? There are two principal organizational strategies to employ based on the relative novelty. At an institution where the use of technology is novel, motivate with the goal that there is much awareness, much interest, much familiarity: use subjective norms, create dependencies, and create infrastructure. Where technology use is typical and not novel, manage use per institutional needs. Identify expectations, plan staffing and curricula accordingly. At such institutions, technology is integrated and the strategic goal is to maintain the integration through management of it.

Technology Integration as Novel

For an institution where technology is new, the goals are widespread awareness building and motivation. The strategies are to use subjective norms, create dependencies, and create infrastructure.

Subjective Norms

A series of studies (Marcinkiewicz, 1996, 1995/1995, 1995, 1993/1994) revealed that the most predictive personological variable of teachers' use of instructional computing was subjective norms. Subjective norms refers to the perception that teachers use technology because they believe that significant constituents expect them to use technology. They use technology because they believe that students, administrators, learned societies, and their colleagues expect them to. It is similar to "peer pressure" in that the incentive is meeting the perceived expectations of others. Subjective norms are operationalized by communicating the expectations to faculty. The research has shown that faculty will use technology if they believe that the constituent groups expect it of them. It supports the need for excellent communication. They need to know that students expect LMS in instruction. Students can be surveyed to know their minds on the matter. Faculty need to know that administration expects them to use LMS. This coincides with the prediction of the model of human competence discussed above. Faculty need to know that their colleagues and learned societies expect them to use LMS. These groups are the support system of faculty; they are the peers and colleagues with whom faculty identify.

Create Dependencies and Infrastructure

One knows that one is responding to a dependency for technology when a task cannot be accomplished without it, or the completion of a task would be done differently than typically expected. An example of this is the cessation of departmental memos on paper; memos will only be posted online via e-mail or perhaps via an LMS. New course offerings will be availed if they are conducted as hybrids with some percentage of them requiring online LMS instruction; otherwise, the courses are not run. Many occurrences exist in professional and personal life including the upgrading of technical services, price changes for needed services, etc. The creation of dependencies is not a goal, but rather a strategy that provides the incentive of completion of a necessary task. The tasks to be performed ought to be a part of the infrastructure of an institution. An example of the complete use of an LMS as a part of the infrastructure of an institution is an LMS for an online degree. In this instance, completion of the degree is made possible or required by the use of an LMS because it is a fundamental part of the infrastructure of the institution offering the degree. Make the use of the technology necessary for the performance of activities that are parts of the infrastructure.

Technology Integration as Mature

An institution that can post employment announcements for faculty requiring knowledge and experience in the use of LMS demonstrates maturity in the integration of technology for instruction. Under such conditions, an institution has defined technology and its expectations for its use; faculty, staff, students, and administration accept and expect the use of the technology. There is sufficient instrumentation available and accessible and there are continuous opportunities for professional development. There are also incentives for the successful use of the technology and faculty are motivated by the incentives. This level of technology integration is the ideal goal state for institutions. In this state the strategy for the integration is management of expectations. This is accomplished by hiring appropriately and providing professional development opportunities. Furthermore, there is continual planning for technology integration.

SUMMARY

The purpose of this set of processes is to guide organizational planners for the integration of technology into instruction. A model for human competence is used to specify the deficient areas, those not supporting competence in the integration of technology. Typically, the deficiencies are the lack of knowledge or skills. An organizational strategy for the introduction of new technology is to begin to create dependencies on it for the completion of necessary tasks. Another strategy is to communicate the expectation that the faculty are expected to use technology by their peers, students, learned societies, and administration. For organizations where technology integration is mature or not novel, integration can be managed by the administration as by institutionalizing job descriptions that require integration.

REFERENCES

Bransford, J. D. (1979). *Human cognition: Learning, understanding and remembering* (pp. 6-9). Belmont, CA: Wadsworth Publishing.

Chevalier, R. (May/June, 2003). Updating the behavior engineering model. *Performance and Improvement, 42*(5).

Clark, D., & Redmond, M. (1982). *Small group instructional diagnosis: Final report.* University of Washington, Seattle. FIPSE. (ERIC Document Reproduction Service. No. ED 217 954).

Gilbert, T. F. (1978). *Human competence: Engineering worthy performance.* New York: McGraw Book Company.

Marcinkiewicz, H. R., & Regstad, N. G. (1996). Using subjective norms to predict teachers' computer use. *Journal of Computing in Teacher Education, 13*(1), 27-33.

Marcinkiewicz, H. R. (1994/95). Differences in computer use of practicing versus preservice teachers. *Journal of Research on Computing in Education, 27*(2), 184-197.

Marcinkiewicz, H. R., & Wittman, T. K. (1995). From preservice to practice: A longitudinal study of teachers and computer use. *Journal of Computing in Teacher Education, 11*(2), 12–17.

Marcinkiewicz, H. R. (1993/94). Computers and teachers: Factors influencing computer use in the classroom. *Journal of Research on Computing in Education, 26*(2), 220-237.

Molenda, M. (May/June, 2003). In search of the elusive ADDIE model. *Performance and Improvement, 42*(5).

Rossett, A. (1987). *Training needs assessment.* Englewood Cliffs, NJ: Educational Technology Publications.

Shrock, S. (1991). A brief history of instructional development. In G. Anglin (Ed.), *Instructional technology: Past, present, and future* (pp. 11-18). Englewood, CO: Libraries Unlimited, Inc.

KEY TERMS AND DEFINITIONS

Dependency: The need for using technology in order to complete one's work.

Integration: The condition in which technology is used in instruction so that without it instruction would not be possible as intended.

Learning Management System (LMS): A set of online processes focused on instruction that function together.

Subjective Norms: The personal belief that others have expectations that one should behave in a certain way. The belief influences one to behave that way.

Technology: The materials, processes, or tools used to solve problems.

Chapter XXV
University Task Force Deepens Academic Involvement in ERP

Michael Crow
Kansas State University, USA

ABSTRACT

Kansas State University has ensured greatly increased academic involvement in the implementation of its new student information system through the use of an Academic Task Force. Consisting of Associate and Assistant Deans, each college of the university is represented on the task force to work directly with project management to review and revise university procedures as well as suggest system enhancements with the goal of melding the new system into the long term objectives of the university. This case study explores the evolution of the task force from its beginnings, springing out of an update session with an academic policy and procedure committee to the point that the task force eventually supplanted the Project Steering Committee as the primary conduit of information exchange between the project team and the academic community.

INTRODUCTION

Why do some IT projects result in success while others can range from "troubled" to outright failure? The stark contrast in results has been all the more obvious in the higher education environment where most institutions are moving from decades old legacy systems that were regularly modified according to user needs to prepackaged software available from a limited number of vendors. These monolithic Enterprise Resource Planning systems are performing mission critical functions to matriculate, enroll and process records for university students/customers but meet with varying degrees of success in their implementation.

Though many factors contribute to the success or failure of an IT project, more than any other organization type, higher education is especially dependent on collaborative implementation involving key stakeholders. As opposed to hierarchical structures in private enterprise, many universities are heavily oriented to the concept of shared governance and the notion of a student information system being unilaterally imposed upon the university community by the central administration would be anathema to that fundamental concept of shared governance.

The challenge is getting a truly collaborative environment. A steering committee is usually the chosen route for project governance, especially in the higher education environment. Steering committees tend be great for oversight, but also operate at such high levels that true collaboration often does not take place. They can be perceived, as the name implies, to be more autocratic than collaborative. K-State found that the best way to ensure collaboration was through a task force that would operate at a closer level to the decision ramifications. At the outset, both the steering committee and the task force were able to co-exist at different levels within the project. The steering committee addressed the broad questions ranging across all of the modules while the task force focused on preparing for the initial student enrollment in the new system. The foci of the two groups would merge as the first major implementation milestone of launching student admissions approached.

BACKGROUND

The LASER (Legacy Applications System Replacement) project was born out of an overarching vision of data sharing to replace the traditional silo effect of legacy systems (Fitzgerald, Rivenbark & Schelin, 2003). This vision was formalized into the Integrated Information Initiative, a ten-year plan to distribute information more widely among users with the appropriate "educational need to know". By breaking down silos of information and transforming the culture from one of data ownership to one of data stewardship, information could be more readily accessed by decision makers to better forecast and plan for future trends. The centerpiece of this initiative was the LASER project, an effort to replace the aging, mainframe-based conglomeration of disparate pieces including a student information system, a billing and receivables system and a financial aid management system among others.

Like most of its peer universities, K-State had maintained and modified these robust but functionally constrained systems for a quarter century or more and the core operating system had long since exceeded its useful life. Only by constant innovation and customization had the institution been able to maintain its cutting edge delivery of services to students and faculty. However, with the natural limitations of the application, combined with an ever-shrinking pool of labor with the necessary skill-set to maintain and push the boundary of the system's ability to deliver new functionality, it became clear that a replacement system would be necessary and a fully integrated ERP would be the system of choice. This choice would fulfill the desires of the administration for a comprehensive approach to data administration that would allow the university to break out of the silo mentality and make data available to far more users more effectively and efficiently.

The original system of choice was the Oracle Student System (OSS), which held the promise for adaptability in line with the vision of the Integrated Information Initiative. Although the OSS application held high Gartner scores for innovation, it was not sufficiently developed at the time to meet all of the needs of a "Top 25 Connected" university with an aggressive implementation timeline (Harris, & Zastrocky, 2005, K-State Media Relations, 2004).

Therefore, Kansas State turned to Oracle's sister product, PeopleSoft Campus Solutions™

with the knowledge that many of the OSS innovations would likely be incorporated into the PeopleSoft product as part of the upcoming Fusion program. In August 2006, the PeopleSoft Campus Solutions system implementation was initiated with the goal of June 2007 for the first go-live milestone for the Admissions module. The first student enrollment in the new system was slated for March 2008.

ORIGINS OF THE TASK FORCE

The academic community had become involved early on in the project with the Business and Engineering Colleges serving as pilot schools for testing the OSS application. However, the task force proper did not become a major factor as an entity until January of 2006. At that point the outgoing chair of the Committee on Academic Policy and Procedure (CAPP) formalized the task force and transitioned to the chairmanship of this newly formed sub-committee known formally as the iSIS Task Force (iSIS was the name chosen for the new system).

The Task Force consisted of Associate and Assistant Deans from the eight colleges, the Division of Continuing Education and the Veterinary and Graduate Schools plus select members representing the Provost, Registrar, and the Faculty Affairs Chair, among others (*see Exhibit 1*). This group began meeting periodically, moving to monthly gatherings in late 2006 to discuss policy and procedural matters related to the new system. During the same time frame they also met weekly for a two hour hands on lab session to learn the system functionality.

The weekly lab session and the monthly policy and procedure meeting were both extremely well attended. This was quite astonishing considering the high level constituency with so many wide-ranging obligations. Yet the dedication was akin to a mandatory attendance seminar for honors students. If a committee member could not attend a meeting or lab session, a designee was nearly always present and three of the colleges regularly sent both the committee member and the designee to both meetings and lab sessions. When the project was a little more than a year from going live with the enrollment module it was decided that the policy and procedural issues yet to be decided were substantial enough in number and complexity to warrant meeting weekly. These weekly one hour sessions were always running past the allotted time and were soon expanded to ninety minutes where still no meeting ever let out early.

Concurrently, the two-hour lab sessions were regularly hosting from two to five staff from each College Dean's Office in highly interactive hands on experimentation and discussion sessions where new functionality such as automatic enrollment from wait lists, requisite checks and electronic class permissions were tested to see how they would perform in various real life campus scenarios.

As testing progressed, the lab sessions were occasionally led by the task force members themselves. They evaluated the various alternatives for deploying functionality before deciding on the option that all could support and live with. The role-based security methodology employed by the application further encouraged the task force philosophy of standardizing all major facets of system functionality. Although sufficient flexibility often existed in the application to allow for differences in the manner in which each college did business, the Task Force felt it would be more efficient to administer and easier for faculty and students to understand if major aspects of system functionality were standardized across the colleges and schools. This required a true spirit of cooperation and sacrifice to often abandon long-time practice in favor of consistency, but the momentum of the collective was always aimed forward toward standardization (Corbitt &Peszynski, 2006).

In this way, consistency was maintained across the campus in the way common functions were performed such as how class permissions were granted. Communications of a single methodology meant that all a student had to know was that he or she would only have to go to the class instructor for class permission. Conversely, the faculty only had to know that they needed to communicate said permission decision to the academic department staff for entry into the system. The academic department staff were then responsible for evaluating the effect that granting the permission would have on the class enrollment capacity and more importantly the room capacity as determined by the fire marshal. If such was the case that room capacity were to be exceeded, the department staff had the authority to deny the permission until the actual capacity was in alignment with code capacity (*see Exhibit 2*).

By maintaining consistency across the campus in wide-ranging and universally applicable areas such as class permissions, more individuality could then occur in areas more specific to an individual college or at the department level. For example, with the advent of electronic validation of prerequisites, such requisites were scrutinized by every curriculum committee on campus for applicability in a variety of situations. It was determined that wide variation would be necessary in the administration of prerequisites. Therefore, colleges and departments were allowed to code requisites as either 'hard' or 'soft', rather than all hard as could be interpreted from the catalog. A soft requisite was defined as a requisite class that was not required but that was strongly recommended as the best preparation for student success in the target course. The system would allow for a note in the class schedule recommending the soft requisite be taken for a class but validations were not activated that would preclude enrollment in the class for those not having taken the requisite (Davis, & Lippert, 2006).

This mix of standardization and individualization according to the outcomes associated with application functionality had to be determined on a case by case basis by the task force and the background necessary to make such informed decisions could only come from immersing themselves in the vagaries of the system through regular testing and experimentation.

TASK FORCE BECOMES A MAJOR PLAYER IN THE PROJECT

By the summer of 2007 the steering committee and project had attained it first major milestone of a successful launch of the admissions module. The decisions from that point forward would demand a deeper familiarity with the system itself than what a group meeting monthly with no hands-on experience could deliver. Therefore, the steering committee metamorphosed into a two-part decision-making body. The key data stewards of the system (Registrar, Admissions, Financial Aid, Cashier) along with the team leads of the respective modules and other affiliated staff regularly met with the project sponsor while the Task Force maintained its rapid pace and high volume of meetings and laboratory sessions to become the primary conduit of information to the academic community. These two groups would share guidance of the project through the impending milestone of enrollment of the student body.

To ensure that a broad dissemination of information and representation of input occurred regarding the upcoming wide-ranging decisions, the first of two forums was scheduled in June 2007 to address major areas of change associated with the implementation of the new system. The June session was a four hour marathon with more than sixty attendees representing various constituencies across the university. During this forum, an open discussion of the first twenty of thirty-six key topics occurred with what at times was a spirited dialogue. Issues such as wait list management, class permission procedures, requisite enforcement and new security access limitations were deliberated, with preliminary decisions on many issues made right at the forum. Other more intricate issues were discussed and evaluated but decisions were then deferred to later task force meetings following additional review and polling of the respective college faculty and administrations.

THE TOUGHEST DECISIONS

The most difficult decisions regarded the degree to which technology would be allowed to affect policy without effecting policy (Dery, Hall, Harley, & Wright, 2006). In one such case, it was decided that the Dean's Offices would retain the right to reposition students on the wait lists when, in their judgment it was deemed necessary to do so. In the past, wait lists were administered in a greatly varied manner, used by some departments and not by others and rarely in the same manner from department to department, even within the same college. In fact, a Faculty Senate ad hoc committee had investigated wait list options a couple of semesters prior to the initiation of the project, in anticipation of the new system and the student representatives on the committee strongly characterized the haphazard application of wait list practices as perceptually unfair to the student populace.

Though the task force agreed with the precept that the student perception of fairness in wait list administration was a goal of the new functionality, they did not agree to cede total control of the wait lists to the new technology. Therefore, it was determined that the system would be allowed to auto-enroll students from the wait list and their position on the wait list would be clearly delineated by the system. However, the Dean's Office would have the capability to reposition students when extenuating circumstances dictated such a course of action. In this way, the manipulation of

wait lists was limited in scope and occurrence, thus giving a more fair perception of the process to students, while still allowing the Deans to intervene in situations where it was appropriate and necessary. Thus, the task force was able to prevent the new technology from dictating procedural change counter to the needs of the campus, while still harnessing the positive aspects of said technology.

Another area where the potential of system rigidity was mediated by collaborative decision-making was in the administration of requisites. Up to the point of the new system implementation, requisites were listed in the catalog, but were not in the legacy system. Therefore, enforcement occurred in a multitude of ways which may have ranged from non-enforcement in some cases, to rigid enforcement in others. We say "may have" because there was no way to know or audit the enforcement ratio as it was left up to colleges, departments or individual faculty to enforce requisites without documentation as to the disposition of any individual case.

With resolution inconsistent from college to college and not formalized into the legacy system's technology, some requisites could potentially exist for years without serious review as to their applicability to a target course. The fact that requisites would be dispassionately enforced by the new system implied the need to review all requisites for relevance and applicability. Again it was decided that the technology could not be the sole arbiter of how business would be conducted. Hence, the compromise to allow 'hard' and 'soft' requisites according to departmental dictates.

Even then, the individual decision to override a requisite presented a philosophical dilemma for the task force to work through. Should the decision to override a requisite be made by the faculty alone as final, as a vestige of academic freedom or should the college be final arbiter as it held the responsibility for ensuring accreditation standards were met and liability (room capacity violations) was minimized. After numerous discussions over a longer period than that of any other topic, it still took an eleventh hour decision by three colleges to join the majority and standardize the procedure for overriding requisites via class permission. The compromise adopted would allow the student to interact with the class instructor only for requesting an override of the requisite. However, the instructor would forward his or her recommendation to the department or Dean's Office where it would be subject to room capacity or accreditation constraints. In this manner the decision was shared without usurping the faculty's control over their own classes (Schwarz, Watson, 2005).

THE TASK FORCE DIVES IN

The task force could methodically evaluate and make the multitude of difficult decisions because it understood the basic logic of a highly complex system. This knowledge could only come from the many hours devoted to testing the way the application processed enrollments when a certain level of academic standing was used as a class requirement or how a savvy staff member could bypass the wait list by granting permission through the class permissions functionality. In addition to the scenario testing, this same group, along with their staff in the Dean's Office, was responsible for creating and testing the 2000 plus enrollment

Exhibit 1. An Associate or Assistant Dean from each college served on the Task Force, but in the case of two colleges the designees became the de facto members by their heavy involvement in the committee. Several regular guests to the meetings such as the LASER Project Manager, interim Vice Provost for IT and Team Leads from other modules were readily welcomed to contribute as the committee was able to operate formally, but in an informal manner. Protocol was followed for votes on major issues but for the most point a mere shaking of the heads was sufficient to accomplish objectives. This relaxed approach allowed the committee to be highly collaborative and more often than not, achieved consensus on decisions large and small.

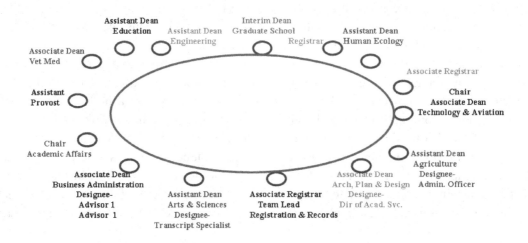

Exhibit 2.Class Permission was a very complex, even convoluted subject for discussion and decision, but the Task force distilled it to simple directions for the faculty, staff and students by focusing each group on their role in the process only and leaving the responsibility for the overall methodology at Deans Office level.

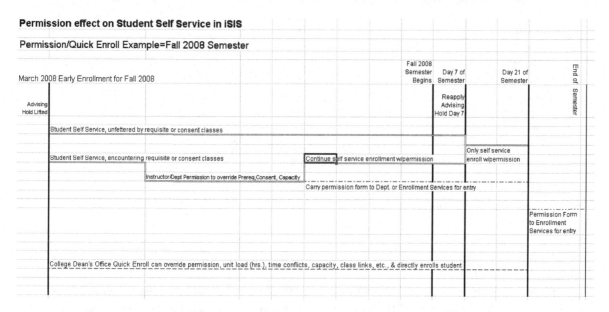

requirements to be used as pre- and co-requisites throughout the system. (*see Exhibit 3*) One of the Associate Deans in the Technology and Aviation College determined that 1,096 different scenarios existed for a given requisite and he deduced the 4-6 scenarios most likely to be encountered, in order to reduce the testing burden to an attainable objective. He documented and presented his methodology to the rest of the task force in one of the lab sessions. The Task Force also took a lead role in orchestrating the Enrollment Pilot during a hectic time of activity.

The degree audit system was shut down for one week in mid-February 2008 to install an interface and perform a complete restructuring and conversion. Advising for the upcoming enrollment would begin immediately afterward and run through the end of March, when enrollment would be in full swing. The Task Force decided to engage in a full-scale enrollment pilot with approximately three hundred students about

two weeks before the beginning of enrollment. This pilot would last one week and would take place in the production system where it could potentially involve any instructor or advisor to remove advising flags or approve permission to enter a class among other things. The coordination of such an event was challenging during this normally tumultuous time, but it was successful and revealed system and practice flaws that could then be corrected during the following week of the student spring break.

The close proximity of the pilot to the actual enrollment was partly due to lessons learned from the dry run for the class schedule. In that case, the dry run took place in July 2007 but the actual class schedule was not assembled until later in October. By that time, many of the lessons learned had been quickly forgotten. There also was such a distance until the real event that the practice session did not attain the same level of relevance, hence participation was lower and

Exhibit 3. Each College created and tested every requisite in a test instance and then individually approved them by checking the 'processed indicator' box so that all checked requisites could be periodically moved to the Production instance.

Requirement Group	Subject Area	Catalog Nbr	Description	Processed Indicator
1 008037	ACCTG	231	ACCTG 231	☐
2 008108	ACCTG	241	ACCTG 241	☐
3 008036	ACCTG	331	ACCTG 331	☐
4 008045	ACCTG	342	ACCTG 342	☐
5 008139	ACCTG	431	ACCTG 431	☐
6 008129	ACCTG	432	ACCTG 432	☐
7 008140	ACCTG	433	ACCTG 433	☐
8 008141	ACCTG	434	ACCTG 434	☐
9 008148	ACCTG	631	ACCTG 631	☐
10 008128	ACCTG	641	ACCTG 641	☐
11 008144	ACCTG	642	ACCTG 642	☐
12 008043	MANGT	420	MANGT 420	☐
13 008132	MANGT	421	MANGT 421	☐
14 008285	MANGT	440	MANGT 440	☐

less intensive. The sense of urgency in the enrollment pilot was markedly higher and the value of the effort was evident from the post-pilot survey results (Dulebohn, Liang, & Marler, 2006).

The task force has been the primary conduit of information between the project team and the academic community for the past year and its authority has been rooted in hard-earned knowledge and the willingness to take action.

FUTURE TRENDS/CONCLUSION

The longevity of the task force has been due, among other things, to the surprising stability of its membership. The task force chair has only changed once during the project, that following the retirement of the original chair, who coincidentally was instrumental in the implementation of the original legacy student information system twenty-five years prior to the LASER project. One of the original members will be leaving as he returns to teaching, but otherwise, the group is expected to remain intact and maintain a presence as the new system grows and matures. The steering committee is being revived to help guide the project through the remaining implementation milestones and the task force chair will serve as a member of the steering committee. The success of the iSIS Task Force has spawned a complimentary task force to guide the implementation of the university's new electronic catalog and peer universities have expressed an interest in enlisting a similarly structured committee. The goals of the task force were to improve communication and form a genuine partnership with the academic community in the implementation of the largest and most complex IT initiative in university history. Those goals were clearly met and this is a big reason for the success of the K-State LASER Project.

REFERENCES

Corbitt, K. J., & Peszynski, B. J. (2006). Politics, complexity, and systems implementation: Critically exposing power. *Social Science Computer Review, 24*(3), 326-341.

Davis, S. K., & Lippert, M. (2006). A conceptual model integrating trust into planned change activities to enhance technology adoption behavior. *Journal of Information Science, 32*(5), 434-448.

Dery, K., Hall, R., Harley, B., & Wright, C. (2006). Management reactions to technological change: The example of enterprise resource planning. *The Journal of Applied Behavioral Science, 42*(1), 58-75.

Dulebohn, J. H., Liang, X., & Marler, J. H. (2006). Training and effective employee information technology use. *Journal of Management, 32*(5), 721-743.

Fitzgerald, K. M., Rivenbark, W. C., & Schelin, S. H. (2003). Analyzing information technology investments in state government. *Social Science Computer Review, 21*(4), 497-505.

Harris, M., & Zastrocky, M. (2005). *Magic quadrant for higher education administrative suites.* From http://www.gartner.com/7_search

K-State Media Relations (2004). *Kansas State University achievements: 2004 all-university* from http://www.k-state.edu/media/achievements/04allaccomplishments.html

Schwarz, G. M., & Watson, B. M. (2005). The influence of perceptions of social identity on information technology-enabled change. *Group & Organization Management, 30*(3), 289-318

KEY TERMS AND DEFINITIONS

Educational 'Need to Know': Concept for determining who should have access to a student's educational records as regulated by the *Family Educational Rights and Privacy Act of 1974,* known as FERPA.

Matriculation: A specific process in the PeopleSoft application that allows the student record to move from under the aegis of the Admissions process to the Records process, thus enabling term activation and enrollment.

Shared Governance: Higher education concept of university management as a bilateral responsibility of both the central administration and the faculty.

Silo Effect: Lack of information exchange between data base systems within an entity or with outside entities. The silo may be limited to the technical deficiencies of the system, but the effect encompasses the larger human problem of the silo mentality, which includes a predisposition away from sharing such information.

ENDNOTES

* Fusion, OSS and PeopleSoft Campus Solutions are trademarks of the Oracle Corporation
** Gartner is the trademark of Gartner Inc.

Chapter XXVI
Production, Publication, and Use of Educational Multimedia Content in Brazil:
Challenges and Opportunities in Real World Technology Projects

Joni A. Amorim
Universidade Estadual de Campinas (UNICAMP), Brazil

Carlos Machado
PST Electronics, Brazil

Rosana G. S. Miskulin
Universidade Estadual Paulista "Júlio de Mesquita Filho" (UNESP), Brazil

Mauro S. Miskulin
Universidade Estadual de Campinas (UNICAMP), Brazil

ABSTRACT

The production of quality educational multimedia content involves both its publication and its use, considering aspects ranging from metadata standards to teachers' guides. In Brazil, there are many challenges and opportunities in real world technology projects; particularly, in the field of education. Challenges may involve not only strategy and project engineering issues, but also the management of change in the creation of virtual groups focused on multimedia production. This scenario has created a platform from which it was possible to suggest a framework for an educational multimedia factory virtual group interaction. Thus, both software implementation for the proposed framework and the management of change are discussed from the perspective of a large-scale multimedia production, at UNICAMP, Brazil. This chapter intends to bring about some of the complexities involved in a pioneer project that can provide High School students with free content by simply connecting to the Internet.

INTRODUCTION

Digital convergence is finally happening (Amorim, 2003): all separate media now become digital and come to be delivered via global network, improving education quality. In this new context, change management comes into play (Bates, 1999; Conner, 1993; Frame, 1994): teachers demand both digital content and training in order to incorporate multimedia in their daily practice. After considering topics such as accessibility, change management and multimedia, this chapter presents two initiatives from the Universidade Estadual de Campinas (UNICAMP), Brazil. One is related to teacher training in educational technology (CENP, 2007), while the other involves large-scale multimedia production for teaching (MEC, 2007). This chapter discusses the production, publication and use of educational multimedia content, presenting, at the same time, a Brazilian perspective on the many challenges and opportunities experienced in real world technology projects.

In education, digital technologies are becoming increasingly important. The use of multimedia can combine text, images, full-motion video, and sound into an integrated package. The authoring process grows in complexity with time due to the increasing multitude of possibilities available: from traditional hypertext to Web-based audio broadcast via RSS (Really Simple Syndication) feed. This growing complexity of modern educational projects and the need for a more efficient production of quality courses stimulates the development of new instructional design approaches.

Improving quality in distance, flexible and ICT-based education turned out to be a priority for most institutions in developing countries, where the digital divide is just one of the many challenges. UNICAMP was established in 1966, as a public university funded by the State of São Paulo, Brazil. In 2007, the University had 6.200 fiber optics-connected computers, 1.800 professors, 15.696 undergraduate students and 17.275 graduate students enrolled in different courses. UNICAMP is one of the most distinguished Brazilian academic institutions and seeks to contribute to solving social problems, through education and research, as well as through services to the community at large. The University accounts for 15% of the total scientific production in Brazil and manages projects both in technology development and in technology education. In 2007, the Graduate Programs obtained the best evaluation among Brazilian universities by the National Coordination for the Improvement of Graduate Professionals (CAPES), accounting for 11% of the Ph.D. degrees granted in Brazil.

The incorporation of the best methods and practices is now mandatory in order to achieve a balance among time, cost, scope, quality, risk and customer satisfaction (Mulcahy, 2006). Improving quality and productivity standards in an organization is a difficult challenge; especially because it is also difficult for people to accept changes.

Change is a transformation, a modification, an alteration, a variation or a deviation. It is a transition from one state, condition, or phase to another. Never before has that changed so fast with such a continuous intensification. In the field of education, massive change comes from ever-advancing technology such as personal digital assistants (PDAs) and interactive digital television (iDTV), suggesting that learning how to better manage change is an important goal to be achieved. A better Management of Change (MoC) would enhance the chances of increasing organizational efficiency and effectiveness even when changes are attempted. The literature on MoC (Bates, 1999; Conner, 1993; Frame, 1994) indicates that there is a basic axiom according to which individuals operate: life is most effective and efficient when people move at a speed that allows them to appropriately incorporate changes, absorbing them with minimum dysfunctional behavior. In education, what happens when teachers are overwhelmed by more change than they can absorb?

The answer could be fatigue, frustration, or apathy resulting from prolonged stress, overwork, or intense activity. This phenomenon is referred to as Burnout Syndrome (Carlotto, 2002). The seriousness of this syndrome tends to get higher in the field of education as additional pressure is put on teachers to learn how to teach under new paradigms such as those of technology-based education without appropriate preparation through specific training. The unsuccessful management of change may cause the display of dysfunctional behavior, a fact that may bring a decrease in the quality of education.

This way, this study also discusses how to apply the concepts of resilience and change to continuing education for teachers. The many changes under consideration when the focus is the massive use of technology could be too drastic or too threatening to institutions and individuals, demanding the determination of the level of resilience that exists among the key people involved. The main intent of such approach would be the application of correct resilience principles to build up the basic strength in individuals, thus preventing problems rather than dealing with them after they arise. In other words, steps taken early in the project prevent problems later on (Mulcahy, 2006).

After this brief literature review, this study presents some aspects of an educational technology teacher training project (CENP, 2007), which, then, suggested important elements to be considered while producing multimedia for public High Schools in Brazil. In the sequence, a large-scale educational multimedia production project (MEC, 2007) is presented in a scenario where the authors recognize the significant interplay between the fields of project management (PM) and knowledge management (KM). This scenario suggests a potential synergy (Regsdell, 2006) between project teams and social networks derived from the KM arena, known as communities of practice (CoPs). Based on this scenario, a framework for an educational multimedia factory virtual group interaction is discussed while

software customization that implements this framework is proposed.

BACKGROUND

Greenfield (2004) defines a software factory as a "development environment configured to support the rapid development of a specific type of application" (p. 1). As this author proposes, software factories promise to change the characteristics of the software industry by introducing patterns of industrialization. In the same way, a multimedia factory would be a development environment configured to support the rapid development of different types of digital media, which may include audio, video, software or hypertext, among others. While a mature software factory would intend to have high levels of code reuse, a mature digital multimedia factory would intend to reuse as many parts of products as possible. As a tendency, future may present increasing cases of systematic family-based product development, with product line practices getting better understood both in the software industry and in the educational digital multimedia industry.

Previous works presented potential advantages and disadvantages of multimedia usage in Brazilian schools (Amorim, 2003; Amorim & Pires & Ropoli & Rodrigues, 2004). The following brief literature review is a basis from which to start a discussion that involves multimedia production, communication management in virtual groups and the role of ICT in organizational groups.

Virtual groups may now benefit from the Internet due to many technological solutions, which include the existence of new tools for e-learning (Horton & Horton, 2003). The tools may be categorized into Learning Management Systems (LMS), Learning Content Management Systems (LCMS) and Collaboration Environment (CE). An LMS is used by managers, administrators, instructors and learners. It allows learners to find and enroll on courses, start a course, track and measure their progress in the courses. Teachers can monitor learners' activities, the environment tools used by each learner, the time of login and logout. Managers can create, change and remove educational programs and produce reports about the ongoing programs. The focus of LMS is on the supply of courses and on tracking learner progress in these courses. The courses must be created with the use of content creation tools. An LCMS, on the other hand, offers tools for the creation, management and reuse of learning content kept in a database. Instructional designers can organize the courses and the authors can manage the learning objects. The focus of LCMS is on content creation and display tools. With a full-featured LCMS, an organization can create courses with some level of customization, manage projects with many authors and different types and levels of content, track user access through the LCMS in different levels and deliver content in different formats and media. Differently, a CE helps people to collaborate with each other at a distance. Collaboration involves sharing content (related to work or study) and inter-participant communication (messages, discussions, classes, meetings, etc). Support tools can be simple emails, instant messengers, whiteboards, forums, audio and video conference, application sharing, virtual machines, etc. Some tools perform synchronous collaboration that may occur in real time. Other tools perform asynchronous collaboration, that is, interactions, not in real time. The interaction in response to another interaction can occur any time later, depending on the constraints of the learning program schedule.

New tools for e-learning require the production of educational multimedia. For many reasons, this production is still a challenge in developing countries. As to people with accessibility needs, the occasional use of assistive technologies and adaptive strategies to access the Web, for example, is an additional challenge that cannot be ignored while producing multimedia products to users geographically dispersed in a continental country like

Brazil. As a consequence, the production of audio, video, software and hypertext to be published on and used via Internet portals has to consider metadata standards like the IEEE Standard for Learning Object Metadata or the Dublin Core Metadata Standard. In this study, metadata should be understood as data describing data, resources or multimedia content. From this perspective, the Resource Description Framework, which uses the eXtensible Markup Language (XML) as its encoding syntax, is of special relevance since it intends to be a foundation for processing metadata while stimulating interoperability among applications on the Web.

The need for representing and transporting metadata in a manner that maximizes the interoperability of independently developed Webservers and clients is evident and brings additional steps to the production of multimedia. Due to that, the educational multimedia production process in large-scale projects must properly define quality standards to be reached that involve not only pedagogical, but also technical aspects that interfere with the project management (Mulcahy, 2006).

In large-scale PM with people who communicate electronically, the use of the best methods and practices for communication management in virtual groups turns out to be of great importance. While considering the role of ICT (Hustad & Munkvold, 2006), a comparison of different organizational groups, like Community of Practice, Knowledge Network, Workgroup and Team, would suggest that the former supports the creation and maintenance of distributed communities, and is the choice of ICT because it is user-friendly and efficient. For a Knowledge Network, the occasional linking of different knowledge networks together, implementing boundary practices through ICT initiated by management, would contrast with a Workgroup. In a Workgroup, characterized by a high degree of formality and a membership mandated from job descriptions and organizational hierarchy, the distributed workgroups depend on ICT for interaction purposes aiming at fulfilling organizational objectives. For a Virtual Team, where the degree of formality is high, there is a dependency on ICT for creating a shared space and for coordinating and performing common tasks with team members selected by management.

Since a Community of Practice (CoP) tends to be informal, or to have a low degree of formality, in a context of self-selected assignment and voluntary participation, it tends to be the best option for educational multimedia production groups that necessarily consist of professionals with complementary profiles. On the other hand, joint enterprises and the subsequent mutual engagement are not necessarily in favor of a shared repertoire or a common vocabulary for communication (Mulcahy, 2006), which intensifies the interplay between the fields of PM and KM. According to Regsdell (2006), the reference material to compare CoPs and project teams should be taken from the Second-Generation Knowledge Management Movement, which emphasizes the discussion of human and social factors with special interest in the generation of new knowledge. This perspective would contrast with the so-called First-Generation, for which the focus would be technological issues related to knowledge management. In the production of educational multimedia, where there is a need for transcending disciplines and bring in different perspectives, resources should be used to cope with new situations and to create new knowledge.

With the objective of communicating electronically in virtual groups, it is necessary to move into a new way of interacting to better use ICT. This transition would be just one more stressing factor in a world where changes are more and more dynamic (Bates, 1999; Frame, 1994). A discussion on the intensification of change would involve, according to Conner (1993), seven fundamental issues: faster communication and knowledge acquisition; a growing worldwide population; increasing interdependence and competition; limited resources; diversifying political and religious ideologies; constant transitions of power;

and ecological distress. Due to this intensification, the ability to successfully manage change has become one of the most important skills needed for personal happiness and organizational prosperity. The negative response to change may come in the form of resistance. Different models exist in the literature (Conner, 1993). The emotional response may go from a passive to an active state, from stability to immobilization, to denial and to anger. Other phases may include bargaining, depression, testing and acceptance. On the other hand, the positive response to change may involve at least five phases: uninformed optimism, informed pessimism, hopeful realism, informed optimism, and completion.

While considering the intensification of change not only in the world in general, but in education as well (Bates, 1999), resilience may be understood as the ability to recover readily from illness, depression, adversity, or the like. One can enhance resilience (Conner, 1993) by understanding the basic mechanisms of individuals resistance, viewing resistance as a reaction to the disruption of expectations, interpreting resistance as a deficiency of either ability or willingness, encouraging and participating in open expressions of resistance and understanding that reactions to change may be managed. This study argues for applying the concepts of resilience and change to continuing education for teachers in order to better prepare them for a technology-based society. The training of teachers is quite fundamental in a context where their students would be getting prepared to deal with a dynamic environment while taking advantage of mechanisms that would boost resilience from a micro to a macro environment.

TEACHER TRAINING IN EDUCATIONAL TECHNOLOGY

The pace of change nowadays has put a premium on an organization's ability to learn. In order to increase the speed of change while having minimal dysfunctional behavior, poor habits that hinder resilience must be reviewed and altered. People must recognize and learn the many mechanisms involved in this process. But if the intent is learning, training is the solution. The literature on the subject (Bates, 1999; Conner, 1993; Frame, 1994) advocates that staff development should be embedded in a broad range of strategies related to the context of workers. From this perspective, UNICAMP establishes collaborations with different kinds of organizations, which include the Government of the State of São Paulo, Brazil, in actions involving teachers from public schools. As an example of teacher training that considers MoC, this section briefly describes a project for teacher training in educational technology, part of a program (CENP, 2007) in which researchers and PhD candidates from UNICAMP participated.

In the program mentioned above, 64-hour courses fostered pedagogical innovation in public schools, while considering the National Curriculum Parameters from the Brazilian Ministry of Education. Out of a total of sixty-four hours, a minimum of eight hours focused on training in educational technology. Having an Internet Portal as a way to deliver part of the multimedia material to the teachers in public schools, the researchers and PhD candidates involved in the project also prepared printed material to be used during the classes.

For the specific training in educational technology, an average of 30 participants per group attended an 8-hour class, given on Saturdays, in a computer laboratory, specially equipped for this activity. Most of the participants were teachers of senior and high schools from locations neighboring Campinas, the city where UNICAMP is based (main campus). All classes started with a discussion about the transition to the Information Society where schools start having ICT-based education in order to foster quality learning. After an introduction to basic concepts like synchronous and asynchronous communication tools, hypertext authoring tools were presented emphasizing publication of multimedia files on blogs. The pedagogical aspects behind the potential educational use of languages like the HyperText Markup Language (HTML), Mathematical Markup Language (MathML) and the eXtensible Markup Language (XML) were presented so that innovations like RSS news feed and video search engines would be discussed. The context brought up discussion themes such as the authoring of accessible multimedia and the possibility of device-independent access to the Internet. The access to public domain images, software, video and audio pleased most groups since they noticed the possibility of enriching their classes with multimedia available on the Web.

Not only the program mentioned above (CENP, 2007), but many others that involved UNICAMP were fundamental to help researchers and PhD candidates to better understand the reality of Brazilian public schools. This knowledge turns out to be fundamental to the quality production of educational multimedia and the accompanying teachers' guide. Some of the many challenges and opportunities in this real world project are presented in the next section.

EDUCATIONAL MULTIMEDIA: CHALLENGES AND OPPORTUNITIES IN A REAL WORLD PROJECT

In order to make it easier for people with disabilities to use the Web, some organizations have developed guidelines, like the World Wide Web Consortium's Web Accessibility Initiative. As far as education is concerned, guidelines for accessibility of Web sites, browsers, and authoring tools should receive special attention due to the need for including students with disabilities in the Information Society. There are general requirements for Web access by people with physical, visual, hearing, and cognitive or neurological disabilities to be considered. As to the production of multimedia for public High Schools in Brazil, to be discussed in this section, the requirements for Web access, prioritized by the government, were related to visual and hearing disabilities.

In 2007, there was a request from the government for large-scale research project proposals for the production of educational multimedia (MEC, 2007), involving different Brazilian organizations, especially Universities. In UNICAMP, proposals in three different fields were approved, the projects planned the creation of almost 900 multimedia products of four types: audio for digital radio, video for digital TV, educational experiments based on hypertext and software with animations and simulations. Researchers in UNICAMP saw these projects as a way to influence High School teaching in Brazil with potential pedagogical innovation stimulated by accompanying teachers' guide for each product. According to the original request for proposals, the guides should consider the possibility of having students with visual and/or hearing impairment in the classroom, a fact that made the production of this material even more challenging.

Large-scale projects on educational multimedia production are especially important to a public institution like UNICAMP, since it represents a way to involve both graduate and undergraduate students in interdisciplinary groups where new knowledge may be created while considering the characteristics of the Brazilian population. The experience is a way to develop human resources in new professional areas and to conduct interdisciplinary research, which includes aspects of management, technology and pedagogy as well. The content would come from the three different high school teaching subjects, in previously approved proposals, namely: Biology, Mathematics and Portuguese. The technology for the production of material, on the other hand, would come from the research areas of arts, languages, semiotics, audio, video, software, and many others. As to management, research turned out to be necessary

on how to properly plan, execute, monitor and control the project process, with an integrated change control that should compile data from many sources to generate spreadsheets with budget control and timetables. The multitude of professional profiles turned the interaction into a defying time-consuming objective.

The need for transferring information and knowledge while carrying out the project was an additional aspect to be considered in the formation of a scenario where the authors identified the relevant interplay involving the fields of PM and KM. As mentioned before, this scenario suggested a potential synergy (Regsdell, 2006) between project teams and CoPs. According to Kisielnicki (2006), the communication system within the team significantly influences its effectiveness, with the key question to be answered being: "What conditions does the project leader need to create in order to maximize the positive and minimize the negative aspects of teamwork?" Without presenting decisive conclusions, the author advocates the hypothesis that the network communication system, where the communication among all members is direct and cross-divisional, provides the most effective framework for the management of information technology projects. The author also expresses that the ideal research would require the same team to replicate the same project twice with the only difference being the communication method. Since all projects are unique, the conclusions of this and related research should be based on estimates.

Among the many challenges, the first one was related to the proposals themselves, since the group of researchers at UNICAMP involved in the projects had no previous experience in preparing project proposals. Another challenge would be the possibility of extending the 18-month duration, originally stated in the proposal, to almost two years, without increasing the budget. In this case, human resources management asked for additional monthly incomes that were planned for eighteen months only, a situation where the desired increase in duration was limited by the budget constraint. The main challenge was the integration of subprojects on Biology, Mathematics and Portuguese, a difficult task that would eventually bring benefits, such as the transfer of knowledge (Paquette, 2006) across these three communities that would necessarily respect the same technological requirements, to say the least.

Paquette (2006) defines a community of creation as: "a community of practice where members mainly focus on the sharing and generation of new knowledge for the purpose of creating new ideas, practices, and artifacts (or products). They can be legitimized through involvement in a company-sponsored product development effort, or may be informal through various practitioners with similar experience and knowledge meeting, and new innovations arise from this interaction" (p. 73). The author also indicates that technologies may expand the horizon of observation that a participant can monitor by allowing for the identification of additional knowledge sources. For the author, sharing asks for the flow of knowledge to be two-way through process, structural, or social means.

From the perspective that an organization is a community made up of smaller communities, the close alignment of CoPs with organizational strategies may increase their functional contributions. Understanding safe enclaves as being shared electronic and non-electronic social spaces that allow for underlying views to be expressed, Paquette (2006) suggests that CoPs may provide safe enclaves from organizational social-political pressures, a fact that would eventually encourage further knowledge sharing. This additional way of sharing is fundamental in a large-scale educational multimedia production project since the many smaller communities must interact somehow to find better solutions to problems at hand.

Ensuring the presence of a truly collaborative culture brings many challenges in terms of communication management, KM and MoC with virtual group building. Smith (2006) believes in a people-centered approach to KM in which CoPs provide a practical framework for the nurturing of collaborative relationships. The author also confirms that KM frequently fails to deliver on its promise as a viable means to favor knowledge creation and sharing. With the intention of guaranteeing a greater chance of success on large-scale projects for educational multimedia production, where there may be conflicting demands of cost, scope, quality, etc., establishing, facilitating and supporting CoPs is a relevant topic to be researched. Based on this scenario, a framework for an educational multimedia factory virtual group interaction is discussed while a software customization that implements this framework is proposed.

FRAMEWORK PROPOSAL

According to Archer (2006), the growing complexity in products, services, and processes requires more specialization and collaboration among the people involved. At the same time, orchestrating the involvement of groups asks for equilibrium in differentiation and integration. The author believes that CoPs "can create both codification and personalization channels to distribute knowledge and support learning" (p. 22) once they have a defined objective and scope. This way, tacit knowledge that is personal, context-specific, and hard to formalize and communicate would eventually be transformed into documents that could be replicated in order to benefit all those involved in a certain project. The author also confirms that KM is related to management in general, in activities like learning and innovation, benchmarking and best practice, strategy, culture, and performance measurement.

Different frameworks for KM are presented in the literature. Gupta & McDaniel (2002) synthesize a framework from an extensive literature review hypothesizing that five components should be considered essential to producing effective management of knowledge: harvesting, filtering, configuration, dissemination, and application. Harvesting means that knowledge must be harnessed from within the organization or acquired in some sense from outside the firm. Filtering means that some mechanism most logically exist to separate unnecessary or distracting knowledge from useful and applicable knowledge while configuration would be related to the development of mechanisms for organizing and storing this knowledge. In the last case, software may augment the management process by allowing better organization, cataloging, searching and sharing of files that are mostly represented by some form of text-base document. Dissemination involves creating a culture appropriate for transforming tacit knowledge into explicit knowledge through tools and tactics that will encourage collaborative and productive exchange within the group. At last, application, a component that should be considered essential to producing effective management of knowledge due to the fact that the best use of knowledge is more important than having knowledge available and failing to use it. The authors indicate that only rigorous hypothesis testing may yield empirical results that would draw on conclusions regarding KM practice.

Thus, this chapter suggests a framework for an educational multimedia factory virtual group interaction that would grow from a framework with five components: harvesting, filtering, configuration, dissemination, and application. This suggested framework should also incorporate the group organization possibilities of CoPs to distribute knowledge and support learning from the perspective that KM is related to management in general and that KM is involved in activities going from innovation to strategy. With the objective of confirming, verifying, or disproving by observation or experiment, a software implementation for the framework in question is proposed from the perspective of the large-scale multimedia production undertaken.

The software implementation to be considered suggests how to adapt existing software called Sakai, a collaboration and learning environment for education. This environment is a free and open-source product built and maintained by the Sakai community (Sakai, 2008). A set of generic collaboration tools forms the core of Sakai: Announcements, Drop Box, Email Archive, Resources, Chat Room, Forums, Threaded Discussion, Message Center, Message of the Day, News/RSS, Preferences, Presentation, Profile/ Roster, Repository Search, Schedule, Search, Web Content, WebDAV, Wiki and Site Setup. Sakai was chosen by the authors since it is already in use at UNICAMP in a project called TIDIA (FAPESP, 2008), an information technology program focused on the development of advanced Internet solutions. This program, created in 2001, involves different organizations in cooperative projects with approximately 600 researchers, out of which 168 are doing research on distance education. The fact that Sakai is in use at UNICAMP and that it has tools to help organize communication and collaborative work were mandatory for it to be chosen. Despite this, other similar software would also be adequate as platforms to test the proposed framework.

Dagger et al., (2007) considers Sakai a traditional e-learning platform, or LMS, suggesting that open-source LMSs are typically built on extensible frameworks that allow implementers to adjust and to modify systems. Dagger et al., (2007) indicates that, with Sakai, Web services were designed to expose a limited set of functionality supported within. If the free model of the Internet is considered, rigid frameworks and boundaries for e-learning platforms will not fit. This chapter suggests a framework for an educational multimedia factory virtual group interaction that may be implemented through the customization of Sakai (Sakai, 2008). The table summarizes the use of collaboration tools to support communication and the proposed enhancement changes.

Table 1. Use of collaboration tools to support communication

Tools	Use to support communication	Enhancement changes
Announcements Tool	Can be useful for posting announcements about important changes in deadlines, meeting times, or meeting locations.	Defines groups of participants by project and communication sessions and allows the announcement tool to target the sessions and their specific times and locations.
Drop Box Tool	Can be useful to upload and organize documents produced in meetings.	No remarkable changes needed.
Email Archive Tool	Provides information of messages exchanged during the project.	Provides e-mail addresses for projects and sessions to allow message exchange among participants of the project or session.
Home	Provides portal page for project.	Allows the definition of portal pages for projects and integrates with announcements, drop box and email archive tools.
Membership Tool	Manages subscriptions for projects and sessions.	Changes the site concept to include project and sessions. The site would represent a project or a past/future session.
Message Center	Can be a support for the project communication matrix.	No remarkable changes needed.
My Workspace	Provides online project site or online session site in case of distant participants.	Evolves the worksite concept to include project and sessions.
Permissions and Roles	Allows the configuration of participants roles when they have access to the project or session site.	No remarkable changes needed.
Schedule Tool	Considering the use of project and session concept. The schedules could be applied to them like posting group deadlines, meetings, tasks, etc.	No remarkable changes needed.
Synoptic Tool	Allows participants to quick look at recent updates on the environment (announcements, messages, emails, resource, etc.)	No remarkable changes needed.
Web Content Tool	Helps in the scenario where the project team has already a website and wants to link to the SAKAI environment.	No remarkable changes needed.

FUTURE TRENDS

Dagger et al., (2007) discuss core challenges to achieve information interoperability in next-generation e-learning platforms. For greater interoperability, environments must exchange both the information's syntax and its semantics while creating frameworks and standards to support plugability. The authors believe that "service composition will let these e-learning platforms dynamically discover and assemble e-learning services to achieve a given user's specific purpose" (p. 30). This way, next generation systems will support targeted personalization, with services interoperating to contextualize the content and activities of an e-learning experience.

Artificial intelligence based performance support systems, in a context of digital convergence and ubiquitous computing, may allow greater customization of the interface and easier communication for virtual groups. Electronic Performance Support Systems (EPSS) will have their importance increased with time since knowledge workers need access to data, information and knowledge all the time and everywhere (Rossett & Schafer, 2006). It is expected that an LMS will interface with the EPSS to supply the knowledge base and/or multimedia content.

For students with disabilities, the potential customization of multimedia products according to the student profile may enhance the access to these products, bringing education to a new standard of more democratic access. Due to the fact that technologies like the Internet provide the access to portals for an international audience, research is needed on metadata solutions for the automation of translation of interface and documents, eventually allowing teachers and students from one country to access products of other countries even when the original language of the product is another one.

While discussing software mass customization and supply chain formation, Greenfield (2004) suggests that the software factory vision will be developed gradually within several years. One of the reasons would be that software factories are based on the "convergence of key ideas in systematic reuse, model driven development, development by assembly and process frameworks" (p. 1). The synthesis into an integrated approach is new, but may benefit organizations in different ways. The multimedia factory, as a proposal based on the concept of software factory, is a new paradigm that demands further research; particularly, if the characteristics of the educational field are considered.

CONCLUSION

The production of quality educational multimedia content involves considering both its publication and its use, keeping in view aspects ranging from metadata standards to teachers' guides.

This chapter presented part of the behind-the-scenes work of a large-scale project on the production of educational multimedia. The scenario showed a significant interplay between the fields of PM and KM, which suggests a potential synergy between project teams and CoPs. Based on this scenario, a framework for an educational multimedia factory virtual group interaction was discussed while a software customization was proposed.

Researchers on issues and trends in technology project management in education organizations may benefit from the perspective presented in this chapter, which considered a project in a Brazilian University, faced with many challenges while producing quality educational multimedia. The implications for technology in education easily justify the research on subjects like accessibility and metadata standards.

Integrated educational and project management Webenvironments can tackle two important aspects: one refers to the use of existing open-source e-learning environments, so that management functionalities can be included via software engineering methodologies; the other aspect refers to bringing up project management practices and methods to large-scale educational initiatives.

ACKNOWLEDGMENT

The authors would like to thank Professor Fernando Antonio Arantes and Mrs. Miriam Cristina Chinellato de Oliveira from GGPE (Grupo Gestor de Projetos Educacionais), GR (Gabinete do Reitor), UNICAMP (Universidade Estadual de Campinas), for fostering research to advance the state of the art of the knowledge of project management. The authors also thank Dr. Adauri Brezolin for careful English revision of the manuscript.

REFERENCES

Amorim, J. A., Pires, D. F., Ropoli, E. A., & Rodrigues, C. C. (2004). O Professor e sua Primeira Página na Internet: Uma Experiência de Uso do Ambiente TelEduc. *Revista Brasileira de Informática na Educação, 12*(1), 37-42.

Amorim, J. A. (2003). A Educação Matemática, a Internet e a Exclusão Digital no Brasil. Educação Matemática em Revista. *SBEM, 10*(14), 58-66.

Archer, N. (2006). A Classification of Communities of Practice. In Coakes, E. & Clarke, S. (Eds.), *Encyclopedia of communities of practice in information and knowledge management* (pp. 21-29). Hershey, PA: IGI Global Publishing.

Bates, A. W. (1999). *Managing technological change.* San Francisco: Jossey-Bass.

Carlotto, M. S. (2002). A síndrome de Burnout e o trabalho docente. *Psicologia em Estudo, 7*(1), 21-29. ISSN 1413-7372. Retrieved December 30, 2007, from http://www.scielo.org/

CENP (2007). *Programa de Formação Continuada "Teia do Saber" - 2007, Capacitação Descentralizada Mediante Contratação de Instituições de Ensino Superior, Projeto Básico.* Portal do Governo do Estado de São Paulo, Secretaria de Estado da Educação, Coordenadoria de Estudos e Normas Pedagógicas. Retrieved December 30, 2007 from http://cenp.edunet.sp.gov.br/Forcont2007/

Conner, D. R. (1993). *Managing at the speed of change.* New York: Random House.

Dagger, D., O'Connor, A., Lawless, S., Walsh, E., & Wade, V. P. (2007). Service-oriented e-learning platforms: From monolithic systems to flexible services. *IEEE Internet Computing, Institute of Electrical and Electronics Engineers, 11*(3), 28-35.

FAPESP (2008). *TIDIA - Programa de Tecnologia da Informação no Desenvolvimento da Internet Avançada.* Portal da Fundação de Amparo à Pesquisa do Estado de São Paulo. Retrieved May 01, 2008 from http://www.tidia.fapesp.br/portal.

Frame, J. D. (1994). *The new project management: Tools for an age of rapid change, corporate reengineering, and other business realities.* San Francisco: Jossey-Bass. ISBN 155542662X.

Greenfield, J. (2004). *Software factories: Assembling applications with patterns, models, frameworks, and tools.* Microsoft Corporation MSDN Architecture Center Portal. Retrieved May 13, 2008 from http://msdn.microsoft.com/en-us/library/ms954811.aspx

Gupta, A., & McDaniel, J. (2002). Creating competitive advantage by effectively managing knowledge: A framework for knowledge management. *Journal of Knowledge Management Practice, 3*(1), 1-9. ISSN 1705-9232.

Horton, W., & Horton, K. (2003). *E-learning tools and technologies: A consumer's guide for trainers, teachers, educators, and instructional designers.* Indianapolis, IN: Wiley Publishing.

Hustad, E. & Munkvold, B. E. (2006). Communities of practice and other organizational groups. In E. Coake s,& S. Clarke, (Eds.), *Encyclopedia of communities of practice in information and knowledge management* (pp. 60-62). Hershey, PA: IGI Global Publishing,

Kisielnicki, J. (2006). Transfer of information and knowledge in the project management. In E. Coakes, & S. Clarke, (Eds.), *Encyclopedia of communities of practice in information and knowledge management* (pp. 544-551). Hershey, PA: IGI Global Publishing.

MEC (2007). *Chamada Pública para Produção de Conteúdos Educacionais Digitais Multimídia.* Portal do Ministério da Educação, Secretaria de Educação a Distância, Departamento de Produção e Capacitação em Programas de EAD. Retrieved December 30, 2007 from http://portal.mec.gov.br/seed/

Mulcahy, R. (2006). *PM crash course: Premier edition.* Minneapolis, MN: RMC Publications, Incorporated.

Paquette, S. (2006). *Communities of practice as facilitators of knowledge exchange.* In E. Coakes, & S. Clarke, (Eds.), *Encyclopedia of communities of practice in information and knowledge management* (pp. 68-73). Hershey, PA: IGI Global Publishing.

Ragsdell, G. (2006). The contribution of communities of practice to project management. In E. Coakes, & S. Clarke, (Eds.), *Encyclopedia of communities of practice in information and knowledge management* (pp. 104-107). Hershey, PA: IGI Global Publishing.

Rossett, A., & Schafer, L. (2006). Job aids and performance support: The convergence of learning and work. *International Journal of Learning Technology, Inderscience Enterprises Limited, 2*(4), 310-328.

Sakai (2008). *The Sakai project.* Sakai Foundation Portal. Retrieved May 04, 2008 from http://sakaiproject.org

Smith, P. A. C. (2006). Organisational change elements of establishing, facilitating, and supporting CoPs. In E. Coakes, & S. Clarke (Eds.), *Encyclopedia of communities of practice in information and knowledge management* (pp. 400-406). Hershey, PA: IGI Global Publishing.

KEY TERMS AND DEFINITIONS

Community of Practice (CoP): KM social network that tends to be informal, or to have a low degree of formality, in a context of self-selected assignment and voluntary participation.

E-Learning: The process of learning online, especially via the Internet.

Framework: A basic conceptual structure used to solve or address complex issues; values, assumptions, concepts, and practices that constitute a perspective of viewing reality.

Management of Change (MoC): Management methodologies to prevent, predict, track, estimate impacts of changes on a system.

Metadata: May be understood as data describing data, resources or multimedia content.

Multimedia Factory: Based on the concept of software factory, it would be a development environment configured to support the rapid development of different types of digital media, which may include audio, video, software or hypertext, among others; while a mature software factory would intend to have high levels of code reuse, a mature digital multimedia factory would intend to reuse as many parts of products as possible.

Resilience: May be understood as the ability to recover readily from illness, depression, adversity, or the like in a context of impacting change.

Software Factory: Development environment configured to support the rapid development of a specific type of application.

Chapter XXVII
Instructional Technology Plans for Higher Education

Hasan Tinmaz
Educational Technologist, Turkey

ABSTRACT

Technology planning is an indispensable activity for all higher education institutions nowadays. The major purpose of the technology planning is to utilize technologies effectively and implement them for communicative, managerial and instructional purposes. This chapter offers a dynamic and adaptable framework for technology planning project in higher education institutions. Basically, the framework compares the mission and vision in terms of three dimensions; Peopleware, Hardware and Software. Peopleware focuses on all people within faculty organizations such as students, academicians and administrators and analyze their current situation in terms of four different interrelated points (technology knowledge, value, belief and attitude) to depict their levels (naïve, apprentice, professional and experienced). In the hardware analysis, the author analyzes personal computers, networking tools, other peripherals (printers, scanners, and etc...) and the building. For software analysis, starting with the operating system, entire software required for instructional and professional purposes are documented. In the last step, project team analyzes the data holistically and creates yearly developmental activities in terms of applicable recommendations.

INTRODUCTION

In parallel to innovations in the world, our societies are continuously developing and evolving.

As a result, both governmental and industrial organizations begin to work out the restructuring ways for increasing their effectiveness and productivity. For the adaptation of societies into modern era and for their preparations for the innovations, "education" is the reality and the necessity for us. As the technology has emerged in the field of education and reflected its effects on educational systems (Westera, 2004), technologies are perceived as a panacea for all instructional problems. Moreover, as Whelan (2004) pointed "today's teens view technology not only as a part of life, but as a way of life" (p. 48).

After a certain time, scientific research studies have shown that there is no significant difference between technologically furnished environments and their counter parts. For instance, well-known educational technologist; Clark (1983) frequently emphasizes that there is no evidence showing that utilization of any medium for delivering instruction yields better learning benefits. On the other hand, the same studies demonstrated that there are certain benefits in terms of instructional and managerial time efficiency, enrichment of instructional contexts in terms of materials, easy student record-keeping activities. Similarly, Clark argues that media utilization offers some opportunities for performance and time savings. In that sense, the scholars from different disciplines have started scrutinizing the underlying reasons in subsequent to those non-significant study results.

The most significant result of these scientific attempts is that we must focus on how technological processes and tools are integrated into teaching-learning environments rather than how much technology is utilized in those environments. Therefore, the history of technology in education might be summarized in one sentence; just bringing the technology, no matter how much it is qualified, into instructional settings and allowing it to be used by the teachers or students mean nothing in terms of learning efficiency. Stakeholders of educational activities must spend more time and energy on technology-enriched contexts so that the return-on-investment will be maximized (Huber, 2005). Otherwise, technology implementation will not be provided in a broad sense.

Instructional Technology is a set of systematic and planned activities to arrange learning and teaching environments for that maximization purpose. In 1994, Seels and Richey defined the field of Instructional Technology "... as theory and application of design, development, utilization, management and evaluation of processes and resources for learning and teaching" (p.1). Such a definition of Instructional Technology comprises each and every individual before, during, and after the related processes and all the Information and Communication Technologies (ICTs) in both micro and macro levels. Each country spends a great amount of money for technological investments. Out of that budget, a huge percentage is dedicated to educational use of technologies in schools, universities or any other institutions.

Improving the efficiency and the generalization of information and communication technologies' usage in education are the ultimate aims of each national development plan. In all levels of education, instructors are encouraged to utilize audio-visual tools in their teaching activities; such as, computers, televisions, videos, overhead projectors, and etc. As Roblyer (2003) identified, the crucial duty of our modern teachers is to establish and to put the effective technology integration plans into practice. Hence, schools and universities are provided with the Internet connections and information technology classrooms for computer-aided-instruction. For instance, according to Eurydice (2008) which is an information network on education in Europe, for the years 2006-2007, Turkey has provided 294.000 computers for its schools, information technology classes for 19.000 schools and ADSL type Internet connection for 25.000 schools. However, in year 2005, 48 students shared one computer in schools where this ratio is decreasing each fiscal year.

Planning is the most vital tool for managing these investments issues on education (Roblyer, 2003). "Instructional technology planning", as a tool of instructional technology, is a technique for making it clear to individuals the current and prospective positions of their technological infrastructure in relation to learning, teaching and managerial activities of an instructional environment. It is a way of "technique" of using both qualitative and quantitative research methods to portray the current situation in order to foresight the prospective needs of organizations. It is a "tool" mostly in the form of written documents for identifying the gap between the available and required sources. In that manner, an instructional technology plan prepared in this essence should act as an indication for cognitive, affective and psychomotor knowledge, skills and abilities in any type of organization.

The instructional technology planning could be in different levels like school, campus, county or country. Roblyer (2003) offers two different levels; district and school saying that there might be overlapping points for their planning activities. This planning process must be prepared and implemented by a committee including all groups of people who will be affected by the results of this planning action; e.g. teachers, academicians, technology specialists. This intensely designed process will increase the possibility of taking the full advantage of technologies in relation to teaching and learning (Roblyer, 2003).

If we specifically concentrate on higher education institutions, we realize that the scope of the plan is highly complicated. For instance, affection of students' beliefs, values, and attitudes towards technology, development of skills and abilities related to ICTs, augmentation of quality of learning environments which faculty members are dealing with, improvement of current technology infrastructure and resources, enhancement of the efficiency of technology implementation in both academic and administrational settings are some of the major considerations. Technology planning is an extensive process which demands on this tremendous effort. It is the profound determination of organizational needs regarding technological and human resources. In addition to determining

needs, it also provides solutions to satisfy those pre-determined needs. Planning process analyzes antecedents, processes and consequences of the given organization. Moreover, it reveals and covers general problems of an organization as a result of a sensitive scrutiny. For future recommendation, it produces precautions for the organization's current system.

Higher education institutions require a specific concern in relation to ICTs and human resources due to their enormous budgets. For instance, the total budget for Turkey's Ministry of National Education and The Council of Higher Education is nearly 21.494.096.000 $ which is 13.6 percent of central government budget in 2007 (National Education Statistics - Formal Education, 2008). Hence, researchers, experts or academicians prepare different reports on current and prospective situations of technological and human resources. Most of these reports stay on shelves for years without implementation. In some cases, even the recommendations of such reports are implemented, they create unexpected and negative results. In general, stakeholders do not consider the entire framework covering all inner dynamics of a system. Consequently, some essential parts of the organization might be neglected which may result in totally negative consequences on the system. This problem can be overcome with a systematic approach working on a well-designed framework.

In the planning process, both improvement of technology usage level and the restructuring of managerial decision process to address the requirements of adjustments must be arranged for overall body of organization. The technology plan should be based both on updating technologies and on flexibility and quality of technological support services provided for learning and teaching activities. Otherwise, planning activities could be a waste of time and money and the entire processes may become inefficient. Most universities develop these technology plans as a futuristic guideline for their own development. On the other hand, technologies have an enormous pace of change and are full of innovations. Thus, individuals must spend too much time to delineate current situation and to foresight the next one, and the next three or five years' time, or even more. That necessitates the existence of a general framework for assessing instructional technology infrastructure of an institution. This chapter presents the pre, the while and post stages of these planning projects in relation to describing a general framework for guiding people to design, implement and assess such projects.

In this chapter, an analysis of a higher education institution's "instructional technology planning" process is presented in accordance with input, process, and output resources. The chapter initially presents the definition of technology planning and its basic stages. Afterwards, the proposed general framework is demonstrated and each framework stage is scrutinized and explained in terms of functional operations. The fundamental purpose of the framework is (a) to diffuse technology utilization in every part of the institution, (b) improve the institution's attitude toward technology, (c) to promote the common usage of the current educational technology resources, and (d) to reveal students' value, beliefs and attitudes.

To achieve these goals, suggestions and methods influencing each group of people in higher education institutions like students, managers and instructors, positive attitudes toward technology are defined as the underpinnings of that framework. Moreover, the interaction among departments in any faculty is taken into consideration within the framework questioning the relational issues and expressing recommendations to increase it. The recommendations must be effective to improve the institution's situation positively in terms of technology implementation. At the end of this process, the main purpose is to set desired conditions in a frame regarding technology integration for all faculties.

BACKGROUND

Many times, we complain about the higher education and have a consensus on the idea that the academic system must change. On the other hand, the question of "what should be changed" clearly shows a variation for different people. Some concerns about the curriculum, some other complains about the technology utilized in the courses, or some other suffers from the negative attitudes of the instructors. For the accomplishment of these changing attempts, the necessity of reformation must be stated within the faculties, not from outsiders (Laurillard, 2002). Therefore, the managers of "changes" should consider too many things together so that they can address the different problems simultaneously (McCormick, 2006).

In that proposed framework, the "changes" in any faculty concentrates on four different issues of faculty stakeholders including students, lecturers, administrators and so forth... These four mutually dependant issues are technology KSAs (Knowledge, Skills and Abilities), Values, Beliefs and Attitudes of the stakeholders. By these four points, we will address the cognitive, affective and psychomotor needs of them. Within the framework, we will attempt to reveal the levels of different stakeholders in relation to these four issues. In this background section, we will first focus on technology planning itself and then the importance of these four issues in relation to technology planning will be explained from the literature.

The changes in tertiary education institutions are not straightforward due to several factors such as technological infrastructure, organization culture, and values (Laurillard, 2002). The activities aiming a profound change in faculties must control different variables together. Hence it is significant to comprehend the aims, focus and the process of technology planning. There are several definitions for technology planning. Here is a very exploratory one;

Technology implementation and planning refers to the extent in which the organization has strategically approached the deployment of new technologies and the manner in which it has prepared for the execution of the technologies prior to their implementation (Bellamy, 2007, p. 33).

The main purpose of the technology planning is to control the implementation of technologies within the body of faculties. We must comprehend these activities like a wide scale project or like a business action. On the other hand, we should always remember that all these activities focus on better education for our students (Huber, 2005). Additionally, for the effective use of new technologies into organizational settings, technology planning is an indispensable issue (Bellamy, 2007). As the innovative technologies have been functionalized in the education sector and their effects reflected on higher education institutions, as Laurillard (2002) suggested, the necessity of careful planning in terms of standardization and management of technologies is unquestionably appeared.

Technological adaptation to new innovations for educational activities is placed at the top of the agenda's of universities (Westera, 2004). Since that technological adjustment is a complicated process, it must be realized formally and carefully. Technology planning is a tool for managing this process where initiates from the current mission of the faculty and assist to reach the objectives stated in the vision (Watson, 2004; Masi & Winer, 2005). In the technology planning process, we simultaneously concentrate on different interrelated faculty aims; budgetary, instructive, human resource management, and etc…

As Watson (2004) outlined, a well-qualified technology planning process will cover a careful analysis of external resources (both technological and human resources) which requires performing several researches. There are several points that should be taken into consideration in that process; formation of project team, preparation of

timeframes of action, setting deadlines for project stages, alternative plan if any crisis occurs, better knowledge on scientific researches and so on.

Each technology plan must be in a form of case study which is very unique to that situation. Technology plan must describe the current situation in a very comprehensive and extensive manner. It should assist faculty to utilize the necessary technological instruments into learning-teaching processes. These planning actions will infuse the technology into organization and changing the culture and will integrate the technology in the required processes effectively. This includes not only instructional activities but also managerial and communication actions. Furthermore, all these attempts must serve a purpose of creating "a dynamic technological environment" (Watson, 2004, p. 35). Similarly the prepared technology plan must be adaptable and flexible for unexpected situations and sudden alterations.

A technology plan is a road-map for giving detailed and clear recommendations to faculties on "what and how to do" about technology implementation in different process for different times. Sometimes, it provides how to embed a knowledge management system for managerial issues; sometimes it offers opportunities for instructors on evaluation purposes. Planning activities covers different monthly or yearly timelines which means we depict the current situations and foresight the future (Huber, 2005). For instance, Masi and Winer (2005) summarize technology planning activities in a university and conclude with a five-year time of action with the following recommendations; installations of hardware and a campus-based course management system, facilitation of technology learning activities for instructors and students, and offering a reward system for instructors in terms of encouraging technology use in courses.

Technology planning requires action – just preparing a report is not magical tool to change everything suddenly. Several factors will affect its impacts on organizations:

- Each stakeholders must be informed about the study results and the activity plan earlier than the implementation,
- Certain and enough time must be dedicated to implementation activities,
- The cost of implementation activities including the process and alterations within the faculties must be arranged in accordance with the idea of return-on-investment.

To compete within the highly dynamic business sector, students must learn about both their subject matters and technological knowledge. Watson (2004) urges that students should spend their times and efforts on being more competent about technology literacy. We must always remember that the students' existing knowledge will profoundly impact on their future learning (Laurillard, 2002). However, even though students utilize the same technological infrastructure or are exposed to the same instruction, their skills fluctuate to a great extent (Wach, 2004).

Technology is not only for students, but also their lecturers as well. The instructors use technologies for their learning and teaching activities as key determinants for better quality (Masi & Winer, 2005). The knowledge or the existence of technology does not guarantee that instructors will functionalize it. Instructors must also know the possible benefits of that technology as well as its limitations. It is significant for higher education institutions that instructors know what they do and why they do for effectiveness and quality (Laurillard, 2002). They must comprehend, as Bellamy (2007) argues, the aims of using that technology for any process.

Furthermore, as Whelan (2004) stated our students utilize the technology in their lives and possess a slightly positive attitude toward technology where it is the proper time for educators to benefit from those favorable attitudes. In order to take the full advantage of technology utilization or integration, we should be aware of each stakeholder's belief on both how learning occurs and how technology affects on our lives, especially on instructional activities (Watson, 2004). Additionally, a well-qualified technology planning project modify the current values of the organization in a way that all organization members merits more on technology for appropriate cases when needed (McCormick, 2006). Therefore it is a good effort to depict the current situation of people about how much they value technology itself and its integration to current inner processes of the organization.

As a conclusion, technology planning is a long-term process and demonstrates a real progress in higher education organizations for academicians, students and administrative staff in terms of increasing the effectiveness of their activities. In the following section, we will focus on how these planning activities are realized within the faculty structure.

MAIN FOCUS OF THE CHAPTER

Technology planning projects are dynamic and adaptable processes. Thus, the main idea of this chapter is to provide higher education faculties with a general framework for conducting technology planning studies. The readers should always remember that all planning activities are unique implying that framework must be adjusted in terms of resources, situation, budget and etc... In the Figure 1, you can see the illustration of the proposed framework. The dashed lines represent the dynamic nature of the framework and the direction of arrows show the flow of tasks to be performed.

Step 1: Team Building

The success of any project strongly depends on the characteristics of project team members. There must be a project manager and vice-managers who will dedicate their times and efforts to that project. Afterwards, there will be several people

Figure 1. The general proposed technology planning framework

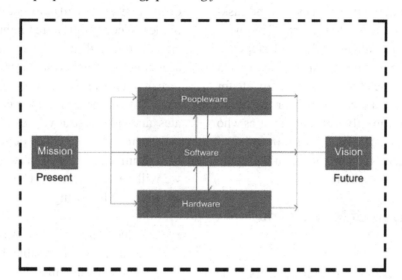

working within that team. The possible roles in any technology project depend on the scope. On the other hand, the alternatives for duties are; curriculum specialist, technology analyst, media specialist, quantitative and qualitative researchers, and etc…

I agree with McCormick's (2006) grouping these roles as; project committee and operational stakeholders. Project committee works like theoretical and managerial orientation of the project whereas operational stakeholders work in the field. They supply each other with the necessary information throughout the process. For the success of the technology planning project, all stakeholders must perceive it not as a task-by-task action, but the owner of all actions. As McCormick emphasizes stakeholders must comprehend the organization culture and behave accordingly for that project.

It is a fundamental concern to include right people for technology planning projects. If you are an outsider of the organization, you should ask the possible project team members to fulfill a CV for you. This CV should briefly include the following headings;

Name – Profession – Years in the Profession - Key Qualifications – Educational Background – Employment Background – Experiences on Technology Planning (if any) – Knowledge & Experiences on Quantitative and Qualitative Data Analysis - Foreign Languages.

Step 2: Meetings and Deadlines

For the quality assurance of the technology planning projects, a weekly meeting of team members is highly crucial. The reports of each meeting must be clearly written down so that team members will check the weekly tasks needed. Moreover, each meeting should start with the controlling the items of previous meeting reports. If the scope of the project is big, there should be some committee meetings earlier than the whole group meeting.

Each project member should fulfill a simple table one day before the meeting so that the manager and/or vice managers could have a general understanding on their personal works about project. This table should be in four columns; name, tasks planned, tasks accomplished, and the revisions on tasks.

Having predefined deadlines (Watson, 2004) a clear work-flow schema is essential for the success of technology planning. Since the planning process will take a long time, it is a good activity to prepare your derivative framework and task-analysis including work-flow charts. This way, each team member will know what will happen in each step, or who is in charge of conducting that step and or how much time they will dedicate for that task. We should always consider that these team members are mostly from our faculties who have other responsibilities as well. In order to prevent from agenda crashes, we should prepare a timeframe of actions beforehand.

Step 3: Analysis of Mission and Vision

At the first kick-off meeting, team members come together to scrutinize the mission and vision statements of the entire higher education system of the country, their university, the faculty (or faculties), departments and related programs. The mission statement which focuses on the current activities of organization will be starting point for us. We will search for to what extent that faculty matches with the activities stated in mission. Afterwards, we will see the future plans of that organization in terms of vision statement which we will attempt to foresight the possible steps to reach that prospective situation effectively. We will carry out a need-assessment with which we will depict the current situation and forecast the future, and identify the reasonable gaps that we can fulfill.

In that step, the major problem might be the lack of concrete and certain mission and vision statements. For some newly established departments or faculties, we might realize this problematic issue. If the case is like that, we should start with our project by creating a realistic, up-to-date and fit-with-faculty mission and vision statements.

Step 4: Peopleware Analysis

This is the most important, difficult and time-spending stage of the entire planning process.

Peopleware is a term for all people in the faculty or university who will be affected from the results of the project. Peopleware might cover managers (such as rector, deans, and head of departments), academicians (such as lecturers, professors, and research assistants), students from different departments and grades and sometimes even graduates and administrative personnel (secretaries and technical clerks). The decision of who will be scrutinized in the project is a threshold wheren we will be very careful. The recommendations are as in the following:

- Include deans and vice-deans and all head of departments, if possible. But be aware that their data sometimes cannot reflect the whole picture of the situation. Moreover, if the team member who will analyze their ideas is a subordinate, s/he cannot act normally for data gathering.

- Use statistical representation and sampling methods for entire faculty. Of course, it is perfect to collect data from each and every person within faculty, but, it sometimes becomes a huge work and the project might fail from that stage.

- For more in-depth knowledge about faculty and departments, establishing interviews with the academic staff are essential. On the other hand, it is a huge work-load for conducting interviews with all faculty members, transcribing and their data analysis. In that sense, the selection of key informers for interviewing is indispensable. The biggest mistake for that selection might be that inclusion of only the dean and head of departments. The proper way is to comprise a group of key informers from different academic levels, such as; deans, head of departments, lecturers, research assistants, students, clerks and etc...

Having such a heterogeneous group will offer an opportunity to compare the ideas of academicians from different levels and different understanding of educational activities and technologies. With the help of that, misunderstandings or different perspectives among the faculty members might be revealed.

Figure 2 shows the illustration of the Peopleware analysis steps. As shown in the figure, stakeholders must be scrutinized from four interrelated points; their knowledge, skills, and abilities (KSAs) in terms of technology, their beliefs, values and attitudes toward technology. The triangles demonstrate the individuals' four different levels on those interrelated points. These four levels from bottom to top are naïve, apprentice, professional and experienced. This framework offers that each individual should be assessed to find his/her level on KSAs, belief, value and attitude which might vary for that person. For instance, an individual might appreciate the technology and its usefulness; however s/he doesn't know how to work with technology.

We will firstly define the four major concerns of the Peopleware. Technology knowledge, skills and/or abilities (KSAs) are the fundamental competencies that a person must possess to functionalize the technological tools and processes. For different departments, different KSAs are required to be acquainted during the higher education. Therefore, the basic, middle and the advanced levels of technological competencies must be overtly defined for each department. The following steps might be:

- Analyzing your students on their stages with respect to predefined competencies,

Figure 2. The peopleware analysis

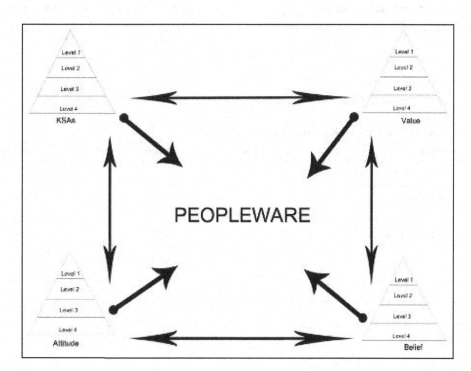

- Checking your departmental curriculum to what extent your department offers opportunities to learn those KSAs in terms courses, or any other activities,
- Checking your departmental courses to what extent your students are experienced in terms of using those KSAs before their graduation,
- Analyzing your academicians about their technology literacy levels in general or in departmental differentiations,
- Checking your academicians about their technology implementation into instruction; e.g. how much they integrate technology into their instructional activities, how much they encourage students to use technologies, which tools mostly utilized in instruction,
- Analyzing the administrative employees' current technological knowledge and try to depict the gap between what they know and what they should know for effectiveness.

For all these analyses activities, both quantitative and qualitative research methods must be applied for all stakeholders. It is a good start to establish a quantitative survey within the faculty by including all possible stakeholders. In order to collect data from students and in order not to disturb the on-going instruction, the weekly schedules of each department in faculties must be investigated. The most available sessions should be identified and the data collection for the same instrument should be conducted in the same week. A time-table derived from the weekly schedule must be readily available including the days, hours, class name and location, number of the students, the name of the instructor and the data collector (Table 1). In the same table, from freshmen to senior years should be written together for each department.

In the student survey, following questions should be asked:

- **Demographics:** Gender, department, grade, possession of a personal computer, Internet connection, the year of computer experiences,
- **Competency levels (Experienced, Inexperienced, Unknown)** on following daily office tools; word processor, spreadsheet,

Table 1. An Example of Data Gathering Schedule

2008-2009 Spring Semester – ABC Department - Data Collection Schedule				
Days	**9.00-9.50**	**10.00-10.50**	**11.00-11.50**	**12.00-12.50**
Monday	32 Sophomore Students Instructional Design Course Mr. Hasan Tinmaz A 201 2nd Floor – 4th Door By Ilker YAKIN			
Tuesday				
Wednesday				
Thursday				
Friday				

presentation, database, web browser, e-mail, web page development, and any other department-specific tools,

- KSAs on technology literacy in a more detailed-fashion (on a five point Likert scale from "I am very good at" to "I am very bad at"). The KSAs should be decided by a group of experts for identifying the real needs on technological competencies. There are several web pages and articles on technology competencies for different sectors which might be a starting point for the needs identification. For instance, "The University of Northern Iowa, Pre-Service Teacher Technology Competencies" offers taxonomy for KSAs of students for faculty of educations (Krueger, Hansen, & Smaldino, 2000). Similarly, ISTE (International Society for Technology in Education) provides educators with "National Educational Technology Standards" each year. Those ISTE standards are quite helpful for creating surveys and interviews. Some possible examples for those competencies are:

  - I can transfer the pictures and videos recorded with a camera to my computer,
  - I can install the drivers of different hardware,
  - I can write formulas in a spreadsheet programs,
  - I can use any operating system,
  - I can solve the computer problems by myself...

- Technology access and technical assistance questions; if the people don't have any technological tools or the problems of these tools cannot be solved, and people will not be able to apply what they know. Therefore, on a five point Likert scale (from strongly agree to strongly disagree), we ask their ideas about technological facilities of the faculty. Some possible questions are;

  - The available faculty infrastructure supports my technology utilization,
  - The number of computer per student is adequate for me,
  - The Internet speed is good for me,
  - The technical assistance for the problems is satisfactory for me,
  - Our faculty computers are updated in a regular manner,
  - I am satisfied with the functions our library,
  - I believe that students' needs are taken into consideration when technological up-dates are implemented.
  - I can access printers in the faculty,
  - I can use scanner in the faculty...

For the instructor survey, we can use similar questions or their adapted versions. We can add some questions like:

- The year of experience in teaching and the year of working in that faculty,
- The preferred teaching methods (from purely teacher-centered to purely student-centered),
- The preferred in-class activities (discussions, role plating, presentations and etc...),
- The personal and professional developmental activities,
- The ways of technology integration to instructional activities,
- The knowledge on technology implementation...

If there are some gaps between departments, lecturers or among students, in order to get in-depth knowledge, possible interviews could be scheduled. As a remark, the anonymity of the survey data must be strongly provided. Especially, the data of administrative employees and academicians must be collected by an outsider, if possible. It is an offer to establish semi-structured process with the lecturers in accordance with the results of the survey which will be a guide for the interview schedule. The possible questions are:

- Can you please describe the mission and vision of your faculty?
- Do you personally perceive yourself as capable in using computers?
- In which topics or content do you want to enhance your technology KSAs?
- Do you want to join any technology oriented training in the faculty?
- When you face a technology related problem in your office, or in your daily life or in the classroom, which ways do you prefer to overcome that problem?
- Do you integrate technologies in your courses? (If yes, please describe, if no, why?)?
- How do you decide in the ways of technology implementation or what is the inner force that you want to use them?
- How do you describe the effects of technologies on you?

Up to this point, we have the data of faculty survey and the transcription of interviews. In order to triangulate the data, we should focus on the realities in action. For that reason, several unobtrusive observations must be conducted. Randomly some courses should be selected and observed with permission. In that observation, a simple "yes", "no", "inapplicable" answer should be used and several notes should be taken when necessary. The possible observation points are:

- Does the instructor use any technological tool? (If yes, what are they?)
- Does the instructor face any technological problem? (Please describe the problem first and then write what s/he did)
- Does the instructor encourage the students to actively participate the course?
- Does the instructor attempt to be a role model in relation to technology use?

- Do the students use the technology? (If yes, how and when?)

The other three vital points for Peopleware issues are; technology attitude, technology beliefs and technology values emphasizing the affective domain of personal development. Unfortunately, students or instructors mostly focus on the learning in cognitive domain and neglect their affective standpoint on the topic. In other words, an instructor might know the technology very well, but the same instructor might think that it is useless for the learning-teaching process. That is why, it is essential to understand both the cognitive and affective situations of the stakeholders.

Technology value stands for the worth assessment in terms technology and its effects on ethics, society, education and etc... Afterwards believing in technology occurs implying that a person accepts or relies on technology and its usefulness on different settings and processes. In the last stage people form their attitude towards technology which means the internal perceptive representation of technology in individual's mind. These terms are used interchangeably for many contexts; yet, they both reflect on affective domain.

The number of questions in the KSAs survey sometimes becomes a huge paper work. Therefore, I suggest preparing and applying another affective domain survey in the following weeks so that people don't get bored with filling the surveys for hours. When organizing such kind of affective surveys, you can check the literature and identify possible questionnaires and their subscales. Subsequently, you can select the questions which strongly correlated with the subscale or the questions which directly related to your purposes. Otherwise, stakeholders will fulfill an enormous number of questions in each survey. For instance, the well known "Computer Attitude Scale" of Loyd and Gressard (1984) could be adapted to survey which addresses four subscales; (a) computer anxiety or fear of computers, (b) liking of computers, (c) confidence in ability to use or learn about computers, and (d) and usefulness (importance) of computers in life. In the affective survey, we may use a five point Likert scale (from strongly disagree to strongly agree) and the following questions are possible:

- Technological tools make me scared (attitude question),
- I feel tensioned when I use any technology (attitude question),
- It is time-consuming to learn something about technology (attitude question),
- Computer technologies are useful for me (belief question),
- Computer technologies can be used for increasing the quality of instruction (belief question),
- Use of technologies in classrooms increases the academic success of students (belief question),
- I know ethical rules for using any technology (value question),
- I will use technologies in my prospective job (value question),
- I need to learn more about technologies for my professional development (value question)…

The last subject about the "Peopleware" is the triangles representing the levels on four major interrelated points. I named these four levels from bottom to top as naïve, apprentice, professional and experienced. Following points are the remarks:

- Since this is a dynamic and adaptive framework, the names of the levels might be changed in accordance with the contexts.
- Those levels could be diminished to three or increased to five, if needed. The levels are organized by statistical cut points, e.g., the mean scores from 1.00 to 1.99 might be named as naïve…
- Since it is too difficult to address the each unique need of student or instructor, we calculate average scores and assess accordingly. In that assessment, it is beneficial to have certain taxonomies. Each department or faculty could create its own taxonomy and adapt it in parallel to innovations. In the finalization of the technology planning process, we will consider those levels and try to identify the ways of moving stakeholders one or more levels further.

There are several different technology taxonomies in the literature. For example, in the work of "The University of Northern Iowa, Pre-Service Teacher Technology Competencies", the entire competencies are leveled in five; pre-novice, novice, apprentice, practitioner, and expert (Krueger, Hansen, & Smaldino, 2000). For further information, the famous book of Tomei (2005), "Taxonomy for the Technology Domain" should be read earlier

Table 2. The sample level of peopleware

Level 1: Naive: Students demonstrate a sound understanding of technology and concepts.			
Values	**Beliefs**	**Attitudes**	**KSAs**
▪ They do not feel a need to learn new technologies. ▪ They understand the social, ethical and legal issues about technology.	▪ They believe that technology is useful.	▪ They are forming their attitudes towards technology. ▪ They assumed to have nearly from negative to slightly neutral attitude toward technology.	▪ They only know fundamental tools of technology ▪ They recognize strengths and weaknesses of technologies ▪ They need always assistance of others.

than creating faculty oriented taxonomy. Tomei states that for the well-qualified instruction, we must add "technology domain" among the other well known domains of learning; cognitive, affective and psychomotor. In the Table 2, you can see a simple example for "Naïve" level.

As a last comment, after all these data gathering activities, the entire data set must be both quantitatively and qualitatively analyzed. Advanced analysis techniques (discourse analysis, discriminative function analysis, and etc…) could be utilized; however, since it is not the scope for that chapter, we will not go into details.

Step 5: Hardware Analysis

For technology use, it is evident that there must be certain technological tools in hand. However the existence of those technologies does not guarantee that they functionalize fully. In order to analyze hardware, entire resources must be grouped into four; (a) the PCs, (b) networking infrastructure and tools, (c) other computer related tools, such as scanner, printer, DVD writer, (d) building infrastructure including classrooms, laboratories, and etc…

Each faculty should have an inventory for hardware resources. On the other hand, many times, these inventories are not up-to-date or include insufficient information. As a result it is a reliable step to create a new and detailed list of hardware resources. For the PC analyses, there is certain software which lists the entire hardware resources and their features connected computer main-board. One can easily prepare an inventory for all hardware utilized in the faculty or university. "Belarc Advisor" is such software which creates a profile of your computer including all installed software and hardware (http://www.belarc.com/free_download.html).

When we want to prepare the inventory for networking, we can still use some computer programs. NetworkView, for example, is a pro-

gram for managing and discovering the tools and software in relation to infrastructure (http://www.networkview.com/) providing users with a network map and its report.

The profile of other technological tools is also important for faculties. In brief terms, it is important to know how many TVs, printers, scanners, digital cameras, overhead projectors, projectors and etc there are… and their accessibility for each stakeholder in the faculty. If our faculty requires more specialized tools such as experiment materials, or maps, or skeletons, we must identify them as well.

Visualization of the faculty infrastructure is essential for both analyzing and providing further recommendations. Hence, the pictures of all classrooms, laboratories and all other buildings should be taken when they are empty. These pictures should be added as an appendix for the last report. Using this appendix, the developments or changes in the infrastructure could be identified in the future. Moreover, the photos of the network elements like hubs, switches, or routers should also be taken.

What is more, interviews with the technical assistants (if exist) on how and when updates for those hardware is done. Similarly, with some separate interviews or with some additional questions to Peopleware interviews, we can learn the ideas of academicians, secretaries and students on the current situation of hardware as well. Most of the time, the major problems are the lack of accessibility and up-to-date technologies.

As a last statement, technology planning process should also delineate the technological tools and access of academicians and students in their personal life. To do that, in surveying, some questions should be added to see whether or not they have personal computers and Internet access in their homes, dormitories or any other place. It might help us for designing for alternative education methods like online courses.

Step 6: Software Analysis

Software is the part computer in which end-users interact with. Therefore people want to use user-friendly computer programs to work with. End users initially interact with the operating system which mainly organizes the entire computer system. Therefore, the selection of operating systems is important for the faculties. There are several points that should be considered in that selection:

- The budget,
- The adaptability of computer programs with the operating system,
- The system security,
- The adaptability of the hardware with the operating system.

When you check the Internet, you can find a long debate on which operating system works better for which system. Yet, we must always remember the issue stated in Salvage Server Project Report (2003):

Computer systems are designed, produced and marketed to have a limited operational life. Although the hardware may last four or five years before total failure, the software used on it may only be supported for two to three years. When regenerating any computer equipment, it is important to select the right operating system to avoid problems with usability of the system (p. 1).

Thus, the extent to which software fits the hardware is a major issue that technology planners consider. For example, in some computers operating system uses the virtual memory a lot in which other useful programs cannot work on the system. Similarly, certain faculty specific programs can only work with a predefined operating system.

Next issue about software is the computer programs for the personal and instructional purposes. Firstly, the departmental curriculum must be carefully scrutinized with the instructors in order to list the required computer programs for all courses. The list should be compared with the current software installed on the computers and budgetary issues should be discussed in terms of fulfilling the gap. If possible, software must be altered with their freeware or shareware equivalences.

Software installation is a must but not sufficient condition for higher education. User rights on working on these programs, their updating, and upgrading are important for technology planning process. In some faculties, instructors are not allowed to install new programs to their office computers. On the other hand, this creates problems for instructors when they want to try new software on check their students' computer based homework. Furthermore, software like operating systems and antivirus has to be updated in a regular manner. If the instructors are not allowed to install programs, they cannot also make updates in their computers which yield problems for end-users. Shortly, faculties should have a decision about such installations and upgrading issues.

Faculties' and instructors' web pages are also a significant concern for the technology planning process. Each faculty must possess a web site including web site links to all departments and all academicians. It should also include faculty's mission and vision, contact information and announcements.

Generally, academicians upload their lectures notes, assignments and announcements to their web sites. Therefore it is important to design usable and effective web sites to facilitate instructional processes. In the technology planning project, the usability of academicians' web sites is also important. For that purpose, several volunteer students must be selected and asked to asses those web pages with the help of a usability inventory. There are several heuristics and inventories for assessing web pages, like Jakob Nielsen's Website (http://www.useit.com/). The following questions are preferable:

- Web site publishes contact information (email, office phones and etc…),
- Web site includes academician's CV,
- Web site includes a updating time,
- All the links are working,
- Web site includes syllabus,
- Web site covers all lectures notes,
- Web site offer alternative learning resources for students,
- The visual design of the web site is good for me,
- There is no grammar mistake on writings…

Step 7: General Assessment – Finalization

After a long journey on planning process, we come to the final and most significant step for finalizing our project. We have a huge set of data from stakeholders and technologies which we will analyze for finding the gap between the current (mission) and the desirable (vision) situations. Now, we should arrange a large-scope meeting with the project team on the major findings and possible recommendations which will be summarized in terms of a road-map plan. The following points are the stages of finalization:

- List the major findings for Peopleware, Hardware and Software,
- For each finding, fulfill a table including the following headings;
  - Proposal Number – X,
  - The time duration for actualizing the proposed idea,
  - The findings for supporting this proposal,
  - The step-by-step sub-processes to actualize the proposed idea;
- Prepare a three-year development plan by filling such a timeframe of action (Table 3)
- Prepare a well-explained technology planning report like a scientific research paper but with less jargon so that each reader can understand it easily.
- Prepare a meeting to share the findings and recommendations for both stakeholders, because changes should start with approval of all people.

Noticeably, it is not enough to write a hundred-pages report without its proper implementation. After all those efforts and time, the decision makers of higher education faculties must be motivated to be eager to implement the plan as produced.

FUTURE TRENDS

Technology planning is a broad project management activity and is becoming more a formal and organized endeavor for different organizations. There are two interconnected trends pertaining

Table 3. Timeframe of action

Year 1	Peopleware	Hardware	Software
Month 1			
Month 2			
Month 3			
Month 4			
Month 5			
….			

to technology planning activities; implementation oriented frameworks and scientific research studies. Here, I want to concentrate on these new trends separately and make some comments and recommendations on them.

For the implementation oriented approaches, we should always remember that each proposed framework needs modifications for the implementation in different settings like elementary and secondary education. There are certain differentiations among those education levels where new adaptable frameworks must be built. Therefore, new scholars should work on how to adapt this framework to those different education levels. From my point of view, new frameworks must be created and implemented for all levels and for all different schooling types like vocational high schools.

In addition to this, it is evident that there are differences among faculties as well; for instance, the technological needs of the "Health and Medicine Faculty" will be deviated than "Educational Sciences Faculty". Establishment of faculty-specific technology planning process is a prospective and necessary step for higher education institutions. With the help of this faculty-oriented specification, we will have a chance to address the specific and fundamental needs of students, managers, and academicians.

Another major issue is the training of qualified researchers about technology planning process. There are certain disciplines and master/Ph.D. programs such as instructional /educational technology and human performance technology. Within those disciplines and programs, there are some technology leadership and management courses. However, a particular master or Ph.D. program should be established for educating well-qualified decision makers and project managers in technology planning.

As a fourth point, the understanding of "organization culture" and "change management" will affect the technology management issues in any organization. In technology planning,

by surveying the all stakeholders, we actually try to understand the inner culture of faculty and related departments. The finalization and implementation of the technology planning process is strongly related with the management of changes and diffusion of innovations in higher education. Hence in parallel to the development of the idea; "comprehension of organization as a culture", the technology planning issues will be more worthwhile.

The power of Information and Communication Technologies (ICTs) are indispensably growing each minute. Accordingly, ICTs become an integral part of our daily activities. Thus the use ICTs in education will affect us strongly. The institutions which adapt themselves to those innovations will survive in the competitive education sectors. Controlling the ICTs infusion into education is a major concern of both governments and scientists. Under the light of this fact, it is obvious that there will occur a new brunch of any organization for focusing on technology implementation, management and planning activities. "Technology planning offices" will offer faculties great opportunities to utilize and implement ICTs at their best performance. These offices might fulfill another obvious need of the higher education institutions; the continuous training of academicians about the new ICTs tools and their integration into instruction.

The design of a digital library will assist all technology planning and management issues. By the development of standardized and instructional Reusable Learning Objects (RLOs) and their embedment into digital libraries, lecturers will have a common database for their technology integrated course activities. Thus, lecturers will have an enriched environment and students will have different content sources. This digital library will assist the planning process in terms of offering alternative learning sources for students and providing academicians with the alternative ideas for their instructional activities

Those instructional assistance actions will yield a more student-centered education where most technology integration efforts aim, too. Hence as the technology management and planning activities implement into higher education faculties at their best, we will have a better student-centered instructional context. Moreover, those mutual effects will also help the formation of new and alternative ways of teaching methods and learning resources. With the possibilities and the capacities of ICTs, more problem-based, authentic and individualized learning contexts will be designed.

Another possible effect of technology management and planning processes is the realization of ICTs about their effects on social, ethical and health concerns. A relatively new discipline, social information technology, deals with how ICTs tools impact on human as individual and the society. With the invention of new tools on social communication, such as blogs, wikis, chatting programs and etc..., we will start to make use of them in technology management and planning projects. Similarly the relationship between technology and ethics will be more common debate issue in any organization. As with the legal sanctions, higher education institutions will form or upgrade new regulations against unethical use of technologies. Licensing issues will be a vital concern in software analysis for technology managers. Besides, in the technology planning processes, project team will start to focus on ergonomics of technologies in hand. As the adverse effects of technologies on human health become clearer, decision makers of any organization will have to find solutions to care of them.

One last point for the technology planning is the necessity of building a continuous evaluation mechanism within the faculty. Our aim with the technology planning is to form a yearly based action plan for the proper implementation of the technologies into faculty dynamics. To assess the extent to which we have succeeded in realization of those plans, there must be a team for frequently scanning the progress and share the findings with entire faculty stakeholders. Additionally, following the first technology plan, this permanent assessment activity should provide the latter one as being an input data.

The other trend for technology planning is to apply and create new scientific research tools and processes. The initial possible donation of technology planning process is the sharing of experiences in the conferences, seminars, journals and so forth... As a result, other initiatives might learn from the success and failure stories to nourish themselves. However, we should be careful about sharing the experiences in terms of data confidentiality and anonymity.

Throughout the scientific efforts on planning, we should clearly depict the adaptive and complementary data gathering methods so that we have more beneficial and unambiguous depiction of the situation. In other words, we should prepare guidelines for when to use quantitative and qualitative data gathering techniques and their analysis methods. For instance, we talk about the surveying as data gathering techniques for higher education institutions. However, when the age group decreases like in elementary or secondary schools, the surveying approach will not be suitable for younger students.

To sum up, technology planning activities will stimulate several trends for theory and application which will affect each other throughout the process. It is clear that technology management and planning activities are getting more important for the higher education institutions of futuristic world. The faculties which are left behind those actions will be disadvantaged in the potential.

CONCLUSION

After the great explosion of ICTs in last decades, all humanity has tried to adapt itself to those innovations. In parallel, the extension of ICTs utilization reflected on teaching and learning processes for different education levels. This chapter focuses on technology utilization efforts within the higher educations structures. It is evident that if we don't manage the technologies in faculties, we will only spend our money for nothing advantageous. Technology planning is both a tool and a process for assisting organizations to manage technology implementation effectively.

This chapter proposes a dynamic and flexible framework for higher education faculties. The framework is like a guideline where you can change its parts to make best use of it. Framework initially requires a team which will work together for months under the carefully arranged deadlines. This team will compare and contrast the current state of the faculty in terms of mission statements with the expected position as declared in the vision. Next step is the analysis of three important faculty aspects; Peopleware, Hardware and Software. For all three points, the perspectives of all stakeholders (academicians, students, secretaries, managers and so on) should be gathered. After in-depth quantitative and qualitative data analysis, several activity oriented recommendations are produced and shared with all stakeholders. The yearly timeframes of action must be implemented sensitively so that the technology increases its effectiveness in terms of communicative, managerial and instructional processes. For better achievements, the approval of all stakeholders and the continuous process assessment are indispensable.

ACKNOWLEDGMENT

I wish to express my profound thanks to my family. Moreover, my deepest heartfelt gratitude is extended to my advisor Mr. Soner Yildirim. I show my appreciations to my best friend, Ilker Yakin.

REFERENCES

Bellamy, A. (2007). Exploring the influence of new technology planning and implementation on the perceptions of new technology effectiveness. *The Journal of Technology Studies, 33* (1), 32-40.

Clark, R. E. (1983). Reconsidering research on learning from media. *Review of Educational Research, 53*(4), 445-459.

Eurydice (2008). *Eurybase: The information database on education systems in Europe: The education system in Turkey.* Retrieved April 23, 2008, from http://www.eurydice.org/portal/page/portal/Eurydice/

Huber, J. (2005). T. C. O. and R. O. I.: The business of technology planning. *Library Media Connection, August-September,* 62-64.

ISTE (International Society for Technology in Education). *National educational technology standards.* Retrieved April 12, 2008, from http://www.iste.org/nets

Krueger, K., Hansen, L., & Smaldino, S. (2000). Preservice teacher technology competencies. *Tech Trends 44*(3), 47-50.

Laurillard, D. (2002). *Rethinking university teaching* (2nd Ed.). New York :Taylor & Francis Group.

Loyd, B. H., & Gressard, C. (1984). Reliability and factorial validity of computer attitude scales. *Educational and Psychological Measurement, 44*(2), 501-505.

Masi, A. C., & Winer, L. R. (2005). A university-wide vision of teaching and learning with information technologies. *Innovations in Education and Teaching International, 42*(2), 147-155.

McCormick, I. (2006). Same planet, different worlds: why projects continue to fail. A generalist review of project management with special reference to electronic research administration. *Perspectives, 10(4)*, 102-108.

National Education Statistics – Formal Education 2007-2008. A publication of official statistics programme. Republic of Turkey – Ministry of National Education.

Roblyer, M. D. (2003). *Integrating educational technology into teaching* (3rd Ed.). Merrill-Prentice Hall: New Jersey.

Salvage Server Project Report (2003). Selecting operating systems for and upgrading older computers. Retrieved April 11, 2008, from http://www.fraw.org.uk/download/ssp/ssp-01.html

Seels, B. B., & Richey, R. C. (1994). *Instructional technology: The definition and domains of the field*. Bloomington, IN: Association for Educational Communications and Technology.

Tomei, L., A. (2005). *Taxonomy for the Technology Domain*. New York: McGraw-Hill.

Wach, H. M. (2004). A case study in technology planning. *Community College Week, 10*.

Watson, L. W. (2004). Access and technology. *New Directions for Community Colleges, 128*, 31-38.

Westera, W. (2004). On strategies of educational innovation: Between substitution and transformation. *Higher Education, 47*, 501–517.

Whelan, D. L. (2004). Generation Tech. *School Library Journal*, (pp. 48-50). Retrieved April 25, 2008, from http://www.schoollibraryjournal.com/

KEY TERMS AND DEFINITIONS

Hardware: Is a general term for tangible computer apparatus functionalized for using computer programs or controlling the networking.

Mission: The commitment of any organization to its responsibilities, purposes, predefined works for achieving short or long terms objectives. Mission frames the current activities of the organization in terms of ideal depictions.

Peopleware: Is a general term for implying all stakeholders who will be affected from the results of the technology planning activities.

Software: Is a general term for the computer programs utilized in any personal computers, in courses, in entire faculty, or in networking infrastructure.

Stakeholder: Is a group or group of people who might be affected by the activities of any organizational structure.

Technology Attitude: Is the internal perceptive representation of technology in individual's mind.

Technology Belief: Is the acceptance or reliance on technology and its usefulness on different settings and processes.

Technology KSA (Knowledge, Skill and Ability): Are the necessary and required competencies for using technologies.

Technology Planning: Or 'instructional technology planning', is a technique for assessing the current and prospective situations of any organization's technological infrastructure in relation to communicative, instructional and managerial activities.

Technology Value: Is the assessment of worth in terms technology and its effects on ethics, society, education and etc…

Vision: An imagination of any organization's prospective situation. Vision is the depiction or prediction of futuristic context in terms of possible successes and aims to be reached.

Chapter XXVIII
Shifting from Classroom to Online Delivery

Patricia McGee
The University of Texas at San Antonio, USA

Veronica Diaz
Maricopa Community Colleges, USA

ABSTRACT

The rapid proliferation of e-learning tools that offer low or no cost investment and are not housed on institutional servers, has made it very attractive for faculty to move learning experiences online. Yet institutions are often unaware of the technology practices of instructors or learners, thereby investing time, effort, and funding into tools and infrastructure than may not be the best support for learning outcomes. This chapter describes shifts in the use of learning technologies, illustrates a high level overview for assessing current use and practice, and provides a framework for selecting delivery solutions and tools that can best support instructional goals.

INTRODUCTION

Instructional technologies and new delivery models have changed the university classroom since the mid-1990s. Since that time, use of the Internet was becoming integrated into teaching, primarily though text-based access, and computers were becoming truly multi-media capable, while faculty members began creating course Web pages. The general adoption of technology, however, was not universal and, for the higher education classroom, technology has not always been readily available or easily accessible. As we approach the end of the first decade of the 21st century, access to technology for teaching and learning is almost ubiquitous and expectations regarding learning outcomes and student success of accrediting agencies, funding organizations, learners, and performance evaluators are high (Kobulnicky & Rudy 2002).

The authors believe that technology adoption and implementation must be driven by an appreciation and understanding of the learner as well as the instructor (Ludema, Cooperrider, & Barrett, 2001). Faculty members are vested in the long-term success of the work of the university and their success and productivity is an indicator of a healthy institutional culture. Without participation and consideration of faculty practice, planning is limited at best, and short sighted at worst. The learner is equally important, however the learner is transitory, and therefore planning around current learners can result in poor infrastructure and other investments. The authors advocate ongoing, reflective, and iterative analysis of the use of instructional tools, instructional delivery models and support services to best capture the present status of what instructors and students are really doing. This provides an appreciation from which planning can commence.

The focus of this chapter is to present an overview of how institutions can best determine the needs of the instructor, and the learner, as they shift from the traditional classroom to online learning. Further, we provide a high-level overview of institutional assessment processes, strategies for determining current teaching and learning activities, support of instructors and learners, and frameworks for moving learning experiences to online environments. We conclude with a discussion about future trends for distributed learning and the probable impact on teaching and learning.

BACKGROUND

Institutions and their faculty are faced with multiple challenges as they move forward in planning for five, ten, or even fifteen years. These include (McGee & Diaz, 2007):

- **The technology-adoption cycle:** Under ideal circumstances, a faculty member may require anywhere from three to four terms to adopt a learning technology tool; even more time may be needed to produce positive results in teaching and learning. Many faculty members are hesitant to experiment with several tools at once and prefer a "one-at-a-time" approach to adoption and integration. The ever-changing array of available tools and the lack of information related to adoption and use together act as a de-motivator.

- **Lack of integrated technology tools:** Although course management systems (CMS) have become standard, many emerging tools are not easily integrated into the CMS. When isolated tools are added on to the CMS course, users are confronted with "multiple log-ins, data input, and results tracking. In other words, tools that are not centrally integrated require an additional "use and management" investment that is otherwise unnecessary. "

- **Learners' changing expectations:** Students have different expectations, skills, abilities, and knowledge about the technology themselves and how the technologies should be best used in teaching and learning. Increasingly intergenerational issues segment classes and challenge a coherent use of technology.

- **Institutional changes to technology commitments:** Faculty members adopt technology at different rates in different ways. This adoption cycle is often at odds with, or even unconsidered, by the institutional adoption of technology. For faculty and students, the sudden or cyclical change of technology (such as upgrades in CMS) can appear as an unstable and unpredictable environment that results in dissonance and relearning, often contributing to the reluctance of faculty to adopt new technologies.

Although there is disagreement on how technologically savvy today's students really are (Kennedy, Judd, Churchward, & Gray, 2008), indicators suggest that what learners truly value, regardless of their generation, is effective pedagogy (Garcia & Qin, 2007). Dede (2005) notes that students now entering college have a neomillennial learning style that is comfortable with, if not prefers, an environment that includes fluency in multiple media and in simulation-based virtual settings. Neomillennial students prefer communal learning involving diverse, tacit, situated experience, with knowledge distributed across a community and a context as well as within an individual. For these reasons, a learning environment that is balanced and includes experiential learning, guided mentoring, and collective reflection is highly desirable to the 21st century learner.

Most critical for institutional planning, evidence suggests that today's learner differs from students of the mid-1990s, see Table 1. Prensky (2001) describes digital natives as anyone born after 1980 who grew up playing digital games, watching non-stop television, incessantly using instant messaging (IM) and email, and not reading books. Students born in 1980 were just graduating from high school in the late 1990s and the impact of this generation was not really felt until the early 2000s. Given the rapid advancements and changes in technology along with institutional expectations for the faculty to use technology in their teaching, it is no wonder that a generational gap exists in the use and perceived value of technology. Table 1 illustrates the way in which faculty member use of technology and expectations of their use of technology has dramatically shifted.

Even with the increased prevalence of technology for teaching and learning, there is limited research that documents what the faculty is really doing with technology in the classroom and online (Mitra, Steffensmeier, & Lenzmeier, 1999). Faculty members have experienced even a greater shift in their practice with technology, The mid-1990s saw an increase in faculty member use of technology, but more importantly, a growing expectation that technology be infused into teaching and learning (Baldwin, 1989). By the mid-2000s, faculty members cannot escape the

Table 1. Higher education students: Then and now (Netday, 2006; Prensky, 2001; Salaway, Katz, Caruso, Kvavik, & Nelson, 2006; Tapscott, 1998)

Mid-1990s	Late 2000s
Digital divide is pronounced, little use of technology in K12 and Higher Education	Access to technology has become more widespread in educational institutions, but some still experience a digital divide
Some students have their own computers	Many own a computer, laptop, and cell phone
Prevalent use of email, no instant message or VoIP	Pervasive use of email, instant messaging, Short Message Service, and other mobile technologies
Existence of single-function technologies (phone, camera, video, music player)	Emergence of multi-function technologies (music + video + phone + camera)
Sporadic, limited access to low-speed Internet	Ubiquitous access to high-speed Internet and also wireless environments
Little classroom technology available	Extensive out-of-class technology use with moderate use of in-class technology
Emergence a few course management systems, mostly home-grown	Pervasive use of enterprise-level course management systems
Course assignments are primarily paper-based and not electronic	Many assignments are electronic and administered via course management system

use of technology, and their students are the ones expecting them to use it, see Table 2.

Gaps in technology uses and preferences between instructor and learner are typical, but are not often considered when making decisions about institutional technology adoption and implementation, or when determining how best to support each group in instructional settings. In order to support the use of emerging technologies, institutions must understand and be aware of the needs, preferences, and practices of both learners and instructors. Using data-driven decision-making increases the likelihood of success, and contributes to an amenable and collaborative attitude of all involved.

INSTITUTIONAL ASSESSMENT

Institutions that have engendered a climate for ongoing assessment are more likely to recognize and understand the deficits and successes of instructional processes (Loacker & Mentkowski, 1993). Assessment can occur at any level, but when it stems from institutional values, it is more likely to be utilized. At a high level, assessment can be used to implement the transformation of learning environments with learning technology: experimentation, extension and transition, standardization of support, integration into curriculum, and diffusion (Diaz & McGee, 2007). Throughout these phases of change, institutions may collect data, communicate consistently with the campus community, and nurture an innovative culture.

The Transformative Assessment Process (TAP)[1] framework below provides a high-level 'map' of assessment points within a process-oriented flow designed to discover and transform practice. Figure 1 below is organized with general (on the left) to more specific processes (on the right) illustrating the drilling down nature of assessment. As institutions or units follow TAP, they may elect to enter other processes, such as assessment at any point in the diagram. This can be especially useful as institutions assess current teaching and learning practices, align goals and priorities, identify and involve stakeholders, and plan future initiatives.

Table 2. The Faculty: Then and now (Baldwin, 1998; Campus Computing Project; EDUCAUSE Core Data Project; NSOPF, 2002; NSOPF, 2005)

Mid-1990s	Late 2000s
Email with students is a little used option	Email with students is the predominant form of communication for the faculty and institutions
Some faculty use home-grown course websites to distribute some course information	Many, if not most, faculty members use a course management system to communicate with students
Most universities do not provide resources or services that can be accessed from home via the Internet	Most universities provide online resources and services accessible from off-campus locations (library, advising, tutoring)
Most faculty members do not have home Internet service and only use a phone in the office	Most faculty members have high-speed home Internet service, cell phones, and other mobile devices
Few universities offer student email accounts	Most universities require, and also offer, student email accounts
Few, if any, classrooms have Internet access	Most campuses have wireless high-speed Internet access throughout
Very few classrooms have computers or overhead projectors	About half of classrooms have computers, projectors, and document cameras
Few universities provide technical support to students and the faculty	Most universities provide faculty and student support for technology, both technical and instructional

Figure 1. Transformative assessment process (TAP)

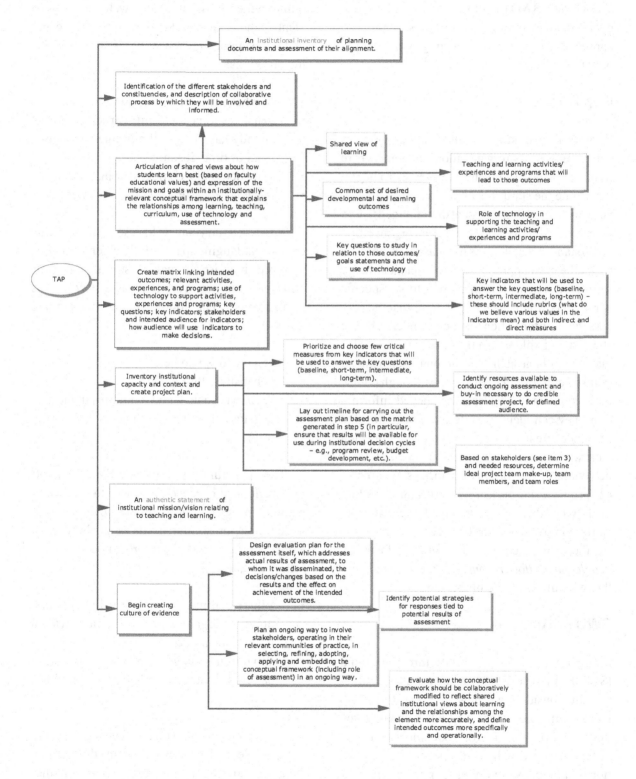

Within a transformative assessment process, a GAP and SWOTT, other analysis tools, can operationalize steps for institutions or units to approach assessment of teaching and learning with technology.

Gap Analysis

In order to plan strategically, it is necessary to determine where an organization is now and where it intends to be in a given time period. To begin, determine the status quo and areas of interest—perhaps areas of improvement that emerged from a recent accreditation review. Once an organization understands what it needs to measure, it can then select the most appropriate and efficient strategy for measurement. It is important to set specific parameters when collecting data so that the process yields information that helps understand the status quo. Explore data that already exists– this may be available at the institutional, department, or instructor level. For example, although course evaluations are considered privileged information, they can identify patterns of behavior that are otherwise invisible. Once you have collected data, write specific statements that include human behaviors, levels of performance, standards of performance, and measures or indicators for future goals. Once this step is completed, the status quo can be compared with the future desired outcome. As the articulated gap is identified, focus on *people, time, effort, resources,* and *infrastructure* that will allow closing of the gap.

SWOTT Analysis

Strength, weakness, opportunity, threat, and trend (SWOTT) (Ansof, 1980) analyses are useful if you are considering a new initiative for which there is little precedent. A SWOTT should draw upon what is known from documentation and observation and will require some data collection and possibly surveying of relevant units or departments.

Start with your strengths. This is a positive reinforcement of what is done well and helps to identify the areas that do not require change and that will support the new effort. Ask the following questions:

- In what ways are we unique?
- What resources and infrastructure do we already have that will minimize an investment of time, resources, or people?
- Why do people come to our institution?
- What do we offer that others do not?

Next, focus on your weaknesses. Although this can be challenging, particularly when change is involved, it assists in making sure that a stumbling block is not overlooked as a new plan is implemented. The following questions guide this step:

- What can we do better?
- What should we avoid?
- What has contributed to failures in the past (e.g. loss of resources, students, infrastructure)

The opportunity portion of a SWOTT is often overlooked because units tend to view their planning as specific to them. However, it is not uncommon for similar needs or goals to exist across a program, division or campus. Ask the following questions:

- What recent mandates, partnerships, funding flows, re-organizations, etc. can provide a new opportunity?
- What trends suggest a new strategy (social patterns, policy, technology, demographics, etc.)?

Determine potential threats that may interfere with your desired outcomes. By going through this step, you can better prepare to develop a convincing rationale and understand the perspectives of those with whom you will need to work to meet your goals.

- What barriers and obstacles do we face?
- How does our competition differ from us?

The last step is critical because it articulates the importance of identifying and preparing for future needs and opportunities. In collaboration with various other units that may be in contact with your constituents, ask

- What are some emerging trends in teaching and learning, are any specific to key discipline areas, colleges, or departments?
- What trends are we seeing in our learner and faculty member characteristics; how can we better support these groups?
- What about what we do has changed in the past five years or is changing now?

The institutional analysis processes we propose, TAP, Gap and SWOTT analyses are easily modifiable and applicable at various levels of planning, see Figure 2. Once these or similar processes have occurred, effective strategies for change can be selected and implemented.

Strategies for Ascertaining Status of Practice

Both institutional assessment strategies described above suggest that collecting data regarding fac-

ulty member and learner practice is critical; an institution must know what is happening *now*. In this section, we describe a general process for collecting data. This process is not intended to be comprehensive, but rather a general framework in order to accommodate the needs and constraints of individual institutions and the units that are involved in planning to support online learning and corresponding technologies. This suggested approach follows a design-based strategy derived from the research approach articulated by Wang and Hannafin (2005): "a systematic, but flexible methodology aimed to improve educational practices through iterative analysis, design, development, and implementation, based on collaboration among researchers and practitioners in real-world settings, and leading to contextually-sensitive design principles and theories" (p. 6).

Step 1: Collecting Information

Capturing baseline data. Capturing current faculty member and student practice offers a point of reference and measurement as initiatives are implemented. It also addresses existing assumptions about current practice, when there may be subtle factors at play.

- Student and faculty member surveys about current practices (e.g., use of tools, where tools are used, teaching approaches, etc; include demographic information)
- Student and faculty focus groups

Figure 2. An overview of the assessment and planning process

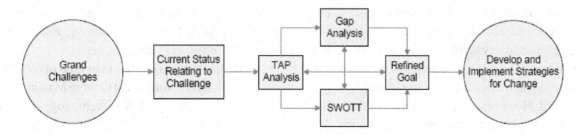

- Observation (e.g., classroom use of technology, use of course management systems)
- Document analysis (e.g. annual reports, review for tenure, lesson plans, Web pages, Power Point™ presentations, handouts)
- Surveys (teaching, adoption, motivation, etc.)
- Document analysis
- Snapshot interviews

Breadth, depth and frequency assessment strategies. Capturing the tools and strategies faculty members are using, and when they use them may be challenging, but revealing. Course management systems have tracking functions that are useful and computer-based tracking software is another option. These strategies go beyond simple collection of existing data and require that the data relate to a time-based context. The intent of these strategies is to explore what instructors are doing in relation to time and place to better understand how much time and what effort they are expending in a given teaching and learning situation.

- Software tracking
- Self-reporting (e.g., time-based surveys, logs)
- Shadowing
- Observation over time or in different settings (e.g. classroom, course management systems)

Step 2: Analyzing Data

Comparative strategies. Different rubric-based tools can assist in determining where an educator lies on a learning technology adoption continuum. Designed for K-12 teachers, these rubrics can be readily used or revised for higher education faculty members. These tools are designed on an assumption that more sophisticated use of technology is desired. However, they can be used to determine faculty use patterns, and set goals and align with

technology adoption models that illustrate where the individual resides on a continuum of technology use (see Table 3).

- CEO Forum at http://www.ceoforum.org/
- TEA Teacher Star Chart at http://starchart.esc12.net/

Descriptive analysis strategies. Similar to a case study, descriptive analysis strategies use multiple sources of information to create a comprehensive picture of faculty members' use of instructional technologies. Descriptive analysis strategies result in a faculty member profile that is dynamic and multi-dimensional. Faculty members can use these profiles in promotion and annual review materials, and they can assist in identifying specific needs to be articulated into individual goals. Although time-consuming, they tend to be the most accurate and reliable.

Step 3: Designing and Implementing Support

Although faculty members have similarities, their unique motivations, experiences, habits, preferences, needs, abilities, and obligations affect what type of support they need and will accept. By setting specific goals for different types of faculty needs, support strategies can be designed or offered in multiple formats at different times.

- **One-on-one training or mentoring:** The Iowa State University (2003) mentoring that offers case studies, student mentors, and results from the initiative.
- **Skills specific training:** Tufts University (2008) offers courses, group/individual coaching, Web-based training, and "learn while you eat" sessions, see
- **Fellow programs that provided project or goal-based outcomes:** George Mason University (2007) offers a Technology Across the Curriculum Faculty Fellows program that

Table 3. Technology teaching and learning continuum

Pedagogical Objective[2]		Demonstrated Skills of the Learner	Possible Instructional Technology Uses	Instructor Expertise Required	Level of Learner Engagement
Student Pedagogical Objective	*Remembering*	• Observation and recall of information • Knowledge of dates, events, places • Knowledge of major ideas • Mastery of subject matter • *Application:* list, define, tell, describe, identify, show, label, collect, examine, tabulate, quote, name, who, when, where	ELMOs, electronic presentations, Internet, email, video, clickers, podcasts	Medium, Low	Medium, Low
	Understanding	• Understanding information • Grasp meaning • Translate knowledge into new context • Interpret facts, compare, contrast • Order, group, infer causes • Predict consequences • *Application:* summarize, describe, interpret, contrast, predict, associate, distinguish, estimate, differentiate, discuss, extend	Tutorials, animation, interactive video, simulations, web pages, streaming video, podcasts, discussion boards	High, Medium	Medium
	Applying Material	• Use information • Use methods, concepts, theories in new situations • Solve problems using required skills or knowledge • *Application:* apply, demonstrate, calculate, complete, illustrate, show, solve, examine, modify, relate, change, classify, experiment	Discipline-specific software applications, simulations, games, student presentations, wikis, collaborative editing/writing	High, Medium	High
Student Pedagogical Objective	**Develop Ability to Conduct Analysis**	• Seeing patterns • Organization of parts • Recognition of hidden meanings • Identification of components • *Application:* analyze, separate, order, explain, connect, classify, arrange, divide, compare, select, explain, infer	ePortfolios, learning objects, discipline-specific software applications, simulations, student presentations	High, Medium	High, Medium
	Develop Ability to Evaluate	• Compare and discriminate between ideas • Assess value of theories, presentations • Make choices based on reasoned argument • Verify value of evidence • Recognize subjectivity • *Application:* assess, decide, rank, grade, test, measure, recommend, convince, select, judge, explain, discriminate, support, conclude, compare, summarize	ePortfolios, simulations, role-plays, Learning Content Management Systems, collaborative editing/writing	High, Medium	High
	Develop Ability to Create	• Use old ideas to create new ones • Generalize from given facts • Relate knowledge from several areas • Predict, draw conclusions • *Application:* combine, integrate, modify, rearrange, substitute, plan, create, design, invent, what if?, compose, formulate, prepare, generalize, rewrite	Wikis, Learning Content Management Systems, Virtual Learning Worlds, ePortfolios, discipline-specific software applications, simulations, games	High	High

supports deeper learning and integration.

- **Communities of practice:** Education Commons is a non-profit organization that supports higher education professionals committed to improving teaching and learning with technology.
- **Self-directed learning:** The Australian Universities Teaching Committee (AUTC) (2003) offers an assortment of exemplars, guides, and tools for use by staff and faculty members to improve practice.
- **Faculty and student research programs:** Ohio State University (2008) sponsors a Research on Research: Student-Faculty ePartnerships through which research outcomes are disseminated through technology.
- **Self assessment:** The Self and Peer Assessment Resource Kit (SPARK) provides a venue for learner and peer critique.

Considering Student Practice

Although we focus on faculty member practice, this is but one half of institutional assessment. The learner's habits, preferences, expectations, and skill level and abilities are equally relevant to supporting the faculty. A large body of literature exists regarding the Millennial or Net Generation Learner, but it is not good practice to use national data to make generalizations about any group of learners when making local decisions. It is critical to include student baseline data about your students in your planning for several reasons:

- Faculty members are motivated to change when they have an understanding of students' teaching and learning needs;
- Understanding the characteristics of students and how they are changing over time will help in selecting solutions that improve student success toward learning objectives;
- Faculty members may be more willing to consider the implementation of discipline-specific technologies to increase the

competitiveness of their curriculum and programs.

Although surveys and focus sessions are good tools to assess practice and needs, institutional and academic departments may already collect this type of information. For example, student academic support centers often have a deep understanding of student needs. Additionally, academic departments or units can identify the technology uses, requirements, and needs of their students.

FRAMING INITIATIVES THROUGH MODELS AND TOOLS

Once a clear picture of faculty and student practice is determined, an organization can decide how to best shift from classroom to online experiences. Understanding tested strategies will save the time and effort of determining what can and will work given the circumstances. The following models of distributed learning draw upon research-based frameworks from the National Center for Academic Transformation[3], Sloan-C[4], and the authors' research. Following the models of distributed learning is a description of emerging technologies that can support and be integrated into the models. Connecting a model with tools should be an interactive process that occurs through careful consideration of the instructor, learner, and institutional infrastructure.

Models of Distributed Learning

Given the proliferation of learning/course management systems (L/CMS) and Web 2.0 applications, the possibilities of instructional delivery are now only limited by the imagination, mission, and resources of the institution. When planning to shift courses from the traditional classroom to technology-mediated designs, it is important to be familiar with the implications of different delivery models. The following delivery models are not exhaustive, but provide a starting point to consider how to move from traditional to distributed course delivery.

Web Enhanced Course Approach. Web Enhanced courses include between-class meeting activities using learning management systems or other information communications technology. One example of this approach is the NCAT's *Supplemental Model*[5]. The supplemental model retains the basic structure of the traditional course and (a) supplements lectures and textbooks with technology-based, out-of-class activities, or (b) also changes what goes on in the class by creating an active learning environment within a large lecture hall setting.

The Web-enhanced approach is probably the most frequently used model and has many advantages. This approach extends the learning experience by actively involving the learner between class meetings, reinforcing classroom experience and preparing for the subsequent class meeting. It can also support independent learning and increase learner-to-learner interaction through extended online activities. Redesigning a course to be Web-enhanced may require reconsidering some course activities and some learner abilities and skills.

Distributed Engagement Approach. This approach allows the learner to complete instructional modules at his or her own pace, in various learning environments and with various supports. Usable for both face-to-face and online environments, the intent is to allow students to progress through material in the way and speed that is most appropriate for the individual. This approach is often structured in a modular format and has success with underprepared students. For instance, a course may have no class meetings and replace them with a learning resource center with online materials and on-demand personalized assistance, using (a) an open attendance model

or (b) a required attendance model depending on student motivation and experience levels. Another example is the buffet model[6] that customizes the learning environment for each student based on background, learning preference, and academic/professional goals and offers students an assortment of individualized paths to reach common learning outcomes.

Advantages to the distributed engagement model are compelling. This approach supports individual learning needs and can promote peer learning as students work independently and collectively to achieve pre-determined goals. Additionally, this model distributes the cost and maintenance of campus resources in a centralized repository. It also provides for ready re-use of learning resources across programs, disciplines, and courses. Some campuses will see some drawbacks to this approach as it may require redesigning spaces, robust hardware and software, and just-in-need student resources and services. This model also redefines the instructional role of tutor, coach, and instructor, which may create resistance and stress for the instructor as well as those who support the instructor. Finally it requires higher levels of discipline and commitment from the learner. Students must be academically prepared and supported in this model in ways that may not otherwise be necessary.

Blended/Hybrid Approach. The blended or hybrid approach involves dividing class experiences between face-to-face and online meetings, thus reducing actual seat time. The National Center for Academic Transformation's Replacement Model[7], a variation of the blended approach, reduces the number of in-class meetings and (a) replaces some in-class with out-of-class time, online, interactive learning activities, and/or (b) makes significant changes in remaining in-class meetings.

The blended approach offers many learner and institutional benefits: it supports classroom instruction through active learning as it engages the learner in thinking and through interaction with others and/or course content and it has the potential to relieve classroom space demand, often at premium. The blended approach does require commitment and new skills from the learner and supports for both the instructor and learning, specifically in between class meetings. Instructors must go through an extensive course re-design process that can improve course outcomes, but requires a commitment of time and effort.

A variation of the blended/hybrid and distributed engagement approach is the HyFlex model (Reigeluth & Frick, 1999). A HyFlex course design enables a flexible participation policy for students as they may choose to attend face-to-face synchronous class sessions or complete course learning activities online without physically attending class. This is also referred to a blended learning environment (Bonk & Graham, 2006). In a HyFlex course, the instructor provides instructional structure, content, and activities to meet the needs of students participating both in class and online. These are not necessarily completely separated sets of activities, and are typically not the same activities for both types of student participation, but must be equivalent sets of activities selected so that student learning can be effective in either participation format.

100% Online Course Approach. In this approach, all course activities, resource use, interactions, and communications take place online, typically through an institutional learning/course management system. NCAT's Fully Online Model[8] eliminates all in-class meetings and moves all learning experiences online, using Web-based, multi-media resources, commercial software, automatically evaluated assessments with guided feedback and alternative staffing models.

As evidenced by the growth of online courses, this strategy presents many advantages as it adds convenience as learning is independent of location and time and engages the learner in a way that does not occur in a classroom. The curriculum can be modularized or self-paced and requires reusable content, making use of existing course materials and reducing repeated investment. This model may reduce evaluation and grade calculation efforts when a CMS is used and centrally documents learner effort. This approach comes with additional investment and design considerations. Ideally online learning requires 24/7 Internet access for faculty members and students as well as technical and instructional support for the learner. It is most successful when the learner has a certain level of technical expertise, motivation, and time management skills, a quality not always evident in learners. All course materials should be developed prior to the course start date, which can create a burden on the instructor and support staff.

Pedagogical Applications of Emerging Technologies

Once you have determined the model most appropriate for the instructor, the course, and the learner, selecting appropriate tools is next. Most technologies used in college classrooms were developed as information communication tools rather than tools intended to support teaching and learning. The proliferation of Web 2.0 and other emerging technologies presents a challenge for institutions as they try to manage the tools and offer faculty development and student support of these tools. Implementing these tools frequently involves replacing or purchasing new hardware and software and poses new demands on infrastructure to support bandwidth and wireless capacities and address issues of security. Today's emerging technologies, however, are low or no cost, are available both on- and off-campus, and require little, if any, infrastructure or investment on the part of the institution. These tools include systems, some user-generated, and Web 2.0 applications that are Web-based, typically free to the user, support collaboration and interaction, and are highly responsive to the user. The proliferation and migration of emerging technologies makes it difficult to include a comprehensive list here, so we offer the following as an illustration of how tools can and should be used within a learning experience, see Table 4.

The authors have analyzed a variety of emerging technologies and created an open wiki for visitors to add to the resources reviewed (see http://elearningtools.wetpaint.com/).

SUPPORTING FACULTY AND LEARNERS

As institutions transform and adopt new instructional delivery models, any of the ones described above, they encounter the challenge of supporting faculty throughout a course design or re-design process and throughout the implementation of these new courses. We believe that support mechanisms based on what is known and understood about faculty and the learner from a comprehensive institutional assessment process, will be more likely to result in faculty and student technology adoption, smoother transitions

between classroom and online activities, and a satisfying teaching and learning experience for both the instructor and learner.

Faculty Styles, Adoption, and Support

Faculty member support must be constructed around faculty member characteristics and behavior, i.e., what they do and how they teach. Faculty members differ in a variety of ways in their learning preferences and application of instructional designs by gender, age, subject of expertise, technology aptitude, technology ability, motivation, and rank. Keeping this diversity in mind will allow more flexibility in how tasks are achieved and how faculty members may be supported. A faculty member does need to be fluent in a given technology in order to create effective pedagogical applications and the more closely the technology matches the context to which it will be applied, the more likely learning will occur and be transferred. The faculty support models described below are not intended to be exhaus-

Table 4. Web 2.0 applications (McGee & Diaz, 2007)

Type	Function	Tools
Communicative	To share ideas, information, and creations	• Blogs • Audioblogs • Videoblogs • IM-type tools • Podcasts • Webcams
Collaborative	To work with others for a specific purpose in a shared work area	• Editing/writing tools • Virtual communities of practice (VCOPs) • Wikis
Documentative	To collect and/or present evidence of experiences, thinking over time, productions, etc.	• Blogs • Videoblogs • e-portfolios
Generative	To create something new that can be seen and/or used by others	• Mashups • VCOPs • Virtual Learning Worlds (VLW)
Interactive	To exchange information, ideas, resources, materials	• Learning objectives • Social bookmarking • VCOPs • VLWs

tive, but rather a sampling of the approaches to consider when thinking about faculty development and learning technologies.

Reeves (2002) notes several common approaches to teaching in higher education: objectivist, instructivist, behavioralist, constructivist, and cognitive. The objectivist approach (see Thorndike, 1913 as cited in Reeves, 2002) separates knowledge from the knower. Knowledge exists outside of a recipient. Instructivists believe that pre-determined instructional goals and outcomes should be determined regardless of the learner. These goals come from disciplinary experts and are organized from simple to complex concepts that are taught through direct instruction. A constructivist approach to teaching is characterized by the belief that knowledge lies with the individual and although meaning is negotiated with others, it is ultimately self-constructed. This approach can be evaluated by behaviors of the learner that demonstrate their understanding. Behavioralists (see Skinner, 1968 as cited in Reeves, 2002) see learning as manifested behaviors that can be shaped by the teacher through stimulus and response. Cognitivists go beyond behavioralism to consider the mental operations of the learner that may or may not be observable. Specific learning strategies are implemented depending on the type of knowledge to be learned. Therefore, approaches to teaching (and learning) are most likely derived from discipline-specific modeling that have come to be institutionalized over time, and that are understandably an expression of how best to develop expertise in students. To illustrate the influence of disciplinary teaching that results in a style, we use Anthony Grasha's work in teaching and learning styles.

Grasha (1996) developed an integrated model of teaching and learning style in order to provide a model for faculty members to set about creating a learning experience that addresses the range of needs and traits present in a classroom. Through extensive research Grasha identified five teaching styles that he then clustered into four groups, an acknowledgement that the five styles are always somewhat blended together. Grasha's (1996) research indicates that faculty members teaching style is viewed as a particular pattern of needs, beliefs, and behaviors that faculty display in the classroom. His research shows that several patterns describe the stylistic qualities of college teachers: *Expert* (transmitter of information); *Formal Authority* (sets standards and defines acceptable ways of doing things); *Personal Model* (teaches by illustration and direct example); *Facilitator* (guides and directs by asking questions, exploring options, suggesting alternatives); and *Delegator* (develops students ability to function autonomously). Figure 4 builds on these styles by adding strategies that may be used to support faculty members in technology adoption based on their instructional preferences.

Approaches to teaching may be related to disciplinary content; although the most common style in university instructors is the *Personal Model*, there are disciplinary differences. For example, Arts and Humanities faculty members typically fall in the *Expert* category, while faculty members who teach Foreign Languages tend to be *Formal Authorities*, and Education has the most *Facilitators*. Although not intended to be prescriptive, style can reveal the underlying perspective of the faculty member and her/his approach to the instructional process.

The classifications and strategies provided above are starting points for developing and conceptualizing your own support mechanisms. One size does not fit all – consider faculty member support to be a smorgasbord where the faculty is supported in a manner that is most satisfying and productive to them. Foremost in planning is making sure to align faculty member support with learner support.

Learner Styles, Adoption, and Support

Just as the faculty members have unique styles, levels of adoption, and support needs, so does the

Figure 4[9]. Teaching style and support

Cluster	Teaching Style	Preferred Approach to Learning/ Support	Strategies
1	Expert/Formal Authority (38%)	Dependent/Participant/Competitive	One-on-one, hands-on, reward/ acknowledgement
2	Personal Model/Expert/Formal Authority (22%)	Participant/Dependent/Competitive	Hands-on, one-on-one, reward/ acknowledgement
3	Facilitator/Personal Model/Expert (17%)	Collaborative/Participative/Independent	Small group or peer/mentor, hands-on, tutorial/reference materials
4	Delegator/Facilitator/Expert (15%)	Independent/Collaborative/Participant	Tutorial/reference materials, small group or peer/mentor, hands-on

Table 5. Learning style and support possibilities

	Preference	Technology	Support Possibilities
Independent	Works alone, at his or her own page	Portal, web site, portfolio, blog, L/CMS	FAQ, walk-in help, email, video tutorial
Dependent	Requires explicit instructions, just-in-need feedback from instructor	L/CMS, IM, email	FAQs, help forum, phone help, walk-in help
Competitive	Desires to be the best at what they do, and exceed the performance of others, with acknowledgement of authority for their achievement.	Portfolio, blog, presentation tools	Mentor others, contribute to FAQ
Collaborative	Works in a team or group in which there is a high level of interaction and communication	Discussions, chat, wiki, L/CMS, VOIP	FAQs, email, phone help, walk-in help
Avoidant	Wants to work alone, does not like to engage in class activities, and is not easily engaged in learning in general	Portfolio, VOIP,	FAQ, walk-in help, email, video tutorial
Participant	Open in communication and interaction with peers and teacher.	Open forums, IM, VOIP, wiki	Walk-in help, email, phone help

learner. Just because a learner uses technology for their personal use does not mean they can intuitively use technology to learn. Technology skills, knowledge, and abilities are often over-estimated in college students (Kennedy, Judd, Churchward, & Gray, 2008). We advocate analyzing student preferences and needs, offering supports that are continuously evaluated, and aligning student supports and services with those of the faculty.

Student learning styles may or may not be a good fit with instructor teaching styles. Although we do not suggest that every learner can or should be accommodated to the fullest degree, we do be-lieve that institutions can offer multiple supports that address style. Grasha and Yangarber-Hicks[10] indicate that learning styles and teaching styles interact in complex ways to guide the selection of instructional technology, see Table 5.

The level and type of student support should be somewhat related to the instructional delivery model(s) to be implemented. Nationally, we know that current student populations have vastly different learning needs and preferences from older student generations. However, your institution's learner may be significantly different from the national stereotype - not all students are Millennials and therefore students may require different types of support. Collect specific data regarding technologies that support individual disciplines and types of learners (e.g., math, English, under prepared students, etc.).

Learners will need support in different areas, deliver through different media, and for different purposes. Five key aspects of support include:

- Technical (basic computer setup; connecting to networks, wireless, printers; virus protection; basic maintenance)
- Online access to information and communication technology services (Internet, email, server, course management system)
- Production (assignments, presentations, projects)
- Online access to resources (library, helpdesk, computer-based training)
- Learning technologies (tools, applications, software)

There are a variety of approaches to offering supports to students proven to be effective. Support for learners can be channeled through the different encounters students have with the institutional staff, faculty members, peers, and resources. Support can be embedded in the educational experiences of the learner. For example, individualized learning that allows the learner to proceed at their own pace or in alternative modalities can greatly increase achievement and satisfaction. For example, Franklin and Marshall have developed self-paced learning materials in a video format appealing to the 21st century learner. The University of Arizona also offers computer based training via video online and on CD-ROM. Tutorials are another version of informal learning that appeal to students. Glendale Community College offers animated online tutorials as does Tufts University and the University of Louisville.

Another successful strategy is to offer support through access to information. Students often require assistance when university staff is not

available or campus services are not open. The following tactics are options to traditional nine-to-five services.

- **Helpdesk Systems:** Traditionally offered via phone, helpdesk services have moved into other media. The University of Arizona's Office of Student Computing Resources (OSCR) Underground offers support in a center as well as a mobile help desk, an emergency CD, and an online trouble-shooting service. Yale University provides campus kiosks Rio Salado Community College offers 24.7 online supports for the student who requires anytime problem solving.
- **Frequently Asked Questions (FAQ):** FAQ pages are a straightforward approach to responding to questions that are ubiquitous. Glendale Community College offer a simple Web page that answers questions and provides links to other solutions. Although a simple solution, FAQ can provide a quick response to problems.

Finally, many institutions have found success by actively seeking out continuous feedback and engaging students. We believe that solicitation of input from students can diminish, if not eliminate, service and support demands. Several successful practices can be utilized:

- **Scanning the learner experience:** This requires that information is collected during a program of study so that attitudes, opinions, and experiences can be compared. A starting place can be the ECAR Study of Undergraduate Students and Information Technology (Salaway, Katz, Caruso, Kvavik, & Nelson, 2006) that can provide a normative snapshot of current students' use of and preferences for information technology. The Distance Education Learning Environment Survey offers a student and faculty member component that can plot differences along a continuum.

- **Support during learning:** Engagement is particularly crucial in blended/hybrid and online courses where the learner can quickly become disengaged. For example, the K-12 Youth Technology Support is a consortium of non-profit, for-profit and professional organizations dedicated to providing best practices in students support services. The University of Louisville's Student Tutorial Online Module Program (STOMP) offers student-generated learning objects through which students are teaching other students. The Free Assessment Summary Tool allows faculty to survey students periodically throughout a course and discuss perceptions and reports with students.

The demand for ongoing and responsive support will no doubt shift, as will the technologies that predicate the need for support. Therefore, just as collecting data for planning is critical, so is ongoing evaluation of support needs and efficacy.

FUTURE TRENDS

Although we believe it is not possible to reliably predict the future of technology use in higher education, we are proponents of scanning the educational and workplace environment to observe and watch faculty member and learner behaviors and characteristics, business trends, and technology developments. How do future trends help solve today's challenges? What new challenges might we create for ourselves? The Knowledge Works Foundations (KWF) and the Institute for the Future (IFTF) have created an interactive tool to consider change: *Map of Future Forces Affecting Education* (http://www.kwfdn.org/map/) that articulates the drivers, impact areas, hotspots, dilemmas, and trends that affect planning. Most directly related to higher education, we have found the following areas to have the greatest impact on

how students learn, how courses are delivered, and how the planning process is shifting.

The open knowledge framework[11] (Norris, Lafrere, & Mason, 2003) is a natural outcome of search engines and the plethora of published information on the Internet. Today, students can "Google™" while instructors lecture, copy and paste while they construct products, and publish their thoughts and lives captured in pictures and video on My Space™. The boundaries of the classroom, much less the campus, no longer exist. Branding of an individual's personal identity rather than their institutional affiliation has become more feasible now that territory and projects such as Epsilen™(http://www.epsilen.com/) are attempting to capture this phenomenon. Epsilen™ is a community-based system that allows institutions to provide social networking, news and events, courses, eportfolio, and repositories of learning objects for the life of the learner, not just for the life of the learner's involvement with the institution. Given that technologies are increasingly offering mobile, transparent, and ubiquitous access to services and information, institutions must expect this trend to continue and plan accordingly.

Shifts in where and how we interact through online communities, simulations, virtual worlds via avatars, and games require us to examine how these activities can inform how we design instruction and use systems to deliver instruction. Beck and Wade (2006) argue that gamers think differently and have much to offer the workplace. According to gamers, the "received wisdom" of the baby boomer generation doesn't have much to offer compared to the trial and error strategies that gamers know to be successful in competitions and winning is key to motivation. We do not suggest that game pedagogy is the answer, but rather ask that we consider how best to utilize the components of games to engage and support the learner and how can we draw upon the learner's unique skills to participate in planning and decision making.

The way in which digital materials are conceptualized and disseminated has changed dramatically since the end of the 20th century and continues to offer new possibilities for interoperable content formats, reusability, and the re-distribution of learning materials. Much more content is available from publishers and other vendors, and increasingly institutions are generating and tagging their own content for re-use and revision. Publishers are seeking new ways to use the content they own and seeking partnership with organizations that may not own content, but understand the instructional process.

Accrediting agencies are also shifting their priorities with an increasing focus on assigning value to continuous quality improvement, not just baseline indicators of change. We see a blurring of lines between K-12, higher education, and the workplace with the rise of early entrance programs and workplace degrees. The learning that takes place today must relate to the learner's experience in school, work, and home, not just the classroom. For higher education, this suggests that technology planning must consider the preparation of the learner in K-12 education, and the expectations of the graduate in the workforce, more so now than ever before.

CONCLUSION

In the late 1990s, five and ten-year planning was possible and reasonable, but today's rapidly changing learning environment and demanding workplace makes this practice obsolete. Institutional planning processes have to reach out farther into the future than they did in the past and that implementation and adoption cycles are shorter. In other words, instead of having a five-year plan, an organization might have a two-year plan and instead of projecting needs two or three years into the future, they might consider needs five to seven years in the future. Given the shortened time for planning, higher education leaders have

an opportunity to re-think the 20th century model of providing services and resources to the student. Students now bring much to the educational experience: their own technology, a post-20th century view of the world and communication methods, and expectations of multiple careers. As technology increasingly invades our personal, social, professional, and educational experiences, we should look for ways to plan for diverse alternatives, rather than a singular experience.

REFERENCES

Ansoff, H. I. (1980). Strategic issue management. *Strategic Management Journal, 1*(2), 131-148.

Australian Universities Teaching Committee (AUTC). (2003). *Information and communication technologies and their role in flexible learning.* Retrieved March 22, 2008 from http://www. learningdesigns.uow.edu.au/

Baldwin, R. (1998, Winter). Technology's impact on faculty life and work. *New Directions for Teaching and Learning, 76* , 7-21.

Beck, J. C., & Wade, M. (2006). *The kids are alright: How the gamer generation is changing the workplace.* Boston: Harvard Business School Press.

Campus Computing Project, see http://www. campuscomputing.net

Chase, M., Macfadyen, L., Reeder, K., & Roche J. (2002). Intercultural hard technologies meet soft skills. *First Monday* 7(8). Retrieved June 21, 2005 from http://firstmonday.org/issues/issue7_8/chase/

Davis, F. D., Bagozzi, R. P., & Warshaw, P. R. (1989). User acceptance of computer technology: A comparison of two theoretical models. *Management Science, 35,* 982-1003.

Dede, C. (2005). Planning for neomillennial learning styles. *EDUCAUSE Quarterly, 28*(1). Available at http://www.educause.edu/ir/library/pdf/EQM0511.pdf

Distance Education Learning Environment Survey. Retrieved April 15, 2008 from http://www.tcet.unt.edu/insight/ilib/deles/actual/

EDUCAUSE *Core Data Project*, see http://www.educause.edu/coredata/

EDUCAUSE. (2006). *Student guide to evaluating information technology on campus.* Retrieved February 22, 2008 from http://www.educause.edu/consumerguide/

Education Commons. (2008). Retrieved April 16, 2008 from http://www.educationcommons.org/commons/

Franklin & Marshall College. (2008). *Self paced learning materials.* Retrieved April 15, 2008 from http://ats.fandm.edu/resources/learning/splm/

Garcia, P., & Qin, J. (2007). Identifying the generation gap in higher education: Where do the differences really lie? *Journal of Online Education, 3*(4). Retrieved on January 17, 2008 from http://innovateonline.info/index.php?view=article&id=379

George Mason University. (2007). *Technology across the curriculum.* Retrieved February 21, 2008 from http://tac.gmu.edu

Glendale Community College. *Popular Questions, for New and Returning Students.* Retrieved April 10, 2008 from http://Web.gccaz.edu/studenthelpdesk/

Grasha, A. F. (1996). *Teaching with style: A practical guide to enhancing learning by understanding teaching and learning styles.* San Bernardino, CA: Alliance Publishers. See http://www.iats.com/publications/TSI.html

Iowa State University. (2003). *Faculty technology mentoring.* Retrieved March 23, 2008 from http://www.public.iastate.edu/%7Emstar/mentor/home.html

K-12 Youth Technology Support Collaborative. Retrieved April 15, 2008 from http://www.studenttechsupport.org/index.cfm

Kennedy, G. E., Judd, T. S., Churchward, A., & Gray, K. (2008). First year students' experiences with technology: Are they really digital natives? *Australasian Journal of Educational Technology, 24*(1), 108-122. Retrieved March 15, 2008 from http://www.ascilite.org.au/ajet/ajet24/kennedy.html

Kobulnicky, P., & Rudy, J. (2002). Third annual EDUCAUSE survey Identifies current IT issues. *EDUCAUSE Quarterly, 25*(2), 2002. Available from: http://www.educause.edu/ir/library/pdf/eqm0222.pdf

Loacker, G., & Mentkowski, M. (1993). Creating a culture where assessment improves learning. In T. W. Banta (Ed.), *Making a difference: Outcomes of a decade of assessment in higher education,* (pp. 5-24). San Francisco: Jossey-Bass.

Ludema, J., Cooperrider, D., & Barrett, F. (2001). Appreciative inquiry: The power of the unconditional positive question. In P. Reason & H. Bradury (Eds.), *Handbook of action research: Participatory inquiry and practice.* Thousand Oaks, CA: Sage.

McGee, P., & Diaz, V. (2007). Blogs, wikis, and podcasting, oh my! What is a faculty member supposed to do? *EDUCAUSE Review.* Retrieved April 10, 2008 from http://connect.educause.edu/Library/EDUCAUSE+Review/WikisandPodcastsandBlogsO/44993

Mitra, A., Stefensmeier, T., Lenzmeier, S., & Massoni, A. (1999). Institutional implications of changes in attitudes towards computers and use of computers by faculty. *Journal of Research on Computing in Education, 32*(1), 189-202.

National Center for Education Statistics. (2002). *1999 National study of postsecondary faculty methodology report.* Washington DC: Department of Education.

National Center for Education Statistics. (2005). *2004 National study of postsecondary faculty methodology report.* Washington DC: Department of Education.

Netday. (2006). *2005 speak up event national highlights: Students and teachers. Project Tomorrow.* Retrieved on December 6, 2006 from http://www.netday.org/SPEAKUP/speakup_reports.htm

Ohio State University. (2008). *Research on research (r²).* Retrieved April 15, 2008 from http://digitalunion.osu.edu/r2/about.htm

Prensky, M. (2001). Digital natives, digital immigrants. *On the Horizon, 9*(5), 1–2. Retrieved February 15, 2008 from http://www.marcprensky.com/writing/Prensky%20-%20Digital%20Natives,%20Digital%20Immigrants%20-%20Part1.pdf

Reeves, T. (2002). *Evaluating what really matters in computer-based education.* Retrieved October 10, 2002 from http://www.educationau.edu.au/archives/cp/reeves.htm

Rogers, E. M. (1995). *Diffusion of innovations* (4th ed.). NY: The Free Press.

Romiszowski, A. J. (1981). *Designing instructional systems.* London: Kogan Page (reprint 1992).

Salaway, G., Katz, R. N., Caruso, J. B., Kvavik, R. B., & Nelson, M. R. (2006). *The ECAR study of undergraduate students and information technology.* Boulder, CO: EDUCAUSE. Available from http://www.educause.edu/LibraryDetailPage/666?ID=ERS0607

Self and Peer Assessment Resource Kit. (n.d.). Retrieved April 15, 2008 from http://www.educ.dab.uts.edu.au/darrall/sparksite

Sherry, L., Billig, S., Tavalin, F., & Gibson, D. (2000). New insights on technology adoption in schools. *T.H.E. Journal, 27* (7), 43-46. Available at http://www.thejournal.com/articles/14594

Tapscott, D. (1998). *Growing up digital: The rise of the net generation.* NY: McGraw Hill.

Tufts University. (2008). ITS training. Retrieved March 18, 2008 from http://ase.tufts.edu/its/training.htm

University of Arizona, Computer Based Training. Retrieved April 15, 2008 from http://uacbt.arizona.edu/what_is.htm

University of Arizona, Office of Student Computing Resources (OSCR). Retrieved February 22, 2008 from http://www.oscr.arizona.edu/about

University of Louisville, *Student Tutorial Online Module Program (STOMP) Technology Module.* Retrieved April 15, 2008 from http://www.s4.louisville.edu/stomp/technology.swf

Wang, F., & Hannafin, M. J. (2005). Design-based research and technology-enhanced learning environments. *Educational Technology Research and Development, 53*(4), 5-23.

Yale University. *Email Kiosks.* Retrieved April 15, 2008 from http://www.yale.edu/its/media/computing/kiosks.html

KEY TERMS AND DEFINITIONS

100% Online Course Approach: All course activities, resource use, interactions, and communications take place online, typically through an institutional course management system.

Blended/Hybrid Learning: Involves dividing class experiences between face-to-face and online meetings, thus reducing actual seat time.

Distributed Engagement Approach: This approach allows the learner to complete instructional modules at his or her own pace, in various learning environments and with various supports.

Usable for both face-to-face and online environments, the intent is to allow students to progress through material in the way and speed that is most appropriate for the individual.

GAP Analysis: Compares the status quo with intended outcomes of a desired change.

Neomillennial Learning Style (Dede, 2005): 21st century learners who prefer an environment that includes fluency in multiple media and in simulation-based virtual settings, communal learning involving diverse, tacit, situated experience, with knowledge distributed across a community and a context as well as within an individual.

SWOTT Analysis: Involves examining the strengths, weaknesses, opportunities, threats, and trends (SWOTT) (Ansof, 1980) associated with the results of a GAP analysis or a planned initiative. SWOTT analyses draws upon what is known from documentation and observation and requires data collection and possibly surveying of relevant units or departments.

The Transformative Assessment Process (TAP): Provides a high level 'map' of assessment points within a process-oriented flow designed to discover and transform practice.

Web Enhanced Course Approach: Offers between class meeting activities using learning management systems or other information communications technology.

ENDNOTES

[1] Source: EDUCAUSE National Learning Infrastructure Initiative (NLII) currently the EDUCAUSE Learning Initiative (ELI) in 2003 by Gary Brown, Washington Statue University, Darren Cambridge, George Mason University, Steve Erhlman, Flashlight Program/TLT Group, Joan Lippincott, CNI, Patricia McGee, University of Texas at San Antonio, Vicki Suter, Pepperdine University, and Robin Zuniga, TLT Group.

[2] Based on Benjamin S. Bloom Taxonomy of educational objectives. Allyn and Bacon, Boston, MA. Copyright (c) 1984 by Pearson Education.

[3] Adapted from the National Center for Academic Transformation Five Course Models, http://www.thencat.org/PCR/Proj_Model.htm

[4] Sloan-C Blended Learning Research Perspectives, http://www.blendedteaching.org/

[5] Examples of the Supplemental Model: http://www.center.rpi.edu/PlanRes/R2R_Model_Sup.htm and http://www.thencat.org/PCR/model_supp.htm

[6] Emporium examples from NCAT: http://www.thencat.org/PCR/model_emporium.htm and http://www.center.rpi.edu/PlanRes/R2R_Model_Emp.htm
Buffet examples from NCAT: http://www.thencat.org/PCR/model_buffet.htm and http://www.center.rpi.edu/PlanRes/R2R_Model_Buffet.htm

[7] Examples of NCAT's Replacement Model: http://www.center.rpi.edu/PlanRes/R2R_Model_Rep.htm and http://www.thencat.org/PCR/model_replace.htm

[8] Examples of the Online Model from NCAT: http://www.thencat.org/PCR/model_online.htm and http://www.center.rpi.edu/PlanRes/R2R_Model_Online.htm

[9] http://www.lcc.edu/cte/resources/teachingexcellence/packets/packet4/teaching_with_style.html#return

[10] Grasha, A. F., & Yangarber-Hicks, N. (2000). Integrating teaching styles and learning styles with instructional technology. *College Teaching,* 48 (1), 2-10.

[11] The Open Knowledge Definition defines open knowledge as any material that allows the user to " use, reuse, and redistribute it" see http://opendefinition.org/

Chapter XXIX
Lean and Global Product Development in Auto Industry

Bimal P. Nepal
Texas A &M University, USA

Leslie Monplaisir
Wayne State University, USA

ABSTRACT

Original equipment manufacturers (OEMs) in automotive industry are faced with the conflicting goals of creating vehicles with higher reliability, increased feature content and quality while lowering model runs, reducing costs, and shorter developmental times. However, to achieve these goals is very difficult in a global product development environment that involves globally distributed OEMs and suppliers working on the components and subsystems of the same but a complex product like an automobile. This is especially true with regard to electronic systems in automotive industry due to the continued and significant increase in overall electrical content in a vehicle, and the historical short lifecycle of enabling technologies. For example, in the last three decades, electrical/electronics control has gone from 100% analog to primarily digital microprocessor based controls (Paras et al., 2004). As the level of integration occurs, automotive electronics are going to be challenged by software development and integration. As a result, it is going to increase overall product development time and cost. While it has been a growing concern for both academician and practitioners, the prior literature is still very limited in terms providing a clear or sufficiently structured framework to address the issues of global product development system. This chapter attempts to narrow down this gap by presenting a lean and global product development (GPD) framework and the necessary enablers to achieve this end. The framework is demonstrated through an automotive industry case study.

1. INTRODUCTION

An efficient product development processes is key to success of any new product. If managed and executed properly, it enables the manufacturing company to develop newer products at a lower cost faster speed than its competition. An article published in *Auto insider* describes that the American car companies General Motors, Ford Motor Company, and DaimlerChrysler, have seen their US market share decline steadily over the past ten years. Similarly, their stock values have tumbled by nearly fifty percent. On the other hand, consumer's demand for newer features and more varieties at lower price is on the rise (Yadav et al., 2007). Research shows that the innovative companies with respect to both product and process are consistently becoming more profitable (Kearney, 2005) than those that are less innovative.

In addition to innovativeness, another important attribute of a successful enterprise is the flexibility of its product development and manufacturing processes. Sobek et al. (1998) suggest that the flexibility of PD system is an important enabler to success in the current volatile and rapidly changing environment. Thomke (2007, page. 194) implies that the widely used stage gate PD process becomes very rigid and expensive if we fail to thoroughly understand customer requirements early on. According to Yadav et al. (2207), "flexibility and effectiveness of PD processes depend on various other factors such as design activities and tools used, their planning and scheduling, information flow structure, quality and availability of information, and decision making approaches". While design tools and techniques are the critical enablers, an integrated product development process or system is pivotal to the overall success of any PD factory. Past studies have revealed that individual best practices and tools are helpful, but in order to reap the full benefits, such practices should be implemented across the board including suppliers and customers (Nepal et al., 2007).

Global auto leaders such as General Motors and Ford are no longer a vertically integrated company. A significant amount of components and sub-systems used in their vehicles are developed by globally distributed suppliers. As the pressure to reduce the time-to-market, and improve quality and reliability of the vehicle is ever increasing, it calls for an efficient overall product development system including suppliers to achieve these objectives. Further, automotive product development is more complex than it seems from outside given the fact that much of the larger OEMs such as GM and Ford own other smaller companies with totally different cultural background. For example, Ford currently owns Mazda, and Volvo in addition to its traditional Ford, Lincoln and Mercury brands. Therefore to optimize its global PD resources and reduce the development time and cost, it has to create a process that allows sharing the components across its different brands. It requires an ability to process reconfiguration, new product architectures, and powerful technology and tools to connect globally distributed teams (Howell and Shu, 2002). Such effort not only provides an economy of scale but also improve the product quality hence reduces its warranty expenditures. In other words, the emphasis on product development process of the global product development company should be to develop innovative, unique, relevant products that can fill real customer needs in terms of variety, and yet, make the company more profitable by taking waste out of its PD process. Nevertheless, the challenge is how one can deal with the increased proliferation of product offerings that makes the supply chain network more complex (Mikkola and Skjoett-Larsen, 2003). Therefore, a lot of hard work and significant investment is required early on in order to take full advantage of global product development.

While there is ample discussion in the published literature on the development of products for global market (Graber, 1996; Howell and Shu, 2002; Thomke and Nimgade, 2001) or global product development teams related issues such as culture and performance (Barczak and Mc-Donough III; www.ptc.com; Lovelace et al., 2001), there is very little precedent in the literature on the global PD process and tools to reduce time-to-market and improve quality.

Another important aspect of global product development is project management and control. In order to cope with increasingly pressure for time and cost reduction, companies are now leaning towards applying lean principles in PD projects. "Lean Thinking" is a business strategy that seeks to eliminate waste to create the most value for customers while consuming the fewest resources (Walton, 1999). The lean principles have been successfully embraced within manufacturing. Recently, there is a growing recognition that these same principles can be equally applied to product development (Walton, 1999; Morgan, 2005). In particular, the reduction in excessive process variability, the creation of flow, and the elimination of waste are seen as key elements of lean product development. While application of these techniques offer the potential for significant improvements in development cycle time and cost, in reality this transfer is far more complex than it sounds (Karlsson and Ahlstrom, 1996). Unlike manufacturing, PD is a non-repetitive, non-sequential, unbounded activity that produces information, and where cogent risk taking might be a key to adding value. Variability is inherently and necessarily, higher in product development than manufacturing. Similarly, due to low expense and high cycle time, the relative economic importance of wasted cycle time compared to wasted expenses can be much higher in PD than it is in manufacturing.

The purpose of this chapter is to present a lean and global product development (GPD) framework and the necessary tools set to achieve this end. It aims to narrow down the gap of current PD literature in two aspects. First, it provides a formal definition of a "global product development system" and tools to reduce time-to-market

and improve quality by applying lean principles in a PD environment. Second, a real world case study that unraveles many hidden and complex issues of a global product development system, which have not been fully explained in the prior literature. The remainder of the chapter is organized as follows. Section 2 presents the evolution of PD process including a brief review of global product development literature. The topics include formal definition GPD, its managerial issues, and application of lean thinking in product development. In section 3, a case study is presented from a global auto industry. The case study demonstrates the proposed framework for lean product development. Section 4 summarizes the results and benefits of case study. Finally, few concluding remarks along with directions for future research are highlighted in section 5.

2. EVOLUTION OF PRODUCT DEVELOPMENT PROCESSES

2.1 Stage Gate Product Development Process

The most generic PD process, widely described as "Stage-Gate" process, was developed and implemented in many US industry during late eighty's and early ninety's (Holmes and Campbell, 2004; Yadav et al., 2007). This process, popularly known as "waterfall" or "phase-gate", is also being used currently in automotive industry. It consists of discrete phases from product planning to product release as illustrated in Figure 1. At the end of each phase is a stage gate that consists of a design review process. Based on the status of earlier milestone (and also inputs from the senior management), the course for next development stage is determined.

The major goal of the stage gate process is to improve the business performance and develop high quality product in order to improve the revenue growth. It also aims to provide a struc-

Figure 1. A generic stage-gate product development process (Yadav et al., 2007)

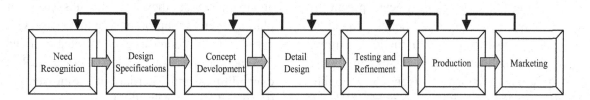

tured process for managing and coordinating the development tasks so that there are no unprecedented outcomes that would hinder the process (Thomke, 2007, p.193). The stage-gate process is driven by the requirements or goals of quality and reliability rather than cost or schedule requirements. Therefore, this type of process provides a mechanism for controlling quality and reliability issues during the gate reviews. However, there is no feedback or cross-stage iteration planned in the stage gate process that makes it inflexible. The other limitation is it is not efficient because it does not control the time and schedule. This is a serious limitation in the today's globalized competition, where time-to-market is a winning strategy in addition to traditional factors such as quality and reliability (Rosas-Vega and Vokura, 2000). Following are the other major pitfalls of traditional stage-gate product development process (Minderhouds, 1999; Unger, 2003).

Difficulty in handling parallel tasks and cross-phase iteration

- Long design review process and rigid milestones prolongs the cycle time that sometimes even leads to skipping of milestones by milestones.
- Excessive amount of documentation overwhelms the engineers and increases non-value added time.
- Less attention to early stages of the PD process that causes late engineering changes and design reworks.

2.2 Concurrent Engineering

Concurrent Engineering is a product development philosophy that requires the involvement of a cross functional teams right since early stage in order to plan for product development and manufacturing processes simultaneously (Quesada *et al.,* 2006). The larger automotive companies like Ford and Toyota have their own PD systems. Ford PD system is currently shifting from traditional phase-gate system and adapting to lean PD processes developed by its Japanese subsidiary Mazda. Toyota has been implementing set-based concurrent engineering that helped the company to reduce impact of late engineering changes and in delaying the product differentiation (Sobek *et al.,* 1999).

PD processes can also be classified as "point-based concurrent engineering" and "set-based concurrent engineering" depending upon how soon the initial set of conceptual ideas converge to a "final design" (Ford and Sobek, 2005). In the point-based approach that the most US OEMs follow, the best conceptual design is selected and frozen early on during the "end of the stage" design review based on various criteria to minimize the complexity and limit the production cost. On the other hand, in the second approach that Toyota pursues, rather than selecting the so-called the best alternative design they develop a set of "viable alternatives" from multiple perspectives. As they progress on to next stage, they gradually eliminate the relatively "poor" alternative based on multiple criteria such as quality, reliability, manufacturability, cost etc. and eventually converge to a "final design" (Ford and Sobek, 2005).

Over the years, the product development literature has evolved from traditional "sequential technology push/market pull models to more overlapped and integrated processes, employing internal cross-functional teams and early supplier involvement to reduce the time-to-market" (Yadav et al., 2007). In nutshell, the companies are now moving more towards lean thinking and looking at the product development from the system's perspective (Cooper and Edgett, 2008), the case this chapter is presenting. Further, the case study highlights the typical issues of global product development and approach to cope with them.

2.3 Global Product Development: Definition and Management Perspectives

Although "globalization" is almost a universal terminology in any business and management literature, the global product development is not as widely discussed. At least, the authors are not aware of any formal definition of "global product development (GPD)" as yet in the past literature. Depending upon the context it has been defined differently. Often it is related to a development of a global product (Graber, 1996) or product development system that involves teams from across the globe (Thomke and Nemagin, 2001). In this chapter, the global product development is defined as "a globally distributed product development process that integrates OEMs and suppliers in order to develop a complex product". In this case, the suppliers are also known as "full service suppliers" who are responsible for design, development, and manufacturing of the components/subsystems they are supplying to an OEM. The suppliers may be in-house or globally distributed. The OEM may have multiple products that require a common subsystem. For example, in automotive industry the traditional North

American "Big Three" corporations Ford, GM and Chrysler have alliances with other global OEMs and in many cases they share the subsystems and platform across their brands. In that sense, GPD can also be considered as global strategic alliance that encompasses capital investment such as R&D expenditures and international joint ventures (Ojah and Monplaisir, 2003).

The various aspects of GPD have been studied in the past. Graber (1996) describes how Black and Decker® developed their products that are used globally by forming a global team representing the members from the different parts of the world. The author quotes, "a global product that fails to meet real consumer needs in the areas of innovation, relevance, and uniqueness is doomed to failure". It also mentions that a "support of top management and global business team structure" were other key factors for successful implementation of GPD in that company. Salhieh et al. (2001) presents a computer supported collaborative methodology for planning the global product development. Howell and Shu (2002) provide a very good insight on global alliance strategy adopted by GM to explore new global market and to develop new products. In the earlier research, it was found that the global product design and development had positive impact on the investor's valuation of a multinational company (Ojah and Monplaisir, 2003). Other researchers have focused on global product development teams. Barczack and McDonough III (2003) argue that building trust and constant efforts to increase communication among team members have strong positive impact on the success of a global PD team. An empirical study shows that there is significant impact of national culture on global team performance (Sivakumar and Nakata, 2003). While there has been a growing research interest on various aspects GPD, there is not as much precedent in the literature about the processes and tools to achieve the ultimate paradigm of global product development.

Challenges in Global Product Development

The prior PD literature has highlighted many challenges in new and global product development that involve multiple players. Handfield and Lawson (2007) have presented a survey of 134 global product development companies. The survey has found many challenges facing the industries in terms of early supplier integration into NPD and improving the efficiencies of product development teams and processes. Among others, the authors recommend to focus on lean product development process and design reuse. Cooper (2007) proposed "seven tools of innovation" for best practices in product development, which include *customer focus, front end loading, spiral development, cross functional teams, effective product development metric system, and flexible, adaptable, and scalable NPD process.*

One of the widely cited problems in global PD factories is late design changes and its impact on the overall development time and cost. As a major step to minimize these problems, researchers and practitioners have underscored the need of early tracking of the problems through collaboration and front loading (Brown and Eisenhardt, 1995; Griffin and Hauser, 1996; Thomke and Fujimoto, 2000). Kohn (2006) presents a case study of a European car company in which he characterizes the concept creation phase in an NPD process as "difficult", especially at the early stages, due to the "negative conflicts" between engineering and marketing functional departments. The author argues that interdependence between the two departments is the major cause for the conflict, which in his views can be resolved by recognizing and having a better understanding of the "relationship". In another extensive empirical study, Quesada et al. (2006) have examined the relationship among the extent of involvement of suppliers in design, concurrent engineering, and the perceived supplier's performance by Japanese and the US automotive OEMs. Their findings suggested that there was a positive correlation between the supplier's involvement and the other two variables- concurrent engineering and the OEM's perception about the supplier's performance.

Supplier's performance has far reaching affects beyond PD time and cost in terms of OEM's overall success in the market. For example, in automotive industry, suppliers' contribute more than 70% of the vehicle content, or total vehicle value (Leenders et al., 2002). Therefore, the quality of parts supplied by the supplier significantly determines the final vehicle quality (Froker, 1997). Womack et al. (1991) suggest that working simultaneously with suppliers can not only shorten product development time but also improve product quality and product costs. Binder et al. (2007) highlights the paradigm shift in the automotive product life cycle practices in the recent time. The authors argue that after "Fordism" and "Toyotism", the current business philosophy in automotive industry is characterized by "partnership and relational model" as opposed to traditional "adversarial and contractual model". While the prior research works have succinctly identified the need for a focus on inter-organizational performance improvement efforts as opposed to traditional local optimization of individual organization's performance, the precedent literature falls short in terms providing a structured framework for such collaboration (Binder et al., 2007).

Analysis of uncertainty in the product development projects is another challenge that needs a credible attention in the technology project management body of knowledge. Although various models have been proposed by academicians and companies such as Ford and Toyota for PD process, a detailed analysis of underlying uncertainty in the PD process such as due to late engineering changes is still a subject under study. Ford and Sobek (2005) have applied real option models to validate the "set-based development" approach that they suggest for managing the uncertainty in product design and development. Rozenes et al. (2006) provide a state-of-the art review of project control that encompasses project risk management, total quantity management among multiple dimensions of project control. Having new set of tools and technologies isn't enough for successful implementation of innovative ideas. Thomke (2006) presents few "common pitfalls" related to automotive companies while adopting a new technology or research and development tools. The pitfalls include *"using new tools merely as substitutes, adding (instead of minimizing) interfaces, and changing tools, but not people's behavior"*. Therefore, the global industry such as automotive has also challenging task in terms of integrating (at the systems level) various kinds of technology, knowledge and hardware/software supplied by the suppliers (Hobday et al., 2005).

2.4 Lean Thinking in Product Development

Lean Thinking is a business strategy that seeks to eliminate waste to create the most value for customers while consuming the fewest resources. Lean focuses on system efficiency over point efficiency, and seeks to identify and remove waste from everything (Womack and Jones, 2003). The lean principles have been successfully embraced within manufacturing. Recently, there is a growing recognition that these same principles can be equally applied to product development (Morgan, 2005). In particular, the reduction in excessive process variability, the creation of flow, and the elimination of waste are seen as key elements of lean product development. While application of these techniques offer the potential for significant improvements in development cycle time and cost, in reality this transfer is far more complex than it sounds. Unlike manufacturing, PD is a non-repetitive, non-sequential, unbounded activity that produces information. In PD, taking a well defined risk is often considered as a key strategy to adding value. Likewise, variability is inherently and necessarily, higher in product development than manufacturing. Lastly, due to low expense and high cycle time, the relative economic importance of wasted cycle time compared to wasted

expenses can be much higher in PD than it is in manufacturing.

The roadmap to lean starts with an organization's culture. The first step is to train everyone on lean concepts: value streams; waste; customer rate of demand (Takt time); one-piece flow; and pull process or system. Value Streams are all activities, both value-adding and non-value-adding, required to take a product, service or transaction from an unfinished state to the hands of its customers. Examples of value streams include: order fulfillment, product development, and hiring. Non-value-add activities are waste, and should be removed from the value stream. Examples of waste in product development include (Liker, 2004; Morgan, 2005, Ohno, 1995):

- **Overproduction:** Designs turning faster than testing capabilities
- **Defects:** Mistaken requirements or specifications
- **Transportation:** Many handoffs of information and too many approvals required
- **Over Processing:** Not invented here; rework as a result of late problem discovery
- **Inventory:** Queues of unprocessed information
- **Unnecessary movement:** Poor data organization
- **Waiting:** Resource conflicts; late information, hardware, software
- **Underutilization of people's knowledge and skills:** Problems not solved at the lowest levels; decisions taken without consulting local experts; customer and employee feedback ignored in new designs.

In summary, the companies are currently moving towards embracing lean principles to achieve the new PD paradigms to compete in the global market. Although this topic has created immense interest in academia and industry, there is not as much precedent in the literature about the processes and tools to achieve the ultimate paradigm of global product development. The prior literature falls short in terms providing a structured framework to realize system level optimization of product development activities. Further, the global industry such as automotive has daunting task to integrate various subsystems that are of heterogeneous characteristics such as different technology, knowledge and hardware/software supplied by different suppliers. This chapter attempts to address these issues through a case study research based on development of an automotive electrical body module.

3. AUTOMOTIVE ELECTRICAL BODY MODULE CASE STUDY

3.1 Background

Automotive software and electronic module development is increasingly adding a new layer of architecture complexity as OEMs continue to increase the feature content across the vehicle programs. IBM research suggests that over 30 percent of these costs are attributable to software and electronics defects and as electronic content increases, this portion of warranty cost will continue to grow (Blake, 2004).While in one hand, there are numerous efforts going on in every manufacturing company to minimize the product cost so as to become more competitive in the global market, on the other hand today automotive manufacturers in the U.S. pay over $700 in warranty costs per vehicle (Arnun, 2004). Therefore, in order to improve product quality and reliability, the traditional "Big Three" North American Auto manufacturers are pursuing various strategies to turn their businesses into profitability. This chapter presents a case study on implementation of lean and global product development framework at Ford Motor Company adopted from Nepal et al. (2007).

According to Nepal et al. (2007), in year 2004, Ford Motor Company has created a global product development system, known as GPDS that has an efficient process, tools, and culture in order to reduce time-to-market, lower development costs and improve product quality. It emphasizes commonality and reusability, including reuse of architecture, system, parts and computer-aided engineering models. The GPDS had been launched as a truly a cross-functional led effort, with executive champions and task force leaders from home organizations across all areas of the business. In order to ensure the buy-ins of all the stakeholders, it involved multiple players including the relevant OEM functional organizations and suppliers. The GPDS had been developed to meet customer and business expectations using one global product creation system adapting the proven Mazda[1]* product development system's benchmark of speed and efficiency by:

- Implementing a lean, standardized manufacturing process-lead approach
- Engaging cross-functional, technical people
- Reusing parts and knowledge
- Working with fewer, more competent and efficient suppliers

While GPDS was being implemented across the Ford, Nepal et al. (2007) focused on just one small case study from electrical electronics systems engineering (EESE) department. However, we believe that the lessons learned and insights from the case study can be generalized to represent the broader context of overall product development process beyond electrical body module, in fact, even beyond the automotive context. The scope of the case study was defined as per the result of the gaps identified by an *'Electrical Task Force'* between Mazda's processes and Ford's existing processes that needed to be addressed to facilitate GPDS implementation. The two major gaps identified were in the areas of implementation of model based systems engineering and developing and improving the current electrical/electronics

(E/E) test capability by incorporating highly accelerating life testing methods.

3.2 Proposed Lean Product Development Framework

A four-step framework is proposed to create a lean product development process as a roadmap to achieve the objectives of global product development system (see Figure 2). As mentioned earlier, the proposed framework is presented within the context of GPDS of Ford as described in Nepal et al. (2007). However, its tools and processes are applicable to any global product development setting beyond automotive. The four steps are problem definition, analysis of current state value stream map, optimization of the process performance, implementation of improved or new process.

Notice that the information flow is two sided between the steps essentially indicating that this is not a sequential process in the strict sense. A lot of activities within these steps can be performed concurrently to a certain extent and may require inputs from each other. For example, the scope and problem definition may be revised and fine-tuned based on the initial findings of as-is value stream mapping and analysis. Similarly, implementation constraints may guide the process optimization efforts and vice-versa. Furthermore, as shown in

Figure 2, it is a continuous improvement process – a pursuit to perfection.

3.2.1 Problem Definition

A key step in the problem definition phase is to identify the gaps in the as-is process with respect to the 'best-in-class' industry leaders. As mentioned in the problem background, this case study primarily focuses on the product development tasks that are related to requirements definition and design verification & testing procedures of electrical body module of a car. In other words, the first step in problem definition is really about knowing your own process and its standing with respect to industry best practices. Therefore, this case study was also begun with benchmarking of both OEMs and suppliers. The benchmarking of suppliers had helped the project team to understand and analyze the process from the system's perspective as advised in the 'lean thinking' (Wommack and Jones, 2003). The following paragraphs briefly outline the outcomes of benchmarking with respect to improvement opportunities.

Benchmarking of suppliers
As mentioned earlier, the purpose of benchmarking suppliers' processes was to identify areas for mutual improvement and develop a

Figure 2. Proposed lean product development framework

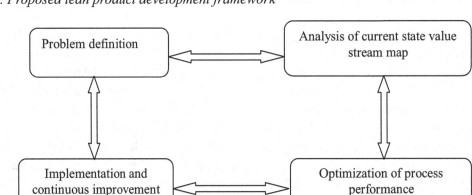

new level relationship needed to support GPDS implementation. The benchmarking was focused on three major elements that are: process, people and tools. The benchmarked suppliers included both domestic and foreign tier one companies. A number of opportunities for improvement were identified during this process, which are grouped into following three categories namely process, people, and tools (Nepal et al., 2007).

i. Process

- **Communication opportunities for improvement:** Need to have single point of contact, authority for D&R engineering, strict commitments to milestones deadlines, and a defined interface ownership.

- **Purchasing opportunities for improvement:** Early sourcing, long-term relationship, one-on-one vision sharing between the executives (OEM and Supplier).

- **Organization opportunities for improvement:** Need to have better vehicle and core alignment, and discipline around commonality and standardization

ii. People: Need to reward innovators and engage suppliers upfront to provide opportunity to contribute more.

iii. Tools - opportunities for improvement: Less engineering by checklist; clarity of specifications; disciplined design freeze; and accept surrogate data from other OEM customers

Benchmarking of other OEMs

As Toyota is considered as the industry leader in automotive product development, especially in lean PD, this section mainly presents the findings of Toyota study. The major sources of this benchmarking were the published literature (Ward et al., 1998; Liker, 2004; Morgan, 2005) and the interview with the researchers in Toyota product development system. There are three primary subsystems within Toyota product development systems that form a social and technical system which interacts to a complex whole. The first

subsystem, the process, contains all the tasks and the sequence of tasks required to bring the product from concept to start of production i.e. information, customer needs, past product characteristics, competitive product data, engineering principles, and other inputs that get transformed through the product development process into the complete engineering of a product that will be built by manufacturing (Liker, 2004).

The second subsystem element is 'people system'. This includes recruiting and selecting engineers, how they are trained and developed, the leadership style, how the organization is structured, how the organization learns, and other subtle things (but very critical for success) such as culture. A measure of the strength of the culture is the degree in which these things are truly shared across the members of the organization. Toyota has a very strong culture compared to most companies (Liker, 2004). Toyota develops a chief engineer system to lead product development and its PD teams are composed of cross-functional experts including suppliers. The final subsystem consists of 'the tools and technology' employed in order to bring a vehicle into being. This subsystem not only includes CAD systems, machine technology and digital manufacturing and testing technologies, but all the tools that support the effort of the people involved in the development project whether it be for problem solving, learning or standardizing best practices and values(Liker, 2004). In summary, the lessons learned from benchmarking of Toyota product development system was certainly one of the major motivating factors behind this study.

3.2 .2 Analysis of Current State Value Stream Map

Value stream mapping (VSM) is a process improvement tool that is used in lean manufacturing. The value stream map captures processes, material flows of a given product family and helps to identify waste in the system. It has proven to be a powerful analytical tool for reducing waste and synchronizing activities in manufacturing and product development in order to: visualize the entire process or system, identify the sources of waste, serve as a common language, and identify "hidden" relationships. This case study was launched as a pilot on a smart junction box of electrical body module for a car. A typical picture of smart junction box is shown in Figure 3. It may be noted that this SJB does not represent the actual Ford component and is included in this chapter just for the readers' benefit. Before mapping the current value stream of any process, it is important to define the "value" of activities based on process objectives and the role of each activity in satisfying the customer requirements. For example in the *Smart Junction Box* case, it had been learned that the original intent of the program management was to use carry over module by maintaining the same supplier. That means, it was merely an 'application change' case and there was no intention of redeveloping of existing component. Therefore, any unintended additional design or engineering work would not add any value to the customer (either internal or external) hence was considered as waste. With that

mindset, the VSM exercise was focused on the activities that start from Confirmation Prototype (CP) through Launch Readiness (LR) milestones within the current Ford Product Development System (FPDS) process (Nepal et al., 2007).

For data collection, several face-to-face interviews were conducted with the corresponding supplier and with Electrical Body Module engineers who were part of the development team of this SJB (Smart Junction Box). An engineering activity log was used to collect the process data (see Table 1).

In the given list, the suppliers' names are not disclosed here to protect the confidentiality. The activity log captured the list of activities that have occurred during the development of any component or subsystem. The activities are listed in a chronological order. Further, two types of timings: total time in system and activity time are documented in the activity log. The total time in system is the time between when information was received and when the design was actually delivered to the next level of customer. The difference (Time in system –Activity Time) gives the 'wait time' for that activity. Apart from Ford engineering, the activity log also captures the

Figure 3. A typical smart junction box used in electrical body module (Source: www.autosplice.com)

Table 1. A select portion of engineering activity log for Smart Junction Box (source: Nepal et al., 2007)

Month	Week	Design Status Summary	Engineering Activity	Activity Time (Hrs.)	Total Time (Hrs.)	Value Added Ratio
Nov '02	1	Convert software to new microcontroller from *Brand A* to *Brand B*	Convert software to new microcontroller *Brand B*	400	480	83%
Feb '03	1	Verify software for CP Bread Board MRD	Tier 1 Supplier Bench Testing on software to verify functionality for CP Bread Board delivery (Not full test)	120	120	100%
	2	3/5 Bread Board MRD	Milestone	0	0	N/A
Mar '03	1	Software verification by Systems Independent Test & Verification (IT&V) group	Software verification by Systems Independent Test & Verification (IT&V) group	240	280	85.7%

activities by the Tier 1 supplier that supplied the SJB. The name of the supplier is not disclosed to protect the proprietary information. The 'as-is' process steps shown on the activity logs were transferred into VSM icons as shown in Figure 4. All the tasks were classified into the following categories as described below (Wommack and Jones, 2003):

- **Category I:** Tasks that actually create value as perceived by customer.
- **Category II:** Tasks that don't create any value but are currently required by the product development, order filling etc. thus can't be eliminated just yet (Type I Muda).
- **Category III:** Tasks that don't create any value as perceived by the customer and so can be eliminated immediately (Type II Muda).

The VSM examined four important areas where the development activities took place: Ford engineering, supplier's electrical/mechanical hardware design, systems IT& V, and software groups. In the first portion of the development it was found that an issue of the obsolescence of the microprocessor (electrical/mechanical design)

had a major impact in delaying the hardware and software of the module as well as generating rework and delays down the stream. As a result of the microprocessor change, the component DV (Design Verification) started late in the development process which in the end generated more engineering changes and rework post 'confirmation prototype' <CP> event. Ford engineering was also driving a lot of rework by issuing late specification revisions to the supplier for the "convertible" version after the <CP> milestone as depicted in Figure 4 (Nepal et al., 2007). The VSM provides us with mainly two types of information: First, the value ratio for each activity which is defined as the ratio of activity time and total time in system; and second, the rework of which value ratio is "zero". It is important to note here that regardless of ratio of actual activity time to total time in system, the value ratio for rework (or any other type of waste such as waiting) is zero. In the given VSM, all the shaded activities represent "rework" or *type II muda*.

Although purposefully not shown in this chapter, according to Nepal et al. (2007), such types of rework examples were identified at various stages even few weeks before the job 1. As a result, continuous fix and testing loops were happening,

Figure 4. Current state value stream map of 'Smart Junction Box' of electrical body module for a vehicle of MY 2005 (Source: Nepal et al., 2007)

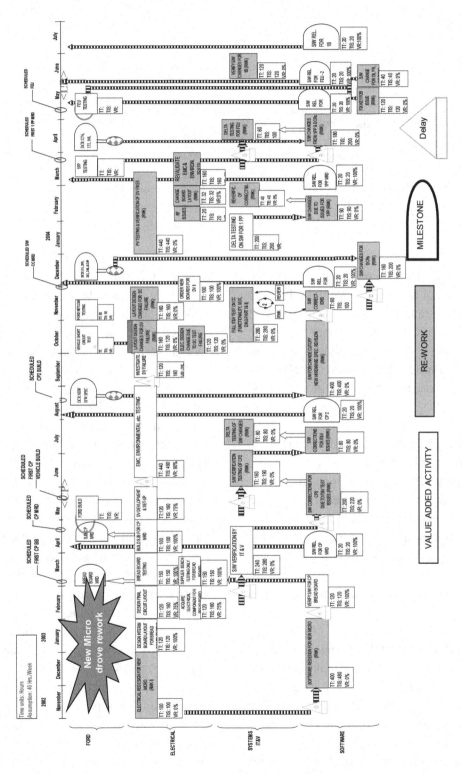

which drove continuous delays and failures. The paper reports that miscommunication among all the parties involved generated confusion during the microprocessor's selection process. The abovementioned situation strongly indicated a need for a standardized process with checklist for making selection decision of components like microprocessors. Further, it was also reported that the design change requests happened late in the process have driven major reworks.

3.2.3 Optimization of Product Development Process

The optimization phase deals with creation of future state value stream map by eliminating the *type II muda* and minimizing *type I muda* from the current process as far as possible. In this case study, it was done so by identifying the enablers of global product development. Two types of enablers were identified in this study. The enablers identified within the GPDS systems are called internal enablers and those adapted from the 'lean manufacturing' concepts are called the external enablers. Following paragraphs provides the highlights of these enablers. However, the sensitive company information is excluded from the discussion to protect the confidentiality.

Internal enablers to reduce the DV/PV Testing Time

Although there were many areas within the product development process that were analyzed for potential reductions in development time and resource utilization. This study was mainly focused on non- geometric engineering design and development which encompassed requirements development, hardware and software specification development, and the design verification and testing. At Ford, a strong emphasis is increasingly placed on reliability requirements which eliminate early-life failures. Early life failures are often the result of poor manufacturing and inadequate design. A substantial proportion of

the early life failures are also due to variation of strength which is a complex function of material properties, design configuration and dimensions (Todinov, 2005). Considerable effort, time and resources are required in both design verification and process verification of an electronics module. The environmental test time alone typically takes 14 to 16 weeks to complete. For example, testing of an electronic module alone takes over 700 hours to accomplish. In addition, there are other tests needed for thermal shock endurance, high temperature endurance and high humidity endurance. All of these tests are very time consuming. These tests in many ways can be considered as attribute testing. Currently, to perform these tests, a specification/test bogey is defined and the electronic component/module is required to meet or exceed this bogey. If the modules do not fail prior to reaching the defined bogey, the test is considered a success and the module may move to a production state assuming the other relevant testing has been successfully accomplished.

Although this test methodology has been employed for many years, it falls short in several regards. For one, it is very time consuming to perform. And secondly, it tests only to a bogey or specification value and nothing more. Even if the electronic module passes the specification limit of the test, it is difficult to estimate the strength or weakness of the product or how robust it really is to the environmental stress in an automobile. To overcome the current test limitations methodology, this research proposed not only to revise the existing environmental test specification with the introduction of highly accelerated life testing (HALT) but also to change the culture of testing to a bogey to testing to failure to acquire significantly more data on the robustness of the electronic module design.

External enablers to Lean Product Development Process

Based on the benchmarking and the lessons learned from the VSM, it has been found that the critical piece for closing the gaps between GPDS and FPDS milestones was the lean policy deployment. Or in other words, the objective is to eliminate completely the *Type II muda* (rework) and minimize the *Type I muda* such as transportation and other logistics related activities.

Further, it is important to examine the entire value chain for implementing lean thinking. For example, we have found that although the micro selection was a supplier responsibility, there were major set-backs to Ford's body module development process when the wrong micro was selected as evidenced in the current state value stream maps. In summary, following tools are suggested for lean product creation (Morgan, 2005; Nepal et al., 2006) in a complex supply chain environment. Those are: value stream mapping of entire PD chain including suppliers, front loading of design activities, standardized processes and check lists, clearly specified requirements, continuous flow of information, early involvement of suppliers, and modular design. The details of improvement initiatives and Ford practices are not disclosed in the chapter to protect the propriety information. Readers are encouraged to see Nepal et al (2007) for more information on external enablers suggested in the case study.

3.2.4 Process Implementation

In order to validate the benefits of both internal and external enablers, the proposed lean PD framework suggests to implement them; first on a pilot basis and upon initial success on a full scale basis. Nepal et al. (2007) mention that several pilot programs were established to validate the benefits of the enablers proposed for the electrical body module case study. The first pilot program on internal enablers was conducted for the front wiper motor with integrated electronics. The pilot program consisted of both normal Ford design verification (DV) testing and HALT testing simultaneously. The results were subsequently analyzed and compared with each

other. A HALT test profile was developed to the motors that could be used for future testing. More examples of HALT test in other product can also be found in Coit et al. (2005).

Similarly, to implement the lean or external enablers several initiatives were taken. Amongst all, the first and foremost step in implementing lean principles is finding the right leaders with the right knowledge and beginning with the value stream itself. The most difficult step may be overcoming the inertia present in the organization. In other words, it creates a need for a change agent plus a core of lean knowledge; and some type of crisis (loss of market share) may also serve as a lever for change. Following steps were recommended for the implementation of lean principles. That are: i) identify a change agent, ii) get the knowledge of lean thinking, iii) create a core lean promotion function, iv) define targets, and v) establish organizational alignment (Nepal et al., 2007). For interested readers, a comprehensive material on lean principles is provided in Wommack and Jones (2003).

4. RESULTS AND BENEFITS OF THE CASE STUDY

From the pilot implementation described in Nepal et al. (2007), Ford could realize the savings in many areas. The study concentrated on two metrics: process improvement metric, and tools & technology metrics. In terms of process improvements, a huge savings resulted from the value stream mapping analysis through identification and elimination of engineering design rework. The pilot study alone was able to identify 25 weeks of engineering design rework which attracted a lot of attentions of upper management. Similarly, due to standardization of applicable hardware and software specifications there was reduction in time for requirements definition by 4 weeks. On the tools and technology front, the HALT testing provided better design robustness testing method. For example, it reduced the testing time by 3 weeks. In addition, there was significant improvement in product performance and warranty due to the attainment of variable test data. The revised environmental DV test process incorporating HALT reduced 6-8 weeks in test time for both DV and PV (process verification). Another benefit of HALT testing is that the product is mature at introduction. At introduction, the product will have few, if any, field failures since the failures were discovered during testing and resolved. This has a two-pronged benefit. First, the warranty costs, repair costs, and warehouse space for replacement parts will dramatically decrease. Second, the in-house rework time will decrease. Since there is ample design margins, one can tolerate shifts in processes to avoid production shut downs, rework, customer notifications and recalls. Increased customer satisfaction is another advantage of performing HALT testing. There is also a potential for overhead reduction and reassignment due to the reduced test times and the reduction in retesting due to early field failures which result in redesigns. Since HALT testing requires fewer test units, there is a reduction in prototype costs associated with the parts.

5. CONCLUSION

In order to stay competitive in the business, manufacturing enterprises are under tremendous pressure to increase the product variety and feature contents while continuously reducing the development time and cost. It is very difficult in a global product development environment that involves globally distributed OEMs and suppliers working on the components and subsystems of the same but a complex product like an automobile. The auto manufacturers are currently moving towards embracing lean principles to achieve the new PD paradigms to compete in the global market. Although this topic has created immense interest in academia and industry, there is no substantive description in the published literature about the processes and tools to achieve the ultimate paradigm of global product development. This chapter has narrowed that gap by presenting a framework for lean product development that was demonstrated through a case study of a global auto manufacturer. It showed how product development can leverage the knowledge and best practices from lean manufacturing processes and analysis techniques.

Further, the chapter has identified many challenges facing the global product development systems. The global product development system at Ford (or any automotive OEM for that matter) is much more complex than what has been presented in this study. Nepal et al. (2007) just focused on two metrics: process improvements and technology improvements. There are other challenges that can directly impact the end results of a global product development process hence need a credible attention in the PD literature. For example, how a global company should tackle the non-technical issues like cultural and other human related issues when it comes to a change management or implementation of a new system. Further, the transition from one product development system to another product development system is a gradual and evolving process that requires a reasonably longer time frame particularly in a global and large corporation like Ford. Therefore, there are several avenues which can lead to many potential research problems beyond just the lean process creation discussed in this case study. While the case study was focused on a car company, the proposed lean PD framework and insights gained from value stream mapping can be applied to any other global product development setting beyond automotive.

REFERENCES

Arnun, E. (2004). Automotive Warranties. *Warranty Week,* April 13th, 2004-07-29

Barczak, G., & McDonough, E. F. III. (2003). Leasing global product development teams. *Research Technology Management, 46*(6), 14-18.

Binder, M., Gust, P., & Clegg, B. (2007). The importance of collaborative frontloading in automotive supply networks. *Journal of Manufacturing Technology Management, 19*(3), 315-331.

Blake, D. (2004). Your business needs to change to succeed with embedded systems. *Society of Automotive Engineers*, 2004-21-0092.

Brown, S. L., & Eisenhardt, K. M. (1995). Product development: past research, present findings, and future directions. *Academy of Management Review, 20*(2), 343-78.

Buczkowski, J., Means, & M. F. (2004). Vehicle Electronics to Digital Mobility: The Next Generation of Convergence. *Product Insider,* 27, November 24th.

Coit, D., Thompson, J. E., & Vogt, N. (2005). Correlating field requirements to accelerated life testing for vehicle electronics. *Society of Automotive Engineers*, 2005-01-1492.

Cooper, R. G., & Edgett, S. C. (2008). Maximizing productivity in product innovation. *Research-Technology Management*, March-April, (pp. 47-58).

Cooper, R. G. (2007). Seven "principles" of innovation- a lack of focus. *Strategic Direction, 23*(1), 38-40.

Ford, D. N., & Sobek, D. K. (2005). Adapting real options to new product development by modeling the second Toyota paradox. *IEEE Transactions on Engineering Management, 52*(2), 175-185.

Forker, L. B. (1997). Factors affecting supplier quality performance. *Journal of Operations Management, 15*(4), 243-269.

Graber, D. R. (1996). How to manage a global product development process. *Industrial Marketing Management, 25*, 483-489.

Griffin, A., & Hauser, J. R. (1996). Integrating R&D and marketing: a review and analysis of the literature. *Journal of Product Innovation Management, 13*(3), 191-215.

Handfield, R. B., & Lawson, B. (2007). Integrating suppliers into new product development. *Research-Technology Management*, Sept.-Oct., (pp. 44-50).

Hobday, M., Davies, A., & Prencipe, A. (2005). System integration: a core capability of the modern corporation. *Industrial and Corporate Change, 14*(6), 1109-1143.

Howell, L. J., & Hsu, J.C. (2002). Globalization within the auto industry. *Research Technology Management, 45*(4), 43-49.

Kohn, K. (2006). Managing the balance of perspectives in the early phase of NPD. *European Journal of Innovation Management, 9*(1), 44-60.

Larlsson, C., & Ahlstrom, P. (1996). The difficult path to lean product development. *Journal of Product Innovation Management, 13*, 283-295.

Lee, J., Lee, J., & Souder, W. E. (2000). Differences of organizational characteristics in new product development: cross-cultural comparison on Korea and the US. *Technovation, 20*, 497-508.

Leenders, M. R., Fearon, H. E., Flynn, A. E., & Johnson, P. F. (2002). *Purchasing and supply chain management*. New York: McGraw-Hill.

Liker, J. K. (2004). *The Toyota Way*. New York: McGraw Hill.

Lovelace, K., Shapiro, D. L., & Weingart, L. R. (2001). Maximizing cross functional new product teams' innovativeness and constraints adherence: a conflict communication perspective. *Academy of Management Journal, 44*(4), 779-793.

Morgan, J. (2005). Lean Product Process Development. *Certificate Program Binder*. Center for Professional Development, University of Michigan, Ann Arbor, MI, May 2-5, http://cpd.engin.umich.edu.

Nepal, B., Monplaisir, L., & Singh, N. (2006). A methodology for integrating design for quality in modular product design. Journal of Engineering Design, *17*(5), 387-409.

Nepal, B. P., Monplaisir, L., Hammond, R., Wrobel, M., D'hondt, A., Herr, G., (2007, Nov. 7-10). Lean product development: An approach to achieve Ford's global product development system milestones. In *Proceedings of the American Society for Engineering Management (ASEM) National Conference,* Chattanooga, TN.

Ojah, K., & Monplaisir, L. (2003). Investor's valuation of global product design and development. *Journal of International Business Studies, 34,* 457- 472.

Ottosson, S. (2004). Dynamic product development-DPD. *Technovation, 24,* 207-217.

Perez, M. P., & Sanchez, A. M. (2000). Lean production and supplier relations: a survey of practices in the Aragonese automotive industry. *Technovation, 20,* 665-676.

Prasas, V., Baltusis, P., Greenberg, J., Rasin, V., Nelson, E., Shulman, M., Simonds, C., McNamara, D., Quesada, G., Syamil, A., & Doll, W. J. (2006). OEM new product development practices: the case of the automotive industry. *Journal of Supply Chain Management, 42*(3), 30-39.

Rozenes, S., Vitner, G., & Spragget, S. (2006). Project control: literature review. *Project Management Journal, 37*(4), 5-14.

Salhieh, S. M., Monplaisir, L., & Singh, N. (2001). A flexible planning methodology to support global product development using CSCW tools. *Global Journal of Flexible Systems Management, 2*(4), 1-13.

Sivakumar, K., & Nakata, C. (2003). Designing global new product teams: optimizing the effects of national culture on new product development. *International Marketing Review, 20*(4), 397-445.

Thomke, S. H. (2007). *Managing Product and Service Development: Text and Cases.* New York: McGraw-Hill/Irwin.

Thomke, S. H. (2006). Capturing the real value of innovation tools. *MIT Sloan Management Review, 47*(2), 24-32.

Thomke, S., & Fujimoto, T. (2000). The effect of 'front-loading' problem solving on product development performance. *Journal of Product Innovation Management, 17*(2), 128-42.

Thomke, S., & Nimgade, A. (2001). Siemens AG: global development strategy. Harvard Business School Case, No. 9-602-061. In *Managing Product and Service Development: Text and Cases.* New York: McGraw Hill.

Todinov, M. (2005). *Reliability and Risk Models.* John Wiley & Sons LTD.

Ward, A., Sobek, D. K. II, & Liker, J. K. (1998). Another Look at How Toyota Integrates Product Development. *Harvard Business Review,* August.

Walton, M. (1999). Strategies for lean product development. *The Lean Aerospace Initiative Working Paper Series,* WP99-01-91. Massachusetts Institute of Technology, Cambridge, USA.

Womack, J. P., & Jones D. T. (2003). *Lean Thinking: Banish waste and Create Wealth in Your Corporation.* Simons and Schuster -Audio Book.

Womack, J. P., Jones, D. T., & Ross, D. (1991). *The machine that changed the world: the story of lean production.* New York: Harper Collins.

KEY TERMS AND DEFINITIONS

Concurrent Engineering: Concurrent Engineering is a product development philosophy that requires the involvement of a cross functional teams right since early stage in order to plan for product development and manufacturing processes simultaneously

Global Product Development: A globally distributed product development process that integrates OEMs and suppliers in order to develop a complex product.

Lean Thinking: A business strategy that seeks to eliminate waste to create the most value for customers while consuming the fewest resources.

Muda: A Japanese term for "waste", widely used in lean manufacturing. In PD environment, it represents the task that does not add value to customer.

Type I Muda: Tasks that don't create any value but are currently required by the product development, order filling etc. thus can't be eliminated just yet

Type II Muda: Tasks that don't create any value as perceived by the customer and so can be eliminated immediately

Value Stream Mapping: A process improvement tool that is used in lean manufacturing. The value stream map captures processes, material flows of a given product family and helps to identify waste in the system.

Value Ratio: Ratio of Actual Task Time to Total Time in System. Ideally, the value ration should be 100% for each task in any process if there is no delay or rework of any time.

ENDNOTE

[1] * Mazda is a Japanese subsidiary of Ford Motor Co.

Section VI
Issues & Trends in Technology Project Management, Planning, and Operations

Chapter XXX
Future Trends:
Global Projects and Virtual Teaming

Debra D. Orosbullard
PMP, USA

ABSTRACT

The business world is running at a faster pace than ever before. Globalization has partnered the world and new ways of doing business to meet increasing demands are inevitable. Teams now have members dispersed around the globe, distanced by location and brought together by technology. Where these geographically dispersed teams work is known as a "virtual" world. The "virtual" team is different from the traditional team many are familiar with requiring that new skills be learned to be a successful member. This chapter will introduce the virtual team and discuss how it is different from traditional teams. The skills required of the leadership and members of a virtual team will be identified and detailed. The various types of virtual teams will be examined to determine how they are utilized in today's business world.

PROJECTS TODAY AND FUTURE TRENDS

Globalization and Project Teams

The integration of the world's people, markets, culture, economies, technology, politics, processes, resources, and services gives birth to "Global-ization". Even though the concept of merging international economies seems new, it has been in development for many centuries.

Worldwide trade and exploration had its beginnings in the 16th century as Portugal began what is known as the "Age of Discovery" in the mid 1400s. As those adventurous early explorers began to venture further and further beyond the known, they began the integration of the world's civilization and gave birth to globalization. It has only been in our lifetime, during the past 75 years or so, that the acceleration of globalization has touched everyone's life on a personal level making it seem a modern phenomena.

In examining how globalization has changed the world it can be safely said that it has influenced every facet of our lives. It has changed our economies; brought together the world's cultures, developed technology, improved health care, led to human rights, and influenced ecology.

This chapter studies the effect globalization has on projects and the project team. Just as it has an impact on our everyday lives, globalization has changed how we manage projects and the structure of the project team and how they interact. Globalization, integration, and multinational corporations all represent a major tend in the twenty-first century (Lientz & Rea, 1998). Teams have changed from the members being co-located organizationally and geographically to the team members being distributed organizationally and geographically (Kimball, 1997).

The way we interact with each other on a project and at the team level has been greatly influenced by today's technological advances. The geographically dispersed team needs a way to communicate and share information in real-time. Technology has provided the means to enable communication globally. The way we work is changing and just like the early explorers we are expanding our horizons and learning new ways to work with the future landscape that is being developed. As Smagg (2008), points out there is an "abundance of technology available today for collaboration including instant messaging, web conference, collaboration technologies, unified communications…" we still need to adjust to this new way of doing business. The roles have changed and the idea of the project team and members roles has changed.

As globalization fosters increased partnering relationships between our organization and those outside such as partners customers, vendors, etc. becomes more complex and important. As technology allows immediate access to partners across the globe and the ability to share electronic project data files real time it brings us together and makes our lives easier, but it also further complicates things. The boundaries between organizations and countries disappear and new challenges arise; to be effective in today's business world the pressure is to be more productive. The virtual or geographically dispersed team has been born out of the need for teams from all over the world to work together.

Work began in the virtual world during the late 1980's when the distance education field began to use computers to connect students. As Pauleen points out, the "Current notion of the Virtual Team has been around since the mid 1900's: First addressed by the practitioner literature… research on virtual teams in organizations has only emerged in the last few years" (Pauleen, 2004).

First, let's define what a virtual team is. There are many definitions of virtual teams, but they all have one thing in common: the "Virtual team members are physically separated (by time and/or space) and the virtual team members primarily interact electronically." ("Virtual", 2008). The quest of business to gain new markets on a worldwide or global level has been the driving force behind the development of virtual teams. As Kimball (1997), points out "Although the technology that supports these new teams gets most of the attention when we talk about virtual teams, it's really the changes in the nature of the teams- not their use of technology – that creates new challenges for team managers and members." There are challenges faced by virtual teams that are usually not a factor in tradition teams, virtual team members usually have never met each other in person, they often live in different countries, are from different cultures, work for different organizations, and they usually do not share the same first language.

Collaboration Across Culture and Time Zones

In the ever-changing world of business those who don't keep up the pace quickly fall out of the race. In looking back, Cantu (1997) describes where the idea of *virtual* came from "virtual was born in the computer industry, describing virtual memory, which is hard disk space used as temporary memory." Looking at where *virtual* is today, Egea (2006) appropriately describes today's virtual business world by saying "working virtual means working together apart."

As organizations have expanded due to increased globalization the concept of working virtually has taken hold along with it. The business world is not the only group to have embraced the virtual world education and social networks have also gone virtual. Many schools and Universities offer courses via online delivery and there are many forms of social networks (message boards, blogs, etc.) that millions participate in on a daily basis.

Like it or not, virtual is here to stay and many would argue, why not, it makes their life easier. Many things can now be accomplished from the comfort of your home or office such as banking, paying bills, ordering dinner, purchase of a new car, …the list goes on and on. Anything that is happening via a computer over the Internet is happening in the virtual world.

As businesses merge and take on projects that are multinational, global competition increases. The need to work faster and more efficiently is paramount. Just as the pony express would be an unacceptable mean's of transporting mail today the modern postal system offering over night delivery isn't able to meet the demand for the instant exchange of information today. Everyone needs information faster and faster and there is an even greater need to work together across the world. Duarte & Snyder (2001) point out that as multinational companies become the norm "the business justification for virtual teams is strong. They increase speed and agility and leverage

Figure 1. Virtual Teaming

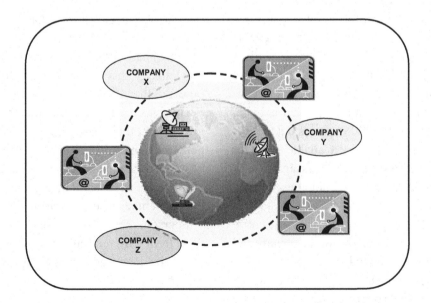

expertise and vertical integration between organizations to make resources readily available." Business strategy today requires organization's to successfully collaborate across all boundaries. Keeping the pace and erasing the boundaries does not come cheap for any organization. The cost of travel in time and dollars has been a driving force in the development of virtual teams. In today's business environment "seconds" do count with the increasing velocity of the marketplace. A project team may need to meet immediately with their partners located oceans away; they don't have the time to travel. Today's technology can make a meeting happen in the time it takes to login to a virtual meeting center. Time is a more precious commodity than ever before. Everyone is strapped for time; there are never enough hours in the day to accomplish everything that needs to be done.

As virtual teaming brings people from different countries and cultures together, working as a team presents new challenges. Change itself is difficult to manage. As workplaces become more "virtual" the people working in them may not be changing and accepting of the new technology at the same rate. Human nature likes to keep things just the way they are, what is familiar is the most comfortable.

Cultural influences on virtual teaming come from corporate cultures as well as geographical or regional cultures. Every organization has a deeply rooted system of behavior's and beliefs each being highly individual in nature. Whether the organization's culture is weak or strong will have an impact on how the team operates in a virtual setting. A weak organizational culture lacks strong beliefs that all conform to, and may be more likely to adopt something new such as virtual teaming. But this weak culture may not provide necessary structure to support virtual teaming. A strong organizational culture may be so formalized in its policy that it could impede the team's ability to adapt and make the necessary changes for virtual teaming.

An individual's culture has a large impact on how they think, feel, and interact with others. Cultural influences bring differing work practices, ideas of power, and trust to virtual team environments. Due to these differences, collaboration of two or more cultures, corporate and geographical will not happen over night. The virtual team may be electronically linked in seconds but linking them on a social level that results in collaboration will take special effort and time.

THE BENEFITS AND DRAWBACKS OF VIRTUAL TEAMING

The transition from working in a collocated team to a virtual team doesn't happen overnight and presents as many new challenges as opportunities. The technology that supports the virtual team environment is growing rapidly, providing access, making extensive data file sharing possible, linking virtual team members via video, audio conferencing, and electronically.

The tools are available, but learning to use them and embrace the technology takes time and is not for everyone. Many people still want to sit in the same room with their team; they feel that's how real work gets done. If someone doesn't feel comfortable using the technology they will resist it and hold on to the old way of doing things. The only way for someone to become comfortable with a new way of doing something is to try it and over time they will become more comfortable. It is important to provide virtual team members with adequate training on the use of the technology, don't assume that just because some team members know how to participate in a web conference that everyone does. Take the time to explain all of the tools your team will be using and make sure that all software is installed and working correctly. Conduct several mock videoconferences if possible, practice uploading data files to a File Transfer Protocol (FTP) site.

Some people may feel that the use of web conferencing is only for a special event and not for weekly team meetings. The real benefits of virtual teaming are recognized as new and innovative ways of communicating and conducting business are experienced. Once a team experiences a successful web conference with team members from around the world from their home office, they are hooked. Meetings conducted via web conferencing software can facilitate experts from all over the world to meet and work together to solve a problem that benefits many. When a remote team can join their colleagues at the home office via a videoconference to work on and solve a problem in the field they are experiencing the value of virtual communication.

The way business is managed, relationships, rules. Conducting business in the virtual world requires skills that are different, that like anything new, carries a learning curve.

The management of a virtual team requires a new set of skills. As pointed out by Duarte and Snyder (2006) there are seven factors they believe critical to success:

- Human resource polices
- Training and on-the-job education and development
- Standard organizational and team processes
- Use of electronic collaboration and communication technology
- Organizational culture
- Leadership support of virtual teams
- Team leader and team member competencies

A successful virtual team must have a global mindset with openness in regards to other cultures and ways of conducting business. They must be sensitive to the needs and beliefs of others to work as a team. This is a very different way of working than most teams are used to traditionally a team is made up of members from the same organization.

Traditional teams usually share a similar culture, background, and the same first language making working together easier and familiar.

Traditional Teaming vs. Virtual Teaming

Traditional teams and virtual teams have many of the same attributes; each require that members work together toward a common goal, leadership is crucial to the success of any team, both have a unique project to manage, schedule to meet and a good or service to be delivered. What makes the teams different is that the virtual team conducts most if not all of its work via technology, rather than being co-located and working face-to-face as in a traditional team environment.

Traditional Team

A traditional team environment brings team members together regularly on a face-to-face basis. The team members are usually colleagues if not working in the same office at a minimum working for the same company. They operate within a corporate culture they are familiar with. Often the members of a traditional team have previously worked on a project together they are familiar. Potentially communication is easier due to co-location and shared language. As Smith (2008), points out "Nonverbal communication can account for as much as 60% of the message a person conveys." Body language can be a indicator to if a person understands what you are saying. Nonverbal communication, which includes body movements or gestures, can communicate as much or more than verbal communication.

A specific example is eye contact or lack of can convey a powerful signal of approval or disapproval during a meeting. In many Eastern cultures (i.e. China) it is disrespectful to look the dominant person in the eye, but in Western culture if you do not look the person directly in the eye when talking to them it can be interpreted that you are hiding something or that you have low self esteem.

The cost and logistics required to co-locate team members from distant offices for face-to-face meetings is significant. When a team member needs to travel thousands of miles to attend a meeting it takes away from their productive in office time. Often meetings that are attended by members from various locations are not productive due to the team members attending not having access to data files, etc.

Virtual Teams

Communication is the most important factor leading to a virtual team's success. The virtual team member will be required to navigate through multiple organizational and often cultural boundaries with acute interpersonal awareness. The virtual teaming environment is different from traditional teaming; the absence of face-to-face communication is often downplayed and is a factor in virtual team failure.

When conducting business globally team members rarely share the same first language, miscommunication due to language barriers is a common complaint when working on an international team. When conducting business on an international level the common language used is English. How fluent the members are in English will influence the teams' ability to effectively communicate. When the team members are having difficulty knowing what each other needs it leads to frustration and has a negative effect on the project. The team member's soft skills, i.e. work etiquette, cultural sensitivity, conflict resolution, and negotiation will aid in closing the gap between virtual team members.

As discussed in *"Virtual Teams"* (2008) virtual teams may be formed to deal with "new realities facing organizations such as:

- Organization-wide projects or initiatives

- Alliances with different organizations, some of which may be in other countries
- Mergers and acquisitions
- Emerging markets in different geographical locations
- The continuing need for business travel and information and communication technologies available to support this travel
- A need to reduce costs
- A need to reduce time to market or cycle time in general

As more people become aware of and/or are involved in virtual teaming more opportunities present themselves, organizations now have the opportunity to hire people to work on their project from all over the globe, and they are not restricted to the local talent pool.

Other advantages include; when working virtually from a home office there is no commute to deal with. Many physical handicaps that may prevent someone from traveling to and from an office disappear, opening a new world of opportunity. With scheduling between different time zones, virtual business allows around the clock productivity between dispersed project teams.

In today's business world organizations have a mix of traditional and virtual teaming. Teams meet in-house, face-to-face everyday to collaborate on projects and they communicate via virtual means, e-mail, teleconference, file sharing, etc. daily. The options are available; you only need to choose which approach works best for your situation.

Global Communication: What Makes it Work

There are several needs that teams have, virtual or traditional, the most significant being a sense of trust among its members. As Smith (2008) discusses, "Teams with higher levels of trust blend more readily, organize more quickly, and manage themselves better." Building trust on a virtual team is difficult, trust is usually developed over time, from familiarity, face-to-face interaction, historical reference, and common ground. A virtual team will rarely have these opportunities towards building trust available. What can a virtual team and its members do to establish trust? On a virtual team each team member being reliable, doing what they say they will do helps to build trust. Since time is of the essence in a virtual environment and often why the team was formed, producing deliverables when you say will is important. Care must be taken to allow each team member to contribute. Members of the team need to stand behind each other and acknowledge outstanding performance. Everyone doing their best and maintaining a positive attitude will help in building trust on a virtual team.

Every team requires a strong leader to be successful, this especially critical in a virtual teaming environment. Joyce Thompson, PhD. (2000) points out, the following "five core categories of effective leadership skills in virtual project teams":

1. Communicating effectively and using technology that fits the situation
2. Building community, based on mutual trust, respect, fairness and affiliation, among project team members
3. Establishing clear and inspiring shared goals, expectations, purpose and vision
4. Leading by example with a focus on visible, measurable results
5. Coordinating/collaborating across organizational boundaries

Virtual teams members are often from different cultures, roles and responsibilities may be interpreted differently. To make a virtual team work ground rules that all team members understand and agree to must be established immediately. Some ground rules to consider are below:

*   Team member roles and expectations

*   Turn around times for communication and data deliveries
*   Types of communication tools and when they are to be used
*   Handling of conflict, including resolution
*   Guidelines of how decisions will be made

When establishing a virtual team it helps to have at least one face-to-face kick off meeting lasting a few days if possible. During this meeting time should be spent getting to know each other, leadership should be established, a communication plan developed, and ground rules as covered earlier discussed.

Careful consideration needs to be given to this initial meeting to allow adequate team building to take place. Modern technology provides the tools to make virtual teaming possible but the success of the team still relies on how well the team interacts and communicates. Time should be included in the agenda for the team members to get to know each other; there are many forms of team building exercises that facilitate this type of exercise. The group should discuss and agree on the ground rules outlined above, bringing the team together and allowing all to participate in the development of the team will help the members to connect and have a stake in the team.

DEVELOPING A VIRTUAL TEAM

The development of a virtual team is different from a traditional team. Not everyone has the ability or even the desire to work in a virtual team environment this can make it difficult when establishing a virtual team. When organizing the members of a virtual team you must make sure that everyone understands the goal of the team and they understand their role is in meeting the goal. Team members need to have excellent interpersonal as well as technical skills, if they are weak in any area training needs to be provide to bring them up to the level required in the virtual teaming environment.

The lack of human contact can lead to feelings of isolation for some. In fact today some of the people who switched to a telecommute position sometime ago are now forming groups with other telecommuters and getting together, renting a office in some instances and working independently together, sharing resources and conversation, they missed the human side of the office.

To be effective virtual team members need to be flexible and have the ability to adapt to new situations quickly. The virtual team member needs to work well as a member of a team and independently. As Kimball (1997) reminds us, "Although the technology that supports these new teams gets most of the attention when we talk about virtual teams, it's really the changes in the nature of teams- not their use of technology- that creates new challenges for team managers and members."

As globalization continues and more businesses turn to virtual teaming to bridge the gap between their partners around the world they need to be aware of the preparation required to pull it off and be successful. Purchasing a state-of-the art video conferencing center by itself won't make it happen. Pauleen (2004) offers this observation, "Virtual leaders and team members are in the thick of it, operating "from the seat of their pants," often without the virtual communication and team skills that are required for the virtual teaming environment and without organizational support..."

Management needs to provide specialized training for the leaders and members of virtual teams for them to be successful. There is a requirement for policies and procedures that govern the virtual team environment. Special consideration is required when teaming with members from other countries and cultures, differences in business etiquette need to be addressed and consideration given to cultural differences.

Selection of the technology required to do business virtually also require planning and consultation with experts in the field. Consideration needs to be given to what technology those you will be teaming with employ or will be adopting. Many times virtual teams are stopped dead in their tracks due to incompatibility issues of software platforms and software versioning.

The Members

As discussed virtual teaming is not for everyone and there are many things that need to be considered before considering this option. Some of the area's requiring careful thought and planning are listed below:

- The type of virtual team
- Virtual team members roles & responsibilities
- Keys to effective communication and participation
- Special challenges for leadership
- What makes a virtual team successful
- Future Trends
- Advantages of virtual teaming

Virtual teams come in many shapes and sizes with no two teams being exactly alike. Their ability to be dynamic and meet the needs of ever changing requirements is what makes them special. Table 1 identifies a sampling of virtual teaming scenarios.

The virtual team member's roles and responsibilities are similar to a traditional team with added emphasis in the operation of the technology that supports them. The virtual team member may have more responsibility for their actions and be held more accountable for their individual contribution. With each team member working independently if they do not provide their contribution on time the entire team will be aware immediately, there will not be a co-worker picking up the slack for the home office.

The keys to effective participation on a virtual team are strong leadership and organization of the team. The ground rules for participation must be established and each member needs to understand and fulfill their role.

Because team members are not co-located special effort is required to coordinate the team and build effective participation and communication. The team can be viewed as "a set of nodes and links..." nodes being the team members and the links communication channels ("Virtual," 2008). A solid team foundation is built on team members who understand their roles and fulfill their responsibilities.

As if leading a team of any type is not enough of a challenge, adding "virtual" elements to the mix makes it just that much more difficult. "Virtual teams need somebody (or something) to bring its members together and guide them to achieve a common goal (Xhauflair & Rorive, 2003). As pointed out by Duarte and Snyder (2006) there a certain competencies that are seen as being essential to a virtual team leader, as detailed in the list below:

1. Coaching and managing performance without traditional forms of feedback
2. Selecting and appropriately using electronic communication and collaboration technology
3. Leading in a cross cultural environment
4. Managing the performance, development, and career development of team members
5. Building and maintaining trust
6. Networking across hierarchical and organizational boundaries
7. Developing and adapting organizational processes to meet the demands of the team

What does it take to make a virtual team successful? The leader and team members must be competent, they need to be supported by their organization and have polices and processes that are specific to virtual teams and their special requirements. All members of the team must have a feeling of trust between themselves. The team must have the use of appropriate technology that supports their communication and work sharing requirements.

Table 1. Types of virtual teams

TYPES	FUNCTIONS
Executive	Business and Administrative
Project	Management of a project within an organization
Remote	Management of an organizations project from a remote location
Global	Management of a project with members and stakeholders located in two or more countries
Local	Management of a project with all members co-located
Community of Practice	To bring members of a particular discipline (i.e. nuclear physicists) together for knowledge sharing & brainstorming

When looking towards the future the trend of "partnering" with organizations over the globe will surely continue and new ways of managing these alliances will take place through virtual teamwork. The success of virtual teaming will remain dependent on how well organizations are able to adapt to the developing technology and provide organizational support to the effort.

The advantages of virtual teaming include more efficient use of time, which leads into the fact that there is a reduction in some of the costs of doing business such as travel. There is an

Table 2. Virtual teaming tools

TOOL	STRENGTHS	LIMITATIONS
Telephone SYNCHRONOUS NON-VISUAL	• Most people have a telephone	• No body language or facial cues are visible; makes it hard to interpret subtle cues from the other person. • Expensive for international calls • Cannot share documents. • Cannot demonstrate anything visual. • Usually limited to one-on-one conversation (unless a conference call)
Mail, courier ASYNCHRONOUS NON-VISUAL	• May be the only way to transmit original documents when a copy will not suffice.	• Slow delivery • Sensitive information may be at risk • May be lost in transit • Expensive
Email ASYNCHRONOUS NON-VISUAL	• Can attach large documents or any computer file • Can be sent or collected from any place with an internet connection • Easy to use mailing lists to send one email to many people; groups of people can follow and contribute to a threaded discussion. • Copies of received and sent messages form a valuable archive of communications. • Very cheap, even with BIG attachments	• Requires an internet connection (may be a problem in remote areas or when in transit) • Can't see facial cues • Destination mailbox may be full or email might be too big to send. • Risk of viruses

continued on following page

Table 2. continued

Videoconferencing SYNCHRONOUS VISUAL	• Instant 2-way communication • Video and audio allows better reading of people's body language and tone of voice • Can have group-to-group meetings • A cheaper alternative to meeting in person • Documents can be exchanged • Being able to see team mates can build team solidarity • Free or cheap software	• Requires a web cam and microphone • Equipment involves cost. • All participants must be available at the same time.
Web Forum, Discussion Boards ASYNCHRONOUS NON-VISUAL	• A structured way to discuss issues • Accessible from any internet-equipped PC • Can allow attachments • Threaded discussions can be archived so a topic can later be referred to • Cheap	• Requires an internet connection • Requires rules or conventions so participants know what is appropriate and what is not • Lack of visual cues can lead to misunderstandings • Requires some setting up and maintenance
Live Chat Rooms SYNCHRONOUS NON-VISUAL	• Immediate • Groups can chat • Cheap • Easy to access	• All participants must be available at the same time • Risk of viruses or hacking
Wiki ASYNCHRONOUS NON-VISUAL	• Allows collaborative knowledge collation, organisation and editing. • Software is open source (free)	• Requires internet connection • May be hard to control what individuals do to shared documents • Requires some setting up
Blogs ASYNCHRONOUS NON-VISUAL	• Quick and easy way for individuals to publicly post timely information	e.g. *b2evolution, Nucleus, pMachine Free, WordPress*

continued on following page

Table 2. continued

Remote Access	• Allows one member to remotely control a distant PC to fix a problem, demonstrate a procedure or carry out a task	• Security must be tight to prevent unauthorized access
Instant Messaging SYNCHRONOUS NON-VISUAL	• Immediate (as soon as you hit the ENTER key at the end of the line) • Discussions can be saved and referred to later • Files can be transferred	• Both parties need to be present at the same time

Note: From: "Tools for Virtual Teams," lecture by M. Kelly, 2006. Copyright by Mark Kelly 2001-2008. Reprinted with permission.

increased availability of resources for the virtual team, experts located elsewhere can be easily made part of the team. There is also the factor of increased response time, which leads to organizations being more competitive.

Tools Available for Virtual Teaming

There are many tools available to the virtual team to conduct day to day business, exchange information and deposit data. With so many choices in collaborative software to facilitate team interaction it is difficult to know which one to choose. The same is true when deciding on type of email, discussion forums, chat rooms and instant messaging, teleconferencing, video conferencing, File Transfer Protocol (FTP) site for secure file exchange, web based portals to employ. Here are some basic questions to answer before deciding which applications or platforms to use:

- Size of your organization, local and remote requirements
- Security and backup requirements
- Size of data files
- Ease of user interface
- Time required to deploy
- What applications are the people I will be working with using
- Compatibility

The following table adapted from Kelly (2006) is very comprehensive and helpful in describing the type of virtual teaming tool and its advantages as well as disadvantages. When a type is described as *synchronous* it means it is happening in real-time and *asynchronous* means the communication or transfer of information happens at different times.

FUTURE TRENDS

In many of today's organizations virtual teams are becoming the norm, "to virtual team or not virtual team" is hardly a choice due to the fast paced environment. The trend will continue into the future making the virtual world seem ordinary because it will eventually be woven into our everyday lives at work, school, and within our community.

What will make a difference as we charge head on into this virtual world where virtual teaming is taking hold is how well we are prepared for the journey. The world of virtual teaming as discussed in this chapter holds endless opportunity for those who have learned how to navigate through it. As the trend continues for organizations to become multinational and partner around the world they will continue to rely upon virtual teaming to get their work accomplished. Virtual teaming facilitates multinational partnering and provides the tools to work together apart, Egea (2006).

REFERENCES

Cantu, C. (1997). *Virtual teams.* CSWT Papers, Center for the Study of Work Teams, University of North Texas. (http://www.workteams.unt.edu/Literature/paper-ccantu.html). Retrieved 27 Feb 2008.

Duarte, D. L., & Tennant Snyder, N. (2001). *Mastering virtual teams: Strategies, tools, and techniques that succeed,* second edition. San Francisco: Jossey-Bass.

Egea, K. (2006). Relationship building in virtual teams: An academic case study. *Informing Science and IT Education Joint Conference.* (p. 81). Central Queensland University, Rockhampton, Australia.

Kelly, M. (2006). *Tools for virtual teams.* Taken from IPM Lecture notes. (http://www.mckinnonsc.vic.edu.au/vceit/virtualteams/tools.htm). Retrieved 12 Apr 2008.

Kimball, L. (1997, April). *Managing virtual teams.* Speech given at Team Strategies Conference, Toronto, Canada.

Lientz, B. P., & Rea, K. P. (1998). *Project management for the 21st century.*

"Managing Groups and Teams / How Do You Build High-Performing Virtual Teams?" (http://en.wikibooks.org/wiki/Managing_Groups_ and_Teams/How_Do_You_Build_High-performance_teams). Retrieved 14 Mar 2008.

Pauleen, D., (2004). *Virtual teams: Projects, protocols, and processes,* (p. viii). Hershey, PA: IGI Global Publishing.

Rad, P., & Levin, G., *Achieving project management success using virtual yeams.* Florida: J. Ross Publishing.

Smagg, C. (2007). *Unleashing the power of remote collaboration & virtual team management.* [Weblog entry]. Marketing & Strategy Innovation Blog. 20 Nov 2007. (http://blog.futurelab.net/2007/11/unleashing_the_power_of_remote.html). Retrieved 19 Mar 2008

Smith, R. O. (2008). *Learning in virtual teams: A summary of current literature."* (http://www.msu.edu/~smithre9/Project12.htm). Retrieved 14 Mar 2008.

Thompson, J. (2000). *Five essential skills will help you lead any project – no matter how distant.* (http://www.qualitydigest.com/sep00/html/teams.html). Retrieved 12 Apr 2008.

Virtual Teams. *Fifth generation work- virtual organization.* (http://www.seanet.com/~daveg/vrteams.htm). Retrieved 27 Feb 2008.

Xhauflair, V., & Rorive, B. (2003). What binds together virtual teams? Some answers from three case studies. *XIth European congress on Work and Organisational psychology 14-17 May 2003- Lisboa.*

KEY TERMS AND DEFINITIONS

Collaboration: To work jointly with others or together especially in an intellectual or business endeavor.

Globalization: The development of an increasingly integrated global economy marked especially by free trade, free flow of capital, and the tapping of cheaper foreign labor markets.

Organizational Culture: Organizational culture, or corporate culture, comprises the attitudes, experiences, beliefs and values of an organization Partnering- to join or associate with another as partner.

Real Time: When an event or function is processed instantaneously, it is said to occur in real-time. To say something takes place in real-time is the same as saying it is happening "live".

Virtual Team: A group of employees using information and communications technologies to collaborate from different work bases. Members of a virtual team may work in different parts of the same building or may be scattered across a country or around the world. The team can be connected by technology such as groupware, e-mail, an intranet, or videoconferencing and can be said to inhabit a virtual office. Although virtual teams can work efficiently, occasional face-to-face meetings can be important to avoid feelings of isolation and to enable team building.

Chapter XXXI
Wiki Enabled Technology Management

Geoffrey Corb
Johns Hopkins University, USA

Stephen Hellen
Johns Hopkins University, USA

ABSTRACT

Social networking technologies—such as Wikis, blogs and instant messaging—are increasingly being employed in business settings to support communication, collaboration and knowledge management. In this chapter, the authors discuss how a Wiki was used to facilitate project management in a large system implementation for a decentralized organization. Further, they show how it continues to add value to the organization after the project's completion, supporting operational management activities while at the same time providing a platform for fostering and promoting innovation. They introduce important implementation considerations for deploying a Wiki in your organization, in addition to sharing observations from our own implementation that saw both successes and failures.

INTRODUCTION

During the implementation of a student information system at Johns Hopkins University, we faced challenges of communication, knowledge management and information overload that are hallmarks of large system implementation projects and magnified in significantly decentralized organizations such as ours. We struggled with these challenges and tried a number of approaches and tools to address them before succeeding with a Wiki. Our first use of a Wiki was to facilitate communication with other universities that were implementing the same student information system software. This use was largely unsuccessful mainly due to lack of adoption and use by would-be collaborators. Since we had already purchased the Wiki software and deployed it in our enterprise, we decided to use it internally to reduce the aforementioned challenges. This began as a very gradual effort with just a few users adding content. Several months later, adoption increased dramatically and, ever since, the Wiki has simplified and greatly improved our approaches to project management and operational management of information technology (IT) systems and services for the university.

This chapter provides a case study on the use of Wiki to support technology project management, planning and operations. It begins with a brief introduction of Wiki concepts, features and the product landscape as of early 2008. We then explore the use of Wiki in project management and in supporting IT systems. Specific examples are shared of successfully using a Wiki as the core repository of project artifacts during the implementation of our student information system. This is followed by discussion of using a Wiki for strategic and operational planning. Many lessons learned are shared from the experience of first attempting to use a Wiki, seeing it fail and subsequently repurposing it and watching its use and adoption grow exponentially.

The conclusion of these lessons is that Wikis provide a number of benefits to all involved. They are simple, efficient and easy to learn, use and implement. Their content is highly accessible for users with varying levels of technical competency. Since they are web based, access is ubiquitous. They are flexible and, generally speaking, inexpensive. These benefits, however, only describe advantages in relation to other collaboration tools. The real power of a Wiki in this domain is derived from its ability to draw people into content rather than push content out. They dramatically change how documents are created and can help to reduce e-mail overload.

The chapter concludes with a discussion of transparency—Wikis allow a broad audience to have insight into details of a project or organiza-

tion. Such openness forces a more disciplined approach to management in some ways but much more significantly fosters trust among all involved.

BACKGROUND

Managing IT has evolved during the past several decades as success factors relevant to the type of technology being managed are refined. Simultaneously, the tools available to support these endeavors have also evolved. While management methodologies cycle from predictive to adaptive and back again—and take on new variations and buzzwords such as spiral, agile or extreme programming—the available supporting tools are continuously improving. These supporting tools include those intended specifically for operational or project management as well as those adapted for this purpose. Wikis are an example of the latter where a general knowledge sharing tool can be leveraged for technical management.

WHAT IS A WIKI?

A Wiki is a set of interlinking dynamic web pages that is specifically designed so that anyone can easily contribute and modify content. They are very often used as the basis for a collaborative community or in business as an inexpensive intranet or knowledge repository. Wikis maintain a history of changes to their content so that it is quickly and clearly evident who is responsible for what changes and content evolution. The power of the Wiki comes from its ability to facilitate knowledge discovery through interlinked and interrelated content. Wikipedia is the best-known Wiki, popular for its community-driven content that has become a fairly reliable collaborative encyclopedia.

Wikis are natural solutions for nurturing an online community in which all members of the community have the ability to learn from one another and contribute their own ideas. They facilitate what we call "collaboration of thought" as opposed to "collaboration of product" which is commonplace in other collaborative environments, such as Microsoft's SharePoint and Google Documents. The idea behind collaboration of thought is that a contributor can quickly and easily deposit an idea in the Wiki in the form of a web page. Other contributors might be drawn to the webpage, and hence the idea, through provision of a unique URL, search results within the Wiki, or consuming the content via RSS feed or dashboards which feature lists of recently-updated content. From here, the idea might be elaborated, invalidated, celebrated and so on by any number of others, providing the opportunity to leverage the collective intelligence discussed by Surowiecki (2004).

In contrast, collaboration of product refers to circumstances when contributors are collaborating for the purposes of producing an article, a presentation, a budget spreadsheet or other asset.

Platforms which provide for advanced file management capabilities, such as version management ("check-in, check-out"), may be more natural for this type of collaboration. Some Wiki products are beginning to incorporate these features as their management of document attachments evolve. At the same time, existing platforms are increasingly beginning to incorporate Wiki features to couple these two forms of collaboration in a single environment.

WIKI ADVANTAGES

Wikis are simple and efficient. They are easy to use, easy to learn and easy to implement. Their content is highly accessible even for those who do not consider themselves to be particularly savvy with technology. As a web-based medium, Wikis provide ubiquitous access to anyone with internet access. Wikis are extremely flexible and can play a variety of roles. They are relatively inexpensive or, for non-enterprise grade solutions, free.

Figure 1. Describing a Wiki advantages

WHAT CAN A WIKI DO FOR YOU?

A Wiki can be used to dramatically improve and capture communications. A Wiki can provide an escape from document management difficulties by eliminating the need to send documents around as attachments to e-mail messages. By eliminating complex e-mail threads, you will always know what the latest version is and be able to review version history. Besides removing the inefficiency of tracking and merging versions and revisions, Wikis promote collaboration, whether incidental or accidental, through progressive elaboration. Through a series of edits to a Wiki page, the content is gradually improved by a broader set of participants than may occur through other mediums. Wikis can help you find what you are looking for by indexing both page content and content contained in common file types attached to Wiki pages.

A Wiki can diminish the boundaries and limitations of time and space. It can help remote workers feel less remote. One can feel more connected with what is transpiring when not physically present. To some extent, it can reduce the frustration of not being up-to-date or not being able to participate more fully. Wikis allow contributors to contribute at the time and place they are able to do so. Wiki pages are progressively elaborated asynchronously. Thus, coherent and accurate content evolves without attending a meeting, joining a conference call, or reacting to an e-mail. At a time and place that is convenient for the user, he or she can go to the Wiki. The user may go to the Wiki with a specific goal in mind only to stumble upon, and perhaps contribute to, other interesting content.

Finally, a Wiki can improve customer service or product quality. By inviting your customers or stakeholders to use the Wiki, you may discover opportunities to better serve, or provide better service to, your customers. Both you and your customers will have a means to learn more about your respective operations, thus fostering greater

understanding and appreciation for the challenges that you each face.

CONSIDERATIONS FOR IMPLEMENTING A WIKI

Products

Dozens of Wiki products are available and the authors do not endorse or promote any particular one. Resources such as (www.Wikimatrix.org) *WikiMatrix* can assist in selecting a product that best meets your needs. The products are typically so inexpensive that cost is almost not an issue. Of course, as with all systems, there is more to the total cost of ownership than the retail price of the product. Two important considerations—true in the selection of almost any software application these days—are open-source versus commercial and local hosting versus application service provider (ASP) hosted. Open-source Wiki products tend to rely on open-source technology stacks such as Linux/Apache/MySQL/PHP (LAMP), Java/Tomcat, Ruby, etc., while commercial products tend to provide better support for commercial technology stacks such as Microsoft's .NET, Oracle and so on. In general, locally-hosted Wikis provide more flexibility including the ability to customize and integrate with existing on-premise systems such as a directory or single sign-on. However, they do require traditional operational considerations such as backup, storage and monitoring. ASP-hosted are quick and easy to get started but may raise questions about who owns the content and what happens if the ASP ceases operations. For our purposes, we selected an enterprise-grade, commercial product which we host locally.

Content and Access

On the surface, it may seem easier to closely manage and shape all project communications. In reality, news travels quickly, bad news seemingly fastest, and there is often no easy way to control the flow of information. With few exceptions such as sensitive personnel data, we have made as much information about our projects and operations available to a very broad base of stakeholders and other constituents. This includes internal status reports, meeting minutes, defect lists and other details that are typically held within a team and appropriately spun for external audiences. There were a few cases where we were surprised at who actually read some of this content. For example, stakeholders asked about contingency plans when they saw an internal meeting agenda mention the recent resignation of a key staff member. Overall, however, we have found it to be beneficial to all involved to push the limits on what is public, thus evolving into a highly transparent and highly trusted organization.

Responsibility and sensitivity are two factors to consider when deciding how open your Wiki should be and thus how transparent your content will be. Responsibility depends on the degree to which you can trust and rely on your authors and contributors, including those who may be within your team or part of a larger realm of interested individuals. Sensitivity refers to the nature of your content such as the potential ramifications of status reports, detailed agendas, work lists, personal blogs and the like being widely accessible. Sensitivity in this context does not refer to data that should otherwise reside in our actual systems. For example, we never allow our Wiki to be used as a place to post or exchange secure data. We do, however, have reserved parts of our Wiki for exclusive use by our management team, so access to this content is specifically controlled.

It is important to consider how much about your project or operations you are willing to share. You must weigh if you really need to restrict access to certain content. If you find that you do need to restrict access, keep asking why and challenging assumptions to make as much content available to as broad an audience as feasible. Our Wiki is closed to the general public but widely open to those even tangentially involved with our projects and initiatives. In general, anyone with access can create new content and improve or comment on existing content. There are very few spaces with access restrictions. We placed a great deal of trust in our authors and make nearly all project assets accessible. Such openness is a core tenant of responsible management practices (Stahl,

Figure 2. Factors to build a transparent and collaborative environment

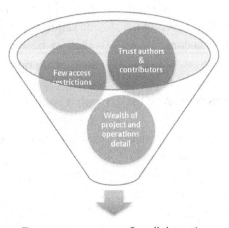

Transparency, trust & collaboration

2004). The result we have observed is far greater transparency that directly fosters trust and leads to genuine collaboration.

Structure

At the outset, it is important to decide whether to build a skeleton or scaffold for content or let it grow organically. In general, it is our opinion that a Wiki should start out with the least amount of structure necessary and structure should only be added over time, when needed. Adoption is far more pervasive when you let people contribute in a way that satisfies them, as we have witnessed first-hand. There have been, and there will no doubt be, successful Wiki implementations which follow a rigid structure and others which have no inherent structure. Far more important than structure of content, however, is that related content be linked together to facilitate knowledge discovery.

WIKI IN ACTION

The History of Our Wiki

We initially implemented a Wiki to provide an environment for online collaboration between institutions implementing the same new-to-market student information system. This was an outright failure as there was not sufficient adoption or use and it never gained traction. Wikis are not guaranteed to succeed for any purpose and particularly not as a tool for managing technology. Ebersbach (2006) points out themes that are common causes of Wiki failures among which several need particular attention when the Wiki is used for technology management: lack of interest; introducing an open, social system in the working world; and quality assurance.

Although our first attempt with the Wiki failed, we already owned and had installed the software so we decided to use it to address a variety of long-standing problems plaguing our project: ineffective document management; communication (simultaneously too much and too little) and knowledge loss (or, perhaps more appropriately, a lack of knowledge retention).

Nambisan (2008) identifies four areas where web-based tools such as a Wiki can support network-centric innovation: process management to bring rigor and stability; project management such as scheduling and coordinating; information sharing among members; and communication support for a community to interact. These characteristics were very similar to the improvements we ultimately realized through a Wiki.

Figure 3. Areas where a Wiki can support innovation

Project Management

The Project Management Institute suggests that project managers are ultimately responsible for adequate and effective communication (2004). Lack of effective communications can doom a project while effective and appropriate communications have even been known to resurrect projects that are in trouble. A Wiki is a platform for communicating and can be the foundational technology in the communication strategy of any well-planned project.

The history-tracking capabilities of a Wiki can be integral in journaling the life of a project. By providing a repository of project artifacts, it can be the basis of in recreating history during essential project post-mortem reviews as part of project closure. Although they track history, Wiki products on the market today do not provide inherent features to fully navigate the time dimension (like Apple's Time Machine feature of its OS X operating system). You cannot view the entire Wiki site as it appeared at a particular point in time, but it is not hard to imagine the introduction of such a capability in the future.

Document Creation and Management

Document management and versioning are perpetual challenges particularly when a group is trying to asynchronously make contributions. All too often, a document gets attached to an email which is sent out to multiple recipients for review and revision. As the changes come back, a significant inefficiency occurs trying to merge multiple, potentially conflicting, changes. Alternatively, network drives may be used to share files only to find versions branching in several directions. In recent years, significant improvements to groupware tools became available, many of which gained substantial traction. The Wiki inverts the most basic concept of group document preparation. Instead of pushing content out, it pulls

contributors in, including both intentional and unintentional participants. Intentional participants are often pulled in by sending a quick link from the Wiki to selected recipients. Unintentional but interested parties often stumble upon content and more often than not offer meaningful contributions or perspectives from different viewpoints that might otherwise not be considered.

A similarly compelling case for using Wikis to create and store content is their ability to search that content. While search features vary by Wiki, the product that we have implemented indexes and searches both page content and attachments in common formats such as Microsoft Word and Adobe PDF. We have found this feature to be exceptionally useful to discover, access and ultimately link to content that exists in various mediums.

Communications

The Wiki affects e-mail use in two ways. First, it establishes an institutional memory by bringing e-mail conversations public and archiving them for posterity. Institutional memory is the collective knowledge and learned experiences of a group. As turnover occurs among group members, it is important to preserve these concepts. As a communications medium, e-mail is fairly closed in that only the recipients are privy to the discussion. There are often others excluded from the carbon-copy lists that have valuable insight to contribute to the conversation. By moving away from e-mail threads and into Wikis—either as evolving content or threaded comments—the discussion becomes as public as the Wiki's security model is configured to permit. Thus, non-obvious or unintentional participants are brought into the conversation often influencing it in tangibly beneficial ways. Second, the Wiki can help reduce what is now commonly referred to as organizational spam. In the workplace it is all too typical to copy many participants on a message. As inboxes are flooded with content that may be irrelevant, e-mail overload develops and the stress that all too frequently accompanies an overflowing inbox. E-mail is an inefficient communication mechanism for collaborative needs because it functions as a single-threaded conversation rather than allowing progressive elaboration and branching. Wikis, on the other hand, allow individuals to choose which content they wish to dive into while avoiding that which is not applicable. Wikis are not, however, a replacement for e-mail but rather serve a distinct purpose. Their strength is an area where e-mail is weak as a communication medium. E-mail can complement a Wiki, specifically as a means to notify a contributor to changes in interesting content in the Wiki.

Most Wikis today also provide for distributing content via really simple syndication (RSS) or similar feeds which can be consumed by an ever-increasing collection of applications (including some Wikis themselves) and devices. These syndications are often subscription-based, allowing the user to specify precisely the types of content that they want to be made aware of, based on keywords, tagging, other taxonomies or search results.

Stemming Knowledge Loss

Our Wiki is a comprehensive knowledge base. All of our generally accessible project assets originate, evolve and are archived in the Wiki. Documentation is iteratively developed and progressively elaborated by a number of contributors from different parts of the organization. The Wiki acts as an ultimate repository for documentation and project assets. Further, the Wiki facilitates knowledge discovery. Content is linked across pages forming a web of interrelated information. The search feature covers pages, blogs, attachments, e-mail messages and comments. Some team members initiate their own blogs which further both knowledge discovery and a sense of community.

Like many organizations, we relied on consultants and contractors for our project and suffered from too frequent staff turnover. In parallel with these changes, the product that we were implementing evolved rapidly and also went through a series of acquisitions. With each departure, new face or new product vendor we lost context and knowledge that can only be rebuilt over time. We have found the Wiki to meaningfully reduce the loss of knowledge and preserve historical context.

Figure 4. Wikis have a direct effect on e-mail habits

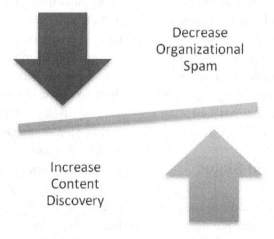

Decrease Organizational Spam

Increase Content Discovery

Similarly it provides a springboard for new team members to more rapidly develop applicable knowledge and context.

Brainstorming and Raw Collaboration

Changes are inevitable in all software projects and the need to balance rigid project scope with stakeholder satisfaction typically dictates that changes will occur. Projects are often jeopardized not only when the customer requires a change but when the customer is unsure of what they want (O'Connell, 2007). Our project began by following a fairly traditional waterfall methodology but over time—and in order to succeed in the culture of our organization—evolved to a highly adaptive approach. While we do not yet follow a specific agile methodology, our approach embraces some core features of the agile strategy by creating an "environment that enables the breakdown and reinvention of traditional functional boundaries" (Chin, 2004, p. 148). Our Wiki facilitates an adaptive methodology by acting as a sounding board for feature designs, screen mock-ups and other efforts where a wide and representative group of stakeholders can quickly view and comment on ideas allowing changes to be made incrementally and customers to have a sense of ownership having influenced the design. This process involves more individual contributors and reviewers than is often the case in a traditional waterfall methodology where requirements gathering sessions are followed by design specifications and so on. We have observed the adaptive approach to be both more efficient and more effective. As Surowiecki asserts, "there's no guarantee that groups will come up with smart solutions. What's striking, though, is just how often they do" (p. 86).

Monitoring Progress and Status

Wikis can provide a number of tools to monitor the progress and status of projects. For example, our Wiki provides a listing of recently updated pages on the dashboard, RSS feeds and an optional daily summary e-mail. The daily e-mail digest is particular useful to keep up with progress when it is not possible to be physically present. It shows what pages were added and changed in the past day which gives insight into both topics germane to your work as well as a view into topics that may only be peripherally of interest. The latter is one element that makes a Wiki particularly useful— by having exposure to topics that you may not otherwise be involved, you have greater context and may also have something meaningful to contribute. In addition, if your organization makes the use of the Wiki pervasive in your work, reading the daily e-mail digest is very much like reading the diary or journal of the day's activities.

OUTCOMES AND OBSERVATIONS

Adoption

Adoption of our Wiki was influenced by three main factors. First, a reason to collaborate is necessary to drive adoption. As discussed earlier, our initial attempt failed because there was not sufficient reason to collaborate. Instead, our project which involved a substantial number of active participants was a good reason to collaborate and provided an automatic audience. Second, the Wiki must build a critical mass of participants and content. We made the Wiki mandatory for certain business functions (agendas, minutes, etc) as well as made it the exclusive source of some content such as contact lists and vendor documentation. All of the technical and functional staff involved on our project ultimately used our Wiki on a routine basis but the degree of use still varies by individual and role. Finally, adoption is enabled when the Wiki is easy to use with a low barrier to entry. Initially, the Wiki we used did not have a WYSIWYG/rich-text editor, thus required writing content using its unique markup

Table 1. Content creation and updates by month suggesting that a critical mass of content and partici-pants was reached in late summer 2005 followed by a spike in updates

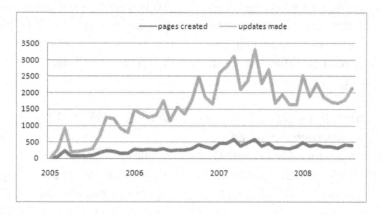

Figure 5. The top graph shows that circulating documents has periods of creative work separated by logistics. The bottom graph indicates that Wikis allow for uninterrupted creativity after doing logistical work at the start. These graphs were originally published in Stewart Mader's Using Wiki in education (2006) and are reprinted here with permission.

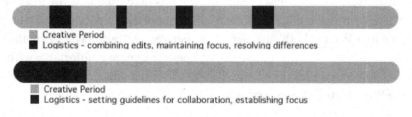

syntax. Additionally, it did not integrate with our single sign-on system. These were not hurdles for our technical staff that have experience with HTML, XML and the like, but were a challenge for some functional staff. As our Wiki software matured, it introduced a rich-text editor and now integrates with our single sign-on system. These enhancements lower the barrier to use and have further increased adoption.

Changes in Work Habits

With the wide-spread use of the Wiki, we see far fewer Word documents created as the Wiki provides an opportunity for earlier collaboration—there is no need to wait for a document to be circulated by e-mail. Now, rather than pushing separate copies of a document to each person, all collaborators are pulled in to a central place where everyone sees the same text. Circulating an e-mail or document has bursts of creativity separated by logistics such as combining edits. A Wiki shifts the logistics to a brief period at the outset followed by uninterrupted creativity and knowledge construction (Mader 2006). Tantek Çelik, Technorati's chief technologist observes that with a Wiki "everyone can make incremental progress without having to wait for everyone else. It's like parallel processing for people rather than computers" (Tapscott, 2006, p. 254).

With a Wiki, meetings frequently evolve into work sessions with a Wiki page created on the fly to capture ideas. The Wiki may act as a whiteboard when projected onto a screen to capture notes and lists, but current Wiki technology is not a useful replacement for capturing diagrams or drawings on the fly. When a Wiki page originates in a meeting, content and ideas continue to evolve afterwards, pulling in more participants. This process typically requires effort to regroup or otherwise make a decision from often varying options.

Finally, a Wiki drastically reduces the volume of conversations taking place over e-mail and provides an improved medium for collaboration. We now see lots of links to Wiki content being sent around by e-mail rather than Word documents.

FEATURE USAGE

As with most applications, use of Wiki features grows over time. However, we have observed a barrier that most users do not cross. Working below that threshold in a Wiki is both sufficient and effective.

Everyone derives value regardless of whether they use advanced Wiki features. Some of our least technically savvy constituents fully embrace our Wiki. While Liebowitz (2007) suggests that "Wikis can be excellent ways to foster collaboration among generations" (p. 70) we have observed the fastest adoption and advanced feature usage by the "net-gen" staff.

WIKIS ARE NOT . . .

While this chapter espouses the virtues of using a Wiki to manage technology, Wikis are not the right answer for all content and are not an overnight solution. They do not replace the rich features or task specific functions in various applications such as using Excel for calculations. Similarly, Wikis are not a file share. In fact, it is recognized as a misuse of a Wiki to simply store documents. Wikis take time to grow to a useful point and it is important to pace their use to ensure a balance between a healthy Wiki growth rate and ensuring people remain comfortable with the process and associated changes (Mader 2008).

Figure 6. Feature usage showing barrier that most users do not cross. Users less comfortable with technology tend to work at the lower half of the spectrum while the more technically savvy users work across the spectrum. The break depicts the threshold that most Wiki users do not cross.

BENEFITS

Wikis help to keep our entire staff better informed. Further, those on the periphery of the project or organization also stay as informed as they choose. Keeping this larger group engaged can greatly improve innovation. For example, global companies in a variety of industries report an average of nearly half their innovation comes from external sources (Sawyer 2007).

Wikis encourage ad hoc community or team formation that leads to both unanticipated interactions and more interactions across organizational boundaries. They have a flattening effect on organizations—at least in terms of culture. Flat organizations inherently lend themselves towards innovation and encourage more cross-functional interaction (Gouge 2003).

Wikis augment the speed and efficiency of work by having information in one place, owned and maintained by everyone. Mader (2006) observes that "unlike many software tools that have a steep learning curve, require training to use and are advertised on the number of features included, Wiki developers take the opposite approach. The resulting simplicity of the Wiki has a compounding effect, that is, the more people use it, the more they want to keep using it and their contributions become vital to the growth of information and community."

FUTURE TRENDS

Wikis fill a gap by tying together various information technology management and knowledge management functions. With the current state of technology, they are the best tool to serve this purpose. As groupware continues to improve, however, it is certainly possible they will be supplanted in the years ahead. Wikis' advantages, particularly in cost, ease of use and familiarity to the "net generation", are significant enough to suggest their traction in this space will continue to grow for quite some time.

A drawback to near exclusive use of a Wiki for management is the connectivity requirement. An author needs to be perpetually connected to the Wiki server in order to author content. This prevents offline editing, such as when working in environments in which broadband internet access is not available. Couple this with rudimentary reviewing capabilities—such as spell checking available only to the extent it is supported in some browsers—and browser-based content authoring may not seem either ideal or suitable under some circumstances. With increasing browser functions, offline caching capabilities and improved data synchronization resources, we remain optimistic that these limitations will be overcome in the near future.

CONCLUSION

Wikis powerfully and adeptly help address a number of the most common technology management challenges surrounding communication, knowledge management and collaboration. In short, Wikis work at work but they also take some work to be successful. Wikis provide a relatively inexpensive solution to common management needs and will be—or perhaps already are—a pervasive part of the IT landscape and for many are considered the most recent "killer app" for technology management.

REFERENCES

Chin, G. (2004). *Agile project management*. New York: AMACOM.

Ebersbach, A., Glaser, M., & Heigl, R. (2006). *Wiki Web collaboration*. Berlin: Springer.

Gouge, Ian. (2003). *Shaping the IT organization*. Leeds, UK: Springer.

Liebowitz, J. (2007). *Social networking: The essence of innovation.* Lanham, MD: Scarecrow Press.

Mader, S. (2008). *Wikipatterns.* Indianapolis, IN: Wiley Publishing.

Mader, S. (2006). Four letter words: How Wiki and edit are making the Internet a better teaching tool. In S. Mader (Ed.), *Using Wiki in education.* Retrieved May 27, 2008, from http://www.Wiki-ineducation.com

Nambisan, S., & Sawhney, M. (2008). *The global brain.* Upper Saddle River, NJ: Pearson Education Inc. As Wharton School Publishing.

O'Connell, F. (2007). *Fast projects.* Harlow, UK: Pearson Education Limited.

Project Management Institute. (2004). *A guide to the project management body of knowledge* (3rd ed.). Newtown Square, PA.

Sawyer, K. (2007). *Group genius: The creative power of collaboration.* New York: Basic Books.

Stahl, B. (2004). *Responsible management of information systems.* Hershey, PA: IGI Global Publishing.

Surowiecki, J. (2004). *The wisdom of crowds.* New York: Anchor Books.

Tapscott, D., & Williams, A. D. (2006). *Wikinomics: How mass collaboration changes everything.* New York: The Penguin Group.

KEY TERMS AND DEFINITIONS

Adaptive: The adaptive approach to software and systems development encourages incremental implementation through a series of iterations, embracing changes and refinements along the way. Traditional phases such as design, develop and test still occur but with blurred boundaries and less rigidity.

ASP: An application service provider (ASP) is an organization that hosts software as a service. Many blog, Wiki and web based e-mail providers are considered ASPs.

Blog: A blog, or web log, is a chronological series of content typically created by an individual. Blogs are most often commentary or observations captured as text but may also include other media such as pictures or video.

Institutional Memory: Institutional memory is the collective knowledge and learned experiences of a group. As turnover occurs among group members, these concepts must be transitioned. Knowledge management tools aim to capture and preserve these memories.

Net-Generation: The net-generation or "net-gen" are those born between 1977 and 1996, inclusive. This group is often stereotyped as having grown up with, and is constantly connected to, many of the technologies that are pervasive today.

Organizational Spam: Organizational spam is the e-mail overload that occurs as e-mail threads grow excessive or recipient lists and carbon copies are overused. E-mail is an inefficient communication mechanism for collaborative purposes because it functions as a threaded conversation rather than allowing progressive elaboration.

Social Networking: Social networking is a technology enabled means to develop communities based upon shared interests. Social networks utilize one or more of an array of mediums such as blogs, messaging, discussion threads and others. Social networking sites are typical examples of web 2.0 applications.

Waterfall: The waterfall methodology for software and systems development is a series of cascading steps of requirements gathering, design, development, testing and support. Each phase has a strict sign-off. Changes that would necessitate reverting to a prior phase are strongly discouraged.

Web 2.0: Web 2.0 is a broadly used term that may be applied to a number of web technologies but at its most basic level describes interactive and often editable web content that encourages information sharing and collaboration.

Wiki: A Wiki is a set of interlinking web pages designed for anyone to easily contribute or modify content. They are very often used as the basis for a collaborative community or in business as an inexpensive intranet or knowledge repository. *Wikipedia* (www.Wikipedia.org) is among the best-known Wikis, popular for its community driven content that has become a fairly reliable collaborative encyclopedia.

Chapter XXXII
Mining User Activity Data in Higher Education Open Systems

Owen G. McGrath
University of California at Berkeley, USA

ABSTRACT

Higher education IT project managers have always relied on user activity data as logged in one form or another. Summarized counts of users and performance trends serve as essential sources of information for those who need to analyze problems, monitor security, improve software, perform capacity planning, etc. With the reach of the Internet extending into all aspects of higher education research and teaching, however, new questions have arisen as to how, where, and when user activity gets captured and analyzed. Tracking and understanding remote users and their round-the-clock activities is a major technical and analytical challenge within today's cyber-infrastructure. As open content publishing and open source development projects thrive in higher education there are some side effects on usage analysis. This chapter examines how data mining solutions – particularly Web usage mining methods– are being taken up in three open systems project management contexts: digital libraries, online museums, and course management systems. In describing the issues and challenges that motivate data mining applications in these three contexts, the chapter provides an overview of how data mining integrates within project management processes. The chapter also touches on ways in which data mining can be augmented by the complementary practice of data visualization.

INTRODUCTION

Before the advent of the Web and of large cross-institutional open source and open content projects, the job of tracking and reporting use was typically accomplished with commercial or home-grown utility software. An academic technology group at a university could confine its efforts to meeting the reporting needs of the local institution by using the features of in-house systems (McGrath, 2005). With today's global access to open content via open source applications on the Web, however, crucial questions arise as to how usage information can be captured and managed, how to ensure that the analysis of this information gets integrated into key management processes, and how to address the sheer scale and pace of usage as they outstrip conventional methods.

Higher education project managers still need to gather and analyze user activity information within contemporary open content or open source Web frameworks, but find themselves increasingly faced with unpredictable access patterns from unknown numbers of unseen users coming from who knows where. This chapter describes a range of higher education efforts – in digital libraries, online museums, and course management systems -- to develop practical approaches towards building and managing distributed capture and analysis systems for large Web-based production deployments. Moving beyond pure research, these projects meet a wide range of real tracking, monitoring, and reporting needs by applying data mining techniques in practice.

BACKGROUND

For decades, automatically generated logs have been a vital source of information within academic computing. From timeshare minicomputers to lab-based workstations, logs have provided data at the heart of acquisition, recharge, licensing, security, usability, and capacity planning processes. In the Internet era, Web log data becomes an even more essential and often sole source of information for all of these same reasons together with the added urgency of supporting round-the-clock, remote access. Tracking users' interactions with digital library content, online museum collections, or e-learning material is crucial. Tools for making sense of usage within these systems depend heavily on the underlying Web technology. The monitoring features available to administrators of these systems rely heavily on Web application server logs as a record of the visitor's access. Further complicating the usage analysis problem is the trend within higher education towards open content, open source application frameworks, distance learning and a more general embrace of open online research collaboration (Lynch, 2007). Academic institutions are also increasingly involved in collaborative efforts to develop open source alternatives to commercial applications such as repositories, portals, and collaboration environments (Olsen, 2003). This shift in the locus of software development away from commercial companies and into loosely organized consortia of higher education institutions, however, ends up with noticeably different processes and results.

Behind open source projects such as Dspace, Fedora, uPortal, Sakai and Moodle are evolving organizations still experimenting with management structures that might allow them to coordinate distributed software development better (Wheeler, 2007). Many of the same technical principles - simple services, loose-coupling, lightweight data standards - that make these open source projects realizable also present challenges to building out full-featured Web analytic tools like those found in commercial systems. In particular, the lightweight distributed design can make it more difficult to develop comprehensive features in areas such as user event logging and usage analysis. To facilitate the development of new tools by loose-knit communities of developers, these consortia aim at minimal overhead and lean requirements in order for applications to plug into the frameworks easily. Consequently, functionality for monitoring and analyzing usage information often gets overlooked. In the case of the National Science Digital Library (NSDL), for instance, a separate Web metric tool had to be tacked on as an after-thought in order to allow for even basic 'canned' reports (Khoo & Donahue, 2007). Collecting, transforming, and analyzing disparate log information through data mining processes is hard work, but opens up the possibility for finding patterns, clusters, associations and commonalities within the usage patterns of open systems. When it succeeds, this approach can result in surprising insights about near and long-term usage patterns, thereby giving support personnel, usability researchers, instructional designers, and many other decision makers a handle on what is really going on in their institution's digital library, online museum, or course management system.

Web Usage Mining Research

Many of the approaches put forward in the general Web usage analytics research literature focus on online retail settings and how to develop comprehensive profiles of e-commerce customers (Sen, Dacin & Pattichis, 2006). The typical concern is with analyzing the so-called clickstream trails left behind by people visiting, browsing, and purchasing in an online shopping Websites. These visitors' navigational patterns are pored over extensively in order to classify them based on the activities, roles, and timing involved. Behaviors are organized into groupings that might shed light on how to improve a site's business activity. In a Web site redesigned based on this sort of analysis, visitors (especially those who are identified as repeat customers) might be presented with a specially tailored content that includes an opportunity to consider buying suggested items. Customers' behavior patterns can also lead to further iterative refinement of the overall site structure when analysis reveals,

for instance, that abandoned shopping cart patterns are due to navigational complexity. A major outcome of the Web usage analysis is that the profiles and patterns can be used to create customized user experiences - shopping suggestions and referrals - based on a customer's profile. In short, the e-commerce usage analysis process involves fairly calculated focus on site visitors in the shopping context where the improved system would potentially boost sales.

Higher Education Data Mining

As a newer sub-field of data mining, educational data mining encompasses its own unique range of concerns and approaches. Romero & Venture provide an excellent literature review of the field (Romero & Ventura, 2007). A fair generalization can be made that much of the inquiry and practical wisdom developed center on applying computational techniques to large institutional data sets, typically those pulled together from disparate sources. For instance, data mining processes in a higher education setting have served as the basis for discovering categories and characteristics in student enrollment patterns (Chen, Hsieh, & Hsu, 2007). Useful for institutional planning, monitoring and decision making, data mining analyses can yield insights at different levels of granularity, such as identifying predictors for graduation rates, course articulation problems within a particular major, or individual students who might benefit from special forms of tutoring (Daradoumis, Martinez-Mones, Xhafa, 2006).

Other recent entries in the higher education data mining field reflect growing interest in understanding the activities carried out online in education-related Web applications. As more teaching, research, administrative processes are moved online, there arise both needs and opportunities for tracking, analyzing, evaluating and improving these online extensions of the institution. Important to making these online environments work is an increasing demand on institutions to document educational outcomes. Even as the distance between students, faculty, and administrators increases online, demands for more detailed and rigorous accounting of teaching activities, curricular progress, and learning outcomes are increasing (Olsen, 2006). In the context of online learning environments, data mining projects have been undertaken in order to examine similarities across thousands of online sessions to reveal useful characteristic aspects of students' interaction with e-learning content (Berendt & Spiliopoulou, 2000). These analyses identified common conceptual error sequences that then informed pedagogical re-design issues, such as whether subgroups of students share similar difficulties, and how content and sequencing might be re-ordered. Obviously, for the approaches to succeed, the issue of what gets logged and what tools are available to analyze those logs become vitally important. Usage logs are at center stage throughout these data mining processes.

Mining Usage in the Digital Library Context

Over the past decade, higher education library technologists have worked hard to create and manage Web search portal access into their rapidly changing and expanding collections. These real and virtual library collections often include open access reference databases, online journals, and even digitized versions of public domain books. In the case of the Arizona Health Sciences Library at the University of Arizona, the move beyond the traditional library interaction model of information access to online systems ushered in a fundamental change in the way users relate to the library as an institution (Bracke, 2004). In the older online card catalog model, sophisticated searching and exploration was usually the domain of the skilled professional reference librarian, not the end-user. Today, Web-based digital library access often allows users to execute natural language queries across huge, heterogeneous networked collections

of full text. No longer is online searching carried out predominantly by professional intermediaries. Moreover, the computing devices involved are no longer just walk-up dedicated terminals within a library building, but powerful and portable personal computers. In the Internet era, the ability to search and retrieve from the outside the walls of the physical library (e.g., from offices, classroom, or off campus) on powerful and inexpensive computing devices means that users find and read electronic documents and books without ever physically visiting the library.

When deciding whether and how to license and support new digital collections, it becomes difficult then for library administrators to anticipate adoption by users – a situation which, in turn, can make production and support planning seem arbitrary (Lynch, 2005). No longer able to rely solely upon face-to-face interaction or circulation and shelving counts for physical volumes, library services groups must extend their deployment projects for Internet environments to include new forms of online user research. Recently, digital library centers have begun to explore new models for tailoring services to their Internet users. The success of these projects rests upon answering key questions about online users in terms of who they are, where they came from, and what different ways they take up the tools, reference resources, and content available to them. Online libraries at schools such as Notre Dame University and North Carolina State University offer personalized MyLibrary Web portals (Jeevan & Padhi, 2006). Unlike traditional user–tailored approaches that require a great deal of face-to-face observations, these new techniques require insights into the online behavior of the digital library's unseen clientele. For Bracke's investigation within the Arizona Health Sciences Library, key questions to answer were about how resource access differed between on-campus and external users. In the case of the UK's National Electronic Library for Health, Alesia Zuccala and colleagues were interested in knowing more about where users were entering from and whether any hidden patterns could be discovered among these electronic referrals (Zuccala et al., 2008).

Mining Usage in the Online Museum Context

While the opening up of university libraries on the Internet has garnered a good deal of publicity, digitization has also begun to transform other core university institutions: museums and archival collections (Lynch, 2002). Just as online information retrieval enables vast access to texts, it can allow for expanded access to digital representations of art work, scientific specimens, cultural artifacts, etc. In the case of the Tokyo University Digital Museum, for example, the kinds of information technology environments deployed in a virtual museum setting represent not just improving technical capacities, but also radical changes to traditional museum notions of curation, exhibits, visitor interaction, information display, and context (Koshizuka & Sakamura, 2000). Until the rise of the Web, there had been an implicit and understandable disciplinary boundary separating information technologists, who were interested in how information could be searched and browsed online, from museum curators, who were interested what happens when visitors enter a physical museum or archive. The dramatic technological changes brought on by the spread of networked information access now enable new configurations of archival collections and museums as online venues, thereby inviting a fundamental reconsideration of the of how collections and artifacts can be made available.

Projects within this new cross-disciplinary field of museum informatics have drawn upon state-of-the-art technologies to create virtual museum experiences available to many thousands of users world-wide. The practical questions these projects raise for those who need to plan and manage the online museums range from understanding the expanded audience to building personalized

museum experiences based on visitor profiles. As with the library, the archetypal museum scenario in the Internet era changes dramatically from the curious patron walking through the door during open hours. As university museums and archives have now moved towards digitization, virtual visitors often out-number real ones. In making sense of this situation from his vantage point of as a maintainer a museum meta-portal, Jonathan Bowen has mapped out the strengths and possibilities of many different Web analytic approaches for online museums (Bowen, 2002). The key questions, in his view, are about who the virtual visitors are and how museums can personalize the online experience (Bowen & Filippini-Fantoni, 2004). Likewise, in considering next steps towards personalization, Darren Peacock and Jonny Brownbill ask how the needs and behaviors of virtual visitors to the Australian National Museum can not only be understood but even anticipated better as they inevitably change over time (Brownbill & Peacock, 2007).

Mining Usage in the Course Management Systems Context

The familiar online course management systems can be found at most colleges and universities today. Called by different names (e.g. virtual learning environment) around the world, the products in this category are either home-grown, commercially licensed, or open source software. Regardless of their provenance, these systems all tended to pull together in one package the same sorts of tools and functions (e.g., mailing list, bulletin board, and chat programs). While annual licenses for commercial systems range into the hundreds of thousands of dollars, a typical user would see very little difference in functionality between commercial and open source products. However, unlike the commercial counterparts, open source course management systems tend to lack full-featured usage tracking tools for administrative users. The consortia of higher education institutions building open source software with and for each other face unique organizational and project management issues. A large cross-institutional project such as Moodle, for instance, consists of scores of developers around the world using and contributing to a shared code base. To facilitate distributed development, the Moodle framework design places minimal requirements on those who might want to create or integrate a new tool. By minimizing the overhead of tool creation and re-writes, however, the Moodle framework ends up with little out-of-the-box functionality in the area of usage reporting, as Romero points out in his data mining study of Moodle use at the University of Cordoba (Romero, Ventura, & Garcia, 2008).

A similar situation exists in the Sakai Project. Whether configured for use as a course management system or more generic collaboration environment, the Sakai platform offers a basic set of tools along with the capacity to easily add or adapt new tools. The Sakai source code can be downloaded and installed by anyone anywhere for free. And pre-existing Web applications have been adapted easily to work within Sakai in a loosely-coupled fashion. Yet, while the Sakai end-user sees a harmonious arrangement of tools that interoperate and share a common interface style, the behind-the-scenes view of Sakai in operation reveals a piecemeal and heterogeneous affair. In particular, responsibility for logging information about users' interaction within is largely left up to individual tool developers. Moreover, the actual logging of the data is spread across several locations in a production instance of Sakai.

Worst of all, Sakai like Moodle provides administrators with no core tools for gathering and analyzing the data. Each user in Sakai is assigned to membership in system-wide roles (e.g., instructor, teaching assistant, and student) and every time they log in they see a personal workspace and collection of course sites to which they belong. Moving within a particular course site, the user has access to content and tools (e.g., calendar, group discussion, email archive, chat, quizzing, and a grade book). After logging into the Sakai framework and using tools and accessing content, the user eventually logs out. In a typical production installation, the user's contact and interactions are logged in various Web server logs, a Tomcat server log, and across many tables of a relational database. Because Sakai provides core tools for collecting and analyzing this session information, copies of the usage data must be gathered and studied externally in order to yield even the simplest usage insights, as McGrath notes in his data mining study of Sakai use at UC Berkeley (McGrath, 2007).

MANAGING DATA MINING PROJECTS

Commonalities Across Three Contexts

In considering commonalities across the data mining projects in the three contexts described above, it's worth noting that data mining methodologies have become more formalized in recent years. Data mining practitioners in many industries, for instance, adhere to a six step methodology known as the Cross-Industry Standard Process for Data Mining (CRISP-DM). From the perspective of balancing the extra work and potential digressions posed by data mining, CRISP-DM not only brings order to the project planning, execution, and monitoring phases, but also explicitly requires an initial understanding phase focused on clarifying objectives (Larose, 2002). Although CRISP-DM itself is not yet widely adopted in the kinds of nascent higher education data mining efforts surveyed in this chapter, the sensible emphasis on good initial planning is not disputed. Indeed, the core planning processes addressed by CRISP-DM rank among the most significant processes of good project management in general. As detailed in the case studies that follow, the benefits that data mining can yield for day-to-day functioning of large online production systems are most likely to occur if one devises some sort data mining objectives, scope, and strategy as early as possible.

Preparation Phase: Gathering and Pre-Processing

Process-wise, data mining of user activity requires that project managers integrate several key steps into the larger workflow of their analysis projects: capturing, aggregating, pre-preprocessing, and exploring usage data. While basic reports and summary statistics can be generated from a few sources, a more complete picture requires aggregating and preprocessing the data first. In the Arizona Health Sciences Library context, this step involved harvesting and coding the various data from the gateway data base sources. In the cases of Moodle and Sakai, the preparation phase involved gathering varied data, file and log formats while also analyzing the differences in their information models. For example, merging semi-structured common log format files from Web servers, the status messages generated by Java classes in application servers, and the structured relational data captured in a relational database can require a range of transformations such as de-normalization and dimensionality reduction. At this stage differences in logging approaches across the distributed systems involved also becomes a key issue. Not all systems even log activity in the database and among those that do so, what qualifies as a user session or action can be difficult to determine.

Nevertheless, once the available data sources are merged, an exploratory data analysis phase can help chart a course for choosing among data mining approaches (e.g., clustering, classification, and affinity). In the case of Bowen's online museum meta-portal, summary statistics served as first steps towards getting to know and manage the huge volume of data. The sheer size of the user activity data generated by any Web-based production system might require carving up the dataset with an initial set of coding categories. In the case of the digital library portal, for instance, Bracke used the exploratory process to devise a multi-variable scheme by which to organize his digital library user types: the kinds of resources they access, their access levels, where they came from, and what they did. In the context of the Moodle study, Romero's university setting involved thousands of students accessing material in almost 200 course sites. Likewise, in the online museum, the various forms of user activity data grew by quickly by the day. In most contexts, questions that arise from finding initial connections within and across the dataset might point to access time and content location patterns as starting points for further investigation. Summarizing the data in an exploratory fashion is almost always a useful first step towards organizing prioritizing questions to pose next (Trant, 2006).

Analysis Phase: Finding Patterns

As mentioned, data mining algorithms look for inherent patterns and similarities in large data sets and can uncover groupings and relations that might otherwise prove impossible to detect. Clustering analysis makes for a good first step in data mining, as the various techniques available can be tuned across a range of variables in processing huge datasets (Markov & Larose, 2007). In the area of clustering algorithms, data mining software packages usually offer a choice of algorithms that work well with different kinds of multi-dimensional data sets. Selecting some time span of session instance data from the flat file as input to a clustering algorithm, one explores for a specific number of clusters or lets the algorithm decide. Romero performed a clustering analysis of student Moodle user variables covering mean session time and the percentage assignments. In his case, three main clusters emerged around groupings that revealed quick, medium, and extended visits.

Similarly, the main goal of Bracke's regression analysis phase was to test modeled groupings generated from his initial coding of the online library log usage data. To provide a baseline, his initial modeling coded users by location and the type of library resource they sought. The regression analysis approach to analyzing user navigation paths through the resources provided a gauge for discerning different kinds of user navigation strategies. After testing his hypothesis on a large volume of data, Bracke's rough initial modeling was confirmed as a useful way to partition users into finer types based on both location and resource use.

One might also wonder about patterns within user sessions, such as common activity sequences. As an aid in answering such questions, data mining software usually provides functions for finding association rules as a method of revealing co-occurrence relations among and across item sets. The goal of this affinity analysis is to discover association patterns in sequences of data, i.e., things that tend to go together. Unlike in clustering where items are grouped based on their inherent similarity, an association rule discovery can often reveal surprising co-occurrences of sequences within large data sets. Sometimes referred to as market basket analysis, affinity analysis can give results that resemble correlations. In the case of Sakai usage data, McGrath's participants' activities were mined for associations, as revealed by event messages logged during each session. Looking at cross-classified counts of tool activity events initially revealed cases where the session activities that co-occur were unsurprising: content reads going together with content reads, login events going together with announcement reads. But further analysis revealed some less obvious co-occurrences: document editing events often co-occurring with discussion forum reading events within sessions, for example.

Since the relevance of any association is easy to misinterpret, their true usefulness comes into play mainly when they are considered in context.

Tool activity associations in their own right mean little until combined with some further empirical investigation of, say, the course sites in which they occur. For example, a major challenge to cultivating institutional best practices for using a system like Moodle or Sakai is to understand how instructors are employing it in the first place. With hundreds of instructors, thousands of sites, and tens of thousands of students, it can be very difficult to know how tools are actually being taken up and used. The clusters and associations offered up through data mining analyses essentially become a launch pad for collecting, analyzing, and inquiring further about how features and content are being accessed. With this information as a starting point for understanding usage of any system, more traditional techniques - direct observation, polls, and interviews - can be pursued, as was also the case in the Peacock and Brownbill's study. Though not to be relied upon solely for documenting activity, data mining results can offer focused indicators of the usage patterns that, if confirmed, ultimately help inform planning and support decisions.

As a summary of the data mining process discussion, the table below provides a synopsis across the three project contexts mentioned—digital library, online museum, and course management system—of how the project's particular questions influence the selection of data sources and methods of analysis. That data sources and methods were varied—is understandable given the range of contexts and systems involved. Still, the processes have much in common.

Future Trends: Project Monitoring and Control With Mining Visualization

The hard work of capturing, aggregating, and unifying varied and distributed activity logs for data mining can also serve as the starting point for a complementary kind of data exploration that is more oriented towards visual analysis. Data

Table 1. Selective overview of Web usage mining approaches in the three contexts

Questions	Data Sources	Methods of Mining Analysis	References
Digital Library 1. How do Web navigational routes into the Arizona Health Sciences digital library users vary by type of resource sought? 2. What hidden associations might there be among the referral access points into the NeLH digital library?	• Web log files • gateway database • Web log files • link extraction data	• Multinomial logistic regression (MLR) analysis • Colink mapping	(Bracke, 2004) (Zuccala et al., 2008)
Online Museum 3. How can online museums be personalized? How do we build user profiles across vast differences in location of origin, platform, querying abilities, etc.? 4. In relation to online museums, how can the needs and behaviors of virtual visitors be understood and their needs better anticipated?	• Web log files • link extraction data • Web log files	• Classification analysis based on live navigation activity • Web metrics, simple correlation • Correlation of coded session, search, and participation metrics	(Bowen & Filippini-Fantoni, 2004) (Bowen, 2002) (Brownbill & Peacock, 2007)
Course Management System 5. How can students users of a Moodle course site be grouped in terms of their Moodle activities and performance in the course? How can Moodle activity be used as a gauge to identify students who would benefit from intervention during the course? 6. How might users of the UC Berkeley Sakai environment be characterized in terms of their session types and tool usage within the system?	• Moodle database tables • Web log files • Sakai database tables	• Clustering analysis of student sessions • Classification analysis student grades • Affinity analysis of tool events • Clustering analysis of student sessions • Affinity analysis of tool events	(Romero, Ventura, & Garcia, 2008) (McGrath, 2007)

visualization approaches represent a major area of research across several intersecting fields. The data mining approaches described in this chapter provide ways to explore huge system usage data sets numerically, their graphical capabilities are limited to traditional approaches to numerical display. Beyond focused presentations of data subsets, the presentation capabilities in data mining software as well as most spreadsheet and statistical packages reveal basic obstacles encountered in presenting huge amounts of data on a screen. As mentioned, the main goals of data mining analyses are usually about the discovery of inherent groupings and co-occurrence within and across the large usage data sets with many variables. The dimensionality of the data -- with attributes ranging across users, sites, activity types, content structure, and time cycles etc. -- often outstrips the display capabilities of most traditional graphical coordinate systems. Problems of over-plotting and dimensional clutter are particularly common in time-based data sets like those mentioned in this chapter.

In recent years, innovative data visualization efforts to overcome such limitations have spawned visualization techniques such as the parallel coordinate plot type found in the visualization software suite Mondrian (Theus, 2002). Rather than trying to represent multiple dimensions using orthogonal axes, the parallel coordinate plot creates equal sized segments with the axes as uniformly spaced vertical lines. These plots are increasingly being used, for instance, in visualizations for stock performance and commodity pricing trends. For visualizing a system's complex usage patterns, it is possible with parallel coordinate plots to present the output results from a data mining analysis such that associations among variables show up very obviously. Highlighting particular temporal relations and historical changes for clusters, such as mean value across time is possible as well.

The approach of using an innovative data visualization system for exploring user activity allows a data mining analyst to get a complementary visual overview of the number of ranges for samples, how many samples fall within those ranges, outlier residence, and groupings within class/attribute pairs. Here a scatter plot matrix display can also be used to provide a quick check for possible relationships among variables. Sizing and coloring controls make it is possible to drill down into any of the plots for further analysis. Other visualization capabilities being explored by data mining projects involve giving users themselves views onto resource access patterns as a way of offering community history and visual recommendations.

CONCLUSION

This chapter has been intended mainly as an overview several higher education efforts to address the particular usage reporting needs of open systems by employing basic techniques and tools of Web usage mining. Even with these

Figure 1. A Mondrian parallel coordinate plot of Sakai user event data

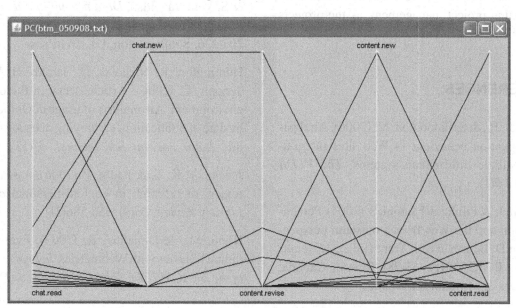

mining techniques in hand, gathering and comprehending usage activity obviously remains a very time consuming project. The combination of data mining approaches and project management disciplines have enabled a basic set of exploratory approaches to pattern discovery in the enormous amounts of data involved in the three contexts described here.

As the field of usage analysis matures, new opportunities to be explored beyond data mining will come from attempts at integrating complementary techniques such as data visualization. Project management of the data visualization process would, of course, involve similar planning, monitoring, and execution. If successful, the results could lead towards repeatable processes that truly leverage the potential and promise of knowledge discovery methodologies for institutional reporting and analysis. Singly or together data mining and data visualization offer potential benefits for assisting those in higher education who are responsible for implementing and deploying online open environments in support of research, teaching, and learning. For user-oriented projects in higher education to keep up with the increasing service demands that the Internet era has brought on, our deployment of analytical tools and processes will require a balance of creativity and sound project management, as the projects described here demonstrate.

REFERENCES

Berendt, B., & Spiliopoulou, M. (2000). Analysis of navigation behaviour in Web sites integrating multiple information systems. *The VLDB Journal 9*(1).

Bowen, J., & Filippini-Fantoni, S. (2004). Personalization and the Web from a museum perspective. In D. Bearman & J. Trant (Eds.), *Museums and the Web 2004* (pp. 63-78). Toronto, Canada: Archives & Museum Informatics.

Bowen, J. (2002). Weaving the museum Web: The virtual library museums pages. *Program: Electronic Library and Information Systems, 36*(4), 236–252.

Bracke, P. J. (2004). Web usage mining at an academic health sciences library: an exploratory study. *Journal of the Medical Library Association, 92*(4), 421-428.

Brownbill, J., & Peacock, D. (2007). *Audiences, visitors, and users: Reconceptualising users of museum online content and services*. Museums and the Web, San Francisco, CA, 11 - 14 April 2007, Toronto, Canada: Archives and Museum Informatics.

Chen, C., Hsieh, Y., & Hsu, S. (2007). Mining learner profile utilizing association rule for Web-based learning diagnosis. *Expert Syst. Appl., 33*(1).

Daradoumis, T., Martinez-Mones, A., & Xhafa, F. (2006). A layered framework for evaluating online collaborative learning interactions. *Int. J. Hum.-Comput. Stud., 64*(7).

Gaudioso, E., & Talavera, L. (2006). Data mining to support tutoring in virtual learning communities: Experiences and challenges. In C. Romero & S. Ventura (Eds.), *Data mining in e-learning, Advances in Management Information Series, 4*, 207-226. Southampton, UK: WitPress.

Huntington, P., Nicholas, D., Jamali, H. R., & Tenopir, C. (2006). Article decay in the digital environment: An analysis of usage of OhioLINK by date of publication, employing deep log methods. *J. Am. Soc. Inf. Sci. Technol., 57*(13).

Jeevan, V. K. J., & Padhi, P. (2006). A selective review of research in content personalization. *Library Review, 55*(9), 556-586(31).

Khoo, M., & Donahue, R. (2007). Evaluating digital libraries with Webmetrics. *In Proceedings of the 7th ACM/IEEE Joint Conference on Digital*

Libraries (Vancouver, BC, Canada, June 18 - 23, 2007). JCDL '07. New York, NY: ACM.

Koshizuka, N., & Sakamura, K. (2000). Tokyo university digital museum. Digital Libraries: Research and Practice. *2000 Kyoto, International Conference,* (pp. 85-92).

Larose, D. T. (2006). *Data mining methods and models.* Wiley-Interscience. Hoboken, NJ.

Lynch, C. (2007). The shape of the scientific article in the developing cyberinfrastructure. *CTWatch Quarterly, 3*(3).

Lynch, C. (2005). Where do we go from here? The next decade for digital libraries. *D-Lib Magazine, 11*(7/8).

Lynch, C. (2002). Digital collections, digital libraries and the digitization of cultural heritage information. *First Monday, 7*(5). Retrieved May 10, 2008, from http://www.firstmonday.org/issues/issue7_5/lynch/index.html

Markov, Z., & Larose, D. T. (2007). *Data mining the Web: Uncovering patterns in Web content, Structure, and Usage.* Hoboken, NJ: Wiley-Interscience.

McGrath, O. (2007). Seeking activity: on the trail of users in open and community source frameworks. *In Proceedings of the 35th Annual ACM SIGUCCS Conference on User Services* (Orlando, Florida, USA, October 07 - 10, 2007). *SIGUCCS '07* (pp. 234-239). New York, NY: ACM.

McGrath, O. (2006). Balancing act: community and local requirements in an open source development process. *In Proceedings of the 34th Annual ACM SIGUCCS Conference on User Services* (Edmonton, Alberta, Canada, November 05 - 08, 2006). *SIGUCCS '06* (pp. 240-244). New York, NY: ACM.

McGrath, O. (2005). Gauging adoptability: a case study of e-portfolio template development. *Proceedings of the 33rd annual ACM SIGUCCS*

conference on User services, (pp.214-217), November 06-09, 2005, Monterey, CA, USA .

Mei, Q. (2004). A knowledge processing oriented life cycle study from a Digital Museum system. *In Proceedings of the 42nd Annual Southeast Regional Conference* (Huntsville, Alabama, April 02 - 03, 2004). ACM-SE 42. (pp. 116-121). New York, NY: ACM.

Olsen, F. (2003). Sharing the Code: More colleges and universities see open-source software as an alternative to commercial products. *The Chronicle of Higher Education: Information Technology,* August, 2003.

Paganelli, L., & Paterno, F. (2002). Intelligent analysis of user interactions with Web applications. *In Proceedings of the 7th international Conference on intelligent User interfaces* (San Francisco, California, USA, January 13 - 16, 2002). IUI '02 (pp. 111-118). New York, NY: ACM Press.

Peacock, D. (2002). Statistics, Structures and Satisfied Customers: Using Web Log Data to Improve Site Performance. In D. Bearman & J. Trant (Eds.), *Museums and the Web 2002: Proceedings. Pittsburgh: Archives and Museum Informatics.*

Romero, C., Ventura, S., & Garcia, E. (2008). Data mining in course management systems: Moodle case study and tutorial. *Computer & Education, 51.*

Romero, C., & Ventura, S. (2007). Educational data mining: A survey from 1995 to 2005. *Expert Syst. Appl. 33*(1).

Sen, A., Dacin, P. A., & Pattichis, C. (2006). Current trends in Web data analysis. *Communications of the ACM, 49*(11), 85-91.

Theus, M. (2002). Interactive data visualization using mondrian. *Journal of Statistical Software, 7*(11).

Trant, J. (2006). *Understanding searches of an online contemporary art museum catalogue.* A preliminary study: http://conference.archimuse.com/system/files/trantSearchTermAnalysis061220a.pdf

Wang, W., & Zaiane, O. R. (2002). Clustering Web sessions by sequence alignment. *In Proceedings of the 13th international Workshop on Database and Expert Systems Applications* (September 02 - 06, 2002). DEXA. IEEE Computer Society, Washington, DC, 394-398.

Wheeler, B. C. (2007). Open source 2007: How did this happen? *Educause Review, 39*(4), 12-27.

Zuccala, A., Thelwall, M., Oppenheim, C., & Dhiensa, R. (2008). Web intelligence analyses of digital libraries: A case study of the national electronic library for health (NeLH). *Journal of Documentation, 63*(4), 558-589.

KEY TERMS AND DEFINITIONS

Affinity Analysis: Affinity analysis is one kind of data mining investigation. In this approach, the goal is to see what association rules if any exist, i.e., what actions co-occur. In the context of Web usage, an affinity analysis might yield a rule such as 'if page A is visited, then page D is visited' which might indicate a previously unknown navigational path popular among users. Affinity analysis is also sometime referred to as market basket analysis, as it can provide retailers with information about products that consumers purchase together.

Clustering Analysis: Clustering analysis is another common kind of data mining investigation. Often performed as part of an initial exploration of data, the goal is to see what natural groupings if any exist, i.e., what items in the data are alike. In the context of Web usage, a clustering analysis might reveal that the site's users fall into two distinct groupings: those who use the site's menu and those who go directly to specific pages within the site.

Data Mining: In common parlance, data mining often refers generally to the idea of probing deeply into some mountain of data. This informal use of the term usually says little about the techniques used to do the probing. In contrast, the more formal use of the term refers specifically to using computational techniques to uncover patterns in huge data sets. Here the techniques range widely from statistics to artificial intelligence. The range of data mining investigations is also varied and ever increasing, but some of the better-known approaches include clustering, classification, and affinity analysis.

Data Warehouse: A data warehouse is typically a second home for data. In large corporate or institutional settings, data deemed important for reporting purposes is copied out of various production systems and brought together in the data warehouse where is can be preserved and analyzed. In a university setting, a student data warehouse might contain historical data gathered from a variety of systems (admissions, housing, advising, degree audit, etc.).

Open Content: Open content usually refers to research or educational material that can be distributed and re-used freely. The types of content can range from previously published books and articles to educational software simulations and lesson plans. Key concerns for those who provide or use open content include ensuring that the material can be easily adapted, integrated, and reconfigured in new online settings.

Open Source: Open source is a term used generally for software created by the programmers who allow then allow the source code to be distributed freely. This form of distribution encourages other programmers to take up, modify, and contribute back improvements to the software. There are many variations on the openness involved in open source. In some cases, the code can be re-used in any way. In other cases, use of the code brings with it a requirement that any new system of which it becomes a part will, in turn, become open to all. Due to the aggregate nature of contributions, the major challenges for open source software product development involve organizational coordination and oversight. The community source process brings to open source a model of governance via an institutional consortium.

Open Systems: Many computing devices that people encounter and use nowadays are not isolated. Especially in the Web era, the computing involves systems of software applications, databases, personal computers, servers, etc. all working together. The openness of such system refers in part to their accessibility by users throughout the world, but also to the ease in which the underlying system components are brought together. Rather than try to design entire systems from the top down, it has proven very powerful to design potential system components so that they can share and understand universal protocols and common services – allowing them to be combined in new and unanticipated ways later on.

Web Usage Mining: As a sub-field of data mining, Web usage mining focuses specifically on finding patterns relating to users of a Web based system: who they are, what they tend to do, etc. In contrast, other types of Web data mining (e.g., Web text mining) might focus on finding patterns in the content itself. Web usage mining relies on data captured behind the scene in server logs and databases.

Compilation of References

A guideline to the project management body of knowledge (2000). (3rd ed.). *An American national standard* (ANSI/PMI 99-001-200).

AAHE Assessment Forum. (1992). *Principles for good practice for assessing students' learning.* Washington, DC: American Association for Higher Education.

Abetti, P. A. (1997). Birth and growth of Toshiba's laptop and notebook computers: A case study in Japanese corporate venturing. *Journal of Business Venturing, 12,* 507-529.

Abran, A., Moore, J., Baourque, P., Dupuis, R., & Tripp, L. (2004). *Guide to the software engineering body of knowledge.* Los Alamitos, CA: IEEE Computer Software.

Abras, C., Maloney-Krichmar, D., & Preece, J. (2004). User-centered design. In B. W. Sims (Ed.), *Berkshire encyclopedia of human-computer interaction,* (pp. 763-767). Great Barrington, MA: Berkshire Publishing Group.

Abu-Taieh, E. El-Sheikh A., Abu-Tayeh, J. (2008). Methodologies and approaches in discrete event simulation relay race methodology (RRM): An enhanced life cycle for simulation system development. In *Simulation and modeling: Current technologies and applications.* Hershey, PA: IGI Global Publishing.

Adair, J. (1983). *Effective leadership: A self-development manual.* Adershott, UK: Gower.

Agarwal, R. Nayak, P., Manickam, M., Suresh, P., & Modi, N. (2007). Virtual quality assurance facilitation model.

IEEE International Conference on Global Software Engineering (ICGSE 2007), IEEE Computer Society.

Air NZ has no option: Norris. (22-23 Oct 2005). *Otago Daily Times.*

Alcorn, P. A. (1986). *Social issues in technology: A format for investigation.* Englewood Cliffs, NJ: Prentice-Hall, Inc.

Alter, S. (2000). Same words, different meanings: Are basic IS/IT concepts our self-imposed Tower of Babel? *Communications of the Association for Information Systems, 3*(April), 2-87.

Alter, S., & Ginzberg, M. (1978). Managing uncertainty in MIS implementation. *Sloan Management Review, 20*(1), 23-31.

American Evaluation Association. (2004, July) *Guiding principles for evaluators.* Retrieved April 1, 2008, from http://www.eval.org/Publications/GuidingPrinciples.asp

Amorim, J. A. (2003). A Educação Matemática, a Internet e a Exclusão Digital no Brasil. Educação Matemática em Revista. *SBEM, 10*(14), 58-66.

Amorim, J. A., Pires, D. F., Ropoli, E. A., & Rodrigues, C. C. (2004). O Professor e sua Primeira Página na Internet: Uma Experiência de Uso do Ambiente TelEduc. *Revista Brasileira de Informática na Educação, 12*(1), 37-42.

Anbari, F. (2003). Earned Value Method and Extensions. *Project Management Journal, 34*(4), 12-23.

Anderson, E. S., Dyrhaug, Q. X., & Jessen, S. A. (2002). Evaluation of Chinese projects and comparison with Norwegian projects. *International Journal of Project Management* 20, 601-609.

Anonymous. (2004). CHAOS Chronicles. Retrieved February 5, 2008, from http://www.softwaremag.com/L.cfm?Doc=newsletter/2004-01-15/Standish

Ansoff, H. I. (1980). Strategic issue management. *Strategic Management Journal, 1*(2), 131-148.

Antilla, J. (2004). *Tacit knowledge as a crucial factor in organizations' quality management.* Paper presented at the Quality Conference, Ostrava, Czech Republic.

Antilla, J. (2006). *Modern approach of information society to knowledge work environment for management.* Paper presented at the IEEE International Conference on Industrial Technology (ICTT 2006), Mumbai, India.

Antilla, J., Savola, K., Kajava, J., & Lindfors, J. (2007) *Fulfilling the needs for information security awareness and learning in information society.* Paper presented at The 6th Annual Security Conference, Las Vegas.

Archer, N. (2006). A Classification of Communities of Practice. In Coakes, E. & Clarke, S. (Eds.), *Encyclopedia of communities of practice in information and knowledge management* (pp. 21-29). Hershey, PA: IGI Global Publishing.

Arnun, E. (2004). Automotive Warranties. *Warranty Week,* April 13th, 2004-07-29

Artto, K. (2000). What do you manage: Processes or personnel's competencies for managing the processes? *Project Management, 6*(1), 4-9.

Athey, T., & Orth, M. (1999). Emerging competency methods for the future. *Human Resource Management, 38*(3), 215-225.

Atkinson, R. (1999). Project management: cost, time and quality, two best guesses and a phenomenon, it's time to accept other success criteria. *International Journal of Project Management, 17*(6), 337-342.

Austin R., Nolan R., & Cotteler, M. (1999). *Cisco Systems, Inc.: Implementing ERP.* Harvard Business School case no. 9-699-022, Boston: Harvard Business School Publishing.

Australian Universities Teaching Committee (AUTC). (2003). *Information and communication technologies and their role in flexible learning.* Retrieved March 22, 2008 from http://www.learningdesigns.uow.edu.au/

Avison, D. E., & Myers, M. D. (1995). Information technology and anthropology: An anthropological perspective on IT and organizational culture. *Information Technology & People, 8*(3), 43-57.

Babcock, D., & Morse, L. (2007). *Managing engineering and technology.* Upper Saddle River, NJ: Prentice Hall.

Baccarini, D. (2001). The future of project management. *Australian Project Manager, 20*(2), 28-9.

Bailey, J. P., & Bakos, J. Y. (1997). An exploratory study of the emerging role of electronic intermediaries. *International Journal of Electronic Commerce, 1*(3), 7-21.

Bailey, R. W. (1989). *Human performance engineering: Using human factors/ergonomics to achieve computer system usability* (2nd ed.). Englewood Cliffs, NJ: Prentice-Hall, Inc.

Bajaj, A. (2006, Fall). Large scale requirements modeling: An industry analysis, a model and a teaching case. *Journal of Information Systems Education, 17*(3), 327-339. Retrieved September 21, 2007, from Proquest database.

Baker, E. R. (2001). Which way, SQA? *IEEE Software,* January/February 2001, 16-18.

Balci, O. (2003). Verification, validation, and certification of modeling and simulation applications. *ACM Transactions on Modeling and Computer Simulation, 11*(4), 352–377.

Balci, O. (1994). Validation, verification, and testing techniques throughout the life cycle of a simulation study. *Annals of operations research, 53*, 215-220

Balci, O. (1995). Principles and techniques of simulation validation, verification, and testing. In C. Alexopoulos, K. Kang, W. R. Lilegdon, & D. Goldsman, (Eds.), *Proceedings of the 1995 Winter Simulation Conference.* (pp. 147-154). New York: ACM Press.

Balci, O. (1997, December 7-10). Verification, validation and accreditation of simulation models. In S. Andradóttir, K. J. Healy, D. H. Withers, & B. L. Nelson (Eds.), *Proceedings of the Winter Simulation Conference* (pp. 135-141), Atlanta, Georgia, USA.

Baldwin, R. (1998, Winter). Technology's impact on faculty life and work. *New Directions for Teaching and Learning, 76* , 7-21.

Banco Central do Brasil (2006). Evolution of accountable values of financial institutions in Brazil. Retrieved jun,13, 2006, from http://www.bcb.gov.br/fis/TOP50/port/Top502005030P.asp

Barczak, G., & McDonough, E. F. III. (2003). Leasing global product development teams. *Research Technology Management, 46*(6), 14-18.

Barki, H., Rivard, S., & Talbot, J. (1993). Toward an assessment of software development risk. *Journal of Management Information System, 10*(2), 203-225.

Barkley, B. (2008). *Project management in new product development.* New York: McGraw-Hill.

Barnard, C. I. (1938). *The functions of the executive.* Cambridge, MA: Harvard University Press.

Barnes, M. (2000, May 22-25). A better model for project management in the 21st century. *Congress 2000. 15th IPMA World Congress on Project Management.* AIPM. Zurich, Switzerland: International Project Management Association.

Barnes, M. (2002). A long term view of project management - Its past and its likely future. *16th World Congress on Project Management*, Berlin.

Barr, R. B., & Tagg, J. (1995, November/December). *From teaching to learning: A new paradigm for undergraduate education.* Change, (pp. 13-24).

Barua, A., Kriebel, C. H., & Mukhopadhyay, T. (1995). Information technologies and business value: An analytic and empirical investigation. *Information Technology Research, 6*(1), 3-24.

BaseCamp. http://www.basecamphq.com/

Bashein, B., & Markus, M. L. (1997). A credibility equation for IT specialists. *Sloan Management Review,* 35-44.

Baskerville, R. L., & Pries-Heje, J. (2001). A multiple-theory analysis of a diffusion of information technology case. *Information Systems Journal, 11*, 181-212.

Bass, B. M. (1985). *Leadership and performance beyond expectations.* New York: Free Press.

Bass, B.M. (1990). From transactional to transformational leadership: Learning to share the vision. *Organisational Dynamics, 18*(3), 19-31.

Bassellier, G., Benbasat, I., & Reich, B. H. (2003). The influence of business managers' IT competence on championing. *Information Technology Research, 14*(4), 317-337.

Bassellier, G., Reich, B., & Benbasat, I. (2001). Information technology competence of business managers: A definition and research model. *Journal of Management Information Systems, 17*(4), 159-182.

Bates, A. W. (1999). *Managing technological change.* San Francisco: Jossey-Bass.

Bates, A. W., Bobrow, D. G., Ernst, R., & Hutch, D. (2003). *Intermediate evaluation of the ETH world programme: Report of the peer review committee submitted to the executive board of the ETH Zurich.*

Baumann, T., Cruse, A., Poli, F., & Asum, H. (2002). The evolution of PM: Status and trends. *16th IPMA World Congress on Project Management*, Berlin. Notes: PowerPoint Presentation.

Beale, R. (2007). Slanty design. *Communications of the ACM, 50*(1), 21-24.

Beck, J. C., & Wade, M. (2006). *The kids are alright: How the gamer generation is changing the workplace.* Boston: Harvard Business School Press.

Behn, R. D. (2003). Why measure performance? Different purposes require different measures. *Public Administration Review, 63*(5), 586-606.

Belbin, R. M. (1986). *Management teams.* London: Heinemann.

Bellamy, A. (2007). Exploring the influence of new technology planning and implementation on the perceptions of new technology effectiveness. *The Journal of Technology Studies, 33* (1), 32-40.

Benaroch, M. (2001). Option-based management of technology investment risk. *IEEE Transactions on Engineering Management, 48*(4), 428-445.

Benaroch, M., & Kauffman, R. (1999). A case for using real options pricing analysis to evaluate information technology project investments. *Information Technology Research, 10*(1), 70-87.

Benbasat, I., Dexter, A., & Mantha, R. (1980). Impact of organizational maturity on information system skill needs. *MIT Quarterly, 4*(1), 21-34.

Benbasat, I., Goldstein, D. K., & Mead, M. (1987). The case research strategy in studies of information technology. *MIT Quarterly, 5*(4), 369-386.

Bennis, W. (2003). *On becoming a leader.* Cambridge, MA: Perseus Publishing.

Bennis, W., & Nanus, B. (1985). *Leaders: The strategies for taking charge.* New York: Harper and Row.

Berendt, B., & Spiliopoulou, M. (2000). Analysis of navigation behaviour in web sites integrating multiple information systems. *The VLDB Journal 9*(1).

Bernstein, P. (1998). *Against the gods: The remarkable story of risk.* New York: John Wiley.

Berny, J., & Townsend, P. R. (1993). Macrosimulation of project risks – A practical way forward. *International Journal of Project Management, 11*(4), 201-208.

Bersoff, E., & Davis, M. A. (1991). Impact of life cycle models on software. *Communication of the Association for Computing Machinery, 34*, 104-117.

Best, R. J. (2004). *Market-based management: Strategies for growing customer value and profitability.* Upper Saddle River, NJ: Pearson Education Inc.

Besterfield, D. H., Besterfield-Michna, C. B., & Besterfield-Sacre, M. (2003). *Total quality management* (3rd ed.). Upper Saddle River, NJ: Pearson Prentice Hall.

Besterfield, H. D. (2004). *Quality control,* 7th ed. Upper Saddle River, NJ: Prentice Hall.

Beyono-Davies, P. (1995). Information systems 'failure': the case of the London ambulance service's computer aided despatch system. *European Journal of Information Systems, 4*, 171-184.

Bigelow, D. (2002). The reality of virtual project management. *PMI Seminars and Symposium Proceedings AIPM (CDRom).* USA: PMI.

Binder, M., Gust, P., & Clegg, B. (2007). The importance of collaborative frontloading in automotive supply networks. *Journal of Manufacturing Technology Management, 19*(3), 315-331.

Birrell, N. D., & Ould, M. A. (1985). *A practical handbook for software development.* UK: Cambridge University Press.

Black, E., & Dehoney, J. (2008, January). *Opening the door: Academic Technology and Library Collaborations at Ohio State.* Paper presented at the annual meeting of the Educause Learning Initiative (ELI), San Antonio, TX.

Black, H. (2001). U.S. aerospace risk analysis survey. *Journal of Cost Analysis & Management*, Winter issue.

Blaikie, N. (2000). *Designing social research.* Cambridge: Polity.

Blake, D. (2004). Your business needs to change to succeed with embedded systems. *Society of Automotive Engineers*, 21-0092.

Blake, R. R., & Mouton, S. J. (1978). *The new managerial grid.* Houston, TX: Gulf.

Block, R. (1983). *The Politics of projects.* Yourdon, NY.

Bodie, Z., Kane, A., & Marcus, A. J. (1999). *Investments* (4th ed.). Irwin / McGraw-Hill.

Boehm, B. (1988). A spiral model of software development and enhancement. *IEEE, May.*

Boehm, B. (2006). *A view of 20th and 21st century software engineering.* Paper presented at the International Conference on Software Engineering.

Boehm, B. W. (1991). Software risk management: Principle and practices. *IEEE Software, 8*(1), 32-41.

Boehm, B., & Basili, V. R. (2001). Software defect reduction top 10 list. *Computer, 34*(1), 135-137.

Boland Jr., R. J. (2002). In M. D. Myers & D. Avison (Eds.), *Qualitative research in information systems: A reader* (pp. 225-240). London: Sage Publications.

Bowen, J. (2002). Weaving the museum web: The virtual library museums pages. *Program: Electronic Library and Information Systems, 36*(4), 236–252.

Bowen, J., & Filippini-Fantoni, S. (2004). Personalization and the web from a museum perspective. In D. Bearman & J. Trant (Eds.), *Museums and the Web 2004* (pp. 63-78). Toronto, Canada: Archives & Museum Informatics.

Boyatzis, R. E. (1982). *The Competent Manager: A model for effective performance.* New York: John Wiley & Sons Inc.

Bplans (2006). *Performing a SWOT analysis.* Retrieved January 12, 2006, from http://www.bplans.com/ma/swotanalysis.cfm

Bracke, P. J. (2004). Web usage mining at an academic health sciences library: an exploratory study. *Journal of the Medical Library Association, 92*(4), 421-428.

Brandenburger, A. M., & Stuart, H. W. (1996). Value-based business strategy. *Journal of Economics and Management Strategy, 5*(1), 5-24.

Branscomb, L. (2000). *Managing technical risk.* US Department of Commerce, NIST GCR 00-787.

Bransford, J. D. (1979). *Human cognition: Learning, understanding and remembering* (pp. 6-9). Belmont, CA: Wadsworth Publishing.

Briggs-Myers, I. (1992). *Gifts differing.* Palo Alto, CA: Consulting Psychologists Press.

Brochta, M. (2002). Project success - What are the criteria and whose opinion counts. *PMI Seminars and Symposium Proceedings, AIPM* (CDRom). USA: PMI.

Broh, R. A. (1982). *Managing quality for higher profits.* New York: McGraw-Hill.

Brown, K. (2000). Developing project management skills: A service learning approach. *Project Management Journal, 31*(4), 53-58.

Brown, S. A., Chervany, N., L., & Reinicke, B. A. (2007). What matters when introducing new information technology. *Communications of the ACM, 50*(9), 91-96

Brown, S. L., & Eisenhardt, K. M. (1995). Product development: past research, present findings, and future directions. *Academy of Management Review, 20*(2), 343-78.

Brownbill, J., & Peacock, D. (2007, April 11-14). Audiences, visitors, and users: Reconceptualising users of museum online content and services. *Museums and the Web*, San Francisco, CA. Toronto, Canada: Archives and Museum Informatics.

Bryce, D. (2005). *Tao-Te-Ching / Lao-Tzu.* New York: Gramercy Books.

Brynjolfsson, E. (1993). The productivity paradox of information technology. *Communications of the ACM, 35*(12), 66-78.

Brynjolfsson, E., & Hitt, L. M. (1996). Productivity, business profitability and consumer surplus: Three different measures of information technology value. *MIT Quarterly.*

Brynjolfsson, E., & Hitt, L. M. (2003). Computing productivity: Firm level evidence. *Review of Economics & Statistics, 85*(4), 793-809.

Buczkowski, J., Means, & M. F. (2004). Vehicle electronics to digital mobility: The next generation of convergence. *Product Insider, 27*, November 24th.

Bunn, M., Savage, G., & Holloway, B. (2002). Stakeholder analysis for multi-sector innovations. *Journal of Business & Industrial Marketing, 17*(2/3), 181-203.

Burrell, G., & Morgan, G. (2005). *Sociological paradigms and organisational analysis: Elements of the sociology of corporate life*. Ardershot: Ashgate Publishing Limited.

Bussen, W., & Myers, M. (1997). Executive information system failure: A New Zealand case study. *Journal of Information Technology, 12*, 145-153.

Bygstad, B. (2005). Managing the dynamics of mutual adaptation of technology and organisation in IS development projects. *Software Process: Improvement and Practice (SPIP), 10*(3), 341-353.

Cadle J., & Yeates D. (2004). *Project management for information systems*, 4/E. NJ: Prentice Hall.

Caldwell, B. (6 July 1998). Andersen sued on R/3. *InformationWeek*.

Campus Computing Project, see http://www.campuscomputing.net

Canfield, J. (2005). *The success principles: How to get from where you are to where you want to be*. New York: Harper Collins Publishers Inc.

Cantu, C. (1997). *Virtual teams*. CSWT Papers, Center for the Study of Work Teams, University of North Texas. (http://www.workteams.unt.edu/Literature/paper-ccantu.html). Retrieved 27 Feb 2008.

Carlotto, M. S. (2002). A síndrome de Burnout e o trabalho docente. *Psicologia em Estudo, 7*(1), 21-29. ISSN 1413-7372. Retrieved December 30, 2007, from http://www.scielo.org/

Carlson, P. (2007, September 4). The flop heard round the world. *Washington Post* (p. C01). Retrieved March 29, 2008, from http://www.washingtonpost.com/wp-dyn/content/article/2007/09/03/AR2007090301419.html?sub=new

Casson, M. C. (1994). Why are firms hierarchical? *Journal of Economics of Business, 1*(1), 47-77.

Castellano, J. F., Rosenzweig, K., & Harper, A. R. (2004). How corporate culture impacts unethical distortion of financial numbers: Managing by Objectives and Results could be counterproductive and contribute to a climate that may lead to distortion of the system, manipulation of accounting figures, and, ultimately, unethical behavior. *Management accounting quarterly*. Retrieved on 13 November, 2006.

Catchpole, P. (1986). Requirements for a successful methodology in information systems design. *Data Processing, 28*(4), 207.

Cattell, R. B., Eber, H. W., & Tatsuoka, M. M. (1970). *Handbook for the 16PF*. Illinois: IPAT.

Cavaye, A., & Cragg, P. (1995). Factors contributing to the success of customer oriented interorganizational systems. *Journal of Strategic Information Systems, 4*(1), 13-30.

CCTA (1995). *An introduction to managing project risk*. London: HMSO.

CCTA (1997). *The management of risk*. Central Computer and Communications Agency. Retrieved November 13, 1997, from http://www.open.gov.uk/ccta/pubcat/riskkey.htm

CCTA (2001). *Managing successful projects with PRINCE2*. Central Computer and Communication Agency, UK.

CENP (2007). *Programa de Formação Continuada "Teia do Saber" - 2007, Capacitação Descentralizada Mediante Contratação de Instituições de Ensino Superior, Projeto Básico*. Portal do Governo do Estado de São Paulo, Secretaria de Estado da Educação, Coordenadoria de Estudos e Normas Pedagógicas. Retrieved December 30, 2007 from http://cenp.edunet.sp.gov.br/Forcont2007/

Cerbin, W. (1993). Fostering a culture of teaching as scholarship. *The Teaching Professor, 7*(3), 1-2.

Cerbin, W. (1994). The course portfolio as a tool for continuous improvement of teaching and learning. *Journal on Excellence in College Teaching, 5*(1), 95-105.

Chandler, A. D. J. (1990). *Sale and scope - The dynamics of industrial capitalism.* London: Harvard University Press.

Chandler, A. D. J. (1997). Strategy and structure - Chapters in the history of the industrial enterprise. In N. J. Foss (Ed.), *Resourses firms and strategies* (pp. 40-51). New York: Oxford University Press.

Chang, T., Wysk, R. A., & Wang, H. (1998). *Computer-aided manufacturing* (2nd ed.). Upper Saddle River, NJ: Prentice Hall.

Charette, R. N. (1989). *Software engineering risk analysis and management.* New York: McGraw-Hill.

Charette, R. N. (2005). Why software fails. *IEEE Spectrum,* September, 2005, *42.*

Chase, M., Macfadyen, L., Reeder, K., & Roche J. (2002). Intercultural hard technologies meet soft skills. *First Monday* 7(8). Retrieved June 21, 2005 from http://firstmonday.org/issues/issue7_8/chase/

Checkland, P., & Scholes, J. (1999). *Soft systems methodology in action.* John Wiley & Sons.

Cheetham, G., & Chivers, G. (1998). The reflective (and competent) practitioner: A model of professional competence which seeks to harmonize the reflective practitioner and competence-based approaches. *Journal of European Industrial Training, 22*(7), 267-276.

Chen, C., Hsieh, Y., & Hsu, S. (2007). Mining learner profile utilizing association rule for web-based learning diagnosis. *Expert Syst. Appl., 33*(1).

Chen, M. (1994). Sun Tzu's strategic thinking and contemporary business. *Business Horizons, 37*(2), 42.

Cheng, M.-I., Dainty, A. R. J., & Moore, D. R. (2005). What makes a good project manager. *Human Resources Management Journal, 15*(1), 25-37.

Chevalier, R. (May/June, 2003). Updating the behavior engineering model. *Performance and Improvement, 42*(5).

Chin, G. (2004). *Agile project management.* New York: AMACOM.

Chin, W. W., & Gopal, A. (1995). Adoption intention in GSS: Relative importance of beliefs. *The Data Base for Advances in Information Systems, 26*(2 & 3), 42-64.

Chittiser, C., & Haimes, Y. (1993). Risk associated with software development: A holistic framework for assessment and management. *IEEE Transactions on Systems, Man and Cybernetics, 23*(3), 701-723.

Chow, T. W. (1985). *Software quality assurance: A practical approach.* Silver Spring, MD: IEEE Computer Society Press.

Christensen, M. J., & Thayer, R. H. (2001). *The project manager's guide to software engineering best practices.* Los Alamitos, CA: IEEE Computer Society.

Clark, D., & Redmond, M. (1982). *Small group instructional diagnosis: Final report.* University of Washington, Seattle. FIPSE. (ERIC Document Reproduction Service. No. ED 217 954).

Clark, R. E. (1983). Reconsidering research on learning from media. *Review of Educational Research, 53*(4), 445-459.

Clayton, M. J. (Dec 1997). Delphi: A technique to harness expert opinion for critical decision-making tasks in education. *Eduational Psychology, 17*(4), 373-386.

Clegg, S. R., Kornberger, M., & Rhodes, C. (Mar 2004). Noise, parasites and translation: Theory and practice in management consulting. *Management Learning, 35*(1), 31-44.

Cleland, D. I., & King, W. R. (Ed.), (1988). *Project management handbook* (2nd Ed.). John Wiley.

Clemons, E. K., & Hitt, L. M. (2004). Poaching and the misappropriation of information: Transaction risks of information exchange. *Journal of Management Information Technology, 21*(2), 87-108.

Clemons, E. K., & Row, M. C. I. (1992). Information technology and industrial cooperation: The changing economics of coordination and ownership. *Journal of Management Information Technology, 9*(2), 9-29.

Coakes, E., & Elliman, T. (1999). The role of stakeholders in managing change. *Communications of the AIS, 2*(4).

Cohen, M. D., & March, J. G. (1974). *Leadership and ambiguity: The American college president.* Princeton, NJ: The Carnegie Foundation for the Advancement of Training.

Coit, D., Thompson, J. E., & Vogt, N. (2005). Correlating field requirements to accelerated life testing for vehicle electronics. *Society of Automotive Engineers,* 2005-01-1492.

Collins, J. (2001). *Good to great.* New York: Harper-Collins.

Computergram International, July 20, 1998. Article's URL <a href="http://findarticles.com/p/articles/mi_m0CGN/is_n143/ai_20920858">

Conner, D. R. (1993). *Managing at the speed of change.* New York: Random House.

Conrad, J., & Sirel, Y. (2005, October). Learning project management skills in senior design courses. In *Proceedings of the 35th ASEE/IEEE Frontiers in Education Conference,* Indianapolis, Indiana.

Cooper, R. B. & Zmud, R. W. (1990). Information technology implementation research: a technological diffusion approach. *Management Science, 36*(2), 123-139.

Cooper, R. G. (2007). Seven "principles" of innovation-a lack of focus. *Strategic Direction, 23*(1), 38-40.

Cooper, R. G., & Edgett, S. C. (2008). Maximizing productivity in product innovation. *Research-Technology Management,* March-April, (pp. 47-58).

Copeland, T., Koller, T., & Murrin, J. (2000). *valuation: Measuring and managing the value of companies* (3rd ed.). New York: John Wiley & Sons.

Corbitt, K. J., & Peszynski, B. J. (2006). Politics, complexity, and systems implementation: Critically exposing power. *Social Science Computer Review, 24*(3), 326-341.

Cotteller, M., Austin, R. D., & Nolan, R. L. (1998). *Cisco System, Inc.: Implementing ERP.* Boston: Harvard Business School Publishing.

Cox, M. D., Grasha, A., & Richlin, L. (1997, March). *Town meeting. Between teaching model and learning model: Adapting and adopting bit by bit.* Lilly Atlantic Regional Conference.

Crawford, L. (1998a, June 10 - 13). *Project management competence for strategy realization.* Paper presented at the Strategy and Startup: Proceedings of the 14th World Congress on Project Management, Ljubljana.

Crawford, L. (2001). *Project management competence: The value of standards.* Uxbridge, UK: Brunel University.

Crawford, L. (2005). Senior management perceptions of project management competence. *International Journal of Project Management, 23*, 7-16.

Crawford, L. H. (2003). Assessing and developing the project management competence of individuals. In J. R. Turner, (Ed.), *People in project management.* Aldershot, UK: Gower.

Cua, F. C., & Garrett, T. C. (in press). The role of business case development in the Diffusion of Innovations theory for enterprise information systems. In B. Cameron & P. Weaver (Eds.), *Encyclopedia of information technology, accounting, and finance.* Hershey, PA: IGI Publishing.

Cua, F. C., & Theivananthampillai, P. (2006, 29 Jun - 2 Jul 2006). *Value management of sourcing decisions: The cost of ownership in performance management systems.* Paper presented at the Pacific Asian Consortium for International Business Education & Research (PACIBER) 2006, Cebu, Philippines.

Cummings, T. G. (1978). Self-regulating work groups: A socio-technical synthesis. *The Academy of Management Review, 3*(3), 625-634.

Cunningham, M. (1999). It's all about the business. *Information, 13*(3), 83.

Daft, R. L. (1978). A dual-core model of organizational innovation. *Academy of Management Journal, 21*, 193-210.

Dagger, D., O'Connor, A., Lawless, S., Walsh, E., & Wade, V. P. (2007). Service-oriented e-learning platforms: From monolithic systems to flexible services. *IEEE Internet Computing, Institute of Electrical and Electronics Engineers, 11*(3), 28-35.

Dainoff, M. J., & Dainoff, M. H. (1986). *People and productivity.* Toronto, Ont: Holt, Rinehart, and Winston of Canada, Limited.

Damanpour, F. (1991). Organisational innovations: A meta-analysis of effects of determinants and moderators. *Academy of Management Journal, 34,* 555-590.

Damanpour, F. (1992). Organisation size and innovation. *Organization Studies, 13,* 375-402.

Daradoumis, T., Martinez-Mones, A., & Xhafa, F. (2006). A layered framework for evaluating online collaborative learning interactions. *Int. J. Hum.-Comput. Stud., 64*(7).

Davenport, T. H. (1993). *Process innovation: Reengineering work through information technology.* Boston: Harvard Business School Press.

Davenport, T. H., & Short, J. E. (1990). The new industrial engineering: Information technology and business process redesign. *Sloan Management Review,* 11-27.

Davenport, T., Harris J. G., & Cantrell, S. (2004). Enterprise systems and ongoing process change. *Business Process Management Journal, 10*(1), 16-26.

Davern, M. J., & Kauffman, R. J. (2000). Discovering potential and realizing value from information technology investments. *Journal of Management Information Technology, 16*(4), 121-144.

Davidson, E. (2006, March). A technological frames perspective on information technology and organizational change. *The Journal of Applied Behavioral Science, 42*(1), 23-40. [Electronic version] Retrieved September 10, 2007, from Proquest database.

Davis, F. D. (1986). *A technology acceptance model for empirically testing new end-user information systems: Theory and results.* Unpublished Doctoral dissertation, Massachusetts Institute of Technology.

Davis, F. D., Bagozzi, R. P., & Warshaw, P. R. (1989). User acceptance of computer technology: A comparison of two theoretical models. *Management Science, 35,* 982-1003.

Davis, G. (1982). Strategies for information requirements determination. *IBM Systems Journal, 2*(1), 4-29.

Davis, G. B., Lee, A. S., Nickles, K. R., Chatterjee, S., Hartung, R., & Wu, Y. (1992). Diagnosis of an information system failure: A framework and interpretive process. *Information & Management, 23*(5), 293-319.

Davis, J., & Cable, J. (2006). *Positive workplace: Enhancing individual and team productivity.* Retrieved July 21, 2007, from http://www.allpm.com/print.php?sid=1634

Davis, S. K., & Lippert, M. (2006). A conceptual model integrating trust into planned change activities to enhance technology adoption behavior. *Journal of Information Science, 32*(5), 434-448.

Davis, W. S., & Yen, D. C. (1999). *The information system consultant's handbook: System analysis and design.* Boca Raton, FL: CRC Press.

DCAMS (1996). *Strategic asset management: Project risk management guidelines, risk management section.* Department of Contract and Management Services, Western Australia.

De Lorenzi, M. (2004). *Report – ETH Zurich Study Tour.* Retrieved from ETH World Web site: http://www.ethworld.ethz.ch/events/explore/study_trip/Report_Study_Tour_ETHZ_050207.pdf

De Lorenzi, M., & Baur, M. (2004). *Live broadcasts.* Retrieved from ETH World Web pages: http://www.ethworld.ethz.ch/technologies/live_broadcast

De Lorenzi, M., & Baur, M. (2005). *sipETH: Internet telefonie for the ETH Zurich.* Retrieved from ETH World: http://www.ethworld.ethz.ch/technologies/sipeth

De Lorenzi, M., & Baur, M. (2005). *Web Services an der ETH Zürich.* Retrieved from ETH World Web pages: http://www.ethworld.ethz.ch/technologies/web_services

De Lorenzi, M., & Wunden, T. (2006). *tRoom - Collaboration space for team.* Retrieved from ETH World

Web Pages: http://www.ethworld.ethz.ch/technologies/tRoom

Dearnaley, M. (2005). Air NZ engineers plead for their jobs. *The New Zeland Herald.*

Dede, C. (2005). Planning for neomillennial learning styles. *EDUCAUSE Quarterly, 28*(1). Available at http://www.educause.edu/ir/library/pdf/EQM0511.pdf

DeGarmo, E. P., Black, J. T., & Kohser, R. A. (1999). *Materials and processes in manufacturing* (8th ed.). New York: John Wiley & Sons

Dery, K., Hall, R., Harley, B., & Wright, C. (2006). Management reactions to technological change: The example of enterprise resource planning. *The Journal of Applied Behavioral Science, 42*(1), 58-75.

Dettmer, H. W. (2003). *Strategic navigation: A systems approach to business strategy.* Milwaukee, WI: ASQ Quality Press.

Dietz, T. (1987). Methods for analyzing data from Delphi panels: Some evidence from a forecasting study. *Technological Forecasting and Social Change, 31*(1), 79-85.

Distance Education Learning Environment Survey. Retrieved April 15, 2008 from http://www.tcet.unt.edu/insight/ilib/deles/actual/

DoD (1988). *Military standard, defense system software development.* DoD-STD-2167A.Washington, DC: Department of Defense.

Dominick, P., Aronson, Z., & Lechler, T. (2007). Transformational leadership and project success. In R. R. Reilly (Ed.), *The human side of project leadership,* (pp. 1-30). Newton Square, PA: Project Management Institute.

Downs Jr, G. W., & Mohr, L. B. (1976). Conceptual issues in the study of innovation. *Administrative Science Quarterly, 21*(4), 700-714.

Drejer, I. (2004). Identifying innovation in surveys of services: A Schumpeterian perspective. *Research Policy, 33*(3), 551-562.

Drucker, P. F. (1995). *Managing in a time of great change.* Oxford, UK: Butterworth-Heinemann.

Drummond, H. (1996). The politics of risk: Trials and tribulations of the taurus project. *Journal of Information Technology, 11,* 347-357.

Drummond, H., & Hodgson, J. (2003, September). The chimpanzees' tea party: A new metaphor for project managers. *Journal of Information Technology, 18*(3), 151. Routledge, Ltd. [Electronic version] Retrieved March 29, 2008, from Academic Search Complete database.

DSMC (1989). Risk management, concepts and guidance. FT. Belvoir, VA: Defense Systems Management College.

Duarte, D. L., & Tennant Snyder, N. (2001). *Mastering virtual teams: Strategies, tools, and techniques that succeed,* second edition. San Francisco: Jossey-Bass.

Dubash, M. (2005). *Moore's Law is dead, says Gordon Moore.* Retrieved April 20, 2008, from http://www.techworld.com/opsys/news/index.cfm?NewsID=3477

Dulebohn, J. H., Liang, X., & Marler, J. H. (2006). Training and effective employee information technology use. *Journal of Management, 32*(5), 721-743.

Dulevicz, V., Turner, J. R., & Müller, R. (2006). *Assessment of project managers using the leadership dimensions questionnaire: An international study* (Henley Working Paper Series). Henley Management College, Henley-on-Thames, UK.

Dulewicz, & Higgs, M. (2005). Assessing leadership styles and organisational context. *Journal of Managerial Psychology, 20*(1), 105-123.

Dulewicz, V., & Higgs, M. J. (2000). Emotional intelligence: a review and evaluation study. *Journal of Managerial Psychology, 15*(4), 341–368.

Dvir, D., Sadeh, A., & Malach-Pines, A. (2006). Project and project managers: The relationship between project manager's personality, project types and project success. *Project Management Journal, 37*(5), 36-48.

Ebersbach, A., Glaser, M., & Heigl, R. (2006). *Wiki Web collaboration.* Berlin: Springer.

Edgerton, R., Hutchings, P., & Quinlan, P. (1991). *The teaching portfolio: Capturing the scholarship in teaching.* Washington, DC: American Association for Higher Education.

Education Commons. (2008). Retrieved April 16, 2008 from http://www.educationcommons.org/commons/

EDUCAUSE *Core Data Project,* see http://www.educause.edu/coredata/

EDUCAUSE. (2006). *Student guide to evaluating information technology on campus.* Retrieved February 22, 2008 from http://www.educause.edu/consumerguide/

Edwards, C. D. (1968). The meaning of quality. *Quality Progress,* October 1968.

Egea, K. (2006). Relationship building in virtual teams: An academic case study. *Informing Science and IT Education Joint Conference.* (p. 81). Central Queensland University, Rockhampton, Australia.

Eisenhardt, K. M. (1989). Building theories from case study research. *Academy of Management Review, 14*(4), 532-550.

Ellul, J. (1967). *The technological society.* New York: Knopf.

Elmaghraby, S. E., & Herroelen, W. S. (1980). On the measurement of complexity in activity networks. *European Journal of Operational Research, 5,* 223-234.

Elrod, P. D., & Tippett, D. D. (2002). The "death valley" of change. *Journal of Organizational Change Management, 15*(3), 273-291. Retrieved September 8, 2007, from Proquest database.

El-Sabaa, S. (2001). The skills and career path of an effective project manager. *International Journal of Project Management, 19*(1), 1-7.

Ely, D. P. (1990). Conditions that facilitate the implementation of educational technology innovations. *Journal of Research on Computing in Education, 23*(2), 298-305.

Ely, D. P. (1999). Conditions that facilitate the implementation of educational technology innovations. *Educational Technology, 34*(6), 23-27.

Essinger, J., & Gay, C. L. (2000). *Inside outsourcing.* London: Nicholas Brealey.

Ettlie, J. E. (1980). Adequacy of stage models for decision on adoption of innovation. *Psychological Reports, 46,* 991-995.

Eurydice (2008). *Eurybase: The information database on education systems in Europe: The education system in Turkey.* Retrieved April 23, 2008, from http://www.eurydice.org/portal/page/portal/Eurydice/

Evans, J. R., & Lindsay, W. M. (1993). *The management and control of quality.* St. Paul, MN: West Publishing Company.

Evans, P. B., & Wurster, T. S. (2000). *Blown to bits - How the economics of information transforms strategy.* Boston: Harvard Business School Press.

Evaristo, R., & van Fenema, P. C. (1999). A typology of project management: Emergence and evolution of new forms. *International Journal of Project Management, 17*(5), 275-281.

Ewusi-Mensah, K. (1997). Critical issues in abandoned information systems development projects. *Communications of the ACM, 40*(9), 74-80.

Ewusi-Mensah, K. (1997). Critical issues in abandoned information systems development projects. *Communications of the Association for Computing Machinery, 40*(9), 74-80.

Ewusi-Mensah, K., & Przasnyski, Z. (1991). On Information systems project abandonment: An exploratory study of organizational practices. *MIS Quarterly,* Mar, 67-85.

Ewusi-Mensah, K., & Przasnyski, Z. (1995). Learning from abandoned information systems development projects. *Journal of Information Technology,* (10), 3-14.

Fairley, R. E. (1994). Risk management for software projects. *IEEE Software, 11*(May), 57-67.

FAPESP (2008). *TIDIA - Programa de Tecnologia da Informação no Desenvolvimento da Internet Avançada.* Portal da Fundação de Amparo à Pesquisa do Estado de

São Paulo. Retrieved May 01, 2008 from http://www.tidia.fapesp.br/portal.

Febraban, F. d. B. B.-. (2006). *Asset ranking of Brazilian banks.* Retrieved June, 13, from http://www.febraban.org.br/Arquivo/Servicos/Dadosdosetor/2006/item13.asp

Feeny, D., Ives, B., & Piccoli, G. (2003). Creating and sustaining IT-enabled competitive advantage. In J. N. Luftman (Ed.), *Competing in the Information Age* (2nd ed., pp. 107-136). UK: Oxford University Press.

Feldman, K. A., & Newcomb, T. M. (1969). *Impact of college on students.* San Francisco: Jossey-Bass.

Feldman, S. (2005). Quality Assurance: Much More than Testing. *ACM Queue,* February 2005, (pp. 27-29).

Fichman, R. G., & Kemerer, C. F. (1993). Adoption of software engineering process innovations: The case of object orientation. *Sloan Management Review, 34,* 7-12.

Fiedler, F. E. (1967). *A theory of leadership effectiveness.* New York: McGraw-Hill.

Fitzgerald, B. (1998). An empirical investigation into the adoption of systems development methodologies. *Information & Management, 34*(6), 317.

Fitzgerald, K. M., Rivenbark, W. C., & Schelin, S. H. (2003). Analyzing information technology investments in state government. *Social Science Computer Review, 21*(4), 497-505.

Fleming, Q., & Koppelman, J. (2005). *Earned value project management,* 3rd Edition. Newtowns Square, PA: Project Management Institute.

Flowers, S. (1996). *Software failure: Management failure.* Chichester, UK: John Wiley.

Foo, S. W., & Muruganantham, A. (2000, November 12-15). Software risk assessment model. In *Proceedings of IEEE ICMIT 2000 International Conference on Management of Innovation,* (pp. 536-544). Singapore.

Ford, D. N., & Sobek, D. K. (2005). Adapting real options to new product development by modeling the second Toyota paradox. *IEEE Transactions on Engineering Management, 52*(2), 175-185.

Foreman, M. (2007). *Fonterra to offshore IT jobs to India?* Retrieved 19 Nov 2007, from http://www.zdnet.com.au/news/software/soa/Fonterra-to-offshore-IT-jobs-to-India-/0,130061733,339274389,00.htm

Forker, L. B. (1997). Factors affecting supplier quality performance. *Journal of Operations Management, 15*(4), 243-269.

Forrest, A. (1990). *Time will tell: Portfolio-assisted assessment of general education.* Washington, DC: American Association for Higher Education.

Foti, R. (2001). Forecasting the future of project management. *PM Network, 15*(10), 28-31.

Fowler, A., & Gilfillan, M. (2003, December). A framework for stakeholder integration in higher education information systems projects. *Technology Analysis & Strategic Management, 15*(4), 467-489. [Electronic version] Retrieved February 5, 2008, from Academic Search Complete database.

Frame, D. (1999). *Building project management competence: Building key skills for individuals, teams, and organizations.* San Francisco: Jossey-Bass.

Frame, J. D. (1987). *Managing projects in organizations.* San Francisco: Jossey Bass.

Frame, J. D. (1994). *The new project management: Tools for an age of rapid change, corporate reengineering, and other business realities.* San Francisco: Jossey-Bass. ISBN 155542662X.

Franklin & Marshall College. (2008). *Self paced learning materials.* Retrieved April 15, 2008 from http://ats.fandm.edu/resources/learning/splm/

Freeman, R. (1984). *Strategic management: A stakeholder approach.* Pitman, MA.

Gale, A. (1999, November 17 - 20). *How to know what: Setting the project management competency agenda.* Paper presented at the PM Days '99: Projects and Competencies, Vienna, Austria.

Galin, D. (2004). *Software quality assurance: From theory to implementation.* Harlow, UK: Pearson Education Limited.

Gallivan, M. (2001). Meaning to change: How diverse stakeholders interpret organizational communication about change initiatives. *IEEE Transactions on Professional Communication, 44*(4), 243-266.

Garcia, P., & Qin, J. (2007). Identifying the generation gap in higher education: Where do the differences really lie? *Journal of Online Education, 3*(4). Retrieved on January 17, 2008 from http://innovateonline.info/index.php?view=article&id=379

Gardner, C. (2000). *The valuation of information technology.* New York: John Wiley & Sons.

Gardner, H. (1993). *Multiple intelligences: The theory in practice.* New York: Basic.

Gardner, H. (2000). *Intelligence reframed: Multiple intelligences for the 21ˢᵗ century.* New York: Basic.

Gareis, R., & Huemann, M. (1999, November 17 - 20). *Specific competences in the project-oriented society.* Paper presented at the PM Days '99: Projects and Competencies, Vienna, Austria.

Gartner. (2008). *Understanding hype cycles.* Retrieved from Gartner Web pages: http://www.gartner.com/pages/story.php.id.8795.s.8.jsp

Garvin, D. A. (1988). *Managing quality.* New York: The Free Press.

Gaudioso, E., & Talavera, L. (2006). Data mining to support tutoring in virtual learning communities: Experiences and challenges. In C. Romero & S. Ventura (Eds.), *Data mining in e-learning, Advances in Management Information Series, 4*, 207-226. Southampton, UK: WitPress.

Gehring, D. R. (2007). Applying traits theory of leadership to project management. *Project Management Journal, 38*(1), 44-54.

George Mason University. (2007). *Technology across the curriculum.* Retrieved February 21, 2008 from http://tac.gmu.edu

Geraldi, J., & Adlbrecht, G. (2007). On faith, fact, and interaction in projects. *Project Management Journal, 38*(1), 32-43.

Gilbert, T. F. (1978). *Human competence: Engineering worthy performance.* New York: McGraw Book Company.

Gill, N. S. (2005). Factors affecting effective software quality management revisited. *ACM Sigsoft Software Engineering Notes, 30*(2), 1-4.

Gilmore, H. L. (1974). Product conformance cost. *Quality Progress,* June 1974.

Giroux, H., & Landry, S. (1998). Schools of thought in and against total quality. *Journal of Managerial Issues, 10*(2), 183-202.

Gitman, L. J. (2003). *Principles of managerial finance, brief edition* (3rd ed.). Boston: Addison-Wesley.

Glass, R. L. (1997). *The software runaways.* NJ: Prentice Hall and Yourdon Press

Glass, R. L. (2006). The Standish report: Does it really describe a software crisis? *Communications of the ACM, 49*(8), 15-16.

Glendale Community College. *Popular Questions, for New and Returning Students.* Retrieved April 10, 2008 from http://Web.gccaz.edu/studenthelpdesk/

Godbole, N. S. (2004). *Software quality assurance: Principles and practice.* Pnagbourne, U.K.: Alpha Science.

Goldratt E. (1997). *Critical chain great barrington.* MA: North River Press.

Goleman, D. (2002). *Primal leadership: Emotional intelligence.* Boston: Harvard Business School Press.

Goleman, D. (2006). *Social intelligence: The new science of human telationships.* London: Hutchinson.

Goleman, D., Boyatzis, R., & McKee, A. (2002). *The new leaders.* Boston: Harvard Business School Press.

Gorrino-Arriaga, J. P., & Eraso, J. C. (2000). Future trends of project management. Congress 2000. *15ᵗʰ IPMA World Congress on Project Management.* Additional Papers. Zurich, Switzerland, International Project Management Association.

Gouge, Ian. (2003). *Shaping the IT organization.* Leeds, UK: Springer.

Graber, D. R. (1996). How to manage a global product development process. *Industrial Marketing Management, 25,* 483-489.

Grady, R. B. (1993). Practical results from measuring software quality. *Communications of the ACM, 36*(11), 62-68.

Graham, I., Henderson-Sellers, B., & Younessi, H. (1997). *The OPEN process specification.* ACM Press/Addison-Wesley Publishing Co.

Grant, D. (2002). A wider view of business process reengineering. *Communications Of The ACM, 45*(1).

Grasha, A. F. (1996). *Teaching with style: A practical guide to enhancing learning by understanding teaching and learning styles.* San Bernardino, CA: Alliance Publishers. See http://www.iats.com/publications/TSI.html

Greenfield, J. (2004). *Software factories: Assembling applications with patterns, models, frameworks, and tools.* Microsoft Corporation MSDN Architecture Center Portal. Retrieved May 13, 2008 from http://msdn.microsoft.com/en-us/library/ms954811.aspx

Greenhalgh, T., Robert, G., MacFarlane, F., Bate, P., & Kyriakidou, O. (2004). Diffusion of innovations in service organizations: Systematic review and recommendations. *The Milbank Quarterly, 82*(4), 581-629.

Greenwood, C., & Maheady, L. (1997). Measurable change in student performance : Forgotten standard in teacher preparation? *Teacher Education and Special Education, 20*(3), 265-275.

Griffin, A., & Hauser, J. R. (1996). Integrating R&D and marketing: a review and analysis of the literature. *Journal of Product Innovation Management, 13*(3), 191-215.

Grix, J. (2002). Introducing students to the generic terminology of social research. *Politics, 22*(3), 175-186.

Gruenwald, G. (1995). *New product development* (2nd ed.). Lincolnwood, IL: NTC Business Books.

Gulliksen, J., Lantz, A., & Bovie, I. (1999). User centered design – Problems and possibilities. *SIGCHI Bulletin, 31*(2), 25-25.

Guntamukkala, V., Wen, H. J., & Tarn, J. M. (2006). An empirical study of selecting software development life cycle models. *Human Systems Management, 25*(4), 265-278.

Gupta, A., & McDaniel, J. (2002). Creating competitive advantage by effectively managing knowledge: A framework for knowledge management. *Journal of Knowledge Management Practice, 3*(1), 1-9. ISSN 1705-9232.

Haab, M. (2007). Relationship between modes of participation and satisfaction of implementation of enterprise resource planning systems in higher education. *Dissertation Abstracts International,* 68/11, May 2008.

Hall, E. M. (1995). *Proactive risk management methods for software engineering excellence.* Florida Institute of Technology..

Hammer, M. (1996). *Beyond reengineering: How the process-centered organization is changing our work and our lives.* New York: HarperCollins Publishers, Inc.

Hammond, R. (2007, September). Party lines, Wikis, and project management. *Online, 31*(5), 30-33. [Electronic version] Retrieved March 18, 2008, from Professional Development Collection database.

Hample, D. (1992). The Toulmin model and the syllogism. In W. L. Benoit, D. Hample & P. J. Benoit (Eds.), *Readings in argumentation: Pragmatics and discourse analysis* (pp. 225-237). Berlin: Foris Publications.

Handfield, R. B., & Lawson, B. (2007). Integrating suppliers into new product development. *Research-Technology Management,* Sept.-Oct., (pp. 44-50).

Handy Understanding Organizations (Penguin Business) (3rd Edition) (Paperback)

Handy, C. B. (1982). *Understanding organizations.* London: Penguin

Harris, M., & Zastrocky, M. (2005). *Magic quadrant for higher education administrative suites.* From http://www.gartner.com/7_search

Hartman, F. T. (2001). The key to enterprise evolution - Future PM. *PMI Seminars and Symposium Proceedings AIPM (CDRom)*. USA: PMI.

Hartman, F., & Skulmoski, G. (1999). Quest for team competence. *Project Management, 5*(1), 10-15.

Harvey, T. R. (1990). *Checklist for change: A pragmatic approach for creating and controlling change*. Boston: Allyn and Bacon.

Heerkensm G. R. (2001). How to become the successful project manager of the future - Be business savvy! *PMI Seminars and Symposium Proceedings AIPM (CDRom)*. USA: PMI.

Hefner, D., & Malcolm, C. (2002, February). 15 essential steps of IT project management. Healthcare financial management. *Journal of The Healthcare Financial Management Association, 56*(2), 76-78. [Electronic version] Retrieved March 18, 2008, from MEDLINE with full text database.

Hefner, R. (1994). Experience with applying SEI's risk taxonomy. In *Proceedings of 3rd SEI Conference on Software Risk Management*. Pittsburgh, PA: SEI.

Henderson-Sellers, B., & Edwards, J. M. (1990). The object-oriented systems life cycle. *Commun. ACM, 33*(9), 142-159. DOI= http://doi.acm.org/10.1145/83880.84529

Henderson-Sellers, B., France, R., Georg, G., & Reddy, R. (2007). A method engineering approach to developing aspect-oriented modelling processes based on the OPEN process framework. *Inf. Softw. Technol. 49*(7), 761-773. DOI= http://dx.doi.org/10.1016/j.infsof.2006.08.003

Hersey, P., & Blanchard, K. H. (1984). *Management of organizational behavior* (4th ed.). Englewood Cliffs, NJ: Prentice-Hall.

Hershey, P., & Blanchard, K. H. (1988). *Management of organizational behaviour,* 5th ed. Englewood Cliffs, NJ: Prentice Hall.

Hevner, A., March, S., Park, J., & Ram, S. (2004). Design science in information systems research. *MIS Quarterly 28*(1), 75-105.

Hobday, M., Davies, A., & Prencipe, A. (2005). System integration: a core capability of the modern corporation. *Industrial and Corporate Change, 14*(6), 1109-1143.

Hoffman, T. (2005, July 11). After THE Fact. *Computerworld, 39*(28), 39-40. [Electronic version] Retrieved March 29, 2008, from Academic Search Complete database.

Holman, D., & Hall, L. (1996). Competence in management development: Rites and wrongs. *British Journal of Management, 7*(2), 191-202.

Hopelain, D., & Loesh, B. (1985). Automated development methodologies: Overview and conclusions. *Data Processing, 27*(2), 43.

Horenstein, M. (2005). *Design concepts for engineers,* 3rd edition. Upper Saddle River, NJ: Prentice Hall

Horn, L. (1994). *SWOT analysis and strategic Planning - A manual*. Hamburg, Germany: GFA.

Horton, W., & Horton, K. (2003). *E-learning tools and technologies: A consumer's guide for trainers, teachers, educators, and instructional designers*. Indianapolis, IN: Wiley Publishing.

House, R. J. (1971). A path-goal theory of leader effectiveness. *Administrative Science Quarterly*, September, 321-338.

House, R. J. (1996). Path-goal theory of leadership: Lessons, legacy, and a reformulated theory. *Leadership Quarterly, 7*, 323-352.

Howard, A. (2002). Rapid application development: Rough and dirty or value-for-money engineering? *Communications of the ACM, 45*(10).

Howell, L. J., & Hsu, J.C. (2002). Globalization within the auto industry. *Research Technology Management, 45*(4), 43-49.

Huber, J. (2005). T. C. O. and R. O. I.: The business of technology planning. *Library Media Connection, August-September,* 62-64.

Huemann, M., Turner, J. R., & Keegan, A. (2004, July 11 - 14). *The role of human resource management in project oriented organizations.* Paper presented at the PMI Research Conference, London.

Huisman, M., & Iivari, J. (2006). Deployment of systems development methodologies: Perceptual congruence between IS managers and systems developers. *Information & Management, 43*(1), 29-49.

Hulett, D. T. (1996). Schedule risk analysis simplified. *PM Network,* (pp. 23-30).

Humphreys, W. S. (2004). *The software quality profile,* Retrieved September 12, 2004, from http://www.sei.cmu.edu/publications/articles/quality-profile/index.html

Hunt, S. D. (1997). Evolutionary economics, endogenous growth models, and resource-advantage theory. *Eastern Economic Journal, 23*(4).

Hunter, M. G., & Beck, J. (1996). A cross-cultural comparison of 'excellent' systems analysts. *Information Systems Journal, 6*(4), 245-260.

Huntington, P., Nicholas, D., Jamali, H. R., & Tenopir, C. (2006). Article decay in the digital environment: An analysis of usage of OhioLINK by date of publication, employing deep log methods. *J. Am. Soc. Inf. Sci. Technol., 57*(13).

Hurt, H. T. & Hubbard, R. (May, 1987). *The systematic measurement of the perceived characteristics of information technologies: Microcomputers as innovations.* Paper presented at the ICA Annual Conference, Montreal, Quebec.

Hustad, E. & Munkvold, B. E. (2006). Communities of practice and other organizational groups. In E. Coakes,& S. Clarke, (Eds.), *Encyclopedia of communities of practice in information and knowledge management* (pp. 60-62). Hershey, PA: IGI Global Publishing,

Hutson, N. J. (2002). Top four components of successful future organisations. *PMI Seminars and Symposium Proceedings.*

Hylton, P. (2006). Technical risk management as the connectivity in a capstone design course. *ASEE Journal of Mechanical Engineering Technology, 23*(1), 48-53.

Iacovou, C., & Dexter, A. (2005). Surviving IT project cancellations. *Communications of the ACM, 48*(4), 83-86.

IEEE (1987). *IEEE standards for software project management plans*, Std 1058.1-1987. New York: IEEE.

IEEE (1992). *IEEE standards for software quality metrics methodology.* IEEE Std 1061-1992. NY: IEEE.

IEEE Std1012 (1998). IEEE standard for software verification and validation. IEEE standards Software Engineering, Vol. Two, Process Standards, 1999 Edition, IEEE

IEEE Std730 (1998). IEEE standard for software quality assurance plans Std 730-1998. *IEEE standards software engineering,* Vol. Two, Process Standards, 1999 Edition, IEEE, (pp. 1-16).

Igbaria, M., & Iivaria, J. (1995). The effects of self-efficacy on computer usage. *Omega: International Journal of Management Science, 25*(6), 587-605.

Igbaria, M., Kassicieh, S., & Silver, M. (1999). Career orientations and career success among research, and development and engineering professionals. *Journal of Engineering and Technology Management, 16*(1), 29-54.

Iivari, J., & Huisman, M. (2007). The relationship between organizational culture and the deployment of systems development methodologies. *MIS Quarterly, 31*(1), 35-58.

Iivari, J., & Maansaari, J. (1998). The usage of systems development method: Are we stuck to old practices? *Information & Software Technology, 40*(9), 501.

Im, I., El Sawy, O., & Hars, A. (1999). Competence and impact of tools for BPR. *Information & Management, 36*(6), 301-311.

InfoTech Group. (2008, March 18.) Ensure user satisfaction with user acceptance testing. *Research Notes.*

Iowa State University. (2003). *Faculty technology mentoring.* Retrieved March 23, 2008 from http://www.public.iastate.edu/%7Emstar/mentor/home.html

IPMA (2006). *International Competence Baseline version 3.0.* ISBN 0-9553213-0-1, IPMA, Nijkerk, The Netherlands.

IPMA (2007). *ICB: IPMA competence baseline* Version 3.0. In C. Caupin, H. Knöpfl, G. Koch., H. Pannenbäcker, F- Pérez-Polo, & C. Seabury (Eds.), Njkerk, The Netherlands: International Project Management Association.

ISO (1991). *Information technology software life cycle processes* ISO/IEC (JTC1)-SC7.Geneva, Switzerland: ISO.

ISTE (International Society for Technology in Education). *National educational technology standards.* Retrieved April 12, 2008, from http://www.iste.org/nets

J. Hoffer, J., George, J., & Valacich, J. (2005). *Modern systems analysis & Design,* 4th edition.NJ: Prentice Hall

Jaafari, A. (1998). Project managers of the next millenium: Do they resemble project managers of today? *14th World Congress on Project Management, Proceedings, Volume 2,* AIPM. Slovenia: International Project Management Association.

Jackson, R. (2006). *Fonterra puts SAP project on ice.* Retrieved 5 Oct 2006, from http://computerworld.co.nz/news.nsf/news/3C182BBD1B82A2C1CC2571F80016AEF1?Opendocument&HighLight=2,fonterra

Jacob, D. (2003). Forecasting project schedule completion with earned value metrics. *The Measurable News, 1,* 7-9.

Jacob, D. S., & Kane, M. (2004). Forecasting schedule completion using earned value metrics revisited. *The Measurable News, 1,* 11-17.

Jarrett, E. (2000). Effect of technical elements of business risk on decision making. *Managing technical risk.* US Department of Commerce, NIST GCR 00-787.

Jawahar, I., & McLaughlin, G. (2001, July). Toward a descriptive stakeholder theory: An organizational life cycle approach. *Academy of Management Review, 26*(3), 397-414. [Electronic version] Retrieved March 30, 2008, from Business Source Complete database.

Jeevan, V. K. J., & Padhi, P. (2006). A selective review of research in content personalization. *Library Review, 55*(9), 556-586(31).

Jesitus, J. (1997). Broken promises?; FoxMeyer 's Project was a disaster. Was the company too aggressive or was it misled? *Industry Week,* November 3, 31-37.

Jiang, B. (2002). Key elements of a successful project manager. *Project Management, 8*(1), 14-19.

Jiang, J., & Klein, G. (1998). Important behavioral skills for IT project managers: The judgments of experienced IT professionals. *Project Management Journal, 29*(1), 39-44.

Jiang, J., Klein, G., & Balloun, J. (1996). Ranking of system implementation success factors. *Project Management Journal, 27*(4), 23-30.

Jiang, J., Klein, G., & Means, T. (1999). The missing link between systems analysts' actions and skills. *Information Systems Journal, 9*(1), 21-33.

Johansson, S., Löfström, M., & Ohlsson, Ö. (2007). Separation or integration? A dilemma when organizing development projects *International Journal of Project Management, 25*(5), 457-464.

Johnson, J., Boucher, K. D., Connors, K., & Robinson, J. (2001). The criteria for success. *Software magazine, 21*(1), 3-11.

Johnson, R. R. (1998). *User-centered technology: A rhetorical theory for computers and other mundane artifacts.* Albany, NY: State University of New York Press.

Jones, T., & Wicks, A. (1999, April). Convergent stakeholder theory. *Academy of Management Review, 24*(2), 206-221. [Electronic version] Retrieved April 10, 2008, from Business Source Complete database.

Juran, J. M. (Ed.). (1974). *Quality control handbook,* 3rd edition. New York: McGraw-Hill.

Juran, J. M., & Godfrey, A. B. (1998). *Juran's quality handbook.* . New York: McGraw-Hill.

K-12 Youth Technology Support Collaborative. Retrieved April 15, 2008 from http://www.studenttechsupport. org/index.cfm

Kansala, K. (1997). Integrating risk assessment with cost estimation. *IEEE Software* (May/June), 61-67.

Kant, I. (1934). *The critique of pure reason* (J. M. D. Meiklejohn, Trans.). London: J M Dent.

Kaplan, R. S., & Norton, D. P. (1996). *The balanced scorecard: Translating strategy into action.* Boston: Harvard Business School Press.

Kaplan, R. S., & Norton, D. P. (1996). Using the balanced scorecard as a strategic management system. *Harvard Business Review, 76*(5), 134-142.

Kaplan, R. S., & Norton, D. P. (2001). *The strategy-focused organisation: How balanced scorecard companies thrive in the new business environment.* Boston: Harvard Business School Press.

Kaplan, R. S., & Norton, D. P. (2004). *Strategy maps: Converting intangible assets into tangible outcomes.* Boston:Harvard Business School Press.

Kappelman, L., McKeeman, R., & Zhang, L. (2006). Early warning signs of IT project failure: The dominant dozen. *Information Systems Management, 23*(4), 31-36.

Karolak, D. W. (1996). *Software engineering risk management.* Los Alamitos, CA: IEEE Computer Society Press.

Katsikas, Sokratis (1998). *Risk analysis and risk management CRAMM methodology.* University of Aegean S Navy. Retrieved September 13, 1998, from http://epic. onion.it/workshops/w08/slides13/

Katz, E. (1962). The social itinerary of social change: two studies on the diffusion of innovation. *Human Organization, 20*, 70-82.

Katz, E. (Ed.). (1961). *The social itinerary of social change: Two studies on the diffusion of innovation.* CA: Institute for Communication Research, Stanford University.

Kautz, K., Hansen, B., & Jacobsen, D. (2004). The utilization of information systems development methodologies in practice. *Journal of Information Technology Cases and Applications, 6*(4), 1.

Kaye, R., & Crowley, J. (2000). Medical device use-safety: Incorporating human factors engineering into risk management. *U.S. Dept. of Health and Human Services Guidance for Industry and FDA Premarket and Design Control Reviewers.* U.S. Dept. of Health and Human Services, Washington D.C.

Keegan, A. E., & Den Hartog, D. N. (2004). Transformational leadership in a project-based environment: a comparative study of the leadership styles of project managers and line managers. *International Journal of Project Management, 22*(8), 609-618.

Kelly, M. (2006). *Tools for virtual teams.* Taken from IPM Lecture notes. (http://www.mckinnonsc.vic.edu.au/ vceit/virtualteams/tools.htm). Retrieved 12 Apr 2008.

Kendall, R., Post, D., Carver, J., Henderson, D., & Fisher, D. (2007). A proposed taxonomy for software development risks for high-performance computing (HPC) scientific/engineering applications. *Software Engineering Institute* (Technical Note CMU/SEI-2006-TN-039).

Kennedy, G. E., Judd, T. S., Churchward, A., & Gray, K. (2008). First year students' experiences with technology: Are they really digital natives? *Australasian Journal of Educational Technology, 24*(1), 108-122. Retrieved March 15, 2008 from http://www.ascilite.org.au/ajet/ ajet24/kennedy.html

Kerr, J. (2006, October 2). The ten commandments of project management. *Computerworld, 40*(40), 44-44. [Electronic version] Retrieved March 18, 2008, from Computer Source database.

Kerzner, H. (2006). *Project management: A systems approach to planning, scheduling, and controlling.* Hoboken, NJ: John Wiley & Sons.

Khalifa, M., & Verner, J. M. (2000). Drivers for software development method usage. *IEEE Transactions on Engineering Management, 47*(3), 360.

Khanna, O. (n.d.). *Industrial engineering and management* (2nd edition). Dhanpat rai publications.

Khazanchi, D., & Sutton, S. (2001). Assurance services for business-to-business electronic commerce: A framework in implications. *Journal of the Association for Information Systems, 1*(11).

Khoo, M., & Donahue, R. (2007). Evaluating digital libraries with webmetrics. *In Proceedings of the 7th ACM/IEEE Joint Conference on Digital Libraries* (Vancouver, BC, Canada, June 18 - 23, 2007). JCDL '07. New York, NY: ACM.

Kidder, S. (1999). I Ching: The classic of change / The classic of changes: A new translation of the I Ching as interpreted by Wang Bi / The Columbia I Ching on CD-ROM. *Philosophy East and West, 49(3), 377.*

Kimball, L. (1997, April). *Managing virtual teams.* Speech given at Team Strategies Conference, Toronto, Canada.

Kirkpatrick, S. A., & Locke, E. A. (1991). Leadership traits do matter. *Academy of Management Executive,* March, 44-60.

Kisielnicki, J. (2006). Transfer of information and knowledge in the project management. In E. Coakes, & S. Clarke, (Eds.), *Encyclopedia of communities of practice in information and knowledge management* (pp. 544-551). Hershey, PA: IGI Global Publishing.

Kitchenham, B., & Linkman, S. (1997). Estimates, uncertainty, and risk. *IEEE Software, 14*(3), 69-74.

Klein, G., Jiang, J., Shelor, R., & Balloun, J. (1999). Skill coverage in project teams. *Journal of Computer Information Systems, 40*(1), 76-81.

Kliem, R. L., & Ludin, I. S. (1999). *Tools and tips for today's project manager.* Pennsylvania: PMI Project Management Institute.

Kliniotou, M. (2004, September). Identifying, measuring and monitoring value during project development. *European Journal of Engineering Education, 29*(3), 367-376. [Electronic version] Retrieved April 8, 2008, from Academic Search Complete database.

Kloppenborg, T. J., & Opfer, W. A. (2002). The current state of project management research: Trends, interpretations, and predictions. *Project Management Journal, 33*(2).

Kloppenborg, T. J., Bycio, P., Cagle, J., Clark, T., Cunningham, M., Finch, M. et al. (2000). Forty years of project management research: trends, interpretations and predictions. Project management research at the turn of the millenium. In *Proceedings of PMI Research Conference, AIPM.* Pennsylvania: Project Management Institute.

Kobulnicky, P., & Rudy, J. (2002). Third annual EDUCAUSE survey Identifies current IT issues. *EDUCAUSE Quarterly, 25*(2), 2002. Available from: http://www.educause.edu/ir/library/pdf/eqm0222.pdf

Kohli, R., & Devaraj, S. (2003). Measuring information technology payoff: A meta-analysis of structural variables in firm-level empirical research. *Information Technology Research, 14*(2), 127-146.

Kohn, K. (2006). Managing the balance of perspectives in the early phase of NPD. *European Journal of Innovation Management, 9*(1), 44-60.

Koshizuka, N., & Sakamura, K. (2000). Tokyo university digital museum. Digital Libraries: Research and Practice. *2000 Kyoto, International Conference,* (pp. 85-92).

Kouzes, J., & Posner, B. (2007). *The leadership challenge.* San Francisco: John Wiley and Sons Publishing.

Kozar, K. A. (1989). Adopting systems development methods: An exploratory study. *Journal of Management Information Systems, 5*(4), 73-86.

KPMG (2002). *Programme management survey.* Retrieved February 13, 2003. from http://www.theregister.co.uk/2002/11/26/it_project_failure_is_rampant/

Krech, D., Crutchfield, R. S., & Ballachey, E. L. (1962). *Individual in society.* New York: McGraw-Hill.

Krueger, K., Hansen, L., & Smaldino, S. (2000). Preservice teacher technology competencies. *Tech Trends 44*(3), 47-50.

K-State Media Relations (2004). *Kansas State University achievements: 2004 all-university* from http://www.k-state.edu/media/achievements/04allaccomplishments.html

Kumamoto, H., & Henley, E. (1996). *Probabilistic tisk assessment and management for engineers and scientists.* New York: IEEE Press.

Kwon, T. H., & Zmud, R. W. (1987). Unifying the fragmented models information systems implementation. In R. J. Boland Jr. & R. J. Hirschheim (Eds.), *Critical issues in information systems research* (pp. 227-251). New York: John Wiley & Sons.

Lambert, L. R. (2002). The future of project management. *Business managers and project managers working as a team.* ESI Horizons.

Larlsson, C., & Ahlstrom, P. (1996). The difficult path to lean product development. *Journal of Product Innovation Management, 13*, 283-295.

Larose, D. T. (2006). *Data mining methods and models.* Wiley-Interscience. Hoboken, NJ.

Laurillard, D. (2002). *Rethinking university teaching* (2nd Ed.). New York :Taylor & Francis Group.

Lechler, T. (1998, July 6 - 8). *When it comes to project management, it's the people that matter.* Paper presented at the IRNOP III: The Nature and Role of Projects in the Next 20 Years: Research Issues and Problems, Calgary, Canada.

Lee, D., Trauth, E., & Farwell, D. (1995). Critical skills and knowledge requirements of IT professionals: A joint academic/industry investigation. *MIT Quarterly, 19*(3), 313-340.

Lee, J. (2001). The Tao of Business. *Asian Business, 37(8), 48.*

Lee, J., Lee, J., & Souder, W. E. (2000). Differences of organizational characteristics in new product development: cross-cultural comparison on Korea and the US. *Technovation, 20,* 497-508.

Leenders, M. R., Fearon, H. E., Flynn, A. E., & Johnson, P. F. (2002). *Purchasing and supply chain management.* New York: McGraw-Hill.

Lei, D., Hitt, M., & Bettis, R. (1996). Dynamic core competences through meta-learning and strategic context. *Journal of Management, 22*(4), 549-569.

Lemon, W. Leibowitz, J. Burn, J., & Hackney, R. (2002). Information systems project failure: A comparative study of two companies. *Journal of Global Information Management, 10*(2), 28-39.

Leonard-Barton, D. (1988). Implementation as mutual adaptation of technology and organization. *Research Policy, 17:5,* 251-267.

Lerouge, C., Newton, S., & Blanton, J. E. (2005). Exploring the systems analyst skill set: Perceptions, preferences, age, and gender. *The Journal of Computer Information Systems, 45*(3), 12-24.

Levene, R. (2002). Service delivery - preparing for a new future in projects. Frontiers of project management research and application. In *Proceedings of PMI Research Conference, AIPM.* USA: PMI.

Levin, G., & Rad, P. (2006). *Successful motivational techniques for virtual teams.* Retrieved July 21, 2007 from http://www.allpm.com/print.php?sid=1637

Leybourne, S. A. (2007). The changing bias of project management research: A consideration of the literatures and an application of extant theory. *Project Management Journal, 38*(1), 61-73.

Lieberman, M. D., Gaunt, R., Gilbert, D. T., & Trope, Y. (2002). Reflection and reflexion: A social cognitive neuroscience approach to attributional inference. *Advances in Experimental Social Psychology, 34,* 199-249.

Lieberman, M. D., Jarcho, J. M., & Satpute, A. B. (2004). Evidence-based and intuition-based self-knowledge: An fMRI study. *Journal of Personality and Social Psychology, 87,* 421-435.

Liebowitz, J. (2007). *Social networking: The essence of innovation.* Lanham, MD: Scarecrow Press.

Lientz, B. P., & Rea, K. P. (1998). *Project management for the 21ˢᵗ century.*

Liker, J. K. (2004). *The Toyota Way.* New York: McGraw Hill.

Linn, R., Baker, E., & Dunbar, S. (1991). Complex, performance-based assessment: Expectations and validation criteria. *Educational Researcher, 20*(8), 15-21.

Lipke, W. (2003). Schedule is different. *The Measurable News*, (pp. 31-34).

Lipke, W. (2004). Connecting earned value to the schedule. *The Measurable News, Winter, 1,* 6-16.

Lipke, W., Zwikael, O., Henderson, K., & Anbari, F. (2008). Prediction of project outcome: the application of statistical methods to earned value management and earned schedule performance indexes. *To appear in the International Journal of Project Management.*

Lippert, S. K., & Davis, M. (2006, October). A conceptual model integrating trust into planned change activities to enhance technology adoption behavior. *Journal of Information Science, 32*(5), 434. Retrieved September 9, 2007, from Proquest database.

Loacker, G., & Mentkowski, M. (1993). Creating a culture where assessment improves learning. In T. W. Banta (Ed.), *Making a difference: Outcomes of a decade of assessment in higher education*, (pp. 5-24). San Francisco: Jossey-Bass.

Locks, M. O. (1973). *Reliability, maintainability, and availability assessment.* Rochelle Park, NJ: Hayden Book Company, Inc.

Loo, R. (2002). Working towards best practices in project management: A Canadian study. *International Journal of Project Management, 20*(2), 93-98.

Lovelace, K., Shapiro, D. L., & Weingart, L. R. (2001). Maximizing cross functional new product teams' innovativeness and constraints adherence: a conflict communication perspective. *Academy of Management Journal, 44*(4), 779-793.

Loyd, B. H., & Gressard, C. (1984). Reliability and factorial validity of computer attitude scales. *Educational and Psychological Measurement, 44*(2), 501-505.

Ludema, J., Cooperrider, D., & Barrett, F. (2001). Appreciative inquiry: The power of the unconditional positive question. In P. Reason & H. Bradury (Eds.), *Handbook of action research: Participatory inquiry and practice.* Thousand Oaks, CA: Sage.

Luftman, J., & Koeller, C. T. (2003). Assessing the value of IT. In J. N. Luftman (Ed.), *Competing in the information age: Align in the sand* (2nd ed., pp. 77-106). UK: Oxford University Press.

Lynch, C. (2002). Digital collections, digital libraries and the digitization of cultural heritage information. *First Monday, 7*(5). Retrieved May 10, 2008, from http://www.firstmonday.org/issues/issue7_5/lynch/index.html

Lynch, C. (2005). Where do we go from here? The next decade for digital libraries. *D-Lib Magazine, 11*(7/8).

Lynch, C. (2007). The shape of the scientific article in the developing cyberinfrastructure. *CTWatch Quarterly, 3*(3).

Lyttinen, K., & Hirschheim, R. (1987). *Information systems failures- A survey and classification of the empirical literature.* In P. Zorkoczy (Ed.), *Oxford surveys of information technology, 4,* pp. 257-309. UK: Oxford University Press.

MacKenzie, D., & Wajcman, J. (Eds.). (1999). *The social shaping of technology* (2nd ed.). Buckingham, UK: Open University Press.

Madachy, R. J. (1997). Heuristic risk assessment using cost factors. *IEEE Software, 14*(3), 51-59.

Mader, S. (2006). Four letter words: How Wiki and edit are making the Internet a better teaching tool. In S. Mader (Ed.), *Using Wiki in education.* Retrieved May 27, 2008, from http://www.Wikiineducation.com

Mader, S. (2008). *Wikipatterns.* Indianapolis, IN: Wiley Publishing.

"Managing Groups and Teams / How Do You Build High-Performing Virtual Teams?" (http://en.wikibooks.org/wiki/Managing_Groups_and_Teams/How_Do_You_Build_High-performance_teams). Retrieved 14 Mar 2008.

March, S. T., & Smith, G. F. (1995). Design and natural science research on information technology. *Decision Support Systems, (15)*, 251-266.

Marchese, T. J.(1987). Third down, ten years to go. *AAHE Bulletin, 40*, 3-8.

Marchewka, J. T. (2006). *Information Technology Project Management: Providing Measurable Organizational Value*. Hoboken, NJ: Wiley.

Marcinkiewicz, H. R. (1993/94). Computers and teachers: Factors influencing computer use in the classroom. *Journal of Research on Computing in Education, 26*(2), 220-237.

Marcinkiewicz, H. R. (1994/95). Differences in computer use of practicing versus preservice teachers. *Journal of Research on Computing in Education, 27*(2), 184-197.

Marcinkiewicz, H. R., & Regstad, N. G. (1996). Using subjective norms to predict teachers' computer use. *Journal of Computing in Teacher Education, 13*(1), 27-33.

Marcinkiewicz, H. R., & Wittman, T. K. (1995). From preservice to practice: A longitudinal study of teachers and computer use. *Journal of Computing in Teacher Education, 11*(2), 12–17.

Marcolin, B., Compeau, D., Munro, M., & Huff, S. (2000). Assessing user competence: Conceptualization and measurement. *Information Systems Research, 11*(1), 37-60.

Marcolin, B., Munro, M., & Campbell, K. (1997). End user ability: Impact of job and individual differences. *Journal of End User Computing, 9*(3), 3-12.

Marcus, M., & Winters, D. (2004). Team problem solving strategies with a survey of these methods used by faculty members in engineering technology. *Journal of STEM Education, 5*(1,2), 24.

Markoff, J. (2008, February 10). Mashups are breaking the mold at Microsoft. *New York Times Online*. [Electronic version] Retrieved March 29, 2008, from http://www.nytimes.com/2008/02/10/business/10slipstream.html?em&ex=1202878800&en=96a368de807a0923&ei=5087%0A#

Markov, Z., & Larose, D. T. (2007). *Data mining the Web: Uncovering patterns in Web content, structure, and usage*. Hoboken, NJ: Wiley-Interscience.

Markus, M. L., & Keil, M. (1994). If we build it, they will come: Designing information systems that people want to use. *Sloan Management Review, 35*(4).

Martin, P. K., & Tate, K. (2001). *Getting started in project management*. New York: John Wiley & Sons.

Masi, A. C., & Winer, L. R. (2005). A university-wide vision of teaching and learning with information technologies. *Innovations in Education and Teaching International, 42*(2), 147-155.

Mason, J. (1996). *Qualitative researching*. Thousand Oaks, CA: Sage Publications.

Mayer, D. (n.d.). Stakeholder theory. *Encyclopedia of Business*, 2nd ed. [Electronic version] Retrieved March 29, 2008, http://www.referenceforbusiness.com/encyclopedia/Sel-Str/Stakeholder-Theory.html

Mayer, K. J., & Salomon, R. M. (2006). Capabilities, contractual hazards, and governance: Integrating resource-based and transaction cost perspectives. *Academy of Management Journal, 49*(5), 942-960.

McAfee, A. (2003). When too much IT knowledge is a dangerous thing. *MIT Sloan Management Review, 44*(2), 83.

McCormick, I. (2006). Same planet, different worlds: why projects continue to fail. A generalist review of project management with special reference to electronic research administration. *Perspectives, 10(4)*, 102-108.

McFarlan, W. (1981). Portfolio approach to information systems. *Harvard Business Review, 65*, 68-74.

McGee, P., & Diaz, V. (2007). Blogs, wikis, and podcasting, oh my! What is a faculty member supposed to do? *EDUCAUSE Review*. Retrieved April 10, 2008 from http://connect.educause.edu/Library/EDUCAUSE+Review/WikisandPodcastsandBlogsO/44993

McGinn, R. E. (1991). *Science, technology, and society*. Englewood Cliffs, NJ: Prentice Hall.

McGrath, O. (2005). Gauging adoptability: a case study of e-portfolio template development. *Proceedings of the 33rd annual ACM SIGUCCS conference on User services*, (pp.214-217), November 06-09, 2005, Monterey, CA, USA .

McGrath, O. (2006). Balancing act: community and local requirements in an open source development process. *In Proceedings of the 34th Annual ACM SIGUCCS Conference on User Services* (Edmonton, Alberta, Canada, November 05 - 08, 2006). *SIGUCCS '06* (pp. 240-244). New York, NY: ACM.

McGrath, O. (2007). Seeking activity: on the trail of users in open and community source frameworks. *In Proceedings of the 35th Annual ACM SIGUCCS Conference on User Services* (Orlando, Florida, USA, October 07 - 10, 2007). *SIGUCCS '07* (pp. 234-239). New York, NY: ACM.

McGreevy, M. (2003). Managing the transition. *Industrial and Commercial Training, 35*(6/7), 241-246. Retrieved September 9, 2007, from Proquest database.

McManus, J., & Wood-Harper, T. (2003). Information systems project management: The price of failure. *Management Services, 47*(5), ABI/INFORM Global, 16.-19.

MEC (2007). *Chamada Pública para Produção de Conteúdos Educacionais Digitais Multimídia*. Portal do Ministério da Educação, Secretaria de Educação a Distância, Departamento de Produção e Capacitação em Programas de EAD. Retrieved December 30, 2007 from http://portal.mec.gov.br/seed/

Mei, Q. (2004). A knowledge processing oriented life cycle study from a Digital Museum system. *In Proceedings of the 42nd Annual Southeast Regional Conference* (Huntsville, Alabama, April 02 - 03, 2004). ACM-SE 42. (pp. 116-121). New York, NY: ACM.

Meirelles, F. S. (2006). *Administração de Recursos de Informática*. Pesquisa Anual. São Paulo: Centro de Tecnologia da Informação Aplicada - CIA, FGV-EAESP.

Mei-Yeh, F., & Lin, F. (2006). Measuring the performance of ERP system – From the balanced scorecard perspectives. *The Journal of American Academy of Business, 10*(1), 256-263.

Melling, D. (1987). *Understanding Plato*. New York: Oxford University Press.

Melville, N., Kraemer, K., & Gurbaxani, V. (2004). Review: IT and organizational performance: An integrative model of IT business value. *MIT Quarterly, 28*(2), 283-323.

Meredith, J., & Mantel, S. (2002). *Project management: A managerial approach*, 5th Edition. NY: John Wiley. ISBN: 0-471-07323-7.

Merriam Webster (2008). *Merriam Webster online: Assurance*. Retrieved March 17, 2008, from http://www.merriam-webster.com/dictionary/assurance

Meyer, A. D. & Goes, J. B. (1988). Organizational assimilation of innovations: A multilevel contextual analysis. *Academy of Management Journal, 31*, 897-923.

Meyers, P. W., Sivakumar, K., & Nakata, C. (1999). Implementation of industrial process innovations: Factors, effects, and marketing implications. *Journal of Product Innovation Management, 16*(3), 295-311.

Michales, J. V. (1996). *Technical risk management*. Upper Saddle River, NJ: Prentice Hall.

Milgrom, P., & Roberts, J. (1992). *Economics, organization and management*. Upper Side River NJ: Prentice Hall.

Milis, K., & Mercken, R. (2004). The use of balanced scoreboard for the evaluation of information and communication technology projects. *International Journal of Project Management, 22*, 87-97.

Milner, D. (1985). An integrated approach to systems development. *Data Processing, 27*(3), 13.

Milson, M. A., & Wilemon, D. (2007). *The strategy of managing innovation and technology* (1ˢᵗ Edition). Upper Saddle River, NJ: Prentice Hall Publishing.

Ministry of Economic Development. (Feb 2004). *Restructuring to accommodate the "new" model.*

Mitchell, R., Agle, B., & Wood, D. (1997, October). Toward a theory of stakeholder identification and salience: Defining the principle of who and what really counts. *Academy of Management Review, 22*(4), 853-886. [Electronic version] Retrieved April 10, 2008, from Business Source Complete database.

Mitev, N. (1994). The business failure of knowledge-based systems. *Journal of Information Technology, 9*(3), 173-184.

Mitra, A., Stefensmeier, T., Lenzmeier, S., & Massoni, A. (1999). Institutional implications of changes in attitudes towards computers and use of computers by faculty. *Journal of Research on Computing in Education, 32*(1), 189-202.

Modarres, M. (2006). *Risk analysis in engineering.* New York: Taylor and Francis.

Molenda, M. (May/June, 2003). In search of the elusive ADDIE model. *Performance and Improvement, 42*(5).

Mooij, R. de (2006). *Four futures of Europe.* ISBN 90-5833-135-0. CPB, The Hague, the Netherlands.

Moore, G. C., & Benbasat, I. (1991). Development of an instrument to measure the perceptions of adopting an information technology innovation. *Information Systems Research, 2*(3), 192-222.

Moore, L. (2007). *If the sky isn't falling, Why does my head hurt?* Retrieved July 21, 2007, from http://www.allpm.com/print.php?sid=1658

Morgan, J. (2005). Lean product process development. *Certificate Program Binder.* Center for Professional Development, University of Michigan, Ann Arbor, MI, May 2-5, http://cpd.engin.umich.edu.

Morin, R. A., & Jarrell, S. L. (2001). *Driving shareholder value.* New York: McGraw-Hill.

Morris, C. R. (2005). *The tycoons: How Andrew Carnegie, John D. Rockefeller, Jay Gould, and J. P. Morgan invented the American supereconomy.* New York: Times Books.

Morris, P., Jones, I., & Wearne, S. (1998, July 6 - 8). *Current research directions in the management of projects at UMITT.* Paper presented at the IRNOP III: The Nature and Role of Projects in the Next 20 Years: Research Issues and Problems, Calgary, Canada.

Mulcahy, R. (2006). *PM crash course: Premier edition.* Minneapolis, MN: RMC Publications, Incorporated.

Müller, R., & Turner, J. R. (2006). Leadership competences and their successful application in different types of project. In L. Ou & R. Turner (Ed.), *Proceedings of IRNOP VII (International Research Network for Organizing by Projects)*, Northwestern Polytechnic University, Xi'an, China.

Muller, R., & Turner, J. R. (2007). Matching the project manager's leadership style to project type. *International Journal of Management, 25*(1), 21-32.

Müller, R., & Turner, J. R. (2007). Matching the project manager's leadership style to project type. *International Journal of Project Management, 25*(1), 21-32.

Müller, R., & Turner, J. R. (2007). The influence of project managers on project success criteria and project success by type of project. *European Management Journal, 25*(4), 289-309.

Müller, R., Geraldi, J., & Turner, J. R. (2007, September). *Linking complexity and leadership competences of project managers.* Paper presented at IRNOP VIII Conference (International Research Network for Organizing by Projects), Brighton, UK.

Mullins, L. J. (1996). *Management and organizational behavior.* London: Pitman.

Munro, M., Huff, S., Marcolin, B., & Compeau, D. (1997). Understanding and measuring user competence. *Information & Management, 33*(1), 45-57.

Murugesan, S. (1994, Dec. 21-22). Attitude towards testing: A key contributor to software quality. *IEEE's Proceedings of 1ˢᵗ International Conference on Software Testing, Reliability and Quality Assurance,* (pp. 111-115).

Muscatello, J. R. & Parente, D.H. (2006). Enterprise resource planning: A postimplementation cross-case analysis. *Information Resources Management Journal, 19*(3), 61-80.

Mustonen-Ollila, E., & Lyytinen, K. (2003). Why organizations adopt information system process innovations: a longitudinal study using diffusion of innovation theory. *Information Systems Journal, 13,* 275-297.

Myles, B. (1990). *The Theaetetus of Plato* (M. J. Levett & M. Burnyeat, Trans.). Indianapolis, IN: Hackett Publishing Company, Inc.

Nadler, D. A. & Tushman, M. L. (2004). Implementing new design: Managing organizational change. In M. L. Tushman & P. Andersen (Eds.), *Managing strategic innovation and change: A collection of readings* (2nd ed.). UK: Oxford University Press.

Nambisan, S., & Sawhney, M. (2008). *The global brain.* Upper Saddle River, NJ: Pearson Education Inc. As Wharton School Publishing.

Nandhakumar, J., & Avison, J. (1999). The fiction of methodological development: A field study of information systems development. *Information Technology & People, 12,* 176-191.

National Center for Education Statistics. (2002). *1999 National study of postsecondary faculty methodology report.* Washington DC: Department of Education.

National Center for Education Statistics. (2005). *2004 National study of postsecondary faculty methodology report.* Washington DC: Department of Education.

National Education Statistics – Formal Education 2007-2008. A publication of official statistics programme. Republic of Turkey – Ministry of National Education.

Neil, D. (2007, September 17). Edsel Agonistes. *Time,* (p. 28). [Electronic version] Retrieved February 26, 2008, from Academic Search Complete database.

Nelson, R. (2005). Project retrospectives: Evaluating success, failure and everything in between. *MISQ Executive, 4*(3), 361-372.

Nelson, R. R. (2007). IT project management: Infamous failures, classic mistakes, and best practices, *MIS Quarterly Executive, 6*(2), 67-78.

Nepal, B., Monplaisir, L., & Singh, N. (2006). A methodology for integrating design for quality in modular product design. *Journal of Engineering Design, 17*(5), 387-409.

Nepal, B. P., Monplaisir, L., Hammond, R., Wrobel, M., D'hondt, A., Herr, G., (2007, Nov. 7-10). Lean product development: an approach to achieve Ford's global product development system milestones, *American Society for Engineering Management (ASEM) National Conference,* Chattanooga, TN,

Netday. (2006). *2005 speak up event national highlights: Students and teachers. Project Tomorrow.* Retrieved on December 6, 2006 from http://www.netday.org/SPEAKUP/speakup_reports.htm

Neuhauser, C. (2007). Project manager leadership behaviors and frequency of use by female project managers. *Project Management Journal, 38*(1), 21-31.

Newman, M., & Robey, D. (1992). A social process model of user-analyst relationships. *MIS Quarterly.* June, 249-266.

Niazi, M., Wislon, D., & Zowghi, D. (2003, November). Critical success factors and critical barriers for software process improvement: An analysis of literature. In *Proceedings of 14th Australasian Conference on Information Systems,* (pp. 26-28).Perth Western Australia.

Niebel, B. W., & Freivalds, A. (1999). *Methods, standards, and work design* (10ᵗʰ ed.). Boston: WCB/McGraw-Hill.

Nielsen, J. (1993). *Usability engineering.* Boston: Academic Press.

Niven, P. R. (2002). *Balanced scorecard step-by-step.* New York: John Wiley & Sons, Inc.

Nolan, R. (1979). Managing the crisis in data processing. *Harvard Business Review* March/April, 115-126.

Nolan, R. (2005). *Cisco Systems Architecture: ERP and Web-enabled IT*, case no. 9-301-099. Boston: Harvard Business School Publishing.

Nord, G. D., & Nord, J. (1995). Knowledge and skill requirements important for success as a systems analyst. *Journal of Information Technology Management, 6*(3), 47-52.

Nord, R. L., & Tomayko, J. E. (2006). Software architecture-centric methods and agile development. *IEEE Software, 23*(2), 47.

Northouse, P. (2007). *Leadership: Theory and practice*. Thousand Oaks, CA: Sage Publications, Inc.

Norwegian_Research_Council. (2007). Høykom. from http://www.hoykom.no

Nye, D. E. (2005). *Technology matter: Questions to live with*. Cambridge, MA: The MIT Press.

O'Connell, F. (2007). *Fast projects*. Harlow, UK: Pearson Education Limited.

O'Leary, D. E. (2000). *Enterprise resource planning systems: Systems, life cycle, electronic commerce, and risk*. New York: Cambridge University Press.

Ohio State University. (2008). *Research on research (r²)*. Retrieved April 15, 2008 from http://digitalunion.osu.edu/r2/about.htm

Ojah, K., & Monplaisir, L. (2003). Investor's valuation of global product design and development. *Journal of International Business Studies, 34*, 457- 472.

Olsen, F. (2003). Sharing the code: More colleges and universities see open-source software as an alternative to commercial products. *The Chronicle of Higher Education: Information Technology*, August, 2003.

Orlikowski, W. J. (2002). Knowing in practice: Enacting a collective capability in distributed organizing. *Organization Science, 13*(3), 249-274.

Orsburn, D. K. (1991). *Spares management handbook*. Boston: McGraw-Hill.

Orwell, G. (1949). *Nineteen eighty-four*. London: Secker.

Ottosson, S. (2004). Dynamic product development-DPD. *Technovation, 24*, 207-217.

Oudshoorn, N., & Pinch, T. (2005). Introduction: How users and non-users matter. In N. Oudshoorn & T. Pinch (Eds.), *How users matter: The co-construction of users and technology* (pp. 1-25). Cambridge, MA: MIT Press.

Oxford Concise Dictionary (1995). 9th edn. UK: Oxford University Press.

Oz, E., & Sosik, J. (2000). Why information systems projects are abandoned: A leadership and communication theory and exploratory study. *Journal of Computer Information Systems 41*(1), 66-79.

Paganelli, L., & Paterno, F. (2002, January 13-16). Intelligent analysis of user interactions with web applications. *In Proceedings of the 7th international Conference on intelligent User interfaces* (San Francisco, California, USA). IUI '02 (pp. 111-118). New York: ACM Press.

Palmer (2004). Overcoming resistance to change. *Quality Progress, 7*(4), 35-39.

Pan, G., & Pan, S. (2006). Examining the coalition dynamics in affecting IS project abandonment decision-making. *Decision Support System, 42*(2), 639-655.

Pan, G., Pan, S., & Newman, M. (2007). Information systems project post-mortems: Insights from an attribution perspective. *Journal of the American Society for Information Science and Technology, 58*(14), 2255-2268.

Paquette, L. (2003). *The sourcing solution: A step-by-step guide to creating a successful purchasing program*. New York: American Management Association.

Paquette, S. (2006). *Communities of practice as facilitators of knowledge exchange*. In E. Coakes, & S. Clarke, (Eds.), *Encyclopedia of communities of practice in information and knowledge management* (pp. 68-73). Hershey, PA: IGI Global Publishing.

Parry, K. (2004). *The seven sins and the seven virtues of leadership: Which path do we follow?* (The Leading

Matters Symposium Series). Centre for Leadership & Management in Education, Graduate School of Management, Griffith University, Australia, Griffith University EcoCentre.

Partington, D. A. (2003). Managing and leading. In J. R. Turner (Eds.), *People in project management*. Aldershott, UK: Gower.

Pascarella, E. T., & Terenzini, P. T. (1991). *How college affects students: Findings and insights from twenty years of research*. San Francisco: Jossey-Bass.

Patterson, J. H. (1976). Project scheduling: the effects of problem structure on heuristic scheduling. *Naval Research Logistics, 23*, 95-123.

Patton, J. D., Jr. (1994). *Maintainability and maintenance management* (3rd ed.). Research Triangle Park, NC: Instrument Society of America.

Patton, M. Q. (1987). *Qualitative evaluation and research methods*. Newbury Park, CA: Sage Publications.

Pauleen, D., (2004). *Virtual teams: Projects, protocols, and processes,* (p. viii). Hershey, PA: IGI Global Publishing.

Peacock, D. (2002). Statistics, Structures and Satisfied Customers: Using Web Log Data to Improve Site Performance. In D. Bearman & J. Trant (Eds.), *Museums and the Web 2002: Proceedings. Pittsburgh: Archives and Museum Informatics*.

Penrose, E. (1997). The theory of the growth of the firm. In N. J. Foss (Ed.), *Resourses, firms and strategies* (pp. 13). New York: Oxford University Press.

Perez, M. P., & Sanchez, A. M. (2000). Lean production and supplier relations: a survey of practices in the Aragonese automotive industry. *Technovation, 20*, 665-676.

Persig, R. M. (1994). *Zen and the art of motorcycle maintenance*. New York: Bantam Books.

Peterson, D. K., Kim, C., Kim, J. H., & Tamura, T. (2002). The perceptions of information systems designers from the United States, Japan, and Korea on success and failure factors. *International Journal of Information Management, 22*, 421-439.

Pfaffenberger, B. (1992). Social anthropology of technology. *Annual Review of Anthropology, 21*(1), 491-516.

Pillai, K. (1996). The fountain model and its impact on project schedule. *SIGSOFT Softw. Eng. Notes, 21*(2), 32-38. DOI= http://doi.acm.org/10.1145/227531.227536

Pindyck, R. S., & Rubinfeld, D. L. (2006). *Microeconomia* (6ª ed.). São Paulo: Prentice Hall.

Pinto, J., & Kharbanda, O. (1995). *Successful project managers: Leading your team to success*. New York: Van Nostrand Reinhold.

Pinto, J., & Kharbanda, O. (1996, July). How to fail in project management (without really trying). *Business Horizons, 39*(4), 45. [Electronic version] Retrieved March 18, 2008, from Business Source Complete database.

PMBOK (2004). *A Guide to the Project Management Body of Knowledge,* 3rd Edition. Newtown Square, PA: Project Management Institute, Inc.

PMBOK (3rd Ed) (2004). *A guide to the project management body of knowledge*. Newton Square, PA: Project Management Institute.

PMI. (2000). *A Guide to the project management body of knowledge*. PA: Project Management Institute.

Polak, F. L. (1973). *The image of the future*. Amsterdam: Elsevier.

Poppendieck, M. (2002). *Wicked Problems, Software Development Magazine*. http://www.sdmagazine. com/documents/s=7134/sdm0205g/sdonline/authors. html#mpoppendieck, [Accessed 2002]

Porter, M. E. (1980). *Competitive strategy: Techniques for analyzing industries and competitors*. New York: The Free Press.

Porter, M. E. (1985). *Competitive advantage: Creating and sustaining superior performance*. New York: The Free Press.

Porter, M. E. (1985). What is strategy? *Harvard Business Review, 74*(6), 61.

Porter, M. E. (1991). Towards a dynamic theory of strategy. *Strategic Management Theory, 12*(1), 95-117.

Porter, M. E. (2001). Strategy and the Internet. *Harvard Business Review*, 61-79.

Porterhouse, M., & Dulewicz, V. (2007). *Agile project managers' leadership competencies* (Henley Working Paper Series). Henley Management College, Henley-on-Thames, UK.

Posavac, S. S. (2008). Overestimating the importance of the given information in multi attribute consumer judgment. *Journal of Consumer Psycholog*. Forthcoming.

Potter, D. L. (June, 1998) *Powerful partnerships: A shared responsibility for learning*. A Joint Report: American Association for Higher Education, American College Personnel Association & National Association of Student Personnel Administrators.

Pouloudi, A., & Whitley, E. (1997). Stakeholder identification in inter-organizational systems: gaining insights for drug use management systems. *European Journal of Information Systems*, (6), 1-14.

Powell, T. C., & Micallef, A. D. (1997). Information technology as competitive advantage: The role of human, business and technology resources. *Strategic Management Journal, 18*(5), 375-406.

Prahalad, C. K., & Hamel, G.-. (1990). The core competence of the corporation. *Harvard Business Review, to be verified*(May/Jun), 79-92.

Prasas, V., Baltusis, P., Greenberg, J., Rasin, V., Nelson, E., Shulman, M., Simonds, C., McNamara, D., Quesada, G., Syamil, A., & Doll, W. J. (2006). OEM new product development practices: the case of the automotive industry. *Journal of Supply Chain Management, 42*(3), 30-39.

Prensky, M. (2001). Digital natives, digital immigrants. *On the Horizon, 9*(5), 1–2. Retrieved February 15, 2008 from http://www.marcprensky.com/writing/Prensky%20-%20Digital%20Natives,%20Digital%20Immigrants%20-%20Part1.pdf

Prescott, M. B. & Conger, S. A. (1995). Information technology innovations: A classification by IT locus of impact and research approach. *The Data Base for Advances in Information Systems, 26*, 20-41.

Pressman, R. S. (2004). *Software engineering: A practitioner's approach*. The McGraw-Hill Companies. ISBN: 007301933X

Pressman, R. S. (6th Ed.) (2005). *Software engineering: A practitioner's approach,* Boston: McGraw Hill.

Project Management Institute (2004). *A guide to project management body of knowledge,* Third edition. ISBN 193069945X. Newtown Square, PA: Project Management Institute.

Project Management Institute. (2004). *A guide to the project management body of knowledge* (3rd ed.). Newtown Square, PA.

Project Manager (2007). *Project manager: Manage team performance*. Retrieved August 8, 2007, from http://www.method123.com/articles/2007/05/21/Team-Performance

Pulat, B. M. (1997). *Fundamentals of industrial ergonomics*. Prospect Heights, IL: Waveland Press, Inc.

Punter, T., & Lemmen, K. (1996). The MEMA-model: Towards a new approach for method engineering. *Information and Software Technology, 38*(4), 295.

Pyzdek, T. (1996) *The complete guide to the CQE*. Tucson, AZ: Quality Publishing.

Rad, P., & Levin, G., *Achieving project management success using virtual yeams,* (p.42, fig 3.4). Florida: J. Ross Publishing.

Ragsdell, G. (2006). The contribution of communities of practice to project management. In E. Coakes, & S. Clarke, (Eds.), *Encyclopedia of communities of practice in information and knowledge management* (pp. 104-107). Hershey, PA: IGI Global Publishing.

Rappaport, A. (1986). *Creating shareholder value: A guide for managers and investors*. New York: The Free Press.

Raz, T., & Michael, E. (2001). Use and benefits of tools for project risk management. *International Journal of Project Management, 19*(1), 9-17.

Reel, J. S. (1999). Critical cuccess factors in software projects. *IEEE Software*, May/June, 18-23.

Reeves, T. (2002). *Evaluating what really matters in computer-based education*. Retrieved October 10, 2002 from http://www.educationau.edu.au/archives/cp/reeves.htm

Reeves, T., & Hedberg, J. (2003). *Interactive learning systems evaluation*. Englewood Cliffs, NJ: Educational Technology Publications.

Reich, B. H., & Benbasat, I. (2000). Factors that influence the social dimension of alignment between business and information technology objectives. *MIT Quarterly, 24*(1), 81-112.

Richman, L. (2002). *Project management step-by-step*. New York: Amacon.

Rittel, H., & Webber, M. (1973). Dilemmas in a general theory of planning, (pp. 155-169). *Policy Sciences, 4.* Amsterdam: Elsevier Scientific Publishing Company, Inc.

Robbins, S. P. (1997). *Essentials of organizational behaviour*. Englewood Cliffs, NJ: Prentice Hall.

Robertson, I., Gibbons, P., Baron, H., MacIver, R., & Nyfield, G. (1999). Understanding management performance. *British Academy of Management, 10*(1), 5-12.

Robey, D., & Boudreau, M. (1999). Accounting for the contradictory organizational consequences of information technology: Theoretical directions and methodological implications. *Information Systems Research, 10*(2), 167-185.

Roblyer, M. D. (2003). *Integrating educational technology into teaching* (3rd Ed.). Merrill-Prentice Hall: New Jersey.

Robotham, D., & Jubb, R. (1996). Competencies: Measuring the unmeasurable. *Management Development Review, 9*(6), 25-29.

Rogers, E. M. (2003). *Diffusion of innovations* (5th ed.). New York: Free Press/Simon & Schuster, Inc.

Rogers, E. M., & Shoemaker, F. F. (1971). *Communication of innovations: A cross-cultural approach* (2nd ed.). New York: The Free Press.

Rolstadas, A. (2000, January 9 - 12). *Project 2000: A university/industry alliance to develop competence for the projectised business*. Paper presented at the IRNOP IV: Paradoxes of Project Collaboration in the Global Economy: Interdependence, Complexity and Ambiguity, Sydney, Australia.

Romero, C., & Ventura, S. (2007). Educational data mining: A survey from 1995 to 2005. *Expert Syst. Appl. 33*(1).

Romero, C., Ventura, S., & Garcia, E. (2008). Data mining in course management systems: Moodle case study and tutorial. *Computer & Education, 51.*

Romiszowski, A. J. (1981). *Designing instructional systems*. London: Kogan Page (reprint 1992).

Rosenthal, R. (1977). The PONS test: Measuring sensitivity to nonverbal cues. In P. McReynolds (Ed.), *Advances in psychological assessment*. San Francisco: Jossey-Bass.

Rosqvist, T., Koskela, M., & Harju, H. (2003). Software quality evaluation based on expert judgment. *Software Quality Journal, 11*(1), 39-55.

Ross, J. (2003, November). The importance of political influence in explaining project management success factors. In *Proceedings of 14th Australasian Conference on Information Systems*, (pp. 26-28). Perth, Western Australia.

Ross, J. W., & Vitale, M. R. (2000). The ERP revolution: Surviving vs thriving. *Information Systems Frontiers, 2*(2), 233-241.

Rossett, A. (1987). *Training needs assessment*. Englewood Cliffs, NJ: Educational Technology Publications.

Rossett, A., & Schafer, L. (2006). Job aids and performance support: The convergence of learning and work.

International Journal of Learning Technology, Inderscience Enterprises Limited, 2(4), 310-328.

Rowley, T. (1997). Moving beyond dyadic ties: A network theory of stakeholder influences. *Academy of Management Review, 22*, 887-910.

Rozenes, S., Vitner, G., & Spragget, S. (2006). Project control: literature review. *Project Management Journal, 37*(4), 5-14.

Rubin, J. S. (1996). And another thing…Utopia or Dystopia? *LOGOS, 7*(3), 242-244.

Russell, B. D. & Yilmaz, M. R. (2006, Fall). Using gap analysis to improve system acceptance. *Information Systems Management, 23*(4), 37-42. Retrieved September 19, 2007, from Proquest database.

Saarinen, T. (1996). An expanded instrument for evaluating information system success. *Information and Management, 31*, 103–118.

Saaty, T. L. (1990). How to make a decision: The analytic hierarchy process. *European Journal of Operational Research, 48*(1), 9-26.

Sakai (2008). *The Sakai project.* Sakai Foundation Portal. Retrieved May 04, 2008 from http://sakaiproject.org

Saladis, F. (2005). *Positive leadership in project management: Leading through laughter.* Retrieved July 21, 2007, from http://www.allpm.com/print.php?sid=1387

Saladis, F. (2006). *Positive leadership in project management: Leadership lessons learned.* Retrieved July 21, 2007, from http://www.allpm.com/print.php?sid=1635

Saladis, F. (2007). *Positive leadership in project management: Effective project leadership - leading project teams to higher levels of competency and effectiveness.* Retrieved July 21, 2007, from http://www.allpm.com/print.php?sid=1717

Saladis, F. (2007). *Positive leadership in project management: Establishing the roles of the project team.* Retrieved July 21, 2007, from http://www.allpm.com/print.php?sid=1657

Salaway, G., Katz, R. N., Caruso, J. B., Kvavik, R. B., & Nelson, M. R. (2006). *The ECAR study of undergraduate students and information technology.* Boulder, CO: EDUCAUSE. Available from http://www.educause.edu/LibraryDetailPage/666?ID=ERS0607

Salhieh, S. M., Monplaisir, L., & Singh, N. (2001). A flexible planning methodology to support global product development using CSCW tools. *Global Journal of Flexible Systems Management, 2*(4), 1-13.

Salvage Server Project Report (2003). *Selecting operating systems for and upgrading older computers.* Retrieved April 11, 2008, from http://www.fraw.org.uk/download/ssp/ssp-01.html

Sanders, D. (2008). *Built to serve.* New York: McGraw-Hill.

Sandford, B. (1988). *Strategies for maintaining professional competence.* Toronto, ON: Canadian Scholar's Press, Inc.

Santas, G. X. (Ed.). (2006). *The Blackwell guide to Plato's Republic.* Malden, MA: Blackwell Publishing Ltd.

Santhanam, R., & Hartono, E. (2003). Issues in linking information technology capability to firm performance. *MIT Quarterly, 27*(1), 125-153.

SAP and Deloitte Sued by FoxMeyer. (27 Aug 1998). The New York Times Retrieved 17 Feb 2007, from http://query.nytimes.com/gst/fullpage.html?res=9A05E7D7123CF934A1575BC0A96E958260

Sauer, C. (1993). *Partial abandonment as a strategy for avoiding failure.* In D. Avison, J. E. Kendall & J. I. Degross (Eds.), *Human, organizational, and social dimensions of information systems development.* North-Holland, The Netherlands: Elsevier Science Publishers.

Sauer, C. (1999). Deciding the future for IS failure: Not the choice you might think. In Currie & Galliers, *Rethinking management information systems: An introductory perspective.* UK: Oxford University Press.

Sauer, C., & Burton, S. (1999). Is there a place for department stores on the Internet? Lessons from an abandoned pilot. *Journal of Information Technology, 14*, 387-398.

Sauer, C., Southon, G., & Dampney, C. (1997). Fit, failure, and the house of horrors: Toward a configurational theory of IS project failure. In *Proceedings of the Eighteenth International Conference on Information Systems*, Georgia, US.

Savage, G., Nix, T., Whitehead, C., & Blair, J. (1991, May). Strategies for assessing and managing organizational stakeholders. *Academy of Management Executive, 5*(2), 61-75. [Electronic version] Retrieved April 10, 2008, from Business Source Complete database.

Sawyer, K. (2007). *Group genius: The creative power of collaboration.* New York: Basic Books.

Sawyer, R. D. (1996). *The complete art of war / Sun Tzu, Sun Pin; translated, with historical introduction and commentary, by Ralph D. Sawyer; with the collaboration of Mei-chun Lee Sawyer.* Boulder, CO: Westview Press.

Schimidt, R., Lytinnen, K., Keil, M., & Cule, P. (2001). Identifying software project risks: An international delphi study. *Journal of Management Information Systems, 17*(4), 5-36.

Schmidt, R. (2001). Identifying project risks: An international Delphi study. *Journal of Management Information Systems, 17*(4), 5-36.

Schniederjans, M. J., Hamaker, J. L., & Schniederjans, A. M. (2004). *Information technology investment.* New Jersey: World Scientific.

Schulmeyer, G. G., & McManus, J. I. (3rd Ed) (1999). *Handbook of software quality assurance.* Upper Saddle River, NJ: Prentice Hall.

Schultz, W. C. (1955). *FIRO: A three dimensional theory of interpersonal behaviour.* New York: Holt, Rinehart, Winston.

Schwalbe, K. (2000). *Information technology project management.* Cambridge, MA: Course Technology, Thomson Learning.

Schwalbe, K. (2006). *Introduction to project management.* Boston: Thomson Course Technology.

Schwarz, G. M., & Watson, B. M. (2005). The influ-ence of perceptions of social identity on information technology-enabled change. *Group & Organization Management, 30*(3), 289-318

Schweber, K. (2004). *Agile project management with scrum.* Redmond, WA: Microsoft Press.

Schweitzer, D. (Sept 2003). Track the true TCO: Watch out for hidden costs over the long term. *Processor, 25*(39).

Scott, J. E. (1999). *The FoxMeyer Drugs bankruptcy: Was it a failure of ERP?* Paper presented at The 5th Americas Conference on Information Systems (AMCIS), Milwaukee, WI .

Scriven, M. (1976). *Reasoning.* New York: McGraw-Hill.

Seels, B. B., & Richey, R. C. (1994). *Instructional technology: The definition and domains of the field.* Bloomington, IN: Association for Educational Communications and Technology.

SEI (1993). *Key practices of the capability maturity model.* Pittsburgh, PA: Software Engineering Institute, Carnegie Mellon University.

SEI (1994). *Proceedings of 3rd SEI Conference on Software Risk Management.* Pittsburgh PA: Software Engineering Institute.

SEI (1995). *Proceedings of 4th SEI Conference on Software Risk Management.* Pittsburgh PA: Software Engineering Institute.

SEI (1997). *Proceedings of 5th SEI Conference on Software Risk Management.* Pittsburgh PA: Software Engineering Institute.

Self and Peer Assessment Resource Kit. (n.d.). Retrieved April 15, 2008 from http://www.educ.dab.uts.edu.au/darrall/sparksite

Sen, A., Dacin, P. A., & Pattichis, C. (2006). Current trends in web data analysis. *Communications of the ACM, 49*(11), 85-91.

Senge, P., Kleiner, A., Roberts, C., Ross, R., Roth, G., & Smith, B. (1999). *The dance of change: The challenges to sustaining momentum in a learning organization.* New York: Doubleday.

Seppanen, V. (2002). Evolution of competence in software contracting projects. *International Journal of Project Management, 20,* 155-164.

Shapiro, C., & Katz, M. L. (1986). Technology adoption in the presence of network externalities. *Journal of Political Economy, 94*(4), 822-842.

Sherry, L., Billig, S., Tavalin, F., & Gibson, D. (2000). New insights on technology adoption in schools. *T.H.E. Journal, 27*(7), 43-46. Available at http://www.thejournal.com/articles/14594

Shneiderman, B. (1986). *Designing the user interface: Strategies for effective human-computer interaction.* Reading, MA: Addison-Wesley Publishing Company.

Shrock, S. (1991). A brief history of instructional development. In G. Anglin (Ed.), *Instructional technology: Past, present, and future* (pp. 11-18). Englewood, CO: Libraries Unlimited, Inc.

Siau, K., & Tan, X. (2005). Special theme of research in information systems analysis and design - IV Evaluation criteria for information systems development methodologies. *Communications of AIS, 2005*(16), 860-876.

Simchi-Levi, D., Kaminsky, P., & Simchi-Levi, E. (2003). *Designing and managing the supply chain: Concepts, strategies, and case studies* (2nd ed.). Boston: McGraw-Hill Irwin.

Simon, H. A. (1978). Rationality as process and as product of thought. *The American Economic Review, 68*(2), 1-17.

Simon, P., & Murray-Webster, R. (2005, December). Making sense of stakeholder mapping. *Project Manager Today, 8.* [Electronic version] Retrieved April 8, 2008 from Project Manager Today journal Web site.

Singh, N. (1996). *Systems approach to computer-integrated design and manufacturing.* New York: John Wiley & Sons.

Sisti, F. J., & Joseph, S. (1994) *Software risk evaluation method.* Pittsburgh PA: Software Engineering Institute.

Sivakumar, K., & Nakata, C. (2003). Designing global new product teams: optimizing the effects of national culture on new product development. *International Marketing Review, 20*(4), 397-445.

Skulmoski, G., Hartman, F., & DeMaere, R. (2000b). Superior and threshold project competencies. *Project Management, 6*(1), 10-15.

Slevin, D. P. (1989). *The Whole Manager.* New York, NY: Amacom.

Smagg, C. (2007). *Unleashing the power of remote collaboration & virtual team management.* [Weblog entry]. Marketing & Strategy Innovation Blog. 20 Nov 2007. (http://blog.futurelab.net/2007/11/unleashing_the_power_of_remote.html). Retrieved 19 Mar 2008

Smith, P. A. C. (2006). Organisational change elements of establishing, facilitating, and supporting CoPs. In E. Coakes, & S. Clarke (Eds.), *Encyclopedia of communities of practice in information and knowledge management* (pp. 400-406). Hershey, PA: IGI Global Publishing.

Smith, R. O. (2008). *Learning in virtual teams: A summary of current literature."* (http://www.msu.edu/~smithre9/Project12.htm). Retrieved 14 Mar 2008.

Soderlund, J. (2004). Building theories of project management: Past research, questions for the future. *International Journal of Project Management, 22*(3), 183-191.

Sommerville I. (2004). *Software engineering,* 7th Edition. Addison-Wesley Publishing Company, USA

Sower, V. E. Savoie, M. J., & Renick, S. (1999). *An introduction to quality management and engineering.* Upper Saddle River, NJ: Prentice Hall.

Spencer, L., & Spencer, S. (1993). *Competence At work: Models for superior performance.* New York: John Wiley & Sons, Inc.

Stacey, R. (1996). *Complexity and creativity in organizations.* San Francisco: Berrett-Koehler.

Stahl, B. (2004). *Responsible management of information systems.* Hershey, PA: IGI Global Publishing.

Stake, R. E. (2005). Qualitative case studies. In N. K. Denzin & Y. S. Lincoln (Eds.), *The Sage handbook of qualitative research* (3rd ed., pp. 443-466).

Stalk, G., Evans, P. B., & Shulman, L. E. (1992). Competing on capabilities: The new rules of corporate strategy. *Harvard Business Review, {to be verified} Mar/Abr,* 57-69.

Standards Australia (1995). *AS/NZS 4360:1995 risk management standards.* Homebush, NSW Australia.

Standards Australia (1999). *AS/NZS43660:1999 Risk management standards.* Melbourne, Australia.

Standish Group (1994). *The CHAOS report.* Retrieved March 1, 2004, from http://www.standishgroup.com/sample_research/chos_1994_1.php

Standish Group (1995). *The scope of software development project failures, CHAOS Report.* Retrieved March 15, 1997, from http://www.standishgroup.com/chaos.html

Standish Group (1998). *CHAOS '98: A summary review.* A Standish Group Research Note. The Standish Group, USA.

Statistical Process Control: the Founders' Way - www.statistical-process-control.org

Stein, T. (31 Aug 1998). SAP sued over R/3. *InformationWeek.*

Stewart, R., Sherif, M., & Daet, R. (2002). Strategic implementation of IT/IS projects in construction: a case study. *Automation in Construction, 11*(6), 681-694.

Stockman, S. G., Todd, A. R, & Robinson, G. A. (1990). A framework for software quality measurement. *IEEE Journal on Selected Areas in Communications, 8*(2), February, 224-233.

Straub, D., Gefen, D., & Boudreau, M.-C. (2005). The IS World quantitative, positivist research methods Website, (Ed.) D. Galletta. Retrieved from http://www.dstraub.cis.gsu.edu:88/quant

Subramaniam, G. H., Jiang, J., & Klein, G. (2006). Software quality and IS project performance improvements from software development process maturity and IS implementation strategies. *The Journal of Systems and Software, 80,* 616-627.

Suh, N. P. (1998). Axiomatic design theory for systems. *Research in Engineering Design., 10,* 189-209.

Summers, D. C. (2006). *Quality,* 4th edition. Upper Saddle River, NJ: Pearson/Prentice Hall.

Surowiecki, J. (2004). *The wisdom of crowds.* New York: Anchor Books.

Surry, D. W., & Farquhar, J. D. (1997). Diffusion theory and instructional technology. *Journal of Instructional Science and Technology, 2*(1) [online].

Surry, D. W., Ensminger, D. C., & Haab, M. (2005). A model for integrating instructional technology into higher education. *British Journal of Educational Technology, 36*(2) 327-329.

Survey Monkey. http://www.surveymonkey.com/

Symon, G., & Clegg, C. (2005, September). Constructing identity and participation during technological change. *Human Relations, 58*(9), 1141-1167. Retrieved September 20, 2007, from Proquest database.

Tagg, J. (2003). *The learning paradigm college.* Bolton, MA: Anker.

Tallon, P. P., Kraemer, K. L., & Gurbaxani, V. (2000). Executive's perceptions of business values of information technology: A process-oriented aproach. *Journal of Management Information Technology, 16*(4), 145-174.

Tannenbaum, R. & Schmidt, K. H. (1958). How to choose a leadership style. *Harvard Business Review,* March-April.

Tapscott, D. (1998). *Growing up digital: The rise of the net generation.* NY: McGraw Hill.

Tapscott, D., & Williams, A. D. (2006). *Wikinomics: How mass collaboration changes everything.* New York: The Penguin Group.

Tavares, L. V., Ferreira, J. A., & Coelho, J. S. (1999). The risk of delay of a project in terms of the morphology of its network. *European Journal of Operational Research, 119*, 510-537.

Tavares, L. V., Ferreira, J. A., & Coelho, J. S. (2004). A surrogate indicator of criticality for stochastic networks. *International Transactions in Operational Research, 11*, 193-202.

Ted, L. (2002). Managing the chaos of change. *The Journal of Business Strategy, 23*(5), 11.

Teece, D. J. (1987). Profiting from technological innovation: Implications for integration, collaboration, licensing and public policy. In D. J. Teece (Ed.), *The competitive challenge.* New York: Harper & Row.

Teece, D. J. (1992). Competition, cooperation, and innovation: Organizational arrangements for regimes of rapid technological progress. *Journal of Economic Behavior and Organizations, 18*(1), 1-26.

Telaro, D. (1999). The "next generation." *Project Manager. PM Network, 13*(1), 43-5.

ten Have, S., ten Have, W., Stevens, F., van der Elst, M., & Pol-Coyne, F. (2003). *Key management models: The management tools and practices that will improve your business.* Harlow, Essex: Financial Times Prentice Hall/ Pearson Education Limited.

Thamhain, H. (1991). Developing project management skills. *Project Management Journal, 12*(3), 39-44.

Thayer, R. H., & Fairley, R. E. (2nd Ed.) (1999). Software engineering project management: The silver bullets of software engineering. *Software Engineering Project Management*, (pp. 503-504). Los Alamitos, CA: IEEE Computer Society,.

The Royal Academy of Engineering (2004). The challenges of complex IT projects. *The Royal Academy of Engineering and the British Computer Society.* Retrieved April 08,2008, from www.bcs.org/server. php?show=conWebDoc.1167

Theus, M. (2002). Interactive data visualization using mondrian. *Journal of Statistical Software, 7*(11).

Thomke, S. H. (2006). Capturing the real value of innovation tools. *MIT Sloan Management Review, 47*(2), 24-32.

Thomke, S. H. (2007). *Managing product and service development: Text and cases.* New York: McGraw-Hill/ Irwin.

Thomke, S., & Fujimoto, T. (2000). The effect of 'front-loading' problem solving on product development performance. *Journal of Product Innovation Management, 17*(2), 128-42.

Thomke, S., & Nimgade, A. (2001). Siemens AG: global development strategy. Harvard Business School Case, No. 9-602-061. In *Managing product and service development: Text and cases.* New York: McGraw Hill.

Thompson, J. (2000). *Five essential skills will help you lead any project – no matter how distant.* Retrieved April 12, 2008, from http://www.qualitydigest.com/ sep00/html/teams.html.

Tidd, J., & Hull, F. M. (2003). *Service innovation. Organizational responses to technological opportunities & market imperatives.* London: Imperial College Press.

Todd, P., McKeen, J., & Gallupe, R. B. (1995). The evolution of IT job skills: A content analysis of IT job advertisements from 1970 to 1990. *MIT Quarterly, 19*(1), 1-27.

Todinov, M. (2005). *Reliability and risk models.* John Wiley & Sons LTD.

Tomei, L., A. (2005). *Taxonomy for the technology domain.* New York: McGraw-Hill.

Tornatzky, L. G. & Fleishcher, M. (1990). *The process of technological innovation.* Lexington, MA: Lexington Books.

Tornatzky, L. G. & Klein, K. J. (1982). Innovation characteristics and innovation adoption-implementation: A meta-analysis of findings. *IEEE Transactions on Engineering Management, 29*, 28-45.

Toulmin, S. (1969). *The uses of argument.* UK: Cambridge University Press.

Trant, J. (2006). *Understanding searches of an online contemporary art museum catalogue*. A preliminary study: http://conference.archimuse.com/system/files/trantSearchTermAnalysis061220a.pdf

Treacy, M. & Wiersema, F. (1996). *Discipline of market leaders: Choose your customers, narrow your focus, dominate your market*. London: HarperCollins.

Tripp, S., & Bichelmeyer, B. (1990). Rapid prototyping: An alternative instructional design strategy. *Educational Technology Research & Development, 38*(1), 31-44.

Trompenaars, F. & Prud'homme, P. (2004). *Managing change across corporate cultures*. Chichester, UK: Capstone.

Tsui, Y.-K. A. (1999). *A holistic model for driving improvement*. Dominguez Hills: California State University.

Tufts University. (2008). ITS training. Retrieved March 18, 2008 from http://ase.tufts.edu/its/training.htm

Turk, W. (2005). *Defense AT&L. Workforce development: Quality management - a primer*. (pp. 30-33).

Turner, J. R. (1999). *The handbook of project-based management: Improving the processes for achieving strategic objectives*. London: McGraw-Hill.

Turner, J. R., & Muller, R. (2003). On the nature of the project as a temporary organization. *International Journal of Project Management, 21*, 1-8.

Turner, J. R., & Müller, R. (2006). *Choosing appropriate project managers*. Newton Square, PA: Project Management Institute.

Umbach, J. (2006). Working with stakeholders: How to avoid the traps. *Feliciter, 52*(2), 47-47. [Electronic version] Retrieved March 30, 2008, from Academic Search Complete database.

University of Arizona, Computer Based Training. Retrieved April 15, 2008 from http://uacbt.arizona.edu/what_is.htm

University of Arizona, Office of Student Computing Resources (OSCR). Retrieved February 22, 2008 from http://www.oscr.arizona.edu/about

University of Louisville, *Student Tutorial Online Module Program (STOMP) Technology Module*. Retrieved April 15, 2008 from http://www.s4.louisville.edu/stomp/technology.swf

US Department of Defense (1984). *MIL-STD-882B, system safety program requirements*.Washington D.C., AMSC F3329.

US Economic Development Administration. (n.d.). *New growth theory, learning and technology*.

Van de Ven, A. H., Polley, D. E., Garud, R., & Venkataraman, S. (1999). *The innovation journey*. New York: Oxford University Press.

Van Grembergen, W. (Editor) (2002). *Information systems evaluation management,* (p. 285). Hershey, PA: IGI Global Publishing. [Electronic version] Retrieved March 7, 2008, from eBrary database.

Vandevoorde, S., & Vanhoucke, M. (2006). A comparison of different project duration forecasting methods using earned value metrics. *International Journal of Project Management, 24*, 289-302.

Vanhoucke, M. S. (2008). *The effect of rework in a project's activities on the forecasting accuracy of earned value metrics*. Working paper, under review.

Vanhoucke, M., & Vandevoorde, S. (2007). A simulation and evaluation of earned value metrics to forecast the project duration. *Journal of the Operational Research Society, 58*, 1361–1374.

Vanhoucke, M., & Vandevoorde, S. (2007). Measuring the accuracy of earned value/earned schedule forecasting predictors. *The Measurable News*, Winter, (pp. 26-30).

Vanhoucke, M., & Vandevoorde, S. (2008). Earned value forecast accuracy and activity criticality. *The Measurable News*, Summer, (pp. 13-16).

Vanhoucke, M., Coelho, J. S., Debels, D., Maenhout, B., & Tavares, L. V. (2008). An evaluation of the adequacy of project network generators with systematically sampled networks. *European Journal of Operational Research, 187*, 511-524.

Varian, H. R. (1999). *Intermediate microeconomics* (5th ed.). New York: W.W. Norton & Company.

Varian, H. R., & Shapiro, C. (1999). *Information rules - A strategic guide to the network economy.* Boston: Harvard Business School Press.

Venkatraman, N., & Henderson, J. (1998). Real strategies for virtual organizing. *Sloan Management Review, 40*(1).

Venturi, G, Troost, J., & Jokela, T. (2006). People, organizations, and processes: An inquiry into the adoption of user-centered design in industry. *International Journal of Human-Computer Interaction, 21*(2), 219-238.

Vessey, I., Ramesh, V., & Glass, R. L. (2002). Research in information systems: An empirical study of diversity in the discipline and its journals. *Journal of Management Information Systems, 19*(2), 129-174.

Virtual Teams. *Fifth generation work- virtual organization.* (http://www.seanet.com/~daveg/vrteams.htm). Retrieved 27 Feb 2008.

Visscher-Voerman, I., & Gustafson, K. (2004). Paradigms in the theory and practice of education and training design. *Educational Technology Research & Development, 52*(2), 69-89. [Electronic version] Retrieved April 1, 2008, from Academic Search Complete database.

Voas, J. (2003). Assuring software quality assurance. *IEEE Software,* May/June, 48-49.

Volti, R. (2006). *Society and technological change* (5th ed.). New York: Worth.

Vredenburg, K., Mao, J., Smith, P. W., & Carey, T. (2002). A survey of user-centered design practice. *CHI Letters, 4*(1), 471-478.

Wach, H. M. (2004). A case study in technology planning. *Community College Week, 10.*

Wade, M., & Hulland, J. (2004). Review: Resource-based view of IT research. *MIT Quarterly, 28*(1), 107-143.

Wagner, J. A., & Hollenbeck, J. R. (2005). *Organizational behavior: Securing competitive advantage* (5th ed.). Mason, OH: Thomson South-Western.

Wallmueller, E. (2004). *Software quality assurance - A practical approach.* NJ: Prentice Hall.

Walls, J. G., Widmeyer, G., & El Sawy, O. A. (1992). Building an information system design theory for vigilant EIS. *Information Systems Research, 3*(1), 36-59.

Walsham, G. (1993). *Interpreting information systems in organizations.* Chichester, UK: Wiley.

Walton, M. (1999). Strategies for lean product development. *The Lean Aerospace Initiative Working Paper Series,* WP99-01-91. Massachusetts Institute of Technology, Cambridge, USA.

Wang, F., & Hannafin, M. J. (2005). Design-based research and technology-enhanced learning environments. *Educational Technology Research and Development, 53*(4), 5-23.

Wang, W., & Zaiane, O. R. (2002, September 2-6). Clustering Web sessions by sequence alignment. In *Proceedings of the 13th international Workshop on Database and Expert Systems Applications.* DEXA. IEEE Computer Society, Washington, DC, 394-398.

Ward, A., Sobek, D. K. II, & Liker, J. K. (1998). Another look at how Toyota integrates product development. *Harvard Business Review,* August.

Wastell, D., & Newman, M. (1996). Information system design, stress and organizational change in the ambulance services: A tale of two cities. *Accounting, Management and Information Technology, 6*(4), 283-300.

Watkins, A. F. (2005). Using learning styles in college teaching. *Journal on Excellence in College Teaching, 16*(3), 83-101.

Watson, L. W. (2004). Access and technology. *New Directions for Community Colleges, 128,* 31-38.

Weber, R. (1999). *Information systems control and audit.* Upper Saddle River, NJ: Prentice-Hall, Inc.

Webster's new world dictionary (3rd college ed.). (1988). New York: Webster's New World.

Wee, C. H. (1994). Sun Tzu's art of war: Selected applications to strategic thinking and business practices. *International Review of Strategic Management, 5,* 83.

Weill, P., & Ross, J. (2005, Winter). A matrixed approach to designing IT governance. *MIT Sloan Management Review, 46*(2), 26-34. [Electronic version] Retrieved April.

Wejnert, B. (2002). Integrating models of diffusion of innovations: A conceptual framework. *Annual Review of Sociology, 28*, 297-326.

Westera, W. (2004). On strategies of educational innovation: Between substitution and transformation. *Higher Education, 47*, 501–517.

Westerman, Cotteleer, Austin & Nolan. (1999). *Tektronix, Inc.: Global ERP Implementation*, Harvard Business School, case no. 9-699-043. Boston: Harvard Business School Publishing.

Westerveld, E. (2003). The project excellence model: Linking success criteria and critical success factors. *International Journal of Project Management, 21*, 411-418.

Wheeler, B. C. (2007). Open source 2007: How did this happen? *Educause Review, 39*(4), 12-27.

Whelan, D. L. (2004). Generation Tech. *School Library Journal*, (pp. 48-50). Retrieved April 25, 2008, from http://www.schoollibraryjournal.com/

Whelan, J. W. (1985). *Cases and materials on federal government contracts*. Mineola, NY: The Foundation Press, Inc.

White, T. S. (1998). Next generation project management: Back to the future. *Tides of Change '98 PMI. Proceedings of the 29th Annual Project Management Institute 1998 Seminars and Symposiums*. AIPM. PMI.

Wiek, J. (2007). *Parasites are the agents of progress: Interview with Michel Serres*. Retrieved 2 May 2008, from http://www.philippwente.com/daten/philipp-wente_200708_hpc_serres_artikel.pdf

Williamson, O. E. (1975). *Markets and hierarchies*. New York: Free Press.

Williamson, O. E. (1979). Transaction cost economics: The governance of contractual relations. *Journal of Law and Economics, 22*(2), 233-262.

Williamson, O. E. (1986). *Economic organization - Firms, markets and policy control*. New York University Press.

Williamson, O. E. (1996). *The mechanisms of governance*. UK: Oxford University Press.

Winter, M., Andersen, E. S., Elvin, R., & Levene, R. (2006). Focusing on business projects as an area for future research: An exploratory discussion of four different perspectives. *International Journal of Project Management, 24*(8), 699-709.

Wolfe, R. A. (1994). Organizational innovation: Review, critique and suggested research directions. *Journal of Management Studies, 31*(3), 405-431.

Womack, J. P., & Jones D. T. (2003). *Lean thinking: banish waste and create wealth in your corporation*. Simons and Schuster -Audio Book.

Womack, J. P., Jones, D. T., & Ross, D. (1991). *The machine that changed the world: The story of lean production*. New York: Harper Collins.

Wong, B., & Tein, D. (2004). Critical success factors for enterprise resource planning projects. *Journal of the Australian Institute of Project Management, 24*(1), 28-31.

Wong, Y. Y., Thomas, M., & George, L. (1998). The strategy of an ancient warrior: An inspiration for international managers. *Multinational Business Review, 6(1), 83*.

Wood, R. C. (2007). How strategic innovation really gets started. *Strategy & Leadership, 35*(1), 21. Retrieved September 9, 2007, from Proquest database.

Woollett, J. (2000). Innovate or die - The future for project management. Prosperity through partnership. *World Project Management Week. Incorporating Project Management Global Conference, AIPM (CD-Rom)*.

Wu, W. Y., Chou, C. H., & Wu, Y. A. Wu (2004). A study of strategy implementation as expressed through Sun Tzu's principles of war. *Industrial Management + Data Systems 104*(5/6), 396.

Wyatt, S. (2005). Non-users also matter: The construction of users and non-users of the internet. In N. Oudshoorn &

T. Pinch (Eds.), *How users matter: The co-construction of users and technology.* (pp. 67-79). Cambridge, MA: The MIT Press.

Wysocki, R. K. (2004). *Project management process improvement.* Artech House Publishers.

Wyssusek, B. & Schwartz, M. (2003). *Towards a socio-pragmatic-constructivist understanding of information systems.* Hershey, PA: IRM Press.

Xhauflair, V., & Rorive, B. (2003). What binds together virtual teams? Some answers from three case studies. *XIth European congress on Work and Organisational psychology 14-17 May 2003- Lisboa.*

XP (2007). http://www.extremeprogramming.org/Kent.html, [accessed 2007]

Yale University. *Email kiosks.* Retrieved April 15, 2008 from http://www.yale.edu/its/media/computing/kiosks.html

Yates, J. C., & Arne, P. H. (2004). Balancing the scales: Managing risks in IT projects. The *Computer & Internet Lawyer Journal, 21*(8), 1-6.

Yeo, K. T. (2002). Critical failure factors in information system projects. *International Journal of Project Management, 20*, 241-246.

Yin, R. K. (2002). *Case study research: Design and methods* (3rd ed.). Newbury Park, CA: Sage Publications.

Yukl, G. A. (2002). *Leadership in organizations.* 4th Ed. Englewood Cliffs, NJ: Prentice-Hall.

Zajonc, R. B. & Markus, H. (Sept 1982). Affective and cognitive factors in preferences. *Journal of Consumer Research, 9*, 123-131.

Zaltman, G., Duncan, R., & Holbek, J. (1973). *Innovations and organizations.* New York: John Wiley and Sons.

Zandin, K. B., & Maynard, H. B. (n.d.). *Maynard's industrial engineering handbook.* 5th ed. McGraw-Hill Professional.

Zuccala, A., Thelwall, M., Oppenheim, C., & Dhiensa, R. (2008). Web intelligence analyses of digital libraries: A case study of the national electronic library for health (NeLH). *Journal of Documentation, 63*(4), 558-589.

Zwerman, B. L., Thomas, J. L., & Haydt, S. M. (2002). Exploring the past to map the future: Investigating the development of established professions to understand the professionalisation of project management. *Frontiers of Project Management Research and Application: Proceedings of PMI Research Conference, AIPM .*

About the Contributors

Terry T. Kidd received his graduate education training from the Texas A&M University. He has presented at international conferences on technology diffusion and adoption and on issues dealing with faculty and staff development. His research interests include technology diffusion and adoption within an educational and community context to support teaching, learning, and human capital development and in the critical perspectives on the intersection of gender, race and class in shaping the adoption and use of ICT's within community and educational context. Dr. Kidd is an experienced educators, consultant, and researcher. He is the co-author of the *Handbook of Research on Instructional Systems Technology, Social Information Technology: Connecting Society and Cultural Issue, and Wired for Learning: An Educators Guide to Web 2.0.*

* * *

Jeihan M. Auda Abu-Tayeh is a head of the International Agencies & Commissions Division at the Jordanian Ministry of Planning and International Cooperation. In her capacity, she has the opportunity to maintain sound cooperation relations with the World Bank Group, as well as the UN Agencies, in order to extend to Jordan financial and technical support for developmental projects through setting appropriate programs and plans, building and improving relations with those organizations. This is achieved through loans and aids programs, by means of designing *project proposals*, conducting *Problem & Needs Assessment* for the concerned Governmental and Non-Governmental Jordanian entities, followed by active participation in extensive evaluation processes, conducted by either the UN Country Team, or the World Bank Group Country Team. She acquired her bachelor's in Pharmaceutical Science and Management from Al-Ahlyya Amman University. Furthermore, in 2002, she got her MBA with emphasis on *"International Marketing & Negotiations Technique"*, with an outstanding GPA of 3.87 out of 4 *(with honors)* from Saint Martin's College, State of Washington; U.S.A.

Evon M. O. Abu-Taieh is a PhD holder in simulation. A USA graduate for both her Master of Science and Bachelor's degrees with a total experience of 19 years. Author of many renowned research papers in the airline and IT, PM, KM, GIS, AI, simulation, security and ciphering. She is the editor/author of the book: *Utilizing Information Technology Systems Across Disciplines: Advancements in the Application of Computer Science* (IGI Global Publishing); the editor/author of *Handbook of Research on Discrete Event Simulation Environments: Technologies and Applications* (IGI Global Publishing); guest editor of the *Journal of Information Technology Research (JITR);* editorial board member in: *International Journal of E-Services and Mobile Applications* (IJESMA) and *International Journal of Information Technology Project Management (IJITPM)* and *International Journal of Information Sys-*

tems and Social Change (IJISSC). She is the author of *Simulation and Modeling: Current Technologies and Applications* (IGI Global Publishing).

Ali Alavizadeh, PhD is an assistant professor in the Department of Industrial and Engineering Technology at Morehead State University. He received his PhD from Indiana State University in technology management (manufacturing systems). He has taught various courses in the areas of quality control, time and motion study, industrial management, hydraulics, and total quality improvement. His research interests include nonlinear dynamical systems, and complex systems modeling and simulation.

Fayez Albadri is a well established consultant, manager and educator for over two decades. He is recognized as an information technology specialist and management expert for his distinguished skills and sound experience in managing IT projects and the implementation of ERP systems and e-business solutions. Dr. Albadri is a pioneer researcher and academic with important contributions in the areas of innovative entrepreneurship, IT strategic planning, management modeling, esolutions, information security, risk management, knowledge management and performance management. He is renowned in the academic circles for his development of (IPRM) the Integrated Project Risk Model and for the introduction of (IELCM) the Integrated ERP Life-Cycle Management approach. Throughout his career, Dr. Albadri has undertaken major professional business and management consulting & training assignments, and important research works in Australia, Japan, Thailand, Hungary, India, Mexico, USA, UK, UAE, Ireland, Morocco and Jordan. This included the delivery of numerous seminars, workshops and training courses to hundreds of academics and professionals from government and non government organizations in Australia and the Middle East region.

Joni A. Amorim, PhD has received his undergraduate degree in mathematics from UNICAMP (Universidade Estadual de Campinas), Brazil. He is a MSc in engineering and a PhD candidate at FEEC (Faculdade de Engenharia Elétrica e de Computação) at UNICAMP. His research interests involve project management, multimedia production and ICT-based education. He works as a project manager and as a teacher in distance education projects at UNICAMP. He develops research with the Universidad Politécnica de Valencia, Spain, on CALL (Computer Assisted Language Learning).

Sohail Anwar, PhD, is currently serving as an associate professor of engineering at The Penn State University Altoona College. In addition, Dr. Anwar is a professional associate for the Management Development Programs and Services at Penn State University, University Park. He is also serving as the chair of the EET Advisory Faculty Committee for Excelsior College, New York. Since 1996, he has been an invited professor of electrical engineering at Universite d' Artois, France. Dr. Anwar is also serving as the editor-in-chief of the *Journal of Engineering Technology* and as an associate editor of the *Journal of Pennsylvania Academy of Science*. Dr. Anwar is a senior member of IEEE and serves as a reviewer for the *IEEE Transactions in Education*.

Bendik Bygstad holds a PhD in computer science from Aalboard University and a Masters of Sociology from the University of Oslo. He worked 15 years in the computer industry, mostly as an IT manager. He is currently an associate professor at the Norwegian School of Information Technology. His main research interest is the relationship between information systems and innovation. Other research interests include project management and research methods. He has published in several IS journals.

Geof Corb is the senior director of enterprise applications at Johns Hopkins University. He is responsible for the university's student systems and educational technologies and has recently assumed responsibility for the support of the SAP implementation at the university and health system. Prior to Hopkins, Corb managed software and systems development for an e-business consultancy, specializing in the development of highly-usable internet, intranet, and extranet web systems. Corb is a graduate of the Whiting School of Engineering at the Johns Hopkins University, holding a Bachelor's degree in computer science, and is currently pursuing an MBA from the Carey Business School, also at JHU. He is also a certified Project Management Professional (PMP). In his spare time, he is a certified Emergency Medical Technician (EMT) and volunteers with his local fire department.

Chad Cray, after leaving the US Army in 2004, Cray was hired on with L-3 communications as a systems engineer. During his time at L-3, Cray graduated from the Keller Graduate School of Management of DeVry University with a Master's in information systems management. Upon graduation, he immediately enrolled in Capella University's organization and management PhD program and is currently in the process of writing his dissertation.

Michael L. Crow is an associate registrar at Kansas State University. He is the Registration and Records Team Lead for the LASER Project to replace the mainframe-based legacy student information system with a new enterprise system from Oracle Corporation. Past projects include the implementation of a shared-services imaging system at K-State, finance and payroll systems for Management and Training Corporation and the start-up of a new Job Corps campus. He holds a BA degree in political science, a BSc in business administration-marketing and a Master's in business administration, all from Kansas State University.

Francisco C Cua, PhD has more than twenty years of experience in accountancy, enterprise systems, consultancy, and teaching. During the writing of this chapter, he was a senior lecturer at the School of Applied Business, Otago Polytechnic, New Zealand. He has worked internationally in Hong Kong, Shanghai, and Beijing as a consultant of Asian Development Bank's project and taken part in various projects as a business analyst, functional analyst, systems manager, and Oracle systems administrator in New Zealand. Diffusion of information systems, business models, supply chain, innovation, and entrepreneurship are his research areas of interest.

Michele De Lorenzi, PhD, has been the head of technology exploration of the strategic program ETH World at ETH Zurich from 2004 until 2005. Currently he is member of the ICT-Commission, a body consulting the executive board of ETH Zurich about the ICT strategy and the use of ICT resources in all application areas. De Lorenzi studied computer science at ETH Zurich where he received his PhD in 1996. Until 2004 he was a partner of a consultancy company for information and telecommunication systems in Zurich, Switzerland. He is also manager of Swiss IT Intelligence Community, a vendor-independent peer-to-peer network for fostering an exchange of ideas and experience among IT departments of large Swiss companies.

Pamila Dembla, PhD, is currently an assistant professor and program coordinator of information systems in the Computer Science and Information Systems (CSIS) Department at Kennesaw State University. She received her PhD in management information systems from University of Memphis,

Tennessee in 2003. She has taught a variety of graduate and undergraduate IS courses such as systems analysis and design, human computer interface design, project management, and database design. Her research interests include innovation adoption, electronic commerce, and global information technology management. She has published book chapters and in journals in addition to presenting at many national and international conferences.

Veronica Diaz is the instructional technology for the Maricopa Community College District, Maricopa Center for Learning and Instruction (MCLI). In that capacity, she leads learning technologies faculty professional development initiatives for the ten colleges. She is also the co-principal investigator of the Achieving Technological Literacy in Arizona for Students and Teachers, and the National Science Foundation Grant. Previously, she was responsible for the University of Arizona's College of management teaching and learning with technology initiatives, Principal Investigator for the HP Technology for Teaching Grant and their Tablet PC Initiative. She also serves as an adjunct professor at the University of Arizona and Northern Arizona University where she teachers various marketing, organization development, technology, and research courses at the undergraduate and graduate level.

Katy E. Ellis, CSP, is an assistant professor in the Department of Information Systems and Technology within the College of Business and Technology at Northeastern State University located in Tahlequah, Oklahoma. She has over twenty years of industry and Department of Defense experience in the field of integrated logistics support specializing in safety systems and the cognitive as well as physical aspects of human factors engineering. She has received recognition from industry as well as the US Air Force for her work in facilitating employee adoption of new and enhanced software systems.

Maha Thamer El-Maheid is a lecturer in the Institute of Traditional Islamic Art and Architecture in The World Islamic Science and Education University. She earned her Master's Degree in management information system. El-Maheid holds two Bachelor degrees: one in interior design, and the second in business management and accounting. She has worked as an interior designer specializing in Islamic arts. El-Maheid enjoys research in the knowledge management field and management information systems. She has published a paper on the reason of failure of information systems in underdeveloped countries and a chapter titled "*Discovering Knowledge Channels in Learning Organization- Case study of Jordan*" in the book *Utilizing Information Technology Systems Across Disciplines: Advancements in the Application of Computer Science.*

Lauren Fancher is director of GALILEO Support Services, for the Board of Regents of the University System of Georgia in their Office of Information and Instructional Technology in Athens, Georgia. With a background in fine arts and digital media, the author has worked in the field of information and instructional technology as a project manager, administrator, designer, and evaluator for over 11 years. Libraries and learning are special interests. She gratefully acknowledges Dr. Thomas Reeves of the University of Georgia College of Education, major professor for her Master's in instructional technology and chief influence on the development of her evaluation practices.

Tony Garrett is a visiting professor at Korea University Business School, Seoul. Prior to his arrival in Korea, he was a senior lecturer in marketing at the University of Otago, Dunedin. Tony's research interests are focused on national differences in new product development and product development for fast moving goods areas, and he has presented and published several papers in this area. He has worked on collaborative research projects with Jilin University (China), the National University of Singapore, HEC (Paris), Chulalongkorn University (Bangkok) and the University of Alabama in Huntsville and has strong links with the New Zealand food and agribusiness industries and is a member of several New Zealand agrifood industry and rural associations, including acting as chair of the Marketing Division of the New Zealand Institute of Food Science and Technology, and the Topoclimate Otago Steering Committee. He also has experience in the food industry, where he was involved in market development activities for several international brands.

Francis T. Hartman, PhD, Dr. Hartman is a professor at the University of Calgary in the project management specialization. He brings over 30 years of experience coupled with more than a decade of practice as a researcher and teacher. Hartman has worked on over $80 Billion worth of projects around the world and has published extensively on project management. Publications include four books (including the national best seller *Don't Park Your Brain Outside*) and numerous international invited book chapters related to creativity, technology management and project management. He is involved in the exploration and development of new and emerging concepts with the leading researchers in the world.

Steve Hellen is the director of Academic Applications at Johns Hopkins University. He is responsible for the university's portfolio of centrally-managed educational technology offerings as well as the records and registration aspects of the student information system. Before Hopkins, he was a consultant with Accenture where he focused on technical architecture and enterprise applications for clients in the telecom, pharmaceutical and insurance sectors. Hellen holds a Bachelor's degree in engineering science from Loyola College in Maryland, a Post Baccalaureate Certificate in Geographic Information Systems from Penn State University, a Master's degree in environmental science and policy from Johns Hopkins University and is a Microsoft Certified Solution Developer. In 2006, Steve and his wife became the proud parents of a wonderful daughter.

Robert K. Hilbrand is the executive director of Project White Hat, an information securities and technology project management consulting firm. He has over 15 years of experience in information systems administration, information security, and IT project management. He has Bachelor's of Arts in sociology from Southwest Texas State University and a Master's of Science in technology project management - information systems security from the University of Houston, where his expertise lies within in the concept of the LiveCD as a desktop platform for general-purpose computing needs within a public access environment.

Peter Hylton is the director of Motorsports at the Indiana University Purdue University Indianapolis (IUPUI) where he also teachers course in mechanical engineering technology. He has previous experience in both the aerospace and motosports industries. He has experience in managing technical risk management programs as a chief design engineer on the Comanche helicopter design program and an integration manager on the Joint Strike Fighter development effort.

Deepak Khazanchi, PhD, is the professor of Information Systems and Quantitative Analysis and associate dean for Academic Affairs in College of Information Science & Technology (IS&T) at the University of Nebraska in Omaha (UNO). Dr. Khazanchi's current research interests are focused in the areas of virtual project management, project management best practices, B2B assurance services and risk analysis in extended enterprise environments and the application of philosophy of science in the information systems discipline. His research has been published in numerous peer-reviewed journals and conferences including *Journal of the Association of Information Systems (JAIS), Decision Support Systems and Information Processing and Management.*

Melanie Karas earned her Executive MBA from Texas Woman's University in 2007. She currently resides in Ohio, where she is a manager at a leading health insurance company. As part of her role, Karas is responsible for leading her team to achieve success in a number of projects.

Gjermund Lanestedt holds a Master's of Management from the Norwegian School of Management (BI) and a Master's of Technology from the Norwegian University of Life Sciences (UMB) Oslo. He worked 10 years in different governmental bodies, both as a project management and as a line manager. After that, he has been associated with different ICT consultancy firms in 10 year. Currently he is chief consultant at the Norwegian IT and telecom consultancy firm Teleplan. E-government, ICT policies and service innovation in the public sector are Lanestedt's main field of interest as a consultant and as a research.

Carlos Machado, DEng has received his undergraduate degree in applied mathematics from UNICAMP (Universidade Estadual de Campinas), Brazil. He has got his Master's degree in engineering, from UNICAMP, focused on business process modeling and simulation applied to industrial systems. He has got his Doctor's degree in engineering, from UNICAMP, focused on supply chain management. He has worked for a telecommunication company designing operation support software for digital convergence networks. He works with business process analysis for an electronic industry in Brazil.

Patricia McGee is an associate professor of instructional in the Department of Educational Psychology at the University of Texas-San Antonio. With over 20 years of experience in distributed learning, she is the recipient of the US Distance Learning Association (USDLA) Gold Award Online Technology. She has been awarded research fellowships with the National learning Infrastructure Initiative (EDUCAUSE Learning Initiative), American Society of Engineering Education/Navy and the ASEE/Force. A prolific author, Dr. McGee publishes in the area of learning objects, faculty support of technology utilization, and learning systems and tools.

Ralf Müller, PhD is an associate professor in Business Administration at Umeå University in Sweden and adjunct professor of Project Management at the Norwegian School of Management BI and the Graduate School of Management in Lille, France. He lectures and researches in project, program, and portfolio management, in project governance, leadership, and in research methodologies. His more than 60 scientific publications include four books, a number of book chapters, journal and conference papers. He frequently speaks at academic and practitioner conferences, such as those of the Project Management Institute, the International Project Management Association, and NASA. Prior to his academic career he worked in a variety of consulting and management positions in the IT industry, including a time as worldwide director of Project Management at NCR Teradata. During that time he consulted corporations and governments in 42 different countries to improve their project management and governance capabilities.

Henryk R. Marcinkiewicz is an educator who has served as a senior university administrator, director, and professor. He has also worked as an instructional designer and teacher in diverse locales in the United States and internationally. He studied the conditions necessary for the adoption of technology in particularly among faculty members. He was award the doctorate in instructional systems from the Pennsylvania State University.

Owen McGrath, PhD, is technical operations manager for Educational Technology Services at the University of California (UC) Berkeley. During the past twenty years, he has led development and support efforts for multimedia courseware, collaborative on-line tools, and more recently the Sakai environment. He has a PhD in education from UC Berkeley and Bachelor's degrees in english and computer science.

Rosana G. S. Miskulin, DEd, has a Doctoral degree in education and is a researcher at IGCE (Instituto de Geociências e Ciências Exatas) at UNESP (Universidade Estadual Paulista), Brazil. Her research interests involve teacher training, mathematics education and ICT-based education.

Mauro S. Miskulin, DEng, has a Doctoral degree in engineering and is a researcher at FEEC (Faculdade de Engenharia Elétrica e de Computação) at UNICAMP (Universidade Estadual de Campinas), Brazil. His research interests involve distance and ICT-based education. He is the president of the Ibero-American Science and Technology Education Consortium.

Jaby Mohammed received his PhD in industrial engineering from University of Louisville in 2006. His research interest includes advanced manufacturing; project management, computer aided design, six sigma, and enterprise resource planning. He is a member of IIE, ASQ, SME, POMS, ITEA, NAIT, KAS, and Informs. He received honorable "Kentucky Colonel" title in 2007.

Leslie F. Monplaisir is an associate professor and director of the Engineering Management Masters Program that is offered exclusively to Ford Motor Company and Visteon with an annual budget of over one million dollars. His research interests include: collaborative product design and development (CPDD), manufacturing optimization, computer integrated manufacturing, and supply chain modeling. Dr. Monplaisir has over thirty publications in these areas and directs a NSF funded laboratory in collaborative engineering. He has research grants from the NSF and Industry (Ford, Sun Microsystems and Motorola) to conduct ongoing research in global product development. He has recently published a book in *Collaborative Engineering for Product Design and Development*. He holds graduate degrees in integrated manufacturing systems and engineering management for University of Birmingham (UK) and University of Missouri-Rolla. He is a senior member of the Institute of Industrial Engineering (IIE), Society of Manufacturing Engineering (SME) and Institute of Electrical Engineering (UK).

Mysore Narayanan, PhD, obtained his doctorate from the University of Liverpool, England. Since joining Miami University in 1980, he has been invited to contribute dozens of articles to several encyclopedias and works of reference. Over the past 28 years, Dr. Narayanan has published and presented more than a hundred papers at local, regional , national and international conferences. He has also designed, developed, organized and chaired conferences for Miami University and dozens of conference sessions for a wide variety of organizations.

Bimal Nepal, PhD, is an associate professor at the Texas A&M University in the Industrial Distribution Program. He earned his PhD in industrial engineering from Wayne State University and his MS in industrial engineering from the Asian Institute of Technology. His research interests include design optimization, systems engineering, operations research techniques in new product development, product architecture and supply chain design, lean product creation, applied operations research and statistics.

Dawn Owens is a doctoral student in the Department of Information Technology at the University of Nebraska at Omaha. Owen's research interests are in project management, software quality assurance, virtual teams, and IT leadership. She has extensive experience in both industry and the academic world. She has worked as a part-time instructor at the University of Nebraska at Omaha teaching MIS related topics. In addition to teaching, she has worked in the professional environment with industry experience encompassing both technical and management expertise. Her background includes all aspects of software development – analysis, design, implementation, testing, maintenance, and project management.

Debra OrosBullard, PMP, began her career in 1984 at Mare Island Naval Shipyard in Vallejo, California as an engineering technician involved in nuclear submarine overhaul. She remained with the Department of Defense for 21 years working at Navy, Air Force and Army installations. In 2005, she moved to the private sector as a project manager after earning her Master's of Science in project management. Her current project is located in Thailand and requires use of virtual teaming to manage the project team.

Gary Pan is a practice assistant professor in the School of Accountancy at Singapore Management University. His research focuses on the area of IT project management and control, and IT capability development. His article have appeared in leading IS related journals including *Management Information Systems Quarterly Executive* (MISQE), *IEEE Transactions on Engineering management* (IEEETEM), *European Journal of Operations Research* (EJOR), *Journal of American Society Information Science and Technology* (JASIST), *Communications of ACM* (CACM), *Information and Management* (I&M), and *Decision Support Systems* (DSS).

James Price is the founder of Taiji Consulting LLC, a boutique project management consulting firm. Though an economist by training, Mr. Price has more than 10 years of experience in the information technology domain, including Fortune 500 consulting, project managing enterprise IT systems, and corporate training. He received his Master's degree in information systems from Kennesaw State University and PMI's Project Management certification in 2008.

Mahesh S. Raisinghani, PhD, is an associate professor in the Executive MBA program at the TWU School of Management. He is a Certified E-Commerce Consultant (CEC) and a Project Management Professional (PMP). Dr. Raisinghani was awarded the 2008 Excellence in Research & Scholarship award and the 2007 G. Ann Uhlir Endowed Fellowship in Higher Education Administration. He was also the recipient of TWU School of Management's 2005 Best Professor Award for the Most Innovative Teaching Methods; 2002 research award; 2001 King/Haggar Award for excellence in teaching, research and service; and a 1999 UD-GSM Presidential Award. His research has been published in several academic journals such as *IEEE Transactions on Engineering Management, Information & Management, Information Resources Management Journal, International Journal of Innovation and Learning, Journal of IT Review, Journal of Global IT Management* among others and international/national conferences.

Otavio Prospero Sanchez, PhD is full professor of Decision Sciences and Information Systems at Sao Paulo Methodist University and Fundacao Getulio Vargas - FGV-EAESP, in Brazil. His research and consulting interests include IT management, Outsourcing, IT investment analysis and information economics. He has been serving as reviewer for *MIS Quartely* - MISQ, *Journal of Management Information Systems* - JMIS e *Brazilian Administration Review* - BAR and is the current editor of *Revista Organizacoes em Contexto* (http://mjs.metodista.br/index.php/roc) a Brazilian journal edited in Portuguese. Professor Otavio holds a Doctorate and an MBA degree from FGV-EAESP and electronic engineering degree from Faculdade de Engenharia Industrial.

Asim Abdel Rahman El Sheikh was awarded his Master's degree in operational research from London School of Economics & Political Science, University of London, London, England. Later he was awarded his PhD in simulation and modeling. He is currently the dean of Faculty of Information Systems & Technology, The Arab Academy for Banking & Financial Sciences, Jordan. Further, he is the author of two books and more than 35 papers. His research interest areas: software piracy, software outsourcing, simulation modeling, SW engineering.

A. J. Gilbert Silvius, PhD (1963) is professor of Business, ICT and Innovation at Utrecht University of Applied Sciences. Silvius has over 20 years experience as a consultant in the area of business and IT. He joined Utrecht University in 2003 and has since published on IT business value, business IT alignment and project management.

Gregory J. Skulmoski, PhD, Dr. Skulmoski teaches project management in the College of Information Technology at Zayed University in the United Arab Emirates. He has published in leading journals and other professional publications. His career spans both academic and hands on project experiences. He has project experience on over $5 billion projects in IT, government, health care, retail, and, oil and gas sectors. Skulmoski has been actively involved in developing project management standards such as the influential PMBOK Guide®, Work Breakdown Structure Standard (2001), the Organizational Project Management Maturity Model and the Project Manager Competency Model (1999) all from PMI. He continues to assist businesses through his consulting practice.

Daniel W. Surry, PhD, serves as a professor in the Instructional Design & Development program at the University of South Alabama in Mobile. He teaches courses related to instructional design, performance technology, and the development of macro level training systems. His research and consulting interests focus on factors that enable the implementation of innovations in organizations. He holds a Doctor of Education degree from the University of Georgia and previously served on the faculty at the University of Southern Mississippi, the University of Alabama, and California State University, Fresno.

Hasan Tinmaz is a doctoral student in the Computer Education and Instructional Technology program at Middle East Technical University, Turkey. His research interests include educational technologies, instructional design, instructional technology planning, adult education and e-learning environments. He received his BS degree (2001) in computer education from Middle East Technical University, Faculty of Education, and his MSc degree (2004) in curriculum and instruction program of Department of Educational Sciences from Middle East Technical University. His master thesis is entitled as *"An Assessment of Preservice Teachers' Technology Perception in Relation to Their Subject Area"*.

Mario Vanhoucke, PhD, is a professor at Ghent University and the Vlerick Leuven Gent Management School in Belgium. He teaches courses in project management, business statistics and applied operations research. He is the program director of the Commercial Engineers (Ghent University), program director of the Project Management course (VLGMS) and partner of the OR-AS (www.or-as.be). His main research interest lies in simulation and optimization models in project scheduling and scheduling in the health case sector. He is an advisor of various PhD project, in collaboration with different universities hospital and international universities. He has published articles in international journals such as *Annals of Operations Research, Management Science, Operations Research*, the *Accounting Review, International Journal of Production Research, Journal of the Operational Research Society, Journal of Scheduling, International Journal of Project Management, Project Management Journal, European Journal of Operational Research*, and *Lecture Notes on Computer Science*.

Kerry S. Webb, PhD, is an assistant professor in the MBA program at the TWU School of Management. He is also the founder and chief consultant for Peak Leadership, LLC, a management consulting firm. Webb has coached, trained, and motivated hundreds of leaders to create high performance work teams and to develop positive organizational cultures. His research has been published in several academic journals and for the past twenty years, he spoken to corporate, government, and non-profit audiences across the United States and internationally. His research includes increasing employee performance, maintaining worker satisfaction, the impact of emotional intelligence in management, creating leadership strategies, enhancing communication, and the utilization of conflict management strategies.

Index